ENCYCLOPEDIA OF BRITISH WRITERS

20TH CENTURY

ENCYCLOPEDIA OF BRITISH WRITERS

20TH CENTURY

Dr. George Stade
GENERAL EDITOR
Department of English and
Comparative Literature
Columbia University

Dr. Karen Karbiener
GENERAL EDITOR
Department of English
Colby College

Dr. Thomas Recchio
ADVISER
Department of English
University of Connecticut, Storrs

Debra Rae Cohen
ADVISER
Department of English
University of Arkansas

Dr. Christine L. Krueger
ADVISER
Department of English and
Comparative Literature
Columbia University

☑®
Facts On File, Inc.

Encyclopedia of British Writers, 20th Century

Facts On File, Inc.
132 West 31st Street
New York NY 10001

Library of Congress Cataloging-in-Publication Data

Encyclopedia of British Writers [written and developed by Book Builders LLC].
    p. cm.
    Includes bibliographical references and indexes.
    Contents: v. 1. Encyclopedia of British Writers, 19th Century / edited by Christine L. Krueger—
v. 2. Encyclopedia of British Writers, 20th Century / edited by George Stade.
    ISBN 0-8160-4670-0 (set : alk. paper)—ISBN 0-8160-4668-9 (v. 1 : alk. paper)—
ISBN 0-8160-4669-7 (v. 2 : alk. paper)
    1. English literature—19th century—Bio-bibliography—Dictionaries. 2. English literature—
20th century—Bio-bibliography—Dictionaries. 3. Authors, English—19th century—Biography—
Dictionaries. 4. Authors, English—20th century—Biography—Dictionaries. 5. English literature—
19th century—Dictionaries. 6. English literature—20th century—Dictionaries. I. Title: Encyclopedia
of nineteenth and twentieth century British writers. II. Krueger, Christine L. III. Stade, George. IV.
Book Builders LLC.

PR451 .E55 2003
820.9'008'03—dc21   2002033920

Facts On File books are available at special discounts when purchased in bulk quantities for businesses, associations, institutions, or sales promotions. Please call our Special Sales Department in New York at (212) 967-8800 or (800) 322-8755.

You can find Facts On File on the World Wide Web at http://www.factsonfile.com

Text design by Rachel L. Berlin
Cover illustration by Smart Graphics
Cover design by Cathy Rincon

Written and developed by Book Builders LLC

Printed in the United States of America

VB Hermitage 10 9 8 7 6 5 4 3 2 1

This book is printed on acid-free paper.

CONTENTS

PREFACE

The articles in *Encyclopedia of British Writers, 20th Century* are designed to introduce the student or general reader to British writers who in the editors' opinion deserve to be read and studied. The articles vary in length, from a few hundred words to more than a thousand words, according to the editors' understanding of an individual writer's present or potential importance. The relative value of these writers continues to be a matter of debate, but the editors have tried to arrive at a consensual ranking by considering such matters as the size of the writer's readership, the quality of the critical and academic interest, and the writer's impact on other writers. There is nothing stable about rankings based on such criteria. During their own era, for example, Marie Corelli had a much larger readership than Joseph Conrad (although Corelli is largely forgotten now), and 43 publishers rejected Samuel Beckett's first novel. The editors hope that the readers of this volume will participate variously in this constant process of reevaluation. There is something very satisfying in discovering just the writer one needs and telling the world about it.

Typically, the articles will tell the reader about the writer's background, parents, education, private life, and above all, his or her writing. They also will provide a sampling of critical responses and suggestions for further reading. Readers should have no trouble finding the writers they need to read, whether traditional or avant-garde, classicist or extremist, highbrow or lowbrow, obvious or arcane, minimalist or maximalist, imperialist or anti-imperialist, feminist or misogynist, homophobic or homophiliac, writers whose politics are on the left, the right, the center, or beyond the pale. Finally, despite a number of movements, mostly short-lived, in which like-minded writers came together, 20th-century writers, in accordance with the modernist injunction to "make it new," were more likely to cultivate their differences than their similarities. The result is a rousing diversity—and the likelihood that you will find just the writer you need.

George Stade
Karen Karbiener
General Editors

INTRODUCTION

From where we stand at the onset of the 21st century, it is hard to see clearly the shape of 20th-century British literary history. Certainly we are not able to see the writers as spread out neatly in historical space according to some transcendent master plan. We perhaps know too much about them, or too little, and in any case what we think we know about them does not always jibe with what they thought about themselves. The result is that the closer we look at the writers of the last century, the more they seem to be in motion, changing places and shifting allegiances.

For all that, certain landmarks appear to have held their ground. World War I, for example, accelerated a process, whereas World War II put a brake on it. That process has come to be called "modernism." Although hints and premonitions of modernist styles and attitudes began to appear in the 1880s and 1890s among aesthetes, Decadents, and symbolists, by around 1910, when, according to Virginia Woolf, "human nature changed," modernism had become self-conscious and argumentative. Although Woolf was alluding to an exhibition of "postimpressionist" paintings by artists such as Cézanne, van Gogh, Gauguin, Matisse, and Picasso, 1910 was also the year of Ezra Pound's imagist manifesto, after which poetry in English was never the same. A year later

Arnold Schoenberg published his theory of harmony, and three years later Igor Stravinsky's *The Rite of Spring* was performed to rioting audiences; music too had changed. Three years before, Picasso had shown his *Demoiselles d'Avignon,* and two years later Marcel Duchamp exhibited his *Nude Descending a Staircase,* both evidence that painting had changed. Four years later World War I began, and nothing at all was ever the same.

As a reaction to the establishment that had drawn them into the war, young English men and women, like their European and American counterparts, cut loose. As women threw off their stays, artists threw off forms and conventions. By 1922, the year of T. S. Eliot's *The Waste Land* and James Joyce's *Ulysses,* modernism had become established. At the time, although its practitioners were united by their interest in experimentation, cultural relativism, and the workings of the unconscious, modernism seemed like a break with all traditions.

Of course, Eliot and Joyce, authors of the exemplary texts of British modernism, were not English but in one case American and in the other Irish. It would not be an exaggeration to say that the great English literature of the modernist era was written mainly by Irishmen, Americans, a Welshman, and a Pole. If one were to construct a model of what was considered the prevailing type of Briton—

someone who openly qualified for membership in the caste that set the styles, determined the values, and wielded the power that showed the world just what it meant to be British—he would be English, male, middle-class, Protestant, and heterosexual. However, by these criteria, none of the great modernists qualified. If the writers were not American or Polish or from one of John Bull's other islands, they were Catholics (usually by conversion rather than by birth), as were Ford Madox Ford, Evelyn Waugh, and Graham Greene; or from the working class, like D. H. Lawrence; or were women, like Virginia Woolf and Katherine Mansfield (who was born in New Zealand); or homosexual, like E. M. Forster and W. H. Auden.

Although the prevailing type in actuality still prevailed, he seemed somehow to have outlived his historical moment. The ideas, values, and practices that constituted his typicality and guaranteed his prevalence no longer seemed those from which anything of moment could be written. When he appeared in modernist fiction, it was as a figure of fun. To write anything new seemed to require at least the adversary edge of Irishmen or Americans trying to cut themselves loose from the cultural imperialism of a mother country whose language was the one they had perforce to use. Or, it required the implacable antagonisms of class conflict, the cool refusals of feminist resentment, the satirical disenchantments of homosexuality, a hatred of the present and a nostalgia for the past, or a burden of guilt, deep enough to drive one into the arms of the church. The modernists saw themselves as on the margin of the literary world, their exile no less real for being inside themselves.

Analogies could be drawn wherever advanced Western civilization had taken a firm enough hold for its modernist writers to tear it apart. Latin American writers, for example, seem to have been in a modernist phase for at least the last quarter of the last century. Their self-perceived relation to Spanish and Portuguese must be something like the Irishman's or American's relation to English during the days of James Joyce and Ezra Pound. But the resentful love and reciprocated hate that

modernist writers feel toward their own countries were especially keen among English moderns, perhaps because in the period just prior to the onset of modernism, England was by many standards the greatest nation in the world, master of an empire on which the sun never set. Its decline, or perhaps appearance of decline, was that much more dramatic.

The decline of nations may be likened to the decline of fathers, at least to boys and girls growing up. The children of discredited fathers and fatherlands seem both more free and more driven to do unheard-of things—and to imagine compensatory worlds more attractive—than are solid citizens assured of their succession. A surprising number of great writers—among them Shakespeare, Dickens, and Joyce, to name three of Britain's greatest—had fathers whose fortunes declined as the sons were growing up. Similarly, Western modernists born near the end of the 19th century clearly felt that their fatherlands were coming down in the world, that the very principle of authority had compromised itself, that their release from filial piety had only delivered them into the anxious compulsions of a world whose center no longer held, and that the aesthetic order of their work would have to compensate for the actual chaos of the world their fiction represented. During the modernist period, although fathers, fatherlands, principles of authority, and conventions and traditions were still there, they were discredited. The insistent presence of these symbols, and the itch to subvert them, is one thing that distinguishes modernist literature from what followed it.

The most common general characteristic of the modernist writers, then, was an adversarial or alienated relationship to their own cultures. The most general common characteristic of their writing was an inverse relation between the rendered aesthetic order and the represented chaos. The more disordered the world represented, the more ordered the rendering of the work. It is in this respect that *The Waste Land* and *Ulysses* are exemplary, but so are the novels of Ford, Conrad, Woolf, Forster, and Waugh. The very techniques used to represent a world of dissolving appearances and crumbling institutions are also the techniques that bind part to part with an unprecedented adhesive force.

These techniques are not simply those of 19th-century writers brought up to date. British modernists did not look toward their immediate past. Rather, they looked around at new situations calling for new practices, or they looked toward the literature of France, America, and Russia. They looked at postimpressionist painting, Russian ballet, Chinese ideograms, Japanese drama, African masks, and American movies. They looked toward psychology, anthropology, and physics. "We are sharply cut off from our predecessors," said Virginia Woolf. ". . . Every day we find ourselves doing, or saying, or thinking things that would have been impossible to our fathers." As a result, she continued, "No age can have been more rich than ours in writers determined to give expression to the differences which separate them from the past and not to the resemblances which connect them with it."

In the late 1920s and through the 1930s, modernism began to tire of its own success. As part of their sustained polemic against Victorianism, the early modernists had asserted the autonomy of art, according to which art ceased to be art when it was designed to serve a moral or political end. But slogans about the independence of art had ceased to hold up in the face of a ruinous inflation, a devastating depression, and the gathering storm that became World War II. Writers were increasingly encouraged to direct art's energies toward the defeat or victory of fascism or communism, though not all writers responded in the same way. Amid much straightforward political writing and alongside a kind of overripe modernism, as written by, say, Wyndham Lewis and David Jones, other writers "as diverse as W. H. Auden, Stephen Spender, Cecil Day-Lewis, George Orwell, and Rex Warner . . . found ways of holding in tension political and literary demands," says Tyrus Miller, author of a book on what he calls "Late Modernism."

Writers who came into prominence in England after World War II were polemically antimodernist: "For me the highest point of literature was the novel of the nineteenth century. . . . I hold the view that the realist novel, the realist story, is the highest form of prose writing; higher than and out of reach of any comparison with expressionism, symbolism, naturalism, or any other ism," said Doris Lessing in 1957. Contemporaries like John Wain, John Braine, Angus Wilson, Kingsley Amis, and Iris Murdoch would have agreed about the realistic novel. Poets like John Betjeman and Philip Larkin, who wrote in rhymed stanzas, seemed to agree that the age of experiment was, or should be, over.

Just as the revulsion against the establishment that followed World War I justified artists in their search for foreign models, so the chastened patriotism that followed World War II encouraged writers to choose English themes, English characters, English settings, sentiments, and techniques. Befitting the literature of an empire that had shrunk radically, large ambitions and world-historical themes were considered bad form.

This went on until the 1970s: "It was axiomatic in Britain that interesting novels came from somewhere else—usually America. British fiction was domestic realism, often about adultery; as for the prose, the rule was that you could have any color you wanted, so long as it was gray." So wrote John Lanchester, himself an interesting novelist, one whose prose is anything but gray. According to Lanchester, three writers—Martin Amis, Julian Barnes, and Ian McEwan, all born during the 1940s—helped bring British English back to life as a literary language. They were helped by writers who published in London but came to it from the outside, such as Anita Desai, Salman Rushdie, Derek Walcott, and V. S. Naipaul, who are now world famous. A number of strong Irish poets and hard-eyed Scottish novelists also enriched the mix. As the century ended, the result was that British fiction, poetry, and drama were all thriving.

In retrospect, it appears that the vicissitudes of modernism comprise the main literary fact of 20th-century British literature. No movement of equal scope or staying power has emerged to replace it. Instead, there has been a large increase in the number of writers who did not go to Oxford or Cambridge or Eton and have a different perspective on things from those who did. There has been an energizing influx of writers from former parts of the British Empire, writers from the Caribbean, India, and the Near East who are not likely to see England (or anything else) quite the way writers from London have seen it. The absorption of forms of popular fiction such as whodunits, science fiction, and the romance into the art novel has made it more robust.

British literary history presents young writers in English with an immense and various repertoire of plots, characters, themes, and techniques with which to work. If one wants to be a modernist, the materials are there. If one wants to be an antimodernist or postmodernist, there are models available. Best of all, when writers go their own ways, there are inspiring "predecessors." Concurrent historical events encouraged British writers of the modernist era to smash traditions and produce new forms. It will be interesting to see what post-September 11 history encourages 21st-century British writers to produce in their place.

George Stade
Karen Karbiener
General Editors

AUTHORS' TIMELINE

Dates	Author	Dates	Author
1843–1926	Doughty, Charles	1872–1963	Powys, John Cowper
1852–1932	Gregory, Lady	1873–1939	Ford, Ford Madox
1854–1941	Frazer, Sir James G.	1873–1956	de la Mare, Walter
1856–1939	Freud, Sigmund	1873–1957	Richardson, Dorothy
1857–1924	Conrad, Joseph	1874–1922	Shackleton, Ernest
1858–1949	Somerville, Edith	1874–1936	Chesterton, G. K.
1859–1932	Grahame, Kenneth	1874–1965	Churchill, Sir Winston
1860–1937	Barrie, J. M.	1874–1965	Maugham, W. Somerset
1861–1931	Tynan, Katharine	1875–1932	Wallace, Edgar
1862–1915	Ross, Martin (Violet Florence Martin)	1875–1940	Buchan, John
		1875–1950	Sabatini, Raphael
1862–1936	James, M. R.	1875–1953	Powys, T. F.
1863–1946	Sinclair, May	1875–1956	Bentley, E. C.
1865–1939	Yeats, William Butler	1877–1946	Granville-Barker, Harley
1865–1947	Orczy, Baroness	1878–1917	Thomas, Edward
1866–1934	Fry, Roger	1878–1957	Coppard, A. E.
1866–1943	Potter, Beatrix	1878–1957	Dunsany, Lord
1866–1946	Wells, H. G.	1878–1967	Masefield, John
1867–1931	Bennett, Arnold	1879–1970	Forster, E. M.
1867–1933	Galsworthy, John	1880–1932	Strachey, Lytton
1867–1935	Russell, George William (A. E.)	1880–1946	O'Casey, Sean
1868–1947	Belloc Lowndes, Marie	1880–1958	Noyes, Alfred
1869–1951	Blackwood, Algernon	1880–1969	Woolf, Leonard
1870–1916	Saki (H. H. Munro)	1881–1958	Macaulay, Rose
1870–1953	Belloc, Hilaire	1881–1964	Bell, Clive
1871–1909	Synge, J. M.	1881–1972	Colum, Padraic
1871–1962	Hodgson, Ralph	1881–1975	Wodehouse, P. G.

Dates	Author	Dates	Author
1882–1941	Joyce, James	1893–1957	Sayers, Dorothy L.
1882–1941	Woolf, Virginia	1893–1968	Read, Herbert
ca. 1882–1950	Stephens, James	1893–1970	Brittain, Vera
1882–1956	Milne, A. A.	1893–1973	Cannan, May Wedderburn
1883–1917	Hulme, T. E.	1893–1978	Warner, Sylvia Townsend
1883–1959	Rohmer, Sax	1893–1993	Stark, Freya
1883–1972	Mackenzie, Compton	1894–1963	Huxley, Aldous
1884–1941	Walpole, Hugh	1894–1983	Bryher (Annie Winifred Ellerman)
1884–1957	Lewis, Wyndham		
1884–1958	Squire, J. C.	1894–1984	Priestley, J. B.
1884–1969	Compton-Burnett, Ivy	1895–1915	Sorley, Charles
1884–1982	Swinnerton, Frank	1895–1972	Hartley, L. P.
1885–1930	Lawrence, D. H.	1895–1974	Jones, David
1886–1926	Firbank, Ronald	1895–1977	Williamson, Henry
1886–1943	Hall, Radclyffe	1895–1978	Leavis, F. R.
1886–1945	Williams, Charles	1895–1985	Graves, Robert
1886–1950	Stapledon, Olaf	ca. 1896–1952	Tey, Josephine
1886–1958	Robinson, Lennox	1896–1967	Ackerley, J. R.
1886–1967	Sassoon, Siegfried	1896–1972	Prescott, H. F. M.
1886–1980	Travers, Ben	1896–1974	Blunden, Edward
1887–1915	Brooke, Rupert	1896–1975	Sherriff, R. C.
1887–1959	Muir, Edwin	1896–1984	O'Flaherty, Liam
1887–1964	Sitwell, Edith	1896–1990	Smith, Dodie
1888–1923	Mansfield, Katherine	1897–1968	Blyton, Enid
1888–1935	Lawrence, T. E.	1897–1988	Sitwell, Sacheverell
1888–1951	Bridie, James	1897–1992	Pitter, Ruth
1888–1957	Cary, Joyce	1897–1999	Mitchison, Naomi
1888–1965	Dane, Clemence	1898–1935	Holtby, Winifred
1888–1965	Eliot, T. S.	1898–1963	Lewis, C. S.
1889–1975	Toynbee, Arnold	1899–1966	Forester, C. S.
1890–1918	Rosenberg, Isaac	1899–1973	Bowen, Elizabeth
1890–1937	Gurney, Ivor	1899–1973	Coward, Noël
1890–1976	Christie, Agatha	1899–1974	Linklater, Eric
1890–1979	Rhys, Jean	1899–1982	Marsh, Ngaio
1891–1973	Gunn, Neil	1899–1996	Travers, P. L.
1891–1986	Jameson, Storm	1900–1954	Hilton, James
1892–1962	Aldington, Richard	1900–1976	Hughes, Richard
1892–1962	Sackville-West, Vita	1900–1985	Bunting, Basil
1892–1969	Sitwell, Osbert	1900–1988	Household, Geoffrey
1892–1973	Tolkien, J. R. R.	1900–1991	O'Faolain, Sean
1892–1978	MacDiarmid, Hugh	1900–1997	Pritchett, V. S.
1892–1983	West, Rebecca	1901–1978	Davies, Rhys
1893–1918	Owen, Wilfred	1901–1980	Collier, John

Dates	Author	Dates	Author
1901–1984	Johnston, Denis	ca. 1908–1980	Manning, Olivia
1901–1990	Lehmann, Rosamond	1908–1984	Ashton-Warner, Sylvia
1902–1971	Smith, Stevie	1908–1992	Calder-Marshall, Arthur
1902–1989	Gibbons, Stella	1908–1992	Liddell, Robert
1903–1950	Orwell, George	1908–1999	Crisp, Quentin
1903–1966	O'Connor, Frank	1908–	Raine, Kathleen
1903–1966	Waugh, Evelyn	1909–1957	Lowry, Malcolm
1903–1969	Wyndham, John	1909–1977	Pudney, John
1903–1973	Plomer, William	1909–1995	Spender, Stephen
1903–1974	Connolly, Cyril	1909–1998	Ambler, Eric
1903–1990	Callaghan, Morley	1910–1979	Monsarrat, Nicholas
1903–1990	Muggeridge, Malcolm	1910–1992	Naughton, Bill
1904–1962	Hamilton, Patrick	1910–	Cooper, William
1904–1966	Allingham, Margery	1910–	Graham, Winston
1904–1972	Day Lewis, C.	1910–	Jesse, F. Tennyson
1904–1973	Mitford, Nancy	1911–1966	O'Brien, Flann
1904–1986	Isherwood, Christopher	ca. 1911–1966	Treece, Henry
1904–1989	Buchanan, George	1911–1968	Peake, Mervyn
1904–1991	Greene, Graham	1911–1977	Rattigan, Terence
1904–1996	Keane, Molly (M. J. Farrell)	1911–1993	Golding, William
1905–1973	Green, Henry	1911–	Bedford, Sybille
1905–1974	Bates, H. E.	1912–1975	Taylor, Elizabeth
1905–1980	Snow, C. P.	1912–1976	Sansom, William
1905–1983	Koestler, Arthur	1912–1981	Johnson, Pamela Hansford
1905–1983	Renault, Mary	1912–1989	Dennis, Nigel
1905–1986	Warner, Rex	1912–1989	Menen, Aubrey
1905–1987	Williams, Emlyn	1912–1990	Durrell, Lawrence
1905–1991	Sharp, Margery	1912–1991	Fuller, Roy
1905–2000	Powell, Anthony	1912–1994	Symons, Julian
1906–1964	White, T. H.	1912–1996	Lavin, Mary
1906–1967	Watkins, Vernon	1912–	Jenkins, Robin
1906–1984	Betjeman, John	1913–1980	Pym, Barbara
1906–1989	Beckett, Samuel	1913–1986	Smart, Elizabeth
1906–1994	Stewart, J. I. M. (Michael Innes)	1913–1991	Barker, George
1907–1963	MacNeice, Louis	1913–1991	Wilson, Angus
1907–1973	Auden, W. H.	1913–1995	Davies, Robertson
1907–1975	Hutchinson, R. C.	1914–1953	Thomas, Dylan
1907–1989	du Maurier, Daphne	1914–1983	Masters, John
1907–1997	Huxley, Elspeth	1914–1986	Reed, Henry
1907–1998	Godden, Rumer	1914–1997	Lee, Laurie
1907–1999	Jones, Gwyn	1915–1944	Lewis, Alun
1907–	Fry, Christopher	1915–1948	Welch, Denton
1908–1964	Fleming, Ian	1915–1992	Dickens, Monica

Dates	Author	Dates	Author
1915–2001	Hoyle, Fred	1925–1994	Wain, John
1916–1986	Chaplin, Sid	1925–1995	Durrell, Gerald
1916–1990	Dahl, Roald	1925–	Aldiss, Brian
1916–1995	Ewart, Gavin	1925–	Bawden, Nina
1916–2000	Fitzgerald, Penelope	1925–	Finlay, Ian
1916–2001	Gascoyne, David	1926–2002	Cowper, Richard
1917–1993	Burgess, Anthony	1926–	Berger, John
1917–	Clarke, Arthur C.	1926–	Brooke-Rose, Christine
1917–	Causley, Charles	1926–	Donleavy, J. P.
1917–	Conquest, Robert	1926–	Fowles, John
1918–1997	Newby, P. H.	1926–	Fraser, George MacDonald
1918–1999	Mortimer, Penelope	1926–	Jennings, Elizabeth
1918–	Barker, A. L.	1926–	Kops, Bernard
1918–	Heath-Stubbs, John	1926–	Morris, Jan
1918–	Spark, Muriel	1926–	Shaffer, Peter
1919–1943	Hillary, Richard	1927–1981	Holden, Molly
1919–1999	Murdoch, Iris	1927–2001	Raven, Simon
1919–	Lessing, Doris	1927–	Freeling, Nicholas
1919–	Middleton, Stanley	1927–	Jhabvala, Ruth Prawer
1920–1944	Douglas, Keith	1927–	Murphy, Richard
1920–1978	Scott, Paul	1928–1998	Smith, Iain Crichton
1920–2000	Comfort, Alex	1928–	Barstow, Stan
1920–	Enright, D. J.	1928–	Brookner, Anita
1920–	Francis, Dick	1928–	Gardam, Jane
1920–	James, P. D.	1928–	Kinsella, Thomas
1921–1978	Crispin, Edmund	1928–	Sillitoe, Alan
1921–1996	Brown, George Mackay	1928–	Trevor, William
1921–1999	Moore, Brian	1929–1994	Osborne, John
1921–	Norris, Leslie	1929–1995	Brophy, Brigid
1922–1985	Larkin, Philip	1929–	Alvarez, A.
1922–1986	Braine, John	1929–	Deighton, Len
1922–1995	Amis, Kingsley	1929–	Friel, Brian
1922–1995	Davie, Donald	1929–	Gunn, Thom
1922–	Scannell, Vernon	1929–	Waterhouse, Keith
1923–1964	Behan, Brendan	1930–1997	Silkin, Jon
1923–	Abse, Dannie	1930–1998	Hughes, Ted
1923–	Gordimer, Nadine	1930–	Arden, John
1923–	Mortimer, John	1930–	Ballard, J. G.
1923–	Rubens, Bernice	1930–	Brathwaite, Edward
1924–1995	Bolt, Robert	1930–	Feinstein, Elaine
1924–	Aiken, Joan	1930–	Fisher, Roy
1924–	Bowen, John	1930–	Pinter, Harold
1924–	White, Jon Manchip	1930–	Rendell, Ruth

Dates	Author	Dates	Author
1930–	Thwaite, Anthony	1938–	Murray, Les
1930–	Walcott, Derek	1938–	Raworth, Tom
1931–	Colegate, Isabel	1939–2001	Waugh, Auberon
1931–	Kavanagh, P. J.	1939–	Atwood, Margaret
1931–	le Carré, John	1939–	Ayckbourn, Alan
1931–	Munro, Alice	1939–	Bragg, Melvyn
1931–	Weldon, Fay	1939–	Delaney, Shelagh
1931–	Wilson, Colin	1939–	Drabble, Margaret
1932–1993	Gilliatt, Penelope	1939–	Greer, Germaine
1932–1999	Hill, Geoffrey	1939–	Heaney, Seamus
1932–2000	Bradbury, Malcolm	1939–	Longley, Michael
1932–	Ellis, Alice Thomas	1939–	Moorcock, Michael
1932–	Fraser, Antonia	1940–1989	Chatwin, Bruce
1932–	Naipaul, V. S.	1940–1992	Carter, Angela
1932–	O'Brien, Edna	1940–	Coetzee, J. M.
1932–	O'Faolain, Julia	1941–	Mahon, Derek
1932–	Wesker, Arnold	1942–	Hill, Susan
1933–1967	Orton, Joe	1943–	Barker, Pat
1933–1973	Johnson, B. S.	1943–	Carey, Peter
1933–	Bainbridge, Beryl	1943–	Ondaatje, Michael
1933–	Duffy, Maureen	1943–	Tremain, Rose
1933–	Frayn, Michael	1944–	Durcan, Paul
1933–	Lively, Penelope	1944–	Raine, Craig
1933–	Storey, David	1945–	Boland, Eavan
1934–1995	Brunner, John	1945–	Cope, Wendy
1934–	Adcock, Fleur	1946–	Barker, Howard
1934–	Bennett, Alan	1946–	Barnes, Julian
1934–	Bond, Edward	1946–	Kelman, James
1934–	McGahern, John	1947–	Hare, David
1935–1979	Farrell, J. G.	1947–	Hulme, Keri
1935–2002	McGrath, John	1947–	Rushdie, Salman
1935–	Griffiths, Trevor	1947–	Russell, Willy
1935–	Keneally, Thomas	1948–	Gee, Maggie
1935–	Lodge, David	1948–	McEwan, Ian
1935–	Sinclair, Clive	1948–	Sinclair, May
1935–	Thomas, D. M.	1949–	Ackroyd, Peter
1936–	Byatt, A. S.	1949–	Amis, Martin
1936–	Caute, David	1949–	Fenton, James
1936–	Dunn, Nell	1949–	Swift, Graham
1937–	Harrison, Tony	1950–	Jordan, Neil
1937–	Stoppard, Tom	1950–	McGuckian, Medbh
1937–	Tennant, Emma	1951–	Muldoon, Paul
1938–	Churchill, Caryl	1952–	Motion, Andrew

A

Abse, Dannie (1923–) *poet, playwright, novelist*

Dannie Abse was born in Cardiff, Wales, the son of Rudy Abse, a movie theater owner, and his wife Kate. Abse fell in love with the lyricism of Welsh English, particularly as expressed in the political speeches of his brother Leo. After studying at the University of Wales, he trained at Westminster Hospital in London to become a doctor.

Abse's poems describe the struggle between his role as a doctor and his feelings as a human being. In the last line of "X-ray," a poem about a doctor's reluctance to view his own mother's X ray, he laments, "I still don't want to know," even as he lifts the photo to the viewing screen.

In his 40s, however, Abse began to reconcile the two halves of his life. "Gradually my mind, as it were, became prepared to write poems with medical themes," he recalled. With the publication of *A Small Desperation* (1968), Abse's voice had matured into that of a confident physician whose view of the world is permanently altered because of what he sees as a doctor. The lines "I know the colour rose, and it is lovely, but not when it ripens in a tumour" from "Pathology of Colours" reflects this altered point of view.

Abse has also written four novels and several plays ranging from the semiautobiographical tale of a young Jewish boy growing up in South Wales in the 1930s (*Ash on a Young Man's Sleeve*, 1954) to musings on medical research (*The Dogs of Pavlov*, 1990) and even on the mentally ill (*Pythagoras [Smith]*, 1990). From 1973 to 1974 he was writer-in-residence at Princeton University, and from 1978 to 1992 he served as president of the Poetry Society, a prestigious organization in Britain that exists to help poetry and poets thrive. Writer Nicholas Wroe points out that Abse "not only became one of the country's leading poets, but did so while maintaining a career as a doctor in a London chest clinic."

Other Works by Dannie Abse

The View from Row G: Three Plays by Dannie Abse. Chester Springs, Pa.: Dufour Editions, 1990.
White Coat, Purple Coat: Collected Poems 1948–1988. New York: Persea Books, 1991.

Ackerley, Joseph Randolph (1896–1967) *playwright, memoirist, editor*

J. R. Ackerley was born in Herne Hill, Kent, England, to Alfred Roger Ackerley, a fruit importer known as the "Banana King." Ackerley received a degree from Magdalene College, Cambridge, in 1921, after serving in the Royal Artillery from 1914 to 1918. In World War I he was wounded twice and held as a prisoner of war in France.

Shortly after the war, Ackerley wrote a three-act play, *The Prisoners of War* (1925), which earned praise from the British poet Siegfried SASSOON. It is widely considered one of the best plays ever written about World War I for its close look at soldiers' personal interactions. Based on Ackerley's own experience, the play is set in a Swiss prison camp and obliquely tells the story of an officer's love for a young soldier.

In addition to several minor novels about his relationship with his dog, Ackerley wrote several pieces of nonfiction. *Hindoo Holiday: An Indian Journal* (1932) is his memoir about his experiences as the personal secretary for a local Indian maharajah in the 1920s. His autobiography, *My Father and Myself* (1968), published posthumously, reveals an extremely unconventional but interesting life riddled with numerous sexual affairs with a wide array of men, including waiters and soldiers, as well as an almost spousal relationship with his dog Queenie, of whom he writes, "The fifteen years she lived with me were the happiest of my life."

Ackerley's literary output was relatively small, but he became profoundly influential as the editor of the *Listener* (1935–59), the literary journal of the BBC (British Broadcasting Corporation). During his years as editor he encouraged the work of such well-known writers as W. H. AUDEN, Clive BELL, Christopher ISHERWOOD, Wyndham LEWIS, Louis MACNEICE, Stephen SPENDER, and Leonard and Virginia WOOLF.

Ackerley is also remembered for leading the way toward the recognition of homosexual writers and for fighting for homosexual civil rights in England. The critic David Yezzi has remarked that Ackerley's "substantial gift was his ability to pronounce sentence on [criticize] himself with inimitable wit and charm," and that he was "lauded as a minor master by contemporaries and friends such as Evelyn Waugh, Elizabeth Bowen, Vita Sackville-West."

Other Works by J. R. Ackerley

My Dog Tulip. 1965. Reprint, New York: New York Review of Books, 1999.

We Think the World of You. 1960. Reprint, New York: New York Review of Books, 2000.

A Work about J. R. Ackerley

Parker, Peter. *Ackerley: A Life of J. R. Ackerley.* New York: Farrar, Straus & Giroux, 1989.

Ackroyd, Peter (1949–) *novelist, biographer, poet*

Peter Ackroyd was born to Graham and Audrey Ackroyd, a Catholic working-class couple, in London, a city that he has used as the setting for most of his novels and nonfiction works and lovingly describes in *London: The Biography* (2000). He attended Cambridge and Yale, and though he wrote some poetry in his youth, he quickly abandoned it for prose.

Ackroyd became known as a nonfiction writer with such biographies as *Ezra Pound and His World* (1979) and *T. S. Eliot* (1984), which won him the Whitbread Award for Biography. His biography of Oscar Wilde, *The Last Testament of Oscar Wilde* (1983), a fictitious representation of Wilde's journal, won the Somerset Maugham Award for its stunningly accurate reproduction of Wilde's voice. Critic Ukko Hänninen observes that Ackroyd "re-create[s] not only the humour but also the poignancy that is so characteristic of Wilde," as demonstrated in the following quote: "I had appealed to the world to save my reputation, and it crushed me."

This postmodernist style of borrowing from previously published sources to mix fact with fiction and the past with the present carries over to Ackroyd's novels. Writer Nick Gevers describes the structure of a typical Ackroyd novel as "history interacting with and finding a mirror in the present." Ackroyd's first novel, *The Great Fire of London* (1982), purports to be a continuation of Charles Dickens's *Little Dorrit,* in which a cast of characters tries unsuccessfully to reenact Dickens's novel. The moral of the story is that it is impossible to reconstruct the past.

Hawksmoor (1985), which won the Whitbread, Guardian Fiction, and Goncourt awards, also brings the past into the future, alternating between chapters set in early 18th-century London and those set in the 20th century. Church architecture and a mystery involving serial killers tie the two story lines together. *Chatterton* (1987) is another mystery, based on three poets in three centuries. According to editor Nancy K. Miller, "The paradox in Ackroyd's writing is that in re-examining the literary past and in imitating others, he is not actually imitating anybody."

Other Works by Peter Ackroyd
Blake. New York: Knopf, 1996.
First Light. New York: Grove Press, 1996.
The Life of Thomas More. New York: Anchor Books, 1998.

A Work about Peter Ackroyd
Onega, Susana. *Metafiction and Myth in the Novels of Peter Ackroyd.* Rochester, N.Y.: Camden House, 1999.

Adcock, Fleur (Kareen Fleur Adcock)
(1934–) *poet, translator*
Fleur Adcock was born in Papakura, New Zealand, but spent several years (1939–47) in England. Her mother, Irene Adcock, is also a writer, as is her sister, Marilyn Duckworth. After her return to New Zealand, in 1954 Adcock received a Classics degree at Victoria University at Wellington. For several years she was married to the poet Alistair Campbell, with whom she had two sons. She has worked as a librarian and university lecturer in both New Zealand and Britain. For the last 20 years she published poetry and translated and edited poetry collections. She also talks about poetry for the BBC (British Broadcasting Corporation).

Adcock has been referred to as the "expatriate poet" because she lives and writes in England and New Zealand, and both countries claim her. She is considered one of the best women poets writing in Great Britain now. Her first book of poetry, *The Eye of the Hurricane* (1964), is filled with poems about her life in New Zealand and gives evidence of her training in the classics. She has commented: "The content of my poems derives largely from those parts of my life which are directly experienced, relationships with people or places; images and insights which have presented themselves sharply from whatever source, conscious or subconscious; ideas triggered off by language itself." In a poem called "For a Five-Year-Old," she tries to explain the strangeness of adult behavior toward animals, admitting that she has trapped mice and shot wild birds: "But that is how things are: I am your mother, And we are kind to snails." In "Richey," a poem published in *The Scenic Route* (1974), Adcock examines her Irish ancestry: "My great-grandfather Richey Brooks began in mud: at Moneymore; 'a place of mud and nothing else' he called it. . . ." The poems in this collection are shorter and filled with more images than her usual style. The collection *The Inner Harbour* (1979) deals with love and loss and the ways in which Adcock was able to accept changes in her life.

In addition to her many volumes of poetry, Adcock has translated other poets, such as Grete Tartler's *Orient Express: Poems* from Romanian. Adcock was also the editor of *The Faber Book of 20th Century Women's Poetry* (1987) and of *The Oxford Book of Contemporary New Zealand Poetry* (1982). Her many awards include the New Zealand National Book Award in 1984, and she was made an Officer of the Order of the British Empire (OBE) in 1996.

A Work about Fleur Adcock
Bleiman, Barbara, ed. *Five Modern Poets: Fleur Adcock, U. A. Fanthorpe, Tony Harrison, Anne Stevenson, Derek Walcott.* New York: Longman, 1993.

A. E.
See RUSSELL, GEORGE WILLIAM.

Aiken, Joan (1924–) *novelist, short story writer*
The daughter of American writer Conrad Aiken, Joan Aiken was born in Sussex after her family moved to England. Her children's books and fan-

tasies reflect the countryside where she grew up and her love of authors like John MASEFIELD, Mervyn PEAKE, and C. S. LEWIS. Homeschooled until she was 12, Aiken left boarding school when she was 17. In 1941 she began work as a clerk at the BBC (British Broadcasting Corporation), and four years later she married Ronald Brown, a press officer at the United Nations Information Center.

Aiken's first book of short stories, *All You've Ever Wanted*, was published in 1953. After her husband died of lung cancer in 1955, she stopped working on her first novel and took a job at *Argosy* magazine to support her two children. When *The Wolves of Willoughby Chase* was finally published in 1962, its success allowed Aiken to become a full-time writer. Set during the imaginary reign of James III of England, this fantasy tells how Simon, a brave and self-reliant gooseboy, helps two girls escape menacing wolves and a cruel governess. Simon discovers his noble parentage in *Black Hearts in Battersea* (1964), the second book in the series, which introduces the resourceful Dido Twite. Though Twite was intended to drown at the end of the book, a letter from a young reader persuaded Aiken to rescue her, and Dido's adventures continued in several other books.

Aiken has written for adults and children in several other genres, including fantasies, thrillers, plays, and short stories. In 1965 the *Willoughby Chase* quartet won the Lewis Carroll Shelf Award. *Nightfall* (1971) received the 1972 Edgar Allan Poe Award. Commenting on why she writes alternative histories that describe England as it might have been, Aiken said, "Why do we want to have alternate worlds? . . . If you write about something, hopefully you write about something that's better or more interesting than circumstances as they now are, and that way you hope to make a step towards it." Aiken's alternative histories combine elements of fairy tales, adventure stories, and humor so creatively that critic Patricia Craig credits her with inventing the "unhistorical romance, . . . a new genre which far outdoes its conventional counterpart in inventiveness and wit."

Other Works by Joan Aiken

The Cockatrice Boys. New York: Tor, 1996.
Dangerous Games. New York: Delacorte, 1999.

Aldington, Richard (1892–1962) *novelist, poet, critic, biographer, translator, screenwriter*

Richard Aldington was born in Portsea, England, to Albert Edward Aldington, a lawyer's clerk, and Jessie May Godfree Aldington. Although he was named Edward Godfree Aldington, he early chose to be called Richard. His family was not well off, and he had to leave University College, London, because of lack of funds. His brilliance in languages and literature was manifest early on, however, and by the age of 20 he was publishing elegantly written poetry. Aldington, Ezra Pound, and Hilda Doolittle ("H. D.") became the leaders of the IMAGISM movement, which Aldington defined: "To present an image (hence the name, imagist). We are not a school of painters, but we believe that poetry should render particulars exactly and not deal in vague generalities, however magnificent and sonorous." He married H. D. in 1913.

About this time Aldington became literary editor of *The Egoist*, a London magazine; published substantial amounts of poetry; and, as secretary to the novelist Ford Madox FORD, transcribed the latter's novel *The Good Soldier*. He enlisted in 1916 as a private in the army but was rapidly commissioned and saw combat as an officer. After the war he devoted himself to the literary life, continuing to publish poetry and book reviews for *The Times Literary Supplement*, as well as criticism and translations of French and Italian works. He worked with T. S. ELIOT on *The Criterion* but, becoming restless, he began to travel abroad. *Death of a Hero* (1929), a novel based on his war experiences, made Aldington an instant celebrity.

He continued to publish almost to the end of his life. Significant works include several novels (*Death of a Hero*, 1929, and *All Men Are Enemies*, 1933); many poems; his autobiography *Life for*

Life's Sake (1941); a biography of Waterloo's hero, *Wellington* (1946), which won the James Tate Black Memorial Prize; biographies of D. H. LAWRENCE and the French poet Frederic Mistral; translations of Greek and Latin poets; and Hollywood screenplays while he lived in the United States from 1935 to 1947. He nearly ruined his reputation with his controversial biography of T. E. LAWRENCE (Lawrence of Arabia), which attempted to prove that Lawrence was not the hero that he was believed to be.

Aldington spent three weeks in Russia as a guest of the Soviet Writers Union in 1962 and died suddenly upon his return to France. Critic Richard Smith stresses the difficulty in summarizing Aldington's literary career: "Though he began his career as an imagist poet, his subsequent writings are the work of a strong individualist whose attitudes and techniques cannot be consistently identified with a particular school or movement."

A Work about Richard Aldington

Smith, Richard E. *Richard Aldington*. Boston: Twayne, 1977.

Aldiss, Brian W. (1925–) *science fiction novelist, short story writer, nonfiction writer*

Brian Aldiss was born in East Dereham, Norfolk, England, to department store owner Stanley Aldiss and his wife Elizabeth. He was a soldier, poet, film critic, and bookseller before becoming a full-time writer.

Among Aldiss's noteworthy science fiction novels are *Barefoot in the Head* (1969), about a future war whose weapons are psychedelic drugs; and *Helliconia Spring* (1982), *Helliconia Summer* (1983), and *Helliconia Winter* (1985), a trilogy that traces the history of a society on a planet with centuries-long seasons. Among his other novels, the semiautobiographical *The Hand-Reared Boy* (1970), *A Soldier Erect* (1971), and *A Rude Awakening* (1978) follow a character named Horatio Stubbs through school and war.

Aldiss has also retold the Dracula, Dr. Moreau, and Frankenstein stories. His *Frankenstein Unbound* (1973) was turned into a 1990 film, and his short story "Supertoys Last All Summer Long" (1969) was filmed as *A.I.* (2001). The former concerns a time traveler meeting both Victor Frankenstein and Mary Shelley, while the latter tells of a lifelike robot boy whose "parents" debate whether to get rid of him as if he were merely an appliance, though he clearly is a sentient being.

Aldiss's history of science fiction, *Billion Year Spree* (1973), treats the genre with serious critical scrutiny instead of the usual fan recollections. He argues that science fiction was born in the 19th century when the mystery and suspense of the Gothic romance was wedded to the scientific and technological wonders of the Industrial Revolution. For Aldiss, Mary Shelley's *Frankenstein* is the first true science fiction novel. He adds that "[t]he greatest successes of science fiction are those which deal with man in relation to his changing surroundings and abilities: what loosely might be called *environmental fiction*." Although Aldiss's work employs familiar science fiction elements, such as robots, lasers, and spaceships, he places a high value on philosophical and sociological questions, as in the Helliconia books' examination of how a culture adapts to its physical environment.

In 1962 Aldiss won a Hugo, the Science Fiction Achievement Award, for *Hothouse* (1962), a collection of stories about humans of the far future living in a huge tree that covers a continent. Three years later his "The Saliva Tree," in which H. G. WELLS foils an alien takeover, won a Nebula Award from the Science Fiction and Fantasy Writers of America. In 1999 that group proclaimed him a "Grand Master." Biographer Tom Henighan credits Aldiss with "a history of science fiction that at one stroke demolished nearly half a century's parochial reading of the genre."

A Work about Brian Aldiss

Henighan, Tom. *Brian Aldiss*. Boston: Twayne Publishers, 1999.

Allingham, Margery (Maxwell March)
(1904–1966) novelist

Margery Allingham was born in London. Her father, Herbert, wrote detective stories and family serials for the popular penny weekly magazines; her mother, Emily, wrote stories for women's magazines. When Allingham was seven, "Mother presented her with a big bottle of Stephen's blue ink, a handful of paper and a nib, and Father outlined a plot for her," reported her sister Joyce. Allingham's first story was published when she was eight. She wrote and produced a play while a student at Cambridge.

Allingham's first novel, a romantic adventure called *Blackerchief Dick* (1923), was published when she was 19. She insisted that fellow student Philip Youngman Carter design the cover. She and Carter married four years later, and he became her frequent writing partner, completing *Cargo of Eagles* (1968) after her death.

After her marriage Allingham adapted silent films into stories for *The Girl's Cinema,* a magazine owned by her aunt. She also began writing mystery novels. *The Crime at Black Dudley* (1929) introduced her detective, Albert Campion. At first the mild-mannered Campion is characterized as "that silly ass," but he matures into a witty, urbane troubleshooter who takes on villains from blackmailers to spies with the help of his manservant, Magersfontein Lugg.

Campion's 24 cases earned Allingham a place among the "Big Four" of the Golden Age of crime fiction, along with Agatha CHRISTIE, Ngaio MARSH, and Dorothy L. SAYERS. The *Observer* review of *The Fashion in Shrouds* (1938) noted that "to Albert Campion has fallen the honour of being the first detective to feature in a story which is also by any standard a distinguished novel." Scholars praise Allingham's consistently ingenious puzzles and engaging characters. *Tiger in the Smoke* (1952), featuring the villainous Jack Havoc, has been rated her best work by both Allingham and her critics. "The killer is known, and the mystery lies in finding him and discovering his motivation, which allows Allingham to create an almost allegorical story of the battle between good and evil," notes critic Paula M. Woods. Commenting on Allingham's enduring appeal, the mystery novelist H. R. F. Keating notes that her later books "say much that is penetrating and wise about men and women, perhaps especially women," which "makes them still immensely readable."

Other Work by Margery Allington
Mind Reader. 1965. Reprint, New York: Avon, 1990.

Alvarez, Alfred (1929–) poet, novelist, critic

A. Alvarez was born to Bertie and Katie Levy Alvarez, members of a well-established Jewish family in London. In 1952 he graduated from Oxford with a degree in English. He spent the following years alternately as a researcher at Oxford, a research fellow at three different universities in America, and a freelance writer in London.

Although Alvarez started writing poetry as an undergraduate, he never produced a large body of verse. In 1961 a group of poems about his failed first marriage won the Vachel Lindsay Prize for Poetry from *Poetry* magazine. These poems, which include the titles "Love Affair," "Waking," and "The Survivor," combine violent and natural images to describe feelings of alienation and separation. His last poetry collection, *Autumn to Autumn, and Selected Poems, 1953–1976* (1978), contains a seven-sequence poem, "Autumn to Autumn," that depicts a cycle of loss and renewal. The sense of renewal is evident in the sequence "Snow," which concludes with the lines "Already the wind is turning, spring patrols the street, / The first buds stir under the snow on the hill."

Although Alvarez's emotionally intense poetry earned him a moderate level of recognition, he attained his greatest status as a critic. His first critical study, *The Shaping Spirit* (1958), analyzed modern English poetry, which he viewed as too academic and lacking in purity and personal strength. Alvarez continued this theme in his anthology *The New Poetry* (1962), in which he calls for English poets to "remain immune from the disease so often found in English culture: gentility." He went on to establish himself as one of the foremost critics of poetry in the 1960s. Scholar Christopher Ricks gave him a limited accolade by opining that Alvarez is a good reviewer because "he can tell the difference between a good poem and a bad one. . . . You can usually trust his choices but not his arguments."

Alvarez turned to novels in the 1970s, writing the highly regarded *Hunt* (1978), about a poker player who is unlucky in love; and *Day of Atonement* (1991), describing the London underworld. His nonfiction works include *Feeding the Rat* (1988), a biography of mountaineer Mo Anthoine; and *The Savage God* (1971), a widely read discussion of suicide. Critic Stephen Pile summarized Alvarez thus: "A bit of a poet and a bit less of a novelist, he is best known for . . . writing *The Savage God,* a celebrated study of that whole dark subject."

Other Works by A. Alvarez

Night: An Exploration of Night Life, Night Language, Sleep and Dreams. New York: Norton, 1995.
Where Did It All Go Right? An Autobiography. New York: Morrow, 1999.

Ambler, Eric (Eliot Reed) (1909–1998)
novelist, screenwriter

Born in London, Eric Ambler was the oldest of three children. His parents, Alfred Percy and Amy Madeleine Andrews Ambler, performed in theatrical reviews. While studying engineering at the University of London, Ambler wrote songs and sketches for vaudeville acts and performed in a comedy double act.

In 1935 Ambler shifted his focus to writing thrillers, which were not then considered real literature. However, realizing that spy novels could deal with current issues and ideological conflicts, Ambler built the plot of his first book, *The Dark Frontier* (1936), around the development of a nuclear weapon. In *The Mask of Dimitrios* (1939), generally considered his masterpiece, an English mystery writer investigating the death of a spy gets caught up in arms deals and Balkan politics. Ambler's first six books, says critic Peter Lewis, "effected a virtual rev-olution of the thriller, making it a vehicle for thoughtful political fiction for the first time."

Soon after his marriage to American fashion reporter Louise Crombie, Ambler joined the army in 1940 and produced nearly 100 films for the British War Office. After the war, in addition to novels, he wrote and produced movies. In 1958 he moved to Hollywood, where he created a television series about private investigators called *Checkmate.* Several of his novels, including *The Mask of Dimitrios* and *Topkapi,* were made into films.

Considered the father of the modern spy thriller, Ambler received several awards for his novels, which are peopled with believable characters and driven by real-world politics. In 1953 his screenplay for *The Cruel Sea* was nominated for an Academy Award. He was named a Grand Master by the Mystery Writers of America in 1975 and received the first Golden Dagger Award from the Veterans of the OSS in 1989. Novelist John LE CARRÉ, also a master of the genre, has described Ambler's novels as "the well into which everybody had dipped." Reviewer George Grella attributes his enduring appeal to "the unique Ambler touch," which is "urbane and ironic" and elevates the spy novel "to a sophisticated examination of the methods and moralities of modern international intrigue."

Other Works by Eric Ambler

Epitaph for a Spy. 1928. Reprint, New York: Vintage, 2002.
Here Lies: An Autobiography. London: Weidenfeld and Nicolson, 1985.
Journey into Fear. 1940. Reprint, New York: Amereon, 1998.

A Work about Eric Ambler

Ambrosetti, Ronald. *Eric Ambler.* New York: Twayne, 1994.

Amis, Kingsley (Robert Markham)
(1922–1995) *novelist, poet, nonfiction writer*

Kingsley Amis was born in London to William Amis, a clerk for Colman's Mustard, and Rosa

Lucas Amis. He was educated at the City of London School and Oxford, where he met his lifelong friend, the poet Philip LARKIN. From Oxford he went on to lecture in English Literature at the University College at Swansea.

While at Oxford and during his early years at Swansea, Amis wrote some well-received poetry, but it was with his first novel, *Lucky Jim* (1954), that he came to public attention. Drawing on his own experiences, Amis wrote of Jim Dixon, an English lecturer at a provincial university who is surrounded by pretentious snobs and wealthy hangers-on of the arts. Jim, who it seems can do nothing right, has a series of comic misadventures and loses his academic job. His fortunes turn for the better when he begins to vocalize his hilariously nasty thoughts: "The bloody old towser-faced boot-faced totem-pole on a crap reservation, Dixon thought. 'You bloody old towser-faced boot-faced totem-pole on a crap reservation,' he said." Jim is representative of a new class of person in postwar England, a member of the hitherto less-privileged classes who by talent and study are beginning to make inroads into the bastions of the traditionally privileged. Novelist David LODGE commented on the novel's significance for him: "*Lucky Jim* was another magic book for me—and for most English readers of my age and background, upwardly mobile, scholarship-winning, first-generation university graduates—for it established precisely the linguistic register we needed to articulate our sense of social identity, a precarious balance of independence and self-doubt, irony and hope." The novel placed Amis in the company of other contemporary writers whom critics labeled ANGRY YOUNG MEN.

Critics are divided about *Take a Girl Like You* (1960). Many believe it is Amis's best work, while just as many feel it is marred by a misogynistic plot. In this book Patrick Standish attempts to seduce virginal Jenny Bunn. He gives her an ultimatum: "I can't carry on any longer as we are. I've tried but it's too much of a strain. I love you and want to sleep with you. I can't go on seeing you and not." He ultimately succeeds only when she is

drunk. The work is fraught with a sort of moral ambivalence and marks a turn in Amis's "comic" fiction toward darker themes. Malcolm BRADBURY praised the work: "It opened the way for Amis to take on a new kind of writing, in which the 1960s mood of sexual liberation and then of growing male-female conflict were to be dominant themes." Around this time, Amis became a public figure, and many critics feel that his time and energies became dissipated in television appearances, literary squabbles with other authors, and side projects such as his "Amis on Drink" column for *Penthouse.*

In the 1960s Amis published many novels, including *One Fat Englishman* (1963), whose titular hero is the obese and disagreeable publisher Roger H. St. John W. Micheldene. Under the pseudonym Robert Markham, he published *The James Bond Dossier* (1964), a mock-scholarly study of the Bond novels, followed under his own name by a spy novel, *The Anti-Death League* (1966), in which he expresses an essentially atheistic world view. *The Green Man* (1969) is a supernatural story set in a country hotel. In 1973 he published a detective story, *The Riverside Villa Murder,* and to end that decade he published *Collected Poems 1944–1979* (1979).

Amis's best novel from the 1980s, *The Old Devils* (1986), takes place among a group of aging drinkers in Wales. Critic James Wolcott describes it as "so dense with booze that the book seems sunken, subaquatic, its retired Welsh sots trying to remain standing in an aquarium stocked with gin and drifting hunks of scenery." It won the BOOKER PRIZE.

Amis was knighted in 1990 and the following year published his *Memoirs,* wherein he settles old scores with his many literary and personal enemies. Amis's son Martin AMIS has been publishing novels since the 1970s and has become nearly as popular and respected as his father. Kingsley Amis will be remembered for his wildly funny comedies and his experiments with genre fiction. As scholar Robert Bell put it, "The funniest writer of our time is also one of the most troubling."

Other Works by Kingsley Amis

Girl, 20. New York: Harcourt Brace, 1972.
That Uncertain Feeling. New York: Harcourt Brace, 1956.

Works about Kingsley Amis

Amis, Martin. *Experience: A Memoir.* New York: Talk Miramax Books, 2000.
Bradford, Richard. *Lucky Him: The Biography of Kingsley Amis.* London: Peter Owen, 2001.
Jacobs, Eric. *Kingsley Amis: A Biography.* New York: St. Martin's Press, 1995.

Amis, Martin (1949–) *novelist, essayist, screenwriter*

Born in Swansea, Wales, and educated in Oxford, Martin Amis is the son of author Kingsley AMIS and his wife, Hilly. Amis's first novel, *The Rachel Papers* (1973), featuring a lusty teenage narrator, earned him the Somerset Maugham Prize. His second novel, *Dead Babies* (1975), is an account of a decadent weekend at an English country house that goes horribly awry. Later stories and novels deal with disasters of a more political nature, including the collection *Einstein's Monsters* (1987), about nuclear war; *Time's Arrow* (1991), a meditation on the Holocaust that created controversy by suggesting memory can distort such historical events; and *The Information* (1995), in which a frustrated novelist decides to ruin his best friend's political ambitions.

Amis prefers to depict emotionally trying situations rather than well-adjusted characters. In the murder novel *London Fields* (1989) he writes, "Who but Tolstoy has really made happiness swing on the page?" Many of Amis's novels depict characters who are emotionally or spiritually numb at the outset but attain some sort of renewal.

Amis makes use of science fiction and fantasy conventions in much of his work. *Dead Babies,* for instance, takes place in the near future and features a protagonist who has become rich running an abortion factory. *Other People, A Mystery Story* (1981) takes place in an afterlife. In *Time's Arrow,* time reverses itself, taking an elderly former Nazi back through the 20th century. More conventional is Amis's screenplay for the 1980 movie *Saturn 3,* in which a madman and his killer robot attempt to destroy a research station on Saturn's moon Titan.

Amis has been likened to a rock star by the British press, who watched closely as in recent years he secured unprecedented large advances from publishers, learned he had an illegitimate daughter, divorced his wife, married fellow writer Isabel Fonseca, and expressed a preference for inventive America over stodgy England. In his memoir *Experience* (2000), Amis laments the exhausting pace that comes with being a famous novelist: "You arrive in each city and present yourself to the media; after that, in the evening . . . you appear at the bookshop and perform."

Early in Amis's career, he held editorial positions at the *London Times Literary Supplement,* the *Observer,* and *The New Statesman.* After his novel-writing career began, he regularly contributed essays and reviews to the *New York Times Book Review, Vanity Fair, Atlantic Monthly, Esquire,* and *The New Yorker.* Many of these essays are collected in *The Moronic Inferno* (1986) and *Visiting Mrs. Nabokov and Other Excursions* (1993). Critic Victoria N. Alexander, writing in *Antioch Review,* argues that Amis has successfully positioned himself as the intellectual heir of Saul Bellow and Vladimir Nabokov and credits him with "ruthlessly brilliant comedy."

Other Works by Martin Amis

Experience: A Memoir. New York: Talk Miramax Books, 2000.
Heavy Water and Other Stories. New York: Harmony Books, 1999.
Money. New York: Viking, 1984.
Night Train. New York: Harmony Books, 1997.
Success. New York: Harmony Books, 1978.

Andrews, Corinne

See WEST, REBECCA.

Angry Young Men

In 1952 the novelist William COOPER denounced the "experimental novel," favored by writers such as Samuel BECKETT. He believed these novels ignored such realistic issues as unemployment and class warfare, diminished the relevance of fiction, and fostered an elitist mentality among writers. His novel *Scenes from Provincial Life* (1950) reintroduced the techniques of the realist novel and emphasized the importance of an individual's own experiences as a way to learn about the world.

Cooper's novel appealed to a group of young writers, including John OSBORNE, Kingsley AMIS, Malcolm BRADBURY, and John BRAINE. These writers were searching for a sense of stability in the turbulent postwar British society and applauded Cooper's rejection of experimental fiction, in addition to his cynical view of middle-class materialism and concern for social status. In 1956 the journalist J. B. PRIESTLEY described Osborne as an "angry young man." The name was soon extended to the entire group who, along with Osborne, despised the bourgeoisie.

The level of their "anger" differed. In Osborne's play *Look Back in Anger* (1956), the main character, Jimmy Porter, though a university graduate, runs a market stall in the working-class community. In Braine's novel *Room at the Top* (1957), the protagonist Joe Lampton derides materialism but privately craves the affluent possessions he lacks. Amis, in *Lucky Jim* (1952), portrays the life of Jim Dixon, who strives to attain a position as a professor even though he views himself as a victim of the system.

Despite their differences, these characters share a helplessness and frustration with the social system. An inability to change British society ultimately unites them. The writers of the Angry Young Men movement, however, did successfully offer an alternative to abstract modern fiction. They led a return to clearly delineated plots, precise character portrayal, and the use of lucid language to communicate ideas. The critic Kenneth Allsop has asserted that the movement had a stronger technical influence than a social one, arguing that "if you accept that a novel's function is to be the image of the society it draws its life from, it is precisely there that the new writing fails." But at the same time, the authors exhibited "an innovating, restless talent . . . that was needed."

A Work about the Angry Young Men
Taylor, David J. *After the War: The Novel and English Society Since 1945*. London: Chatto and Windus, 1993.

Anthony, C. L.
See SMITH, DODIE.

Arden, John (1930–) *playwright, critic, novelist*

John Arden was born in Yorkshire, England, to Charles Alwyn Arden, a glass factory manager, and Annie Elizabeth Arden. Arden was educated at Cambridge and the Edinburgh College of Art, where he studied architecture. In 1957 his first play, *The Waters of Babylon*, the story of a pimp who cleverly deceives those around him, was accepted for production by the Royal Court Theatre. Arden sets up the unappealing nature of his main character, Krank, in the opening scene: "Why don't I wash my cups and plate more often than only once a week? 'Cause I am man of filthy habit in my house, is why."

Arden's early work earned him a place among the ANGRY YOUNG MEN, a group including Kingsley AMIS, John OSBORNE, and John WAIN. This group was characterized by their scorn for both aristocratic tradition and the new British welfare state. Arden's play *Live Like Pigs* (1958), for example, traces the struggle between tenants in a housing project and the British Housing Authority. "Why don't you folk leave us alone?" declares one of the main characters, Rosie, "We didn't come here cos we wanted; but now we are here you ought to leave us be." The *New York Times* called the play "[r]ibald, brawling, roaring."

These early works also reveal Arden's Marxist analysis of class struggle, manifested in the everyday battles that shape the lives of his main characters. In his introductory note to *Live Like Pigs* he states, "When I wrote this play I intended it to be not so much a social documentary as a study of differing ways of life brought sharply into conflict and both losing their own particular virtues under the stress of intolerance and misunderstanding." Arden's first plays frequently have only the barest of sets, so that the focus is on the dialog exchanges between his characters. The lack of elaborate staging often gives these dramas an improvisational feel.

Named the "most promising playwright" by the *London Evening Standard* in 1960, Arden captivated audiences through his examination of the character of English life during and after the turbulent years of the 1960s and 1970s. Much of his later work was greatly influenced by his collaboration with his wife, Margaretta D'Arcy. Together they wrote a number of plays, radio dramas, and documentaries for television. In 1974 they received an award from the British Arts Council for *The Island of the Mighty*. First produced in 1972, this historical play explores the themes of exploitation and oppression in the context of Great Britain's relationship to the rest of the world.

Arden has moved away from the theater because of changing working conditions for playwrights that put profitability above the creative process. These shifts, he claims, have inhibited his ability to express himself fully as an artist. He has, however, continued his interest in the stage, and in 1977 published *To Present Pretence: Essays on the Theatre and its Public,* a critical analysis of the modern theater.

Arden's solo radio play, *The Old Man Sleeps Alone,* (1982) was included in *Best Radio Plays of 1982.* His novel *Silence Among the Weapons* (1982) is set in the period of the Roman Empire and discusses the important influence that Rome had over the people of the Mediterranean. The novel was a finalist for the BOOKER PRIZE in 1982.

Many critics consider Arden one of the most original voices in modern British theater. As John Russell Taylor writes in the introduction to Arden's *Three Plays* (1975), "Arden has continued to shatter any preconceptions we might have about what to expect from him almost before they have formed in our minds. . . . Arden is a genuine original, and far more important than the differences between his plays and those of his contemporaries is the internal consistency which makes them a logical, coherent progression, all first, foremost, and unmistakably the product of one exceptional mind."

Other Works by John Arden
The Business of Good Government. New York: Grove Press, 1963.
Left-Handed Liberty. New York: Grove Press, 1965.
Serjeant Musgrave's Dance. New York: Grove Press, 1960.

Works about John Arden
Malick, Javid. *Toward a Theatre of the Oppressed: The Dramaturgy of John Arden.* Ann Arbor: University of Michigan Press, 1995.
Wike, Jonathan. *John Arden and Margaretta D'Arcy.* New York: Garland, 1995.

Ashton, Winifred
See DANE, CLEMENCE.

Ashton-Warner, Sylvia (1908–1984)
novelist, nonfiction writer
Sylvia Ashton-Warner was born in Stratford, New Zealand, to a father crippled by arthritis, so her mother, Margaret Warner, supported the family by teaching in remote country schools. At first Ashton-Warner resisted becoming a teacher, fearing the profession would stifle her creativity as a writer and painter. However, she graduated from Auckland Teachers' College and, from 1938 to 1955, she worked with her husband Keith Henderson teaching Maori children to read. After Henderson's death in 1969, she was invited to set up an alternative school in Colorado, an experience she described in her nonfiction work *Spearpoint:*

Teacher in America (1972). At her death, Ashton-Warner was recognized as a pioneer in both New Zealand literature and education.

Ashton-Warner's first novel, *Spinster* (1959), is also her most acclaimed. Anna Vorontosov is a single teacher working in a Maori school who tries to integrate the inner world of her emotions with the outer reality of her teaching. Ashton-Warner's decision to tell Anna's story in the present tense, interrupted only by the voices of her young students, "conveys the poetry and color of a special kind of experience from within the mind of a woman of sensibility," according to reviewer Ruth Blackman.

The nonfiction *Teacher* (1963), based on Ashton-Warner's success with teaching struggling learners to read, expresses her philosophy of teaching, which builds on the knowledge students already have and the words that have meaning for them. The book won her international recognition as an innovative educator.

Ashton-Warner's novel *Greenstone* (1967), while also considered innovative, received mixed reviews. To critic Elinor Baumbach, only the Maori characters seem real. However, reviewer Eleanor Dienstag says this fable for adults expresses two themes that recur throughout Ashton-Warner's work: ". . . the channeling of destructive energies into creative ones . . . and her dream of two different but complementary cultures, the Maori and the Western."

Among Ashton-Warner's three autobiographical works, *I Passed This Way* (1979) is the most complete. Reviewer Linda B. Osborne notes that Ashton-Warner "builds her self-portrait through a series of images that hold for her a special meaning," which is consistent with her belief that the "key vocabulary" consists of words that evoke deep feeling and make a child eager to use these words in reading and writing.

In 1982 Ashton-Warner was recognized as a Member of the Order of the British Empire (MBE) for her services to New Zealand education and literature. *Sylvia,* a feature film based on her autobiographies, was produced by Michael Firth in 1985.

A Work about Sylvia Ashton-Warner

Hood, Lynley. *Sylvia! The Biography of Sylvia Ashton-Warner.* New York: Viking, 1989.

Atwood, Margaret (1939–   ) *novelist, poet*

Margaret Atwood was born in Ottawa, Ontario, to Carl Atwood, an entomologist, and Margaret Killam Atwood, a nutritionist. She spent her childhood accompanying her father on his researches in the wilderness of Quebec. She graduated from the University of Toronto with a B.A. in 1961, received an M.A. from Radcliffe in 1962, and did some graduate work at Harvard University, beginning a thesis on Gothic fiction.

Atwood's first published work, *Double Persephone* (1961), was a book of poetry exploring the mythological figure Persephone. Her most important collection of verse, *The Circle Game* (1966), uses Gothic imagery to explore issues of gender. For example, the first poem, "This Is a Photograph of Me," is narrated by a dead woman: "The photograph was taken / the day after I drowned." Her first novel, *Edible Woman* (1969), is a darkly comic tale of a woman who fears marriage and stops eating.

Atwood's most celebrated novel, *The Handmaid's Tale* (1985), is set in a horrifying future society, Gilead, where women are condemned to illiteracy and servitude. The novel purports to be the recorded narration of Offred, a servant: "Where the edges are we aren't sure, they vary, according to the attacks and counterattacks; but this is the centre, where nothing moves. The Republic of Gilead, said Aunt Lydia, knows no bounds. Gilead is within you." Critic Sandra Tomc sees the novel as a critique not merely of male oppression but also of American domination over Canada: "In the nightmare future she imagines, women have succumbed to a totalizing patriarchy. Appropriately, given Atwood's conflation of feminism and nationalism, Canada, in some analogous gesture, has succumbed to its totalizing southern neighbor."

The Robber Bride (1993) focuses on the demonic Zenia's haunting of her three friends, robbing them of their money and men. This book has dark Gothic undertones: "Zenia, with her dark hair sleeked down by the rain, wet and shivering, standing on the back step as she had done once before, long ago. Zenia, who had been dead for five years." *Alias Grace* (1996), which continues Atwood's exploration of gender and power, is based on the true story of Grace Marks, a servant accused of murdering her master in 1843.

Atwood's most recent novel, *Blind Assassin* (2000), tells three interconnected stories, beginning with a woman, Iris Griffin, telling of her sister's death in 1945. This novel won the BOOKER PRIZE. Fellow Canadian writer Alice MUNRO comments: "It's easy to appreciate the grand array of Margaret Atwood's work—the novels, the stories, the poems, in all their power and grace and variety. This work in itself has opened up the gates for a recognition of Canadian writing all over the world."

Other Works by Margaret Atwood

Cat's Eye. New York: Doubleday, 1989.
Power Politics. New York: Harper & Row, 1973.

Works about Margaret Atwood

Cooke, Nathalie. *Margaret Atwood: A Biography.* Toronto: ECW Press, 1998.
Nischik, Reingard M., ed. *Margaret Atwood: Works and Impact.* Rochester, N.Y.: Camden House 2000.

Auden, Wystan Hugh (1907–1973) *poet, dramatist, critic, librettist*

W. H. Auden was born in York, England, the youngest son of George Augustus Auden, a medical doctor with far-ranging interests. His mother, Constance Rosalie Bicknell Auden, was a nurse and a devout Anglican, who passed on her love of music to her son. The Auden family was Scandinavian in origin, and Auden was brought up on the Icelandic sagas. The year after he was born, his father became medical inspector of schools in the industrial city of Birmingham. York and Birmingham both left their mark, for Auden's favorite rural and urban landscapes remained those of England's Pennine

uplands (celebrated in "In Praise of Limestone," 1948) and modern industrial cities.

Auden grew up interested in science and literature and considered becoming a mining engineer, but at 15 he determined to become a great poet, though he remained attracted to science. His broad and erudite reading led to verse abounding in scientific and technical terms. Auden became both a private poet and a public spokesman—the intellectual conscience of the generation that grew up in the 1930s between two world wars.

After his education at St. Edmund's School and Gresham's in Norfolk, Auden entered Oxford in 1925. At St. Edmund's he met his lifelong friend, novelist Christopher ISHERWOOD; at Oxford he met fellow poets Louis MACNEICE and Cecil DAY LEWIS. While at Oxford he fell under the spell of T. S. ELIOT, who exerted a brief influence; but more durable were earlier influences such as Anglo-Saxon and Middle English poetry and the writers Thomas HARDY and W. B. YEATS.

Upon graduating from Oxford, Auden spent 1928–29 in Berlin. He was a natural teacher and returned to become a schoolteacher. During the 1930s he went to Iceland with MacNeice and to Spain and China with Isherwood. On the eve of World War II, he and Isherwood emigrated to the United States, where Auden taught at various universities. America gave him an international point of view and helped him forge a truly international English style.

In 1939 Auden met Chester Kallman, who became his life's companion. The two men collaborated on several opera libretti, including Stravinsky's *The Rake's Progress* (1951). In 1946 Auden became an American citizen. He returned to Oxford late in life to become professor of poetry (1956–61) and writer-in-residence at his old college. He died in Vienna and is buried in Kirchstetten, Austria.

Critical Analysis

Auden was a complex and versatile poet who produced numerous volumes of poetry and criticism. He frequently rewrote his work, thus complicating its study. Auden believed that spheres of action and art are separate and that "poetry makes nothing happen." Nevertheless, he recognized the power of words and wielded them with care. He removed from his canon poems he found less than truthful.

Auden's literary career has three major phases that may be labeled psychological, political, and religious. During the earliest phase, from 1928 through the mid-1930s, his poetry was influenced by the psychologists and psychoanalysts Sigmund FREUD, John Layard, Homer Lane, and Georg Groddeck. As Stephen SPENDER remarked, Auden's early verse diagnoses ills in individuals and the body politic: "Sometimes Auden's poems are more symptomatic than curative; sometimes they concentrate . . . on the idea of a cure." The poem "Petition" (1929), beginning "Sir, no man's enemy," illustrates the difficulty of the early clinical verse. To this period belong *Poems 1930, The Orators,* and *The Dance of Death.*

Auden's second, or political, phase began with *Spain* (1937), written as a result of first-hand experience of the Spanish Civil War. It lasted through the early 1940s and coincides with the period of Auden's world travels, embracing the verse plays written with Isherwood: *The Dog beneath the Skin* (1935), *The Ascent of F6* (1936), and *On the Frontier* (1938). The first is a Brechtian parable, the second about a mountaineering expedition, and the third concerns two families living in hostile states. At this time Auden was strongly influenced by marxist ideas, though he was never a member of the Communist Party.

The third major phase began with Auden's emigration to the United States and his return to religion. He rejoined the Anglican Church in New York, and dominant influences were Søren Kierkegaard and Reinhold Niebuhr. To this period belong the long poems *New Year Letter* (1940), *For the Time Being* (1945), and *The Age of Anxiety* (1947). Also called *The Double Man, New Year Letter* follows the Kierkegaardian division of life into aesthetic, ethical and religious spheres. Auden described *For the Time Being,* written to honor his deceased mother, as a Christmas oratorio. In *The Age of Anxiety* four lone individuals try to make sense of their lives. This period also includes what

many believe was Auden's finest decade, the 1950s, when he published *Nones* (1951), *The Shield of Achilles* (1955), and *Homage to Clio* (1960). An example of the masterly style of this period is "In Praise of Limestone," which ends:

> . . . when I try to imagine a faultless love
> Or the life to come, what I hear is
>   the murmur
> Of underground streams, what I see
>   is a limestone landscape . . .

Some critics subdivide this period, noting that from the 1960s until his death, Auden wrote the cozy, domestic poems contained in *About the House* (1966), *Epistle to a Godson* (1972), and *Thank you, Fog* (1974).

Auden's poetry is, as Auden scholar Richard Hoggart observes, characteristically that of an "abstracting and generalizing intelligence." Auden himself said that his subject was not nature, but mankind in its relation to nature—often a manmade nature. His poems view human life from a distance, as from a great height, set within a dwarfing geological or evolutionary frame. Although his poetry is concrete and specific, it is also abstract and not at all sensuous. Auden's poems contain striking images, but they are images devoid of color, smell, or taste. This is not a visual poetry. Consider, for example, the poem "May," which opens: "May with its light behaving/Stirs vessel, eye, and limb."

Despite their abstractness, however, Auden's poems can be most moving because of, not despite, their complex thought. Consider the famous "Lullaby" (1937), which begins "Lay your sleeping head, my love"; or "Musée des Beaux Arts" (1939), with its seemingly casual colloquial opening, "About suffering they were never wrong,/The Old Masters . . ."

Auden's technical expertise and virtuosity were such that he was able to write poems of all kinds and to bring new luster to complex and outmoded kinds. His elegies for Sigmund FREUD, W. B. YEATS, and Henry JAMES obey classic conventions but are contemporary. He rehabilitated the ode and has left many fine ballads and sonnets. Auden is also celebrated for a form of poem he wrote throughout his career: the *paysage moralisé*, or moralized landscape. From the German poet Rilke he learned to regard the human in terms of the nonhuman. Thus, Auden endows landscape with human characteristics, viewing human beings as products of different kinds of landscape or environment, as in the sequence *Bucolics* (1953), about those who inhabit woods, mountains, lakes, plains, streams, and islands. "In Praise of Limestone" is perhaps the finest example of this genre.

Like his themes, Auden's style changed over the decades. The early poems were riddling and obscure partly because they were studded with references understood only by a few friends. Thus, "Petition" opens with the deliberately snarled syntax of "Sir, no man's enemy, forgiving all/But will its negative inversion, be prodigal." The early poems are also much indebted to Anglo-Saxon poetry. For example, "The Three Companions" begins, "O where are you going?" (1931) with hammer-beat rhythms and striking alliteration and assonance, giving it the vigor of Anglo-Saxon verse.

In his later years, Auden developed a more relaxed and limber style, distinguished by a rich, exuberant, and dazzling vocabulary and by verse often based on syllabics as well as, or instead of, strong and weak accents. Auden is regarded by many as the 20th-century's preeminent poet in English. For 40 years he influenced and inspired generations of poets on both sides of the Atlantic. As John Hollander observed in a tribute on Auden's 60th birthday, he was "the most articulate and cosmopolitan of all English poets born in this century." He was also a perceptive and rewarding critic in volumes such as *The Enchafèd Flood* (1950), *The Dyers's Hand* (1962), and *Selected Essays* (1964).

Works about W. H. Auden

Bahlke, George W. *Critical Essays on Auden*. Boston: G. K. Hall, 1991.

Carpenter, Humphrey. *W. H. Auden: A Biography*. Boston: Houghton Mifflin, 1981.

Davenport-Hines, Richard. *Auden*. New York: Pantheon, 1995.

Haffenden, John, ed. *W. H. Auden: The Critical Heritage*. Boston: Routledge & Kegan Paul, 1983.

Hecht, Anthony, *The Hidden Law: The Poetry of W. H. Auden*. Cambridge, Mass.: Harvard University Press, 1993.

Mendelson, Edward. *Early Auden*. New York: Viking, 1981.

———. *Later Auden*. New York: Farrar, Straus & Giroux, 2000.

Smith, Stan. *W. H. Auden*. New York: Blackwell, 1985.

Ayckbourn, Alan (1939–) *playwright, director*

Alan Ayckbourn is the only son of Horace Ayckbourn, a former first violinist of the London Symphony Orchestra, and Irene Maud Worley, a writer of romances. His mother divorced his father when Alan was five and then contracted a second failed marriage. It is probable these broken marriages contributed, along with Ayckbourn's own first unsuccessful marriage at an early age, to the critical portrayal of marriage in his plays, which show increasing disillusionment with the institution.

Ayckbourn's grandparents were music-hall performers, and early in his own career, he alternated acting with stage direction. He toured with Donald Wolfit's repertory company, but his most important career move was joining the Stephen Joseph Theatre in Scarborough, Yorkshire, in 1959. Stephen Joseph, son of actress Hermione Gingold, encouraged Ayckbourn to write for the stage. On Joseph's death in the late 1960s, Ayckbourn returned to Scarborough as a theatrical director after a few years producing radio drama for the BBC (British Broadcasting Corporation) in Leeds.

Ayckbourn became a prolific and successful writer of sharp, sometimes bittersweet comedies about British middle-class and suburban manners and mores. The Stephen Joseph Theatre serves as an ideal proving ground for his plays. Ayckbourn writes "team" dramas for performance by a known troupe of actors for a familiar audience in an intimate setting. Since the early 1970s, his pattern has been to write a play for summer production in Scarborough, followed by a season in London a year later.

Ayckbourn's first few plays, written under the pseudonym Roland Allen, have not been published. His first published play, *Standing Room Only* (1961) is about overpopulation resulting from a monumental traffic jam. *Relatively Speaking* (1967) established Ayckbourn as a presence on the London stage. Modeled on Oscar Wilde's *The Importance of Being Earnest,* the play substitutes Ayckbourn's own brand of jokes for Wildean wit and epigram.

In Ayckbourn's plays, setting is as important as character. *Relatively Speaking* shows his ingenuity in staging by simultaneously presenting two juxtaposed households. More elaborate staging is deployed in *How the Other Half Loves* (1971), in which an upper-class household is superimposed upon a lower-middle-class one. The audience is able to distinguish the Fosters' tasteful abode from the Phillips' cluttered nest through color and style contrasts. Ayckbourn's sense of timing and sequence are impeccable. The handling of time in this play is unusual, as events do not occur in chronological order. Critic Albert Kalson calls this play, which made Ayckbourn's name on Broadway, one of the playwright's "most felicitous concoctions."

Absurd Person Singular (1973) follows the antics of three couples (upper-, middle-, and lower-class) who join each other in a series of Christmas reunions, each act taking place in one of the couples' kitchens. The play, in which the battle of the sexes is enhanced by class warfare, won the *Evening Standard* Award for the year's best comedy.

Ayckbourn's most popular drama is his trilogy *The Norman Conquests* (1974), which he called his first "offstage action play." The three dramas it comprises—*Table Manners, Living Together,* and *Round and Round the Garden*—take place during a single weekend in different parts of the same country house. Action and conversation that take place "off" in one play are picked up in another. The three interlinked dramas were intended to be presented on three successive days, like the action itself. However, each play is self-contained so they may be viewed in any order.

The success of *The Norman Conquests* is due largely to the in-depth development of its characters. Norman, a scruffy librarian, is a compulsive philanderer, manipulator, and narcissist. Married to practical Ruth, Norman plans to take his sister-in-law, Annie, away for a weekend of illicit passion. (Unmarried Annie could use a break, as her life has been sacrificed to looking after her bedridden mother.) Reg, Ruth's brother, and his wife Sarah come to relieve Annie. However, they are not "in the know," believing that she will be weekending with her dithering old flame, Tom. When she discovers Annie's secret, Sarah resolves to overthrow the lovers' plans, until Norman propositions her as well. At this point Norman's wife returns, intent on retrieving her husband.

The winner of numerous awards, *The Norman Conquests* marked a new mood in Ayckbourn comedy—more bitter and astringent and with more rounded characters than those of his 1960s comedies. The mood of Ayckbourn's comedy has darkened even further since the mid-1980s.

In *Sisterly Feelings* (1981) Ayckbourn explores alternative endings and different permutations and combinations of plot, depending on a coin toss in the second scene. After his wife's burial, Ralph Matthews takes his daughters, Abigail and Dorcas, to the park where he first proposed to his wife. Both girls are unhappily married; both are attracted to young Simon Grimshaw. They toss a coin to see who will walk back to town with him, and the winner of the toss will have an affair with him. After that, each woman must decide what to do, but in the end each returns to her unsatisfactory spouse in the play's unvarying final act. Though the playwright sets out to explore how chance and choice affect our lives, the play's ultimate effect is deterministic.

Ayckbourn's drama combines conventional subject matter with experimental stage techniques in the handling of time and space. Some find a disproportion of manner to matter in his plays. On the other hand, his work shows continuous experimentation and increasing skill, particularly in character development, as well as the ability to distill the essence of what is universally funny in relations between British suburbanites. It seems likely that, of his many plays, some of those discussed here will survive for years to come.

Works about Alan Ayckbourn

Billington, Michael. *Alan Ayckbourn.* New York: Grove Press, 1984.

Dukore, Bernard F. *Alan Ayckbourn: A Casebook.* New York: Garland, 1991.

Page, Malcolm, ed. *File on Ayckbourn.* London: Methuen, 1989.

Aydy, Catherine
See TENNANT, EMMA.

Bainbridge, Beryl Margaret (1933–)
novelist

Beryl Bainbridge was born in Liverpool, England, to Richard Bainbridge, an unsuccessful salesman, and Winifred Bainbridge. The couple quarreled constantly, and Beryl's childhood was tumultuous and unhappy. With some formal training in dance, she ran away to London at age 15 and began an acting career that lasted until 1972.

After years of acting in repertory theaters and on the radio, and after a failed marriage, Bainbridge began her writing career. She has acknowledged the influence of Charles Dickens and Robert Louis Stevenson, whose work she imitated as a child, and her fiction often explores the violence, ambitions, and everyday lives of the lower middle classes. *Harriet Said* (1973), Bainbridge's first novel, includes most of these elements. Based on an Australian newspaper story, the novel retells a complicated murder plot in which a young girl seduces an older male neighbor to kill her mother. Because of its violence and immoral characters, the novel went unpublished for more than a decade.

Later in her career Bainbridge wrote historical novels based on much more well-known events. Her Whitbread Award–winning novel, *Every Man for Himself* (1996), is based on the sinking of the *Titanic*. In a manner very reminiscent of James Cameron's motion picture *Titanic* (1997), Bainbridge's novel places prominent American figures on the ship (for instance, a young man with ties to J. P. Morgan), tells a coming-of-age story, and details the social interactions on the ship before it sank in 1912. In a passage indicative of the novel's attention to social interaction, the narrator comments, "I found Lady Duff Gordon entertaining. . . . She had a long thin face and a haughty expression, but that was just her style."

Bainbridge has been criticized for unbelievable plots that contain often repulsive violence, such as episodes of stalking and rape, but despite this criticism she is a well-regarded novelist. The scholar and critic Frank Kermode has written that Bainbridge is a unique and powerful writer and describes her as "an odd and in a mutated way fantastic talent." Another scholar, Barbara Millard, agrees: "Bainbridge has emerged as one of the most original . . . of contemporary British novelists."

Other Works by Beryl Bainbridge
The Birthday Boys. New York: Carroll & Graf, 1994.
Winter Garden. New York: Braziller, 1981.

A Work about Beryl Bainbridge
Wenno, Elisabeth. *Ironic Formula in the Novels of Beryl Bainbridge.* Göteborg, Sweden: Acta Universitatis Gothoburgensis, 1993.

Ballard, James Graham (1930–   )
novelist

J. G. Ballard was born in Shanghai, China, to James Ballard, a business executive, and Edna Johnston Ballard. In 1937 Japan seized Shanghai, and while other families fled, the Ballards remained, convinced that the British Empire's battle fleet based in Singapore guaranteed them protection. After Japan bombed Pearl Harbor, however, the Ballards were captured and sent to a prison camp outside of Shanghai. Ballard became separated from his family and found himself struggling to survive on his own. Eventually, he chose to join his family in the prison camp at the expense of freedom.

After World War II the Ballards moved back to Shepperton, England. Later he would remark, "Although I've lived in Britain for over 50 years I suspect I still see everything through a visitor's eyes, and I think that gives my fiction its particular perspective, [a] heightened awareness of the ordinary."

The experience of war haunts Ballard's first four novels, in each of which a global catastrophe, linked to the unbalancing of an ecosystem, destroys civilization. In *The Wind from Nowhere* (1962), high-velocity winds literally blow away human civilization and all its surface artifacts. Rising world temperatures cause massive flooding in *The Drowned World* (1962), while drought plagues the Earth in *The Burning World* (1964). Finally, in *The Crystal World* (1966) living creatures are transformed into crystal statues.

Ballard's early novels are steeped in images of desolation that reach back to the stress of his war-ravaged childhood and his separation from his family. (The 1964 death of Mary Matthews, whom he had married in 1953, only deepened his abiding sense of abandonment.) Thus, Ballard's landscapes, vacant of human life (often all life), are strange and terrifying. They are landscapes filled with recurrent images of decay and water, as in the opening of *The Crystal World:* "The darkness of the river . . . impressed Dr. Sanders. . . . [T]he surface of the water was still gray and sluggish, leaching away the somber tinctures of the collapsing vegetation along the banks." The image of the river water eating away at the vegetation on the bank evokes the mysterious crystal plague that is eating away at the living world. Moreover, this passage illustrates Ballard's "unmistakable style," which, according to filmmaker Michel Deville, "alternates between the bald and the baroque, the clinical sanity of the scientist and the raw, convulsive energy of Surrealism [the production of fantastic imagery through unnatural and incongruous combinations]."

Ballard's experiences before and during his Japanese internment formed the basis for two autobiographical novels: *Empire of the Sun* (1984) and its sequel, *The Kindness of Women* (1991). In the first book Ballard describes how numbingly routine death becomes for the barely teenaged boy: "Wars came early to Shanghai, overtaking each other like the tides that raced up the Yangtze and returned to this gaudy city all the coffins cast adrift from the funeral piers of the Chinese [embankment]."

In Ballard's trilogy *Crash* (1973), *Concrete Island* (1974), and *High Rise* (1975), concrete and metal replace water as the dominant image. The landscape, no longer natural, is wholly consumed by the concrete and steel of highways, buildings, and cars. Through graphic images of broken bones and bloody death, *Crash* portrays life as an open wound. The narrator, a fictional James Ballard, is part of a cult whose members purposefully crash their cars as a reaction against the unnaturalness of their lives and their world. While hospitalized from one such crash, the narrator thinks of the many types of wrecks that he and his now-dead mentor, Vaughan (killed in a car smashup), once visualized: "I think of the crashes of psychopaths, implausible accidents carried out with venom and self-disgust . . . the crashes . . . of manic-depressives crushed while making pointless U-turns . . . of sadistic . . . nurses decapitated in . . . crashes on complex interchanges." The litany in part numbs not only the pain of Vaughan's loss but also the narrator's guilt in feeling insufficient pain over that loss. Ballard, critic Peter Briggs writes, "seeks to identify things (and people made into things by the media) as external representations of the inner map of the contemporary psyche."

Other Works by J. G. Ballard

Cocaine Nights. Washington, D.C.: Counterpoint, 1996.
Rushing to Paradise. New York: Picador, 1994.
Super-Cannes. New York: Picador, 2001.

Works about J. G. Ballard

Luckhurst, Roger. *The Angle Between Two Walls: The Fiction of J. G. Ballard*. New York: St. Martin's Press, 1997.
Orr, Ken. *J. G. Ballard*. Vancouver, B.C.: Macmillan Library Reference, 1997.

Barker, Audrey Lillian (1918–   ) *short story writer, novelist*

A. L. Barker was born in St. Paul's Cray, Kent, England. Her father, Harry Barker, was an engineer; her mother, Elsie Dutton Barker, cleaned houses for a living. Barker attended primary and secondary county schools until the age of 16, when her father, who disapproved of her schooling, forced her to take a job with a clock-making firm. In 1949 Barker took a position with the BBC (British Broadcasting Corporation), where she remained employed until she retired in 1978.

Barker's first volume of short stories, *Innocents* (1947), won the Somerset Maugham Award. In "Submerged" she explores the antagonism between adults and youths, one of her favorite themes. Peter Hume, a young boy, decides that "it was his parents who really irritated him by their transparent tact. . . . It confirmed his suspicion that there was nothing but a great deal of willful mystery in adult affairs."

In later collections Barker featured female main characters, of varying age and social position, placed in traditional English settings. For example, in *Femina Real* (1971) she explores the strength and vulnerability of women as daughters, wives, mothers, and friends.

Barker's short story collections have been praised for their fresh vision in describing characters caught in extreme situations. Critic Francis King, reviewing *Life Stories* (1981), wrote that these qualities exist in her stories because Barker is concerned "with the jarring impact caused by a collision between innocence and experience." Reviewers have also described Barker's works as offbeat, surreal, memorable, and written with a commitment to language and craftsmanship. Awards she has won include the Cheltenham Festival Literary Award and the Katherine Mansfield Short Story Prize.

Although best known for her short stories, Barker has also attained limited recognition as a novelist. *The Gooseboy* (1987), her most popular and critically acclaimed novel, describes the dignity and attractiveness of a deformed boy living with a well-off family in southern France. David Profumo, writing in the *Times Literary Supplement*, commented, "If A. L. Barker is . . . 'a writer's writer,' her fiction admired by the few but not perhaps read by the many, it may well be because her novels to date have seldom enjoyed plots as enthralling and quirky as those that have made her short stories so distinctive."

Other Works by A. L. Barker

The Haunt. New York: Virago, 1995.
The Woman Who Talked to Herself. New York: Vintage, 1991.

Barker, George Granville (1913–1991) *poet*

George Barker was born in Loughton, Essex, England, to George Barker, a constable, and Marion Frances Taaffe Barker. He attended secondary school in London but dropped out at the age of 14. He then held a series of jobs ranging from garage mechanic to wallpaper designer. At 16, Barker decided he would be a poet. From 1930 onward he supported himself through writing and teaching at universities around the world. Barker had a long affair with novelist and poet Elizabeth SMART with whom he had four children.

Barker was 20 when he published his first book of poetry, *Thirty Preliminary Poems* (1933). Influenced by the poet Louis MACNEICE, Barker had a despairing concern for the social conditions of the time. In the poem "Elegy Number 1," he writes, "Lovers on Sunday in the rear seats of the cinemas / Kiss deep and dark, for is it the last kiss?"

T.S. ELIOT helped Barker publish his second collection of verse, *Poems* (1935). This volume, like his first, reflects his despair about life and his thoughts of death. The next year William Butler YEATS made Barker the youngest contributor in his *Oxford Book of Modern Verse* (1936).

One of Barker's most successful collections, *Eros in Dogma* (1944), combines love poems with elegiac laments about the burdens that external forces place on individuals. He sparked controversy for his use of erotic images in his long autobiographical poem *The True Confession of George Barker* (1950). This poem covered many of his common themes: the distortion of sex, an impenitent loss of faith in God, and the loss of love for other humans. Critic E. G. Burrows noted that while Barker often treated those themes with a lack of respect, "Behind the clever lines there is a tense battle being waged and it is Barker's genius to show us the value of this struggle and the toll it has taken even in the midst of his most urbane verses."

Although Barker won a handful of poetry awards in his career, including the Guinness prize and *Poetry* magazine's Levinson Prize, he remained overshadowed by the other acclaimed poets of his day, such as Dylan THOMAS. By the 1970s Barker's poetry volumes were attracting little attention.

Neglected for much of his career, Barker finally enjoyed a widespread critical reappraisal of his work four years before his death when he published *Collected Poems* (1987). Reflecting on his merits, biographer Martha Fodaski wrote that Barker created ". . . poetry of conscience. And, as the conscience of his times, he explores the effects of the people, the events, and the ideas of an era and a life upon the human heart."

Other Works by George Barker

III Hallucination Poems. New York: Helikon Press, 1972.

Villar Stellar. Boston: Faber & Faber, 1978.

Works about George Barker

Fodaski, Martha. *George Barker.* Boston: Twayne, 1969.

Heath-Stubbs, John, and Martin Green, eds. *Homage to George Barker on his 60th Birthday.* London: Brian and O'Keefe, 1973.

Barker, Howard (1946–) playwright

Howard Barker was born in Norwood, England, just south of London. His father, Sydney Charles Barker, was a unionized factory worker; his mother, Georgia Irene Carter Barker, was a homemaker. After Barker graduated from Battersea Grammar School, where he often improvised short plays in the back of an army truck during his lunch breaks, he earned a B.A. and M.A. in history from Sussex University.

Nearly all of Barker's plays reflect his belief in socialism while confronting the issues of class conflict and state power. *No End of Blame* (1981)—which the scholar Andrew Parkin assesses as Barker's best production to date for its "acute and varied . . . analysis of state power"—is representative of most of the playwright's work. The protagonist, Bela, is a cartoonist searching for a country or government in which he can express himself as he wishes. During the play, which spans both World War I and World War II, Bela moves from Russia to England and is rebuked for his political beliefs and philosophical outlook in each location. Finally, near the end, he meets his ultimate defeat when his supervisor fires him, commenting, "It is the board's feeling that there is a quality of—depression—in your work—of nihilism—which makes it inappropriate . . . to a national, family newspaper."

The Wrestling School, an acting company, has performed Barker's plays since 1988, and under the playwright's own direction since the mid-1990s. Beginning with the production of his first stage play, *Cheek* (1971), a grotesquely comic play about conflict between a dying father and his adolescent son, Barker has written more than 45 plays that are aimed mostly toward audiences who share his leftist political orientation. In assessing Barker's ultimate contribution to drama, the scholar Liz Tomlin has remarked that he is important for "[d]ismissing contemporary" drama as "obsessed with entertaining" and aspiring to a more political, socially responsible, and "intellectually demanding theatre designed to challenge the prevalent . . . traditions."

Other Works by Howard Barker

Arguments for a Theatre. New York: Manchester University Press, 1986.

The Collected Plays. New York: Riverrun, 1990.

A Work about Howard Barker

Itzin, Catherine. *Stages in the Revolution: Political Theatre in Britain Since 1968.* London: Methuen, 1980, pp. 249–258.

Barker, Pat (1943–) *novelist*

Born Patricia Margaret Drake to a working-class mother and unknown father in Thornaby-on-Tees, Pat Barker was brought up by her grandparents. She was educated at the local grammar school, and in 1965 she earned a B.S. degree from the London School of Economics.

Barker was nearly 40 when her first novel, *Union Street* (1982), won the Fawcett Prize and she was instantly recognized as a strong new voice. Barker has a faultless ear for dialogue, and her language, at once earthy and poetic, is brutally blunt and direct.

Barker's first three novels—*Union Street, Blow Your House Down* (1984), and *The Century's Daughter* (1986)—concern working-class women. *Union Street* comprises seven stories about seven women living on a street in the shadow of a factory in a northern postindustrial town. The characters range in age from 11 to 70, their successive tales representing seven stages of a woman's life from adolescence through old age. This book was followed by a novel based on the serial killer known as the Yorkshire Ripper. *Blow Your House Down* centers on the Ripper's victims, terror-stricken prostitutes; each of four parts presents one woman's story.

The central character of *The Century's Daughter* is Liza Jarrett, the "sole remaining inhabitant of a street scheduled for demolition." Almost as old as the century, she tells her life story to a social worker. Liza figures, says scholar Sharon Carson, as "Barker's barometer to measure the country's afflictions, from the irrevocable losses of war to the unraveling of family ties and the gradual dissolution of community."

Barker next turned to novels addressing the experience of men at war, blending fiction with fact, notably in the trilogy encompassing *Regeneration* (1991), *The Eye in the Door* (1993), and *The Ghost Road* (1995). The *New York Times* rated *Regeneration* one of the four best novels of 1991. *The Eye in the Door* won the Guardian prize, and *The Ghost Road* won the BOOKER PRIZE.

Barker's novels employ a technique she calls the "compound eye," with a possible pun on "I." Characters become multifaceted through a presentation that permits them to tell their own stories yet also indicates how others see and react to them. The view of life that emerges is hardheaded, realistic, unsentimental, and remarkable for its candor and integrity.

Regeneration opens with war hero Siegfried SASSOON's "A Soldier's Declaration," his refusal (in July 1917) to return to the front because of a conviction that the war is evil, unjust, and insane. Persuaded by fellow poet Robert GRAVES to submit to a medical examination, Sassoon is classified "mentally unsound" and sent to Craiglockhart, the military hospital under Dr. William Rivers that specialized in treating shell shock. The fictional character Billy Prior, subject of the succeeding volumes *The Eye in the Door* and *The Ghost Road,* was conceived by Barker as Rivers's alter ego.

Well-chosen imagery unifies the trilogy. In *Regeneration* the "unspeakable" horrors soldiers have witnessed cause some to become mute, like witnesses of the Holocaust. The image of the human eye dominates *The Eye in the Door:* The eye of the title signifies unrelenting surveillance. As *Regeneration* handles hysteria at the front, its sequel addresses hysteria on the home front, showing pacifists, homosexuals, conscientious objectors, and feminists hunted down. In *The Ghost Road,* Prior, returning for his final tour of duty, finds "ghosts everywhere. Even the living were only ghosts in the making."

Battles do not feature in Barker's war novels. Instead, she penetrates the battleground of men's minds, where subterranean forces drive them toward mass slaughter. Carson observes that Barker "has an ingenious capacity to associate differences and similarities, and to demonstrate that it is often the differences that are similar."

Other Works by Pat Barker

Another World. New York: Farrar, Straus & Giroux, 1999.

Border Crossing. New York: Farrar, Straus & Giroux, 2001.

Works about Pat Barker

Alexander, Flora. *Contemporary Women Novelists.* London: Edward Arnold, 1989.

Perry, Donna. *Backtalk: Women Writers Speak Out.* New Brunswick, N.J.: Rutgers University Press, 1993.

Barnes, Julian (Dan Kavanagh)

(1946–) *novelist, journalist, essayist*

Julian Barnes was born in Leicester, England. Both of his parents were French teachers, and the family moved to Northwood, a London suburb, while Barnes was still young. After winning a scholarship, he attended the City of London School. In 1964 he enrolled at Magdalen College, Oxford, to study languages. He spent the 1966–67 school year teaching in France, graduating from Oxford with honors the following year.

After university, Barnes worked for several years as an editorial assistant for the *Oxford English Dictionary.* In 1972 he moved to London, studied law, and was admitted to the bar. During this time he also began writing book reviews for *The New Statesman,* eventually accepting a position there as assistant literary editor. In subsequent years,

Barnes worked as deputy literary editor for the *Sunday Times* and as television critic for *The Observer.* In 1979 he married Pat Kavanagh.

While working as a journalist, Barnes also began writing fiction. His first novel, *Metroland* (1980), reveals his interest in love and jealousy, themes he would pursue in many novels. *Metroland* also introduces Barnes's use of postmodern narrative, characterized by a heavy use of parody, an ironic tone, and a general skepticism toward art's ability to explain life. Barnes repeatedly explores the relationship between life and art, and his narratives question the ability of individuals to understand either one. The main character of *Metroland,* a teenager named Christopher Lloyd, and his friend Toni initially reject the middle-class lifestyle of their parents for a liberated, artistic existence. But as Lloyd ages, he marries, starts a professional career, and shelves his artistic aspirations. Toni, however, becomes an artist, and the novel urges the reader to compare Lloyd's acceptance of a normal life with Toni's rebelliousness.

Barnes's second novel, *Duffy* (1980), written under the pseudonym Dan Kavanagh, is a crime thriller. Its main character, Nick Duffy, is a bisexual private detective who has left the police force after being blackmailed by corrupt officers. Barnes has written three subsequent novels as Dan Kavanagh, each featuring Duffy. These novels, unlike those published under Barnes's own name, employ more conventional plots and narratives and contain many of the characteristics of the hard-boiled American crime thriller.

In 1984 Barnes published his best-known novel, *Flaubert's Parrot,* which is presented as a nonfiction account written by an English doctor named Geoffrey Braithwaite. While in France, Braithwaite sees a stuffed parrot in a museum. The parrot supposedly belonged to Flaubert while he wrote his short story "Un Coeur Simple." But Braithwaite soon sees another parrot bearing the same claim. As Braithwaite continues his research, he discovers more and more stuffed parrots, each supposedly having belonged to Flaubert. Braithwaite is unable to discover any evidence that would allow him to eliminate any of the parrots. The novel highlights Barnes's doubts about ever knowing the truth, but it also reinforces his belief that truth exists. As the critic Merritt Moseley notes, "Braithwaite doubts the possibility of finding out which was the 'real' Flaubert's parrot, but this does not lead him to conclude that there was no real parrot."

Barnes artfully combines the search for truth with his fascination with love and jealousy in the novel *Talking It Over* (1991). The main character, Stuart, marries a beautiful woman named Gillian, but his friend Oliver also falls in love with her and eventually seduces her. This novel provides the best example of Barnes's narrative experimentation, as each character addresses the reader through a first-person account. Stuart, Oliver, and Gillian separately defend their own actions and comment on the motives of the other two. The multiple narratives also raise doubts about each character's veracity, causing the reader to question the truths each offers up during the course of the novel.

Barnes continues to work periodically as a journalist. In 1995 he published *Letters from London,* a collection of essays he had previously written for *The New Yorker.* He was also honored in France as an Officier de l'Ordre des Arts et des Lettres. Although some critics have described his postmodern narrative techniques as disjointed and unstructured, Barnes is repeatedly praised for his narrative variety and is humorously referred to as the best British author never to have won the BOOKER PRIZE. Merritt Moseley claims that Barnes's "unique mixture of literary experimentation, intelligence, and dedication to the truths of the human heart . . . makes every book an adventure."

Other Works by Julian Barnes

Before She Met Me. New York: McGraw-Hill, 1986.
Cross Channel. New York: Knopf, 1996.
A History of the World in 10½ Chapters. New York: Knopf, 1991.
Staring at the Sun. New York: Knopf, 1987.

A Work about Julian Barnes

Moseley, Merritt. *Understanding Julian Barnes.* Columbia: University of South Carolina Press, 1997.

Barrie, James Matthew (1860–1937)
novelist, playwright

J. M. Barrie was born in Kirriemuir, Scotland, to David Barrie, who owned and ran a loom business, and Margaret Ogilvy Barrie. He grew up in the shadow of his older brother David. When David died in a skating accident, six-year-old Barrie tried to earn his mother's affection and ease her pain by dressing up as his deceased brother. As tragic as this death was for Barrie's mother, it served as a kind of inspiration for Barrie. As he acted out the role of David, he realized that his brother would never grow up, that he would always be 13 years old to their mother. When Barrie himself turned 13, he realized that there would come a time when his childhood would be over. This idea frightened him, and as he grew up he discovered that he had a hard time relating to adults, preferring the company of children, whom he felt understood him better.

Barrie studied at Dumfries Academy at the University of Edinburgh, where he received his degree in 1882. The following year he became a journalist for the *Nottingham Journal* and in 1885 he moved to London to work as a freelance writer. His first success came with a series of sketches based on his mother's stories of her childhood in Kirriemuir, which Barrie renamed Thrums. Originally printed in *The St. James's Gazette,* the sketches were published as *Auld licht idylls* in 1888.

Barrie found success as a novelist with such popular titles as *A Window in Thrums,* the further remembrances of his mother's childhood experiences; and such plays as *The Little Minister,* which he adapted from his successful novel about a short minister who angers his neighbors when he falls in love with a gypsy. Both the novel and the play earned Barrie praise. His greatest success, however, came with the 1904 production of his play *Peter Pan or the Boy Who Wouldn't Grow Up.*

Peter Pan is a magical boy from Never-Never-Land, a place where boys and girls stay children forever. "I don't want to go to school and learn solemn things," Peter declares. "No one is going to catch me, lady, and make me a man. I want always to be a little boy and to have fun." He befriends a girl named Wendy and takes her with him to Never-Never-Land to meet the Lost Boys, Peter's band of friends, and to do battle with a team of pirates led by the evil Captain Hook.

The story of Peter Pan grew out of stories Barrie told to the Davies boys, sons of Arthur and Sylvia Llewellyn Davies, whom Barrie had befriended in 1897. He cared deeply for the boys and would spend as much time with them as possible, making up games and telling them stories, many of which were about Peter Pan, who was named after young Peter Davies.

Although Peter Pan began as a children's character, and is certainly considered one today, Barrie did not initially intend his play to be only for children. As Cynthia Asquith writes in her biography of Barrie, "He didn't want children to take Peter Pan seriously. His favorite reaction to his own play was that of the little boy who, favoured by a seat in the author's box, and at the end injudiciously asked what he had liked best, promptly replied: 'What I think I liked best was tearing up the programme and dropping the bits on people's heads.'"

Barrie continued to write both plays and novels, including *The Admirable Crichton* (1902), a play about a butler who saves a shipwrecked family but in the process reverses the roles of servant and master; and his adult novel *The Little White Bird* (1902), the book in which Peter Pan is first introduced as a character in stories told to a little boy. Barrie rewrote his play as a children's book in 1911.

Barrie was famous for his generosity. In his later years he donated all royalties from *Peter Pan* to the Great Ormond Street Hospital for Sick Children in London. He answered his own fan mail and helped people with requests for jobs or advice. He received numerous honors before his death, including the Order of Merit (1922), the Rectorship of St. Andrews University, and the Chancellorship of Edinburgh University.

Barrie never lost touch with the boy within, and his work was consistently shaped by this childlike view. As critic Angel M. Pilkington wrote of Barrie, "He believed in the power of emotion, but he also was possessed of an irrepressible humor. He saw the pathos and beauty in humanity, but just as clearly he perceived the confusions and the cruelties. How else could he have made Peter Pan, Wendy, and Captain Hook?"

Works about J. M. Barrie

Birkin, Andrew. *J. M. Barrie and the Lost Boys: The Love Story That Gave Birth to Peter Pan.* New York: Clarkson N. Potter, Inc., 1979.

Dunbar, Janet. *J. M. Barrie: The Man Behind the Image.* Boston: Houghton Mifflin, 1970.

Wullschläger, Jackie. *Inventing Wonderland.* New York: Free Press, 1995.

Barry, Sebastian (1955–) *playwright, poet, novelist*

Sebastian Barry was born in Dublin, Ireland; his father was an architect and his mother, Joan O'Hara, an actress. He was educated at Trinity College, Dublin, where he received a degree in English and Latin. He has lived in France, Greece, Switzerland, England, and the United States, and currently lives in Wicklow, Ireland.

Barry has won recognition primarily as a dramatist. *Boss Grady's Boys,* a play about two elderly brothers performed at the Abbey Theatre, Dublin, in 1988, won the first BBC/Stewart Parker Award. *The Steward of Christendom,* performed at the Royal Court Theatre, London, in 1995, won the Writers' Guild award as well as many other honors. The critically acclaimed script focuses on Thomas Dunne, a former Dublin police commissioner, ranting, Lear-like, in a nursing home circa 1932 about his memories of Ireland's civil war. Barry was a Writer Fellow at Trinity College, Dublin, in 1995–96. His play *Hinterland* (2002) concerns a retired politician, Johnny Silvester, haunted by his past.

Although Barry's first love is theater, he is also an accomplished poet and novelist and has written several books for children as well. His novel *The Whereabouts of Eneas McNulty* (1998) is about a rural Irish urchin who joins the British army in World War I and finds himself, on his return, branded a collaborator with the hated British. He must spend the rest of his long life wandering, like Virgil's Aeneas; his travels over 70 years take him to places as diverse as France, Texas, and Nigeria. The *Times* of London described the work as "a novel reflecting on Irish history, Irish losses, Irish enmities, with singular force, grace and beauty." His latest novel, *Annie Dunne* (2002), is a much more static work, in which the drama unfolds within the characters over a single summer (1959). Much of the story's joy lies in the sensuous descriptions of rural life. Annie Dunne, the aged daughter of the central character of Barry's play *The Steward of Christendom,* lives with her cousin Sarah in a remote Irish farmhouse. A nephew, who goes to England to seek work, leaves his two children in Annie's care, and her growing love for them opens her to unanticipated pain.

Barry's prolific literary career has been devoted to a rich and complex evocation of Irish history and contemporary life, often told from the point of view of the previously voiceless. John Lahr, reviewing the play *Our Lady of Sligo* for *New Yorker* magazine in May 2000, said that Barry is "probably Ireland's finest living dramatist."

Other Works by Sebastian Barry

The Engine of Owl-Light. Manchester, England: Carcanet, 1987.
Fanny Hawke Goes to the Mainland Forever. Dublin: Raven Arts Press, 1989.
The Only True History of Lizzie Finn/The Steward of Christendom/White Woman Street: Three Plays. Westport, Conn.: Heinemann, 1996.
Prayers of Sherkin/Boss Grady's Boys: Two Plays. Westport, Conn.: Heinemann, 1995.
The Rhetorical Town: Poems. Dublin: Dolmen Press, 1999.
Time Out of Mind; and, Strappado Square. Dublin: Wolfhound Press, 1983.

Barstow, Stanley (1928–) *novelist, short story writer*

Stan Barstow was born in Horbury, Yorkshire, England, to Wilfred Barstow, a coal miner, and his wife, Elsie. Barstow attended grammar school in Ossett and in 1944 went to work as a draftsman for an engineering company in the town. Eighteen years later he left his job to pursue a literary career.

Barstow emerged as a writer in the early 1960s soon after John BRAINE, Kingsley AMIS, and Alan SILLITOE began their literary careers. These authors were part of the ANGRY YOUNG MEN, a group of writers who wrote about heroes with rebellious and critical attitudes toward society. Barstow's first novel, *A Kind of Loving,* (1960) was his most successful. Its hero, Victor Brown, is a Yorkshire coal miner's son who, seeking to do what is right, marries a girl he does not love after she becomes pregnant with his child. Critic Maurice Richardson describes the book as "seductively readable and makes an interesting variation on the much more familiar lower-than-middle-class picaresque genre in which the hero escapes traps by clownish antics."

Barstow wrote two sequels to *A Kind of Loving: The Watchers on the Shore* (1966) and *The Right True End* (1976). These books describe Victor's marital troubles, bitter divorce, and, after many trials, eventual entrance into a more fulfilling relationship. At the end of the latter work, he finally has real hope for the future: "I'm buoyed up by a happiness too powerful now for that tiny seed of anxiety which in the small hours will bloom into terror at what the morning might bring." Barstow later wrote a second trilogy—*Just You Wait and See* (1986), *Give Us This Day* (1989), and *Next of Kin* (1991)—about a Yorkshire family during World War II.

The Desperadoes and Other Stories (1961) was the first of several of Barstow's collections of short stories. As in his novels, Barstow is realistic and compassionate in his depiction of the hardships faced by the working people in northern England's industrial district. His stories are often tragic, like "Gamblers Never Win," which describes an impoverished coal miner whose life unravels as he turns to gambling and drinking. Later collections such as *A Season with Eros* (1971) have similar heartbreaking themes. For example, "Waiting" describes a selfish son who grows impatient while waiting for his aging father to die.

Critics have praised Barstow's true-to-life works for capturing the tragedy of people from his class and region. Scholar Ingrid von Rosenberg writes that in Barstow's novels, he "clearly wished to communicate . . . about a subject of common social interest, thereby showing a social responsibility comparable to that of the bourgeois novelists of the eighteenth and nineteenth centuries."

Other Works by Stan Barstow

B-Movie. London: Michael Joseph, 1987.
Joby. London: Michael Joseph, 1964.

Bates, Herbert Ernest (Flying Officer X)

(1905–1974) *novelist, short story writer*
H. E. Bates was born in Rushden, Northamptonshire, England, to Albert Ernest Bates, who ran a shoemaking shop and later worked in a factory, and Lucy Elizabeth Lucas. Bates had little interest in school until a teacher inspired him to pursue literature. He was accepted at Cambridge, but for financial reasons he was unable to attend. He started writing fiction in the early 1920s while working at a variety of jobs, including newspaper reporting.

Bates's first novel, *The Two Sisters* (1926), depicts the empty lives of two sisters who are each courted by the same man promising to rescue them from their tyrannical father. Bates attained critical and popular success with his fourth novel, *The Fallow Land* (1932), which describes the difficult existence of a woman who has to run a farm and raise her sons while coping with her husband's alcoholism.

During World War II Bates joined the Royal Air Force and wrote several morale-boosting short stories and novels under the pseudonym "Flying Officer X." The best known of these works, *Fair Stood the Wind for France* (1944), describes the efforts of downed British flyers trying to escape from occupied France.

Following the war, Bates wrote *The Purple Plain* (1947), *The Jacaranda Tree* (1949), and *The Scarlet Sword* (1950), a trilogy about British outposts in the Far East. Bates biographer Dennis Vannatta wrote that "[t]he virtue of *The Scarlet Sword* is its single-mindedness. It evokes the violent world of rape, murder, and torture that marked the Indian partition with a relentlessness that forces the reader to keep turning the pages."

After 1950, Bates had more success with short fiction than with novels. He wrote about one of his most popular characters in *Sugar for the Horse* (1957), a comedic collection about the lovable English farmer Uncle Silas. Bates describes him as short and thick-built, with "some gay, devilish spark of audacity which made him attractive to the ladies." Silas also likes to drink: "'God strike me if I tell a lie,' he used to say, 'but I've drunk enough beer, me boyo, to float the fleet and a drop over.'"

The comedy stories in *The Darling Buds of May* (1958) introduced Bates's popular Pop Larkin character, a freelance junk dealer and entrepreneur. Dennis Vannatta holds that Bates's greatest talent was in capturing the heart and soul of a locale and its people: "The farmers and poachers and passionate women and violent young men, the fields and meadows that he captures with a painter's skill are the best guarantee . . . that Bates's fiction will live on."

Other Works by H. E. Bates

Elephant's Nest in a Rhubarb Tree and Other Stories. New York: New Directions, 1988.
A Month by the Lake and Other Stories. New York: New Directions, 1987.

A Work about H. E. Bates

Vannatta, Dennis. *H. E. Bates.* Boston: Twayne, 1983.

Bawden, Nina Mabey (1925–   ) *novelist*

A novelist equally at home writing for adults or children, Nina Bawden was born in London. At

Oxford she studied philosophy, politics, and economics, receiving her degree in 1946. Bawden's first novel, *Who Calls the Tune* (1953), was a murder mystery. She wrote several novels for adults before she attempted one for children, *The Secret Passage* (1963). The story was inspired by her own children after they had found a hidden passage in their basement.

Two subsequent Bawden novels for children, *Carrie's War* (1973) and *The Peppermint Pig* (1975), have become classics. *Carrie's War* is about children being evacuated from London to a Welsh mining town during World War II—an experience the author lived through herself. *The Peppermint Pig* is especially notable for its intense realism, as when Bawden writes: "Old Granny Greengrass had her finger chopped off at the butcher's when she was buying half a leg of lamb." The book received the Guardian Award for Children's Fiction in 1975.

In interviews about her work, Bawden has said that in her writing for children she has tried to compensate for the fact that others underestimate children's feelings and perceptions. A reviewer for the *Times Literary Supplement* agreed: "No writer is better than Bawden at conveying the alienation of childhood."

Bawden's many novels for adults, known for their examination of the drama in middle-class life, have also won awards. *Afternoon of a Good Woman* (1976), which tells the story of Penelope, who has tried hard to be a good wife, mistress, mother, and magistrate, won the *Yorkshire Post* Novel of the Year. *Circles of Deceit* is the story of a painter who is a brilliant copyist, duplicating great works of art, and his tangled relationships with four women: his first wife, his young second wife, his aunt, and his mother. It was nominated for the BOOKER PRIZE in 1987. A reviewer from the *Guardian* newspaper wrote about the later novel that it "[p]lays with time and notions of forgery and fidelity in life and art, as well as tracing with extraordinary exactness and creative tact, the pain and survival of a loved one."

In 1995 Bawden published *In My Own Time: Almost an Autobiography.* This book contains recollections of her childhood, the years during World War II, her education, and family life; and insights into how a writer turns life experiences into works of art. Bawden is a Fellow of the Royal Society of Literature.

Other Works by Nina Bawden
Devil by the Sea. London: Virago, 1997.
Family Money. London: Virago, 1997.
The Finding. New York: Puffin, 1993.
Granny the Pag. New York: Clarion Books, 1996.
Off the Road. New York: Puffin, 2000.
Ruffian on the Stair. London: Virago, 2002.

Beauchamp, Kathleen Mansfield
See MANSFIELD, KATHERINE.

Beckett, Samuel (1906–1989) *playwright, novelist*
Samuel Beckett was born in a suburb of Dublin, Ireland, to William Beckett, a surveyor, and Mary Jones Beckett. He completed his secondary studies at Portora Royal School in Northern Ireland and went from there to Trinity College, Dublin, where he earned a B.A. in French and Italian in 1927 and subsequently earned an M.A. in 1931.

Shortly after receiving his B.A., Beckett accepted a teaching position at the École Normale Supérieure in Paris, where he met his lifelong friend and mentor, James JOYCE. While in Paris and under Joyce's tutelage, Beckett learned the craft of writing. He wrote an essay entitled "Dante . . . Bruno . . . Vico . . . Joyce" (1929), on Joyce's yet unreleased *Finnegan's Wake*.

Beckett eventually abandoned teaching and spent the 1930s in Dublin, London, and Paris, struggling as a writer. In 1933 he published a collection of 10 short stories, *More Pricks than Kicks*, which describe the youth, middle age, and death of Belacqua, a character Beckett took from Dante's epic poem *The Divine Comedy*. Four years later, and after 43 rejections, Beckett finally published *Murphy* (1937), his first novel, which focuses on its title character, a Dubliner living in London, who is so dissatisfied with the chaos of the world around him that he spends the majority of his time strapped in a rocking chair exploring his own mind.

Beckett was awarded the Croix de Guerre and the Médaille de la Résistance for his service to the French Resistance in World War II. After the war, still living in France and writing in French, he began work that would establish him as one of the 20th century's most important novelists and playwrights. The first of his important postwar writings was a trilogy of novels: *Malloy* (1951), *Malone Dies* (1951), and *The Unnamable* (1953). All of these books feature disconnected, alienated narrators living almost entirely within the confines of their own minds or imaginations.

One year later Beckett produced *Waiting for Godot* (1954), a play about two men standing beside a country road waiting for a man called M. Godot. The critic H. A. Smith has praised this as "the most comprehensively and profoundly evocative play of the last thirty years." Beckett went on to write a number of equally provocative plays, including *Endgame* (1957), about the horribly repetitive and almost death-like lives of two disabled characters; and *Krapp's Last Tape* (1960), which tells the story of an elderly man reviewing his life by listening to snippets of a tape-recorded journal that he began in his youth. All of Beckett's plays challenged the dramatic form by reducing casts to one or two characters and sets to the most basic elements, often a single tree or a table and chair on an otherwise empty stage.

Critical Analysis

Beckett's trilogy of *Malloy, Malone Dies,* and *The Unnamable* established his primary themes—disconnection from the world and the artist trapped within his own mind—as well as a stream-of-consciousness style that runs throughout the rest of his work. The main characters of each novel become so disconnected from the world that they even lose track of where they are or how they got there. At the beginning of the first novel, for instance, Molloy remarks, "I am in my mother's room," but goes on to say, "I don't know how I got there. Perhaps in an ambulance, certainly a vehicle of some kind. I was helped. I'd never have got there alone."

Molloy and Malone, the narrator of the trilogy's second novel, share a sense of separation from the world, and both feel compelled to tell their tales or become artists. As they try to do this, however, they fall deeper and deeper into their stories until they can no longer distinguish between themselves and the narratives they are creating. This difficulty progresses through the trilogy until, in *The Unnamable,* as the title suggests, the narrator is entirely subsumed by his narrative and is never even named.

While all of the novels use a stream-of-consciousness style, with the narrators reporting their thoughts to the reader as they occur, the technique dominates *The Unnamable* more than any other. Near the novel's end, the narrator simply pours words upon the reader, stopping, it seems, only for a breath:

> Now I can speak of my life, I'm too tired for niceties, but I don't know if I, ever lived, I have really no opinion on the subject. However that may be I think I'll soon go silent for good, in spite of its being prohibited. The, yes, phut, just like that, just like one of the living, then I'll be dead, I think I'll soon be dead, I hope I find it a change.

Waiting for Godot is one of the landmarks of 20th-century literature. The two-act play is concise—it contains only two important characters, Vladimir and Estragon, and takes place in a single location—and minimalist, with a set composed of only a lone tree and a country road. The play centers on conversations between Estragon and Vladimir, who spend two days waiting beside a country road for a person named M. Godot, who never appears. While waiting, the two discuss issues ranging from their hats and boots to their religions and the possibility of hanging themselves, which flares up only to quickly die, like so many of their topics.

Waiting for Godot, with God embedded in Godot's very name, has been described as a Christian allegory. The critic John Gassner has remarked that it "presents the view that man, the hapless wanderer in the universe, brings his quite wonderful humanity—his human capacity for hope, patience, resilience, and, yes, for love of one's kind, too, as well as his animal nature—to the weird journey of existence." Other critics have praised the play for its manipulation, or breaking, of several dramatic conventions. Beckett's starkly empty set marks a departure from standard 20th-century drama, which typically uses elaborate sets and even multiple settings, but Beckett's more compelling change is his method of developing, or not developing, his characters through action. While conventional drama uses action to create clearly defined, individual figures, Beckett's protagonists engage in mindless, fidgeting action (removing their pants or tugging on pieces of rope to test their strength) that does not distinguish one from the other but, in the words of the scholar David Pattie, "leads inexorably to the blurring of distinctions between characters."

Krapp's Last Tape is Beckett's most concise play, consisting of a single character named Krapp, a 69-year-old man who sits alone in a dark room reviewing his entire life by listening to audio recordings of himself talking at various points throughout his life. As he listens to fragments of tapes from his youth, middle age, and old age, Krapp becomes increasingly drunk and ridicules the images of himself as a younger man, at one point saying, "Just been listening to that stupid bastard I took myself for thirty years ago, hard to believe I was ever as bad as that." While Krapp is a thoroughly pathetic character, the scholar Jean-Jacques Mayoux has observed that he is a poignant clown figure complete with "white face and red nose, the 'rusty black narrow trousers, too short,' the 'surprising pair of dirty white boots, size 10 at least, very narrow and pointed,' with the grotesque near-sighted peerings to match, and the ways of a

habitual drunkard." Indeed, interspersed between snippets of tape and his expostulations of disgust for his younger self, Krapp slips into the clown mode, sticking a banana in his mouth at one point, nearly forgetting that it is there, and later slipping on its peel. Krapp illustrates that near the end of Beckett's dramatic career, the poet was capable of laughing at humanity despite his awareness of all of its problems.

In 1969 Samuel Beckett was awarded the Nobel Prize for, as the committee wrote, "'a body of work that, in new forms of fiction and the theatre, has transmuted the destitution of modern man into his exaltation.'" Scholar Deirdre Bair has remarked that "[t]his comment is probably the most accurate description of Beckett's writing, as in its succinctness it takes into account his prose, his plays, his achievement, his life."

Other Works by Samuel Beckett

Collected Poems 1930–1978. London: John Calder, 1984.
The Complete Dramatic Works. London: Faber & Faber, 1986.
Watt. 1953. Reprint, London: Calder, 1994.

Works about Samuel Beckett

Andonian, Cathleen Culotta. *Samuel Beckett: A Reference Guide.* Boston: G. K. Hall, 1989.
Bloom, Harold, ed. *Samuel Beckett: Modern Critical Views.* New York: Chelsea House, 1985.
Cronin, Anthony. *Samuel Beckett: The Last Modernist.* London: HarperCollins, 1996.
Pattie, David. *The Complete Critical Guide to Samuel Beckett.* New York: Routledge, 2000.

Bedford, Sybille (1911–   ) *novelist, biographer, essayist*

Sybille Bedford was born in Charlottenburg, Germany, to Maximilian and Elizabeth Bernard von Schoenebeck. Her mother came from a wealthy background and it was her money that supported the family during Bedford's childhood. Bedford had an international education and studied at several different private schools located in Italy, France, and England. In 1935 she married Walter Bedford. Her work as a novelist, biographer, and essayist has earned her critical acclaim among contemporary literary scholars and the reading public.

Often drawing from her own experiences as a young girl growing up in Europe, Bedford's writings consider a diverse range of themes including war, aristocratic society, criminal justice, and international travel. Her first novel, *A Legacy* (1956) tells the story of two families, one Jewish and one Catholic, and their attempt to survive in Germany under the Nazis during World War II. Her mentor, Aldous HUXLEY, called the book "[a]n interesting, odd, unclassifiable book—at once historical novel and a study of character, a collection of brilliantly objective portraits." Evelyn WAUGH described the work as "[a] book of entirely delicious quality. . . . Everything is new, cool, witty, elegant."

Jigsaw: An Unsentimental Education was short-listed for the BOOKER PRIZE and continues the theme of Bedford's first novel. It describes the displacement felt by Europeans after the war and the horrors experienced by people living under the Nazi and Fascist regimes. In the novel's opening passage the narrator, Billi, depicts the controlled world of Nazi Germany, recalling memories of her restrained early childhood: "Please be good, please keep quiet," implores Billi's worried mother, "he doesn't like to have a baby in the hall. Please just go to sleep."

Bedford has also written several biographies. Her two-volume biography of Aldous Huxley, published in 1974, offers personal insights into the famous writer's life by recounting her experiences with Huxley and his wife, Maria. This intimate approach to biography earned her admiration among critics such as William Abrahams, who praised her in the *Atlantic Monthly* for her decision to focus on Huxley's private life, although it required the "mastering of a staggering amount of material." Abrahams called the biography "unquestionably a work of art."

Bedford's writings have experienced renewed attention in recent years and previously out-of-print titles have been reissued. Bedford's gift for creating believable and true-to-life characters has been a hallmark of all her writing. Peter Levi, a reviewer for the *Spectator,* has praised Bedford for her ability to write about ordinary, everyday events that in her work "read like a crisp unforgettable honeymoon." He wrote of her talent: "Bedford's genius is for writing about people. [Her] excellence is immortal, her career one of great distinction in literature."

Other Works by Sybille Bedford

A Compass Error. 1968. Reprint, Washington, D.C.: Counterpoint Press, 2001.
A Favorite of the Gods. 1963. Reprint, Washington, D.C.: Counterpoint Press, 2001.

Behan, Brendan (1923–1964) *playwright, memoirist*

Brendan Behan was born in a tenement house in Dublin. Later, when he was famous, he often portrayed himself as a child of the slums, but this was not the case. Both his parents were educated and well-read. His father, Stephan Behan, was a housepainter who once studied for the priesthood, while his mother Kathleen came from a middle-class family. Behan's father was also a republican who was arrested and imprisoned at the end of the Irish Civil War, and Behan's maternal uncle, Peadar Kearney, wrote the Irish national anthem. His upbringing was thus steeped in Irish history, politics, and literature.

At 13, Behan joined the Irish Republican Army (IRA). In 1940, while carrying a bag of explosives, he was arrested in Liverpool and sentenced to three years in juvenile detention in Suffolk. After two years he was released and deported back to Ireland, where, in 1942, he was arrested again for firing at a police detective during an IRA parade. This time he was sentenced to 14 years. During his time in prison, he started to write short stories. Early in his incarceration, the novelist Sean O'FAOLAIN, who was then editor of *The Bell,* published an account of Behan's youthful imprisonment.

A general amnesty provided Behan with his release from prison in 1946. In 1950 he returned to Dublin, where his talent drew attention in literary circles.

The Quare Fellow (1954) was his first successful play. It was well received when it was first performed in 1954, and the 1956 London production made him famous. *The Quare Fellow* is a grim, yet comic, drama about the effects an imminent prison hanging has on warders and inmates alike. The condemned prisoner, the "quare fellow" of the title, is never seen on stage, but his presence is everywhere in the prison. More than just a protest against capital punishment, the play, a blending of comedy, tragedy, and naturalistic language, is a portrait of the human spirit enduring under intolerable pressures. Behan's sympathy with and portrayal of people outcast and marginalized by society would be present in all his best work.

In the play, a prison official reminds one of the warders that the condemned prisoners get a Christian death with benefit of cleric and sacraments. The warder, Regan, responds, "But that's not our reason for hanging them, sir. We can't advertise 'Commit a murder and die a happy death,' sir. We'll have them all at it. They take religion very seriously in this country."

When *The Quare Fellow* opened in London, the drama critic Kenneth Tynan wrote in the *Observer* that "in Brendan Behan's tremendous new play, language is out on a spree, ribald, dauntless, and spoiling for a fight. . . . With superb dramatic tact the tragedy is concealed beneath layer upon layer of rough comedy. . . . I left the theatre overwhelmed."

Behan's next play, *The Hostage* (1958), was first written in Gaelic and then translated by the author. It is the story of an English soldier kidnapped and held in a Dublin brothel by the IRA. Also an enormous success, *The Hostage* continued Behan's exploration of the wounded lives of the down-and-out. He also extended his sympathy to include victims from both sides of the conflict. One of the women the hostage has befriended says over his slain body, "It wasn't the Belfast Jail or the Six Counties that was troubling you, but your lost youth and your crippled leg. He died in a strange land, and at home he had no one. I'll never forget you, Leslie, till the end of time."

Borstal Boy (1958), Behan's memoir of his prison days, was a best-seller in England and America; it demonstrated Behan's exceptional lyrical power and his largeness of spirit. His later work did not equal these early successes. In fact, his later memoirs, like *Brendan Behan's New York* (1964) and *Brendan Behan's Island* (1962), were transcribed from recordings. Though he often said when he was a struggling writer that he was ripe for success, a wild lifestyle led to alcoholism, diabetes, and an early death in Dublin. An IRA guard of honor accompanied his coffin at his funeral.

Critic Declan Kiberd has observed, "To the very end, Behan's fear was that his own formal wildness might be domesticated and misinterpreted," and that Behan's best work is "an organized project of resistance by those in the modern world who stand defeated but not destroyed."

Works about Brendan Behan

Arthurs, Peter. *With Brendan Behan.* New York: St. Martin's Press, 1981.

Kiberd, Declan. *Inventing Ireland: The Literature of the Modern Nation.* Cambridge, Mass.: Harvard University Press, 1996.

Wallace, Martin. *Famous Irish Writers.* Belfast: Appletree Press, 1999.

Bell, Clive (Arthur Clive Howard Bell)
(1881–1964) *art critic, nonfiction writer*

Clive Bell was born in East Shefford, Bedfordshire, England, to William Heyward Bell, a mining engineer. He attended Cambridge, where he was influenced by the moral philosophy of G. E. Moore, which emphasized the enjoyment of conversation and beautiful objects. In 1907 Bell married Vanessa Stephen, daughter of Leslie Stephen and sister of Virginia WOOLF.

In his early career Bell wrote literary reviews for the *Athenaeum* periodical. In 1910 and 1912 he attended postimpressionist art exhibitions organized by his mentor and friend, Roger FRY. These events led Bell to focus his writing on art criticism. His first work on this subject, *Art* (1914), marked the beginning of his career as one of the world's foremost art theorists.

In *Art* Bell sets forth his "significant form" concept in assessing aesthetic quality. Bell writes that in each work of art, "lines and colours combined in a particular way, certain forms and relations of forms, stir our aesthetic emotions. These relations and combinations of lines and colours, these aesthetically moving forms, I call 'Significant Form' . . . the one quality common to all works of visual art." For Bell the focus of an artwork was not the subject but instead the form and design, and the feelings and ideas they expressed.

Art stirred great controversy at the time it was published. Many critics questioned Bell's logic and could not understand why "significant form" is the essential great quality of great art. Critic Randall Davies asked, "But why should Mr. Bell suppose that the forms that move him are the only ones proper to move others?" Despite its detractors, *Art* helped boost popular interest in postimpressionist painters.

Bell's other important works of art criticism include *Since Cézanne* (1922), a discussion of the French artist Paul Cézanne's influence, and *An Account of French Painting* (1932), a history of French art over nine centuries. He also wrote *On British Freedom* (1923), a discussion of British politics and society; and *Civilization* (1928), an analysis of the qualities that comprise a civilized state of society. In one of his later books, *Old Friends: Personal Recollections* (1956), Bell recalls the friendships he had while part of the loose-knit group of writers and intellectuals known as the BLOOMSBURY GROUP. The scholar Donald Laing has written that Bell's works "provide a valuable record, not only of some forty years of English art history, but also of a sensitive and intelligent man's engagement with the major development to take place in the visual arts in the first half of the twentieth century."

Works about Clive Bell

Bywater, William G., Jr. *Clive Bell's Eye.* Detroit: Wayne State University Press, 1975.
Laing, Donald A. *Clive Bell: An Annotated Bibliography of the Published Writings.* New York: Garland, 1983.

Belloc, Hilaire (Joseph Hilaire Pierre Belloc) (1870–1953) *nonfiction writer, essayist, poet, novelist*

Hilaire Belloc is remembered for his vigorous defenses of Catholicism and his poetry for children. He was born in Saint-Cloud, France, the son of French barrister Louis Belloc and British political radical Elizabeth Rayner Parkes. After his father's death, he and his family, including his sister Marie BELLOC LOWNDES, moved to England, where he was educated at Oxford and was elected to Parliament as a Liberal.

Belloc analyzed religion in such volumes as *Europe and the Faith* (1920), *How the Reformation Happened* (1928), *A Conversation with an Angel, and Other Essays* (1928), *Essays of a Catholic* (1930), and *The Great Heresies* (1938). In *The Great Heresies* he went so far as to define entire religions, including Islam, as heretical departures from the true Catholic faith. Belloc's religiosity earned him the friendship of G. K. CHESTERTON and rebuttal essays by the socialist George Bernard SHAW, who parodied Chesterton and Belloc as a hybrid beast, the Chesterbelloc.

Belloc also wrote biographies of such pivotal historical figures as Oliver Cromwell (*Cromwell,* 1927); the French cardinal Richelieu (*Richelieu,* 1929); the English cardinal Wolsey (*Wolsey,* 1930); as well as major figures of the French Revolution. His output furthermore included novels; volumes of essays with such titles as *On Everything* (1910); and books about European places and history, such as *The Path to Rome* (1902). He is perhaps best known for books of children's verse, including *The Bad Child's Book of Beasts* (1896) and *More Beasts for Worse Children* (1897), in which he observes, "The Llama is a woolly sort of fleecy hairy goat/ With an indolent expression and an undulating throat/ Like an unsuccessful literary man." Most critics and readers paid more attention to his poetry than to his philosophical books, although those works continued to sell amongst religious and conservative readers. Arthur Bryant, in his foreword to *Belloc: A Biographical Anthology,* called Belloc "one of the most versatile English writers of our age."

Other Works by Hilaire Belloc
At the Sign of the Lion. 1916. Reprint, Freeport, N.Y.: Books for Libraries, 1964.
The Cruise of the "Nona." 1925. Reprint, New York: Hippocrene Books, 1983.
The Four Men: A Farrago. 1917. Reprint, Oxford, England: Oxford University Press, 1984.

Works about Hilaire Belloc
Speaight, Robert. *The Life of Hilaire Belloc.* Freeport, N.Y.: Books for Libraries, 1957.
Van Thal, Herbert, ed. *Belloc: A Biographical Anthology.* New York: Alfred A. Knopf, 1970.

Belloc Lowndes, Marie Adelaide
(Philip Curtin, Elizabeth Rayner)
(1868–1947) *novelist, short story writer, memoirist*
Born in Saint-Cloud, France, to Louis Belloc, a French barrister, and Elizabeth Rayner Parkes, a prominent English feminist and writer, Marie Belloc Lowndes and her younger brother, writer Hilaire BELLOC, were both raised as Catholics and spent much of their childhood in France. Her French grandmother translated Harriet Beecher Stowe's *Uncle Tom's Cabin* (1852) into French. Following Louis Belloc's death in 1872, Belloc Lowndes's mother brought the two children to live in London, where they lived on a modest income.

Belloc Lowndes later claimed that spending time in both France and England gave her an intimate knowledge of the literatures of both countries, though she insisted that her "heart is all French." She spent her adolescence and adult life mostly in England. She had only two years of formal education, although her brother was sent to school with the help of relatives. She began writing at age 16, and her first job was as a journalist for W. T. Stead at the *Pall Mall Gazette,* writing a guide for the Paris Exhibition of 1889. At this time she traveled frequently to France and socialized with many French writers, including Paul Verlaine, Emile Zola, and Jules Verne. Belloc Lowndes secured a small sum of money from Stead that enabled her brother to travel in France and submit his impressions for publication. In 1896 she married *Times* journalist Frederic Sawry Lowndes, with whom she had two sons and a daughter.

Belloc Lowndes published more than 40 novels, most of which are crime stories or mysteries, many derived from real-life criminal cases. Her daughter Susan wrote that Belloc Lowndes tended to depict "the reactions of ordinary persons to sudden violence in their own circle." Belloc Lowndes also wrote royal biographies and historical novels, and two of her works appeared under pseudonyms (Philip Curtin and Elizabeth Rayner). Her most famous novel, *The Lodger* (1913), is about a woman who realizes that her lodger is Jack the Ripper. This novel inspired several film versions, including one by Alfred Hitchcock in 1926. Belloc Lowndes also wrote several volumes of memoirs. Despite her success, though, she did not entirely relish being known as a writer of crime fiction.

Other Works by Marie Belloc Lowndes
The Diaries and Letters of Marie Belloc Lowndes. London: Chatto & Windus, 1971.
A Passing World. London: Macmillan, 1948.
Where Love and Friendship Dwelt. New York: Dodd, Mead, 1943.

Bennett, Alan (1934–) *playwright, autobiographer*
Alan Bennett was born in Leeds, Yorkshire, to Walter Bennett, a butcher, and Lilian Mary Peel Bennett. He attended Oxford, graduating with honors

in 1957. From 1960 to 1962, he was a junior lecturer in modern history at Magdalen College, Oxford, where he cowrote and performed in the comedy revue *Beyond the Fringe* (1962).

Bennett's first stage play, *Forty Years On* (1968), is about a comic revue being performed at a boys' boarding school. The play was influenced by *Beyond the Fringe* in that it consisted of a series of satiric skits poking fun at well-known cultural and political figures in establishment England. Like much of Bennett's work, the play mocks traditional English manners and mores. In one scene the headmaster describes the English literati: "The silly way of talking they had. How simply too extraordinary they used to say about the most humdrum occurrence. If you blew your nose it was exquisitely civilized." The play also exhibits the blend of regret and nostalgia found in many of Bennett's works about England. This is seen in the headmaster's reflection about the decline of traditional English values: "Once we had a romantic and old-fashioned conception of honour, of patriotism, chivalry and duty. But it was a duty that didn't have much to do with justice, with social justice anyway."

Bennett's other dramatic works include *Getting On* (1971), about a disillusioned member of Parliament; and *Kafka's Dick* (1986), about an insurance salesman who is investigating the famous Czech author Franz Kafka's visit to contemporary England. In one of his most acclaimed plays, *The Madness of George III* (1992), Bennett portrays the political intrigue in England during the American Revolution. Critic Robert Brustein has written that the play's uniqueness "lies in the way it manages to evoke an entire historical epoch. . . . Before long we are deep in the intrigues of Georgian politics."

Bennett has also written many dramatic and documentary works for television as well as numerous reviews for the *London Review of Books*. He combined many of these pieces with play prefaces and humorous commentary in his autobiography *Writing Home* (1994), a critical and popular success. Critic David Nokes describes Bennett as "probably our greatest living drama-tist. . . . His genius lies in an unerring ear for the idioms of lower-middle-class life, the verbal doilies of self-respect and self-repression."

Other Work by Alan Bennett
Say Something Happened: A Play. New York: Samuel French, 1982.

A Work about Alan Bennett
Wolfe, Peter. *Understanding Alan Bennett.* Columbia: University of South Carolina Press, 1999.

Bennett, Arnold (1867–1931) *novelist*
Arnold Bennett was born in the industrial town of Hanley, Staffordshire, northern England, to Enoch Bennett, a lawyer, and Sarah Ann Bennett. He attended public and private schools, including a short tenure at an art school, but never went to college because his father wanted him to join him in his law firm. Bennett studied law only halfheartedly and failed the bar twice before moving to London, where he began his career as a writer.

Bennett secured a position as the editor for the weekly magazine *Woman,* and after writing several pieces for various magazines and literary journals, he published his first novel, *A Man from the North* (1884), an apprentice piece, overshadowed by his later novels. He went on to write more than 35 novels, the best-regarded of which are a series of novels set in the region of Bennett's childhood: *The Old Wives' Tale* (1908), *Clayhanger* (1910), and *Riceyman Steps* (1923).

The best of Bennett's early novels are all unified by their setting, the northern industrial region known as the "five towns," which the author knew well in his youth. From his memory of that area, Bennett wrote *Anna of the Five Towns* (1902), *Leonora* (1903), and *Sacred and Profane Love* (1905), which all unsentimentally examine women whose lives are narrowed by their materialistic pursuits.

The Old Wives' Tale, also set in the five towns, established Bennett's enduring reputation more than any other novel and is still considered a classic of British literature. Its attention to setting cements the five towns as a literary region comparable to Thomas Hardy's Wessex, and its treatment of characters and themes displays Bennett's full literary capability. The novel follows two sisters, Constance and Sophia, from childhood through old age, while developing the themes of change and death. The sisters marry, with Constance remaining in England and Sophia moving with her husband to France. They experience life's full range of emotions—happiness, frustration, and grief—while gradually, and half-unknowingly, growing old. Bennett brings the reader face-to-face with aging and death when Sophia looks upon her once young and beautiful but now dying husband, who had left her years before: "In her mind she had not pictured Gerald as a very old man. She knew that he was old; she had said to herself that he must be very old, well over seventy. But she had not pictured him." The image she encounters makes her shudder and remark, "'Yet a little while . . . and I shall be lying on a bed like that! And what shall I have lived for? What is the meaning of it?'"

Bennett also received critical acclaim for *Clayhanger*, the first novel of a trilogy about the family of Edwin Clayhanger. Clayhanger, modeled after Bennett himself, struggles to free himself from a domineering father who wants him to join the family printing business. In addition to such parent/child conflicts, *Clayhanger* and its sequels, *Hilda Lessways* (1911) and *These Twain* (1916), also explore problems between the sexes.

The last novel for which Bennett earned acclaim is *Riceyman Steps* (1923), which won the James Tait Black Memorial Prize. It is a dark novel with Freudian sexual undertones about an elderly and miserly antique bookseller, Earlforward, who marries a widow named Violet. Largely because of Earlforward's obsession with money and Violet's detestation of that pursuit, the relationship becomes a mixture of love and hate that ends, eventually, in death.

During his lifetime Bennett achieved great commercial success, but many of the nation's literary elite, including Virginia WOOLF and T. S. ELIOT, turned against him late in his career and ef-

fectively pushed his work into near obscurity, mainly because he was old and a careerist. Recent scholarship has reassessed Bennett and led to a resurrection of his reputation. As the writer and Bennett biographer Frank SWINNERTON observes, Bennett's "characters are . . . illustrations of the endless foibles and endurances of mankind. . . . Bennett's novels will live, indeed . . . future generations will see and feel in them the actual life of one part of England in a day that is already past."

Other Work by Arnold Bennett

The Grand Babylon Hotel. 1902. Reprint, New York: Penguin, 1992.

Works about Arnold Bennett

Hepburn, James, ed. *Arnold Bennett.* New York: Routledge, 1997.
Squillace, Robert. *Modernism, Modernity, and Arnold Bennett.* Lewisburg, Pa.: Bucknell University Press, 1997.

Bentley, Edmund Clerihew (1875–1956)
novelist, poet, journalist

E. C. Bentley is best known both as a crime-fiction writer and as the originator of the poetic form known as the clerihew, which he invented as a diversion from his schoolwork when he was 16 years old and attending St. Paul's School in London. A clerihew is a humorous pseudobiographical poem of four lines in which the first two lines and the last two lines rhyme, for example:

> *Wolfgang Amadeus Mozart*
> *Whose very name connotes art*
> *Thought flutes untunable and otophagic*
> *[painful to the ear]*
> *Till he made one that was magic.*

Bentley's first collection of clerihews was published in 1905 under the title *Biography for Beginners.*

Bentley worked as a journalist for the London *Daily News*, the *Daily Telegraph*, and *Punch* from 1901 through 1934. During this time, however, his main success was as a mystery writer. Though he wrote only four mystery novels, he was enormously popular in his time and had a great influence on later mystery writers. His first novel, *Trent's Last Case* (1913), is among the first books of the Golden Age of mystery fiction, which includes such writers as Dorothy L. SAYERS and Agatha CHRISTIE. Philip Trent, in contrast with the stoic and self-important heroes of previous detective stories, is a self-mocking gentleman, an artist and part-time detective who must find the killer of an American capitalist.

One of Bentley's innovations in the mystery genre is a realistic approach to the material. For example, where previous literary detectives were master sleuths who always got their man, Trent finds that his best efforts have led to a completely erroneous conclusion.

Bentley was also influential in his avoidance of melodrama, his use of multiple solutions to the crime, and a humorous approach to characters. As Sayers wrote, ". . . running into little sidestreams of wit and humor, or spreading into crystal pools of beauty and tender feeling, *Trent's Last Case* welled up in the desiccated desert of mystery fiction like a spring of living water."

Bentley's contribution to literature is still strongly felt today. In Sayers's words, his work was that "of an educated man, . . . who was not ashamed to lay his gifts of culture at the feet of that Cinderella of literature, the mystery novel."

Other Works by E. C. Bentley

Trent Intervenes. 1938. Reprint, New York: House of Stratus, 2001.

Trent's Own Case. 1936. Reprint, New York: House of Stratus, 2001.

Berger, John Peter (1926–   ) *novelist, art critic, screenwriter*

John Berger, a committed marxist, is a novelist, painter, and art historian famous for his study of the peasant communities of the French Alps and for his influential studies of perception and art.

Born in London, he attended the Central School of Art and the Chelsea School of Art in London and taught drawing from 1948 to 1955. In 1952 he began writing influential art criticism with marxist overtones for London's *New Statesman.*

Berger's first novel, *A Painter of Our Time* (1958), written in journal entry form, is a character study of an aging, bitter painter who struggles with financial worry and a loveless marriage. The book was praised for its realistic depiction of the life of an artist.

Berger earned the 1972 BOOKER PRIZE for *G.: A Novel.* Set during the failed revolution of Milanese workers in 1898, the novel tells the story of a young man's sexual encounters in Europe. Berger was heralded for the compassion with which he explored how men and women relate to each other and their search for intimacy. The novel also earned him the James Tait Black Memorial Prize.

Berger's most influential work is often considered to be *Ways of Seeing* (1972), a study of art based on the BBC television series of the same name. In this book he analyzes not only art but also the very meaning of perception—what we see and how we see it. In his examination of how image relates to text, Berger writes, "It is seeing which establishes our place in the surrounding world; we explain that world with words, but words can never undo the fact that we are surrounded by it."

Particularly relevant even three decades after the book's publication is Berger's discussion of images in the mass media. He suggests that the images of advertising are "of the moment"—that is, they speed past the viewer and transmit their message of capitalism on a subconscious level. Art, Berger argues, was once an expression of what an artist saw or possessed. Advertising is about what one does not have but thinks one needs.

In the 1970s Berger moved to a small village in the French Alps and became fascinated with the culture of the peasants who lived there. He soon explored this culture in his writing. *Pig Earth* (1979) was the first of Berger's *Into Their Labours* trilogy, which also includes *Once in Europa* (1983) and *Lilac and Flag: An Old Wives' Tale of a City*

(1990). These books are told through the stories passed on to him by French peasants and examine the changes in their way of life as they move from their isolated rural community to the city. Critic Harrington B. Laufman writes that in *Pig Earth* "[t]he 'fiction', that is the re-told tales, are the book's strength. It is unclear where the village story-tellers' tales end and Berger's elaboration (if any) begins. These seamless stories transported me to an earthy, physical world of self- reliance amidst the close community of the village."

In collaboration with the Swiss filmmaker Alain Tanner, Berger wrote the screenplay for *Jonah Who Will Be 25 in the Year 2000* (1983), which film critic Leonard Maltin called a "[s]ensitive, literate, engaging comedy about eight individuals affected by the political events of the late '60s."

Berger continues to write and paint. His paintings have been shown all over the world.

Other Works by John Berger
About Looking. New York: Vintage, 1992.
The Success and Failure of Picasso. New York: Vintage, 1993.
To the Wedding: A Novel. New York: Vintage, 1996.

A Work about John Berger
Dyer, Geoff. *The Ways of Telling: The Work of John Berger.* New York: Pluto Press, 1988.

Betjeman, John (1906–1984) *poet*
John Betjeman was born in London to Ernest Edward Betjeman, a businessman, and Mabel Bessie Betjeman. His parents fought constantly, and Betjeman was raised almost solely by a nanny. He went to a number of private elementary and preparatory schools, even studying under T. S. ELIOT at one point, but left Oxford after failing an important exam. He worked as a teacher at several high schools and for the Ministry of Information during World War II. However, his main goal was to be a poet.

Betjeman spent the better part of the 1930s supporting himself by writing for the magazine *Ar-chitectural Review* and producing several travel guides. In addition he wrote his first two volumes of poetry, *Mount Zion* (1931) and *Continual Dew* (1937), which featured subjects, including architecture, landscapes, religion, and death, that would become standard in his work. This early work also displayed his characteristically nostalgic tone.

With his first two collections virtually unrecognized by both critics and the public, Betjeman's reputation improved only slightly with the appearance of *Old Lights for New Chancels* (1940), *New Bats in Old Belfries* (1945), and *A Few Late Chrysanthemums* (1954). In 1958, however, with the publication of *Collected Poems*, he finally captured the interest of the popular reading public and the literary establishment. In this collection of previously published poetry, he demonstrated himself to be a poet remarkably untouched by the aesthetics of modernist poets such as Eliot. Among his influences was Alfred, Lord Tennyson. Instead of the experimentation and free verse of many of his contemporaries, Betjeman adopted traditional verse forms and presented what critic Louise Bogan described as "an entire set of neglected Victorian techniques . . . immediately acceptable even to our modern sensibilities, grown used to the harsh, the violent, and the horrifying."

Collected Poems contains two of Betjeman's most enduring poems: "Slough" and "The Metropolitan Railway." "Slough" is an example of what some critics call Betjeman's "light," or less serious verse. In great detail, it describes a dull suburban town, that "isn't fit for humans now, / There isn't grass to graze a cow." Regardless of the poem's "lightness," or perhaps because of it, it has been widely anthologized.

"The Metropolitan Railway" confronts progress and the price paid for it. The poem begins with a husband and wife on a bright and shiny metro platform but changes direction with the lines "visualize, far down the shining lines / Your parents' homestead set in murmuring pines." Betjeman shows how this earlier generation might have experienced the railroad on their first ride and describes how it entirely changed the face of the

British countryside. In the last stanza the poem returns to the present, in which the husband has died of cancer and the wife has a bad heart. Both have been abandoned by the promise of progress that seemed so wonderful in their youth.

Another of Betjeman's best poems, "In Willesden Churchyard," appears in *High and Low* (1966). In this poem the speaker walks among the headstones of a cemetery with his "love" and ponders the lives of the people lying beneath his feet. He ultimately arrives at questions about his own death. The poem ends with the lines, "Not ten yards off in Willesden parish church / Glows with the present immanence of God," but it suggests uncertainty rather than reassurance about death, even with the presence of God near at hand.

Betjeman was a popular poet, with his *Collected Poems* selling more than 100,000 copies in a time when poetry was commonly regarded as remote and sometimes unreadable. He was poet laureate from 1972 until his death and received numerous honorary degrees. While some critics question Betjeman's poetic skill, others see him as a worthy heir of 19th-century poetry. As Louise Bogan remarks, "it is a pleasure to let down our defenses and be swept along . . . and to meet no imperfect . . . rhymes . . .; to recognize sincerity so delicately shaded . . . that it becomes immediately acceptable even to our modern sensibilities."

Other Works by John Betjeman

English Cities and Small Towns. 1943. Reprint, London: Prion, 1997.
John Betjeman: Collected Poems. London: John Murray, 1990.

A Work about John Betjeman

Brown, Dennis. *John Betjeman.* Tavistock, England: Northcote, 1999.

Blackwood, Algernon (1869–1951)
novelist, short story writer

Algernon Blackwood was born in Shooter's Hill, Kent, England, the son of the duchess of Manchester and Sir Stevenson Arthur Blackwood. His parents were members of a strict Calvinist sect. Their beliefs exerted great influence on Blackwood's fiction, which he began writing after a series of failed jobs and illnesses.

In 1900 Blackwood joined a mystical secret society, the Hermetic Order of the Golden Dawn, which was dedicated to the study of the occult and magic; its best-known member was William Butler YEATS. Blackwood drew from his experiences with the Golden Dawn and other occult studies to describe strange mystical states of mind in eerie detail in such short-story collections as *The Empty House and Other Ghost Stories* (1906) and novels such as *The Human Chord* (1910).

Blackwood had a special gift for finding the horror in situations in which the line between faulty human perception and true danger is unclear. In "The Transfer" (1912), for instance, the narrator describes a child's beliefs about an unnaturally dead patch in a garden, noting "it was Jamie who buried ogres there and heard it [the ground] crying in an earthy voice, swore that it shook its surface sometimes while he watched it, and secretly gave it food." One of his best-known characters is the physician and occult investigator John Silence, featured in *John Silence: Physician Extraordinary* (1908).

Although Blackwood viewed his fiction as describing mystical and altered states of consciousness, many of his readers regard them as straight horror stories. His greatest impact was on later horror writers, including the American writer H. P. Lovecraft, who wrote of Blackwood, "he is the one absolute and unquestioned master of weird atmosphere." Fellow British writer Hilaire BELLOC, observed that Blackwood was a genius who created "successful literary achievement in the most difficult of literary provinces."

Other Works by Algernon Blackwood

The Best Ghost Stories of Algernon Blackwood. New York: Dover Publications, 1973.
Tales of the Uncanny and Supernatural. New York: Book-of-the-Month Club, 1992.

A Work about Algernon Blackwood

Ashley, Mike. *Algernon Blackwood: An Extraordinary Life.* New York: Carroll & Graf, 2001.

Blair, Eric Arthur

See ORWELL, GEORGE.

Blake, Nicholas

See DAY LEWIS, CECIL.

Bloomsbury Group

The Bloomsbury Group was the name given to a loosely knit group of writers and intellectuals who began meeting in 1905. It started when writer Thoby Stephen brought a group of his friends at Cambridge to meet his sisters, Virginia (who was to become Virginia WOOLF) and Vanessa (who was to marry art critic Clive BELL), at their Gordon Square home in Bloomsbury, a section of London. Eventually a variety of artists, economists, publishers, and writers would become members of the group. Among its original members were Bell, novelist and publisher Leonard WOOLF, historian Lytton STRACHEY, and civil servant Saxon Sydney-Turner. The Bloomsbury group was later joined by literary critic Desmond MacCarthy, novelist E. M. FORSTER, art critic Roger FRY, novelist David Garnett, and economist John Maynard Keynes. In addition to Bloomsbury, the group met at the country homes of its members

The members of the Bloomsbury Group denied having a formal reason to gather. Leonard Woolf stated that "we had no common theory, system, or principles which we wanted to convert the world to." However, the group's members were united in their belief in the importance of the arts, the pursuit of knowledge, and the creation and enjoyment of aesthetic experiences. They were considered the genteel wing of the innovative and progressive writers and artists who made up the avant-garde. Bloomsbury members delighted in offending the English upper classes through their rejection of the aesthetic, social, and sexual norms of traditional Victorian society. They also enjoyed playing pranks such as the Dreadnought Hoax, in which group members disguised themselves as dignitaries from Zanzibar in order to receive an official tour of a British battleship.

Among the important books written by Bloomsbury Group members are Strachey's *Eminent Victorians* (1918), Bell's *Art* (1914), Keynes's *Economic Consequences of the Peace* (1919), Virginia Woolf's *Jacob's Room* (1922), and Leonard Woolf's *Hunting the Highbrow* (1927). In addition, the Woolfs founded the Hogarth Press, which published T. S. ELIOT's *The Waste Land* (1923). Although the group was influential, some writers such as Wyndham LEWIS and F. R. LEAVIS criticized it as effeminate, elitist, pretentious, and shallow. Writer Frank SWINNERTON described the Bloomsbury Group as "intellectually Royalist—royalist you understand, to itself." Critic Dmitri Mirski described the group's liberalism as "thin-skinned humanism for enlightened and sensitive members of the capitalist class."

Bloomsbury's influence waned after Virginia Woolf's suicide in 1941, but critical interest in the group revived after 1960. Poet Stephen SPENDER wrote of the group: "Bloomsbury has been derided by some people and has attracted the snobbish admiration of others: but I think it was the most constructive and creative influence on English taste between the wars."

Works about the Bloomsbury Group

Marler, Regina. *Bloomsbury Pie: The Making of the Bloomsbury Boom.* New York: Henry Holt, 1997.
Rosenbaum, S. P. *Victorian Bloomsbury: The Early Literary History of the Bloomsbury Group ,* vol. 1. New York: St. Martin's Press, 1987.

Blunden, Edmund Charles   (1896–1974)
poet, nonfiction writer
Charles Blunden was born in London to Charles and Georgina Tyler Blunden and grew up in the English countryside of Yalding, Kent. Although

Blunden's family had financial problems, he was able to attend the prestigious private school Christ's Hospital and Queen's College, Oxford, on academic scholarships. During World War I he fought with the Sussex regiment, saw heavy front-line action in France, and survived a gas attack.

A poet and scholar of the same World War I generation as the poets Siegfried SASSOON and Wilfred OWEN, Blunden was deeply influenced by the British romantics throughout his life, and despite witnessing the horrors of war, he wrote poetry that is often set in rustic, rural places and narrated by shepherds. The pastoral qualities so typical of Blunden's work are nowhere more evident than in his major collection *The Poems of Edmund Blunden* (1930). "The Barn," for instance, establishes a highly rustic tone in its first lines: "Rain-sunken roof, grown green and thin / For sparrows' nests and starlings' nests." Blunden's love for the pastoral is so strong that even when he broaches the topic of war, his poetry retains some its elements. After describing a disheveled and disheartened group of soldiers in "An Infantryman," Blunden ends the poem optimistically: "You smiled, you sang, your courage rang, and to this day I hear it, / Sunny as a May-day dance, along that spectral avenue."

Blunden is also remembered for his 1928 memoir of World War I, *Undertones of War,* in which he describes his entire war experience in vignettes that focus largely on daily routines rather than combat. Although written in prose, the scholar Paul Fussel, underscoring Blunden's place in the pastoral tradition, describes Blunden's memoir as "an extended pastoral elegy."

Throughout his career, Blunden taught literature at universities around the world, most notably at Oxford in 1966. He also published biographies of Leigh Hunt, Percy Bysshe Shelley, and Thomas Hardy. He will be best remembered, however, as a traditional and pastoral poet. In the estimation of the scholar G. S. Fraser, "Blunden is a last important survivor of that generation of first world war poets who passed through and surmounted an ordeal of initiation . . . the last surviving poet of the school of Hardy, the last writer of a natively English poetry."

Other Works by Edmund Blunden
English Villages. London: Prion, 1997.
Selected Poems. Edited by Robyn Marsack. 1947. Reprint, Manchester: Carcanet, 1982.

A Work about Edmund Blunden
Webb, Barry. *Edmund Blunden: A Biography.* New Haven, Conn.: Yale University Press, 1990.

Blyton, Enid (Mary Pollock) (1897–1968)
children's author
Born in London, Enid Blyton was the daughter of Thomas Carey and Theresa Mary Harrison Blyton. Her family thought she would grow up to become a pianist, but even before she could write, Enid was telling her brothers stories. When she was 14, the writer Arthur Mee published one of her poems and encouraged her to write more. "All through my teens, I wrote and wrote and wrote . . . poems, stories, articles, even a novel," Blyton recalled in *Story of My Life* (1952).

When Blyton decided she wanted to write for children, she became a kindergarten teacher, and her students acted as her critics. The poems she wrote for them appeared in *Child Whispers* (1922). The following year, she worked on a children's book with editor Hugh Pollock, whom she married in 1924; they had two children. After their divorce, Blyton married Kenneth Waters, a surgeon, in 1943.

Blyton wrote an average of 15 books a year, published several children's magazines, and organized children's charities. Eventually she published more than 700 books, several under the name Mary Pollock, and 10,000 short stories. *Little Noddy Goes to Toyland* (1949), about a little toy man with a talent for getting into trouble, became the first of several popular series. Critic Lucy Clark wrote that Blyton's series retain their appeal because they tell easy-to-read stories about "kids in groups going on adventures away from their parents and eating fabulous feasts." The mystery stories about the Famous Five and the Secret Seven have been translated into more than 60 languages and adapted into several television series.

In the 1950s Blyton's work was criticized for its simple style, sexist stereotypes, and snobbishness. However, critic Sheila G. Ray notes that Blyton's faults make her popular with children: "She was above all a skilled storyteller and many adults today must owe their pleasure in reading to this quality in her work." The scholar Peter Murphy agrees: "Her books are about children in jeopardy, children empowered, children winning through. Enid Blyton is still the world's greatest storyteller for children."

Other Works by Enid Blyton

Five Are Together Again. 1963. Reprint, New York: Galaxy, 2000.
Good Old Secret Seven. 1960. Reprint, New York: Galaxy, 2000.

A Work about Enid Blyton

Rudd, David. *Enid Blyton and the Mystery of Children's Literature.* New York: Palgrave, 2000.

Boland, Eavan Aisling (1945–) *poet, essayist*

Eavan Boland was born in Dublin, Ireland, to the painter Frances Kelley and the diplomat Frederick (Frank) H. Boland, whose various posts led the family to London and New York. Boland graduated from Trinity College, Dublin, and currently directs the creative writing program at Stanford University. She has published more than 10 volumes of poetry, a memoir, numerous pamphlets, and essays and poems in journals in Ireland and America. Her awards include the Lannan Foundation Award in Poetry and the America Ireland Fund Literary Award.

Boland found that as a woman poet she confronted a male-dominated literary tradition filled with crippling preconceptions and expectations. In her essay collection *Object Lessons: The Life of the Woman and the Poet in Our Time* (1995), she recalls a moment when she saw "that everything which has defined my life up to that moment is something which has not happened. . . . Sometimes on my way to college, or making a detour to have a cup of coffee in the morning, I saw my reflection in a shopwindow. I never liked what I saw. A red-headed girl, always self-conscious, never graceful enough. . . . It was a measure of the confusion I felt, the increasing drain on my purpose and clear-headedness that I hardly ever thought I saw an Irish poet."

As with other contemporary women poets—Sylvia Plath, Adrienne Rich, and Anne Sexton, for example—Boland turned these concerns into poetry. *In Her Own Image* (1980), with charcoal drawings by Constance Short, includes poems on anorexia, mastectomy, menstruation, and masturbation. Throughout her poetry Boland challenges herself to make and her readers to follow that difficult and sustaining move from object or icon (Mother Ireland, Housewife) to subject or author.

Another response to Boland's life and times seems especially apt for the daughter of a diplomat: She addresses the seductions and ravages of power, whether deployed by imperial master, nationalist ideologue, or religious authority. Poetry comes in, Boland says, where myth touches history and language reclaims place. For her place is the point of intersection among myth, history, voice, and silence. She avoids writing about the famous Irish nationalist places, usually the sites of catastrophe, and finds her own versions of what William Butler YEATS calls "befitting emblems of adversity: the Dublin suburbs, the workhouse in Clonmel where a Boland ancestor was master, the only "administrative" job a Catholic could get, the charity hospital in Dublin where Boland's grandmother died alone in October 1909.

Boland also composes beautiful, artistic poems rendered as autobiography ("I Remember"), as cautionary tale ("Degas's Laundresses"), or as moments of pure visual and verbal beauty ("Renoir's 'The Grape Pickers'"). In "I Remember" the early memory is captured with imagery drawn specifically from the painter's tools: "porcupining in a jar / The spines of my mother's portrait brushes / Spiked from the dirty turpentine . . ."

Finally, Boland is a fine love poet, writing of sexual, romantic, familial, maternal, and domestic love. Among most resonant sentences in *Object Lessons* is "I want a poem I can grow old in. I want a poem I can die in." Some of her love poetry—"The Black Lace Fan My Mother Gave Me" and "The Pomegranate," for instance—comes very close to meeting that demand.

Other Works by Eavan Boland

Against Love Poetry. New York: W. W. Norton, 2001.

The Lost Land. New York: W. W. Norton, 1998.

An Origin Like Water: Collected Poems 1957–87. New York: W. W. Norton, 1997.

Outside History: Selected Poems 1980–1990. New York: W. W. Norton, 2001.

Bolt, Robert Oxton   (1924–1995)

playwright, screenwriter

Robert Bolt was born in Sale, near Manchester, England, to Ralph Bolt, a shopkeeper, and his wife, Leah, a teacher. From 1943 to 1946 Bolt served with the Royal West African Frontier Force in Ghana. After completing his degree in history in 1949, he taught English at Millfield School in Somerset.

A request to write a school Christmas play became "an astonishing turning point," because it made Bolt realize that "this is what I was going to do." Beginning with *The Master* in 1953, the BBC (British Broadcasting Corporation) aired 15 of his radio dramas. Bolt's first stage play, *The Last of the Wine* (1956), was an adaptation of a radio play about the threat of atomic war. The success of *Flowering Cherry*, about an unsuccessful insurance salesman who dreams of planting a cherry orchard, earned Bolt the 1957 *Evening Standard* Drama Award for Most Promising British Playwright and allowed him to become a full-time writer.

Bolt's most acclaimed work is *A Man for All Seasons* (1960), which won the Tony Award for best

play in 1962. The drama portrays the conflict between King Henry VIII and Sir Thomas More, described by Bolt as "a hero of selfhood," who chose to die rather than betray his conscience. London *Times* reviewer Chris Peachment called the play "a rare and abiding portrait of a virtuous man."

Bolt's skill at creating well-structured plots brought new success when he worked with director David Lean on screenplays. His adaptations of *Dr. Zhivago* (1965) and *A Man for All Seasons* (1966) won Academy Awards. His other films include *The Bounty* (1984); and *The Mission* (1986), which the critic Sheila Benson described as a "spectacle of conscience" about slavers' treatment of the Guarani Indians. *The Mission* won the Palme d'Or at the 1986 Cannes Film Festival.

Some critics consider Bolt's plays old-fashioned because of their traditional plot structure, but others praise his literate, well-crafted works for the questions they raise and for their engaging heroes, who often struggle with compelling ethical dilemmas. Bolt's own explanation was that he used the past "not to give a history lesson but to create an effective, entertaining, possibly disturbing—and truthful—evening in the theatre." According to Chris Peachment, Bolt engages issues that many playwrights would not dare to tackle: "It is our luck that we have a playwright naïve and bold enough to ask large questions about conscience and place them on a national scale."

Other Works by Robert Bolt

Bolt: Plays One. New York: Dimensions, 2001.

Bolt: Plays Two. New York: Dimensions, 2001.

A Work about Robert Bolt

Turner, Adrian. *Robert Bolt: Scenes from Two Lives.* New York: Vintage, 1998.

Bond, Edward   (Thomas Edward Bond)

(1934–   ) *playwright, poet, essayist*

Edward Bond was born in the Holloway suburb of North London. His parents were farm laborers who had moved to London in the 1930s to find work. After quitting school, he worked in a factory before the British Army drafted him and sent him to Vienna.

Bond's first play to be produced was *The Pope's Wedding* (1962), which depicts a married East Anglian farm worker who has an obsessive, and eventually violent, relationship with a recluse. His second play, *Saved* (1965), is set in a South London working-class neighborhood. Bond uses violence in the drama to express his views that industrialized society has a corrupting and dehumanizing influence on urban youths. When one of the characters is asked if he ever killed anyone, his response shows no consciousness of humanity: "Well I did once. I was in a room. Some bloke stood up in the door. Lost, I expect. I shot 'im. 'E fell down. Like a coat fallin' off a 'anger." *Saved* created a firestorm of controversy because of its brutal depiction of thugs stoning a baby to death.

Censorship and critical disapproval did not prevent Bond from writing many more controversial plays on social and public themes. An anarchist, he uses plays such as *The Worlds* (1979), a defense of working-class terrorism set in contemporary Britain, to call for the overturning of what he considers the institutionalized injustice of the capitalist system. Although his dramas have varying geographical and historical settings, Bond consistently uses disturbing and violent scenes to try to shock his audience into seeing a need for change. In a review of *Lear*, Bond's socialist rewriting of the Shakespearean tragedy, critic John Weightman wrote, "The message is that successive regimes behave mistakenly in similar ways in order to preserve their authority, and that improvement can only come through a change of heart."

Bond has won several honors for his powerful works, including the George Devine Award and the John Whiting Award. The scholars Malcolm Hay and Philip Roberts have noted that Bond's plays "explore and investigate the nature of human behaviour in societies which, like our own, inhibit and destroy natural human responses and turn people against each other."

Other Work by Edward Bond
Tuesday. London: Methuen Drama, 1993.

A Work about Edward Bond
Hay, Malcolm, and Philip Roberts. *Bond: A Study of His Plays.* London: Eyre Methuen, 1980.

Booker Prize (Booker McConnell Prize, Man Booker Prize)
Founded in 1969 by the company Booker Mc-Connell, the Booker Prize (recently renamed the Man Booker Prize) is awarded annually to an outstanding novel written in English by a resident of the British Commonwealth or the Republic of Ireland. Each year the Booker Prize Management Committee appoints a panel of judges, including a literary critic, an academic, a literary editor, a novelist, and a major figure in the publishing industry. To help ensure the prize's integrity, a new panel of judges is chosen each year.

The judges first read all of the submitted works for that year—sometimes as many as 120—and decide on a short list of six outstanding novels. The authors of these books receive £1,000 and a leather-bound copy of their book. From the short list the judges then choose the winner, who earns an additional £20,000.

More valuable than the prize money to the writers chosen for the short list and for the Booker Prize itself is the publicity and visibility that come with the honor. An excellent example of the prize's selling power is 1999's winner *Disgrace* by J. M. COETZEE. The novel jumped from number 1,431 to number 6 on the *London Times* best-seller list, a sales leap of 1,784 percent in five days. Of course, with so much at stake, the prize is often the subject of controversy. One recurring question is whether the judges can possibly do justice to the volume of submissions they have to read.

The first winner of the Booker Prize was *Something to Answer For* by P. H. NEWBY. Other winning writers include Bernice RUBENS, David STOREY, Keri HULME, Kazuo ISHIGURO, Michael ONDAATJE, Roddy DOYLE, and Peter CAREY. In 2002 the Man Booker

Prize was awarded to Yann Martel, a Spanish-born novelist now living in Canada.

Bowen, Elizabeth (1899–1973) *novelist, short story writer*

Elizabeth Bowen was born in Dublin, Ireland, to Henry Cole and Florence Colley Bowen, aristocrats who lived at Bowen's Court, an estate that had been in the family since 1653. She was educated at Downe House in Kent, where she came under the tutelage of the novelist Rose MACAULEY, who in turn introduced her to a broader literary community, which included Edith SITWELL, Walter DE LA MARE, and Aldous HUXLEY.

In 1923 Bowen married Alan Cameron and published her first book, *Encounters,* a collection of stories generally about inexperienced young women in difficult situations. She soon followed this with *The Hotel* (1927), a novel that explores similar themes. In 1929 Bowen moved to London and became acquainted with the BLOOMSBURY GROUP, a literary circle whose most prominent member, Virginia WOOLF, became one of her dearest friends. At this time Bowen began to establish a literary reputation. The first of her major novels, *The Last September* (1929), is an engaging study of a young woman attempting to develop her own personality in the confines of an aristocratic family.

Bowen further enhanced her reputation with *Friends and Relations* (1931), a novel set in Britain that focuses on the social interactions of several upper-class characters. However, she reached the peak of her creative abilities with what are still regarded as her finest novels: *The House in Paris* (1935), which describes a day-long friendship between two young children; *The Death of the Heart* (1938), which focuses on a young girl's ill-fated love for an older, more experienced, and villainous man; and *The Heat of the Day* (1948), which is based on Bowen's experiences in World War II.

Although Bowen is primarily remembered as a novelist, she also wrote numerous short stories, of which the most highly acclaimed, including "The Mysterious Kôr" and "Demon Lover," appear in *The Collected Stories of Elizabeth Bowen* (1981).

Late in her career, at the age of 70, Bowen won the James Tait Black Memorial Prize for *Eva Trout* (1968), a novel about an eccentric young woman who is accidentally murdered. Despite the prize it received, critics do not regard this as one of Bowen's best novels. Nevertheless, according to the scholar Siobhán Kilfeather, Bowen will long be remembered for "an extraordinary attention to tradition. Language, conventions, and manners that have been taken for granted she places under stress. She addresses mainstream, middle-class English life as someone sufficiently alienated by race and gender to cast a cold eye upon it."

Critical Analysis

Siobhán Kilfeather mentions that Bowen promulgates tradition because she continued the rich legacy of the British novel of manners, or realistic stories about the social interactions and conventions of a particular social class. For instance, her first novel, *The Last September* (1929), describes the social life of Irish aristocrats as they waltz unsettlingly through parties and tennis matches at Danielstown, an ancestral estate; they are totally impervious to the Irish revolution ravaging the country simultaneously. The novel constantly observes its characters, noting even how they sit or stand. In a typical passage, before the beginning of a tennis match, Bowen writes:

> Everybody was sitting or standing about . . . there were two courts and eighteen players; they were discussing who was to play first . . . Lois was nowhere; Lawrence sat on the ground smoking and taking no part in the argument. Lady Naylor talked eagerly to a number of guests . . . Livvy Thompson was organizing.

Lois Farquar, noticeably absent in this passage but the central character of Bowen's novel, is entirely stifled by this environment and longs for change. That finally comes near the novel's end, when the secondary story of the distant war merges with the actions of the aristocrats at Danielstown as soldiers burn down the old estate. Much of the novel's appeal stems from Bowen's masterful interweaving of these dual plots and her use of the fire to force the inhabitants of Danielstown to acknowledge the war and simultaneously end the boring phase of Farquar's life.

The House in Paris (1935), more than any of Bowen's other novels, reveals Virginia Woolf's influence. As Woolf does in *To the Lighthouse,* Bowen links several disconnected narratives into a single, unified story, and then deftly manipulates time. In *The House in Paris,* the narratives concern a disastrous love affair and its consequences. The novel, divided into three distinct parts, takes place in a single day, but in its second section it branches into an extended flashback to explain events that took place 10 years earlier. In that earlier time, Bowen deals primarily with Karen Michaelis, who becomes engaged to a man she does not love, has an affair with another woman's fiancé, becomes pregnant, and sends the resultant child to live in Paris after her paramour commits suicide. Although Karen's fiancé knows of the affair, he marries her nonetheless, and she doesn't see her child for nine years. The child, Leopold, is the focus of the first and third portions of the novel as he arrives at a house in Paris, where he is supposed to meet his mother for the first time. Leopold spends the day playing with Henrietta, a young girl making a travel stop at the same house, but his mother never comes, leaving Leopold weeping "like someone alone against his will, someone shut up alone for a punishment." According to the scholar Edwin J. Kenney, Jr., Leopold's "loneliness . . . is for Elizabeth Bowen a metaphor for all human loneliness caused by the combination of fate, of external circumstances, and innocence."

The Death of the Heart (1939) is about an inexperienced young woman named Portia. With both of her parents dead, she is forced to live with Thomas and Anna Quayne, a childless couple grown callous because of unfulfilled dreams. Neither of the Quaynes are capable of providing Portia the love and support she needs, and she spends

the novel unsuccessfully searching for love from several men, most notably a philandering young man named Eddie. The novel's greatness, according to the scholar Janet Dunleavy, is "[i]ts narrative mode [which] incorporates an expertly handled multiplicity of viewpoints which evoke a multiplicity of responses to a single event or situation." One such event is Portia's passion for Eddie. While the two are having a conversation, Bowen reveals that Portia is falling in love:

> The force of Eddie's behaviour whirled her free of a hundred puzzling humiliations, of her hundred failures to take the ordinary cue. She could meet the demands he made with the natural genius of the friend and lover. The impetus under which he seemed to move made life fall, round him and her, into a new poetic order.

In an ensuing passage, however, Bowen quickly turns her attention to Eddie, revealing that to him, Portia's love is something of a tool that will allow him to somewhat repair his roguish reputation: "For Eddie, Portia's love seemed to refute the accusations that had been brought against him for years."

In addition to her novels, Bowen is also well known for her short stories. Some of the most noteworthy are found in *The Demon Lover and Other Stories* (1945), a collection of stories about London during World War II. In Siobhán Kilfeather's words, the stories "are justly celebrated for their evocations of the fear in London, as the city comes to terms with danger." "The Mysterious Kôr," for instance, describes a paralyzed and frightening London during the German blitz as two characters, Pepita and Arthur, wander the city's streets pretending that London is a lost city in Africa, dreading their return to a crowded and claustrophobic apartment. Bowen develops the horrible psychological effect of the war by describing what would otherwise be a pleasant moonlit London night in military terms: "Full moonlight drenched the city and searched it; there was not a niche left to stand in. The effect was remorseless." To avoid the feeling of dangerous exposure suggested in this passage, Bowen writes that "People stayed indoors with a fervour that could be felt: the buildings strained with battened-down human life, but not a beam, not a voice, not a note from a radio escaped."

Other Works by Elizabeth Bowen
Little Girls. 1963. Reprint, New York: Penguin, 1992.
A Time in Rome. 1959. Reprint, New York: Penguin, 1990.
To the North. 1932. Reprint, New York: Penguin, 1997.

Works about Elizabeth Bowen
Bennett, Andrew, and Nicholas Royle. *Elizabeth Bowen and the Dissolution of the Novel: Still Lives.* New York: St. Martin's Press, 1994.
Hoogland, Renee C. *Elizabeth Bowen: A Reputation in Writing.* New York: New York University Press, 1994.
Jordan, Heather Bryant. *Elizabeth Bowen: A Study of the Short Fiction.* Boston: Twayne, 1991.

Bowen, John Griffith (1924–   ) *novelist, playwright, screenwriter*

John Bowen was born in Calcutta, India, the son of Hugh Bowen, a factory manager, and Ethel Bowen, a nurse. He earned his degree at Oxford. After publishing three novels while working at an advertising agency, he quit his job and started writing full-time.

Bowen is known for screenplays written specifically for television. Writer Betsy Greenleaf Yarrison describes the themes that Bowen revisits in all of his work as "the manipulation of one human being by another . . . the loneliness and isolation of people not at peace with their surroundings . . . the failure of individuals to form lasting emotional bonds with one another, and the prevalence of self-deception in modern life." Bowen's simple, engaging plots help the average television viewer understand these issues.

Bowen's television work, such as *A Holiday Abroad* (1960), *The Essay Prize* (1960), *The Jackpot*

Question (1961), and *The Candidate* (1961), all explore disillusionment and self-deception. In *A Holiday Abroad,* a week spent at a wealthy friend's home makes a schoolboy resentful of his own poverty. In *The Essay Prize,* an arrogant father confronts his own jealousy and failure when his son turns out to be a talented writer. In *The Candidate,* a successful businessman realizes that he is willing to sacrifice his career and his marriage to obtain a parliamentary seat.

Bowen's most successful stage play, *After the Rain* (1967), based on the novel of the same name (1958), expands on themes of manipulation and self-realization to explore "the making of superstition and myth" in a society 200 years in the future. In this play a professor uses hypnotized prisoners to reenact the story of a group who, having survived a flood that nearly destroys the human race, founds a new society. Betsy Greenleaf Yarrison calls *After the Rain* "an ambitious play: the survivors create a religion and a political system in the course of their voyage, and the drama makes some incisive comments on the political values of contemporary society."

Yarrison believes that Bowen "is noteworthy for his sound craftsmanship, his gift for writing dialogue that is both realistic and theatrically effective, and above all for his discerning portraiture of ordinary human beings struggling to be good in a corrupt, modern world."

Other Work by John Bowen
Plays One: After the Rain/The Disorderly Women/Little Boxes/Singles. London: Oberon Books, 1999.

Bradbury, Malcolm (1932–2000) *novelist, literary critic, screenwriter*

Malcolm Bradbury was born in Sheffield, England, to Arthur Bradbury, a railway employee, and Doris Marshall Bradbury. He earned his B.A. in 1953 from University College Leicester, his M.A. in 1955 from the University of London, and his Ph.D. in 1964 from the University of Manchester. In 1959 he married Elizabeth Salt, with whom he had two children.

Bradbury's fame as a novelist began with *Eating People Is Wrong* (1959). This book relates the adventures of a professor at a provincial university that has taken over the buildings of a former insane asylum; his office is a padded cell. Although Bradbury wrote that he disliked being labeled a writer of "campus novels," he was interested in ideas, and thus he wrote about "a place where people did discuss ideas, theoretical and aesthetic [and] contemplated literary and cultural theory."

From 1961 to 1965 Bradbury served as a lecturer at the University of Birmingham, where he became friends with David LODGE, another "campus novelist." In 1965 he moved to the University of East Anglia, where he helped found a writing program. His most famous novel, *The History Man* (1975), concerns a thoroughly detestable sociology professor, Howard Kirk, who stirs up campus unrest, has affairs with students, and drives his wife Barbara to suicide. This book was adapted into a successful television series. Bradbury himself was a writer of televised series such as *Anything More Would Be Greedy* (1989) and *The Gravy Train* (1990).

Bradbury was also a serious and highly regarded academic, known for his perceptive literary criticism, which runs to dozens of volumes and includes studies of Evelyn WAUGH, E. M. FORSTER, and Saul Bellow. Much of his academic work involves the novel: *The Modern American Novel* (1983); *The Novel Today* (1990), and *From Puritanism to Postmodernism* (1991).

Bradbury's other novels include *Stepping Westward* (1965), which explores the meanings of the word "liberalism"; *Rates of Exchange* (1983), about a British professor sent to Communist Eastern Europe; and *Dr. Criminale* (1992), about television journalists. David Lodge said of him, "He was not only an important novelist, but a man of letters of a kind that is now rare." Bradbury numbered himself among the "many writers for whom writing is not an economic activity but a vocation, the book not a commodity but a site of exploration."

Other Works by Malcolm Bradbury

To the Hermitage. London: Picador, 2000
Unsent Letters: Irreverent Notes from a Literary Life. New York: Viking, 1988.

Bragg, Melvyn (1939–) *novelist, screenwriter*

Melvyn Bragg was born in Carlisle, North Cumbria, England, to Stanley Bragg, who held many jobs, and Ethel Parks Bragg, a factory worker. A gifted student, he won a scholarship to attend Oxford, where he studied history. After graduating in 1961, he worked six years for the BBC (British Broadcasting Corporation) as a writer and a producer.

Bragg published his first novel, *For Want of a Nail,* in 1965. It describes the adolescence and early adulthood of a Cumbrian man from a working-class family. Since he frequently set his books in Cumbria, Bragg gained a reputation as a regional novelist. D. H. LAWRENCE influenced Bragg's use of sensuous images, while Thomas Hardy is his inspiration for writing tragic rural epics. Some critics describe Bragg as a didactic Romantic novelist. He is concerned about the usefulness of his books, as his narrator in *The Nerve* (1971), a novel about a teacher's nervous breakdown, describes: "Where possible, fiction, like all imaginative writing, should be helpful; the very best is beautiful and truthful and instances of those aspects of life are all the help we need."

Bragg's novels often chronicle the economic tensions faced by rural families. In *The Hired Man* (1970), his novel about a rural working-class family in the early 1900s, the character John is forced to hire himself out as a laborer: "He felt his jaws clench at the reply that would have to come through them when, soon, he would stand in the Ring looking for work. But the jaws would have to unclench—work had to be found." Bragg's works also portray the tensions that societal expectations place on individuals and families, as in *Autumn Manoeuvres* (1978), a novel about politics in which a young Member of Parliament struggles with self-doubt: "He felt he had let the people down. They deserved a minister. . . . someone who could begin to have a positive effect on their apparently intransigent problems. Not him."

In 1968 Bragg started writing screenplays, including a collaboration on the film version of the popular musical *Jesus Christ Superstar* (1973). He gained fame in the 1970s as a presenter of television programs on literature and the arts. In 1988 he wrote the well-received biography *Richard Burton: A Life* (1988). In 1989 reviewer Michelle Field summarized Bragg: "His reputation in the States is now chiefly as the producer and presenter of the *South Bank Show* . . . and as the author of *Richard Burton: A Life*. She added, "In England, however, Bragg is immediately put in the traditional 'man of letters' pigeonhole (people who have been great commentators and taste-makers as well as writers)."

Other Works by Melvyn Bragg

A Son of War. London: Sceptre, 2001.
Speak for England. New York: Alfred Knopf, 1976.

Braine, John Gerard (1922–1986) *novelist*

John Braine was born to Fred Braine, a sewage plant superintendent, and Katherine Henry Braine in Bradford, Yorkshire. Braine abandoned his secondary education before graduation and worked in a bookstore, a pharmacy, a factory, and in the Royal Navy before becoming a librarian, a job he would hold for 10 years.

As a novelist Braine is associated with a group of British authors known as the ANGRY YOUNG MEN. The writers of this group, including Kingsley AMIS and John WAIN, shared Braine's rejection of two trends: literary elitism, or the sense that literature should cater to the upper social classes; and an overwhelming avant-gardism, or intense experimentation in form that often alienates audiences. In rejecting these trends, Braine and the other writers of the group often used brash, semiarticulate, and highly sexualized characters to explore themes of class-consciousness and success.

Braine's most enduring novel, and the one most indicative of the Angry Young Men, is *Room at the Top* (1957). The novel follows a young, lower-middle class protagonist, Joe Lampton, as he moves into a wealthy London suburb, struggles to attain prominence, and impregnates the daughter of a wealthy businessman, who gives Joe a business in exchange for never seeing his daughter again. Lampton narrates the entire novel retrospectively, reviewing his life since his arrival in the city. In a passage indicative of Braine's characteristically plain style, Lampton reveals his fall from relative innocence and the guilt he feels for his methods of achieving social success. Looking at a picture of himself, Joe remarks:

[M]y face is not innocent exactly, but *unused*. I mean unused by sex, by money, by making friends and influencing people, hardly touched by any of the muck one's forced to wade through to get what one wants.

As this passages suggests, with the "muck one's forced to wade through," Joe has achieved his success through less than honorable means, often manipulating his love interests and choosing his acquaintances solely for their social rank. Braine subtly condemns his single-minded obsession with success and the means to which he stoops, but Lampton, enraged that the life of the upper class is nearly closed to him and willing to do nearly anything to achieve that elusive goal, emerges as a new and engaging type of character. Largely because of its protagonist, *Room at the Top* it was an instant popular success, selling well in both England and the United States. The critic Kenneth Allsop remarked that "few books have revealed so explicitly the actual shape and shimmer of the fantasy life longings of a Joe Lampton, and certainly no-one until John Braine has described the exact kind of urges operating within the post-war specimen."

Immediately following *Room at the Top*, Braine published *Life at the Top* (1962), an overly obvious and too moralistic continuation of his first novel that features Lampton reaping the bitter fruits of his dubiously achieved success. Braine rebounded, however, with *The Jealous God* (1964). The novel describes a Catholic man, Vincent Dungarvan, who is torn between choosing a life in the priesthood and his very strong love of women. He eventually falls in love with a woman, Laura Heycliff, who forces him to choose between herself and Catholicism because she is divorced, and marrying her would require Dungarvan to leave the church. The novel displays more intricately developed characters, a more appealing Yorkshire setting, and a less abrupt style than Braine's earlier novels. The author's attention to characters and his new style are both evident in one of Dungarvan's first encounters with Heycliff:

> She handed him a form; he took out his pen, then put it back in his pocket again. . . . He cleared his throat. "It isn't long till closing time." He suddenly found himself beginning to stammer, his self-confidence dwindling before her official composure.

Room at the Top established the ruthlessly ambitious protagonist typical of the Angry Young Men and revealed the restrictive social environment of postwar Britain. In assessing Braine's work, the scholar Judy Simons commented, "Braine's work is notable for its directness and continues to claim a steady popular readership. It remains of central academic interest to critics whose main concern is with the social context of literature, and no study of fiction of the 1950s can afford to ignore his earlier books."

Other Works by John Braine

These Golden Days. London: Methuen, 1985.
The Two of Us. London: Methuen, 1984.

Works about John Braine

Lee, J. W. *John Braine.* New York: Twayne, 1968.
Salwak, Dale. *John Braine and John Wain: A Reference Guide.* Boston: G. K. Hall, 1980.
Wilson, Colin. *The Craft of the Novel.* London: Gollancz, 1975.

Brathwaite, Edward Lawson Kamau
(1930–   ) poet, essayist

Edward Brathwaite was born in Bridgetown, Barbados, to Hilton Brathwaite, a warehouse clerk, and Beryl Gill Brathwaite. He attended Harrison College in Barbados, where he cofounded a school newspaper and wrote a column on jazz. Brathwaite won the coveted Barbados Island Scholarship to attend Cambridge, where he earned an honors degree in history in 1953. He returned to the Caribbean in 1962 to take up a series of teaching posts at different universities.

Brathwaite published his first poems as a college student in the Barbados literary journal *Bim*. His interest in complex rhythms of structure and creating long lyrical poems reflects the influence of T. S. ELIOT. His first major works—*Rights of Passage* (1967), *Masks* (1968), and *Islands* (1969)—composed the trilogy called *The Arrivants*. The poems in these works reflect Brathwaite's concern with rediscovering the identity of West Indian blacks through an examination of their African roots. His verse frequently describes the enslavement and transporting of Africans to the Caribbean. In the poem "New World A-Comin" he writes, "the flesh and the flies, the whips and the fixed / fear of pain in this chained and welcoming port." In 1970 he won the Cholmondely Award.

Brathwaite's second major trilogy, consisting of *Mother Poem* (1977), *Sun Poem* (1982), and *X/Self* (1987), continues his search for cultural identity. These works solidified his reputation with many critics as the most important West Indian poet. When reviewing *Mother Poem* David Dorsey noted Brathwaite's "sober, passionate and lucid perception of the beauty and pain black Barbadians are heir to."

Brathwaite promotes the Creole language spoken by most West Indians as an important part of reclaiming the West Indies cultural heritage. In the poem "Calypso" from *Islands* he writes, "Have you no language of your own / no way of doing things."

Brathwaite is also an essayist. In his historical work *Folk Culture of the Slaves in Jamaica* (1970), he writes, "The people danced and spoke their un-English English until our artists, seeking at last to paint themselves, to speak themselves, to sing themselves, returned . . . to the roots, to the soil, to the sources." He also suggests Caribbean blacks should similarly move beyond the religions and other traditions imposed upon them during the colonial age. The scholar June D. Bobb writes, "Brathwaite clearly intends his poetry to speak to members of the Caribbean's black population, so that they may recognize their position in society, become cognizant of their identity, and discover their connectedness to a creolized Caribbean culture."

Other Work by Edward Brathwaite

Words Need Love Too. Philipsburg, St. Martin: House of Nehesi, 2000.

A Work about Edward Brathwaite

Bobb, June D. *Beating a Restless Drum: The Poetics of Kamau Brathwaite and Derek Walcott.* Trenton, N.J.: Africa World Press Inc., 1998.

Bridie, James (Osborne Henry Mavor)
(1888–1951) playwright

Considered the founder of the modern Scottish theater, James Bridie was born Osborne Henry Mavor in Glasgow. He studied medicine and earned his degree from Glasgow University in 1913. After serving as a military doctor during World War I, he set up his own practice in Glasgow in 1919.

During these years, Bridie's interest in the theater grew. In 1922 he wrote his first play, *The Switchback,* about a doctor tempted by fame and fortune. The play was first performed in 1929. Bridie began to devote more energy to his writing and abandoned medicine in 1938 to become a full-time playwright, although he served as an army doctor during World War II.

Some of the most notable traits of Bridie's work are the power of his dialogue, his delight in human beings debating and arguing, and the exploration of human morality. Perhaps his most famous play is *The Anatomist* (1930), based on the true story of a proud and boisterous 19th-century doctor who is

supplied with bodies for dissection by a pair of murderers. The doctor expresses his conflict about this situation: "Do you think because I strut and rant and put on a bold face that my soul isn't sick within me at the horror of what I have done? . . . No, I carry the deaths of those poor wretches round my neck till I die."

To critics who objected to what they saw as unsatisfactory resolutions in his plays, Bridie responded, "Only God can write last acts, and He seldom does. You should go out of the theater with your head writhing with speculations."

Bridie wrote more than 40 plays in all. He was one of the founders of the Glasgow Citizens' Theatre, and helped to found the Royal Scottish Academy of Music and Drama. He was a member of the Arts Council and an adviser to the annual Edinburgh Festival.

Works about James Bridie

Bannister, Winifred. *James Bridie and His Theatre.* Philadelphia: Century Bookbindery, 1980.

Low, John Thomas. *Doctors, Devils, Saints, and Sinners: A Critical Study of the Major Plays of James Bridie.* Edinburgh: Ramsay Head Press, 1980.

Tobin, Terence. *James Bridie (Osborne Henry Mavor).* Boston: Twayne, 1980.

Brittain, Vera (1893–1970) novelist, poet, memoirist, journalist, nonfiction writer

Vera Brittain was born in Staffordshire and raised in the Cheshire town of Macclesfield. Her father was the wealthy owner of a paper mill, and her mother was the daughter of a musician. For the first nine years of her education, Brittain was taught at home by a governess. Later she lamented that she had grown up in a household containing "precisely nine books." Nonetheless, she avidly read what books she could and tried to write novels of her own.

When Brittain was 11 the family moved to Buxton, and she was sent to a private day school. Later she attended St. Monica's, a respected girl's boarding school in Surrey where she excelled in almost every subject. At age 16 she read Percy Bysshe Shelley's elegy for John Keats, "Adonais," and this melancholy poem sealed her determination to become a writer. As a student, she also became committed to the suffragist movement, fighting for women's right to vote.

At Christmas 1913 Brittain met Roland Leighton, her first love and soon her fiancé. She was heartbroken when he and her brother went to fight in World War I. She later recalled that "all through the War poetry was the only form of literature that I could read for comfort, and the only kind that I ever attempted to write." Some of these poems appear in her collection *Poems of the War and After* (1934).

Brittain attended Oxford, but she became increasingly determined to help the suffering soldiers. After a year at Oxford she temporarily left to work as a volunteer nurse with the VAD (Voluntary Aid Detachment). This experience made her a passionate pacifist. She described her time there in her first autobiography, *Testament of Youth* (1933). The most haunting sections of the book are those that describe her bewildered agony when her beloved brother and her fiancé were both killed in action. At first too stunned to understand it or weep, she lives for a while "like a slaughtered animal that still twists after life has been extinguished."

After the war, Brittain returned to Oxford. She had originally enrolled to study English, but now she switched to history in search of facts to make sense of the war. She wrote, "It's my job, now, to find out all about it, and try to prevent it, as far as one person can, from happening to other people."

At Oxford Brittain became close friends with Winifred HOLTBY. After they finished at Oxford the two lived together in London. Brittain worked briefly as a teacher and a journalist. Much of her journalism is passionately feminist and pacifist, and she became known as a stirring speaker for both causes.

Brittain's first novel was *The Dark Tide* (1923). Highly autobiographical, this book describes a woman's struggle to receive an education. Years later Brittain wrote another autobiographical novel, *Born 1925* (1948), a family saga that describes how two generations respond to World War II.

Brittain is best known for *Testament of Youth* (1933). Winifred Holtby said of this book, "Others have borne witness to the wastage, the pity and the heroism of modern war; none has yet so convincingly conveyed its grief." *Testament of Youth* became a best-seller again decades later, when Virago republished it in 1978. Brittain followed the original publication with the autobiographies *Testament of Friendship* (1940), a description of her relationship with Holtby; and *Testament of Experience* (1957).

Brittain wrote extensively on women's issues, including the histories *Women's Work in Modern England* (1928) and *Lady into Woman: A History of Women from Victoria to Elizabeth II* (1953). Her feminist principles became linked to her pacifist ethics. A member of the Peace Pledge Union, she was in demand as a lecturer on the subject around the country. She continued to work for pacifism even during World War II, when popular opinion condemned that philosophy as treacherous. Her book *Seeds of Chaos* (1944) argues strongly against the bombing of Germany.

Brittain wrote more than 25 books in different genres. At the end of her life she was still attending demonstrations and protests, and when she died she was working on a final autobiography, *Testament of Time*. At her request, her ashes were scattered over her brother's war grave in Italy.

Works about Vera Brittain

Berry, Paul, and Alan Bishop, eds. *Testament of a Generation: The Journalism of Vera Brittain and Winifred Holtby*. London: Virago, 1985.

Gorham, Deborah. *Vera Brittain: A Feminist Life*. Cambridge, Mass.: Blackwell Publishers, 1996.

Brooke, Rupert Chawner (1887–1915)
poet

Rupert Brooke was born in Warwickshire, England, to William Parker Brooke, a high school teacher, and Mary Ruth Cotterill Brooke. He earned a B.A. from King's College, Cambridge, and before World War I served as a schoolmaster at Rugby School. He traveled to Germany and America while writing his early poems.

Until the outbreak of World War I Brooke wrote GEORGIAN POETRY, which focused on country settings and youthful love and was similar to the work of Walter DE LA MARE. The most notable of Brooke's Georgian poems is "The Old Vicarage, Grantchester" (1912), which nostalgically describes a small, rural British village.

Despite his contributions to Georgian poetry, Brooke's reputation rests on his status as a "trench poet" like Wilfred OWEN and Siegfried SASSOON, who both earned the title by fighting in World War I. Of all the trench poets, Brooke was by far the most patriotic. His often-anthologized poem "The Soldier" became a rallying cry for Britain near the outset of the war, before poets and the public alike became disillusioned with the conflict (as the poems of Owen and Sassoon reflect). "The Soldier" opens with the remark that when a British soldier dies in battle and is buried abroad, "there's some corner of a foreign field / that is forever England." The rest of the poem glorifies England as a land capable of producing men that, in death, would enrich the soils of any foreign land. Even in the poem "The Dead" (1914), with its ominous title, Brooke remains positive, suggesting that when British soldiers die "honour has come back . . . and nobleness walks in our ways again."

Through the efforts of such prominent figures as Winston Churchill, Henry James and Walter de la Mare, Brooke came to represent ideal British manhood. When he died of sunstroke, dysentery, and blood poisoning near the island of Skyros in the Aegean Sea he was mourned throughout England. When World War I extended into a brutal and wholly unromantic conflict, however, his patriotic, pro-war poems rang hollow, and the public lost interest and even attacked his work. In the words of the scholar William E. Laskowski, Brooke was considered, for a time, "almost criminal in his blind, unconscious" assistance of the "Old Men

who would send an entire generation off to the slaughterhouses of the Marne and the Somme." Despite the backlash against his work, however, the scholar Doris Eder writes that Brooke's "war sonnets perfectly captured the mood" of the war's earliest moments, before the coming disaster could be recognized, and suggests that they are "deserving to be remembered."

Other Works by Rupert Brooke
The Collected Poems of Rupert Brooke. Murrieta, Calif.: Classic, 2001.
The Letters of Rupert Brooke. Edited by Geoffrey Keynes. London: Faber & Faber, 1968.

Works about Rupert Brooke
Laskowski, William E. *Rupert Brooke.* New York: Twayne, 1994.
Lehmann, John. *The Strange Destiny of Rupert Brooke.* New York: Holt, 1980.

Brooke-Rose, Christine (ca. 1926–)
novelist

While there is some discrepancy over Christine Brooke-Rose's birth date (some say 1926, others argue 1923), she was certainly born in Geneva, Switzerland, to Evelyn Blanche Brooke and Alfred Northbrook Rose, a defrocked monk and businessman who abandoned the family while Brooke-Rose was a child. She was educated in Belgium, where she lived with her mother and grandparents; and England, where she received her undergraduate degree from Oxford and a Ph.D. in Middle English from the University College, London.

Brooke-Rose is known as an experimental postmodern British writer who pushes the limits of language and the concept of the novel with nonlinear, often fragmented plots that delve into scientific issues such as genetics and nuclear war. Her first novels, however, are traditional. *The Sycamore Tree* (1959), for instance, is a standard novel of manners that focuses on the social interactions between two literary families in the Chelsea section of London. It mildly satirizes English social life, particularly the characters' concern with fashion, and is told in chronological order by a third-person narrator.

Later in her career, however, Brooke-Rose's writing changed dramatically as she experimented with form and explored science to such an extent that her most noteworthy novels—*Xorandor* (1986), *Verbivore* (1990), and *Textermination* (1991)—are classified as science fiction. *Xorandor*, a novel written totally in dialogue, is narrated by two 12-year-old computer-programming twins, Jip and Zab, who discover a living stone named Xorandor that communicates with computers. They further discover that the stone has been alive for 5,000 years and has a terrorist offspring. The twins spend the rest of the novel attempting to prevent the nuclear destruction threatened by the terrorist stone. The novel is noteworthy not only for its imaginative plot but also for its experimental method of narration. At the beginning of the novel, Brooke-Rose explains that Jib and Zab are telepathic. Their dialogue reveals that they are narrating this story jointly by dictating it into a computer:

[I]t's tough dictating this, Zab. It'd be much easier typing it straight on the keyboard.

But then it'd all come from one of us only, even if we took turns. One, it's important to be two, and two, it's easier to interrupt on vocal than to push hands away. You agreed, Jip, you even dubbed it flipflop storytelling. . . .

Verbivore is a sequel to *Xorandor* in which an unknown force interferes with all electronic transmissions on earth. This situation allows Brooke-Rose to demonstrate how much contemporary society has come to rely on oral communication devices, such as telephones, radios, and televisions, and to imagine the difficulties that would ensue if all means of electronic communication disappeared. In the words of the scholar Sarah Birch, the novel suggests that "we have . . . been immersed for too long in a predominantly oral culture for it

not to have permanently altered our minds," and that even a return to written communication would be extremely difficult.

Textermination is yet another highly imaginative novel that tells the story of a wide range of characters taken from other authors' works assembled in a netherworld of deceased literary figures whose afterlife depends on living people reading their books. Near the beginning of the novel, Jane Austen's Emma explains that the purpose of the assembly of authors and characters is

To pray together for our continuance of being, but also for all our brethren, far more numerous than even we who are here, who remain dead in never-opened books, coffins upon coffins stacked away in the great libraries of the world.

Brooke-Rose's literary career has inspired lively critical debates and a wide range of responses. Although critics admire her experimentation with the novel—her dual first-person narrators in *Xorandor*, for instance—such science fiction elements as talking rocks and mysteriously jammed radio waves often cause critics to view her as an author who writes outside of the British literary tradition. According to the scholar Morton P. Levitt, "[s]he will likely always be something of an exotic, acceptable as an 'experimenter' if only because she is somehow foreign, and undeniably outside the tradition." Other critics, however, such as Tyrus Miller, assert that "her writing, whatever her chosen genre and form, is consistently thoughtful, provocative, witty, and technically masterful" and will therefore "be recognized as one of the essential English-language writers of the end of the twentieth century."

Other Works by Christine Brooke-Rose

Next. Manchester, England: Carcanet, 1998.
Remake. Manchester, England: Carcanet, 1996.
Stories, Theories and Things. Cambridge, England: Cambridge University Press, 1991.
Subscript. Manchester, England: Carcanet, 1999.

Works about Christine Brooke-Rose

Birch, Sarah. *Christine Brooke-Rose and Contemporary Fiction.* Oxford, England: Clarendon, 1994.

Friedman, Ellen J., and Richard Martin, eds. *Utterly Other Discourse: The Texts of Christine Brooke-Rose.* Normal, Ill.: Dalkey Archive Press, 1995.

Brookner, Anita (1928–) *novelist, art historian*

Anita Brookner, the only daughter of Newson and Maude Schiska Brookner, was born in London. Her father was a Polish Jewish businessman; her mother gave up a career as a concert pianist on marrying. In England Brookner felt herself a displaced person although she had been born, was educated, and lived nearly all her life in London. She remained single, and in an interview she observed, "Mine was a dreary Victorian story: I nursed my parents till they died."

Brookner earned a bachelor's degree in French literature at the University of London and a doctorate in art history at the Courtauld Institute of Art. From 1964 to 1987 she was a lecturer and reader at the Courtauld Institute, and she was the first woman to be appointed Slade Professor of Art at Cambridge University (1967–68). Brookner published celebrated studies of the painters Watteau, Greuze, and David. Her *Romanticism and Its Discontents* (2001) is a study of 19th-century romantic painting.

In her novels, Brookner's protagonists are usually sensitive, refined, and lovelorn middle-aged women of foreign background; their search for love often entails freeing themselves from smothering family ties. Her first novel, *A Start in Life* (1981), established the pattern the author would follow in most of her fiction. The story follows Ruth Weiss, a Balzac scholar who goes to Paris to do research on the great French writer. At the outset, at age 40, Ruth "knew that her life had been ruined by literature" and thwarted by her elderly parents. The care and energy she should have lavished on life have instead gone into tending her parents and her studies. In Paris she hopes but fails to find love and freedom. The novel ends with her return to her empty life back home.

Brookner's work in general may be traced to the French *moraliste* tradition of analytical, unsentimental novels. In *Providence* (1982) the protagonist, daughter of a cosmopolitan family (this time British/French), is an academic specializing in French literature. She falls hopelessly in love with an art historian who is scarcely aware of her. In *Look at Me* (1983) Frances Hinton, a medical reference librarian, falls under the spell of a glamorous couple and is attracted to a male colleague, but all three eventually spurn her timid overtures. Frances consoles herself with the thought that although "problems of human behavior continue to baffle us . . . at least in the library we have them properly filed."

Brookner's most successful novel, *Hotel du Lac* (1984), won the BOOKER PRIZE. The protagonist, Edith Hope, is the daughter of an English professor and an Austrian mother who writes romance novels. Insecure in her identity, she feels alienated. For many years she has been mired in a hopeless affair as the self-effacing mistress of a married art dealer, David Simmonds. She becomes engaged to the colorless Geoffrey Long but bolts from marriage at the last moment. Edith takes refuge from her lover and husband-to-be in an off-season Swiss hotel, where a wealthy, attractive fellow guest, Philip Neville, proposes a marriage of convenience to her. Discovering that Neville is having an affair with a beautiful young woman, however, Edith returns to London and her old life. As critic John Skinner observes, *Hotel du Lac* demonstrates that "the juxtaposition of romantic longing with detached analysis of such feelings remains central to Brookner's fiction."

Among Brookner's many novels, *Family and Friends* (1985) is unusual, as it is a family saga based on a series of wedding photographs. Brookner said it was inspired by one of her grandmother's wedding photos. The strong-willed fictional matriarch Sofka is at the center of the novel, which is also the story of her four children and how none of them follows the script she has written for them. Brookner has said that *Family and*

Friends is "the only one of my books I truly like." According to the critic Derwent May, this novel has a strongly visual and spatial quality, much like "some painting, with a group of figures who take on different appearances as you tilt . . . or rotate it, but are always held in exactly the same pattern."

Brookner's work, admired for its lucidity and elegance, nevertheless exhibits considerable sameness and narrowness of plot and character. As the writer Carol Anshaw observes, the author's universe is one "where the meek inherit nothing but the crumbs of the bold and where the bold make rather trivial use of their loaf."

Works about Anita Brookner

Skinner, John. *The Fictions of Anita Brookner: Illusions of Romance.* New York: St. Martin's Press, 1992.
Stadler, Lynn V. *Anita Brookner.* Boston: Twayne, 1990.

Brophy, Brigid (1929–1995) *novelist, short story writer, playwright, nonfiction writer*

Brigid Brophy was born in London. Her mother, Charis Brophy, had been a headmistress and nurse and was an air-raid warden during London's Blitz. Her father, John Brophy, was a novelist, and Brigid herself began writing when young. She won a scholarship to Oxford in 1947 but was soon expelled for drinking in chapel. She subsequently spent several years working as a typist for a publisher of pornographic literature.

Brophy's first book was a collection of six short stories, *The Crown Princess and Other Stories* (1953). The title story describes an imaginary nation that is so obsessed with the private life of their princess that nobody can work. At the same time, the princess herself pores over numerous magazine articles about herself and increasingly feels she is not real. When she thought of who she was, "the imagination groped and encountered nothing. It was led on and on: to more and more nothingness."

In the same year Brophy published her first novel, *Hackenfeller's Ape*, a science-fiction story in which an ape acquires human sexual inhibitions that bewilder and pain him. The ape grows increasingly distressed over "[h]is own puzzling need to be fastidious." The novel was critically acclaimed and won the Cheltenham Literary Festival award. Brophy wrote several more books featuring animals and was a passionate defender of animal rights.

Many of Brophy's novels grapple with two themes: sexual desire and the attraction of death. *The Snow Ball* (1964) features both. The novel, which describes a wild New Year's costume party, caused some controversy for its description of female orgasm: "Suffering, sobbing, swelling, sawing, sweating, her body was at last convulsed by the wave that broke inside it." Lengthy philosophical speculations fill pages in between sexual encounters; one character asks rather peevishly, "Have you noticed what a metaphysical ball this is?"

One of Brophy's most acclaimed books is *The Adventures of God in His Search for the Black Girl* (1973), a collection of modern fairy tales with feminist and philosophical themes. Brophy wrote much that could be described as feminist, but she never fell neatly into any particular school of feminism. For example, she spoke about the way sexism is prevalent in contemporary society but is hard to see: "It appears that cages have been abolished. Yet in practice women are still kept in their place just as firmly as the [zoo] animals are kept in their enclosures." Brophy also felt that monogamy and marriage are archaic, and she spoke out against censoring pornography. She argued that censorship laws can be used to repress social change in unexpected ways. "A society that is not free to be outraged is not free to change." In many ways Brophy's arguments foreshadowed the pro-sexuality feminist movement that became popular after the mid-1980s.

Brophy also wrote several nonfiction books, many with psychoanalytic themes. *Black Ship to Hell* (1962) examines human destructive instincts, while *Mozart the Dramatist* (1964) rereads Mozart as a passionate person who resisted the repressions of his time. Brophy has also written several books on the *fin-de-siècle*, the turn of the century around 1900, when there was much decadent, glamorous poetry and art. Brophy's *Black and White* (1968) discusses one of the artistic stars of this era, the erotic artist Aubrey Beardsley.

Brophy was always alert to the question of why an author writes. She once wrote that she did not believe an author writes a novel in order to communicate: "If one bothers about its reception by others at all, one's wish for the work of art is not that it should be understood but that it should be loved."

Brophy was a daring writer who was impatient with conventions, and her irreverence can be seen in her nonfiction book *Fifty Works of English and American Literature We Could Do Without* (1967). Cowritten with her husband, an art historian, the book dismisses many much-loved works as literarily inept, from Shakespeare's *Hamlet* to Emily Brontë's *Wuthering Heights*. Brophy contends, for example, that Lewis Carroll's *Alice's Adventures in Wonderland* "lurches from one laboured situation to the next," and she dismisses Virginia WOOLF's acclaimed novel *To the Lighthouse* as "reducing human experience to the gossipy level of the shallowest layer of consciousness."

In 1969 Brophy collaborated with Maureen DUFFY to prepare a Pop Art exhibition. Brophy published selections of her earlier journalism in *Don't Never Forget* (1966). Brophy also wrote plays, including *The Burglar* (1967) and a satirical radio play about American life, *The Waste Disposal Unit* (1964). From 1984 onward Brophy suffered severely from multiple sclerosis. She is remembered particularly for her originality and political commitments, and in 1969 *Life Magazine* called her "the best prose writer of her generation."

Other Works by Brigid Brophy

In Transit (1969). Harmondsworth, England: Penguin, 1971.
Reads. London: Cardinal, 1989.

Brown, George Mackay (1921–1996)
poet, novelist

"The Bard of Orkney," as George Mackay Brown was known, was born in Stromness in the Orkney Islands off the north coast of Scotland, the youngest son of John Brown, a postman, and his wife Mhari. Brown suffered from tuberculosis for more than 10 years, during which time he started writing poetry. He attended Newbattle Adult Education College in Midlothian, received honorary degrees from the Universities of Dundee and Glasgow and the Open University, and was a Fellow of the Royal Society of Literature.

The landscape, speech, and rich Norse history of the Orkney Islands, where Brown spent almost his entire life, strongly influenced his writing. His first collection of poetry, *The Storm* (1954), explores these themes in a way that critic Kate Grimond calls "simple, but not naive, lyrical not whimsical," as in these lines from "Further than Hoy" in *The Storm:*

> the legends thicken
> the buried broken
> vases and columns.

Brown's novels continue his explorations of the Orkney Islands. *Beside the Ocean of Time* (1994), which was short-listed for the BOOKER PRIZE and recognized as Scottish Book of the Year, tells the story of a bored schoolboy who escapes into his imagination to dream the history of his remote island home. This passage introduces the reader to the island through the experience of visitors interacting with the locals: "It was to an island satiated with festival that the three mysterious strangers came. In those days, the country people went out of their way to be pleasant and welcoming to visitors, but those men, from first setting foot on Norday, didn't seem to care what the islanders thought of them."

The Golden Bird (1987), which contains two stories about Orkney, won the James Tait Black Memorial Prize. Literary critic Sabina Schmid has praised "Brown's ability to widen his vision and to invest the typically Orcadian consciousness and the often local setting with a universal relevance."

Other Works by George Mackay Brown
A Calendar of Love. 1967. Reprint, North Pomfret, England: Trafalgar Square, 2000.

For the Islands I Sing: An Autobiography. London: John Murray, 1998.

The Sea and the Tower. Calgary, Alberta: Bayeux Arts, 1997.

Works about George Mackay Brown

Spear, Hilda, ed. *George Mackay Brown: A Survey of His Work and Full Bibliography.* New York: Edwin Mellen Press, 2000.

Yamada, Osamu, et al. *The Contribution to Literature of Orcadian Writer George Mackay Brown.* New York: Edwin Mellen Press, 1992.

Brunner, John Killian Houston (Keith Woodcott) (1934–1995) *novelist, short story writer*

Born in Oxfordshire, England, John Brunner was a writer of mysteries, spy novels, and mainstream fiction. He remains best known, however, for his science fiction, which he began publishing in 1951 with *Galactic Storm.*

A prolific writer, Brunner turned out close to 100 short stories and some 40 novels in the next decade and a half. Many of these works were colorful adventure tales, such as *Sanctuary in the Sky* (1960), which concerns the struggle of three interstellar civilizations for control of a mysterious artificial world; and *Times without Number* (1962), which relates the escapades of a time-traveling agent based in a world where the Spanish Armada conquered England.

Major success came with Brunner's novel *Stand on Zanzibar* (1968), which earned him the science-fiction field's Hugo Award for Best Novel. Considered a classic of science fiction, *Stand on Zanzibar* follows a large cast of characters living in a severely overpopulated 21st-century world. This work showcases Brunner's skill for predicting certain aspects and issues of modern life, such as government eavesdropping, genetic engineering, and the influence of mass media. The characters Mr. and Mrs. Everywhere, for example, are two newscasters whose appearance is altered according to the nationality of the individual viewers. "Whatever my country and

whatever my name," goes the corporate line, "a gadget on the set makes me think the same."

This sometimes uncanny knack for predicting future trends and inventions is perhaps shown most clearly in *The Shockwave Rider* (1975), which features an Internet-like global data network. Brunner's observations and extrapolations of the present serve as warnings to readers of dire consequences if various political, social, and environmental trends go unchecked. As he explains in *The Shockwave Rider,* "For all the claims one hears about the liberating impact of the data-net, the truth is that it's wished on most of us a brand-new reason for paranoia."

In addition to the Hugo Award, Brunner also won the British Science Fiction Award, the British Fantasy Award, and the Apollo Award. Fellow science-fiction author James Blish said of Brunner's writing, "The work has beauty, compassion, power, precision, and immediacy. It is not science fiction as we used to know it, but we are all the better for that."

Other Works by John Brunner

The Crucible of Time. New York: Del Rey Books, 1983.
The Jagged Orbit. New York: Ace Books, 1969.
A Maze of Stars. New York: Del Rey Books, 1991.
The Sheep Look Up. New York: Harper & Row, 1972.

A Work about John Brunner

De Bolt, Joseph, ed. *The Happening Worlds of John Brunner: Critical Explorations in Science Fiction.* Port Washington, N.Y.: Kennikat Press, 1975.

Bryher (Annie Winifred Ellerman) (1894–1983) *novelist, poet, film critic*

Born Annie Winifred Ellerman in Kent, England, to Sir John Reeves Ellerman, a wealthy shipping magnate, and Hannah Grover Ellerman, Bryher traveled extensively as a child and read history and classical literature. In 1914 she published a volume of poetry titled *Region of Lutany and Other Poems.* In 1919 Bryher befriended the American poet Hilda Doolittle (H.D.), with whom she subsequently traveled extensively. Bryher took her pseudonym from one of the Scilly Islands they visited. The two women developed a deep friendship that inspired the writing careers of both.

Bryher's first novel, *Development* (1920), a candid exploration of her artistic development and sexual identity as a teenager, became an unexpected success. Although she was a lesbian, the following year she married editor Robert McAlmon. Together they established the Contact Press, which published the works of many important writers, such as James JOYCE, Ernest Hemingway, Dorothy RICHARDSON, and Ezra Pound. Bryher also financed the Egoist Press, which published the works of H.D. and McAlmon. In 1927 she divorced McAlmon and married artist Kenneth Macpherson. The couple founded a film company and a film criticism magazine, *Close Up.* Bryher then wrote *Film Problems of Soviet Russia* (1929), her only work of film criticism. From 1935 to 1950 she published *Life and Letters Today,* a literary review journal. After 1940 she wrote 10 novels and two autobiographies.

Bryher is best known for her historical novels. Many critics consider *Gate to the Sea* (1958), the story of an ancient Italian tribe's defeat of Poseidonia in the fourth century, one of her best works. *This January Tale* (1966) takes a negative view of the Norman conquest of the Saxons in 1066. Critic Richard Winston wrote, "Like all of Bryher's fiction . . . it is both swiftly moving and perfectly static, full of action and yet fixed in time and space, slight yet comprehensive."

Bryher often wrote about friendship and loyalty among men. She believed in these virtues but frequently wrote with a tragic vision. Her characters often face separation and suffering. At the end of *Gate to the Sea,* a slave named Lykos reflects, "Never believe the philosophers who say that we learn through suffering. I have never accepted either my lameness or our slavery. I have endured but resented them, every waking hour." Critics have praised her historical novels for their accuracy, clear descriptions, and relevance. Reviewer Horace Gregory writes that she has "given renewed vitality and meaning to incidents of the past. Her historical novels are short, highly charged analogies to situations and problems that bedevil our days and nights."

Other Works by Bryher
The Roman Wall. New York: Harcourt, 1954.
Visa for Avalon. New York: Harcourt, 1965.

A Work about Bryher
Benstock, Shari. *Women of the Left Bank Paris, 1900–1940.* Austin: University of Texas Press, 1986.

Buchan, John (1875–1940) *novelist, nonfiction writer*

John Buchan (pronounced Buck-an) was born in Perth, Scotland, to Helen and the Reverend John Buchan. He published six books, including his first novel, *Sir Quixote of the Moors* (1895), before completing his classics degree at Oxford University.

Licensed to practice law in 1901, Buchan spent two years in South Africa administering Boer refugee camps. Returning to London in 1903, he wrote an authoritative book on tax law and produced numerous political articles for the *Spectator.* He married Susan Grosvenor in 1907, and soon after, he became literary adviser for Thomas Nelson and Sons. He wrote several books for the publishing company, including *Prester John* (1910), in which a young Scot thwarts a Zulu uprising. This boys' adventure was the first of Buchan's works to gain a worldwide readership.

During World War I Buchan wrote a serial called *History of the War* (1915–19), with a new section appearing every two weeks. Commissioned as an officer in the Intelligence Corps, he became head of the new Department of Information in 1917. After the war Buchan became a director of the Reuters news agency and wrote more than a book a year, even after his election to the House of Commons in 1927. He was created Baron Tweedsmuir and appointed Governor General of Canada in 1935.

Although Buchan wrote in many genres, including history, biography, and literary criticism, his reputation today rests mainly on what he called his "shockers," or thrillers, the best of which feature Richard Hannay or Edward Leithen, decent men who must protect the world from anarchy. Buchan's background in intelligence gives these adventures credibility. His best-known novel, *The Thirty-nine Steps* (1915), introduces mining engineer Richard Hannay, an ordinary man who is pursued across Scotland as he tries to stop a conspiracy to start a war between Germany and Britain. According to reviewer Joyce Park, this first Hannay adventure is a "fast-paced, brilliantly conceived story" from which every subsequent "'innocent man falsely accused, fleeing from both bad guys and police' tale" takes its inspiration. It was made into a movie by Alfred Hitchcock in 1935. Biographer Janet Adam Smith believes the appeal of Buchan's classic thrillers is their ability to "convey a sense of the real possibility of evil and irrational forces breaking through the façade of civilized life."

Other Works by John Buchan

The Four Adventures of Richard Hannay. Boston: Godine, 1988.
The Leithen Stories. Edinburgh: Canongate, 2000.

A Work about John Buchan

Smith, Janet Adam. *John Buchan and His World.* New York: Scribner, 1979.

Buchanan, George Henry Perrott
(1904–1989) *novelist, poet, essayist*

George Buchanan was born in Larne, Ireland, to Henry Buchanan, a country clergyman, and Florence Moore Buchanan. He was educated at Larne Grammar School, Campbell College in Belfast, and the University of Belfast. In 1925 he moved to London and became a journalist, working as a subeditor for the London *Times* and as a columnist and drama critic for the *New Chronicle.*

Buchanan's first novel, *A London Story* (1935), contrasts the careers of two brothers; one resists the oppression of his employer, and the other bows to it. Much of Buchanan's fiction is set in World War II, including *A Place to Live* (1952), a novel about a Royal Air Force pilot who later finds contentment running a hotel after the war. In one of his best-known works, *Rose Forbes* (1937), Buchanan addresses what became a common topic for him: middle-class adult sexuality. The main character is an Irish woman seeking emotional and sexual fulfillment through a series of marriages and affairs. This novel, like many of Buchanan's other writings, also explores how social and political crises wear on people and have brought about the decline of the Victorian middle class. While walking in a London park, Rose sadly reflects, "During the early years of the century, people would walk here feeling . . . that they all were in a smooth carriage, being comfortably borne to well-appointed future. Today they have been robbed of that facile optimism."

Buchanan's poetry also reflects a gloomy outlook on the effects that the social and political convulsions of the 20th century have had on Britain. In "Multiplicity" (*Minute-Book of a City,* 1972 collection), Buchanan writes, "Multiplied Hamlet is the Chamberlain government hesitating before the murderers of Europe." In the poem "Kilwaughter (to C.H.L.B.)" he laments "the poets grew up to be recruited for another war." His pessimistic vision is also seen in the poem "Second Thoughts," in which he writes, "the principal second thought is death." In describing Buchanan, scholar John Foster Wilson notes that it is "the social backcloth, a backcloth of middle class decline, that gives ballast to the lightweight coyness and gnomic affectation that tend to mar his work. . . . Distant explosions and gentle decay at home characterize . . . Buchanan's fiction."

Other Works by George Buchanan

The Green Seacoast. London: Gaberbocchus, 1959.
Possible Being. Manchester, England: Carcanet New
    Press, 1980.

Bunting, Basil (1900–1985) *poet, journalist*

Basil Bunting was born and died in Northumber-
land, England. His father, T. I. Bunting, a physician,
and his mother, Annie Cheesman Bunting, were
Quakers. He attended the London School of Economics and spent much of his life as a journalist
and music critic. He assisted Ford Madox FORD on
the *Transatlantic Review* in Paris.

Bunting's list of published works is short: *Red-
imiculum Metallarum* (1930); *Poems: 1950; The
Spoils* (1965); *Briggflatts: An Autobiography* (1966),
and his *Collected Poems,* published in 1968 and as
Complete Poems in 2000. Although he was a fine
poet, he shunned literary society for most of his
life. He was a disciple of the American poet Ezra
Pound and moved to Rapallo, Italy, where Pound
lived, in 1924. Like Pound's work, Bunting's poetry
shows concreteness and musicality. Bunting also
claimed William Wordsworth as a lifelong influence, sharing Wordsworth's passion for nature and
for spoken verse.

Bunting's poetry is intensely musical. In his introduction to *Collected Poems* he writes: "I have set
down words as a musician . . . not to be read in silence, but to trace in the air a pattern of sound that
may . . . be pleasing." In this volume his long
poems, including *Villon, The Spoils,* and *Briggflatts,* are listed as "Sonatas," free-verse lyrics as
"Odes," and translations as "Overdrafts."

Bunting was particularly attracted to the long
poem, of which his best example and one of his
finest poetic achievements is *Briggflatts.* A poem in
five movements, in its structure and musicality it
recalls T. S. ELIOT's *Four Quartets,* although the
mood is sterner and less transcendental. *Briggflatts*
emulates Anglo-Saxon verse in predominantly
four-stressed lines employing alliteration and assonance (repetition of consonant and vowel sounds,
often in initial or stressed syllables, respectively).

It is filled with Northumbrian local and historical
allusions. The poem begins with the poet calmly
contemplating death as a mason inscribes his
name on his tombstone:

> . . . *the stone spells a name*
> *naming none,*
> *a man abolished.*

Here alliteration is chiefly on the letter *n* and assonance on the vowel *o*—"stone" and "none" set up
a slant rhyme in Northumbrian dialect. In the following lines from Part V, alliteration is on d, l, sh,
and s sounds:

> *The sheets are gathered and bound,*
> *The volume indexed and shelved,*
> *dust on its marbled leaves.*

As the scholar Neil Corcoran observes, "Repeated images, reiterated motifs, the sense of variations . . . on central themes, all help give
[Bunting's] work an integrity of organization rare
in modernist long poems."

Other Works by Basil Bunting

Basil Bunting on Poetry. Edited by Peter Makin. Balti-
    more: Johns Hopkins University Press, 1999.
The Complete Poems. Edited by Richard Caddel. New
    York: Oxford University Press, 1994.

A Work about Basil Bunting

Forde, Victoria, *The Poetry of Basil Bunting.* Chester
    Springs, Pa.: Dufour Editions, 1992.

Burgess, Anthony (John Anthony Burgess Wilson, Joseph Kell)

(1917–1993) *novelist, essayist*

Of Irish descent, Anthony Burgess was born John
Anthony Burgess Wilson in Manchester, England.
His father, Joseph Wilson, was a cashier and a part-
time pianist in a local pub. His mother, Elizabeth
Burgess, a music-hall dancer, died in an influenza
epidemic when Burgess was two years old. Burgess

received Catholic schooling, but at 16 he rejected Roman Catholicism. Graduating from Manchester University in 1940, he joined the Royal Army Medical Corps, although he completed his wartime duty working in intelligence. After the war he taught school. In 1960 Burgess was diagnosed with brain cancer and given, at most, one year to live. Spurred by the diagnosis, he became a prolific writer, and by the time he did die of cancer 33 years later, he had written 50 books and hundreds of essays. A number of the latter, covering writers composers, and history, appear in *One Man's Chorus* (1998).

Burgess's first published novel, *Time for a Tiger* (1956), a novel about the British in Malaysia, introduced his pen name, Anthony Burgess. (Joseph Kell was another of his pseudonyms.) His novels are generally satirical, addressing moral issues and social ills. His impassioned humanism contains lingering accents of his former Catholicism.

Burgess's best-known novel is *A Clockwork Orange* (1962), which critic Esther Petix calls a "horrible [vision] of the future, predicated upon the present"—a projection of "excesses of the Welfare state." As the book opens, a gang of young teenage thugs are on a raping, robbing, and killing rampage. However, the focus shifts to the state's aggressive experiments in behavior modification to render the gang's leader, Alex, no longer a threat. The price of society's safety, the state assumes, is the loss of free will in those whom society "cures." Burgess questions this assumption, placing it in a theological framework that considers the relationship of goodness to the exercise of free will. (The novel's concluding chapter—omitted from U.S. editions until 1988—exposes the state as misguided in its reformative zeal.) Having reverted to his pre-"treated" state, Alex nevertheless has grown tired of his violence, but will his resolve be undone or just sublimated? Scholar Samuel Coale notes that "in [Burgess's] novels[,] good and evil interpenetrate one another. . . . There are moments when good seems to conquer evil, but these are only moments in an endless flux of time and space."

Burgess created Nadsat, the language that the thugs speak, mostly from Russian, English Cockney slang, and inventions of his own. While trying to rob a woman with a house full of cats, Alex thinks, "Among all the cracking kots and koshkas what should I slooshy but the shoom of the old police-auto siren . . . the old forella of the pusscats had been on the phone to the millicents when I thought she'd been govoreeting to the mewlers and mowlers." Nadsat, which derives from the Russian word for teenager, embodies youth's rebellion against the "clockwork" society that offends them. Nadsat is, at once, their own possession and a mark of participation in humanity's drive for liberty across time. American author William Burroughs wrote, "I do not know of any other writer who has done as much with language as . . . Burgess has done here."

Perhaps Burgess's most vivid character is F. X. Enderby, a variously marginalized, humorously idiosyncratic everyman inhabiting four novels: *Inside Mr. Enderby* (1963), *Enderby Outside* (1968), *The Clockwork Testament* (1974), and *Enderby's Dark Lady* (1984). In the first novel a character tells us, "[l]ife . . . has to be lived" rather than turned into adolescent poetry. However, Robert K. Morris writes, "*Enderby* makes the strongest, yet most human case possible for whatever self-possession and indivisibility the artist might yet have in a world doing its damnedest to usurp [him]."

Burgess's novel *Earthly Powers* (1980) is a pseudomemoir that surveys the 20th century. Its narrator, Kenneth Marchal Toomey, draws on Burgess's own past and often echoes the author's views, as when he notes that Nazi Germany "had abdicated the rights and duties of freedom of moral choice." However, Toomey is homosexual, while Burgess was not—a point that both of Burgess's autobiographies, *Little Wilson and Big God* (1986) and *You've Had Your Time* (1990), felt obliged to make. "Burgess, despite the variety of narrators and situations in his fiction," critic William H. Pritchard writes, "speaks to us as one of us: a fallen man with the usual amount of ambition, irritation, guilt, decency and common sense."

Other Works by Anthony Burgess

Byrne. London: Hutchinson, 1995.

A Dead Man in Deptford. New York: Carroll & Graf, 1995.

A Work about Anthony Burgess

Bloom, Harold. *Anthony Burgess*. Broomall, Pa.: Chelsea House, 1992.

Byatt, A. S. (Antonia Susan Byatt)

(1936–) novelist, literary critic

A. S. Byatt was born in Sheffield, England, to John Frederick Drabble, a judge, and Kathleen Marie Drabble, a teacher. She is the sister of novelist Margaret DRABBLE. Although they came from working-class backgrounds, both her parents were educated at Cambridge University, which Byatt also attended, receiving her bachelor's degree in 1957. She also did graduate work in art and literature at Bryn Mawr College and Oxford during the late 1950s. In 1959 she married the economist Charles Rayner Byatt.

Byatt's work as a novelist, literary critic, and lecturer has earned her acclaim as one of Britain's finest contemporary writers. As a critic, she has written about such women writers as Jane Austen, George Eliot, and Iris MURDOCH. Called a postmodern Victorian by one critic, she deals in her fiction with themes that incorporate historical subjects with modern literary forms. She once claimed, "I see writing as a passionate activity, like any other," a sentiment that has carried over into all of her writing.

Byatt drew upon her own early experiences as a young writer for her first novel, *The Shadow of the Sun* (1964), which tells the story of an aspiring female novelist. Like her protagonist, Byatt felt that she had to overcome a great deal as a woman writer: "when you're a woman," she says, "you start with one hand tied behind your back."

Byatt's most acclaimed novel is *Possession* (1990), which won the prestigious BOOKER PRIZE. The book uses historical sources from the late 19th century to tell the story of two English scholars,

Roland Michell and Maud Baily, who are engaged in the obsessive study of two Victorian poets, and the love affair that ultimately results from their work together. Byatt's biographer Kathleen Coyne Kelly comments, "Part academic potboiler, part suspense story, part romance, it is a virtuoso postmodernist exercise that weaves together many strands: a contemporary story of academic conflicts, rivalries and discoveries; a 19th century chronicle of ill-fated love; and a meditation on the imagination and creativity."

Byatt's *Angels and Insects* (1992) is a collection of two novellas, "Morpho Eugenia" and "The Conjugial Angel," which are set in the 19th century and together deal with the clash between faith and reason. "Morpho Eugenia" (the title is taken from the name of a rare butterfly) is a story of metamorphosis and the attempt to unlock the mysteries of the natural world: "When evening came, he had a newly hatching large cocoon, which he took along with him to the conservatory; watching it would be a kind of reasonable employment whilst he waited to see if she would come." "The Conjugial Angel" focuses more on the idea of spiritual transformation by exploring the Victorian interest in séances and the afterlife.

Two other well-known works by Byatt include *Babel Tower* (1996) and *The Biographer's Tale* (2000). The former work is the third novel in a planned tetralogy that includes *The Virgin in the Garden* (1978) and *Still Life* (1987). Set in the 1960s, *Babel Tower* is a memoir of what some critics labeled the "permissive society" of the post–World War II era, a period plagued with political and moral scandals. "You waste your own time, since there is no God," one character proclaims provocatively. *The Biographer's Tale* is a satire of academic life that follows the story of a biographer trying to uncover the details of a minor historical figure.

Although Byatt has described her political affiliation as radical, she has also said she does not use her writing as a vehicle to express her political opinions. "Of course I am a feminist," Byatt has remarked, "but I don't want to be required to write a feminist programme, and I feel uneasy when this seems to be asked of me." For reviewer Donna Seaman, Byatt remains "a dazzling storyteller and a keen observer of the power and significance of her medium."

Other Works by A. S. Byatt

The Djinn in the Nightingale's Eye: Five Fairy Stories. New York: Random House, 1997.

The Matisse Stories. New York: Random House, 1995.

Passions of the Mind. New York: Random House, 1993.

A Work about A. S. Byatt

Kelly, Kathleen Coyne. *A. S. Byatt.* Boston: Twayne, 1996.

Calder-Marshall, Arthur (R. D. Mascott, William Drummond) (1908–1992)
novelist, biographer, screenwriter

Arthur Calder-Marshall was born in Surrey, England, to Arthur Grotjan and Alice Poole Calder-Marshall. He attended Oxford, where he edited the undergraduate magazine *Oxford Outlook*. Calder-Marshall's first novel, *Two of a Kind* (1933), describes the ordeal of a honeymooning couple after they are swept out to sea in a small boat. Critical acclaim came with his fifth novel, *Pie in the Sky* (1937), which explores the various emotional and industrial conflicts of characters in a midlands mill town. As William Drummond, Calder-Marshall wrote several film novelizations, such as *Midnight Love* (1960).

A move to Hollywood prompted Calder-Marshall to try his hand at writing screenplays, including the Academy Award–nominated documentary *The World Is Rich* (1946). He concentrated on nonfiction after World War II, writing several biographies. His biographical subjects ranged from author Jack London (*Lone Wolf: The Story of Jack London,* 1962) to filmmaker Robert Flaherty (*The Innocent Eye: The Life of Robert J. Flaherty,* 1963). His best-known nonfiction work is *No Earthly Command* (1957), the story of an admiral who later became a priest.

Two novels helped establish Calder-Marshall's reputation as a fiction writer: *The Fair to Middling* (1959), a mystery about disfigured orphans whose experiences at a traveling fair teach them that they would have accomplished far less in their lives had they been "normal"; and *The Scarlet Boy* (1961), another mystery with a plot twist. Under the pen name R. D. Mascott, Calder-Marshall wrote *003½: The Adventures of James Bond Junior* (1967), which critic Nick Kincaid called "a beautiful novel, far better than [James Bond series author] Fleming's work, it was—and still is—an intelligently observed, highly literate (and literary) . . . novel." Mascott's description of Auntie Mo, one of the characters in *003½*, demonstrates Calder-Marshall's vividly descriptive writing style: "Life had tautened her like violin catgut till she twanged. She twanged at any and everything; a wasp (which she astonishingly swatted with the swinging head of the chicken and flattened with her rubber-soled shoes), the sound of a shotgun (coming, James thought, from Undercote—somebody shooting pigeons) and the telephone, which she leapt to answer." Critic John BETJEMAN wrote: "Arthur Calder-Marshall has always written lucidly and readably. However dated and unreadable some prose-writers may become who seem to us elegant or contemporary-tough today, he will remain fresh and clear."

Callaghan, Morley Edward (1903–1990)
novelist, short story writer

Morley Callaghan was born in Toronto, Ontario, Canada, to middle-class parents of Irish descent, Thomas and Mary Dewan Callaghan. He received his B.A. from the University of Toronto in 1925 and his law degree from Osgoode Hall Law School in 1928. Callaghan started his writing career as a journalist for the *Toronto Daily Star*. At the encouragement of Ernest Hemingway, whom he met during his time at the *Star,* he soon turned his attention to writing short stories and novels.

A Roman Catholic, Callaghan often used religious subjects and biblical themes in his work while creating characters that champion the struggles faced by the common man. His 1934 novel *Such Is My Beloved,* which tells the story of a young priest who eventually finds redemption in overcoming the challenges of the priesthood and parish life, is widely considered Callaghan's finest novel. Other works, such as *They Shall Inherit the Earth* (1935), reinterpret biblical stories, such as Cain and Abel, using the Great Depression, for example, as a backdrop to explore familial relationships. In examining Callaghan's writing career, Edmund Wilson commented in *O Canada* that he "is today perhaps the most unjustly neglected novelist in the English-speaking world."

Callaghan's reputation rests on his short stories, many of which first appeared in popular U.S. magazines such as the *New Yorker* and the *Atlantic Monthly.* Four stories in his collection *Now That April's Here and Other Stories* (1936) were the basis of the 1958 feature film titled after the lead story. Both "Silk Stockings" and the "Rocking Chair" deal with the theme of unrequited love. "A Sick Call" also involves human relationships as its subject and deals explicitly with the end-of-life decision by a man's spouse to convert from Protestantism to Catholicism. Callaghan's stories have also appeared in the well-known anthology *The Best American Short Stories.*

Callaghan has also written plays, autobiographies, memoirs, and young adult fiction. Despite being labeled once the best "short story writer in the world" by the *New York Times,* Callaghan's works remain all but forgotten today. Some, including Callaghan himself, attribute this neglect to a falling-out he had with Hemingway after an ill-fated boxing match in the 1930s, whereas others have pointed to his relative seclusion in Canada, where he spent the majority of his writing career. Notwithstanding his relative obscurity, according to one reviewer, "Nowhere is the extremity of the individual's situation more evident than in Callaghan's short stories, where the conflict is internalized inside a single character, one who must often choose between personal relationships and his desire to be part of an impersonal society."

Other Works by Morley Callaghan

More Joy in Heaven. 1937. Reprint, Toronto: McClelland and Stewart, 1996.

White Narcissus. 1929. Reprint, Toronto: McClelland and Stewart. 1996.

A Work about Morley Callaghan

Boire, Gary. *Morley Callaghan: Literary Anarchist.* Toronto: ECW Press, 1994.

Camberg, Muriel
See SPARK, MURIEL.

Cannan, May Wedderburn (1893–1973)
poet, memoirist

Born in Oxford, England, May Wedderburn Cannan was the daughter of Charles Cannan, an illustrious professor who was dean of Oxford University's Trinity College and played a leading part in directing the University Press. Cannan shared her father's enthusiasm for literature, and in 1908 she published her first poem in *The Scotsman.*

When Cannan was 18 she joined the VAD (Voluntary Aid Detachment), where she trained as a nurse, and for part of World War I she worked as a nurse in France. The war was tragic for Cannan: her first fiancé was killed at the front, and later in the war her second fiancé died of illness while in the army.

Grief runs through Cannan's poetry collection *In War Time* (1917), a book of poems about the war. Her famous poem "Lamplight" addresses her dead love with quiet grief: "There's a scarlet cross on your breast, my dear / And a torn cross with your name." Her collection *The Splendid Days* (1919) gathers more verses on war bereavement. The poem "Paris, November 11, 1918" closes with the lines: "But I saw Love go lonely down the years, / And when I drank, the wine was salt with tears."

Cannan wrote several memoirs, starting with *The Lonely Generation* (1934). Her autobiography *Grey Ghosts and Voices* (1976), published posthumously, is a poignant salutation to "my friends who were dead and . . . my friends who, wounded, imprisoned, battered, shaken, exhausted, were alive in a new, and a terrible world."

Other Work by May Wedderburn Cannan

The Tears of War: The Story of a Young Poet and a War Hero. Edited by Charlotte Fyfe. Wiltshire, England: Cavalier, 2000.

Carey, Peter (1943–   ) *novelist, short story writer*

Peter Carey was born in Bacchus Marsh, Victoria, Australia. After completing his secondary education at Geelong Grammar School, he enrolled at Monash University in 1961 to study chemistry and zoology. Following a near-fatal car accident in 1962, he left school and went to work in advertising, a field he remained in until 1988. In 1980 he formed his own agency.

In 1974 Carey's fourth attempt at a novel was accepted for publication, but he then withdrew it in favor of a short story collection, *The Fat Man in History* (1974). The stories gained critical recognition for their surrealistic style and their adaptation of the traditional Australian tall tale. They also introduced the major themes of Carey's fiction: a fierce condemnation of capitalism and consumer exploitation, a fear of lingering colonialism, and a criticism of the overly proud Australian character.

Carey explores these themes in his first published novel, *Bliss* (1981). The main character, an advertising executive named Harry Joy, suffers a heart attack. Although he survives, he believes he has died and has been condemned to Hell. Joy's surroundings seem hellish because a freakish cancer epidemic, caused by additives in an American product advertised by Joy's agency, has ravaged the community. To escape, Joy joins a commune.

Carey's third novel, *Oscar and Lucinda* (1988), won the prestigious BOOKER PRIZE as did *The True History of the Kelly Gang* (2001). Set in the 19th century, the story revolves around Oscar, an Anglican priest who emigrates to Australia to suppress his gambling addiction, and Lucinda, an heiress who is also a gambling addict. The novel was praised for its narrative technique. The first of Carey's two narrators, Oscar's great-grandson, romantically describes Oscar and Lucinda's relationship, which for him symbolizes the peaceful Australian countryside. But Kumbaingiri-Billy, an aboriginal storyteller, undermines the myth of the peaceful colonization of the country when he describes the slaughter of an aboriginal tribe.

In addition to winning the Booker Prize twice, Carey has twice won the National Book Council Award, and he has been elected to the Royal Society of Literature. The critic Graham Huggan has written that Carey's indictment of capitalism defines his fiction: "[H]e displays the lethal attractiveness of contemporary consumer culture: he is an assiduous collector and chronicler of its slick utopian myths."

Other Works by Peter Carey

Illywhacker. New York: Harper, 1985.
Jack Maggs. New York: Alfred A. Knopf, 1998.
The Tax Inspector. New York: Alfred A. Knopf, 1992.

Works about Peter Carey

Huggan, Graham. *Peter Carey*. New York: Oxford University Press, 1996.
Woodcock, Bruce. *Peter Carey*. Manchester, England: Manchester University Press, 1996.

Carter, Angela (Angela Olive Stalker Carter) (1940–1992) *novelist, short story writer, essayist, screenwriter*

Angela Carter was born in 1940 in Eastbourne, Sussex, England. During World War II she lived with her grandmother in South Yorkshire near a coalfield, a place her grandmother was certain the Germans would never bomb. Her first job was writing features and music reviews for the Croydon *Advertiser*. She married when she was 20 and studied English at the University of Bristol.

Carter's works embrace a feminist point of view and range from the realistic to the fantastic and erotic. Her writing incorporates magic realism—literature that uses elements of dreams, magic, fantasy, and fairy tales to manipulate or intrude on otherwise realistic settings and characters.

Carter's first novel, *Shadow Dance,* was published in 1966. It introduces readers to Carter's exploration of female subservience in a patriarchal society and the need for both men and women to free themselves from the destructive aspects of such a society. Toward the end of the novel, Carter describes Emily and Morris, two characters on the verge of escape: "She walked as if she had a destination ahead of her of which she was quite sure . . . Morris felt less shadow-like the more they went on together."

The Magic Toyshop (1967), a modern horror myth, reveals Carter's fascination with Freudian thought and fairy tales. As the critic Aidan Day noted, it shows "Carter's persistent interest in the way in which men as well as women may be negatively affected by patriarchy and seek to resist it." In *Heroes and Villains* (1969), set in a post-nuclear-holocaust world where the Professors and the Barbarians vie for control, Marianne, a Professor's daughter, becomes ruler of the Barbarians by adopting the best traits of both groups into her personality.

In 1970 Carter separated from her husband and moved to Japan, where she wrote essays for *New Society,* a current affairs and culture weekly. She lived in Japan for two years but continued writing for *New Society* for 20 years. In 1972 she moved back to England and served as Arts Council Fellow at Sheffield University and as a visiting professor of creative writing at Brown University in the United States.

Carter's experiences in Japan had a profound effect on her writing. She said she "learnt what it is to be a woman and became radicalized." In *The Passion of New Eve* (1977), which Carter called "a feminist tract about the social creation of femininity," Evelyn, a young Englishman, is captured by a feminist group and surgically turned into a woman: "Now first of beings in the world, you can seed yourself . . . that is why you have become New Eve." In 1979 Carter published *The Sadeian Woman,* in which, to the dismay of many feminists, she advanced the seemingly outrageous idea that the wicked and deviant Marquis de Sade was a man ahead of his time who actually liberated woman sexually.

Some critics and authors, including the novelist Salman RUSHDIE, consider *The Bloody Chamber* (1979), a feminist retelling of classic fairy tales, to be Carter's master work. As Rushdie explains, "She opens an old story for us, like an egg, and finds the new story, the now-story we want to hear within." Carter also translated the French fairy tales of Charles Perrault, and she wrote a bloodthirsty screenplay for *The Company of Wolves* (1984), a film retelling of Little Red Riding Hood.

The critic Marina Warner has noted that Carter's "imagination was one of the most dazzling this century, and through her daring, vertiginous plots, her precise, yet wild imagery, her gallery of wonderful bad-good girls, beasts, rogues, and other creatures, she causes readers to hold their breaths as a mood of heroic optimism forms against the odds." *Nights at the Circus* (1984) illustrates Warner's comment. Carter herself described this work as a comic novel. The main character, Sophie Fevvers, is a circus aerialist who has grown wings and is a prototype for the 20th-century woman freeing herself from a patriarchal society.

Carter earned numerous literary awards for her work, including the John Llewellyn Rhys Prize (1967), the Somerset Maugham Award (1968), and the James Tait Black Memorial Prize (1984). She wrote until her death from cancer in 1992. Commenting on her continuing popularity, Rushdie has said, "She has become the contemporary writer most studied at British universities—a victory over the mainstream she would have enjoyed."

Other Works by Angela Carter

Expletives Deleted. London: Vintage, 1993.

Fireworks: Nine Profane Pieces. New York: Viking Penguin, 1987.

The Infernal Desire Machines of Dr. Hoffman. New York: Viking Penguin, 1982.

Love. New York: Penguin, 1988.

Shaking a Leg: Collected Writings. Edited by Jenny Uglow. New York: Penguin, 1998.

Works about Angela Carter

Day, Aidan. *Angela Carter: The Rational Glass.* New York: St. Martin's Press, 1998.

Michael, Magali Cornier. "Angela Carter's Nights at the Circus: An Engaged Feminism via Subversive Postmodern Strategies." *Contemporary Literature* (1995): pp. 492–521.

Roemer, Danielle M., and Cristina Bacchilega, eds. *Angela Carter and the Fairy Tale.* Detroit: Wayne State University Press, 2001.

Tucker, Lindsey, ed. *Critical Essays on Angela Carter.* New York: Macmillan, 1998.

Cary, Joyce (1888–1957) *novelist*

Joyce Cary was born in Londonderry, Northern Ireland. His father was a civil engineer descended from a once-prominent Anglo-Irish family whose fortunes had greatly declined by the time of Cary's birth. After studying in Edinburgh and Paris, Cary received a law degree from Oxford University. In 1912 he joined the British Red Cross and served as an orderly in the Balkan Wars. He then joined the British colonial service in Nigeria, staying there until 1920, at which time he resigned his post and returned to England. It was then that he began to write his novels.

Cary's first four books are set in West Africa and deal with the dramatic, and sometimes tragic, results of the confrontation between traditional African life and the British colonial administration. The last of the four books, *Mister Johnson* (1939), is an especially powerful story of a native clerk torn between loyalties to the place that he comes from and the world in which he is trying to make his way.

During the 1940s Cary produced his most popular and important work, a trilogy of novels whose setting is the world of art. *Herself Surprised* (1941), *To Be a Pilgrim* (1942), and *The Horse's Mouth* (1944) are all told in the first person by characters who also appear in the other novels. The first book is narrated by Sara, who pretends to be an innocent housewife but is in fact a social-climbing thief. The second is told by Wilcher, a member of the landed gentry who pretends to be eccentric but turns out to be malevolent and corrupt. The two novels involve the exploits of the narrator of the third, Gully Jimson, who is without pretense. Gully is described at various points in the trilogy as a "scoundrel," as being "not quite right in the head," and as "a painter of genius." This last description concurs with Jimson's own, even though each painting he sells he describes as "rubbish." This passage from the final scene of the novel, when Jimson is putting the finishing touches on a great mural painting even as his assistant and the authorities argue over whether the building on whose wall he is working has been condemned, gives an idea of the energy and humor in Jimson's voice:

> "It's no good getting irritated against the bureaucracy," I said. . . . I told them, or perhaps I only thought I told them, because I was thinking, what it wants in the top left corner is a lively passage in a strong green. Say a field of cabbage. Yes, curly kale. After all, curly kale, as a work of the imagination, beats Shakespeare. The green, the tender, the humorous imagination. When the old 'un dreamt curly kale, he smiled in his beard.

Writing in the magazine *Saturday Night*, the novelist Robertson DAVIES said of the three novels that "they provide me with the inexhaustible

Gully—the only fully articulate painter I have ever met in fiction."

Cary's next trilogy takes place in the world of politics. *Prisoner of Grace* (1952), *Except the Lord* (1953), and *Not Honour More* (1955) focus on characters whose shifting loyalties and ability to deceive have deadly emotional and physical results. The novels tell the story of Nimmo, a clerk with ambitions beyond his capabilities, who marries Nina, his social superior, who has not given up her love for Jim Latter, who is still pursuing Nina. Matters come to a head and are resolved in a killing.

Cary won critical praise for his ability to present characters that are both true to and larger than life in stories that combine comedy and tragedy. Cary remarked of his creative process, "The center of the plan was character—the books had to be soaked in it. In such a dilemma, whether to stick to my scheme, or stick to my character, the character felt and known in the book, I stuck to my rule, which was character first."

Cary had planned a third trilogy that was to deal with religion, but he died before completing the first book. Critic Kingsley Hart remarks in his introduction to *The Horse's Mouth* that the instinct of religious belief plays as great a role in all Cary's later books as the instinct to create. Hart maintains that with his focus on inspired rebels, Cary carries on the Nonconformist (English, non-Anglican Protestant) tradition of English fiction, following such writers as George Eliot and D. H. LAWRENCE.

Biographer Kinley Roby sums up Cary's achievement thus: "His novels are brimming with life, the lines dance with energy, and his characters have sufficient force to march, frequently, straight off the page into our memories. . . . Cary was a great writer and a great visionary."

A Work about Joyce Cary

Roby, Kinley E. *Joyce Cary.* Boston: Twayne, 1984.

Causley, Charles (1917–) *poet*

Charles Causley was born in Launceston, Cornwall, England, to Charles Samuel and Laura Jane Bartlett Causley. His Canadian-born father was permanently disabled by a German gas attack in World War I and died in 1924. Causley was educated at Horwell Grammar School and Launceston College. After service in the Royal Navy during World War II, he returned to Launceston to teach school.

Causley turned to poetry during World War II to deal with the horrors of that conflict. His collection *Farewell, Angie Weston* (1951) recreates the sailor's life during the war. Many poems in the volume are written in rhyme and meter such as "Nursery Rhyme of Innocence and Experience," which contains the lines "O where is that sailor / With bold red hair? / And what is that volley / On the bright air?" Causley's second collection, *Survivor's Leave* (1953), also covers the harsh reality of war. Written in the traditional ballad form for which the poet is best known, the poems, such as the famous "On Seeing a Poet of the First World War at the Station of Abbeville," reflect the influence of W. H. AUDEN in their use of bold metaphors and archetypal figures.

Causley's later poetry stemmed from his experience as a teacher. Among these works are several highly regarded volumes for children, including *Figgie Hobbin* (1970). Writing from a child's perspective, Causley deals with serious themes, as in the poem "Who," which expresses a vision of lost childhood: "Who is that child I see wandering, wandering / Down by the side of the quivering stream?"

Causley addresses similar themes of self-definition in his adult work *Collected Poems* (1975). In the poem "Wedding Portrait" he sees his past and present in his parents' wedding picture. The poem contrasts the love his parents had on their wedding day with the later horrors they faced and their eventual deaths. At the end of the poem his parents' love is restored, and he describes how he uses the breath they gave him: "I warm the cold words with my day: / Will the dead weight to fly. To fly." Critic Edward Levy writes of this poem, "It is the poet's breath which can, by naming and defining, bring both dead and living to life, reminding the living of the dead and healing the deadness in them." In a tribute to the poet when he turned 70, critic Barry Newport wrote that Causley produced "a body of poetry that, with craftsmanship, compassion and honesty continues to reflect the necessary condition of all human existence."

Other Work by Charles Causley
As I Went Down Zig Zag. New York: Warner, 1974.

A Work about Charles Causley
Chambers, Barry, ed. *Causley at 70.* Calstock, England: Peterloo Poets, 1987.

Caute, John David (John Salisbury)
(1936–) *novelist, playwright, historian*
David Caute was born to Edward and Rebecca Caute in Alexandria, Egypt, where his father was serving as a colonel in the British army dental corps. Caute received a B.A. in history and, with a thesis on communism among French intellectuals, earned a Ph.D. from Oxford.

Caute's thesis led him into a historical work that established his reputation as a scholar of history, *Communism and the French Intellectuals, 1914–1960* (1966). Beginning with the engaging and metaphorical first line, "The international Marxist movement was originally fathered and mothered by intellectuals," the book displays Caute's unique ability to explain why communism appealed to its supporters.

Before Caute went to university, he served 18 months on the African Gold Coast as a soldier in the British army. His most acclaimed novel, *At Fever Pitch* (1959), is set in that region. In this novel, which was awarded the London Authors Club Award and the John Llewellyn Rhys Memorial Prize, Caute explores the issues of Western colonialism, socialism, communism, and sexuality. Laced with sexuality and gruesome violence, *At Fever Pitch* combines the coming of age story of the novel's central character, Michael Glyn, and the story of a British colony's fight for independence.

The issues that Caute confronts in *At Fever Pitch* also appear in his play *Songs for an Autumn Rifle* (1960). Set in Hungary during the Russian invasion of 1956, the drama explains how British socialists who supported the Soviet Union faced a political dilemma when the country invaded Hungary. With his play *The Demonstration* (1970) Caute addresses student revolution: A class of drama students refuses to perform a play assigned by the professor and replaces it with one of their own making, which accuses the university of repressive authoritarianism.

Caute has published more than 30 novels, plays, and pieces of academic writing. He acknowledges Karl Marx, Jean-Paul Sartre, and the German dramatist Bertolt Brecht as inspirations. Although some readers dislike the historical and political dimension of Caute's work, the scholar Gerald Steele has written that Caute "is one of the most intellectually stimulating novelists of recent decades in England."

Other Works by David Caute
Fatima's Scarf. Toronto: Hushion House, 2000.
News from Nowhere. London: Hamilton, 1986.
The Women's Hour. London: Paladin, 1991.

A Work about David Caute
Tredell, Nicholas. *Caute's Confrontations: A Study of the Novels of David Caute.* Nottingham, England: Pauper's Press, 1994.

Cayer, D. M.
See DUFFY, MAUREEN.

Challans, Eileen Mary
See RENAULT, MARY.

Chaplin, Sidney (1916–1986) *novelist, short story writer*
Sid Chaplin was born in Shildon in Durham County, England. His father, Isaiah Chaplin, an

electrician, and his mother, Elsie Charlton, both came from mining families. Chaplin attended six elementary schools as his family moved to different mining villages. He entered the family profession in 1931 but found time to attend the Workers' Educational Association classes of the University of Durham. Chaplin was employed at the Dean and Chapter Colliery until 1950, when he became a public relations officer for the National Coal Board.

Throughout his career, Chaplin drew upon personal experience and his inherited mining tradition for his fiction. His first volume of short stories, *The Leaping Land* (1946), describes the trials of life for mining families in northern England. His subsequent volumes received critical praise for their realistic portrayal of British mining families and the hardships and dilemmas they face. In the title story of *A Thin Seam and Other Stories* (1968), a miner's son is torn between taking an opportunity to attend college to perhaps find a better life or returning to his village to work in the pit: "I saw that the primrose path was open to me and that not a soul would ever condemn me for taking it, just the same I knew that all the time I would be supported on the bowed sweated shoulders of my father and brothers and others like them." When reviewing *The Bachelor Uncle* (1978), a collection of stories told from the viewpoint of a boy whose father was killed in the mines, critic John Mellors wrote, "As one might expect from an ex-collier, the background of the Durham mining village rings utterly authentic."

Chaplin's novels were also noted for their descriptions of British working-class culture. In his best-known novel, *The Day of the Sardine* (1961), he describes a miner's cynicism about seeking to attain a more affluent way of life. In a departure from Chaplin's usual topics, the novel *Sam in the Morning* (1965) describes the personal and professional trials of a corporate executive who is fascinated with the monolithic building that he works in. In *The Mines of Alabaster* (1971), a struggling actor wrestles with issues from his past while pursuing a coal miner's daughter to Italy.

In addition to his fiction, Chaplin also wrote for the National Coal Board, *Coal Magazine,* and *Coal News,* and he was an occasional contributor to the *Guardian* newspaper. Critic Michael Standen, when comparing him to other British writers who have depicted coal miners, such as D. H. LAWRENCE, wrote that Chaplin "with actual underground experience deals with the hidden fractures of English life more directly, more uncomfortably."

Other Work by Sid Chaplin
My Fate Cries Out. New York: Dent, 1949.

Chatwin, Bruce (1940–1989) *travel writer, novelist, journalist*

Bruce Chatwin was born in Sheffield, England, during World War II, the eldest son of his family. His father was a lawyer who spent the war in the navy. Chatwin described his wartime childhood as nomadic: "My father was at sea, my mother and I wandering from place to place, travelling up and down wartime England to stay with relations and friends. Our temporary stopping-places are less clear than the journeys between them."

Chatwin said later that his ancestors were either "solid and sedentary citizens . . . or horizon-struck wanderers who had scattered their bones in every corner of the earth." His own wanderlust was allegedly first piqued when he was nine years old, and a favorite uncle was murdered while traveling in West Africa. Chatwin became fascinated by the continent after this and researched all he could. In this way he learned about Victorian explorers like Richard Burton, who would later inspire him in his own travels. Chatwin was educated at private boarding school. Never a fan of literary classics, he once declared hyperbolically that he had never read anything except art books and encyclopedias until he was 20. But Chatwin did enjoy reading children's books about true-life adventures and travel. He recalled, "I never liked Jules Verne, believing that the real was always more fantastic than the fantastical."

In 1958 Chatwin joined the prestigious London auction firm Sotheby's. He worked his way up to director of the firm's impressionist art section, where he was especially talented at writing descriptions of art objects. The reviewer Jay Currie notes that Chatwin "etched the bones of his writing style describing the loot of empire." Chatwin left Sotheby's in 1966 to study for an archaeology degree at the University of Edinburgh, but he left his studies after two years. He then worked for the London *Sunday Times* for five years as a traveling journalist.

In 1976 Chatwin abandoned his newspaper job to travel to Patagonia in southern South America. His trip produced the travelogue *In Patagonia* (1977), an unusual blend of personal anecdotes, autobiography, imaginative reverie, and travel book. He had a genius for combining random details in illogical but amusing ways. For example, he describes watching a teacher draw a bleak map of cold war Europe on the blackboard: "We saw the zones bump one another leaving no space in between. The instructor wore khaki shorts. His knees were white and knobbly, and we saw that it was hopeless."

Chatwin has been criticized for mixing truth with fiction in his anecdotes, but *In Patagonia* was nonetheless critically acclaimed. The *Guardian* called it "the book that redefined travel writing." It won the Hawthornden prize and the E. M. Forster Award of the American Academy of Arts and Letters.

Chatwin's novel *On the Black Hill* (1982) is set closer to home, in the wild Welsh hills he visited as a child. Chatwin said later, "It always irritated me to be called a travel writer. So I decided to write something about people who never went out." The novel describes the lives of twin brothers who live for 80 years on an isolated farm in Wales, far from the changing civilization of the 20th century. It won the Whitbread Award and became a film in 1988.

One of Chatwin's most famous books is *The Songlines* (1987). On the surface this work is a study of the Australian aborigines' "Dreamingtracks," songs and stories that cover Australia in an invisible sacred web. The book also explores Chatwin's own attachment to a nomadic life. The author has been criticized for spending little time asking aborigines what the Dreaming actually meant to them, but the book is nonetheless ac-

claimed for its haunting depiction of the Australian wilds.

Newsday said of Chatwin, "No ordinary book ever issues from Bruce Chatwin. Each bears the imprint of a dazzlingly original mind." As his biographer Susannah Clapp wrote, "He was famous for being a vivid presence." He was greatly mourned after his early death from AIDS.

Other Works by Bruce Chatwin

Anatomy of Restlessness: Selected Writings, 1969–1989. Edited by Jan Borm and Michael Graves. New York: Viking, 1996.

Far Journeys: Photographs and Notebooks. Edited by David King and Francis Wyndham. New York: Viking, 1993.

Utz. New York: Viking, 1989.

What Am I Doing Here? New York: Viking, 1989.

Works about Bruce Chatwin

Clapp, Susannah. *With Chatwin: Portrait of a Writer.* New York: Knopf, 1997.

Shakespeare, Nicholas. *Bruce Chatwin.* New York: Doubleday, 2000.

Chesterton, G. K. (Gilbert Keith Chesterton) (1874–1936) *novelist, nonfiction writer, poet, playwright*

Born in London, G. K. Chesterton was the son of Edward Chesterton, a realtor, and Marie Grosjean Chesterton. As a schoolboy he spent time dreaming, drawing cartoons, and making the acquaintance of "odd and scrappy sorts of people like myself." After studying art and literature at University College, London, he began writing reviews for the *Bookman.* Described by George Bernard Shaw as "a man of colossal genius," the eccentric, 300-pound Chesterton was a literary legend renowned for his witty essays on religion, politics, and contemporary issues.

Orthodoxy (1908), which Chesterton described as "a sort of slovenly autobiography," traces his journey from agnosticism to faith in Christianity. In 1922 he became a Roman Catholic. Works like *The Everlasting Man* (1925) and other eloquent defenses of Christianity earned Chesterton the title of the father of modern popular spiritual writing. His conservative religious beliefs also influenced his works on economics and politics, in which he advocated widespread ownership of property.

Today Chesterton's fictional detective Father Brown is considered his most enduring creation. The unassuming priest, whom Chesterton described as "shabby and shapeless, his face round and expressionless, his manners clumsy," solves crimes by putting himself into the mind of the criminal. A founding member of the Detection Club, an organization of professional mystery writers, Chesterton shaped the conventions of the classic mystery: "to play fair with the presentation of clues, to battle wits with the reader, to conceal the identity of the criminal until the climactic moment . . ., to construct bizarre puzzles with purely rational solutions, and to encapsulate everything into a concentrated, short-story form," notes scholar, John C. Tibbetts.

Among Chesterton's other works, which include poems and plays, his novel *The Man Who Was Thursday* (1908) and his biographies have received the most critical praise. Critic Patrick Braybrooke thinks *Charles Dickens* (1903) was "its author's best book." Editor A. C. Ward admires his *Robert Browning* (1903) but complains that in *Francis of Assisi* (1923) Chesterton's focus shifted from his subject to word play and "verbal trickery."

Not all of Chesterton's more than 100 works will endure. However, Tibbetts notes that Chesterton's "love of paradox and whimsy, his flashing wit and indomitable optimism, and his impassioned defense of spiritual values place him among the most beloved, oft-quoted literary figures of the twentieth century."

Other Work by G. K. Chesterton

The Penguin Complete Father Brown. New York: Penguin, 1987.

A Work about G. K. Chesterton

Pearce, Joseph. *Wisdom and Innocence: A Life of G. K. Chesterton.* San Francisco: Ignatius, 1997.

Christie, Agatha (Mary Westmacott)
(1890–1976) *novelist, short story writer, playwright*

Born Agatha May Clarissa Miller in Devon, England, Agatha Christie was educated at home by her mother, Clarissa Boehmer Miller, after the death of her American father, Frederick Alvah Miller. She studied music in Paris but did not have a strong enough voice for an opera career. In 1914 she married Colonel Archibald Christie, a fighter pilot. During World War I Christie's work as a volunteer nurse and pharmacist familiarized her with poisons, a knowledge she would use in her novels. She was divorced in 1928 but soon met her second husband, Max Mallowan, an archeologist whom she often accompanied on digs.

Christie's first published novel, *The Mysterious Affair at Styles* (1920), was written on a dare from her sister Mary. It contained several elements of what came to be known as "Golden Age" mysteries: a country house, a puzzle with a logical solution, clues meant both to misdirect readers and to give them a fair chance to solve the crime, and a distinctive detective. "Hercule Poirot, the dandy with the egg-shaped head who is retired from the Belgian police and living in England as a war refugee" became, according to critic David Hawkes, "Christie's most famous creation." Often assisted by his loyal friend Captain Hastings, Poirot uses his "little grey cells" to solve crimes in more than 30 subsequent books.

In Christie's second novel, a thriller entitled *The Secret Adversary* (1920), two charming but naïve adventurers solve a kidnapping and thwart Bolshevik spies. Over the course of five books, Tommy Beresford and Tuppence Cowley marry, have children, and undertake secret missions for British intelligence. In *Partners in Crime* (1929), Tommy and Tuppence solve several mysteries using methods that parody well-known fictional sleuths such as Sherlock Holmes, Father Brown, and even Hercule Poirot.

Christie's other detectives were introduced in short stories. Mr. Parker Pyne becomes a professional problem solver after retiring from his job as a government statistician. The mysterious Harley Quin is described by Christie as a "catalyst" who was always "a friend of lovers, and connected with death."

The only one of Christie's sleuths to rival Poirot in popularity is Miss Marple, a sweet old lady "with a steel-trap mind and a genius for analogy" whose knowledge of village life gives her unerring insight into crime, according to Martha Hailey DuBose. After solving the *Murder in the Vicarage* (1930), Miss Marple appears in 11 subsequent "cozy" mysteries, which are characterized by an amateur detective, a village setting, and a genteel omission of violent details about the crime.

After some of her books were dramatized, Christie felt she could do a better job and began to write her own plays. By the end of World War II she was as well known for her plays as for her mysteries. *The Mousetrap* (1952), in which guests at a country house are snowbound with a murderer, became the world's longest-running play; it is still on stage in London. Director David Turner attributes its longevity to Christie's "knack of making the solving of the crime more important than the crime," so that audiences get caught up in trying to identify the murderer.

While Christie's mysteries made the best-seller lists and were often adapted into stage plays and movies, the six romantic novels she wrote as Mary Westmacott never achieved popularity. Christie's favorite, *Absent in the Spring* (1944), reflects her experiences in the Middle East, while *Unfinished Portrait* (1934) portrays the breakdown of her first marriage.

Christie herself said, "I regard my work of no importance—I've simply been out to entertain," but biographer Mary S. Wagoner wrote that "she dominated 20th-century classic British detective fiction in all three of its forms: the short story, the novel, the play." With other members of the the professional Mystery Writers Organization Detection Club, such as Dorothy L. SAYERS and G. K. CHESTERTON, Christie developed the rules of fair play that defined the novels of the Golden Age of mysteries, which ran roughly from 1920 to 1940.

While Christie has been criticized for her stereotyped characters, the mystery writer Robert Barnard notes that her generalized descriptions allow readers to associate the characters and settings in her books with the people and places they know. Christie scholar Marty S. Knepper considers her "the cleverest whodunit plotter ever, . . . known for fair but surprising endings." *Twentieth-Century Authors* ranks *The Murder of Roger Ackroyd* (1926), a "brilliant *tour de force* with a trick ending" as "one of the few undoubted classics of the modern detective story." In 1954 Christie became the first Grandmaster recognized by the Mystery Writers of America. In 1971 she was made a Dame Commander of the Order of the British Empire (OBE).

Other Works by Agatha Christie
And Then There Were None. 1939. Reprint, New York: St. Martin's Press, 2001.
An Autobiography. New York: Dodd, 1977.
Murder on the Orient Express. 1934. Reprint, New York: Berkley, 2000.

Works about Agatha Christie
Benson, Matthew. *The Complete Christie: An Agatha Christie Encyclopedia.* New York: Pocket, 2000.
Sova, Dawn B. *Agatha Christie A to Z: The Essential Reference to Her Life and Writings.* New York: Facts On File, 1996.

Churchill, Caryl (1938–   ) playwright
Caryl Churchill was born in London but spent much of her early life in Canada. Her father, Robert Churchill, was a political cartoonist distantly related to Sir Winston Churchill; her mother was a model, actress, and secretary. In 1956 the family returned to England, and Churchill was horrified at the class system she found. Many of her plays challenge English class structure.

Churchill attended Oxford, graduating with a B.A. in 1960. She wrote and staged her first plays while there, including a one-act play, *Downstairs* (1958), and the play *Having a Wonderful Time* (1959). After she graduated she wrote many successful plays for radio and television. Radio gave her a chance to use scenes of unusual length, varying conventional scenes with very short ones, and to move through time and space. She continued to use these devices in her later stage plays.

In 1972 Churchill wrote *Owners,* her first major play for the theater. The play is about a woman, Marion, who is a successful property developer and incredibly cruel. Churchill deftly caricatures Marion's husband's jealousy of her success: "She can stand on her own two feet which is something I abominate in a woman."

From 1974 to 1975 Churchill was the Royal Court's resident dramatist. During this time she wrote *Moving Clocks Go Slow,* a science-fiction play; and *Objections to Sex and Violence* (1975), about a female caretaker who is physically and sexually mistreated. This latter play brought her to the attention of a feminist theater group called Monstrous Regiment, which changed Churchill's entire way of writing.

From 1961 to 1976 Churchill had written her plays on her own, and she found this isolation very difficult. From 1976 onwards, Churchill discovered the delight of creating plays while in discussion with producers and actors who shared her political principles. With the aid of Monstrous Regiment, Churchill wrote *Vinegar Tom* (1976), a play arguing that the 17th-century witch trials in England were actually motivated by hatred and fear of women who did not fit conventions in various ways (i.e., unmarried or poor women, or expert healers). The play includes a horrifying scene in which a woman is pierced with needles by a witch-hunter.

The late 1970s saw Churchill becoming increasingly successful and critically admired. In conjunction with the Joint Stock Theatre Group, for whom she wrote several plays, Churchill produced *Cloud Nine* (1979), her famous two-act satire on sexual prejudices. The first act describes a patronizing Victorian big-game hunter on an African safari: "Women can be treacherous and evil. They are darker and more dangerous than men. The family protects us from that." The second act features the same characters, 25 years older, in 1979 London.

The play questions prejudices against women and homosexuals and typifies Churchill's unconventional dramatic strategies. Musical routines are part of the action, and the characters are played by actors of the opposite sex. *Cloud Nine* won a *Village Voice* Obie Award.

In the 1980s Churchill continued to produce clever plays exposing sexism and class prejudice. Her play *Top Girls* (1982), for example, asks what successful women have been required to do throughout history in order to succeed in a male-dominated world. *Softcops* (1984) is a cabaret play set in 19th-century France. The *Times Literary Supplement* reviewed *Softcops* as a "music-hall turn and Victorian freak show." Churchill's plays often use singing and music in unusual ways. The critic Leonard Ashley notes that Churchill's work often uses "popular devices like song in a dance of ideas that emphasize social rather than psychological conflicts."

In the 1990s Churchill produced many diverse plays that challenged the usual conventions of drama. *Mad Forest: A Play from Romania* (1990) was written after she and a group of student actors visited Romania to research the atrocities of the Romanian dictator Ceausescu's political regime. *The Skriker* (1994) is a fantastical blend of folklore and contemporary life depicting a malevolent goblin who chases two women to London, wanting to steal their firstborn children.

Churchill has written scores of critically acclaimed plays. The critic Benedict Nightingale praised her as "a dramatist who must surely be rated among the half-dozen best now writing . . . a playwright of genuine audacity and assurance, able to use her considerable wit and intelligence in ways at once unusual, resonant, and dramatically riveting."

Other Works by Caryl Churchill

Far Away. New York: Theatre Communications Group, 2001.

Plays: One. Owners, Traps, Vinegar Tom, Light Shining in Buckinghamshire, Cloud Nine. London: Methuen, 1985.

Plays: Two. Softcops, Top Girls, Fen, Serious Money. London: Methuen, 1990.

Works about Caryl Churchill

Kritzer, Amelia. *Plays of Caryl Churchill: Theatre of Empowerment*. New York: St. Martin's Press, 1991.

Randall, Phyllis. *Caryl Churchill: A Casebook*. New York: Garland, 1988.

Churchill, Sir Winston Leonard Spencer

(1874–1965) *historian, biographer, journalist, memoirist, essayist, novelist*

Winston Churchill was born at Blenheim Palace, England, to an American mother, Jenny Jerome, whose father was Leonard Jerome, proprietor and editor of the *New York Times* during the Civil War. Churchill's father was Lord Randolph Churchill, a descendant of John Churchill, the first duke of Malborough and one of England's most distinguished soldiers.

Churchill's father was an ambitious politician, and his pursuit of advancement in Parliament left him no time for concern with his son's education. After unhappily enduring a preparatory school young Winston was sent to Harrow, one of the great English public schools, where his academic record was so unpromising that he was not considered a candidate for Oxford or Cambridge. However, he had one teacher at Harrow who taught him to love the structure of the English sentence, a love that would serve him well in his later oratory and written histories. His father decided that he should go to Sandhurst, the British military academy. He was commissioned a second lieutenant in 1895 and was assigned to the 4th Queen's Own Hussars.

Peacetime service in England for aristocratic officers of fashionable regiments was anything but arduous, and Churchill's low threshold of boredom drove him to seek adventure and excitement in a shooting war. There was only one available at the time, a rebellion in Cuba against Spanish rule, so with another adventurous soldier he set sail for Cuba. There, on his 21st birthday, he was involved in combat. He distinguished himself to such a degree that he was awarded the Spanish Order of the Red Cross. He also began his writing career at this time, earning five pounds per dispatch as a reporter for the British newspaper the *Daily Graphic*. Thus began a writing career that would last another 70 years and produce 34 volumes of history, biography, autobiography, and a novel, along with four volumes of essays and eight volumes of speeches.

In the winter of 1896–97 the Hussars were posted to India, where there seemed nothing to do but play polo and read books. At his request, Churchill's mother sent him the eight volumes of Edward Gibbon's *Decline and Fall of the Roman Empire* along with the works of Plato and Aristotle. Among 19th-century British writers, he read Thomas Malthus, Charles Darwin, and historian Thomas Babington Macaulay. Macaulay's choice of subjects, his style, and the example of his life in government service made him probably the single greatest influence on Churchill's future career.

Churchill studied seriously three or four hours a day for months, until he had another opportunity to see combat, in northern India. As before in Cuba, he paid his way by reporting, this time for the Allahabad *Pioneer*. He then wrote his first book, *The Story of the Malakand Field Force* (1898). Soon he sought out yet another war reporting job, this time for the *Morning Post* with General Kitchener in Egypt, also in 1898.

Realizing that he could earn a living with his writing and could have more freedom outside the army, Churchill resigned his commission in 1899 and made his first run for a seat in Parliament. He lost this first election but ran again in 1900 and was elected. Thus began a political career that lasted for 64 years, including two terms as prime minister.

In 1906 Churchill wrote a substantial biography of his father, *Lord Randolph Churchill*. In 1908 he married Clementine Hozier. He subsequently wrote a four-volume history of World War I, *The World Crisis* (1923–31). Churchill described his intentions with that work: "I set myself at each stage to answer the questions 'What happened, and Why?' I seek to guide the reader to those points where the course of events is being decided, whether it be on a battlefield, in a conning tower, in Council, in Parliament, in a lobby, a laboratory, or a workshop." Arthur Conan Doyle praised the history, saying it contained "the finest prose style of any contemporary."

Churchill followed *The World Crisis* with what many consider to be his masterpiece, *Marlborough: His Life and Times* (1933–38). This was a biography of his most famous ancestor, the duke of Marlborough, a war hero from the early 18th century. While writing this work, and throughout the 1930s, Churchill warned his country and the world of the Nazi threat in Germany. His collected speeches from between the two world wars, and particularly in the early years of the second war, represent his best and most stirring prose:

> If we can stand up to him [Hitler], all Europe may be free and the life of the world may move forward into broad, sunlit uplands. But if we fail, then the whole world, including the United States, including all that we have known and cared for, will sink into the abyss of a new Dark Age made more sinister, and perhaps more protracted by the lights of perverted science. Let us therefore brace ourselves to our duties, and so bear ourselves that, if the British Empire and its Commonwealth last for a thousand years, men will still say, "This was their finest hour."

Churchill became Britain's prime minister and led his country to victory in the war. Afterward, he published the monumental *The Second World War* (1948–54) in six volumes. Because he was involved in so many of the major decisions of the war, the work is essentially a long autobiography of those years. Churchill employed the same rhetorical style that made his speeches so memorable to the writing of history: "The citadel of the Commonwealth and the Empire could not be stormed. Alone, but upborne by every generous heart-beat of mankind, we had defied the tyrant in the height of his triumph." The work appealed to a Britain recovering from the devastation of the German attacks and eager to celebrate their victory. Churchill was awarded the Nobel Prize for literature in 1953. Biographer Maurice Ashley praises Churchill's achievements in historiography while explaining away their defects: "He never had either the time or inclination to absorb himself in it completely or to revise his work in detail in the light of later knowledge: he preferred to make history than to write it."

In his 80s, Churchill produced what is possibly his best-known work today, the four-volume *A History of the English-Speaking Peoples* (1956–58). He intended with this work to emphasize the common heritage of Britain, the United States, Canada, Australia, and New Zealand, weaving together their histories from the Middle Ages to the end of the 19th century. His conclusion makes his ideological agenda explicit: "Here is set out a long story of the English-speaking peoples. They are now become Allies in terrible but victorious wars. And that is not the end." His section on the American Civil War is generally considered the strongest part of the book. Although American historians had written volumes about this event, the peculiarities of American politics were still incomprehensible to many Europeans. Churchill condensed this chapter of history, making it accessible to British readers: "It is almost impossible for us nowadays [to realize] how profoundly and inextricably Negro slavery was interwoven into the whole life, economy, and culture of the Southern states." By modern historiographic standards, Churchill's patriotism, his rhetorical flourishes, and his overwhelming belief in progress detract from the ideal of history as the plain narration of facts. Furthermore, his history deals almost exclusively with politics and war, omitting the histories of art, literature, science, and everyday life. However, as scholar Manfred Weidhorn wrote: "It will survive as a contribution to history by a successful man of action, politician, orator, journalist rather than a scholar."

Works about Winston Churchill

Gilbert, Martin. *Churchill: A Life.* New York: Holt, 1991.
Jenkins, Roy. *Churchill: A Biography.* New York: Farrar, Straus & Giroux, 2001.

Clarke, Sir Arthur Charles (1917–)
novelist, nonfiction writer

Arthur C. Clarke is one of science fiction's most important authors. Born to Charles Clarke, a farmer, and his wife, Nora, in Minehead, Somersetshire, England, Clarke later studied physics and mathematics at King's College and worked as a radar technician in the Royal Air Force during World War II.

Clarke's fiction is marked by accurate science and logical extrapolation from current knowledge. His novel *Sands of Mars* (1952), for example, tells in almost documentary fashion the story of the exploration of Mars, while *Islands in the Sky* (1952) gives a guided tour of life aboard a space station.

At times Clarke's science fiction becomes almost mystical, as time and again he employs science to inspire the sort of awe normally reserved for religion. As he notes in his nonfiction book *Profiles of the Future: An Inquiry into the Limits of the Possible* (1984), "Any sufficiently advanced technology is indistinguishable from magic." Thus, in one of his best-known novels, *Rendezvous with Rama* (1973), he depicts human scientists trying to understand a large, wonderous alien space craft that drifts into our solar system. As the critic Peter Nicholls observes, "The spaceship is a symbol of almost mythic significance, enigmatic, powerful, and fascinating."

Influenced by the writer Olaf STAPLEDON, Clarke speculates in a number of his novels on the evolution of the human race. Thus, in *Childhood's End* (1953) all of humanity merges into a single great super-being. Helping in the process are aliens who, ironically, look like demons and devils. The science fiction author Robert J. Sawyer has written that *Childhood's End* inspired readers and writers alike because Clarke ended it with intriguing, unanswered questions, "so that the reader can write the sequel in his or her own mind."

In Clarke's most famous novel, *2001: A Space Odyssey* (1968), the author blends his fascination with the technology of space travel with speculation on the next stage of human development. Based on his short story "The Sentinel" (1951),

about evidence of alien life discovered on the moon, and developed simultaneously with Stanley Kubrick's film version, *2001* tells how an unseen, powerful alien race uses devices shaped like black monoliths first to help early humans develop tools and then to transform a 21st-century astronaut, David Bowman, into a godlike starchild. The novel earned praise beyond the science fiction community, with the *New Yorker* commenting on the novel's "poetry, scientific imagination, and . . . wit." Clarke has written three sequels, of which *3001: The Final Odyssey* (1997) is the last.

Clarke has produced many nonfiction books, most championing science and technology. He was the first writer to propose the creation of telecommunications satellites in 1947. As he would write in *1984, Spring: A Choice of Futures* (1984), he has never shared George ORWELL's fear that new technology would be used to enslave or dehumanize. While others condemn television for corrupting the public, Clarke argues that it is an essential component of a moral world because it allows the entire planet to see wrongdoing and misery and thus act to stop it.

Clarke also has written many books promoting space travel, most notably *The Exploration of Space* (1951), winner of the 1952 International Fantasy Award; and *The Promise of Space* (1968). He has written several nonfiction works on undersea exploration, including *The Challenge of the Sea* (1960) and *Indian Ocean Treasure* (1964), as well as two mainstream novels: *The Deep Range* (1957), about future colonization of the ocean; and *Dolphin Island* (1963), dealing with communication between humans and dolphins. Clarke became so fascinated by scuba-diving that he moved to Sri Lanka, where he could dive year round. Despite his great familiarity with science, Clarke also developed an interest in paranormal phenomena, and he recounted various reports of ghosts and psychic powers as the host of two television series devoted to such claims.

In recognition of the scope and impact of his nonfiction work, Clarke won the 1962 UNESCO Kalinga Prize for science writing. In 2000 he was knighted, in part because for his contributions to telecommunications.

Still, it is for his role in the development of modern science fiction that Clarke remains best known. The American science fiction author Isaac Asimov praised Clarke's ability to create imaginative stories without straying from known scientific principles, saying of him, "Nothing reasonable frightens him simply because it seems fantastic." The scholar Eric Rabkin observes that Clarke's "unique combination of strong plots of discovery and compelling scientific detail mark his work as among the most polished in the genre."

Other Works by Arthur C. Clarke

The Collected Stories of Arthur C. Clarke. New York: Tor, 2000.
A Fall of Moondust. New York: Signet, 1961.
The Fountains of Paradise. New York: Harcourt Brace, 1979.

Works about Arthur C. Clarke

McAleer, Neil. *Arthur C. Clarke: The Authorized Biography.* Chicago: Contemporary Books, 1992.
Reid, Robin Anne, ed. *Arthur C. Clarke: A Critical Companion.* Westport, Conn.: Greenwood Press, 1997.

Coetzee, John Michael (1940–)
novelist

J. M. Coetzee was born in Cape Town, South Africa. Although his parents were Afrikaners, Coetzee attended English schools and studied English literature at the University of Cape Town. This background has allowed him to create realistic characters, both Afrikaner and English—an uncommon achievement in South African fiction.

In 1962 Coetzee moved to England to work as a computer programmer, but he grew dissatisfied with the work. In 1966 he was awarded a Fulbright scholarship to complete his doctoral thesis in English at the University of Texas. While in the United States, he protested the Vietnam War, comparing it to South African apartheid. The comparison continued to trouble him after his 1972 return to South Africa to teach at the University of Cape Town.

Coetzee's first book, *Dusklands* (1974), combines these two concerns. It consists of two novellas. The first, "The Vietnam Project," describes an army propaganda officer who devises a psychological scheme to harm the North Vietnamese. The second, "The Narrative of Jacobus Coetzee," has its title character, an 18th-century explorer, first study then massacre a South African tribe. Although the settings differ, both stories examine the effects of colonialism. In Coetzee's view, colonialism alienates individuals from the world because the process of colonization creates a permanent division between two groups. This alienation is the central theme in Coetzee's fiction.

Many South African reviewers criticized *Dusklands* and subsequent novels because they did not portray the contemporary abuses of apartheid. In response, Coetzee published *Age of Iron* (1990). The novel's protagonist, the terminally ill Mrs. Curren, has two key experiences. First, she encounters a homeless man, Vercueil, whom she tries to shape into an ideal human being; second, she visits an impoverished black township. Both incidents reveal the illusions of many white South Africans. Mrs. Curren, although well-intentioned, fails to recognize Vercueil as an individual upon whom she does not have the right to impose a new identity, and her belief that black South Africans lead pleasant, comfortable lives is overturned.

Coetzee has won many awards, including Britain's BOOKER PRIZE, South Africa's CNA Literary Award, and France's Prix Femina Etranger. According to the critic Kelly Hewson, Coetzee's fiction powerfully demonstrates "that oppression and injustice are not limited to South Africa, that, in some sense, they are eternal."

Other Works by J. M. Coetzee

Disgrace. New York: Viking, 1999.
Life & Times of Michael K. New York: Viking, 1984.
Waiting for the Barbarians. New York: Penguin, 1982.

Works about J. M. Coetzee

Gallagher, Susan. *A Story of South Africa: J. M. Coetzee's Fiction in Context.* Cambridge, Mass.: Harvard University Press, 1991.

Kossew, Sue, ed. *Critical Essays on J. M. Coetzee.* New York: G. K. Hall, 1998.

Colegate, Isabel (1931–   ) *novelist, nonfiction writer*

Born in Lincolnshire, England, Isabel Colegate was part of an aristocratic family. Her father, Sir Arthur Colegate, was a politician, and her mother was Lady Colegate, born Frances Worsley. Colegate's writing reflects much of her childhood experience of class. Many of her novels explore how class has changed in English society throughout the 20th century.

Colegate left school when she was 16. She completed her first novel, *The Blackmailer,* within a year, although it was not published until 1958. *The Blackmailer* describes a war widow who believes her husband died heroically; the villain, who knows that in fact her husband was a coward, threatens to reveal the truth publicly. Soon the relationship between blackmailer and widow becomes complex and passionate. This novel was Colegate's first exploration of a recurring theme: the interconnection between money and power.

Colegate's aristocratic experience enriches her novels *The Great Occasion* (1962) and *Statues in a Garden* (1964). Both novels describe moments of transition in English culture. The first covers the 1950s to 1970s, and the second is set in 1914, with World War I on the horizon. World War I was the catalyst for huge changes to the comfortable, aristocratic way of life that the British landed gentry had enjoyed for centuries.

The Shooting Party (1980) is Colegate's most famous evocation of the aristocracy's vulnerability on the eve of World War I. The novel describes a weekend of flirtation at a country house to which guests have been invited for a shooting party. However, this luxurious environment is doomed by history, its comfortable, ritualized violence fading out after the greater violence of World War I. The shooting party ends in tragedy, and "[b]y the time the next season came round a bigger shooting party had begun, in Flanders." The *Daily Telegraph* called *The Shooting Party* "as vivid and brilliant as painting on glass." The novel won the W. H. Smith Literary Award, and it became a popular film in 1984.

Colegate's novel *A Winter Journey* (1995) is about an elderly brother and sister, Edith and Alfred. Both of them have been successful in their careers, Edith in politics and Alfred in photography, but they are haunted by painful memories from their past. They spend a quiet weekend holiday together, and their proximity forces them to remember and face these painful memories. *Kirkus Reviews* described the novel as "sharp-eyed yet warm-hearted, unfailingly witty, impeccably written."

Colegate recently published her first nonfiction book, *A Pelican in the Wilderness: Hermits and Solitaries* (2002). A reverie on the attractions of solitude, it examines ancient and contemporary loners. But Colegate remains best known as a novelist recording Britain's changes through the 20th century. As the reviewer Claire Dederer notes, "Isabel Colegate has a unique gift for shining the bright light of passing history onto seemingly quiet rural lives."

Other Works by Isabel Colegate

A Glimpse of Sion's Glory. London: Hamilton, 1985.

The Orlando Trilogy. London: Penguin, 1984.

Collier, John (1901–1980) *novelist, short story writer, poet*

John Collier, the son of John George and Emily Noyes Collier, was born in London to an affluent family. Privately educated, he never attended college and published his first poem at age 19.

Yet it is not for his poetry that Collier is remembered, but for his novels and science fiction short stories. His first novel, *Married to a Chimp* (1931), is modeled after Victorian novels that are concerned with familial interactions. It differs from that form, however, in that the main acquaintance of its central character, Mr. Fatigay, is a chimpanzee named Emily, whom he adopts while teaching in the Congo. When he returns to England, he prefers Emily's company to that of his fiancée, Amy, and comes to consider the chimpanzee his true wife.

Married to a Chimp exhibits some fantastic elements, but it cannot be classified as fantasy, as are many of the stories in Collier's collection *Fancies and Goodnights* (1951). Many of the stories in this book, which won the first International Fantasy Award, explore marriage and murder using of a detached tone, omniscient narrators, stock characters, and surprise endings, characteristics suggesting the influence of Aldous HUXLEY, SAKI, and Ronald FIRBANK. The most famous stories in the collection are "The Chaser," a tale in which a young man buys a love potion that will result in his paramour becoming horribly and perpetually obsessed with him; and "Thus I Refute Beezly." In the latter story, Mr. Carter arrives home from work to find his son Simon engaged in a conversation with an imaginary person named Mr. Beezly. Infuriated by this display of imagination, Mr. Carter threatens to beat his son to make him stop, but Simon remarks that Mr. Beezly "'said he wouldn't let anyone hurt me. . . . He said he'd come like a lion, with wings on, and eat them up.'" When Carter goes upstairs to administer the beating, his wife hears screams and finds "on the second floor landing . . . the shoe, with the man's foot still in it, like that last morsel of a mouse which sometimes falls unnoticed from the side of the jaws of the cat."

Although some critics accused Collier of misogyny for his treatment of women in *Married to a Chimp,* his legacy is mostly positive. According to the novelist Anthony BURGESS, Collier "possessed considerable literary skill and a rare capacity to entertain."

Other Work by John Collier

The John Collier Reader. New York: Alfred A. Knopf, 1972.

A Work about John Collier

Richardson, Betty. *John Collier.* Boston: G. K. Hall, 1983.

Colum, Padraic (Patrick Collumb)
(1881–1972) *poet, playwright, children's writer*

Poet and playwright Padraic Colum was born Patrick Collumb in Longford, Ireland. In 1901 he joined the Irish Republican Army and adopted the Gaelic spelling of his name. He spent much of his time at the National Library, where he started a close friendship with fellow poet James JOYCE. At 17, while working as a clerk in the Irish Railway Clearing House in Dublin, Colum began writing in his spare time. Much of his subject matter came from stories told by inmates of his father's workhouse. In 1902 Colum won a competition for his play *The Saxon Shillin',* which dealt with Irishmen joining the British army.

Colum acted in and wrote plays for the Irish National Theatre Society. After his play *Broken Soil* (1903) was staged, he focused on writing. His poems began to appear in newspapers, and he became acquainted with key figures of the Irish Literary Renaissance, including W. B. YEATS, James STEPHENS, and Lady GREGORY, one of the founders of the Abbey Theatre. Colum wrote some of the theater's first plays and found success with his peasant drama *The Land* (1905). The play deals with the emigration of many young Irish to America after Ireland's Land Act of 1903, which allowed families to buy their own land. Martin, a farmer whose daughter is leaving, complains to his son about having no one to talk to. "For when I'm talking to you, Cornelius, I feel like a boy who lends back all the marbles he's won, and plays again, just for the sake of the game." Although filled with humorous dialogue, the play ultimately feels somber, as two young people decide to leave their families. Colum scholar Curtis Canfield writes that "in the final analysis, the play represents a tragic whole, although the parts which make it up are . . . not tragic but humorous."

Colum's first book of poetry, *Wild Earth* (1907), included such famous poems as "A Drover" and "An Old Woman of the Roads." In 1914 Colum traveled to New York, where he wrote children's stories for the *Sunday Tribune*, which were collected in *The King of Ireland's Son* (1916). In 1922 he was asked by the Hawaiian legislature to write three children's volumes based on the islands' folklore.

After spending the early 1930s in France, Colum and his wife Joyce returned to America to teach comparative literature at Columbia University. Colum published more than 50 books before his death. Stopford A. Brooke wrote of him, "To hear him . . . give a reading from his own poems or tales, is to fall under the spell of all Ireland."

Other Works by Padraic Colum

Selected Poems of Padraic Colum. Edited by Sanford Sternlicht. Syracuse, N.Y.: Syracuse University Press, 1989.

The Trojan War and the Adventures of Odysseus. 1918. Reprint, New York: William Morrow & Co., 1997.

A Work about Padraic Colum

Sternlicht, Sanford. *Padraic Colum*. Boston: Twayne, 1985.

Comfort, Alex (1920–2000) *novelist, nonfiction writer, poet, essayist*

Alex Comfort was born in London to Alexander Comfort, an education officer, and Daisy Comfort. He was educated at home and exhibited extraordinary intellectual abilities early on; he blew the fingers off his left hand while constructing a bomb at age 14. Comfort published a travel book at 18, before entering Trinity College, Cambridge. While still an undergraduate he published his first novel, *No Such Liberty* (1941). He published another novel, *The Power House* (1944), set in France, between earning his B.A. in 1943 and his M.A. in 1945.

Comfort's best novel, *On This Side Nothing* (1949), explores the Zionist movement and was published the same year he received his Ph.D. A pacifist and an anarchist, Comfort published *Authority and Delinquency in the Modern State*, a work applying psychiatry and psychological findings to political science, in 1950.

In the 1950s Comfort began research on the genetics and biology of aging, all the while writing and publishing poems, novels, and essays. He published *The Biology of Senescence* in 1961 and *Ageing and the Biology of Senescence* in 1964.

Despite his prolific literary career, it was *The Joy of Sex* (1972) that made Comfort's popular reputation as well as his fortune. This book, which he later said took him two weeks to write, sold more than 12 million copies in dozens of languages. The title was a play on *The Joy of Cooking* and was subtitled *A Gourmet Guide to Lovemaking*. The work captured the spirit of the times, following, as it did, the sexually liberating years of the late 1960s, and its illustrations, which depicted ordinary people rather than young Venuses and Adonises, appealed to a very wide audience.

After *Joy*'s publication, Comfort moved to Santa Barbara, California, where he remained until his return to England in 1985. He updated his work in *More Joy of Sex* (1974) and *The New Joy of Sex* (1991). In his early enthusiasms over life extension he suggested, at a scientific conference in Washington, D.C., in 1969 that within 20 years the human life span might reach 120 years. Comfort died at age 80. His obituary in the *Guardian* newspaper called him "a dazzling intellectual whose prolific output of novels, poetry, and philosophy remains overshadowed by a sex manual."

Compton-Burnett, Ivy (1884–1969) *novelist*

Ivy Compton-Burnett was born in Middlesex, England, to James Compton-Burnett, a homeopathic doctor, and his second wife, Katherine Compton-Burnett. She had 11 siblings and step-siblings. Educated at home by a tutor, she eventually attended the University of London, from which she received a degree in classics in 1902.

Compton-Burnett's father died in 1901, and her beloved younger brother Guy died four years later. When her mother died in 1911, Compton-Burnett became head of the household, but there was much domestic conflict. World War I brought much grief, and by its end she had lost her job, her home, and her closest friends. Her brother Noel was killed in France in 1916, two of her sisters committed suicide in 1917, and Compton-Burnett herself nearly died of influenza after the war. Happiness finally came during the period from 1919 to 1951, when she lived with the historian Margaret Jourdain.

Compton-Burnett's first novel, *Dolores* (1911), is a weak tale about a self-sacrificing heroine. The author dismissed this work as an apprentice piece and never listed it among her publications. Her second novel, however, *Pastors and Masters* (1925), received more critical approval. Set in a boy's boarding school, it describes inept teachers haranguing students, ingratiating themselves with parents, and mocking each other. Much of the dialogue is cynical: "'The sight of duty does make one shiver,' said Miss Herrick. 'The actual doing of it would kill one, I think.'"

Compton-Burnett's third novel, *Brothers and Sisters* (1929), draws heavily on her own life and introduces many features found in her later novels. It is set in the close confines of a late-Victorian household, where a family's secrets and cruelties are revealed in measured, decorous language. Novelist Pamela Hansford JOHNSON wrote that Compton-Burnett's "piercingly wise, discreet, mannered Victoriana conceals abysses of the human personality . . . a gentle tea-cosy madness, a coil of vipers in a sewing-basket."

Compton-Burnett is famous for her dialogue, which fills the bulk of her novels; she gives little space to descriptions of the characters or their unspoken thoughts. The critic Kathleen Wheeler writes, "Compton-Burnett's emphasis upon dialogue in most of the novels virtually creates a new genre of novel, the novel-play." Bitter, witty, and insightful, Compton-Burnett's dialogue is instantly recognizable, in part because it is often

strangely mannered and artificial. For example, Rosebery in *Mother and Son* (1955) declares, "As I am accused of giving preference to women . . . I will deserve the reputation and indulge the propensity." As well as making deft barbs, the dialogue also often leaps from point to point in unaffected tangents. Reviewer W. G. Rogers notes that Compton-Burnett "fills her matchless dialogue with utterly unpredictable remarks, she flits from sense to nonsense, she swings you around and around until, helpless and happy, you hope she'll never let go."

Compton-Burnett's novels are frequently comic. Characters are shockingly candid about disliking each other, being pretentious, wanting to be selfish, and having no sense of meaning in their life. Her brand of comedy is dark and, to some critics, disturbing. The reviewer for the *Church Times,* for example, said of her novel *A House and its Head* (1935): "It is as if one's next door neighbour leaned over the garden wall, and remarked, in the same breath and chatty tone, that he had mown the lawn in the morning and thrust the wife's head in the gas-oven after lunch."

Bullivant and the Lambs (1947) (published in Britain as *Manservant and Maidservant*) was one of Compton-Burnett's favorite novels. In this work, a domineering father, Horace Lamb, terrorizes his children and wife but suddenly undergoes a change of heart and becomes kind and well-meaning. None of his family believe the transformation, and complications ensue. The book has been praised for the way it juxtaposes the world of the upper-class family with the world of their servants.

Similar conflicts occur in *Mother and Son* (1955), which describes an unpleasant, controlling, upper-class woman, Miranda, who seeks a paid woman companion to follow her every whim: "I want someone who will adapt herself to me and accept my words and ways." The novel exposes the tensions within the family and the strangely intense bond between Miranda and her son Rosebery. Rosebery asserts that he is "faithful to the one woman, and that the one who fills the earliest memories." *Mother and Son* won the James Tait Black Memorial Prize.

Compton-Burnett wrote 20 novels. Although they have never been best-sellers, they have always been recognized for their extraordinary originality. Writer Storm JAMESON noted that the novels appeal because of their "repetition of one and the same human situation, an acting-out of the powerful impulses that run counter to an accepted social morality—brutal truth-telling, repressed family hatreds and loves." In Jameson's terms, Compton-Burnett's cynical novels offer a "ritual purgation in a modern idiom."

Other Works by Ivy Compton-Burnett

A God and His Gifts. New York: Simon & Schuster, 1964.

The Last and the First. New York: Alfred A. Knopf, 1971.

A Work about Ivy Compton-Burnett

Spurling, Hilary. *Ivy: The Life of I. Compton-Burnett.* New York: Columbia University Press, 1986.

Connolly, Cyril (1903–1974) *essayist*

Cyril Connolly was born in Whitley, England. His father, Matthew, was an army officer, and his mother, Muriel Maud, came from an affluent Anglo-Irish family. In 1914 Connolly enrolled at St. Cyprian's, a prominent preparatory school. From there, he gained admission to Eton, the leading British private school. At Eton he developed a deep love for Latin poetry and was inspired to write his "Theory of Permanent Adolescence," which argues that the intensity of one's school experiences stunts any future development.

After earning a history degree at Oxford in 1925, Connolly served as secretary to the wealthy American writer and expatriate Logan Pearsall Smith. Through Smith, Connolly was introduced to British literary society, and in 1927 he began writing reviews for the *New Statesman*. In these reviews and in subsequent work, he explored 18th-century fiction; 20th-century modernists including James JOYCE and Marcel Proust; and turn-of-the-century Decadents, such as Oscar Wilde and Charles Baudelaire.

Connolly collected many of his early essays in *The Condemned Playground* (1945). Overall, these essays produce a nostalgic effect and suggest that a time of cultural achievement has passed. Connolly's nostalgia is also coupled with his remorse at his failed attempts to be a fiction writer. The economic recession and social unrest of reconstruction after World War II troubled him, and he believed that gifted, lonely artists willing to defy accepted conventions would disappear.

Connolly edited the magazine *Horizon* from 1940 to 1950. By the time of his final publication, *The Evening Colonnade* (1973), his interests had expanded to include art and the natural world of geology and animal life. But Connolly remains best known for his literary essays that contain a passion for a skill he could never master. The biographer Jeremy Lewis indicates that "his entire output might well be regarded as an extended meditation, essentially autobiographical, on the problems of being a writer."

A Work by Cyril Connolly

Enemies of Promise. New York: Persea Books, 1983.

A Work about Cyril Connolly

Lewis, Jeremy. *Cyril Connolly: A Life.* 1938. Reprint, North Pomfret, Vt.: Trafalgar Square, 1998.

Conquest, Robert (George Robert Acworth Conquest) (1917–) *poet, editor, historian*

Robert Conquest was born in Malvern, England, to Robert Folger Westcott Conquest and Rosamund Acworth Conquest. His British upbringing and education at Oxford influenced his philosophy of poetry. This included an aversion to mystical and deliberately obscure imagery and language, which he regarded as inappropriate for English poetry. He edited the anthology *New Lines* (1956), in which he wrote, "The debilitating theory that poetry *must* be metaphorical gained wide acceptance. Poets were encouraged to produce diffuse and sentimental verbiage, or hollow technical pirouettes." Critics credit Conquest's *New Lines* anthology with creating the loose affiliation of important mid-century poets known as the MOVEMENT.

Another manifestation of Conquest's antimodernist views was his decision to edit a series of science-fiction anthologies with his avowedly "philistine" friend Kingsley AMIS, entitled *Spectrum* (1961–66). In addition to various literary, political, and educational societies and magazines, he became a leading member of the British Interplanetary Society.

Conquest shared Amis's conservative political leanings, and while working as a British diplomat he began writing several books on Soviet history that were highly critical of communism. These included *Power and Policy in the U.S.S.R.* (1967) and *Harvest of Sorrow* (1986), about the mass starvation caused by the collectivization of farming in Ukraine under Stalin.

Conquest combined his interests in poetry and Russia with the collection *Back to Life: Poems from Behind the Iron Curtain* (1958). His book *Reflections on a Ravaged Century* (1999) fused his interests in technology, totalitarianism, and the virtues of clear, simple language by arguing that 20th-century intellectuals had fallen for profound-sounding but authoritarian ideas, in part because the ideas seemed forward-looking and modern. Princeton political scientist Aaron Friedberg says that Conquest's history books make him "the West's leading chronicler of its [communism's] crimes."

Other Work by Robert Conquest
The Great Terror: A Reassessment. New York: Oxford University Press, 1990.

Conrad, Joseph (Josef Teodor Konrad Nalecz Korzeniowski) (1857–1924)
novelist

Joseph Conrad led three separate and distinct lives: his youth in Poland (1857–73); his life at sea (1874–94); and his life as a writer (1895–1924), wherein he drew upon the hoard of his physical and mental voyages to create his fictions. Born in Berdichev in Polish Ukraine, Conrad was the only son of Apollo Korzeniowski and Evelina Bobrowska. (The Poland of that time was not a nation-state, but partitioned among the powers of Russia, Germany, and Austria.) His father, a poet, translator, and patriot, was exiled with his family to Vologda in northern Russia when Conrad was five. The harsh environment broke both parents' health, and Conrad was orphaned at 11. His maternal uncle, the lawyer Tadeusz Bobrowski, then assumed his guardianship, and he was educated by a tutor and at schools in Cracow, Poland.

At 14 Conrad determined to go to sea, in part motivated by the nautical novels of Frederick Marryat, but also to escape Poland and the loss of his parents. At 17 the young Pole, who spoke fluent French and Russian but virtually no English, arrived in Marseilles. He sailed on several French ships to the West Indies before reportedly becoming involved in smuggling (possibly gunrunning for the Spanish Carlist cause), an episode that appears to have ended in shipwreck. In 1877 Conrad was wounded, the result of either a duel over a woman or a suicide attempt after losing all his money at gambling. It is difficult to establish the facts from the highly colored versions in the autobiographical *The Mirror of the Sea* (1906) and the late novel *The Arrow of Gold* (1919).

In 1878, at age 21, Conrad joined the English merchant marine. For the next 20 years he made numerous voyages, mostly to Asia and also to India, Malaysia, Australia, and South Africa. Conrad acquired his master's certificate in 1886 and captained his first ship in 1888. In 1890 he made a fateful voyage up the Congo. His diary of this journey furnished material for his novella *Heart of Darkness* (1902). Though he spent less than six months in Africa, Conrad's experience in the Congo made an indelible impression on him and wrecked his health. Partly due to ill health, he abandoned the sea in 1894. Two years later he married Jessie George and settled in Kent; the couple had two sons. In 1895 Conrad published his first book, *Almayer's Folly*, the story of a Dutchman's failed ambitions in Malaysia, which took five years to write.

Conrad's decision to write in English was an extraordinary but deliberate one. When he first sailed on a British ship, he spoke little English, though according to his autobiography, *A Personal Record* (1912), he had been reading the language since childhood. Because of his temperament (he loved to excel at difficult tasks), but also because English was an adopted tongue, writing was exceedingly arduous for him, despite his assertion that "it was I who was adopted by the genius of the language . . ." Conrad's works are artistic masterpieces, shaped and constructed with extreme care, every word chosen as carefully as though he were writing poetry. As he observes in his preface to *The Nigger of the Narcissus* (1897), "Any work that aspires . . . to the condition of art should carry its justification in every line."

Conrad's major works were composed between 1897 and 1911, a dozen years that saw the publication of *The Nigger of the Narcissus, Lord Jim* (1900), *Heart of Darkness* (1902), *Typhoon* (1903), *Nostromo* (1904), *The Secret Agent* (1907), and *Under Western Eyes* (1911). In all these novels characters are placed in extreme situations that reveal their strengths and weaknesses. His other work, though of interest, has not had the impact of these. One of his minor novels was *Romance* (1903), a collaboration with Ford Madox FORD detailing the Caribbean adventures of a young Englishman.

Critical Analysis

Two of Conrad's most characteristic works are *Heart of Darkness* and *The Secret Sharer*. Both novellas seamlessly blend physical voyages with journeys into the depths of the human mind. Both concern a character's confrontation with his inner or other self. In *Heart of Darkness* Marlow, an Englishman who appears in several of Conrad's novels, emerges out of a narrative frame as the author's representative, testifying to the truth of this horrifying story of European smash-and-grab raids on the African continent.

Conrad's narrators and protagonists are often doubles: The ostensible hero is confronted by someone who is his seeming opposite and who acts as accomplice, witness, and judge. Thus Marlow confronts, bears witness to, and judges Kurtz, once an emissary of enlightenment, who turns out to be hollow and succumbs to his worst instincts. Similarly, in *Lord Jim*, Marlow confronts a younger, "failed" self in the title character, or, as the untried captain of *The Secret Sharer,* confronts the outlaw Leggatt (a legate, or envoy, from his subconscious) as his alter ego.

Not only are characters thus doubles, or doppelgängers, but so are moral values. Conrad himself held to two conflicting codes: the work ethic of the mariner's code embodied in Marlow, and the need to identify with outlaws and outcasts (possibly part of his familial Polish past).

Perhaps Conrad's most symbolic work is *Heart of Darkness*. In addition to the physical voyage up the Congo, to discover the fate of Kurtz, a European trader, the novel is a journey back to the beginnings of time and a descent into the unconscious. This story of penetration into the heart of darkness begins on a vessel awaiting the turn of the tide on the Thames. In the opening and closing paragraphs, London's historic waterway merges with the Congo, both rivers having launched colonial enterprises. Marlow visits Brussels, a city presented as a "whited sepulchre," to ask his aunt's help in securing command of a steamship to sail up the Congo. The journey itself develops in three stages, foreshadowed by a series of omens and marked by Marlow's reaching, successively, the Outer, Central, and Inner trading stations. Everything in the story is both its physical self and a symbol. Thus, the women in the Brussels office resemble the Greek goddesses of fate knitting human destiny. Kurtz himself resembles nothing so much as a skeleton made of the ivory to which he has sacrificed all his ideals. Above all, the land and ocean, wilderness and river, are presented in constant chiaroscuro, alternating light and darkness, and frenetic movement, followed by complete stillness, suggestive of life and death.

The Secret Sharer also seamlessly fuses a sea voyage entailing both physical and psychic adventure. The young captain in his first command confesses to feeling a stranger to himself and his ship when the ship's ladder, unwittingly left dangling overboard, is grabbed by the swimming Leggatt. The captain shelters the stranger who comes aboard, feeling an instinctive sympathy for him. It turns out that Leggatt, mate on the *Sephora,* has killed a man who refused an order while a storm raged and a sail had to be set. Though the captain and his "secret sharer" resemble each other in age and appearance, they are not alike in character, which is the point. A psychological exchange or transfer of personality takes place between them when the captain allows Leggatt to escape by going overboard. In the process he runs his ship so close to land that he risks it, crew, indeed everything he holds dear to enable his other self to go free.

Although Conrad was originally dismissed as a spinner of nautical tales and exotic romances, he was an artful storyteller. His reputation grew posthumously, assuring his place in the pantheon of the 20th century's greatest writers.

Conrad died of a heart attack in Bishopsbourne, Kent, and is buried in St. Thomas's, Canterbury, under an epitaph from Edmund Spenser that he chose for himself: "Sleep after toil, port after stormy seas . . ."

Works about Joseph Conrad

Karl, Frederick R. *A Reader's Guide to Joseph Conrad.* Syracuse, N.Y.: Syracuse University Press, 1997.

Sherry, Norman. *Conrad: The Critical Heritage.* London: Routledge, 1997.

Watt, Ian. *Conrad in the Nineteenth Century.* Berkeley: University of California Press, 1981.

Cooper, William (Harry Summerfield Hoff) (1910–2002) *novelist*

Born Harry Summerfield Hoff in Crewe and educated at Christ's College, Cambridge, William Cooper was a physics teacher. He served in the Royal Air Force during World War II and in 1945 entered the civil service. He became the personnel consultant to the Atomic Energy Research Authority in 1958. He published four novels under the name Hoff before his fifth one, under the Cooper pseudonym, brought him recognition.

Narrated by the young, lower-middle-class schoolteacher Joe Lunn, *Scenes from Provincial Life* (1950) is Cooper's most important work. Praised for its sardonic comedy and artful realism, it influenced younger novelists of the 1950s, including Kingsley AMIS, John BRAINE, and Stan BARSTOW, as well as the ANGRY YOUNG MAN genre of novel. Three sequels continued the story of Joe Lunn, one of which, *Scenes from Metropolitan Life,* was written in 1951 but was suppressed for many years because of the threat of libel.

Cooper is known not only for the literary merit of his works but also for their contribution to the "new realism" school of British fiction. He also wrote *From Early Life* (1990), a memoir.

Other Works by William Cooper

Disquiet and Peace. London: Macmillan, 1956.
Young People. London: Macmillan, 1958.

Cope, Wendy (1945–) *poet*

Wendy Cope was born in Erith, Kent, England, to Fred Stanley Cope and Alice Mary Hand, both of whom were company directors. Cope attended private schools before enrolling at Oxford to study history. After earning a bachelor's degree in 1966, she taught in London primary schools, becoming a deputy headmistress in 1980. Cope later was an arts and review editor for *Contact,* a teachers' magazine, and from 1986 to 1990 she was a television critic for the *Spectator,* a journal that reviews politics and culture.

Cope's poetry collection *Making Cocoa For Kingsley Amis* (1986) parodied many famous poets, including T. S. ELIOT, Ted HUGHES, and Seamus HEANEY. In the poem "Waste Land Limericks" Cope reduced Eliot's most famous work to five limericks, starting the last section with "No water. Dry rocks and dry throats, / Then thunder, a shower of quotes." In addition to parodies, the collection also contains personal love poems. In "Message" Cope describes the frustration of waiting for a potential boyfriend to make the first move and call: "But one more day is more than I can bear - / Love is already turning into hate." Kingsley AMIS joined many critics in praising the volume that bore his name.

In 1991 Cope published *The River Girl,* a long narrative poem that explores a love affair between a goddess and a young poet. Her collection *Serious Concerns* (1992) marked a return to the style that made her famous with its mixture of parodies and humorous, though sometimes anguished, love poems. Although regarded as a talented writer of light poetry, Cope resists being categorized: "I dislike the term 'light verse' because it is used as a way of dismissing poets who allow humor into their work. I believe that a humorous poem can also be 'serious.'" Her poems display craftsmanship and also cover serious issues such as suicide.

Cope has received several honors, including the British Society of Authors' Cholmondeley Award in 1987. In addition to poetry, she has written a children's book, *Twiddling Your Thumbs* (1988), and edited an anthology of poems by women. Reviewer George Szirtes writes, "Wendy Cope is a sensible and witty poet. That is, I suppose, one reason why people who don't necessarily like poetry, like her."

Other Works by Wendy Cope

Does She Like Word-Games? London: Anvil Press, 1988.

If I Don't Know. London: Faber & Faber, 2001.

Coppard, Alfred Edgar (1878–1957) *short story writer, poet*

A. E. Coppard was born in Folkestone, England, the son of a tailor. He attended school in Folkestone and Brighton but had to leave when he was nine due to poor health. He later moved to Whitechapel and held a variety of jobs including tailor's apprentice, paraffin vendor's assistant, auctioneer, and cheesemonger. He supplemented his meager earnings from these jobs with prize money won in athletic competitions.

In 1919 Coppard began writing full-time; he published his first collection of short stories, *Adam and Eve and Pinch Me,* in 1921. The collection was a huge success and established Coppard's name in the literary world. The next year he published his first collection of poetry, *Hips and Haws* (1922), and for the next 30 years he published almost a book a year. His short-story collections include *Fishmonger's Fiddle* (1925), *Silver Circus* (1928), and *Fearful Pleasures* (1946). Among his poetry collections are *Yokohama Garland* (1926) and *Cherry Ripe* (1935).

Coppard saw his writing as part of the tradition of ballads and folklore. Many of his stories, which range from romance to horror, take place in the vividly described English countryside and feature characters who are brought to life through their rural dialects, as in "Thunder p'raps, but 'twill clear; 'tis only de pride o' der morning."

The protagonist of "The Higgler" is a typical Coppard character: a well-intentioned misfit who struggles to make his way in the world. Harvey Witlow is a salesman who becomes deeply infatuated with Mary, a girl on his route. When the girl's mother offers Harvey Mary's hand in marriage as well as a small fortune, Harvey becomes suspicious and confused. His obsession over his almost self-imposed dilemma makes him the type of odd character for which Coppard routinely showed a deep compassion. "The Higgler" is one of his most popular stories.

In addition to his many collections, Coppard also began work on his autobiography. The first volume of this work, *It's Me, O Lord,* was published after his death in 1957. His legacy lives on in the A. E. Coppard Prize for Fiction, awarded to longer short stories that have trouble getting published due to their length. The award is named for Coppard because his first short story was rejected for publication for its 12,000-word length.

Other Work by A. E. Coppard
Collected Tales of A. E. Coppard. North Stratford,
N. H.: Ayer, 1976.

Cornwell, David John Moore
See LE CARRÉ, JOHN.

Coward, Noël (1899–1973) *playwright,*
lyricist, novelist, poet, screenwriter, memoirist

A quintessential man of the theater whose public
image was that of the suave, sophisticated, upper
class, Noël Coward was born into the lower-
middle-class family of Arthur Sabin and Violet
Veitch Coward in Teddington, a suburb of London.
His father was a piano salesman, and the family's
main distinction was its overwhelming musicality.

The young Noël Coward first acted on stage in
1911 and continued to work on the stage or in
films and television for the next 56 years as actor,
director, writer, singer, pianist, and producer. He
wrote musicals, serious drama, comedies, film and
television scripts, poems, a novel, parodies, and his
autobiography, but as one of his biographers
wrote, his "greatest achievement was the creation
and refinement of his own persona, the witty,
charming sophisticate with an elegant disdain for
the crude world of ordinary life."

Coward's first major success was a serious play,
The Vortex (1924), in which the playwright himself
played the lead role of Nicky Lancaster, a young
man whose mother is having an affair with someone his own age. A success in both London and
New York, this play was, as critic Milton Levin
wrote, "a mixture of Ibsen and Maugham [and]
has also a strong suggestion of *Hamlet* in the play's
ancestry." Coward's next play, *Hay Fever* (1925), involves the argumentative Bliss family. Each family
member has, unbeknownst to the others, invited
an overnight guest at the same time. The play involves various pairings off until the constant bick-
ering among the family members drives the guests
away; the family, intent on arguing with each other
at the breakfast table, are unaware of their guests'

departure. The melodramatic Mrs. Bliss, a former
actress, is one of the play's most memorable characters: "I wanted a nice restful week-end, with moments of Sandy's ingenuous affection to warm the
cockles of my heart when I felt in the mood, and
now the house is going to be full of discord—not
enough food, every one fighting for the bath,—
perfect agony! I wish I were dead!"

Never one to slavishly repeat his successes,
Coward a few years later turned to musical comedy
with what he called an "operette," *Bitter Sweet*
(1929). Although *Bitter Sweet* was a huge success,
Coward topped it the next year with a play he
wrote for himself and the noted actress Gertrude
Lawrence, *Private Lives.* Coward and Lawrence
played Elyot and Amanda, a divorced couple, each
of whom has remarried. They meet again on their
respective honeymoons at the same Riviera hotel,
succumb to mutual attraction, and run away to
Paris together. When their spouses follow them to
Paris, all four characters attack each other in turn.
At first glance the plot seems flimsy, hardly enough
for even one act, but reviewers saw ". . . a species of
magic . . . Mr Coward has exactly the right effron-
tery for a first-rate conjurer . . . [and he] is a first
rate artist of the theatre. . . . The seeming spontaneity of the chatter has been attained by the most
industrious stage-craft and a remarkable sense of
timing and of tone."

In the 1930s Coward wrote a series of successful
plays, such as *Design for Living* (1933), about a love
triangle involving an interior designer, a painter,
and a playwright; and *Tonight at 8:30* (1935), a series of one-act plays that included *Still Life,* set in
the refreshment room of a train station.

In 1941 Coward's comedy *Blithe Spirit* was produced. Critic John Gassner called this play "a tour
de force of fancy in which Coward also displays the
cutting edge of his wit." The plot involves one of
Coward's best creations, Madame Arcati, a medium
whom a mystery writer, Charles Condomine, invites to his home as research for a novel. With the
help of a maid with psychic powers, Arcati manages
to call up the spirits of Charles's two late wives, who
continue to battle as Charles makes his exit.

In 1960 Coward published his only novel, *Pomp and Circumstance,* a comic tale set on the island of Samola. He also brought out two collections of short stories in the 1960s, along with a book of verse in 1967, *Not Yet the Dodo.* He published two autobiographics, *Present Indicative* (1937) and *Future Indefinite* (1954), and was engaged in writing a further volume, *Past Conditional,* when he died. He was knighted in 1970. Coward's plays have always been favorites with audiences, but in recent years they have become scholarly favorites as well: "Noël Coward, some quarter-century after his death, [has] become a subject for serious debate," declared the organizer of the first Coward conference in 1999.

Other Work by Noël Coward

The Collected Plays of Noël Coward. London: Methuen, 2000.

Works about Noël Coward

Kaplan, Joel, and Sheila Stowell, eds. *Look Back in Pleasure: Noël Coward Reconsidered.* London: Methuen, 2000.

Levin, Milton. *Noël Coward.* Boston: Twayne, 1984.

Mander, Raymond, and Joe Mitchenson. *Theatrical Companion to Coward.* New York: Theatre Communications, 2000.

Cowper, Richard (John Middleton Murry Jr.) (1926–2002) *novelist*

Richard Cowper is the pseudonym for John Middleton Murry Jr., the son and namesake of the prominent literary critic John Middleton Murry and his second wife, Violet le Maistre. Born in Bridport, Dorsetshire, England, Cowper received a B.A. from Oxford, served in the Royal Navy, and taught English at several British universities. After 1970 he supported himself as a writer of science fiction novels, with a few forays into other genres.

Cowper's first major novel was *The Twilight of Briareus* (1974), in which a celestial supernova irradiates Earth, causing mass infertility and granting some people, called Zetas, strange hallucinatory

powers. As the novel unfolds, it becomes clear that the Zetas are capable of contacting the alien life forms that caused the supernova and possibly saving humanity from extinction.

One of Cowper's most highly praised novels is *The Road to Corlay* (1978), which was nominated for the British Fantasy Award in 1979. The novel is based on an earlier short story, "The Piper at the Gates of Dawn," which sets the stage: England in 2999, after the melting of the polar ice caps. Its central character, a 13-year-old flutist named Thomas, proclaims a new religion called the creed of kinship and inspires followers with his music. In the novel, Britain is ruled by a harsh, dictatorial church that tries desperately to suppress Thomas's new religion. The church eventually kills Thomas, but not the creed of kinship. As Cowper explains in the novel, "the spirit of the Boy had refused to be shackled . . . the spark of the Boy's faith had flown out along the highways of the Kingdoms starting hungry fire in the dry kindling of men's hearts." The critic Duncan Lunan finds the novel remarkable for Cowper's success "in the extraordinary task of portraying a convincing alternative religion whose followers could attract sympathy and admiration."

In assessing Cowper's literary achievement, the critic John Clute compares him to H. G. WELLS, whose work also projected a profound fear of Britain's ultimate destruction sometime in the future. In Clute's words, "Almost all of Cowper's novels make conscious elegiac play on the beleaguered island that Wells, too, despaired of before his death. . . . There is a sense that Cowper writes about England in order that we may remember it, after it disappears for good. This note, whenever he strikes it, makes his work compulsive reading."

Other Work by Richard Cowper

Clone. New York: Pocket Books, 1979.

Crisp, Quentin (Denis Charles Pratt) (1908–1999) *nonfiction writer*

From an early age Quentin Crisp was openly and flamboyantly gay at a time when few others dared be so. Born Denis Charles Pratt in South Wimbledon, Surrey, England, he was the son of a solicitor and a nursery governess, whom he described as "middle-class, middle-brow, middling." Educated at a preparatory school in Derbyshire, he was a journalism student, art student, engineer's assistant, commercial artist, and tap-dancing teacher before being exempted from military service because of his homosexuality.

A job as a nude art model during World War II became the basis for Crisp's autobiographical book *The Naked Civil Servant* (1968), which led to a series of articles and one-man stage shows about style and manners. Crisp was notoriously witty and polite, even asking callers who made death threats whether they would care to make an appointment. At the same time he affected great cynicism—joking, for instance, that he had no fondness for nature and looked forward to the day when the entire Earth would be covered in a uniform concrete slab. He wrote in *The Naked Civil Servant* that in his London apartment, "There was no need to do any housework at all. After the first four years, the dust doesn't get any worse."

Crisp was sometimes at odds with the gay activists of the 1960s and later decades because he believed that dressing like a dandy was a more fitting expression of homosexuality than political activism. To Crisp, having come of age at a time when homosexual acts were a criminal offense, dandyism was a courageous pose. Some later gay activists, however, saw his appearance as debasement and self-parody. Crisp explained his philosophy in such books as *How to Have a Life-Style* (1979), *Doing It With Style* (1981), and *Manners: A Divine Guide to Good Manners* (1984).

Crisp's final two decades were spent on the Lower East Side of New York City, where he lived as though he were impoverished, despite his substantial savings. He accepted lunch invitations from virtually anyone who asked so long as he did not have to pay. He wrote of those years in *Resident Alien: The New York Diaries* (1996).

Crisp died of a heart attack on a trip to England as he prepared to tour the country in another one-man show. Critic Donald Carroll, in his introduction to *Resident Alien*, noted that because of his wit, Crisp was "often spoken of as the Oscar Wilde" of our day. "He had an influence on the young people in England," said linguist Donald Philippi, and he helped inspire the "gender ambiguity in the New Romantic [fashion and music] movement."

Other Works by Quentin Crisp

How to Become a Virgin. New York: St. Martin's Press, 1981.
How to Go to the Movies. New York: St. Martin's Press, 1989.
The Wit and Wisdom of Quentin Crisp. New York: Harper & Row, 1984.

Crispin, Edmund (Robert Bruce Montgomery) (1921–1978) *novelist, composer*

Born in Chesterham Bois, Buckinghamshire, England, as Robert Bruce Montgomery, Edmund Crispin was the son of Robert Ernest Montgomery, a government official, and Marion Blackwood Jarvie Montgomery. He turned to writing and music when ankle problems kept him from playing sports.

After a fellow student at Oxford recommended that he read a locked room mystery by the American author John Dickson Carr, Crispin wrote his first mystery novel, *The Case of the Gilded Fly* (1944), published under the pseudonym Edmund Crispin. This novel introduces Gervase Fen, a tall, eccentric Oxford English professor with great energy, varied interests, and an intuitive ability to solve "impossible" murders. Fen's career as an amateur detective begins when the body of a disagreeable actress is left at his door.

Fen becomes addicted to solving crimes, pursuing murderers through eight more classic mysteries. With Crispin's characteristic irony, Fen seems to be aware that he is a character, describing himself as "the only literary critic turned detective in fiction."

Crispin's last novel, *The Glimpses of the Moon* (1977), was published after a long break from novel writing, during which Crispin wrote choral music, requiem masses, and film scores under his given name. He also established a reputation as a literary critic and edited several distinguished science-fiction anthologies, such as his seven-volume *Best SF* (1956–70), helping to make that field a re spected genre.

In his own work Crispin wrote that he tried to "embody the nowadays increasingly neglected principle of fair play to the reader—which is to say that the reader is given all the clues needed to enable him to anticipate the solution by the exercises of his logic and his common sense." And indeed, although his early works were criticized for poorly constructed plots, he became known for playing fair with his readers. Crispin's mysteries also possessed a comic style. Critic Michael Dirda attrib-utes the "distinctive flavor of a Crispin novel" to "hilarious similes, broad farcical situations, funny names, puns, unexpected actions or statements, humorous characters, zany games, utterly inappropriate behavior, and tongue-in-cheek diction." While other mystery writers have become dated, Dirda believes Crispin's "civilized and compassionate comedy" ensures that he "will always merit a high place in the field."

Other Work by Edmund Crispin

The Moving Toy Shop. 1946. Reprint, New York: Penguin, 1993.

Curtin, Philip

See BELLOC LOWNDES, MARIE.

Dahl, Roald (1916–1990) *short story writer, children's writer, screenwriter*

Roald Dahl was born in Llandaff, Wales, to Harald Dahl, a Norwegian owner of a successful ship-brokering business headquartered in Cardiff, and his second wife Sofie Hesselberg Dahl. He was educated in a local school, St. Peter's, and the Repton boarding school, where he excelled at athletics. During World War II he was a Royal Air Force fighter pilot and his first published magazine stories were about those experiences. These stories were published in the collection *Over to You* (1946). Noël COWARD claimed that these stories "pierced the layers of my consciousness and stirred up the very deep feelings I had during the war and have since, almost deliberately, been in danger of losing."

Dahl began selling his short stories to American magazines, including the prestigious *New Yorker*. One of his most memorable stories is "Taste" (1951), a twisted tale of Michael Schofield, who nearly loses his daughter in a wine-tasting wager. His adversary, Richard Pratt, is vividly described: "The man was about fifty years old and he did not have a pleasant face. Somehow, it was all mouth—mouth and lips—the full, wet lips of the professional gourmet, the lower lip hanging downward in the center, a pendulous, permanently open taster's lip, shaped open to receive the rim of a glass or a morsel of food." This story and others were collected in *Someone Like You* (1953). A critic for *New York Times* said that Dahl "knows how to blend . . . an antic imagination, an eye for the anecdotal predicament with a twist at the end, a savage sense of humor . . . and an economical, precise writing style." The reviewer went on to compare Dahl favorably with SAKI, O. Henry, Guy de Maupassant, and Somerset MAUGHAM.

Throughout the 1950s Dahl wrote other stories that would appear in *Kiss Kiss* (1960). Two of his best known stories from this period, "The Way Up to Heaven" and "William and Mary," deal with tensions between married couples. "The Way Up to Heaven" deals with a conflict over lateness between an elderly American couple, the Fosters: "It is really extraordinary how in certain people a simple apprehension about a thing like catching a train can grow into a serious obsession."

"William and Mary" tells a more bizarre story of the Pearls. Mrs. Pearl believes that her domineering husband has died. He has taken part in a medical experiment, however, whereby his brain and one eyeball remain alive after his body has died. Mrs. Pearl decides to take her husband's brain home to restore the balance of power in their relationship, taunting him by smoking in front of him, a habit of which he disapproved: "'So don't be a naughty boy again, will you, my precious,' she said, taking another pull at the cigarette. 'Naughty boys are liable to get punished most severely nowadays. . . .'" In its review of *Kiss Kiss,* the *Times Literary Supplement* praised Dahl as "a social satirist and a moralist at work behind the entertaining fantast."

Dahl then turned to writing for children. For some time, to entertain his two young daughters, he had made up tales about a little orphan boy, James, who magically enters a giant peach filled with friendly insects. Dahl turned these stories into *James and the Giant Peach* (1961). He followed with his most famous children's novel, *Charlie and the Chocolate Factory* (1964), which retains the darker tones of Dahl's short stories in a work for children. A set of children, including the poor boy Charlie, win a chance to tour Willy Wonka's candy factory. Along the way, the children are punished for their vices, such as excessive television watching and greed. When the gum-chewing Violet Beauregarde swells up to a "gigantic blueberry," Wonka expresses little concern for her rescue: "We've got to squeeze the juice out of her immediately. After that, we'll just have to see how she comes out." A reviewer for the *Times* of London called it "the funniest book I have read in years," noting that, despite apparent debts to Lewis Carroll and Hilaire BELLOC, Dahl was "a great original."

Personal tragedy plagued Dahl; his daughter Olivia died suddenly after a short illness, his only son, Theo, was maimed in a traffic accident, and his wife, Patricia Neal, suffered a massive stroke that left her helpless for several months. Despite this, Dahl continued to produce a series of screenplays and children's books. Among the latter are *Charlie and the Great Glass Elevator* (1972), a sequel to *Charlie and the Chocolate Factory;* and *The BFG* (1982), about a "Big Friendly Giant." The success of his children's books overshadowed his previous career as a short story writer. Scholar Mark West notes, however, continuities between the two halves of his career: "In almost all of Dahl's fiction—whether it be intended for children or for adults—authoritarian figures, social institutions, and societal norms are ridiculed or at least undermined."

Other Works by Roald Dahl

The Best of Roald Dahl. New York: Vintage Books, 1990.
Switch Bitch. New York: Alfred A. Knopf, 1974.

Works about Roald Dahl

Treglown, Jeremy. *Roald Dahl: A Biography.* New York: Farrar, Straus & Giroux, 1994.
West, Mark. *Roald Dahl.* Boston: Twayne, 1992.

Dane, Clemence (Winifred Ashton)

(1888–1965) *novelist, playwright, screenwriter*
Clemence Dane was born Winifred Ashton in Blackheath, England, to Arthur Charles Ashton, a commission merchant, and Florence Bentley Ashton. Her parents sent her to private schools until age 16. After taking time off from school to teach French abroad, she went on to study art in London and Dresden. This decision to study art instead of following a more conventional path deeply upset her parents and possibly led her to adopt the pseudonym Clemence Dane in her writing. Between the world wars she earned a notable reputation as a novelist, playwright, and screenwriter, as well as portraitist, actress, and social critic.

Dane's writings deal with war, feminism, and sexuality, subjects that sometimes shocked both her parents and her middle-class audiences. Her first novel, *Regiment of Women* (1917), tells the story of an intimate relationship between two women teachers at a girls' school. Other works, such as her 1939 allegorical novel *The Arrogant History of White Ben,* describe the disillusionment caused by World War I and offer bleak predictions for the future.

Dane also wrote scathing social critiques. She began her 1926 feminist work *Women's Side* with the following bold remark: "Here are some opinions on subjects that concern women. They are offered not as words of wisdom, but as words of provocation." The book outlines her advanced views on women's independence and supports gender-based legal reforms.

In 1921 she finished her first play, *A Bill of Divorcement,* which was based on her novel *Legend.* The play earned praise from both the public and drama critics, who noted her ability to appeal "broadly to popular audiences" even on difficult subjects such as contemporary divorce laws in Britain. She won an Academy Award in 1946 for her screenplay *Vacation from Marriage.* Despite her controversial tone, Dane achieved a significant following among mainstream audiences.

Davie, Donald (1922–1995) *literary critic, poet*

Donald Davie was born in Barnsley, Yorkshire, England, to George Clarke Davie, a businessman, and Alice Sugden Davie. He earned his B.A., M.A., and Ph.D. degrees from Cambridge and, except for four years spent in the Royal Navy, worked as an academic his entire life. He received numerous awards, including fellowships from the Guggenheim Foundation and the American Academy of Arts and Sciences, and an honorary fellowship from Cambridge.

Davie's landmark book of literary criticism is *Purity of Diction in English Verse* (1952), in which he argues that poets occupy an extremely important societal function as the most elevated users of language in any community. Davie asserts that poets, as language experts, are responsible "for purifying and correcting the spoken language." According to Davie, poets can enlarge their languages by developing new metaphors, but purification comes through giving new meaning to old or dead metaphors. The keystone, for example, a dead metaphor that has lost its initial meaning as the stone at the top of an arch, now simply suggests importance without any reference to an arch.

Davie is also known as a member of the MOVEMENT, a group of like-minded poets in the 1950s who resisted the appearance of extremely abstract and nearly incomprehensible poetry, believing instead that poetry's content should be rational, its

form logical, and its language clear. Davie accomplishes these goals of clarity and rationality in the poem "Remembering the Thirties," in which he explains that his generation hears but does not fully understand the stories of the previous generation. In the clearest of lines, Davie writes that old veterans eventually realize "That what for them were agonies, for us / Are high-brow thrillers."

Throughout his long academic career, Davie published nearly 30 volumes of criticism and verse while also editing more than a half dozen books about 18th-century poets, including a collection of William Wordsworth's poetry. His productivity and the quality of both his scholarship and writing have prompted the critic Michael Schmidt to declare him "the defining poet-critic of his generation" and remark that "Donald Davie's impact as a critic will prove central and durable; his poems will survive in their formal diversity, their intellectual richness and rigour, their emotional honesty."

Other Works by Donald Davie
Older Masters: Essays and Reflections on English and American Literature. New York: Continuum, 1993.
Selected Poems. Manchester, England: Carcanet, 1997.

A Work about Donald Davie
Bell, Vereen, and Laurence Lerner, eds. *On Modern Poetry: Essays Presented to Donald Davie.* Nashville, Tenn.: Vanderbilt University Press, 1988.

Davies, P.
See GODDEN, RUMER.

Davies, Rhys (1901–1978) *novelist, short story writer*

Rhys Davies was born in the mining community of Clydach Vale in the Rhondda Valley of Wales. His father, Thomas Rees Davies, was a grocer and his mother, Sarah Davies, a former teacher. At 12 Davies entered the Porth County School, but after discovering such authors as Gustave Flaubert, Leo Tolstoy, and Anton Chekhov, he developed a passion for literature and left school to devote all of his time to reading. In 1920 Davies moved to London to write professionally.

After gaining recognition as a short story writer, Davies published his first novel, *The Withered Root* (1927), which tells the story of Reuben Daniels, an alienated preacher in the Rhondda Valley who dies of insanity. Davies's novels repeatedly explore the strenuous lives of Welsh miners. Critics praised his blunt, intense depictions of the Welsh people and landscape, but they also noted that he imitated the naturalism of D. H. LAWRENCE and that his characters seemed formulaic. (Lawrence had been a key influence on Davies since the two established a friendship in Paris in 1928, and Davies even smuggled the manuscript of Lawrence's *Pansies* into England to avoid the British censors.)

In 1935 Davies began a trilogy that traces the decline of the Llewellyn family. Originally wealthy landowners, the family fortune diminishes, and they are forced to sell their vast estate to the encroaching mining companies. The new industrialism destroys the idyllic region and saps the people's vitality. The third volume of the trilogy, *Jubilee Blues* (1938), is particularly noteworthy for the realistic characters that populate the vivid settings.

In 1944 Davies published his most acclaimed novel, *The Black Venus*. The book's heroine, Olwen Powell, demands the right to choose her own husband and "cast off her chains." It is significant because Davies creates a strong female protagonist and explores the conflict between Welsh tradition and modern values.

In 1967 Davies was made an Officer of the Order of the British Empire (OBE), and the Welsh Arts Council presented him with an award for his achievements. The critic G. F. Adam has noted that Davies succeeded when he discovered a "regionalism in the wider sense of the term, where the Welsh setting remains, but serves as a means to the expression of problems of universally human value."

Other Work by Rhys Davies

The Collected Short Stories of Rhys Davies. Llandysul, Wales: Gomer, 1996.

Davies, Robertson William (1913–1995)
novelist, playwright, essayist, journalist

Robertson Davies was born in Thamesville, Ontario, Canada, to a newspaper owner. He received a degree in literature from Oxford University in 1938. From a young age he was drawn to the theater, playing small roles outside London. He also acted at the Old Vic Repertory Company in London, and in 1940 he married Brenda Matthews, the company's stage manager. The couple returned to Canada soon after, and Davies began work as a journalist. He was the editor of the *Peterborough Examiner* for 15 years and its publisher from 1955 to 1965.

Davies's love of theater led him to write many plays, which he considered comedies rather than tragedies that criticized Canada's provincial attitudes. He won the 1948 Dominion Drama Festival Award for best Canadian play for *Eros at Breakfast* (1948), which made use of allegory and was more theatrical than realistic. In a similar style, *King Phoenix* (1953) is a fantasy based on the mythical King Cole, while *General Confession* (1959) is a historical comedy of ideas with the main characters serving as Jungian archetypes of self, persona, shadow, and anima. These three plays, with their elaborate costumes and settings and magic transformations, reveal Davies's inclination for spectacle and extravagance.

Although Davies wrote plays, essays, and criticism, he is best known and admired for his many novels. The Salterton Trilogy—*Tempest-Tost* (1951), *Leaven of Malice* (1954), and *A Mixture of Frailties* (1958)—is a social comedy set in a small Ontario university town.

The novel that begins the Deptford Trilogy, *Fifth Business* (1970), is widely considered by most critics to be his finest work, with its blend of myths, magic, freaks, evil, and theatrical elements. It follows a magician whose life is linked to that of the protagonist, Boy Staunton. *The Manticore* (1972), the second Deptford novel, won the prestigious Governor General's Award for Fiction in 1973. The last novel of the trilogy was *World of Wonders* (1975).

Reviewer S. A. Rowland writes that Davies "delights in paradox and is himself an example: among the most innovative of contemporary novelists, he stresses our deep roots in old cultures and 'magical' beliefs."

Other Works by Robertson Davies

The Lyre of Orpheus. New York: Viking Penguin, 1988.

Murther and Walking Spirits. New York: Viking Penguin, 1991.

The Well-tempered Critic: One Man's View of Theatre and Letters in Canada. Toronto: McClelland and Stewart, 1981.

What's Bred in the Bone. New York: Viking Penguin, 1985.

A Work about Robertson Davies

Grant, Judith Skelton. *Robertson Davies: Man of Myth.* New York: Viking, 1994.

Daviot, Gordon

See TEY, JOSEPHINE.

Day Lewis, Cecil (Nicholas Blake)
(1904–1972) *poet, novelist, nonfiction writer, screenwriter*

C. Day Lewis—the surname sometimes appears hyphenated—was born in Ballintubbert, Ireland. His parents, both Anglo-Irish, were F. C. Lewis, a Protestant minister, and Kathleen Blake Squires Lewis, who died when he was four years old. An omission in Lewis's autobiography, *The Buried Life* (1960), speaks volumes. Despite countless references to his father, Day Lewis does not name him, whereas, in the few pages devoted to his mother, he names her twice, both times using her full name.

Day Lewis entered Wadham College, Oxford, in 1923. Two individuals there influenced him: Sir Maurice Bowra, a college tutor; and fellow student W. H. AUDEN, who inspired his interest in both poetry and left-wing causes. Day Lewis graduated from Oxford in 1927, and the following year he married Mary King. About this time his first name

appeared in print as the initial "C" rather than the full "Cecil," a name he hated.

Day Lewis's first two poetry collections, *Beechen Vigil* (1925) and *Country Comets* (1928), consist of apolitical poems, written mostly at Oxford, with classical or biblical themes. Neither book is exceptional, but *Comets* contains the lyrical "Naked Woman with Kotyle," a variation on Percy Bysshe Shelley's "Ozymandias." *Transitional Poem* (1929), written in a more conversational style, suggests a rejection of past poetic practice: "I say it is a bottle / For papless poets to feed their fancy on."

From Feathers to Iron (1931) consists of the long title poem and an epilogue dedicated to Auden. The occasion is Day Lewis's anticipated birth of his first child. Sections of the lyrical poem disclose nature as vibrant: "Now the full-throated daffodils, / Our trumpeters in gold." Sensitivity to nature remained a constant in Day Lewis's poetry throughout his career.

During the 1930s Day Lewis maintained friendships with fellow leftists Auden, Louis MAC-NEICE, and Stephen SPENDER. The four of them, including Day Lewis, were dubbed by detractors of their politics as the "Macspaunday poets," a merger of their names.

Day Lewis's great difficulty in finding a voice recognizably his own perhaps explains his academic obsession with language. In *The Poet's Way of Knowledge* (1957) he wrote, "Poets are compelled to break away from the language of their predecessors."

Day Lewis worked as a teacher until 1935, returning as Clark lecturer at Cambridge in 1946 and professor of poetry at Oxford from 1951 to 1956. He wrote for the *Left Review* and in 1936 joined the Communist Party; disillusioned, he left it two years later.

Reflective of the gathering storm in Europe, the poetry collection *Overtures to Death* (1938) is one of his most gripping books. The title poem directly addresses death with fervor: "You lean with us at street-corners, / . . . Your eyes are the foundry's glare." Louis MacNeice noted that Day Lewis, "whose theme is the modern industrial world, its economics and its politics, takes his images especially from such things as pylons, power-houses, spies, frontiers, aeroplanes, steam-engines."

The post-communist Day Lewis became an increasingly fastidious and traditional poet. In *The Room* (1965), "Who Goes Home?" was occasioned by Winston Churchill's death. A typical stanza begins "Soldier, historian, / . . . Adorned the present and awoke the past." Here Day Lewis was writing as though he were Britain's Poet Laureate, a post to which he was in fact appointed in 1968.

In addition to his poetry, Day Lewis wrote 20 mystery novels under the pseudonym Nicholas Blake. Most featured the detective (and Oxford graduate) Nigel Strangeways, whom some believe Day Lewis based on Auden. The most famous, *The Beast Must Die* (1938), formed the basis for a brilliant film: Claude Chabrol's *Que la bête meure* (1969).

One of Day Lewis's children—with the actress Jill Balcon, whom Day Lewis married in 1951—is the actor Daniel Day Lewis. Fifty-one years separate the Academy Awards that they won: C. Day Lewis's for helping to adapt George Bernard Shaw's *Pygmalion* (1938) to the screen, Daniel Day Lewis's for his passionate enactment of the Irish artist Christy Brown in Jim Sheridan's *My Left Foot* (1989).

As a poet, Day Lewis's best period was the 1930s. According to critic D. E. S. Maxwell, Day Lewis's poems of this decade gave "a flesh and blood presence" to the abstract concepts of "art as propaganda, the *bourgeois* predicament, documentary realism" that "exist in the events, personalities and appearances of the time: in the shabby towns of an industrial wasteland denied the machines of the new technology; . . . in the heartless antics of the complacent or ill-disposed."

Other Work by C. Day Lewis

The Complete Poems. Stanford, Calif.: Stanford University Press, 1995.

A Work about C. Day Lewis

Gelpi, Albert. *Living in Time: The Poetry of C. Day Lewis.* Oxford, England: Oxford University Press, 1997.

Deighton, Len (1929–) *novelist, nonfiction writer*

Born in London, Len Deighton attended St. Martin's School of Art after completing military service with the Special Investigation Branch in 1949. While working as a waiter, he developed an interest in cooking and eventually became a pastry chef at London's Royal Festival Hall. His interest in cooking inspired him to draw a comic strip for the London *Observer* and to write two books on French cooking, including *Ou Est le Garlic?* (1965). In 1960 he married illustrator Shirley Thompson.

Settling in the Dordogne, France, Deighton began his first novel, a thriller about the rescue of a kidnapped biochemist. *The Ipcress File* (1962) was an immediate success. Deighton wrote six more books featuring its nameless hero, who became Harry Palmer in the movie adaptations. "The creation of this slightly anarchic, wise-cracking, working-class hero was Deighton's most original contribution to the spy thriller," wrote London *Times* reviewer T. J. Binyon, who also praised Deighton's "gift for vivid, startling description."

Berlin Game (1983) began the first of several trilogies featuring Bernie Sampson, a British intelligence agent whose survival depends on uncovering double- and triple-crosses during the cold war. Unlike many fictional spies, Sampson has a wife, family, and domestic problems on top of his dangerous business. Deighton's thrillers "display a thorough and intimate knowledge of spies and spying [that] lends considerable realism to his books," says critic George Grella. "Spies, we see, are real people" whose "activities represent a kind of institutionalized deceit."

Like his espionage novels, Deighton's nonfiction is meticulously researched. Scholar George H. Reeves praises *Fighter: The True Story of the Battle of Britain* (1977) for "a profusion of detail . . . that will delight the military history specialist," while its "well-paced narrative and . . . deft characterization will hold the attention of the general reader."

Deighton has also written several best-selling novels that are not thrillers, including *SS-GB* (1979), an alternative history in which the Nazis conquer Great Britain. Although Deighton has worked successfully in many genres, his reputation rests primarily on his thrillers. George Grella calls him "a master of modern spy fiction . . . who creates a convincingly detailed picture of the world of espionage while carefully examining the ethics and morality of that world."

Other Works by Len Deighton

Blood, Tears, and Folly: An Objective Look at World War II. New York: HarperCollins, 1993.

Winter: A Novel of a Berlin Family. New York: Ballantine, 1987.

de la Mare, Walter (1873–1956) *poet, novelist, children's writer*

Walter de la Mare was born to James Edward de la Mare and his wife Lucy Sophia Browning, a descendant of the British poet Robert Browning, in Charlton, Kent, England. He attended St. Paul's Cathedral School but did not attend college because of financial constraints. He instead went to work as a statistical clerk for the Anglo-American Oil Company.

De la Mare resisted most of the concepts of modernism, the antiromantic, realist literary movement that spanned most of his lifetime. He was a romantic author who avoided the problems of the present in favor of the world of the imagination. De la Mare's work was often fantastic and unbelievable and engaged the classically romantic themes of death, dreams, and altered mental conditions.

De la Mare's romantic disposition is evident in the literature he wrote for children, which is widely regarded as his best work. The novel *The Three Mulla-Muglars* (1910), for instance, is set in an imaginary world and tells the story of three young monkeys coming of age while searching for their long-lost father. The novel is successful largely because, as the scholar James Decker writes, it contains "a balance of humor and seriousness atypical of the genre of children's fantasy," leading the scholar Edward Wagenknecht to call the work an "epic of courage."

De la Mare's most celebrated volume of poetry, *Peacock Pie* (1913), is also intended for children and engages his usual range of romantic, supernatural topics, such as witches and fairies. One of the most endearing features of *Peacock Pie* is its intimate and inviting tone. In "The Window," for instance, de la Mare asks the reader to sit beside him and gaze onto the street from behind a curtain, where "not a single one can see / My tiny watching eye."

De la Mare's writing for adult audiences includes the poem "We Who Have Watched," which appeared in the 1953 volume *O Lovely England and Other Poems,* and numerous ghost stories. In "We Who Have Watched" de la Mare ponders where one can find hope in a world of "Mammon, vice and infamy / Cringe, bargain, jape and jeer."

The best of de la Mare's ghost stories appear in the story collection *On the Edge,* which the scholar John Clute regards as "polished, subtle, [and] securely crafted." In "A Recluse," one of the stories in *On the Edge,* the narrator, disregarding cryptic warnings, enters the haunted home of Mr. Bloom, a mysterious, ghostlike, and satanic figure. As the story unfolds, it becomes obvious that Mr. Bloom himself is a ghost and that the other spirits in his home are there as a result of his dabbling in the black arts.

Although de la Mare had moderate success as a "serious" writer for adults, he is remembered for his children's literature. According to the critic J. B. Priestley, de la Mare was a member of "one of that most lovable order of artists who never lose sight of their childhood, but re-live it continually in their work and contrive to find expression for their maturity in it, memories and impressions, its romantic vision of the world." Near the end of his life de la Mare received numerous awards for his literary achievements. He was named Companion of Honour by King George VI in 1948 and received the Order of Merit in 1953.

Other Works by Walter de la Mare

Collected Poems of Walter de la Mare. Boston: Faber, 1979.

Collected Stories for Children. London: Faber & Faber, 1947.

Works about Walter de la Mare

Wagenknecht, Edward. *Seven Masters of Supernatural Fiction.* New York: Greenwood, 1991.

Whistler, Theresa. *Imagination of the Heart: The Life of Walter de la Mare.* London: Duckworth, 1993.

Delaney, Shelagh (1939–) *playwright, scriptwriter*

Shelagh Delaney was born in Salford, England, to Joseph Delaney, a bus inspector, and Elsie Delaney. Her mother read constantly and inspired her with a love of storytelling. Delaney was an indifferent student and left school at 17, but she maintained an interest in literature and began writing a novel.

In 1957 Delaney was so moved by a performance of Terence RATTIGAN's play *Variation on a Theme* that she decided to convert her novel into a play called *A Taste of Honey* (1958). The drama features Jo, who has an affair with a Welsh sailor, gives birth to an illegitimate child after he departs, and then is aided by Geof, a homosexual art student, until her mother returns and drives him away. Although the plot is underdeveloped, the play was highly praised for its realistic and contemporary dialogue and characters who are working-class people facing common problems.

British audiences, bored by the theatrical tradition of genteel drawing-room plays, welcomed these qualities. Delaney's play won the 1958 Charles Henry Foyle Award for best new drama and the 1961 New York Drama Critics Circle Award for best foreign play. However, some critics attributed the play's success to the director, Joan Littlewood, who was famous for improvising and adapting original scripts.

Delaney's next play, *The Lion in Love* (1960), portrays an impoverished family, whose income comes from peddling trinkets, and expertly explores the social problems introduced in *A Taste of Honey*. However, the best qualities of the first play are absent: The language in *Lion* is much more formal, and some of the child characters are not fully developed. The play was largely panned, and it failed commercially. Delaney turned from writing plays to screenplays and radio scripts.

Delaney's plays are frequently compared to those of John OSBORNE and other members of the ANGRY YOUNG MEN movement. Like these writers, Delaney uses working-class slang and portrays working-class lives. But Delaney's characters express an acceptance and optimism not always present in the works of her contemporaries. As the critic John Russell Taylor says about *A Taste of Honey,* Jo "recognizes that her fate is in her own hands, and takes responsibility for the running of her own life."

A Work about Shelagh Delaney

Lacey, Stephen. *British Realist Theater: The New Wave in Its Context.* London: Routledge, 1995.

Dennis, Nigel Forbes (1912–1989) *novelist, playwright, poet, journalist*

Born in Surrey, England, to Michael Beauchamp Dennis, a lieutenant colonel in a Scottish regiment, and Louise Bosanquet Dennis, Nigel Dennis was raised in Rhodesia following his father's death in 1918 and educated partly in Austria and Germany. He worked as a journalist in the United States from 1931 to 1949, but much of his early writing was lost or destroyed due to war and neglect. He was assistant editor and book review editor of the *New Republic* and later joined *Time* as a staff book reviewer.

Dennis published his first novel, *Boys and Girls Come Out to Play* (published in the United States as *A Sea Change*), in 1949, shortly after his return to England. The book is about two Americans who visit Poland in 1939 and become caught up in the outbreak of war. Winner of the Anglo-American Novel Prize in 1949, it demonstrated Dennis's talent for satire and comic invention.

Dennis's reputation as a satiric novelist was established with his *Cards of Identity* (1955), in which he targets the manipulation of mass opinion. Regarded as his finest work, the book satirizes the shallowness of modern human identity, culminating in "The Prince of Antioch," the play within the novel, which is a parody of Shakespeare. Dennis adapted *Cards of Identity* for the stage in 1956. He wrote plays denouncing left-wing totalitarianism and critiquing the debasement of standards under democracies. His play *The Making of Moo* (1957) is aimed at the idolatry of religion.

Known for his witty journalism, Dennis coedited the periodical *Encounter* and contributed reviews and columns to the Australian newspaper *The Sunday Telegraph*. He expressed his love of the Mediterranean in *An Essay on Malta* (1972) and in *Exotics* (1970), a volume of poems mostly set in that region.

Other Works by Nigel Dennis

Dramatic Essays. London: Weidenfeld & Nicolson, 1962.
A House in Order. New York: Vanguard, 1966.

Desai, Anita (1958–   ) *novelist, short story writer*

Daughter of a Bengali businessman, D. W. Mazumdar, and a German mother, Toni Nina, Anita Desai grew up speaking German at home and Hindi in public, but she first read and wrote in English. She received a B.A. with honors from the University of Delhi in 1957. A year later, she married Ashrin Desai. The winner of several literary awards, she lives in Bombay and teaches periodically in the United States.

Desai has been influenced most notably by Virginia WOOLF and Henry James. Essential qualities of her fiction are seeming "plotlessness" (she admits to having only a faint notion of plot when she begins writing); habitual exploration, through stream of consciousness, of the inner states of characters; and use of imagery and symbolism to convey atmosphere and character.

While other writers appreciate her work, the Indian literary establishment has criticized Desai for ignoring India's most pressing problems and socioeconomic realities. In her nine novels and collections of short stories, Desai is concerned with older, upper-middle-class women who, since British rule ended in India, have come down in the world yet continue trying to live as they once did.

Desai's fiction has broadened in scope over the decades, however, and she does portray important realities of Indian life.

Desai's first novel, *Cry, the Peacock* (1963), concerns a marriage so desperate that the wife kills her husband and herself. In *Bye Bye, Blackbird* (1975), set in London, two Indians—one more British than the British, the other an immigrant who detests everything British—reverse stances. *Fire on the Mountain* (1977) centers on two solitary women, Nanda Kaul and her great-granddaughter Raka. Nanda's refusal to take responsibility results in her friend Ila's rape and murder and Raka's torching of the surrounding countryside.

Clear Light of Day (1980), which many critics consider Desai's masterpiece, concerns the reunion of two sisters in a ghostly family mansion in New Delhi. Taking place during the Partition, which split the subcontinent into India and Pakistan, it depicts the family's own partition yet ends in reconciliation and harmony. *In Custody* (1984) portrays India's last great Urdu poet, Nur, and his devotee, Deven. Through a desire to embrace art and poetry, Deven finds himself married to squalor. Desai's darkest work is *Baumgartner's Bombay* (1989), in which the doubly exiled Baumgartner meets in India the fate he went there to escape.

Other Works by Anita Desai

Diamond Dust: Stories. Boston: Houghton Mifflin, 2000.
Fasting, Feasting. Mariner Books, 2000.

A Work about Anita Desai

Bhatanaghar, Manmohan K. *Novels of Anita Desai: A Critical Study.* Columbia, Mo.: South Asia Books, 2000.

Dickens, Monica (1915–1992) *novelist, nonfiction writer*

Although not as famous as Charles Dickens, her great-grandfather, Monica Dickens established her own notable literary career. She was born in London to Henry Charles Dickens, a barrister, and Fanny

Runge Dickens. A Roman Catholic, Dickens was educated at St. Paul's School for Girls, at a finishing school in Paris, and at a dramatic school.

In the 1930s Dickens, bored with her upper-middle-class life, worked as a maid and a cook in private London homes. She wrote about these experiences, often humorously, in the autobiography *One Pair of Hands* (1939). She recounts the following from a day of washing clothes: "There was no one but me to answer the telephone, which always rang when I was covered in soap to the elbow. I accepted a bridge party for the owner of the corsets, and a day's golfing for the wearer of the socks, but did not feel in a position to give an opinion on the state of cousin Mary's health."

Dickens later took up nursing, chronicling her years in that profession in *One Pair of Feet* (1942). She describes her wartime experience in an aircraft factory in the novel *The Fancy* (1943). She became a prolific fiction writer after World War II. Her novel *The Happy Prisoner* (1946) describes a soldier who discovers a series of important truths while recuperating from war wounds.

Dickens often found herself compared to her great-grandfather and frequently received mixed reviews from critics. For example, when reviewing *Winds of Heaven* (1955), a novel about an aging English widow who clashes with her three daughters, critic Dachine Rainer wrote, "Her characters are plausible enough, but the book is as sordid as her forebear's without his brutal social satire, relieving comic sense, or that vast compassion which moves us."

While Dickens's early works were often lightly satirical, her novels became more serious in the 1960s as she addressed topics such as child abuse, alcoholism, suicide, and inner city social problems. Drawing on her extensive journalistic experience writing for *Woman's Own* magazine, Dickens thoroughly researched her topics. She spent numerous hours at juvenile courts, for example, before writing *Kate and Emma* (1964), a novel about the ill-treatment of children.

In the 1970s Dickens became involved with the Samaritans, a group that counsels those considering suicide. She founded the first American branch of Samaritans in Boston in 1974. The scholar Carlton Jackson notes that although Dickens was best known in England as a novelist and best known in the U.S. as a Samaritan, her works were effective tools of reform since she, as "a novelist, sees a difficult life situation, and in reporting it sometimes enlarges it in a way that will, perhaps, garner support for its alleviation."

Other Works by Monica Dickens

Befriending: The American Samaritans. Carlton Jackson, ed. Bowling Green, Ohio: Bowling Green University Popular Press, 1996.
The Room Upstairs. London: Heinemann, 1966.

Doe, John James
See O'BRIEN, FLANN.

Donleavy, James Patrick (1926–)
novelist, playwright, nonfiction writer

J. P. Donleavy was born in Brooklyn, New York, to Irish immigrants James Patrick and Margaret Donleavy. He was raised and educated in the Bronx and attended the Naval Academy Preparatory School, then served briefly during World War II.

Despite his birth and upbringing as an American, Donleavy always considered himself Irish. He took the opportunity afforded by the G.I. Bill to move to Dublin, Ireland, and entered Trinity College. In Dublin he married and began his novel *The Ginger Man*, which, when it was published in 1955, brought him money and a sudden reputation. The idea for the novel, he said, came about in 1949 while he was celebrating an American Thanksgiving in Dublin. The book was published in Paris by Maurice Girodias's Olympia Press. Much to Donleavy's dismay, it was published as part of a pornographic series. This and other details of its publication led to a 25-year-long lawsuit between Donleavy and Girodias. When it ended Donleavy had not only won but found himself owning Olympia Press.

Originally rejected by more than 30 American publishers, *The Ginger Man* has as its hero Sebastian Dangerfield, who was based on Gainer Stephen Crist, a law student at Trinity. The novel details Dangerfield's mostly drunken adventures and misadventures in Dublin and London. The book became a cause célèbre, sold millions of copies, and was translated into dozens of languages. Its proceeds enabled Donleavy to buy an estate in Ireland, and he gave up his American citizenship. The novel's shocking language (for the 1950s) and equally bold characterizations and events were in some part responsible for its fame. (An unexpurgated edition was published in 1963.)

Since *The Ginger Man* Donleavy has written 10 other novels, five plays, and three nonfiction works, but none has had the astounding success of his first. The scholar Charles Masinton writes that Donleavy's fiction is notable for his "accurate ear for the rhythms and intonations of human speech. This talent—along with an ability to populate his novels with a host of interesting comic characters—makes his works quite entertaining."

Other Works by J. P. Donleavy

A Fairy Tale of New York. 1973. Reprint, New York: Atlantic Monthly Press, 1989.

Singular Man. 1963. Reprint, New York: Atlantic Monthly Press, 1989.

A Work about J. P. Donleavy

Donleavy, J. P., *The History of The Ginger Man*. Boston: Houghton Mifflin, 1994.

Doughty, Charles Montagu (1843–1926)
poet, historian, travel writer

Charles Doughty is best known for his epic *Travels in Arabia Deserta* (1888), a two-volume work describing his two-year trek across Arabia and his time among the Bedouins. He was the orphaned son of a Suffolk squarson (a vicar who is also a landowner, i.e., a squire and a parson) and the product of a religious school system. As such he always remained intensely focused on whatever subject he was studying. In fact he spent an entire decade researching his epic poem *The Dawn in Britain* (1906) and another decade writing it.

Doughty's particular passion was for what he thought of as the lost beauty and perfection of the English language found in the writings of the Renaissance. He believed that the language had fallen into disrepair since then and tried to bring about its restoration. The vehicle he chose for this was *Travels in Arabia Deserta* (1888).

In the 1870s Doughty made many trips to North Africa and the Levant. These travels awakened in him an obsessive curiosity, and he eventually turned his attention to Arabia to search for the ruins of a vanished civilization of which he had heard. While his contemporaries often approached foreign lands with many preconceptions, Doughty greeted Arabia with an open mind and soon became fascinated by Arab culture, faith, and history. He spent two years in Rub'al Khali, the "empty quarter" of what is now Saudi Arabia, adapting to the Bedouin culture.

On his return to England, Doughty faced the greatest trial of all: an uninterested public. Scholars frowned on Doughty's insistence that his firsthand knowledge invalidated many of the established beliefs about Arabia, and publishers objected to the intentionally antique style of his writing, as in the following passage: "When the Beduins saw me pensive, to admire the divine architecture of these living jewels . . . they thought it but childish fondness in the stranger."

Although the work received little attention at first, *Travels in Arabia Deserta* proved to have a longer life than expected. The book was used in the planning of operations during Britain's campaigns in Arabia, and in 1921 it was reissued with a forward by T. E. LAWRENCE, who had become a great admirer of the author. Doughty was pleased to accept the adulation of a younger fellow traveler.

Douglas, Keith Castellain (1920–1944)
poet

Keith Douglas was born in Kent to an army officer and his wife, and was educated at Christ's Hospital School in London and at Oxford. His education was cut short by the outbreak of World War II. By 1941 he was serving as a tank commander in North

Africa, where he wrote some of his finest poetry. He was killed in Normandy three days after taking part in the Allied invasion of Europe.

Douglas had written poetry since the age of 10, and his early work was published in *Augury: An Oxford Miscellany of Verse and Prose* (1940). From 1937 onward, his work appeared in a number of periodicals, including Geoffrey Grigson's *New Verse*. The only volume of his poetry to be published in his lifetime was *Selected Poems* (1943). His style became increasingly mature and coldly angry, as is evident in *Alamein to Zem Zem* (1946), his documentary prose account of desert warfare.

Douglas's *Collected Poems* appeared in two editions: edited by J. Waller and G. S. Fraser (1951) and with an introduction by Edmund Blunden (1966), a distinguished soldier poet from World War I and Douglas's tutor at Merton College, Oxford. The poet Ted HUGHES edited and introduced Douglas's *Selected Poems* (1964), which significantly renewed interest in Douglas's poetry. Douglas's poems "How to Kill" and "Vergissmeinnicht," often anthologized, represent his incisive clarity and plainness of diction. Douglas's poetry is known for its ruthlessly unsentimental quality, as well as its candor and detachment. As the following lines from the poem "Aristocrats" demonstrate, he celebrated the last stand of the chivalric hero, recognizing both the folly and glamour of modern-day chivalry: "How can I live among this gentle / obsolescent breed of heroes, and not weep?"

Other Work by Keith Douglas

Graham, Desmond, ed. *Complete Poems*. Winchester, Mass.: Faber & Faber, 2000.

A Work about Keith Douglas

Graham, Desmond. *Keith Douglas: 1920–1944*. New York: Oxford University Press, 1974.

Doyle, Roddy (1958–) *novelist, playwright, screenwriter*

One of the most artistically and commercially successful Irish novelists in recent years, Roddy Doyle was born in Dublin. He was educated at St. Fintan's Christian Brothers School in Sutton and at University College, Dublin. Afterward he taught English and geography for 14 years at Grendale Community School in Killbarrack, on the north side of Dublin. He transformed this area into the fictional Barrytown, which was the setting for his early novels.

His first novel, *The Commitments* (1987), was originally self-published but soon was picked up by a London publisher. The novel tells the story of a group of down-and-out young Dubliners who form a soul band with the hopes of making it big. They almost succeed, but internal conflicts destroy the band. At the center of the novel is the Rabbitte family, who would be the focus of Doyle's next two novels, *The Snapper* (1990) and *The Van* (1991).

All three books are about working-class life, in which people deal with too little money and too much domestic strife. The grim elements of these novels are relieved by moments of high comedy.

Reviews in the Irish press of Doyle's novels have been mixed. Some reviewers are offended by the coarse, often obscene, language the characters use. Doyle has said in interviews that although he feels pressured to present Irish life in a more positive light, he refuses to do so. No matter how raw the portrayal of the working-class Irish, Doyle believes his dialogue-driven stories are true to the source of his inspiration: the life and dreams of the poor and working class who are treated as outcasts by society. The harsh language conveys a vitality of spirit that perseveres in the most oppressive of settings.

Doyle's next novel, *Paddy Clarke Ha Ha Ha* (1993), takes place in the Barrytown of 1968 and concerns the effects of the breakup of a marriage on a 10-year-old boy named Paddy Clarke. As the novel progresses, the boy matures, as reflected in his vocabulary, and by the novel's end he has learned the bittersweet acceptance of pain as an unavoidable constant in life. This novel firmly established Doyle's literary reputation, becoming a best-seller in America and Great Britain, where it was awarded the BOOKER PRIZE.

The Woman Who Walked into Doors (1996) is perhaps Doyle's most ambitious work. It is a first-person narrative about a 39-year-old alcoholic widow who has been a victim of spousal abuse. Doyle also explored the theme of violence in a family in 1993 in a four-part television series that he scripted, called *Family*. The vision in both works is darker than in his earlier novels, but it is no less compelling.

Doyle's recent book, *A Star Called Henry* (1999), is a historical tale that deals with the years preceding and following the 1916 Easter Rebellion of Irish Nationalists seeking independence from Britain and how events of the time affect a young man, Henry Smart. It is the first in a proposed trilogy with the general title *The Last Roundup*.

Doyle has also worked as a screenwriter, adapting his Barrytown trilogy successfully to film. He has also written plays for the Dublin-based theater group Passion Machine.

Though he has taken some critical knocks, Doyle is well thought of by many reviewers and scholars. Speaking of *Paddy Clarke*, reviewer Carolyn See said in the *Washington Post*, "It is a beautifully written novel; it may be one of the great modern Irish novels." She also compared Doyle to Brendan BEHAN. The novelist Fay WELDON writes, "There was Joyce's Dublin and now there is Roddy Doyle's: wholly contemporary, extremely funny, and wonderfully and energetically delinquent. [His work is] irresistible to the modern spirit."

A Work about Roddy Doyle

White, Caramine. *Reading Roddy Doyle.* Syracuse, N.Y.: Syracuse University Press, 2001.

Drabble, Margaret (1939–) *novelist, short story writer, playwright, nonfiction writer, editor*

Born in Sheffield, Yorkshire, Margaret Drabble is the daughter of John Frederick Drabble, who was a lawyer and country court judge as well as a novelist; and Kathleen Marie Bloor Drabble, the daughter of fundamentalist parents who was the first in her family to attend a university and become an atheist. One of four children, Drabble is the younger sister of novelist A. S. BYATT. After attending a Quaker boarding school in York, she studied English at Cambridge University, where she was among the top students in her class.

A prolific novelist, Drabble's writing has given voice to the lives of contemporary British women and their male counterparts. Influenced by the 19th-century novelist Jane Austen, Drabble has written novels, short stories, and plays that emphasize the female voice and experience.

Drabble began her writing career with *A Summer Bird-Cage* (1963), the story of Sarah and her elder sister Louise, as seen through Sarah's eyes when she returns home to attend Louise's wedding. *The Garrick Year* (1964), about the marital struggles of Emma, a young woman married to an egocentric actor, soon followed. *The Millstone* (1966), for which Drabble was awarded the prestigious John Llewelyn Rhys Prize, focuses on the difficulties the unmarried Rosamund Stacey faces when she finds herself pregnant and chooses to keep the child.

From 1967 to 1980, Drabble published seven more novels, including *The Needle's Eye* (1972), considered by some critics to be her best. Focusing on the way money impinges on the emotional relationship of Simon Camish, who grew up poor, and Rose Vassilou, an heiress who has given all her money away, through Rose the novel examines "[h]ow to live without exploiting anyone, and yet to resist the self-satisfaction of being 'good,'" as American novelist and critic Joyce Carol Oates has written. For Oates, "*The Needle's Eye* is an extraordinary work: "It not only tells a story deftly, beautifully, with a management of past and present (and future) action that demonstrates Miss Drabble's total mastery of the mysterious form of the novel, but it succeeds in so re-creating the experiences of the characters that . . . we become them, we are transformed into them, so that by the end of the novel we have lived, through them, a very real, human, yet extraordinary experience."

In *The Ice Age* (1977), influenced by the effects of "Thatcherism" and Britain's oil crisis, Drabble depicts English society as it undergoes its own "ice age" involving the death of tradition.

The Radiant Way (1987), the first of a trilogy about contemporary England, is set in the 1980s and focuses on three friends who attended Cambridge together 25 years before: Liz Headeland, a psychotherapist juggling career and family; Alix Bowen, a wife, mother, and political activist; and Esther Breuer, an unmarried academic with an interesting love life. Moving between the past and present tenses, the novel ends with a picnic celebrating Esther's 50th birthday. As the three women silently watch the sun set, the narrator's final words suggest the symbolic death of life as it had once been: "The sun hangs in the sky, burning. The earth deepens to a more profound red. The sun bleeds, the earth bleeds. The sun stands still." Like *The Radiant Way*, the trilogy's two subsequent volumes—*A Natural Curiosity* (1989) and *The Gates of Ivory* (1991)—depict the decline of Britain, the changing economic and political scene, and the confrontation of each of the friends with herself and her role in a rapidly changing world. As the American novelist Marilynne Robinson has written about *The Radiant Way*, "This novel is a valuable specimen of new consciousness."

While Drabble's next novel, *The Witch of Exmoor* (1997), about the conflicts between the Palmer family and their eccentric and mysterious mother Frieda, focuses on the author's somewhat left-wing politics, her recent novel *The Peppered Moth* (2001) can be seen as a departure from her earlier work in its more autobiographical theme. Drabble draws on her family history to explore the relationships among four generations and the nature of genetic inheritance.

Drabble is also the author of two biographies, of Arnold BENNETT (1974) and Angus WILSON (1995). Other works include *A Writer's Britain: Landscape in Literature* (1979), which explores the way literature is connected to the way landscapes are perceived. Drabble also edited *The Oxford Companion to English Literature: Fifth Edition* (1985, revised 2000). She has received the James Tait Black and the E. M. Forster awards and in 1980 was made a Commander of the Order of the British Empire (CBE). As David Plante notes,

"[Drabble's] fictional people live in terms of their times: her novels can be read . . . as private records of those times." Linda Simon further characterizes Drabble as a writer "concerned with the behavior of individuals within the community and of characters within fictional worlds. She is concerned with the possibilities of fiction itself."

Works about Margaret Drabble

Bokat, Nicole Suzanne. *Novels of Margaret Drabble: "This Freudian Nexus."* New York: Peter Lang, 1998.

Hannay, John. *The Intertextuality of Fate: A Study of Margaret Drabble.* Columbia: University of Missouri Press, 1986.

Wojcik-Andrews, Ian. *Margaret Drabble's Female Bildungsromane: Theory, Genre, and Gender.* Vol. 6. New York: Peter Lang, 1995.

Drummond, William

See CALDER-MARSHALL, ARTHUR.

Duffy, Maureen (1933–) *novelist, poet, playwright*

Maureen Duffy was born in Sussex and raised in London in a poor home. Her father left the family when Duffy was a baby. War and poverty made her early life hard, but hardships gave her determination: In her tough and witty poem "Rejection Slip," she wrote, "blitzkrieg and depression stamped my genes / In a pattern for carrying on."

Duffy worked hard to win a scholarship to attend a good school. She adored poetry but enjoyed novels less, recalling later, "I had more or less given up novel reading at the age of eleven when our girls' school syllabus required us to move on from Sir Walter Scott to Austen and the Brontës, which represented for me a declension from the free imaginative life of the individual to the much narrower world of a woman's supposed place in the marriage stakes." She attended King's College in London, graduating with a B.A. degree in 1956.

Duffy's first novel was the critically acclaimed *That's How It Was.* Heavily autobiographical, it describes the early life of Paddy, an illegitimate girl with two passions: her need for an education and her complex relationship with her mother.

After her first novel Duffy found conventional prose too restrictive: "I wanted to use a language for fiction that was capable of rising to poetry, and that had all the sinewy vigour and flexibility of the London demotic I had been brought up on," she wrote. Duffy strove for this in *The Microcosm* (1966), a novel about the underground lesbian bar scene. The novel opens with melancholy, the narrator, a woman called Matt, mourning a dead lover while spending nights in the dark confines of the bar she calls the "house of shades": "Sometimes I think we're all dead down here, shadows, a house of shades, echoes of the world above where girls are blown about the streets like flowers on young stalks."

The Microcosm opens with a quote from a poem by Louis MACNEICE: "World is crazier and more of it than we think, / Incorrigibly plural." Duffy respected this plurality in her work, creating many characters who were unusual and thus ostracized by others. She worked especially hard to depict alternative sexualities. Duffy herself was one of the first British writers to publicly announce her homosexuality. During the 1950s and 1960s she spoke out actively on behalf of gay and lesbian rights.

Duffy has written about London many times. *Wounds* (1936) is a sensual novel describing various Londoners searching for sexual fulfillment and wounded by the lack of it. *Capital* (1975) spans thousands of years of London's history. The novel opens by introducing the contemporary archaeologist Meepers, obsessed with excavating London: "It was the living who passed ghostly around him, through whose curiously incorporeal flesh he moved without sensation while the dead pressed and clamoured, their cries drowning out the traffic." The novel then plunges back to the distant past of a Neanderthal tribe camped by the Thames River, and it proceeds to dart among various historical periods, all the sections tied together by Meepers's attempts to make a continuous story from London's history.

Duffy offered more of her own experience of the city in *Londoners: An Elegy* (1983), a tribute to the wartime London she knew as a child—"My hometown was danced away round a VJ bonfire"—and to the sheer complexity of contemporary London, full of so many different people, cultures, sexualities, and classes.

Duffy is also passionately committed to the antivivisectionist cause. Her dedication to animal rights is clear in her novels *Gor Saga* (1981), about a half-man half-gorilla hybrid; and *I Want to Go to Moscow* (1973), a novel about antivivisectionists. She expresses her beliefs in *Men and Beasts: An Animal Rights Handbook* (1984).

Duffy has also been involved in improving funding for writers, serving as chair and then president of the Writer's Guild of Great Britain for several years. Her poem "A Letter to Whom It Doesn't Concern" is a savage indictment of those who ignore the plight of struggling authors.

In addition to novels, Duffy has also written plays, such as *The Lay Off* (1962), *The Silk Room* (1966), and *A Nightingale in Bloomsbury Square* (1973).

Other Works by Maureen Duffy

Collected Poems. London: Hamilton, 1985.
England: The Making of the Myth, from Stonehenge to Albert Square. London: Fourth Estate, 2001.
Restitution. London: Fourth Estate, 1998.

A Work about Maureen Duffy

Rule, Jane. *Lesbian Images.* New York: Pocket Books, 1976.

du Maurier, Daphne (1907–1989)
novelist, short story writer

The daughter of the actor, producer, and theater manager Gerald du Maurier and the actress Muriel Beaumont, Daphne du Maurier was born in London. She was educated at home and then later at schools in France. At 20 she visited Cornwall, in southwest England, and immediately felt spiritually connected to the landscape. Du Maurier lived in Cornwall for most of her life. In 1932 she married Frederick Arthur Montague Browning, a major in the Grenadier Guards who was 10 years her senior. They had three children.

Du Maurier's fiction largely consisted of Gothic romances, historical adventures, and tales of the supernatural. She achieved popular success with *Rebecca* (1938), a psychological ghost story. In this novel a wealthy man, and through him his innocent second wife, are haunted by the memory of his first wife, Rebecca. The novel is told in the first person by the second wife (at 21 she is half her spouse's age), who is never referred to by name, despite the novel's abundant dialogue. Rebecca is one of three symbolical forces arrayed against the narrator; the other two are her husband's enormous country estate and its black-clad housekeeper, who still communes with the mansion's former mistress.

Critics attacked the book for its stilted writing ("She waited a moment. I did not say anything. Then she went out of the room. She can't frighten me anymore, I thought"); the thinness of the novel's psychology; and its resemblance to other novels, especially Charlotte Brontë's *Jane Eyre,* which du Maurier had loved since childhood. Still, *The Times* (London) review found such flaws "easy to overlook" because of the novel's "atmosphere of genuine terror." Alfred Hitchcock's first U.S. film, based on the novel, won the 1940 Academy Award for best picture.

Du Maurier tackled the theme of the *doppelgänger* (double) in *The Scapegoat* (1957). Her next novel, *The House on the Strand* (1969), has no lookalikes, but it intriguingly provides the narrator, Dick Young, with *two* variations on the double: Magnus Lane, to whose Dr. Jekyll he plays Mr. Hyde by ingesting the drug his friend has concocted; and Roger Kylmerth, whom he meets in his ensuing time travels to the 14th century, where he also falls in love. The quest for identity here is ambiguous, and the crossing of time reflects the popular interest of the 1960s in expanding consciousness through hallucinogenic means. Du Maurier's writing remains overwrought: "My mind, usually clear when I had taken the drug, was stupefied, baffled; I had expected something akin to the autumn day that I remembered from the previous time, when Bodrugan had been drowned." Yet, as critic Judith Cook writes, the novel "pulled together the threads of much of [du Maurier's] earlier work—recreation of past centuries, descriptions of the countryside, and a mystery—and made out of them a haunting book."

Du Maurier's short story "Don't Look Now" (1972), a much transformed version of "Little Red Riding Hood," even more spookily mixes and corrupts elements of time. It uses a holiday setting, a decaying Venice, to relate a frightening adventure about marital sorrow—the death of a child is involved—and guilt. A comment that biographer Richard Kelly has made about this story applies widely to the author's work: "du Maurier does not develop her characters to the point where we can have any strong feelings of sympathy for them. Instead, we watch with curiosity what *happens* to them."

Many of du Maurier's supernatural short stories are precise and gripping. Exemplary in this regard is "The Birds" (1952), in which masses of birds, rebelling against human exploitation, attack people. In 1965 Alfred Hitchcock turned this story into another film.

Du Maurier's memoir, *Enchanted Cornwall* (1992), was published posthumously. Judith Cook notes that du Maurier's work "developed and matured over the years but, partly as a result of her early success, the development shown in her later writing was underestimated."

Other Work by Daphne du Maurier
The Glass Blowers. 1963. Reprint, Cutchogue, N.Y.: Buccaneer Books, 1999.

Works about Daphne du Maurier
Horner, Avril, and Sue Zlosnik. *Daphne du Maurier: Writing, Identity and the Gothic Imagination.* New York: St. Martin's Press, 1998.

Leng, Flavia. *Daphne du Maurier: A Daughter's Memoir.* Edinburgh: Mainstream Publishing, 1997.

Dunn, Nell (1936–   ) *novelist, short story writer, playwright*

Nell Mary Dunn was born in London and raised on an estate in Wiltshire, England. After attending a convent school, she went to London to study art history. By the 1960s she had left her comfortable life in Chelsea to live in Clapham, where she worked in factories and a nightclub to gather material for her fiction. Dunn's short-story collection, *Up the Junction*, was published in 1963. One critic noted her striking ability to report on the working-class Britons, "built on their dialect, street signs, bits of popular music, the clichéd and repetitious folk-wisdom of ghetto life."

Dunn's first novel, *Poor Cow* (1967), centers on a single character, Joy, a young mother with a failed marriage behind her. She gets involved with men who have nothing to offer her. Critic V. S. PRITCH-ETT wrote that the realistic dialogue revealed "the exposed, unsupported, morally anonymous condition of people who have nothing that can mean much to them."

In addition to her novels, Dunn has written plays. In *Steaming* (1981), the subject again is mainly working-class women, here seen in a London Turkish bath, which is threatened with being closed down. The six female characters vary in age and class, but they are united in their needs and disappointments and galvanized by their successful campaign against closing the bath to take some decisive action in their own lives. One reviewer characterized *Steaming* as "a gentle piece of female consciousness-raising." The play won the Society of West End Theatre Award in 1982, among other awards.

Dunn has also compiled books of interviews with women (*Talking to Women* [1965]) and with people pursuing alternate lifestyles (*Living Like I Do* [1976]). In 1969 she cowrote, with Susan Campbell, a children's story, *Freddy Gets Married*. More recent publications have been *Grandmothers Talking to Nell Dunn* (a sequel to *Talking to Women*) and a sequel to *Poor Cow* called *My Silver Shoes*, in which Joy is now living next door to her mother and coping with growing older. Both books were published in 1991.

A Work about Nell Dunn

Wandor, Michlene. *Drama Today: A Critical Guide to British Drama, 1970–1990*. London: Longman, 1993.

Dunsany, Lord (Edward John Moreton Drax Plunkett) (1878–1957) *novelist, short story writer, playwright, poet*

Lord Dunsany was born in London as Edward John Moreton Drax Plunkett and spent much of his childhood at his ancestral castle near Dublin, Ireland. He became the 18th Lord Dunsany when his father died in 1899. After graduating from Sandhurst, the British military academy, Dunsany achieved the rank of captain. A hunting enthusiast, he traveled to Africa to hunt big game, and his skill at chess earned him the title of Irish champion.

Dunsany's first book, *The Gods of Pegana* (1905), is set in what he called "the country of my dreams." Critic Martin Gardner has compared the "elaborate mythology" of the stories to that of J. R. R. TOLKIEN. *The Book of Wonder* (1913), which contains more tales about "the things that befell gods and men" in Dunsany's imaginary lands, is prefaced with this invitation: "Come with me, ladies and gentlemen who are in any wise weary of London: come with me: and those that tire at all of the world we know: for we have new worlds here."

Dunsany's work is characterized by what he describes as "two lights that do not seem very often to shine together, poetry and humor." Humor dominates his tales about Joseph Jorkens, a notorious liar who appears in five books set in a London club. A complaint from W. B. YEATS spurred Dunsany to write about Irish themes, including a vivid description of his native landscape in *My Ireland* (1937).

Dunsany's fantasy novels are considered classics of the genre. George RUSSELL praised *The King of Elfland's Daughter* (1924), in which a mortal prince goes to Elfland searching for his bride, as "the most purely beautiful thing Lord Dunsany has written," filled with lyrical descriptions of Elfland and characters "symbolic of our own spiritual adventures." Others consider *The Charwoman's Shadow* (1926) Dunsany's masterwork. Both of these novels have recently been reissued.

During this lifetime, Dunsany was best known for his plays. In 1909, at Yeats's request, he wrote a one-act play, *The Glittering Gate,* in which two burglars break into the locked gates of heaven to find nothing but a blue, star-filled void. *If* (1921), in which time travel alters the past to create a new present, is considered his best full-length drama. At one time five of his plays were in production on Broadway.

Dunsany's works include short stories, novels, memoirs, more than 40 plays, and nine books of poetry. Although he received little respect from critics after his death, today he is recognized as an early master of the fantasy genre and the greatest British fantasy writer of the 20th century.

Other Works by Lord Dunsany

Arthur C. Clarke and Lord Dunsany: A Correspondence. Edited by Keith Allen Daniels. Ridgecrest, Calif.: Anamnesis Press, 1998.
The Curse of the Wise Woman. London: Sphere, 1976.

Works about Lord Dunsany

Joshi, S. T. *Lord Dunsany: Master of the Anglo-Irish Imagination.* Westport, Conn.: Greenwood, 1995.
Schweitzer, Darrell, and Tim Kirk. *Pathways to Elfland: The Writings of Lord Dunsany.* Holicong, Pa.: Wildside Press, 1989.

Durcan, Paul (1944–   ) *poet*

Born into a family of lawyers in Dublin, Ireland, Paul Durcan was educated at Gonzaga College and University College, Cork, where he earned his B.A. and studied archaeology and medieval history. Durcan is known as a social critic and satirist. He became known not only through his publications but through his public performances of his poetry. He has gained a reputation for wit, energy, and his attacks on Irish social and religious institutions as

well as abusers of women, the pious, the opinionated, and the violent.

Although Durcan began publishing in the late 1960s, his poetry gained serious critical notice only in 1982 with *The Selected Paul Durcan.* After the breakup of his marriage in the 1980s, his poems became more introspective and overtly feminist. He won the Whitbread Prize for Poetry in 1990 for the poetry collection *Daddy, Daddy,* written in tribute to his late father. As is typical of his work, this collection also touched on his political, religious, and social concerns.

Seamus HEANEY has noted a "tension between the lyrical and the anti-lyrical, between intensity and irony, between innocence and fear" in Durcan's work. Durcan embraces political nonpartisanship (he opposes both the British and Irish Republican Army) and portrays violence as "the outcome of monstrous fantasies that sacrilegiously deny the minutiae on which life and creativity depend." His poetry collections *Crazy about Women* (1991) and *Give Me Your Hand* (1994) are his responses to paintings in the National Galleries of Ireland and Britain.

Other Works by Paul Durcan

Cries of an Irish Caveman. London: Harvill, 2001.
A Snail in my Prime. New York: Penguin, 1995.
Teresa's Bar. Dublin: The Gallery Press, 1976.

A Work about Paul Durcan

Toibin, Colm. *The Kilfenora Teaboy: A Study of Paul Durcan.* Dublin: New Island Books, 1996.

Durrell, Gerald Malcolm (1925–1995)

nonfiction writer, memoirist, children's writer
Gerald Durrell was born in Jamshedpur, India, to Lawrence Samuel, an Anglo-Irish civil engineer, and Louise Florence (Dixie) Durrell. His elder brother was poet and novelist Lawrence DURRELL.

Durrell recalled his happy childhood in the memoirs *My Family and Other Animals* (1956); *Birds, Beasts and Relatives* (1969); and *The Garden of the Gods* (1979), republished as *Fauna and Fam-*

ily. As a toddler he loved to visit the local zoo. Educated by private tutors in Greece, France, Italy, and Switzerland, he recalled the tutelage of naturalist Theodore Stephanides on Corfu in *Fillets of Plaice* (1971).

After World War II, Durrell was an assistant keeper at Whipsnade, a special zoo for the breeding and preservation of animals. While there he kept a detailed diary, which he turned into *A Bevy of Beasts* (1973). After conducting research on imperiled Père David deer, he aspired to acquire his own zoo. A small inheritance received at the age of 21 enabled him to undertake a series of wildlife collecting expeditions. He visited the Cameroons, British Guiana (now Guyana), Argentina, Paraguay, Patagonia, Madagascar, Sierra Leone, Mexico, Australia, New Zealand, and Malaya. BBC-TV films were made of two of these trips; he also hosted TV specials about animals. *Encounters with Animals* (1958) collects his radio talks. In 1979 he married Lee Wilson McGeorge, an American zoologist who collaborated with him on *The Amateur Naturalist: A Practical Guide to the Natural World* (1983).

In the late 1950s income from Durrell's books finally enabled him to establish his own zoo on a 35-acre site in the Channel Islands, including a 17th-century manor house named "Les Augrès." Durrell described how the zoo came into being in *Menagerie Manor* (1965) and *The Stationary Ark* (1976). Still running, the Jersey Zoo is dedicated to saving endangered animals and species and is now a major tourist attraction with more than 200,000 visitors a year. In 1963 Durrell also founded the Jersey Wildlife Preservation Trust.

In addition to his nonfiction books, Durrell published a handful of novels and short-story collections about animals for children, among which are *Rosie Is My Relative,* about a tipsy elephant (1968); and *The Mockery Bird* (1982), which is set on a mythical island.

A Work about Gerald Durrell

Botting, Douglas. *Gerald Durrell: The Authorized Biography.* New York: Carroll & Graf, 1999.

Durrell, Lawrence (1912–1990) *novelist, short story writer, poet, playwright, nonfiction writer*

Lawrence Durrell was born in India, near the Tibetan border, to Lawrence Samuel Durrell, a civil engineer, and his wife, Louisa. Both of Durrell's parents had been born in India, and though of British heritage, they both considered themselves to be more Indian than British. Durrell's younger brother was the naturalist Gerald DURRELL, whose autobiographical works give an amusing view of the young "Larry."

When he was about 12 years old, Durrell's parents sent him to England to study at St. Edmund's School in Canterbury. Durrell was unhappy in England and later described life there as "the English death." When he had completed his secondary schooling, he took but did not pass the entrance examinations to Cambridge University. He then worked for a time as a jazz pianist in a nightclub.

In 1935 Durrell moved to the Greek island of Corfu with the first of his four wives, Nancy Myers. That same year he published his first novel, *Pied Piper of Lovers,* an autobiographical work about his life in Bloomsbury, England. He also read Henry Miller's *Tropic of Cancer,* which so impressed him that he wrote the author a fan letter, beginning a correspondence that lasted for 45 years. When Durrell was about to publish his second novel, *The Black Book: An Agon* (1938), Miller counseled him not to give in to his publisher's suggestion to delete erotic passages.

In 1941 Durrell and his wife and baby daughter were forced to leave Greece to escape from the advancing Nazi army. They settled for a time in Cairo, but in 1942 the couple separated and Durrell moved to Alexandria, Egypt, where he worked for the British Information Office. There he met and married Eve Cohen, who became the model for the character Justine in the 1957 novel of the same name.

In 1952, after living for a period of time in Rhodes, Argentina, and Yugoslavia, Durrell bought a home in Cyprus. He hoped to be able to live out his life there and pursue his writing, but he was driven away by the conflict between Greek and Turkish factions on the island. One of his greatest works, *Bitter Lemons* (1957), describes this period in his life. *Bitter Lemons* is just one among several of Durrell's works, including *Prospero's Cell* (1945) and *Reflections on a Marine Venus* (1953), that have been classified as "island books." These books, though focused on a particular place, are much more than mere travel books. They make each island and its people come alive and evoke the history and the mythology of the place. In *Bitter Lemons*, for example, Durrell describes the island as "full of goddesses and mineral springs; ancient castles and monasteries; fruit and grain and verdant grasslands; priests and gypsies and brigands."

While in Cyprus, Durrell began work on *Justine*, the first volume in the *Alexandria Quartet*, a series of novels set in Alexandria, Egypt, which portray the same series of events from several different perspectives. After he settled in the Provence region of France, he completed *Justine* and its three companions: *Balthazar* (1958), *Mountolive* (1958), and *Clea* (1960). These are widely considered Durrell's finest works of fiction.

In addition to 17 novels, Durrell wrote dozens of volumes of excellent poetry, much of it modeled on ancient Greek verse; and several volumes of short stories, four plays, and numerous works of nonfiction, including *A Key to Modern Poetry* (1952) and his last work, *Caesar's Vast Ghost* (1990), about his adopted home in Provence. In a review of Durrell's collected poems in the *New York Times*, critic Harrison E. Salisbury said of Durrell that

> it is, of course, as a painter with words that his talent finds its highest mark. Here is the witchery of phrase and comparison that makes his pages gleam like new metal. You run through the poems and the phrases leap out and imbed themselves in your memory—"calm as paint," "swarms of golden hair," "kisses leave no fingerprints," "soft as an ant's patrol" or "rosy as feet of pigeons pressed in clay."

Durrell's poetry is sensuous; he revels in images of sound and touch, and he portrays the joy of the erotic in glittering terms. Lovers lie near the Mediterranean "Steeped in each other's minds and breathing there / Like wicks inhaling deep in golden oil . . ."

Durrell is master of the craft of poetry, able to move with ease from the lyric and erotic to dry wit and sarcasm.

Critical Analysis

Deeply influenced by the physics of Einstein and the psychology of Freud, Durrell experimented with the form of the four novels that make up the *Alexandria Quartet* in order to reflect the complexity of modern consciousness and modern existence. Durrell himself said that he wanted to apply the space-time continuum to a novel. He described his intention in greater detail in an interview with *The Manchester Guardian*: "It [*The Quartet*] is really intended to be a four-dimensional dance, a relativity poem, and ideally all four volumes should be read simultaneously as they cover the three sides of space and one of time. You might call it a sort of stereoscopic narrative with stereophonic personality." In this quotation, Durrell is primarily referring to his use of narrative technique, in which the "same" story is retold from different viewpoints. The narrator of *Justine*, *Balthazar*, and *Clea* is novelist L. G. Darley, who tells the story of a love affair that took place in the Egyptian city of Alexandria just before World War II. The basic story is told in the first volume, then kaleidoscopically reexamined and amplified in the subsequent volumes. In *Balthazar* Darley quotes other characters who contradict his original story. *Mountolive* is told by an omniscient narrator who reveals the "facts" of the story. Finally, *Clea* brings the story forward in time. Central characters in the story include Darley; his Greek mistress Melissa; the British ambassador Mountolive; the spy Pursewarden; the artist Clea; and Justine, the Jewish wife of a wealthy businessman, Nessim, and the object of Darley's obsession. The novels are set in Alexandria,

Egypt, and the city itself becomes an important character and an integral part of the sexual and political intrigue that propels the story.

Critics have been sharply divided on the Alexandria Quartet since the beginning. Many thought Durrell should have received the Nobel Prize, while others have objected to Durrell's lush, exotic—some say overwrought—prose, as seen in this passage from *Clea:*

> The whole quarter lay drowsing in the umbrageous violet of approaching nightfall. A sky of palpitating velours which was cut into by the stark flare of a thousand electric light bulbs. It lay over Tatwig Street, that night, like a velvet rind.

Whatever one thinks of the style, however, critics agree on Durrell's ability to evoke a sense of place. In reviewing *Clea,* Orville Prescott of *The New York Times* wrote:

> The Alexandria of Mr. Durrell's powerful imagination will always be far more real to thousands of readers than the actual Mediterranean port, a dream city created by art and poetic language that shimmers on the desert horizon of contemporary fiction like an exotic oasis, repulsive and yet fascinating, reeking of languorous lusts and dreary depravities.

An academic journal devoted to the study of Durrell's work is entitled *Deus Loci,* which translates to local god, or the god of the place. All of Durrell's work is, in one way or another, about the spirit or god of the places he portrays, and he uses his considerable powers of language to evoke that spirit for his readers.

Other Works by Lawrence Durrell
Collected Poems, 1931–1974. New York: Viking, 1980.
Nunquam. New York: Viking, 1979.
Tunc: A Novel. New York: Dutton, 1968.

Works about Lawrence Durrell
Bowker, Gordon. *Through the Dark Labyrinth: A Biography of Lawrence Durrell.* New York: St. Martin's Press, 1997.
Pine, Richard. *Lawrence Durrell: The Mindscape.* New York: St. Martin's Press, 1994.

Eagle, Solomon
See SQUIRE, JOHN COLLINGS.

Eastaway, Edward
See THOMAS, EDWARD.

Eliot, Thomas Stearns (1888–1965) *poet, playwright, essayist*

T. S. Eliot was born in St. Louis, Missouri, the seventh child of Henry Ware Eliot, the president of the Hydraulic-Press Brick Company, and the poet Charlotte Champa Stearns. Educated at Harvard, the Sorbonne, and Oxford, Eliot studied Italian Renaissance and 17th-century English literature; philosophy; and various languages, including Sanskrit. At Harvard he came under the influence of the scholar Irving Babbitt, whose anti-romanticism found a permanent place in Eliot's poetic philosophy. Although Eliot wrote a Ph.D. dissertation, he never took the final oral exam to complete the degree.

In 1915 Eliot moved to England, where he became a British subject 12 years later. He worked first for a bank and then held editorial positions at the literary magazines *Egoist* and *Criterion* and at the publisher Faber & Faber. In 1917 he published his first volume of poetry, *Prufrock and Other Observations*. The title is taken from "The Love Song of J. Alfred Prufrock," whose timid, fearful narrator stumbles along in a world of decaying traditions.

In 1919 *Poems* appeared, containing "Gerontion," a blank-verse interior monologue that reveals an old man's disillusionment with the modern world. The following year Eliot published *The Sacred Wood,* a collection of critical essays, among which is "Tradition and the Individual Talent," an examination of the nature of tradition and its importance to poetry. In 1922 Eliot published his most famous poem, *The Waste Land,* a fragmented, kaleidoscopic presentation of the cultural decay that Eliot saw afflicting the modern world.

In 1927 Eliot joined the Anglican church and, three years later, produced "Ash Wednesday," a poem about the conflict between faith and doubt. His poetic masterpiece, *Four Quartets* (1943), is another religious meditation. Its four sections—"Burnt Norton" (1936), "East Coker" (1940), "The Dry Salvages" (1941), and "Little Gidding" (1941)—originally were published separately, but together they form a unified, though complex, examination of human consciousness, spiritual immortality, and Christian mysticism.

Eliot partly attributed the modern world's inadequacies to the decline of religion. In his essay "A

Dialogue on Dramatic Poetry" (1928), he quipped, "Our literature is a substitute for religion, and so is our religion." In three lectures published collectively as *The Idea of a Christian Society* (1939), he promoted the concept of small, tightly knit, religiously oriented communities as an antidote to the loneliness and alienation individuals feel in the modern world. He further argued that religion and art help to make Europe a unified culture in *Notes Toward the Definition of Culture* (1949).

Eliot also wrote for the stage. His plays, most of them in a tragic-comedic vein, deal with religious themes. *Murder in the Cathedral* (1935), for instance, centers on the 12th-century conflict between King Henry II and Thomas Becket, the archbishop of Canterbury.

In 1948 Eliot was awarded a Nobel Prize in literature. Two decades after his death, his light-hearted poems in *Old Possum's Book of Practical Cats* (1939) inspired the long-running stage musical *Cats* (1981). The American critic Edmund Wilson noted that Eliot immediately and forever changed the tone of literature, that his works "turned out to be unforgettable poems, which everyone was trying to rewrite."

Central to Eliot's work is his appreciation for tradition, which transmits ideas across generations. The numerous allusions to classical works in his poetry are not intended to undermine and mock those works but to remind the reader of the pieces of a once-great culture that are scattered around us at all times.

Eliot wrote of all artists' indebtedness to the past in the essay "Tradition and the Individual Talent," in which he argues that tradition is not a mere repetition of the immediate past. Instead, for a poet tradition is created from a European literary heritage that stretches back to Homer. Poets forge their own individual traditions by using the works from any period and in any language. To Eliot the past is not "dead, but . . . what is already living."

Eliot believed that the poet must be invisible in his work, with the language speaking for itself. Indeed, when Stephen SPENDER confessed to Eliot an interest in becoming a poet, Eliot replied that he understood what it meant to write poetry but not what it meant to be a poet. Rather than use poetry only to give voice to his own feelings, Eliot sought a degree of objectivity. In his 1920 essay "Hamlet and His Problems," he writes,

> The only way of expressing emotion in the form of art is by finding an "objective correlative"; in other words a set of objects, a situation, a chain of events which shall be the formula for that particular emotion; such that, when the external facts . . . are given, the emotion is immediately evoked.

Eliot, however, was conscious of the difficulty of conveying precise meaning through language, lamenting in "Burnt Norton," that "Words strain, / Crack and sometimes break, under the burden."

Critical Analysis

The Waste Land demonstrates much of Eliot's poetic philosophy. Written in five sections, this poem is a relentless portrayal of the blasted, withered cultural landscape of the modern world. According to Eliot, the title, along with much of the poem's symbolism, was suggested by a 1920 book, *From Ritual to Romance* by Jessie L. Weston. He also relied on *The Golden Bough* (1890) by Sir James FRAZER for source material in writing *The Waste Land*.

From Weston, Eliot took the idea of a wasteland ruled by a Fisher King (the fish is an ancient Christian symbol), with both land and king made sterile by an evil spell. Salvation awaits the arrival of a virtuous knight who can lift the spell by finding the Holy Grail, the vessel out of which Christ drank at the last supper, and thus restore life to the land and sexual potency to the king. At the end of *The Waste Land*, however, it is uncertain whether the modern world is capable of salvation—or even willing to receive it.

In *The Waste Land* Eliot combines imagery from his classical education with visions of urban squalor. Thus, the poem opens with lines that echo and parody the beginning of Chaucer's *Canterbury Tales*. Where in Chaucer's prologue April brings life-giving rain, in Eliot's poem it is the "cruellest month."

The poem quickly moves on to the petty details of modern life, such as gossip and memories of a childhood sled ride. Adults in the world of *The Waste Land* bicker in familiar-sounding ways about marriage, children, and money. Behind them is the dreary city backdrop enveloped in "the brown fog of a winter dawn." Scholar Lyndall Gordon says Eliot creates "a psychological hell in which . . . one is quite alone."

The Waste Land also exemplifies Eliot's idea of tradition with its mix of different languages. The poet breaks into German several times in the first section and sprinkles Italian and French quotations throughout. The poem quotes or refers to some 35 writers, including Dante, Baudelaire, Verlaine, Spenser, Shakespeare, and St. Augustine.

The style of *The Waste Land* is fragmented, for at the urging of the American poet Ezra Pound, Eliot cut the original 800 lines down to 400. As a result the poem moves abruptly from the realism of the modern city to the mythological land of the Fisher King and back again. Humor is juxtaposed with the somber. As scholar F. O. Matthiessen observes, Eliot "omitted logical connectives and the reader must find his own way through this 'music of ideas' in a way . . . analogous to associating . . . themes in a symphony."

In the end even the moments of beauty in *The Waste Land* are undermined by reminders of ugliness: Thus "splendour of Ionian white and gold" is followed immediately by a river sweating "oil and tar." Edmund Wilson observes that "Eliot uses the Waste Land as the concrete image of a spiritual drought." The poem leaves one with the sense, says the scholar Gilbert Seldes, that "life had been rich, beautiful, assured, organized, lofty, and now is dragging itself out in a poverty-stricken and disrupted and ugly tedium . . . broken glimpses of what was."

Other Works by T. S. Eliot

The Complete Poems and Plays: 1909–1950. New York: Harcourt Brace, 1952.

Inventions of the March Hare: Poems 1909–1917. Edited by Christopher Ricks. New York: Harcourt, Brace, 1997.

Selected Essays. 1917–1932. New York: Harcourt Brace, 1950.

Works about T. S. Eliot

Bloom, Harold, ed. *T. S. Eliot.* New York: Chelsea House, 1999.

Davidson, Harrit, ed. *T. S. Eliot.* New York: Longman, 1999.

Gordon, Lyndall. *T. S. Eliot: An Imperfect Life.* New York: W. W. Norton, 1999.

Moody, A. David. *The Cambridge Companion to T. S. Eliot.* Cambridge, England: Cambridge University Press, 1994.

Ellerman, Annie Winifred

See BRYHER.

Ellis, Alice Thomas (Anna Haycraft)
(1932–) *novelist*

Alice Thomas Ellis was born in Liverpool to a father of Russo-Finnish ancestry and a Welsh mother. She attended Bangor County Grammar School in Gwynedd and the Liverpool School of Art. Ellis converted to Catholicism at age 19 and was a postulant at a Liverpool convent, but she had to leave because of a back injury. In 1956 she married Colin Haycraft, the chairman of the Duckworth Publishing House. She subsequently worked as a fiction editor at Duckworth for many years.

Ellis's first novel, *The Sin Eater* (1977), describes a family that gathers at their Welsh country estate while the patriarch is dying. Like many of Ellis's works, the book contains manifestations of the Devil, who exerts his influence in causing conflicts among family members. Critic Jeremy Treglown described it as "an impressively self-confident novel, full of uncomfortable jokes and sharp perceptions."

Also in 1977, Ellis published a parents' guide to baby care, *Natural Baby Food*, under the name Anne Haycraft. Her second novel, *The Birds of the*

Air (1980), is a social comedy about Barbara, a woman who has recently lost a father and a son and who has discovered her husband's affair. Ellis frequently writes about moral choices and absurd situations people face, as when, in this book, she describes Barbara's unsuccessful attempt to seduce Hunter, her homosexual publisher.

The 27th Kingdom (1982) describes the struggle between good and evil when a West Indian postulant comes to live at a boardinghouse run by a middle-aged woman and her bizarre nephew. Like many of Ellis's works, the novel contains elements of magic and mysticism, including an anthropomorphized swimming cat and devils that take the form of pigeons.

Ellis is considered a leading member of "the Duckworth Gang," a name given to a group of women writers, including Beryl BAINBRIDGE, whose works were published by the Duckworth Publishing House. These writers have a common style, writing short novels with a touch of the macabre and the bizarre, about women facing domestic crises. In *Unexplained Laughter* (1987) Ellis describes Lydia, a London woman who is staying at her Welsh cottage and seeking to restore meaning to her life after a failed love affair. While out in her garden one evening she hears a mysterious laughter, and then "the soft tread of something moving closer, the susurration of something being unsheathed, the breath of someone hissing through his teeth."

Critic Harriet Waugh characterizes Ellis's works as "short, edged comedies of human failure in the face of some ultimate good," and comments that Ellis "writes intelligent novels that seem not to take themselves too seriously, and . . . writes with clarity and wit."

Other Work by Alice Thomas Ellis

Pillars of Gold. New York: Viking, 1992.

Enright, Dennis Joseph (1920–   ) *poet, essayist, critic, novelist*

D. J. Enright was born in Leamington, Warwickshire, England, to George Enright, a postman, and Grace Cleaver Enright. He studied English at Cambridge under the noted literary critic F. R. LEAVIS and received a B.A. degree in 1944 and an M.A. degree in 1946. In the 1950s and 1960s he held positions at universities in England, Egypt, Germany, Japan, Thailand, and Singapore. In the 1970s Enright worked as a coeditor for *Encounter* magazine and as a director for Chatto & Windus publishers.

Laughing Hyena and Other Poems (1953) is the first of Enright's numerous poetry collections. Like much of his verse that followed, the volume contains poems expressing his admiration of the people and culture of non-Europeans. Poems such as "Standards" and "Akiko San" in the *Bread Rather Than Blossoms* (1956) volume exhibit Enright's talent for empathetic descriptions of working-class peoples who live in poverty around the world. In "Dreaming in the Shanghai Restaurant" in the *Addictions* (1962) collection, he writes of his admiration for an elderly Chinese man he observed: "He is interested in people, without wanting to / convert them or pervert them . . ." When reviewing that volume, a *Times Literary Supplement* critic wrote, "scarcely a poem in the book fails to produce a rewarding image, a satisfactory visual detail, a piece of interesting local colour." Enright's poetry displays an ironic wit and often addresses social problems. In "Elegy in a Country Suburb" in *The Old Adam* (1965), he decries the violence between Chinese and Malaysian gangs: "A party of Malays / Lopping an old man's Chinese head."

In addition to poetry, Enright also wrote literary essays and works of criticism. He frequently discussed German literature, including the authors Goethe, Thomas Mann, and Stefan George. A collection of his book reviews and essays was published in *Man Is an Onion* (1972). He has also written novels, such as *Figures of Speech* (1965), which explore the lives of English people living in Asia. Enright, however, remains best known for his poetry. Literary scholar William Walsh observes that over his career, Enright "matured as a poet, developing a uniquely personal purity of style, extending his scope and preserving in a world working constantly against it an incorruptible wholeness and truth of self."

Other Works by D. J. Enright

Collected Poems. New York: Oxford University Press, 1981.

A Faust Book. New York: Oxford University Press, 1979.

Works about D. J. Enright

Simms, Jacqueline, ed. *Life By Other Means: Essays on D. J. Enright.* New York: Oxford University Press, 1990.

Walsh, William. *D. J. Enright: Poet of Humanism.* Cambridge, England: Cambridge University Press, 1974.

Ewart, Gavin Buchanan (1916–1995)
poet, editor

Gavin Ewart was born in London to George Arthur Ewart, a surgeon, and Dorothy Turner Ewart. He attended Cambridge and received his B.A. degree in 1937. During World War II he saw active duty in the Royal Artillery. After leaving the service, Ewart worked from 1946 to 1952 as an assistant in the book review department of the British Council. He spent the next 20 years as a copywriter at advertising agencies.

At age 17 Ewart published his first poem, "Phallus in Wonderland," an irreverent parody of the Lewis Carroll classic, in the literary magazine *New Verse.* Soon after college he published his first collection, *Poems and Songs* (1939). Foreshadowing his future writings, the volume contained several examples of light verse on sexual themes. The poem "Audenesque for an Initiation" acknowledges the influence of W. H. AUDEN on his work. In "The Fourth of May" he reflects on his unhappy days at a public school.

Ewart's collection *Pleasures of the Flesh* (1966) was banned by the bookstore W. H. Smith & Son for its bold sexual themes. In the poem "Office Friendships" he addresses the issue of sexual urges at the workplace: "It's a wonderful change from wives and work / And it ends at half past five." In his later collections he combines his humorous observations of sexual fantasies with poems about war memories and family life. *The Collected Ewart* (1980) includes "Trafalgar Day," a poem written about his daughter on her 16th birthday: "you'd be soft-hearted; and / the emotion you inspire in me could, loosely, be called love."

Ewart's later verse contains liberal social commentary, as seen in his 1974 poem "The Gentle Sex," describing an incident in which several Belfast women beat a political opponent to death. Even in his later years, however, Ewart never departed from the humorous observations of human behavior and unashamed discussion of erotic themes that made him famous. Critic Anthony THWAITE wrote in 1978, "One of the few bright features about poetry in the late 1970s is that Gavin Ewart is growing old disgracefully. . . . He grows more prolific, wider-ranging, funnier, and more scabrous as the years go by."

Ewart continued publishing volumes of verse through the 1980s, including two collections for children. He also edited numerous anthologies, including the *Penguin Book of Light Verse* (1980). Critic Philip Toynbee wrote that despite Ewart's satire, "what he continually shows is true sympathy; a real fellow-feeling for many kinds of people who are normally despised or, at best, overlooked."

Other Works by Gavin Ewart

Alphabet Soup. Oxford, England: Sycamore Press, 1971.

Like it or Not. London: Badley Head, 1992.

A Work about Gavin Ewart

Stephen W. Delchamps. *Civil Humor: The Poetry of Gavin Ewart.* Madison, N.J.: Fairleigh Dickinson University Press, 2002.

expressionism

Expressionism was a movement that spread from art to literature, notably drama and poetry, exerting considerable influence on modernism. It flourished shortly before and after World War I and was at its height in Germany between 1915 and 1920. Expressionist art portrays a highly subjective vision of life, rebelling against realistic representation in favor of abstract art that conveys individual emotions rather than collective experience. It was a youth movement motivated by anger against the older generation, filled, before World War I, with restlessness and a sense of doom, and afterward with despair and disillusionment.

Artistic forerunners of expressionism were painters Vincent van Gogh, Edvard Munch, and James Ensor, who depicted primal emotions or, avoiding an objective portrayal of nature, rendered her with unprecedented intensity. One of the artworks that best epitomizes expressionism is Munch's *The Scream,* in which nature itself cries out in distress. Principal expressionist artistic groups included *Les Fauves* (1905), *Die Brücke* (1906), and *Der blaue Reiter* (*The Blue Rider*) (1907); principal theorists were Wilhelm Worringer and Wassily Kandinsky.

Expressionist drama is dedicated to expressing internal rather than external reality. It frequently features a protagonist searching for identity, surrounded by stereotypical types. Other features are stylized acting, harsh lighting, and strange musical effects that create a dreamlike atmosphere. August Strindberg was a forerunner of expressionist drama; among other exponents were Reinhold Sorge, Georg Büchner, Walter Hasenclever, and Frank Wedekind. Some early plays by Bertolt Brecht are expressionist—for example, *Baal* and *Drums in the Night* (both 1922). Among German expressionist poets were George Heym, Gottfried Benn, Else Lasker-Schüler, Georg Trakl, and August Stramm.

English-language literature offers few examples of expressionism. One offshoot was the short-lived movement VORTICISM (1912–15), associated with writer/painter Wyndham Lewis, poet Ezra Pound, and sculptors Henri Gaudier-Brzeska and Jacob Epstein. Vorticism was an antimimetic movement contemporaneous with IMAGISM.

The collaborative verse dramas written by W. H. AUDEN and Christopher ISHERWOOD for the Group Theatre in the 1930s—*The Dog beneath the Skin* (1935), *The Ascent of F6* (1927), and *On the Frontier* (1938)—were expressionist, having been influenced by Brechtian epic drama. In the United States several plays in the 1920s, such as Eugene O'Neill's *The Great God Brown* (1922) and *The Hairy Ape* (1923), and Elmer Rice's *The Adding Machine* (1923), were expressionistic. Such drama often protested aspects of modern life such as materialism and industrialization.

A Work about Expressionism
Furness, R. S. *Expressionism.* London: Methuen, 1973.

Fairfield, Cicely Isabel

See WEST, REBECCA.

Farrell, James Gordon (1935–1979)
novelist

J. G. Farrell was born in Liverpool, England, to Anglo-Irish parents; his father was an accountant. Farrell attended Oxford, where he studied French and Spanish. His novel *The Lung* (1965) tells the story of a victim of polio, a disease he contracted while at college. In the 1970s he wrote the three books that compose his "Empire Trilogy" and established his reputation: *Troubles* (1970), *The Siege of Krishnapur* (1973), and *The Singapore Grip* (1978).

Troubles is set at the huge but ramshackle Majestic Hotel in Kilnolough, Ireland, during the Irish uprisings of 1919. The crumbling hotel is a symbol for the collapse of the British Empire, which Farrell portrays with sympathy. Critics noted its lively details and flashes of dark humor. For example, Farrell uses a rotting sheep's head that British major Brendan Archer discovers in his room to represent the decay of the Irish body politic: "In the chamber pot was a decaying object crawling with white maggots. From the middle of this object a large eye, bluish and corrupt, gazed up at the Major, who

scarcely had enough time to reach the bathroom before he began to vomit. . . ."

The Siege of Krishnapur describes a British garrison's defense of a small town during the Indian Mutiny of 1857. Farrell is sympathetic to the virtues of British Empire in this book as he relates the heroic efforts of Mr. Hopkins in defending the town against the sinisterly portrayed Indians. Critic John Spurling praised the book in *The New Statesman:* "For a novel to be witty is one thing, to tell a good story is another, to be serious is yet another, but to be all three is surely enough to make it a masterpiece."

The Singapore Grip covers the Japanese capture of Singapore during World War II. Here the declining empire is treated less sympathetically; the British characters are portrayed as selfish and shortsighted. Near the end of the novel, British businessman Walter Blackett notices spots of soot on his white linen suit as he watches the city burn. Farrell uses his actions to describe his moral corruption: "He tried to brush them off, but that only made them worse. Soon his suit, his shirt and his face were covered in oily black smudges."

In assessing Farrell's significance, the critic Nicholas Shrimpton wrote that his "remarkable trilogy . . . suggests that we too, the British, will not properly understand how we live now until we make some sense of our neglected national memories."

Other Work by J. G. Farrell

A Girl in the Head. New York: Harper, 1969.

A Work about J. G. Farrell

Binns, Ronald. *J. G. Farrell.* New York: Methuen, 1986.

Farrell, M. J.

See KEANE, MOLLY.

Feinstein, Elaine (1930–) *poet, novelist*

Born in Bootle, Lancashire, England, to Isidore and Fay Compton Cooklin, Elaine Feinstein received a B.A. (1952) and an M.A. (1955) in English from Cambridge University. She then served as an editor for Cambridge University Press, lectured at several colleges, and studied for a career in law before her first volume of poetry was published in 1966.

Feinstein is a feminist poet and novelist whose work, according to critic Jennifer Birkett, often presents "landscapes of exile, suffering, and loss." For example, Feinstein's early poetry collection, *In a Green Eye* (1966), explores domesticity and her deep attachment to various people in her life, while also demonstrating the profound influence of the American poet William Carlos Williams with short, terse lines of verse. Her attention to domesticity is nowhere more evident than in the poem "Buying a House for Now," which begins joyfully, "To live here, grace / fills me like sunshine" and goes on to describe the process of moving into a new home. Her attachment to other people is evident in "Dance for a Dead Aunt," which describes her emotions on receiving a small inheritance from an aunt after the woman is nothing but "ashes / scattered." Feinstein is not limited to such emotional, domestic poems and, as *The Feast of Eurydice* (1980) demonstrates, she is capable of using subjects as remote as the classical Greek myth of Orpheus and Eurydice to explore complex themes, such as the effects of past generations on the present.

As a novelist, two of Feinstein's most successful novels are *The Circle* (1970), which follows a character named Lena as she searches for joy in life and ultimately finds it outside of her family obligations in the solitary comfort of literature; and *The Survivors* (1982), a historical novel about two Jewish families who move to England from Odessa at the turn of the 20th century. The two families live vastly different lives (one affluent, one impoverished) in Liverpool, but they are united when their children marry. *The Survivors* is remarkable, according to the critic Neil Philip, for its epic scope and the author's ability to "encompass three generations, to manage such a large cast, without losing sight of the personal, the individual, the sense of the minute as well as the year." According to the scholar Deborah Mitchell, Feinstein is "something of a rarity among writers—equally at home in verse and fiction," achieving a unique "cross-fertilization between narrative and lyric" that allows her to incessantly explore "new and enriching approaches to writing."

Other Works by Elaine Feinstein

Gold. Manchester, England: Carcanet, 2001.
Lawrence and the Women: The Intimate Life of D. H. Lawrence. New York: HarperCollins, 1993.

Fenton, James (1949–) *poet, journalist*

James Fenton was born in Lincoln in eastern England to Mary Hamilton Ingoldby Fenton and John Charles Fenton, an Anglican priest and theologian. He attended both public and private schools, eventually earning his degree from Oxford in 1970. Immediately upon graduation, he began a career in journalism, writing for the *New Statesman*. Initially he wrote literary criticism, but he later shifted to politics. His work took him to both Germany and Indochina, where he served as a foreign correspondent and found a wealth of material for his poetry.

Fenton's interest in poetry began in school when he discovered W. H. AUDEN's poetry. Auden's poetry—highly technical, formalistic (using defined poetic forms like sonnets and haikus), and often political—appealed to the young Fenton. Auden's influence is nowhere more evident than in Fenton's first collection of poems, *Our Western Furniture* (1968). Written specifically for Oxford's Newdigate undergraduate poetry contest (which he won), this sonnet sequence explores the meeting of American and Japanese cultures in the 19th century when America was expanding and Japan was emerging from centuries of isolation.

While *Our Western Furniture* displayed Fenton's promise as a young poet, the work on which his reputation stands grew out of the time he spent abroad. Inspired by his time in Germany, "A German Requiem" (1981) is an elegy both for the German Jews who died in World War II and for the survivors of the war who struggle daily with their memories of the past, trying to forget the horrors they saw and selectively omitting them from the stories they tell. In lines that capture the essence of this poem, Fenton writes, "It is not your memories that haunt you. . . . It is what you have forgotten, what you must forget."

When Fenton wrote about his experiences in Indochina in *The Memory of War* (1982), he found widespread popular and critical acclaim. As is typical with most of Fenton's work, the poems of this collection deal with war and politics in highly structured verse. In "Cambodia," for instance, Fenton discusses war's senselessness in 10 rhymed couplets: "One man shall wake from terror to his bed / Five men shall be dead." The ironic tone imparted by the rhyming couplets describing death in "Cambodia" reappears even more intensely in "Dead Soldiers." In this poem Fenton recounts, in a stark and straightforward style, a disgustingly decadent lunch of frog legs and wine that he had with the military leader of Cambodia on a site overlooking an active battlefield. As the leader describes empty wine bottles as "dead soldiers," it becomes evident that his strange position in the civil war is impossible for the West to understand. Of this war, the West's expectations "were always wrong," Fenton writes, "It was a family war."

Although Fenton has not been a prolific writer, his work has always been of the highest quality and has consistently earned him comparisons to Auden and William Butler YEATS. According to the critic Julian SYMONS, "Fenton's work, ironic, elegant, aware of yet always a little detached from the suffering it deals with, is the truest social poetry of our time."

Other Works by James Fenton

Children in Exile: Poems, 1968–1984. New York: Noonday Press, 1994.
Out of Danger. New York: Penguin, 1993.
The Strength of Poetry. New York: Farrar, Straus & Giroux, 2001.

Finlay, Ian Hamilton (1925–) *poet, artist, short story writer, playwright*

Born in Nassau, the Bahamas, to James and Annie Whitlaw Finlay, Ian Finlay attended school in Scotland until age 13. When World War II broke out, he evacuated to Scotland's Orkney Islands, where he studied philosophy and worked as a shepherd. After briefly attending Glasgow School of Art, he wrote short stories and plays, some of which were broadcast by the BBC (British Broadcasting Corporation).

Finlay's first book of poetry, *The Dancers Inherit the Party* (1960), contains short, rhyming poems about love, the Orkneys, and other subjects: "The hollowness is amazing. That's the way a boat floats" ("Orkney Lyrics 2, The English Colonel Explains an Orkney Boat"). Through the Wild Hawthorn Press, which he founded in 1961, and *Poor. Old. Tired. Horse. (P.O.T.H.)*, a magazine he edited from 1961 to 1968, Finlay published much of his experimental typographical work. He soon emerged as Britain's foremost writer of concrete poetry (in which the arrangement of the words on the page contributes to the meaning) with *Rapel: Ten Fauve and Suprematist Poems* (1963).

Finlay wrote "Star/steer" (1966)—which repeats the word "star" in a curved line from top to bottom, ending in the single word "steer"—on both paper and slate. He cast other "poem-objects" in such materials as wood and even neon lights, as in "Windflower" (1976). "Wave/rock" (1966) was the first poem ever made from sandblasted glass.

Through his work, Finlay explores both wild and cultivated nature as well as themes of war and conflict. "View to a Temple" (1987), one of his open-air installations (multimedia, multidimensional works created temporarily for an indoor or outdoor space), frames a view of a classical temple through an avenue of guillotines, a reference to the French Revolution. Evidence of Finlay's interest in both nature and classical antiquity is seen at Stonypath (also known as "Little Sparta"), an allegorical garden that he and his wife, Sue, began creating in 1967 at their farmhouse in Dunsyre, Scotland. At Stonypath, Finlay sets his inscribed slabs (including one containing the single word "cloud" and another the monogram of the artist Albrecht Dürer, in a setting reminiscent of one of his paintings), benches, fountains, and sundials among trees, water, plants, and flowers. He also has sundials at Canterbury, the University of Kent, and Edinburgh's Royal Botanic Garden.

Finlay has exhibited at the National Maritime Museum at Greenwich, the Max Planck Institute (Stuttgart), and the Scottish National Gallery of Modern Art, winning awards from the Scottish Arts Council bursary (1966–68). In 1990 he installed an inscription from Plato's *Republic* on Glasgow's Bridge Piers (stone blocks that once supported a highway). A fellow author writes, "In Finlay's work, meaning is ultimately dependent upon context. His art explores the limits of what can be said, and it returns us to the daily act of re-creating or re-composing our 'mode of being.'"

A Work about Ian Finlay

Finlay, Alec, ed. *Wood Notes Wild: Essays on the Poetry and Art of Ian Hamilton Finlay.* Edinburgh: Polygon, 1995.

Firbank, Ronald (1886–1926) *novelist*

Ronald Firbank was born in London to Joseph Thomas and Jane Harriette Firbank. His parents were a wealthy couple living off the inherited earnings of Firbank's grandfather, a railway contractor who had amassed a small fortune. Little is known about Firbank's early life other than that he suffered from poor health and was educated almost entirely by tutors. He did spend several years at Cambridge, but the painfully shy and effeminate young man succeeded only in establishing himself as an eccentric. He never received a degree and spent most of his time writing his first major novels.

Firbank's books prepared the way for those of James JOYCE, Virginia WOOLF, and D. H. LAWRENCE. His novel *Vainglory* (1915)—the story of Mrs. Shamefoot, who tries to memorialize herself by having a window in a cathedral dedicated to her—anticipates the rise of modernism with its minimal plot and its fragmented and circular narrative. Firbank followed *Vainglory* with *Inclinations* (1916), a story riddled with suggestions of homosexuality, about two single British women traveling through Greece.

Caprice (1917), a more plot-driven novel, tells the story of a young woman, Sarah Sinquier, who steals her family's silver and runs away from a small town to London in hope of becoming an actress. Selling the silver, she finances a production of *Romeo and Juliet*. The play propels Sarah into stardom, but at the novel's end she dies when she falls from the stage.

Valmouth (1918) is set in an imaginary health spa and filled with elderly characters. This novel contains hardly any action; instead, it is filled with the conversations of an extremely large cast of characters. Dialogue was Firbank's forte. At one point in *Valmouth* he assembles a roomful of characters, whose snippets of speech form a collage. It is as though the reader is standing in the middle of the crowded room and hearing fragments of a dozen different conversations.

Valmouth earned Firbank more critical acclaim than any of his previous work. It is rivaled in its success only by *Sorrow in Sunlight* (1924; published as *The Prancing Nigger* in the United States). This latter novel centers on a West Indian family, the Mouths, who move from their small village to a city in hopes of entering their island's elite social circles. As it turns out, the move to the city is a journey into a world of vice, a place, as the scholar James Merritt notes, where "'Sin' is the major pastime of its inhabitants." The stereotypical "sinfulness" and descriptions of the novel's black characters often turn them into caricatures. Nonetheless, Firbank shows a keen interest in Afro-West Indians and their culture:

[T]he Cunans [the novel's islanders], in their elegant equipages, made, for anyone fresh from the provinces, an interesting and absorbing sight. The liquid-eyed loveliness of the women and the handsomeness of the men, with their black moustaches and their treacherous smiles—these, indeed, were things to gaze on.

During his lifetime Firbank received neither widespread popular appeal nor overwhelming critical praise. Many scholars consider him important only for his paving the way through his narrative experimentation for the next generation of British authors. Merritt, however, disagrees, arguing that "Firbank is a classic, a writer whose chief works are of genuine literary excellence" and whose writing "offers to the reader a constantly diverting view of humanity unlike that offered by any other novelist."

Other Works by Ronald Firbank

Firbankiana: Being a Collection of Reminiscences of Ronald Firbank. New York: Hanuman Books, 1989.
Five Novels. Norfolk, Va.: New Directions, 1989.
Santal. 1921. Reprint, Los Angeles: Sun and Moon, 1995.
3 More Novels. New York: W. W. Norton, 1986.

Works about Ronald Firbank

Brophy, Brigid. *Prancing Novelist: A Defense of Fiction in the Form of a Critical Biography in Praise of Ronald Firbank.* New York: Barnes and Noble, 1973.
Merritt, James Douglas. *Ronald Firbank.* Boston: Twayne, 1969.

Fisher, Roy (1930–) *poet*

Roy Fisher was born in Birmingham, England, to Walter Fisher, a jewelry maker, and Emma Jones Fisher. He attended Wattville Road Elementary School, Handsworth Grammar School, and Birmingham University. After receiving his degree in English, Fisher taught at Dudley College of Education and Bordesley College. He was also a senior lecturer in American Studies at Keele University.

Fisher started writing poetry as a teenager and published his first book, *City*, a collage of poetry and prose, in 1961. Evoking a strong sense of place, his poems describe moments, environments, landscapes, and human lives in an industrial city. The title poem, which appears in revised form in *Collected Poems 1968*, is his best-known work. Fisher describes urban desolation in this poem, which intersperses verse with passages of prose: "The city is asleep. In it there are shadows that are sulphorous, tanks of black bile. The glitter on the roadways is the deceptive ore that shines in coal."

Fisher solidified his reputation as one of the few British masters of prose poetry with *Metamorphoses* (1970), a collection about the unforeseen outcomes of change. His verse most often explores natural occurrences of the world through clear, vivid descriptions. He makes his images memorable by taking real things and making them strange. In "As He Came Near Death" he writes, "Then the hole: this was a slot punched in a square / of plastic grass rug, a slot lined with the white polythene, floored with dyed green gravel."

Fisher published several volumes of verse in the 1960s and 1970s, but because only small presses would handle his early collections, he received limited critical attention before the 1980s. When Oxford University Press published *Poems 1955–1980* (1980), he emerged from obscurity to gain recognition as one of Britain's most original poets. He won the Cholmondeley Award for Poetry the following year.

Fisher's emphasis on sensory details in his poems consistently wins praise from critics. David Zaiss writes that his poems "speak to an awareness; their dark heat raises an ordinary moment in the mind, so that the images almost crunch." Poet and critic Andrew MOTION notes that Fisher's poems "make the act of seeing itself dramatic. Throughout his career he has tried to create an absolutely authentic realism, consistently addressing himself to the world with a latter-day kind of wise passiveness."

Other Works by Roy Fisher

Consolidated Comedies. Heaton, England: Pig Press, 1981.

The Half-Year Letters. Guildford, Surrey, England: Circle Press, 1983.

Fitzgerald, Penelope (1916–2000) *novelist, biographer*

Penelope Mary Fitzgerald was born in Lincoln, England, the daughter of Edmund Valpy Knox, the editor of *Punch*, and Christine Hicks Knox, a moderate suffragette. Educated at Oxford, she subsequently worked as a programmer for BBC (British Broadcasting Corporation), a journalist, a bookshop owner, and a tutor.

Fitzgerald came to writing late: She was 59 when she published her first book, a biography of the Victorian painter Edward Burne-Jones; and 61 when the first of her nine novels, *The Golden Child* (1977), was published. Fitzgerald's fiction is remarkable for its compression and imaginative empathy. She referred to her novels as "microchips." Asked to cut the length of her first work, she made this her standard practice, thus achieving remarkable concision.

Most of Fitzgerald's novels reflect periods of her life when she was engaged in specific activities. For instance, *The Golden Child* (1977) was inspired by a visit to the Tutankhamen exhibition at the British Museum in the winter of 1971–72. This novel, a thriller set in a claustrophobic museum, follows Waring Smith, a junior museum functionary, as he discovers that his world is run by fakes. The first of several Fitzgerald excursions into self-enclosed worlds with special rituals and ways of thinking, here she captures the stifling atmosphere and arch rivalries of the art world and of museum politics and administration. Scholar Catherine Cole sees *The Golden Child* as questioning "value, power, and authority" and demonstrating "the secrecy of their operation."

Out of Fitzgerald's experience as a bookstore owner came *The Bookshop* (1978), set in an East Anglian coastal town that is stagnating socially, economically, and politically. Florence Green's well-meaning efforts to transform the dilapidated Old House into a flourishing bookshop are thwarted by local interests. Green's decision to stock Nabokov's *Lolita* is the last straw: She is evicted from the Old House and from staid and stuffy Hardborough.

Fitzgerald's *Offshore* (1979) won the BOOKER PRIZE. It draws on the years when the author and her family lived on a Thames houseboat, and is both comic and sad. The critic R. E. Hosmer sees it as depicting a kind of "utopian community of houseboat dwellers" living on the tidal Thames around Battersea Reach. In the space of fewer than 150 pages, the author presents a miniature world whose inhabitants spend half their lives mired in mud, the rest drifting on water. In *Offshore*, Catherine Cole notes, "a precisely evoked world is perfectly matched with the apparent inconclusiveness, the hesitancies and reticences, the ebb and flow of the book's construction."

Another novel presenting a miniature world and resembling a controlled experiment is *Human Voices* (1980), which takes place at Broadcasting House, the London headquarters of the BBC, from May through September 1940. France has fallen; Britain awaits invasion, and London is being heavily bombed. In this novel, style is content, for it is a work seriocomically concerned with communication, with what people say and how they say it—and also with what they do not say. The novel's staple is dialogue. In her observation that the BBC prefers truth to consolation, the author comments on her own candid art.

Critics have remarked on Fitzgerald's rare gift for portraying the very young and very old. This is in evidence among the elderly eccentrics and knowing children of *At Freddie's* (1982), which features the

Temple School that trains child actors for the London stage. The novel draws on the author's experiences at the Italia Conti School. On the other hand, *Innocence* (1986), set in Florence in the 1950s, seems to be an excursion into imagination. This love story between the Ridolfis, a family descended from Renaissance midgets, and the Rossis, former peasants, has an allegorical air and somewhat resembles E. M. FORSTER's Italian novels. Fitzgerald was fascinated by the concept of innocence.

Fitzgerald's biographies are remarkable for the way they capture their subjects' milieus and times. Similarly, her historical novels—*The Beginning of Spring* (1988), *The Gate of Angels* (1990), and *The Blue Flower* (1955)—show thorough research and imaginative penetration. Pre-revolutionary Russia comes vividly to life in the first of these, pre-World War I Cambridge in the second, and the life of a late 18th-century German principality is recreated in the third, as in this description of the protagonist's homeland in *The Blue Flower*:

> His life was lived in the "golden hollow" in the Holy Roman Empire, bounded by the Harz Mountains and the deep forest, crossed by rivers . . . proceeding in gracious though seemingly unnecessary bends and sweeps past mine-workings, salt-houses, timber mills, waterside inns. . . . Scores of miles of rolling country bringing forth potatoes and turnips and . . . cabbages . . .

The Blue Flower is the story of poet-philosopher Novalis's love for 12-year-old Sophie Kühn. It won the National Book Critics Circle Award.

All in all, Fitzgerald's work demonstrates, as R. E. Hosmer observes, "a keenly intelligent and analytical insight into human thought and behavior, matched to a remarkable and extraordinary sympathy for the foibles and failures of humankind."

Other Works by Penelope Fitzgerald

Edward Burne-Jones. Phoenix Hill, England: Sutton Publishing, 1975, reprinted 1997.
The Knox Brothers. Washington, D.C.: Counterpoint Press, 2000.

A Work about Penelope Fitzgerald

A Reader's Guide to Penelope Fitzgerald. New York: Mariner Books, 1999.

Fleming, Ian (1908–1964) *novelist, children's writer*

Ian Fleming was born in London, the son of Major Valentine Fleming, a Conservative member of Parliament, and Evelyn St. Croix Rose Fleming. He became a journalist and, during World War II, assistant to the director of Royal Naval Intelligence. His intelligence work, particularly in helping the Americans set up the OSS, the forerunner of the CIA, earned him a pistol engraved with the slogan "For Special Services" and provided him with inspiration for his central character, James Bond, secret agent 007 of the British Secret Service. As critic Tony Buchsbaum notes, the fanciful character Fleming created while on a romantic getaway in Jamaica "would become the most successful action hero of all time," due largely to the film series based on the books.

Bond, first seen in *Casino Royale* (1953), is witty, emotionally detached, and skilled at everything from killing enemy agents to romancing the numerous women who pass briefly through the novels. Bond is more prone to political reflection and moral doubts in *Casino Royale* than is his on-screen incarnation. Noting the excesses of his own government at the conclusion of this first mission, Bond remarks that "this country-right-or-wrong business is getting a little out-of-date. . . . If I'd been alive fifty years ago, the brand of Conservatism we have today would have been damn near called Communism and we should have been told to go and fight that."

Fleming's novel *Live and Let Die* (1954) was set in Jamaica, one of many exotic locations to which the author sent Bond and one to which he would return in *Dr. No* (1958). As described in *From Russia with Love* (1957), Bond is handsome but battle-scarred: "It was a dark but clean-cut face, with a three-inch scar showing whitely down the sunburned skin of the right cheek."

From Russia with Love clearly established Bond as a cold war hero fighting communism. However, his best-known enemies were the criminal mastermind Blofeld and the organization SPECTRE, which appeared primarily in the novels *Thunderball* (1961), *On Her Majesty's Secret Service* (1963), and *You Only Live Twice* (1964).

Shortly before his death, Fleming also wrote *Chitty Chitty Bang Bang* (1964), a children's tale about a flying car. It was also adapted for the screen and stage. After Fleming died, the Bond novels were continued by other authors, including Kingsley AMIS, who wrote *Colonel Sun* (1968) as Robert Markham. Historian Jeremy Black, in his book *The Politics of James Bond,* notes that Bond may be "the most famous Briton of the twentieth century" and concludes that the "Fleming novels are not great literature. . . . Yet the very success of the novels as adventure stories suggests a degree of potency that is worth probing."

Other Works by Ian Fleming

Diamonds Are Forever. New York: Berkley, 1956.
Goldfinger. New York: Fine Communications, 1959.
The Man with the Golden Gun. New York: Signet, 1965.

Works about Ian Fleming

Lycett, Andrew. *Ian Fleming: The Man Behind James Bond*. Atlanta: Turner Publishing, 1995.
Rosenberg, Bruce A., and Ann Harleman Stewart. *Ian Fleming*. Boston: Twayne Publishers, 1989.

Flying Officer X

See BATES, H. E.

Ford, Ford Madox (Ford Hermann Madox Hueffer) (1873–1939) *novelist, fairy tale writer, poet, editor, nonfiction writer*

Ford Madox Ford was born in Merton, Surrey, to Francis Hueffer, the art editor of the *London Times,* and Catherine Madox Hueffer, an artist. He was christened Ford Hermann Madox Hueffer but

changed his name to Ford Madox Ford in 1919. He was educated in private schools and, throughout his youth, felt intellectually insecure around his rather intimidating parents and their friends. He did not receive a university education.

Ford distinguished himself as an editor, a nonfiction writer, a poet, and, most notably, a novelist. In 1908 he founded the journal *English Review,* which published the work of prominent authors like Thomas Hardy, H. G. WELLS, and John GALSWORTHY. In 1924 Ford also started the journal *Transatlantic Review,* which published an even more impressive list of authors, including D. H. LAWRENCE and James JOYCE.

The early years of Ford's career were marked by his close friendship with the novelist Joseph CONRAD, with whom he collaborated on several largely unsuccessful, jointly written novels. These included *Romance* (1903), about a young British man traveling in the Caribbean. Out of his relationship with Conrad, however, Ford developed a theory of the novel that demanded, in particular, clearly drawn characters and a detached narrator.

Ford began his writing career with several books of fairy tales; a book of poetry; some works of nonfiction; *Poems for Pictures and for Notes of Music* (1900), illustrated by his grandfather; and *The Fifth Queen* trilogy, three novels about the life of Katharine Howard, the fifth wife of Henry VIII. The scholar Charles G. Hoffman credits the trilogy with saving "Katharine Howard from the obscurity of history." Nevertheless, success eluded Ford until the publication of *The Good Soldier: A Tale of Passion* (1915), which is regarded as his greatest achievement. In this novel, an American named John Dowell narrates the story of his life as he attempts to fit the disjointed pieces of his memory together like the pieces of a puzzle. Much of the story centers on an affair that Dowell's wife, Florence, had with his friend, Edward Ashburnham, a former British soldier with whom Dowell seems strangely infatuated himself. The most remarkable element of the novel is Dowell, in whom Ford finally achieves the type of powerful, detached narrator that he envisioned with Conrad. Dowell's narration, ironically, utterly lacks any of the passion suggested in the book's subtitle. Even in the description of his wife's suicide the voice seems neither horrified nor sad. He simply relates the event matter-of-factly: "She drank a little phial of prussic acid and there she lay—O, extremely charming and clearcut—looking with a puzzled expression at the electric light bulb. . . . Anyhow there was the end of Florence." This method of narration drew high praise from the critic Rebecca WEST, who felt that Ford's technique of "presenting the story not as it appeared to a divine and omnipresent intelligence, but as it was observed by some intervener not too intimately concerned in the plot" was more successful than Conrad's attempts at the same goal.

The *Parade's End* tetralogy consists of *Some Do Not* (1924), *No More Parades* (1925), *A Man Could Stand Up* (1926), and *The Last Post* (1928). The four novels tell the story of Christopher Tietjens, born into the upper class that initially represents all of the traditional values of pre–World War I Britain. Tietjens first engages in a personal psychological war with his wife before becoming involved in the actual trench warfare of World War I. At the end of the tetralogy, in Ford's words "weary to death—of the Office, of the nation, of the world and people . . . and of the streets," Tietjens rejects the dominant, commercial culture and moves to a subsistence farm with a new wife. According to the scholar Frank MacShane, "Parade's End is "a panoramic work covering many levels of society . . . [and] shows that it is necessary to abandon social forms and privilege to preserve the old values that gave England its character."

Because of his contributions to the literary world as an editor and the quality of his novels, Ford Madox Ford is still highly regarded. According to the scholar Richard Peterson, "Ford is now generally perceived as a legitimate member of an exclusive company of artists who shaped modern literature because of their belief in the autonomy of the artist and the primacy of literature in defining the values of civilization."

Other Works by Ford Madox Ford

Antwerp. 1914. Reprint, Murrieta, Calif.: Classic, 2001.

England and the English. 1907. Reprint, Murrieta, Calif.: Classic, 2001.

The Portrait. 1910. Reprint, Murrieta, Calif.: Classic, 2001.

Works about Ford Madox Ford

Bender, Todd K. *Literary Impressionism in Jean Rhys, Ford Madox Ford, Joseph Conrad and Charlotte Brontë.* New York: Garland, 1997.

Saunders, Max. *Ford Madox Ford: A Dual Life.* New York: Oxford University Press, 1996.

Forester, Cecil Scott (1899–1966) *novelist, screenwriter, short story writer, historian*

C. S. Forester was born Cecil Lewis Troughton Smith to George Smith, an English teacher, and Sarah Troughton Smith in Cairo. He spent most of his childhood in England, and by the time he was seven he had formed his lifetime habit of reading at least one book a day. Although he enrolled in medical school, the "pure, barbaric yearning to tell a story" prompted him to begin writing under the pen name C. S. Forester.

In 1920 Forester wrote his first novel in a two-week burst of inspiration. After its rejection by several publishers, he took a more disciplined approach to writing. The success of *Payment Deferred* (1926), a crime novel which mystery critic Martin Edwards calls "his masterpiece of suspense," enabled him to marry Kathleen Belcher. In the 1930s Forester wrote Hollywood film scripts and served as a foreign correspondent, covering the Nazi occupation of Czechoslovakia. Eventually he moved to Berkeley, California.

Among Forester's best-known works is *The African Queen* (1935), a romantic adventure on which director John Huston based his classic 1951 film about a proper English missionary and a rough engineer who resist the Germans during World War I. Besides novels, Forester also wrote short stories and histories, such as the biography

Josephine, Napoleon's Empress (1935) and *The Age of Fighting Sail: The Story of the Naval War of 1812* (1956).

Forester's most enduring creation is Captain Horatio Hornblower, introduced in *Beat to Quarters* (1937) as a naval genius who fights for England during the Napoleonic Wars. The 10 books of the Hornblower saga, which follow his career from midshipman to Admiral of the West Indies, sold over 8 million copies. Reviewer Sanford Sternlicht attributes the popularity of these romantic historical novels to Hornblower's stature as "the prototype British hero" of his age. "Hornblower leads men.... He causes them to see and do their duty." Former U.S. Secretary of Defense Caspar Weinberger, who praises "the excitement, the scrupulously accurate backgrounds and authenticity of technical detail" in the saga, says, "Forester to a superlative degree has the ability to convey the spray, the color, the wind, and the men molded by the sea."

Other Works by C. S. Forester

The Good Shepherd. 1955. Reprint, New York: Simon & Schuster, 2001.

The Hornblower Companion. Annapolis, Md.: Naval Institute Press, 1999.

A Work about C. S. Forester

Sternlicht, Sanford V. *C. S. Forester and the Hornblower Saga.* Syracuse, N.Y.: Syracuse University Press, 1999.

Forster, Edward Morgan (1879–1970)

novelist, short story writer, essayist, nonfiction writer

E. M. Forster was born in Marylebone, London, England, the son of an architect of the same name who died while his son was a baby. An only child, Forster grew up surrounded by a bevy of imposing women. He lived with his mother, Alice (Lily) Clara Whichelo, until she died in 1945 at age 90. His great-aunt Marianne Thornton, a member of the evangelical, philanthropic Clapham Sect, was the subject of a Forster biography.

Forster was educated at Tonbridge School and at a school in Eastbourne, both of which he loathed. His years at Cambridge University (1897–1901) were idyllic. There he read classics and history; was tutored by Goldworthy Lowes Dickinson, subject of another biography; and absorbed the philosophy of G. E. Moore, which exalted the pleasures of human relationships and the enjoyment of beautiful objects. At Cambridge Forster realized he was homosexual, but he kept this secret for some years.

Most of Forster's life was lived in Hertfordshire, Kent, and Surrey, whose stifling lifestyle he satirized in his early fiction. A legacy from his great-aunt enabled him to travel to Italy and Greece, and travel inspired him to write. The sense of place is strongly developed in Forster; his discovery of the beauty and animation of classic Mediterranean lands liberated his imagination, inspiring novels and short stories. Virtually all of Forster's fiction hinges on contrasting places, manners, and ways of life.

During World War I Forster worked in Alexandria as a volunteer with the Red Cross. Out of this Egyptian experience emerged two books: *Alexandria: A History and a Guide* (1922) and *Pharos and Pharillon* (1923). He also traveled to India three times between 1912 and 1945. From his first two journeys came the travel book *The Hill of Devi* (1953) and the last novel published in his lifetime, *A Passage to India* (1924).

For the remaining 46 years of his life, Forster wrote nonfiction, including his *Aspects of the Novel* (1927). Other literary essays are collected in *Abinger Harvest* (1936) and political ones in *Two Cheers for Democracy* (1951). A liberal humanist, Forster became popular as a broadcaster during World War II. During the final quarter-century of his life, he was invited by King's College to live there as an honorary resident. Refusing a knighthood, he was made a Companion of Honour in 1953 and in 1969 was awarded the Order of Merit. His novel *Maurice,* which addressed homosexual themes, was published posthumously in 1972.

Critical Analysis

If not given to stylistic experiment, Forster is still an original novelist with unusual gifts. He fuses social realism with psychological insight and larger-than-life symbolism, and he has a dry wit and quirky temperament. Scholar John Colmer regards him—together with D. H. LAWRENCE—as "one of the two most original [English] novelists of the first half of this century." As the critic Frederick P. W. MacDowell says, "All of his novels have become classics, and the word Forsterian can alone describe their rich mixture of comedy and poetry, and their luminous . . . style."

Forster began by writing domestic comedies of manners resembling Jane Austen's, but with, as Colmer puts it, "a malicious dash of Samuel Butler" added. While completing *A Passage to India,* he fell under the spell of French novelist Marcel Proust. Forster also had a mystic strain. As scholar Philip Gardner observes, his fiction "moves easily from the realistic into the symbolic or mystical."

Before turning to novels, Forster wrote short stories. These are mostly classical and pantheistic, full of fantasy and the supernatural; they turn on moments of revelation and liberation, or the reverse. A handful are memorable: "The Story of a Panic" (1904), "The Road to Colonus" (1904), and "The Machine Stops" (1909). Forster's stories are collected in *The Celestial Omnibus and Other Stories* (1911), *The Eternal Moment and Other Stories* (1947), and *The Life to Come and Other Stories* (1972).

Forster's novels, by contrast, are realistic, but with melodramatic plots containing considerable contrivance, including frequent sudden, unprepared-for deaths (as many as five in *The Longest Journey*). Forster's first published and first written novels, *Where Angels Fear to Tread* (1905) and *A Room with a View* (1908), both take English travelers to Italy, contrasting the repressed, stuffy, and "proper" manners of English middle-class visitors with Italian naturalness, spontaneity, and vitality. A story of young love triumphing, *A Room with a View* is simpler and lighter-hearted than *Where Angels Fear to Tread,* which involves the kidnap-ping of a baby who is killed when thrown out of a carriage. The latter novel's open ending leaves its principal characters, Philip Herriton and Caroline Abbott, sadder but wiser, largely because, after experiencing Monteriano and Italy, they transcend homegrown Sawston values.

Forster's own favorite among his works was *The Longest Journey* (1907), which he called the book "I was most glad to have written," because it came closest to "saying what I wanted." Both *The Longest Journey* and *Howards End* (1910) take place entirely in England and are quintessentially English; indeed, they are about who shall inherit that country.

Each of *The Longest Journey*'s three parts—"Cambridge," "Sawston," and "Wiltshire"—is presided over by a character or characters: Cambridge by Stuart Ansell, Sawston by Herbert and Agnes Pembroke, and Wiltshire by Stephen Wonham. Rickie Elliot is the central character who links the others. He is an idealist not wholly comfortable with the values by which the others live: Ansell values intellect; Stephen Wonham, instinct; and the Pembrokes, materialism. In his efforts to bridge the radically different worlds of the other characters, Rickie is torn apart; he loses his life trying to save his half-brother, Wonham.

Howards End is more integrated and finished than its predecessor, though it too contains melodramatic elements. Here Forster sets in conflict and reconciles two social classes and ways of life. The Schlegels represent the upper-middle-class life of culture and values, while the Wilcoxes stand for the business or imperial class, inhabiting a world of what Forster calls "telegrams and anger." The means of reconciling the two classes is the marriage of Henry Wilcox to Margaret Schlegel, an attempt to harmonize the external with the internal, or the prose with the passion of existence, through love. Finally, the house Howards End, which the first Mrs. Wilcox bequeaths to Margaret, but which the Wilcox family seek to prevent her from inheriting, becomes a home to her and her sister, and to the child Helen has conceived by lower-class Leonard Bast.

Forster's masterpiece, *A Passage to India* (1924), shows a growth in subtlety and complexity. As in *Where Angels Fear to Tread,* two English people—here the youthful Adela Quested and the elderly Mrs. Moore—travel to a foreign land, India, to prepare for Adela's marriage to Ronny Heaslop, Mrs. Moore's son. In Chandrapore, they meet Cyril Fielding, English principal of Government College, and his Muslim friend Aziz. The impulsive Aziz enthusiastically invites the ladies to visit the "extraordinary" Marabar Caves a short distance away. This proves a fateful expedition: Shortly afterward, Mrs. Moore dies, her previously ardent Christian faith undermined, and Adela accuses Aziz of assaulting and trying to rape her. Although Adela later retracts her charge at Aziz's trial, it is too late: Aziz's life and career are ruined. Fielding's standing in the Anglo-Indian community is also jeopardized because he crossed racial lines to champion Aziz.

Interactions among the major characters are skillfully presented. Thus, Fielding and Aziz are initially drawn to each other through intelligence, goodwill, and mutual respect, while Aziz and Mrs. Moore bond instantly through their instinctual natures. Adela and Fielding, both rationalists lacking the spiritual dimension Mrs. Moore and Aziz possess, merely like each other. However, huge obstacles erected by time and space, race, caste, class, and creed block satisfactory personal relationships in this work.

The novel's title alludes to 19th-century American Walt Whitman's poem "Passage to India." Forster skeptically views Whitman's buoyant optimism calling for "the earth to be spann'd, connected by network, / The races, neighbors, to marry, and be given in marriage," and the soul's passage to union with God. Like other Forster novels, *A Passage to India* embodies a dual vision, presenting physical and social relations within a metaphysical or spiritual context. No other work exemplifies as well Forster's brilliant use of literary leitmotivs or repeated images accompanying specific people, places, events, or ideas, or of what he calls in his *Aspects of the Novel* (1927) pattern and rhythm. Just one example out of many is the echo that haunts the Marabar Caves. (Forster was knowledgeable about music and habitually used rhythmic and musical techniques in his writing.)

A Passage to India is also visually compelling with its panoramic geographical and geological sweep and its vistas down the ages. Like *The Longest Journey, A Passage to India* is tripartite in structure. The architectural and geologic motifs of mosque, caves, and temple symbolize the three principal faiths of India: Islam, Christianity, and Hinduism. Islam is evoked through recurrent images of arches receding into infinity. The caves embody the hollow Christianity practiced by Anglo-Indians. These caves, Forster determined, were "to engender an event like an egg" and breed panic and emptiness. The final redemptive Hindu festival of Gokul Ashtami is represented by the Hindu temple or world-mountain.

The action of *A Passage* also follows the seasonal cycle, opening during the cool season, coming to a climax during summer, and ending with the monsoon. The first part of the narrative comprises principally exposition; the second, the catastrophe; while the third offers an open ending. Since Forster believed less and less in closed endings, he offers here an ending that opens on infinity.

Works about E. M. Forster

Beauman, Nicola. *E. M. Forster: A Biography.* New York: Alfred A. Knopf, 1994.
Furbank, P. N. *E. M. Forster: A Life.* New York: Harcourt Brace Jovanovich, 1981.
Lago, Mary. *E. M. Forster: A Literary Life.* New York: St. Martin's Press, 1995.
Stone, Wilfred. *The Cave and the Mountain: A Study of E. M. Forster.* New York: Oxford University Press, 1966.

Fowles, John Robert (1926–) *novelist, short story writer, essayist*

John Fowles was born in the town of Leigh-on-Sea in Essex, England. His family life was suburban and conventional, and Fowles said later that he has tried to escape his childhood environment ever since. He was educated at Bedford School, a boarding school, and then briefly attended Edinburgh University.

Fowles studied French at Oxford, graduating in 1950. While there he became enthusiastic about the philosophies of French existentialists like Sartre and Camus. His hatred of conventionality meshed neatly with their views.

Fowles is known for his psychologically fraught novels. His first published novel was *The Collector* (1963), which describes a deranged butterfly collector who acquires a different ambition. In a desperate attempt to gain love, he kidnaps an art student and keeps her captive in his basement, where he tries to make her fall in love with him. "It was like not having a net and catching a specimen you wanted . . . you had to nip the thorax, and it would be quivering there. It wasn't easy like it was with a killing-bottle." The novel begins with the kidnapper's story of the experience, a frightening blend of affection for her and deranged cruelty. For the second half of the novel, the imprisoned girl tells her story, and her writing is a painful contrast to the kidnapper's psychotic calm: "I'm so sick, so frightened, so alone." The *Observer* praised the novel as "An intriguing study of warped sexuality." It was made into a film in 1965.

Fowles's second novel, *The Magus* (1965), is one of his most famous books. A blend of detective story and existential speculation, it describes an English schoolmaster's stay on a Greek island, where he gradually realizes that the island's strange millionaire is running the schoolmaster's life, his love affair, and the island in such a way as to make him uncertain of everything, even his own identity. *Newsweek* called it "fast and frightening . . . an emotional maelstrom of high intrigue." The novel has acquired cult status and became a film in 1968.

Fowles's third novel was the best-seller *The French Lieutenant's Woman* (1969). Set in Victorian England, the first 12 chapters resemble a classic Victorian novel, introducing the tragic figure of a woman abandoned by her sailor beloved. The novel's structure recalls classic novels of the 19th century in its realistic narrative and its moral digressions. Then Fowles suddenly and shockingly unsettles these conventions by having an authorial narrator interject commentary: "I do not know. This story I am telling is all imagination. . . . So perhaps I am writing a transposed autobiography. . . . Perhaps it is only a game." American writer Joyce Carol Oates described *The French Lieutenant's Woman* as "[a] remarkable original work in which at least two visions operate simultaneously, the one Victorian and melodramatic, the other modern and wise. An outlandish achievement." Haunting and passionate, the novel was extremely popular and became a film in 1981.

In the 1970s Fowles wrote a novella and several short stories. The stories were collected in *The Ebony Tower* (1974). In 1977 he published the long novel *Daniel Martin.* Partly autobiographical, this book describes the life of a Hollywood screenwriter who has begun to feel his work and life are meaningless: "I feel I've become a man driving through nothingness." The novel shifts repeatedly between past and present, and in the course of it Martin comes to realize how his disillusionment stemmed from the choices he made in his student days: "All those mirrors and masks in my room when I was a student. I think they just about summed it up." Reviewer Paul Gray wrote, "Like Henry James before him, Fowles has created rarefied creatures free enough to take on the toughest question that life offers: how to live?"

Fowles has written many nonfiction essays on topics ranging from philosophy to nature, beginning with his collection *The Aristos* (1964) and, most recently, *Wormholes* (1998). He has also written text to accompany photograph books, such as *Lyme Regis Camera* (1990) and *Tree* (1979). He has lived in the south English coastal town of Lyme Regis since 1968, and he became so fascinated with the local history that he spent 10 years being curator of the Lyme Regis Museum.

In 1999 Fowles was nominated for the Nobel Prize in literature. Hundreds of critics have praised his inventive and astonishing writing. The reviewer John Gardner once declared, "Fowles is the only writer in English who has the power, range, knowledge, and wisdom of a Tolstoy or James."

Other Works by John Fowles

Behind the Magus. London: Colophon, 1994.
The Enigma of Stonehenge. Coauthor Barry Brukoff. London: Cape, 1980.
Figures of the Human: Poems. Middletown, Conn.: Wesleyan University Press, 1964.
Islands. Photographs by Fay Godwin. London: Jonathan Cape, 1978.

Works about John Fowles

Acheson, James. *John Fowles.* New York: St. Martin's Press, 1998.
Aubrey, James R. *John Fowles: A Reference Companion.* Westport, Conn.: Greenwood, 1991.

Francis, Dick (1920–) *novelist*

Dick Francis was born in Pembrokeshire, South Wales, into a family that loved horses. On his mother Catherine Thomas Francis's side, his grandfather bred hunters. His father, Vincent Francis, was a jockey and stable manager who encouraged Francis to develop his riding skills. When he was five, his older brother offered him sixpence to jump a donkey over a fence. "In my heart, from that moment, I became a professional horseman," he recalled. After serving as a pilot during World War II, Francis married Mary Margaret Brenchley in 1947 and became a professional steeplechase jockey. Named Champion Jockey in 1954, he retired after a horse he was riding fell at the 1957 Grand National.

Francis began his writing career as racing correspondent for the London *Sunday Express.* At a friend's suggestion, he wrote an autobiography, *The Sport of Queens* (1957). Then, inspired by "the threadbare state of a carpet and a rattle in my car," he decided to try his hand at a mystery novel. *Dead Cert* (1962), in which a steeplechase jockey investigates the accident that killed his best friend, was an immediate success, and Francis began turning out a novel a year.

Typically, each Francis book features a new hero who is involved with horses or racing. "I usually have a main character who has to fight his way out of tight corners and this main character is learning things all along," he notes. Because each book has a subplot related to the hero's special interest, Francis and his wife Mary spend months researching such topics as flying, photography, and collectible toys. Francis recently acknowledged that his wife has contributed to the writing of the books.

Francis was named a Grand Master by the Mystery Writers of America in 1996. That same year he received the Best Novel award for *Come to Grief* (1995), in which ex-jockey Sid Halley investigates what drives a man to mutilate race horses. *For Kicks* (1965) and *Whip Hand* (1980) received awards from the Crime Writers Association.

While some critics consider Francis's books formulaic, most agree with critic Philip Pelham that "Francis improves with every book as both a writer of brisk, lucid prose and as a concocter of ingenious and intricately worked-out plots." Scholar Rachel Schaffer notes that "he has made lasting contributions to the hard-boiled mystery genre, expanding the formula to highlight the racing world and develop his own vision of what it means to be a moral man in an often corrupt world."

Other Works by Dick Francis

Shattered. New York: Jove, 2001.
Trial Run. New York: Putnam, 2000.

A Work about Dick Francis

Davis, J. Madison. *Dick Francis.* New York: Twayne, 1985.

Fraser, Lady Antonia (1932–)
biographer, novelist

Lady Antonia Fraser was born Antonia Pakenham in London into a family of distinguished writers known as the "Literary Longfords." Her father, Francis Aungier Pakenham, was the seventh earl of Longford. Her mother Elizabeth, also a writer, recalls her firstborn as a "wonder child" who "always wrote, even before she could write—poems, little stories." Fraser also enjoyed competitive sports, playing tennis and joining the soccer team at a boys' school.

Shortly after graduating from Oxford, Fraser published a children's book on King Arthur. She continued to write after marrying Hugh Fraser, a politician with whom she had six children. After a much publicized divorce, Fraser married playwright Harold PINTER in 1980.

Fraser works in broadcasting, having produced scripts for radio and television and having been a regular panelist on several BBC radio quiz shows, including *My Word!* A political activist, she works to free writers imprisoned for their political beliefs.

Fraser's reputation as a biographer was established with *Mary, Queen of Scots* (1969), a lively, carefully researched study that won the James Tait Black Memorial Prize. *The Weaker Vessel* (1984), a vivid portrait of women's varied roles in 17th-century England, won the 1984 Woltzer Prize for history and the 1985 Prix Caumont-La Force.

Fraser began writing mysteries because "there was something in myself that history didn't express." *Quiet as a Nun* (1977) introduced Jemima Shore, a glamorous, independent detective. As Fraser explains, Shore solves crimes "just because the public had got used to seeing her on the telly as 'Jemima Shore, Investigator,' probing juvenile delinquency, housing shortages, women's rights," and other issues. According to critic Anne Tolstoi Wallach, Fraser "writes both history and mystery with zest and verve, and her primary interest is people—foolish queens, military commanders, former wives," all brought to vivid life by Fraser's engaging narrative style.

Other Works by Antonia Fraser

Marie Antoinette: The Journey. New York: Doubleday, 2001.
Political Death. New York: Bantam, 1996.
The Warrior Queens. New York: Vintage, 1988.
The Wives of Henry VIII. New York: Alfred A. Knopf, 1992.

Fraser, George MacDonald (1926–)
novelist, screenwriter, memoirist

George MacDonald Fraser was born in Carlisle, England, near the Scottish border, to Dr. William and Anne Struth Donaldson Fraser. Reading Raphael SABATINI made him realize that history was "an unending adventure story that far outstripped fiction." He left Glasgow Academy at 18 to enlist in the Army. After World War II he became a reporter on the Carlisle paper, which taught him to "write tight and fast." Eventually he became deputy editor of the *Glasgow Herald*.

In 1966, Fraser says, "I suddenly decided I would write a Victorian adventure story and I sat down and wrote it in 90 hours, just two hours a night steadily when I came home from work." His inspiration was Harry Flashman, the school bully in Thomas Hughes's *Tom Brown's Schooldays* (1857), who is expelled from Rugby for drunkenness. *Flashman* (1969) pretends to be a volume in Flashman's memoirs, which deals with Harry's adventures on a British expedition to Afghanistan. According to the introductory note, the ex-bully eventually rises to eminence as General Sir Harry Paget Flashman VC, KCB, KCIE. The author describes his antihero as "an unrepentant old cad," whose only redeeming qualities are his "humour and shameless honesty as a memorialist." Flashman's career, detailed in several novels, spans many of the most significant events of the Victorian era, including the Afghan War and Custer's Last Stand. Fraser captures the history and language of the period so well that some American reviewers were fooled into believing that Flashman's first adventure was nonfiction.

While best known for the Flashman series, Fraser has also written several successful screenplays, including *The Three Musketeers* (1973), an adaptation of his novel *Royal Flash* (1975), and the James Bond film *Octopussy* (1983). The novel *Black Ajax* (1998), based on the life of a 19th-century black boxer who nearly defeated the reigning white world champion, stirred controversy because MacDonald Fraser chose to use language that was historically accurate but is now considered racist.

Novelist Kingsley AMIS called Fraser "a marvellous reporter and a first-rate historical novelist." Critic John Keegan calls his description of his service in Burma, *Quartered Safe Out Here* (1994), "one of the great personal memoirs of the Second World War. Fraser notes that critics consider him a satirist, but he refuses to take his work too seriously. When writing the Flashman books, "the aim is to entertain (myself, for a start) while being true to history, to let Flashman comment on human and inhuman nature, and devil take the romantics and the politically correct revisionists both."

Other Works by George MacDonald Fraser

Flashman and the Tiger. New York: Anchor, 2001.
The Steel Bonnets. North Pomfret, Vt.: Trafalgar Square, 2001.

Frayn, Michael (1933–   ) *novelist, playwright, journalist, screenwriter, nonfiction writer*

Michael Frayn was born in the London suburbs to Violet Alice Lawson and Thomas Allen Frayn, an asbestos company salesman. After training as an interpreter and teaching Russian in the British army, Frayn studied philosophy at Cambridge, where he also wrote stories for *Granta* magazine and most of his first play, *Zounds!* (1957). He then worked as a journalist for the *Manchester Guardian* and later *The Observer* (London). For the former, he wrote "Miscellany," a column intended to showcase significant directors. But citing a lack of directors, Frayn invented material, such as the characters "The Crumbles," an ambitious suburban couple.

Frayn's first novel, *The Tin Men* (1965), a satire about computers that rule people's lives, won the 1963 Somerset Maugham Award for fiction. *In Against Entropy* (1967; released in Britain as *Towards the End of the Morning*) is a comic novel about a 37-year-old newspaper features editor who plans to improve his life by appearing as a television panelist. Frayn also draws on his newspaper background in his play *Alphabetical Order* (1975), about

a hyperefficient employee who tries to bring order to a newspaper office by organizing its library.

Frayn's first produced screenplay, *Clockwise* (1986), stars Monty Python's John Cleese as a headmaster obsessed with punctuality. He also wrote several documentaries about cities for the BBC (British Broadcasting Corporation), and won an Emmy Award for his screenplay for television's *First and Last* (1989), about a man who sets out to walk the length of Britain.

Noises Off (1982), for which Frayn is perhaps best known, is a play-within-a play with an on-stage farce called *Nothing On* and a "real-life" farce that develops backstage as the theater company rehearses and tours. The play has won several awards and was revived on Broadway in November 2001. *New York Times* reviewer Ben Brantley wrote, "'Noises Off' . . . allows you to laugh, loudly and wantonly, at a world in which everything seems out of joint" and noted that Frayn ". . . brings an acute scholarly intelligence to anything he touches."

Frayn also wrote a volume of philosophy, *Constructions* (1974); and translated and adapted several Anton Chekhov plays, including *Wild Honey: The Untitled Play* (1984), originally discovered with its title page missing. He has won 17 awards, and in 2001 he received an honorary doctorate from Cambridge University. He is married to biographer Claire Tomalin and has three children from a previous marriage.

A Work about Michael Frayn

Page, Malcolm. *File on Frayn.* Westport, Conn.: Heinemann, 1994.

Frazer, Sir James George (1854–1941) *nonfiction writer*

Sir James G. Frazer was born in Glasgow, Scotland, to Daniel Frazer, a pharmacist, and Katherine Frazer. He studied classics at the University of Glasgow and later received a scholarship to Cambridge. In 1879 he was elected a Fellow there and began translating and editing classical literature, eventually publishing translations of *Pausanias*

(1898) and *Fasti of Ovid* (1929). In 1907 Frazer accepted the University of Liverpool's first chair in anthropology, created specifically for him, but he soon returned to Cambridge, where he stayed for the rest of his life.

Often considered the founder of modern anthropology, Frazer proposed that cultures progress from magical through religious to scientific thought. He influenced the early 20th-century movement called modernism, in which contemporary science and philosophy were accepted along with historical Christianity, and literary interest shifted from the external world inhabited by fictional characters and focused instead on the characters' internal, psychological states. The scholar Herbert Wesinger has written that along with Charles Darwin, Karl Marx, Sigmund FREUD, and Albert Einstein, Frazer is "a major molder of the modern mind."

A Cambridge professor editing the ninth edition of the *Encyclopedia Britannica* asked Frazer to contribute several articles to the work. One of the articles grew too long for the encyclopedia and was published instead as Frazer's first book, *Totemism* (1887), which proposed that animals, plants, or other natural objects (totems) act as signs of a clan or tribe and repositories for a person's soul. Frazer later republished *Totemism* in *Totemism and Exogamy: A Treatise on Certain Early Forms of Superstition and Society* (1910), an ethnographical (relating to the study and systematic recording of human cultures) survey of totemism.

Frazer's monumental second work, *The Golden Bough: A Study in Magic and Religion* (1890), established him in the field of anthropology. Originally intending the study as two volumes, he expanded it to 12 and then added a supplementary volume, *Aftermath* (1936). Because Frazer himself rarely traveled, he turned to others for the field research for *The Golden Bough*. He developed and distributed, mainly to missionaries, a questionnaire, *Questions on the Manners, Customs, Religions, Superstitions, &c., of Uncivilized or Semicivilized Peoples.*

The Golden Bough was named after the bough in the sacred Arician grove near Lake Nemi in Italy. In the book's opening scene, a doomed priest-king waits at the grove for a rival who will murder him and become the new priest—a rite to renew the vigor both of leadership and of the world. Frazer writes in *The Golden Bough*: "Kings were revered, in many cases not merely as priests, that is, as intercessors between man and god, but as themselves gods. . . . Thus kings are often expected to give rain and sunshine in due season, to make the crops grow, and so on."

Frazer draws parallels between pagan beliefs and the death and resurrection of Christ, writing, "At least it is a remarkable coincidence . . . that the Christian and the heathen festivals of the divine death and resurrection should have been solemnised at the same season and in the same places. . . . it is difficult to regard the coincidence as purely accidental." He proposes that cultures evolved in how they try to control the natural universe, first using magic. In *homeopathic* magic, magicians act out or create a model of what they wish to happen (the Law of Similarity). For example, some dancers believed that leaping high into the air would make their crops grow tall. *Contagious* magic (the Law of Contact) held that a person who has had contact with certain things will continue to be influenced by them, as in the belief that a person could injure an enemy by damaging a piece of hair or clothing removed from the victim.

According to Frazer, after a society dismisses magic as unworkable, it turns to religion, appealing to spirits or gods for help. Then, with a failure of religion, a culture finally embraces science.

With its exploration of primitive thought *The Golden Bough* sparked imaginations and provided background information for such writers as D. H. LAWRENCE and T. S. ELIOT, whose poem *The Waste Land* (1922) contrasts the spiritual void Eliot saw in modern society with values of the past. Author Marc Manganaro writes that Eliot, following Frazer, presented the "cultural 'facts' . . . which apparently first emerged from the cultural fount and are just now receding from our grasp into extinction. Those cultural nuggets—myths, poems, gods, holy books, cathedrals—accumulate to form a last-chance purview of World Culture."

Most of the works Frazer published after *The Golden Bough* expand on themes within it. Frazer twice delivered the Gifford Lectureships on natural theology at St. Andrew's University, published as *The Belief in Immortality and the Worship of the Dead* (1913) and *The Worship of Nature* (1926).

Knighted in 1914 and recipient of the British Order of Merit in 1925, Frazer held honorary doctorates from nine universities. Though anthropologists later debunked many of *The Golden Bough*'s methods and conclusions, the book remains a singular source of comparative data on magical and religious practices. Marc Manganaro writes, "The point is not just that Frazer's contemporaries recognized Frazer's tactic but that they, in large part, were swept away by it even as they recognized his argumentative shortcomings."

Works about Sir James G. Frazer
Ackerman, Robert. *J. G. Frazer: His Life and Work.* New York: Cambridge University Press, 1987.

Manganaro, Marc. *Myth, Rhetoric, and the Voice of Authority: A Critique of Frazer, Eliot, Frye, and Campbell.* New Haven, Conn.: Yale University Press, 1992.

Freeling, Nicholas (1927–   ) novelist
Nicholas Freeling was born in London, England. His father was a farmer who had descended from a family of landowners. After his father died in 1939, his mother struggled financially to raise the family. Starting at age 18, Freeling worked as a cook in European hotels and restaurants. After a period of restless wandering in the late 1950s, he decided to become a writer.

Freeling's literary career began when he introduced the Dutch police inspector Piet Van der Valk in the crime novel *Love in Amsterdam* (1962). The novel describes Van der Valk's investigation of the relationships of a middle-aged woman, Elsa, whose murder he is assigned to solve. Readers were drawn to the flamboyant Van der Valk, a dedicated sleuth who ignores ineffective bureaucratic police procedures and instead relies on his own intuition to solve cases that have stumped other investigators. He mines intimate details from suspects and uses his penetrating character observations to solve crimes. In *Love in Amsterdam*, Van der Valk closes in on the killer after he concludes that Elsa "was a secretive woman. Everything she did, when she could make it so, was underhand, designed to deceive and mislead." The series of novels centered on Van der Valk established Freeling as a top writer of crime fiction. In a review of *The Lovely Ladies* (1971), Freeling's 12th novel, John R. Coyne Jr. wrote, "The pleasure in reading a Freeling novel comes largely from the often-comic contrast between the artificial social demands and the personal code of conduct and point of view of a man who makes his own judgments."

Seeking a wider frame of reference for his fiction, Freeling ended the Van der Valk series with *The Long Silence* (1972). He then created two other detective series with Van der Valk's wife Arlette and the French policeman Henri Castang as the respective heroes. In novels such as *The Widow* (1979), in which Arlette helps break up a professional drug ring in Strasbourg, Freeling gained critical and popular praise for his examination of criminal behavior from a female point of view. In the Castang series, beginning with *Dressing of a Diamond* (1974), Freeling again creates an independent sleuth who solves crimes with keen observations about character and motive. Critic Ian Hamilton has written that Freeling improved crime literature by "heaping such erudition on a maligned genre," in addition to providing "an up-to-standard supply of bleak internationalist wisdom as well as the usual flourish of scarred, aphoristic insights into what makes people love and hate the way they do."

Other Works by Nicholas Freeling
A City Solitary. London: Heinemann, 1985.

Not as Far as Velma. New York: Mysterious Press, 1989.

Friel, Brian (1929–) *playwright, short story writer*

Brian Friel was born in Omagh, County Tyrone, Northern Ireland, to Catholic parents. In 1939 the family moved to Londonderry, when his father became a school principal. From 1941 to 1946, Friel attended St. Columb's College. He then entered St. Patrick's College, graduating in 1948 and eventually becoming a teacher in Londonderry. In 1954 he married Anne Morrison, with whom he had five children.

While teaching, Friel began writing short stories, which appeared in *The New Yorker*. Encouraged by his success, he became a full-time writer and began writing plays.

Friel's plays are rooted in Irish culture. The country and its traditions serve both as the setting for most of his plays and as a silent yet all-embracing figure that exerts a subtly powerful influence on Friel's characters. The plays combine reality, memory, and fantasy to portray a people whose vision of the past violently conflicts with the truths of the present. But Friel rarely condemns his characters for their belief in a benign, peaceful Ireland. Instead, he depicts them with compassion and complexity and avoids the dangers of sentimentality. His perception and development of character are his leading qualities as a playwright.

Friel's first plays, produced between 1958 and 1962, received some critical acclaim in Ireland. However, he was displeased with their overall quality, and therefore he studied at the Tyrone Guthrie Theatre in Minneapolis in 1963. His dramatic skills improved, and the following year, he won the Irish Arts Council McAuley Fellowship, which led to the Dublin Theatre Festival producing his next play.

Philadelphia, Here I Come (1964) established Friel's reputation as a playwright. The drama explores a common conflict faced by Irish emigrants: whether to seek a better life in America or to embrace the familiarity—and limitations—of Ireland. The main character, Gar O'Donnell, waits in an airport to board a plane for Philadelphia, and as he waits, images of family and friends trouble him. He regrets leaving his elderly father, but a vision of a former teacher suggests the mundane, constricted future that Ireland would hold for Gar. Friel uses a unique device to examine Gar's conflict. Two actors perform his role, one representing his public self, the other his private.

Philadelphia, Here I Come earned Friel international recognition, yet subsequent plays, such as *The Loves of Cass McGuire* (1966), did not meet with critical praise. Despite his skills at characterization, these plays lack a unified dramatic action.

However, Friel eventually corrected this problem. His play *Translations* (1980) fully realizes its dramatic potential. The play is set in 1833 in Ballybeg, an Irish-speaking community, at a time when the British have instituted English as the national language of Ireland. The play thus explores the death of the Irish language and the accompanying loss of history and cultural identity. Friel personalizes the loss through the experiences of the fictional O'Donnell family. The play is performed in English, although the Irish characters are ostensibly speaking in Gaelic. Friel therefore creates a double translation, thereby explaining the play's title and its ironies. Friel concludes that problems of language and history cannot be resolved. The critic Nesta Jones has noted that the play "is about the death of language and yet language is vibrant and alive onstage."

In 1990 Friel's best play, *Dancing at Lughnasa*, premiered at the Abbey Theatre in Dublin. Its 1991 New York production won Tony Awards for Best Play, Best Director, and Best Supporting Actress. Partly autobiographical, the drama is again set in Ballybeg, but now in 1936. The area is becoming industrialized, and the encroaching modernization threatens the village's traditions. The five Mundy sisters embody the conflict between past and present. The play also takes place during the fall harvest, and the changing seasons illustrate the disappearing past. As the play progresses, the Mundy family crumbles, and two of the sisters die tragically. The play emphasizes memory as a preservative of the Mundys' history. The critic Richard Pine has noted that "memory, to which the outsider cannot be privy, gives them access to some past that is theirs alone, to a world which they carry within them."

Friel's success as a playwright has led to both theatrical and social prominence. He has won the American-Ireland Fund Literary Award and received a Doctor of Letters degree from the University of Ulster. In 1989 BBC Radio broadcast six of his plays; it was the first time the organization had so honored a living playwright. Friel also served in the Irish Senate from 1987 to 1989. Nesta Jones notes that Friel's plays "have been informed always by a deep compassion for his fellow man and a profound understanding of human frailty."

Other Works by Brian Friel

Brian Friel: Plays Two—Dancing at Lughnasa, Fathers and Sons, Making History, Wonderful Tennessee, Molley Sweeney. Winchester, Mass.: Faber & Faber, 1999.
Selected Plays. Washington, D.C.: Catholic University of America Press, 1986.

Works about Brian Friel

Andrews, Elmer. *The Art of Brian Friel.* New York: St. Martin's Press, 1995.
Jones, Nesta. *Brian Friel.* Winchester, Mass.: Faber and Faber, 2000.
Pine, Richard. *The Diviner: The Art of Brian Friel.* Chester Springs, Pa.: Dufour Editions, 2000.

Fry, Christopher (Christopher Horns)
(1907–) *playwright*

Christopher Fry was born Christopher Harris in Bristol, England, to Charles John Harris, a builder and preacher, and Emma Marguerite Fry. He later adopted his mother's maiden name. As a child, Fry attended the experimental Froebian school and the Bedford Modern School, and after seeing a production of *Peter Pan,* he aspired to a life in theater. He did not attend college but supported himself as a kindergarten teacher; he also held varied positions for various small theater companies.

After World War II Fry's plays began gaining national attention, and he emerged as one of Britain's finest playwrights. His plays are written in verse, having religious themes, and are frequently comic. *A Phoenix Too Frequent* (1946) is a thoroughly comic play that takes place inside a tomb. The central character, Dynamene, plans to die, along with her servant Doto, in order to be with her newly dead husband. Such a plot has tragic potential, but here Fry is making a farce of death. In her first lines, Dynamene says that she is so tired of mourning that she would "rather have to sleep / with a bald bee-keeper who was wearing his boots." In the words of the scholar Glenda Leeming, "Death is reduced to a comic choice."

Fry's next comedy, *The Lady's Not for Burning* (1948), is one of his best known works. The play, set in a 15th-century town, describes the interactions of Thomas, a former soldier, who wants to be hanged; and Jennet, a young, wealthy, orphaned, but life-loving girl whom the town leaders plan to burn at the stake on a false charge of witchcraft in order to steal her fortune. The play is filled with memorable characters, not the least of whom is Thomas. Self-deprecating—"I spit, I am . . . I'm a black and frosted rosebud whom the good God / Has preserved since last October. Take no notice"—he is both pathetic and endearing.

Fry has used comedy masterfully, but he is not limited to it. *The Firstborn,* which he began during World War II but did not finish until 1948, is based on the life of Moses and reveals a much darker side of the playwright. It follows Moses, whom Fry depicts, according to the scholar Audrey Williamson, as "almost Shakespearean," from his childhood to his development as the leader of the Israelites and his role in bringing the plagues upon Egypt. *The Firstborn* is more than a biblical story, however, for it presents Moses as a figure torn between his desire to deliver his people from slavery and his horror at bringing down the plagues upon Egyptian families with whom he also has close connections. The drama also draws parallels between the slave-owning, domineering Egyptians and Hitler's Germany.

After several decades of this more serious work, which also included a play about Henry II, *Curt-*

mantle (1962), Fry returned to comedy in *A Yard of Sun*. The play is set in Italy immediately after World War II and describes problems that arise when a family's rogue son returns mysteriously and extremely wealthy. With its bungled parables, mixed metaphors, and comic reversals, the comedy is not as overt as in Fry's earlier plays, as when the "prodigal" son, initially the family's outcast, becomes the father's pride and joy.

According to Glenda Leeming, Fry's dramas are "valid products of their time," which are still "performed on television, on radio, all over England in provincial theaters, and all over the world."

Other Works by Christopher Fry
Selected Plays. New York: Oxford University Press, 1985.
A Sleep of Prisoners. 1951. Reprint, New York: Dramatist's Play Services, 1998.

A Work about Christopher Fry
Leeming, Glenda. *Christopher Fry.* Boston: Twayne, 1990.

Fry, Roger (1866–1934) *art critic*
Born in London into a well-off Quaker family—his parents were the judge Sir Edward Fry and Mariabella Hodgkin Fry—Roger Fry went to King's College, Cambridge, to prepare for the scientific career his father had urged upon him. While there he won top honors in science, but he also manifested an interest in art, as both a critic and a painter. Although he attempted to comply with his father's wishes for a scientific career, art finally won out. Study and travel in Italy and France in the early 1890s led to Fry's becoming a lecturer in art history and connoisseurship, and he also began to exhibit his own work at the New English Art Club in London, where he met and married fellow student Helen Coombe.

Fry published his first complete work, on Giovanni Bellini, in 1896 and began writing art criticism for the *Athenaeum* in 1900. In 1905 he produced his first major work, an edition of the great English 18th-century painter Sir Joshua Reynolds's *Discourses.* This and his work in the founding of the formidable art periodical *Burlington Magazine* brought him to the attention of the American financier J. P. Morgan. As a result of this association, in 1905 Fry became director of the Metropolitan Museum of Art in New York, a post he held until 1910. Up until that time he had been content with the study of traditional art and of the old masters, but in 1906 his life as a critic underwent a major change when he went to an exhibition of Paul Cézanne's paintings. This caused him to seek out other works by the painters Gauguin, Matisse, and van Gogh. In 1910 and again in 1912 at the Grafton Galleries Fry organized exhibitions of these artists. He gave them the name by which they remain known today, postimpressionists, because they emphasized color and light in the manner of impressionist painters like Monet but placed more emphasis on abstraction and symbolism. These postimpressionist exhibits caused a major break with the traditional art establishment and allied Fry with the painters of the BLOOMSBURY GROUP.

After the war, Fry published a collection of his *Burlington* articles and others as *Vision and Design* (1920). His *Cezanne* (1927) confirmed his preeminence as did his series of lectures at Queen's Hall in later years. In 1933 his career was crowned as he was appointed Slade Professor of Art at Cambridge. Sir Kenneth Clarke called Fry "incomparably the greatest influence on taste since Ruskin."

Other Work by Roger Fry
A Roger Fry Reader. Edited by Christopher Reed. Chicago: University of Chicago Press, 1996.

Works about Roger Fry
Falkenheim, Jacqueline Victoria. *Roger Fry and the Beginning of Formalist Art Criticism.* Ann Arbor: University of Michigan Press, 1980.
Woolf, Virginia. *Roger Fry: A Biography.* 1940. Reprint, New York: Vintage, 2003.

Fuller, Roy (1912–1991) *poet, novelist, memoirist*

Born in Lancashire, Roy Broadbent Fuller attended Blackpool High School and became an articled clerk (a solicitor's apprentice) at age 16. He qualified as a solicitor in 1934, and his law career was entirely concerned with building societies (building and loan institutions). After working as assistant solicitor for 20 years, he became solicitor to the Woolwich Equitable Building Society in 1958. In 1969 he became vice president of the Building Societies Association.

In the late 1930s, Fuller contributed poems to *New Verse,* writing on matters of social and political concern. He published his first collection, *Poems,* in 1939; his poems reflect the influence of W. H. AUDEN. He served in the Royal Navy from 1941 until 1945, during which time he gained credibility as a war poet. His volumes *The Middle of a War* (1942) and *A Lost Season* (1944) reflected his own wartime experiences, particularly in their themes of loneliness, tedium, and fear.

Fuller expressed postwar concerns about modern English life in his poems *Epitaphs and Occasions* (1949) and *Counterparts* (1954). The former depicted left-wing sympathies and man as a social animal, and the latter marks the beginning of his experimentation with poetic devices. His poems tend to reflect logical progressions from particular observations to general reflections, and his later work conveys a more reflective and analytic tone.

Although he was regarded as a master technician, critics claimed that his tone and form were not unique. Although his novel *Fantasy and Fugue* (1954) was melodramatic, his novel *The Ruined Boys* (1959) demonstrated a subtle characterization and quiet evocation of the real world.

In 1968 Fuller became professor of poetry at Oxford, where he remained until 1973, and published his lectures as *Owls and Artificers* (1971) and *Professors and Gods* (1973). He was awarded the Duff Cooper Memorial Prize in 1968. He wrote three volumes of memoirs in the 1980s, and his autobiography, *Spanner and Pen,* was published in 1991. His son, John Fuller, is also a poet and novelist.

Other Works by Roy Fuller

New and Collected Poems, 1934–84. London: Secker and Warburg, 1985.

Spanner and Pen: Post-War Memoirs. North Pomfret, Vt.: Trafalgar Square, 1991.

The World Through The Window: Collected Poems For Children. London: Blackie, 1989.

Works about Roy Fuller

Powell, Neil. *Roy Fuller: Writer and Society.* Manchester, England: Carcanet Press, 1995.

Tolley, A. T. *Roy Fuller: A Tribute.* Northfield, Minn.: Carleton University Press, 1993.

G

Galsworthy, John (1867–1933) *novelist, short story writer, playwright*

John Galsworthy, the oldest of four children, was born in Kingston Hill, Surr\ey, England, to a prosperous family. His father, also named John Galsworthy, was an attorney and real estate investor who had significant international investments in the mining industry. His mother, Blanche Bartleet Galsworthy, was the daughter of a notable businessman. The family lived on a sizable estate outside of London. As prominent society members, Galsworthy's parents shared an overriding Victorian concern for propriety and respectability. Therefore they expected Galsworthy to succeed his father as an attorney and overseer of the family's business interests.

In 1886 Galsworthy entered New College, Oxford, to study law. However, his studies bored him, and for diversion he turned to gambling and romance, continuing in these pursuits even after graduating. His affair with an actress prompted his father to send him on numerous foreign trips to inspect the family's mining investments. During one such trip, he met the novelist Joseph CONRAD. Conrad ignited Galsworthy's passion for writing and eventually introduced him to Ford Madox FORD and Edward Garnett, who edited many of Galsworthy's early novels.

By 1895 Galsworthy had largely abandoned his law practice for writing. He financed his first publication, a collection of short stories entitled *From the Four Winds* (1897). Galsworthy's parents discouraged his writing because they believed it was bohemian. They also feared his blossoming relationship with Ada Cooper Galsworthy, his cousin's wife. Ada believed her marriage was a mistake, and while her husband served in the Boer War, she and Galsworthy began an affair. They married in 1905 after his father died and Ada divorced. Ada served as an editor and model for Galsworthy's fiction.

Galsworthy frequently depicts characters who defy Victorian conventions of propriety and sexuality, then experience subsequent guilt, alienation, and even death. As his fiction developed, he incorporated such situations into a broader indictment of Victorian middle-class life. He deplored the materialism of Victorian society, believing that it fostered social apathy. Wealth, he argued, was the result of good fortune, and prosperous individuals had no cause to judge themselves superior to others. His third novel, *The Island Pharisees* (1904), powerfully presents his social philosophy. The protagonist, a successful attorney, despises the middle class and wanders despondently through London's poorest areas, eventually befriending a French tramp.

Galsworthy also used his plays for his social criticism, beginning with *The Silver Box* (1906). The productions commonly highlighted corrupt government practices.

During World War I, Galsworthy actively supported the war effort, raising funds and supplies for both refugees and troops. The war's severity depressed him, and the Allies' victory reshaped his opinion of English middle-class society. His later novels depict characters who are more humane and socially aware than the materialistic villains of his earlier works.

Galsworthy enjoyed immense popularity during the 1920s. He was awarded honorary doctorates by Manchester, Dublin, Cambridge, Oxford, and Princeton universities. In 1932 he won the Nobel Prize in literature. Two months later he died of a brain tumor. Almost immediately, his literary reputation began to decline. Younger novelists, such as Virginia WOOLF and D. H. LAWRENCE, attacked his novels, arguing that the plots were formulaic and the characters were stereotypes infused with sentimentality. For instance, Woolf quipped that to ask writers like Galsworthy "to teach you how to write a novel—how to create characters that are real—is precisely like going to a bootmaker and asking him to teach you how to make a watch."

Today, however, many critics regard Galsworthy as the last influential Victorian novelist; they praise his ability to create complex narratives and to capture the Victorian character. The critic Sanford Sternlicht notes that Galsworthy's novels express "all the virtues and vices a people choose to see in themselves: integrity, endurance, respect for tradition . . . but also reserve, snobbery, class rigidity, conventionality, and noncommunicativeness."

Critical Analysis

The Man of Property (1906) is Galsworthy's most famous novel. This book introduces the Forsyte family and serves as the foundation for the first trilogy that comprise Galsworthy's celebrated *Forsyte Saga.* The character Soames Forsyte dominates the action. Soames is the prototypical Victorian "man of property": he is arrogant, greedy, and insensitive. Above all, he considers his wife, Irene, a passionate and sensual woman, as a possession. Irene leaves to live with an artist, and in revenge Soames financially ruins the artist and rapes Irene after she returns. The novel exemplifies Galsworthy's bitterness toward the upper middle class and provides his most poignant portrayal of the social penalties that plague lovers who place passion above social convention.

However, Galsworthy also hints at a possible redemption for the bourgeois. Jolyon Forsyte, Soames's cousin, marries a governess and becomes a painter. His actions initially outrage his family and result in his banishment from them. But his father, Old Jolyon, eventually pulls his son back into the family. Old Jolyon initially shares Soames's crass materialism, but as he gradually accepts his son's decisions, he learns to appreciate beauty.

The second book of the saga, *In Chancery* (1920), reintroduces the Forsyte family. It also reflects Galsworthy's softening postwar opinion of British society. The middle-aged Soames, obsessed with fathering an heir, divorces Irene and marries the much younger Annette Lamotte. Ironically, Irene remarries and has a son, while Soames and his new wife have a daughter.

But Galsworthy does not depict Soames as viciously as he does in *The Man of Property.* Rather, the author portrays Soames as much more introspective, and he allows the reader access to Soames's thoughts and emotions. Soames now regrets his cruel treatment of Irene, and in the succeeding novel, *To Let* (1921), his love for his daughter Fleur exceeds his concern for monetary gain.

The second Forsyte trilogy begins with *The White Monkey* (1924), followed by *The Silver Spoon* (1928). In the final novel of the saga, *Swan Song* (1928), Soames appears as a completely sympathetic figure. When Fleur accidentally ignites a house fire, Soames saves her at the cost of his own life.

The Forsyte novels thoroughly entranced contemporary audiences, and Soames's death made headlines in several London newspapers. Galsworthy's increasingly sympathetic portrayal of Soames provoked the criticism that ruined his literary reputation in the 1930s, but these detractors failed to recognize Galsworthy's development as a novelist. His narrative voice reflects a willingness to teach the postwar generation about the failures of the Victorian middle class and to provide them with an example of a better society. As the critic James Gindin has noted, Galsworthy's "work at its best demonstrated a remarkable capacity to reach others, to suggest to them that it is also their own saga."

Other Works by John Galsworthy

The Forsyte Saga. New York: Oxford University Press, 1999.

The Silver Spoon. Amsterdam, The Netherlands: Fredonia Books (NL), 1928, reprinted 2001.

The White Monkey. New York: Scribner, 1924, reprinted 1969.

Works about John Galsworthy

Gindin, James Jack. *John Galsworthy's Life and Art.* Ann Arbor: University of Michigan Press, 1987.

Sternlicht, Sanford V. *John Galsworthy.* Boston: Twayne, 1987.

Gardam, Jane (1928–   ) *novelist, short story writer*

Jane Gardam was born in the small town of Coatham in Yorkshire, England. Her father, William Pearson, was a well-known schoolmaster and her mother, Kathleen Helm Pearson, came from an upper-class background. The theme of class difference came to inform Gardam's later writings. She attended Bedford College for Women in London on a scholarship, receiving a degree in English with honors in 1949. Gardam's literary pursuits earned her a reputation as an award-winning author of both adult and children's fiction.

Gardam's first book was *A Few Fair Days* (1971), a collection of nine short stories. Together, these stories use the coming of World War II to trace the development of the book's female protagonist, Lucy, from childhood to early adolescence. Gardam's novel *A Long Way from Verona* (1971) continued what was to become a recurring theme

in Gardam's work: the female adolescent experience in 20th-century Britain. She subsequently established a reputation as a writer of "adolescent fiction," and she has won several prestigious awards for her work in this genre, including a Whitbread Award for her book about rural life in England, *The Hollow Land* (1981).

Gardam's first work of adult fiction, *Black Faces, White Faces* (1975) won the David Higham Prize for Fiction and the Winifred Holtby Prize. The 10 short stories in this collection deal with the issue of racial tension and describe the clash of black and white cultures in a modern context. "Something to Tell the Girls' is about two retired British female teachers who must confront the reality of their own difference while traveling in Jamaica. "White face, white face" one boy yells at them, "go home." Of her writing for adults, critic Donna Seaman has remarked, "Gardam entertains and enlightens with vibrant descriptions and martini-dry wit."

The Whitbread Award-winning *The Queen of the Tambourine* (1991) is the story of a dissatisfied middle-aged woman on the brink of madness. The book is structured around a series of letters from the main character, Eliza, to a neighbor whom she hardly knows. To help combat her utter loneliness, she writes letters that the reader is made to understand will not be returned: "I wrote you a quick note last week and wonder if it went astray? I know that you and I have not known each other for very long and have been neighbors for a very few years, but somehow I feel I know you very closely." Another Whitbread winner, Anita BROOKNER. praised Gardam for "prose that is witty, vibrant, and off the wall" and called the book "[e]xcellently done."

In her writing, Gardam has worked to break down the divisions between "adult" and "children's" fiction. *God on the Rocks* (1978), for example, chronicles the difficult relationship between a mother and daughter and is told from the point of view of both characters. Gardam has faced constant challenges in merging the adult and juvenile genres of fictions from critics who insist on viewing her primarily as a writer for children. Nevertheless, as the *London Times* reviewer Elaine

FEINSTEIN has noted, Gardam remains "a spare and elegant master of her art."

Other Work by Jane Gardam

Bilgewater. London: Little, Brown, 2001.

Gascoyne, David (1916–2001) *poet, novelist, nonfiction writer*

David Gascoyne was born in Harrow, Middlesex, England. His father, Leslie Gascoyne, worked for the Midland Bank, while his mother was, in Gascoyne's own words, "a frustrated actress." He left school at the age of 16 to dedicate himself to writing and immediately managed to publish his first poetry collection, *Roman Balcony and Other Poems* (1932). The following year Gascoyne published his first and only novel, *Opening Day*, which explores the conflict between a boy and a father who disapproves of his son's aesthetic and cultural yearnings.

Gascoyne's early work is heavily influenced by French SURREALISM, a movement devoted to artistically exploring the depths of the unconscious, especially relating to dreams, sexuality, and madness. While visiting France early in his life, Gascoyne became close friends with such influential surrealist painters as André Breton and Salvador Dalí, and he introduced their work to the British public in his popular *Short Survey of Surrealism* (1935). Gascoyne's collections *Man's Life Is This Meat* (1936) and *Hölderlin's Madness* (1938) show the surrealistic influence. Lines such as "Butterflies burst from their skins and grow long tongues like plants" from *Salvador Dali* (1942) introduced a new and original (if sometimes disturbing and unsettling) voice in English poetry.

Gascoyne spent much of his later life living in France, sometimes feeling himself to be more closely tied to European values and ideas than English ones. Indeed, the surrealist writer Philippe Soupault once said, "David is not an English poet, he is a French poet writing in English." Yet this did not prevent him from obtaining a commission from BBC Radio to write *Night Thoughts* (1956), a long, three-part poem that uses complex, passionate language to explore themes of fear and isolation. Indeed, later in life Gascoyne found himself honored on both sides of the channel, being made a Fellow of the Royal Society of Literature in 1994 and a Chevalier de L'Ordre des Arts et des Lettres in 1996. Poet Allen Ginsberg, an admirer of Gascoyne's work, summed him up as "a Surrealist poet. He belongs to the Paris School of Surrealism of Breton, Eluard, and Ernst, whom he translated when he lived there before the war."

Other Works by David Gascoyne

Collected Poems 1988. Oxford: Oxford University Press, 1988.

David Gascoyne: Collected Journals, 1936–42. Edited by Kathleen Raine. London: Skoob Books Publishing, 1990.

Gee, Maggie (1948–) *novelist*

Maggie Gee was born in Poole, Dorset, England, the daughter of Victor Valentine and Mary Church Gee. She received an M.Litt from Oxford, and in 1980 she completed her Ph.D. at Wolverhampton Polytechnic, where she wrote a thesis on modernist writers. As an author Gee claims to have "felt the same affinity with writers of both sexes" and names Charles Dickens and Jane Austen among her early influences. Named by *Granta* magazine as one of the best young novelists in 1983, Gee has established a reputation as an experimental writer with a talent for characterization who is unafraid to deal with highly charged social issues.

The stories told in Gee's novels range from the sensational to the political. She has achieved her greatest success in revising the crime thriller genre. Her first novel, *Dying, in Other Words* (1981), tells the story of the mysterious death of Moira Penny, a postgraduate literature student at Oxford. Her demise in the early pages of the novel sets off a bizarre series of complicated events that result in the subsequent deaths of several of Moira's friends and acquaintances. In *Lost Children* (1994) Gee turns her attention to more socially conscious themes by using the issue of homelessness to explore questions of selfhood.

Gee's most overtly political works have dealt with the theme of nuclear disarmament, a campaign that she strongly supports as a member of the Campaign for Nuclear Disarmament. *The Burning Book* (1983) takes as its topic the destructive effects of nuclear weapons on the modern world. As a reviewer for the *Times Literary Supplement* claimed, "Maggie Gee's writing, with its constant references to the hidden ugliness of life presages doom. . . . *The Burning Book* is an odd kind of novel but a marvelously cogent anti-war statement." Similarly, her later novel *Grace* published in 1988, uses the murder mystery genre to deal with the issue of nuclear contamination. Described as having a "thriller like conclusion" by the *Library Journal*, *Grace* was not as well received by critics as *The Burning Book*. *Publishers Weekly* called the work "ambiguous" and argued that "The characters are deftly delineated and the issues broached are certainly important, but the novel as a whole neither hangs together nor convinces."

Gee has been recognized as an important contemporary literary figure in Britain. Although some have criticized her story lines as too complicated and overtly political, others have suggested that it is the complexity of her language and characterization that makes her work, in words of one *New York Times* book reviewer, "terribly affecting." Elizabeth Hawes, another *Times* reviewer, has remarked, "Ms. Gee writes easily and perceptively. She gives her characters strong physical presences and she creates tension effortlessly."

Other Works by Maggie Gee

The Ice People. London: Richard Cohen Books, 2000.
Where Are the Snows. London: Trafalgar Square, 2000.

Georgian poetry

Georgian poetry refers to a series of five volumes of poetry issued in England between the years 1912 and 1922. The term "Georgian" refers to George V, the king of England at the time. Edward Marsh edited the volumes, which included poetry by Robert GRAVES, Siegfried SASSOON, Rupert BROOKE, D. H. LAWRENCE, and Harold Monro. Marsh and Brooke began to publish the volumes with the idea of making modern poetry available to the general public. They felt that the poets whose verse they anthologized were the pioneers of a new age of poetry that arose in reaction to Victorian tastes and styles.

While some who would become great contributed to the volumes, the general evaluation of history is that Georgian poetry was not particularly good. Much of it was conventional in verse form and style, pastoral and nostalgic rather than forward looking. For example, these lines by Frances Ledwidge are not much more than bad Romantic poetry:

> *When the clouds shake their hyssops, and the rain*
> *Like holy water falls upon the plain,*
> *'Tis sweet to gaze upon the springing grain.*

The "war" poetry classified as Georgian was conventional and blindly patriotic. These lines, from Brooke's "The Soldier," contrast sharply with the war poetry that emerged from Brooke himself and others who later fought in the trenches:

> *If I should die, think only this of me:*
> *That there's some corner of a foreign field*
> *That is for ever England.*

Ironically, the Georgian poets themselves thought their work was revolutionary. However, when T.S. ELIOT's *The Waste Land* was published in 1922, it made Georgian poetry look thoroughly old-fashioned.

Still, there are some excellent poems in the anthologies. D. H. Lawrence's poem "Cruelty and Love" hints at the passionate encounters that are the hallmark of his later novels. (Many critics, however, do not classify Lawrence as a Georgian poet simply because he was included in the anthologies). Brooke's ironic poem "Heaven" first appeared in a volume of *Georgian Poetry* and satirizes religious belief by imagining a similar metaphysics among fish. Their deity is "Immense, of fishy form and mind, / Squamous, omnipotent, and kind," and heaven is "mud, celestially fair." A delightful little poem by Harold Monro, entitled "Milk for the Cat," is full of funny, apt images. As the cat waits for her saucer of milk, she is "grown thin with desire / Transformed to a creeping lust for milk." Still, most of the poems are unironic, pastoral, and nostalgic and are little read today, though other works by some of the poets certainly are.

Gibbons, Stella (1902–1989) *novelist, short story writer, poet*

Born in London to Irish parents Telfod Charles and Maud Williams Gibbons, Stella Gibbons was the eldest of three children. Her childhood was generally unhappy, and she often spent time entertaining her younger brothers with imaginative stories. Educated by governesses, Gibbons did not attend a formal school until the age of 13, when she went to the North London Collegiate School. When she was 19, she took a journalism course at University College, London, and worked as a decoder of cables for the British United Press, where she claimed she first learned to write. She spent 10 years on Fleet Street in various jobs, including writing dramatic and literary criticism and fashion writing. She was also beginning to publish short stories and poems. In 1933 she married Allan Bourne Webb, an actor and opera singer with whom she had a daughter, Laura.

Having already written an acclaimed volume of poetry, *The Mountain Beast* (1930), Gibbons wrote her first novel, *Cold Comfort Farm* (1932), while traveling on trains to and from her job as an editorial assistant for *Lady* magazine. A biting and humorous satire of the pastoral novel, *Cold Comfort Farm* parodies the conventions used by contemporary writers, including Mary Webb and Sheila Kaye-Smith, as well as Thomas Hardy and D. H. LAWRENCE. The success of this novel prompted Gibbons to leave her job at *Lady* and devote herself to writing full time. *Cold Comfort Farm* is the work she is best known for, but her other work included 25 novels, four volumes of poetry, and three collections of short stories.

Recognized for its comic genius, *Cold Comfort Farm* won the prestigious Femina Vie Heureuse Prixe in 1933. It was adapted for a musical in 1965, for television in 1968, and for film in 1996. Gibbons was also known for treating young love with both sensibility and romance, as well as for her intimate chronicling of ordinary life during the World War II era, as in *The Bachelor* (1944) and *The Matchmaker* (1949). In 1950 she was elected a Fellow of the Royal Society of Literature. She published her last novel in 1970, still writing for her own pleasure.

Other Works by Stella Gibbons

Conference at Cold Comfort Farm. New York: Longman, 1949.
Here Be Dragons. London: White Lion, 1972.

Gilliatt, Penelope (1932–1993) *novelist, short story writer, screenwriter, film critic*

Penelope Gilliatt was born in London, England, to Cyril Conner, a lawyer, and Mary Douglass Conner. Gilliatt attended college in both England and America, starting first at Queen's College in London and later studying at Bennington College in Vermont. She married a college professor, Roger William Gilliatt, in 1954 and decided to write under her married name even after the two divorced. Gilliatt was best known for her work as a film and drama critic for the *New Yorker* magazine, a position that she held in conjunction with Pauline Kael from 1968 to 1979. Her work as a novelist, short story writer, and screenwriter, however, also earned her much acclaim during her lifetime.

The themes expressed in Gilliatt's writing include issues of class and social change as depicted through the telling of stories about contemporary places and events. Many of Gilliatt's short stories first appeared in the *New Yorker*. Published collections of her stories include *What's It Like Out? And Other Stories* (1968) and *Quotations from Other*

Lives (1981). Her first novel, *One by One* (1965), depicts the lives of individuals deeply affected by the physical and emotional scars left by the German bombing of London during World War II. *A State of Change* (1967), also set in postwar London, continues many of the themes of dislocation introduced in her first novel by relating the memories of the main characters Kakia and Harry as they try to come to grips with an England full of economic deprivation and cultural malaise. Gilliatt paints a grim picture of Kakia's arrival in England after the war: "She arrived in a London that seemed full of closed circles and bitterness about income taxes."

Critic T. Lindvall has characterized Gilliatt's style as "readable, sassy, flippant, and buoyant." In 1971 Gilliatt won awards from the National Society of Films Critics, the New York Film Critics, and the Writer's Guild of Britain for her screenplay *Sunday Bloody Sunday,* which explores the complex relationships forged and broken among the film's three main characters, who find their lives intertwined in contemporary London.

Gilliatt continued her work as a critic throughout her career. *To Wit,* published in 1990, analyzes humor's importance in literature and on the silver screen. "Great comedy, great wit makes the ceiling fly off," claimed Gilliatt, "and suddenly liberates us again as we were when we were much younger and saw no reason not to believed that we could fly, or become someone else, or bound on a trampoline and not come down again."

Gilliatt had an exciting and highly productive career as a writer that included success as a journalist, novelist, essayist, and critic. Despite criticisms that have labeled her work as "elitist" because of her decision to create primarily upper-class characters, her ability to meld characterization with contemporary experience has earned her the praise of author Anthony BURGESS, who recognized her as a writer of "great originality . . . passion and intelligence."

Other Works by Penelope Gilliatt

22 stories. New York: Dodd, Mead, 1986.

A Woman of Singular Occupation. New York: Scribner, 1989.

Godden, Rumer (Margaret Rumer Godden; P. Davies) (1907–1998) *novelist, children's author, memoirist*

Rumer Godden was born in England but spent almost all of her early childhood in India, a country she loved all her life. She later recalled, "We felt at home, safely held in her large warm embrace, content as we never were to be content in our own country." From her earliest years she meant to be a writer. She would hide her poems and prose in a secret place in the garden: a huge cork tree set about with amaryllis.

In her early teens Godden was sent to school in England, but she was homesick for India. Her English teacher, Mona Swann, quickly noticed Godden's aptitude for writing and offered to help the young woman to develop her talent. Swann wrote later: "Voluntarily Rumer wrote draft after draft and was ever ready to discuss and learn from the most ruthless criticism."

At 18 Godden returned to India for a brief holiday and then returned to England to train as a ballet teacher. A childhood injury had weakened her back, however, so ballet was painful for her, but she persevered and soon returned to India to open a dancing school in Calcutta.

Godden married in 1934, but tragedy soon followed: Her first baby, a boy, died four days after birth. To recover from the grief, Godden wrote frenetically. Neither of her first two novels were accepted by publishers, but her third attempt, *Chinese Puzzle* (1936), was accepted on the same day that her first daughter was born. This whimsical novel is written from the perspective of a Pekingese dog recalling his various incarnations as human and Pekingese. It received some mildly positive reviews but was not a commercial success; nor was *The Lady and the Unicorn* (1937), a ghost story and romance.

Success finally came with Godden's third published novel, *Black Narcissus* (1939), a haunting story about Sister Clodagh, an English nun who founds a convent in the Himalayas. Taking over an abandoned palace, the nun and her comrades struggle with their isolation, the strange palace, and the unremitting wind.

Godden was Catholic, and nuns are her protagonists again in *This House of Brede* (1969), an acclaimed novel about Benedictine nuns; *Five for Sorrow, Ten for Joy* (1979), a lyrical story of an ex-criminal who becomes a Dominican nun; and *The Dark Horse* (1981), a novel about Calcutta's Sisters of Poverty and the horse-racing community in 1930s India.

Godden returned to England in 1938 and spent the first years of World War II in Britain. There she completed her novel *Gypsy, Gypsy* (1940), a story of a bitter and controlling old woman who deliberately tries to corrupt a family of gypsies who come to live nearby. Godden wrote about gypsies again later in her children's book *The Diddakoi* (1972), which describes a half-gypsy girl struggling to adapt to settled life and cruelty from fellow schoolchildren.

Godden returned to Calcutta in 1940 as the war intensified. In India she wrote *Breakfast with the Nikolides* (1942). Like many of Godden's books, this novel has child protagonists who have to struggle against an unsympathetic or strange world. The story describes children struggling with two unhappy parents, race hatred, and an eerie Indian town.

When the war ended, Godden returned to England, where she published several more books. Her next critical success was with *The River* (1946), a poignant elegy of innocence inspired by her childhood in India. The child heroine, Harriet, is growing up, and her world is changing. The *Saturday Review* described the novel as "[S]o intense, so quietly demanding of attention, that at the time there will be nothing in your thoughts but a small girl in India, and the people and places that were her world."

Godden's famous book *The Greengage Summer* (1958) is, like the earlier *Breakfast with Nikolides,* written from the perspective of a teenage girl. The novel describes the protagonist losing her childhood naïveté and entering the complex adult world of attachment and deception.

Godden has also written many books for children. *The Mousewife* (1951) describes a friendship between a mouse and a dove. Godden based the story on a diary entry by Dorothy Wordsworth, which the latter wrote as a story for her brother, the poet William. Several of Godden's children's books have dolls as the main character, for example *The Dolls' House* (1947) and *Impunity Jane* (1954).

Godden remained a prolific writer all her life. At 84 she published the acclaimed novel *Coromandel Sea Change* (1991), which describes a couple's eight-day honeymoon trip to the Coromandel coast. While there, they become estranged from each other and entangled with tragic local events.

Godden also published two volumes of autobiography, *A Time to Dance, No Time to Weep* (1987) and *A House with Four Rooms* (1989). Asked when she would give up writing, she replied, "Not until it gives me up." She was made an Officer of the Order of the British Empire (OBE) in 1993.

Other Works by Rumer Godden

Cromartie v. the God Shiva Acting Through the Government of India. New York: Morrow, 1997.
House with Four Rooms. New York: Morrow, 1989.
Miss Happiness and Miss Flower. New York: Viking, 1961.

A Work about Rumer Godden

Chisholm, Anne. *Rumer Godden: A Storyteller's Life.* London: Macmillan, 1998.

Goff, Helen Lyndon

See TRAVERS, PAMELA LYNDON.

Golding, William Gerald (1911–1993)
novelist, poet

William Golding was born and died in Cornwall, England. His father, Alec Golding, was descended from a long line of schoolmasters, whose ranks his son would join. His mother, Mildred Golding, was an early suffragist. At age 12 Golding began writing a historical novel that he projected would fill 12 volumes. His first published work, *Poems 1930* (1935), was like GEORGIAN POETRY in style. Considering his work a failure, though, he abandoned poetry.

Educated at Marlborough Grammar School, where his father was a master, Golding entered Oxford intending to become a scientist, but after two years he switched his focus to literature, specializing in Anglo-Saxon. In 1939 he married Ann Brookfield, a chemist; the couple had a son and a daughter.

Upon leaving Oxford, Golding worked for the theater for several years as a writer, actor, and producer. The discipline of playwriting contributed to the economy and structure of his novels. Golding then taught English and philosophy at Bishop Wordsworth School, Salisbury, from 1939 to 1940 and again from 1945 until 1961, when he became a full-time writer.

The author was 43 when his first novel, *Lord of the Flies* (1954), was finally published after having been rejected by 21 publishers. The book at first received mixed reviews, particularly in England, where it was compared unfavorably to a charming but more literal tale of life on a tropical island, Richard HUGHES's *A High Wind in Jamaica*. However, Golding's dark tale found favor on the college campus, becoming a world classic: It was translated into 26 languages and had sold 7 million copies by 1980. In 1966 Golding was made a Commander of the Order of the British Empire (CBE), and in 1988 he was knighted. In 1983 he was awarded the Nobel Prize for literature.

Critical Analysis

Golding is an author whose each successive work deals with a different subject in a different time and place. His techniques are distinctive, and his novels are intensely visual, highly patterned, and well articulated. They possess allegorical elements and mythic qualities. The myth they illustrate most powerfully is that of the Fall, in which humanity loses freedom while gaining knowledge of good and evil.

A major influence on Golding's writing were classic boys' adventures, such as those written by R. M. Ballantyne, Robert Louis Stevenson, and Jules Verne, which he read in youth. He was also influenced by the Greek classics and by his experience serving in the Royal Navy during World War II. He said that war taught him that "man produces evil as a bee produces honey."

Golding's examination of the Fall is the central focus of *Lord of the Flies*. This novel, which tells the story of British schoolboys wrecked on a tropical island during a global war, can be read from a sociological, psychological, political, or religious perspective. It is a powerful parable of the evolution of human society and parodies Ballantyne's *The Coral Island* (1858), in which three shipwrecked English boys, Ralph Rover, Jack Martin, and Peterkin Gay (Golding uses similar names for his central characters) set up a model society on a South Sea island. In Golding's novel, the society formed by his castaways is presided over by "the Lord of the Flies," or Beelzebub, and reveals the innate depravity of human nature. Ralph, a representative of reason, and Piggy, who stands for intellect, are overcome by the brute violence and bloodlust of Jack and his henchmen before Ralph's last-minute reprieve. As critic Stephen Medcalf has noted, Golding's novels draw readers deep into their protagonists' perceptions; engulfed or embedded in this experience, readers are abruptly brought back to reality through a sudden, sharp shift of point of view. Medcalf observed of the end of *Lord of the Flies* that "the naval officer and his cruiser remind us . . . (like the crash landing of the boys at the beginning and the fall of the airman in the middle) that the boys themselves are escaping from a world war." But, as Golding asked, "Who will save the adult and his cruiser?"

Golding's own favorite among his books was *The Inheritors* (1955), which narrates, from the point of view of a Neanderthal survivor, the triumph of *homo sapiens* over his race. The Neanderthals inhabit a ledge above a fall of water, a geological fault that seems to represent the metaphysical fall. The novelist's extraordinary achievement is in devising for this work a language through which a primitive creature incapable of conceptualization can nevertheless express and reveal its consciousness. Novelist A. S. BYATT describes *The Inheritors* as "a tour de force which has not been equalled in my lifetime."

Throughout *Pincher Martin* (1956) the reader is locked within the consciousness of "Pincher" (Christopher) Martin, a voracious egoist stranded on a rock in mid-Atlantic during wartime, who refuses to die. The novel's ending, however, reveals Martin to be physically dead already—what is experienced is the infinitely extended moment of extinction. Thus Golding's fiction presents a postmortem consciousness, which the American title *The Two Deaths of Christopher Martin* made clear were Martin's physical and spiritual deaths. Golding commented on his hero's desperate situation: "The rock . . . is nothing but his own mirage. . . . Before the presence of God everything surrounding Martin vanishes, and he himself is left nothing but a center of consciousness and a pair of claws against which the black lightning of heaven plays . . ."

Free Fall, the most fluid and subtly structured of Golding's works, concerns the painter Sammy Mountjoy, who examines his life, trying to ascertain the exact moment when he fell from grace and lost his freedom. The novel alludes to Dante's *Divine Comedy* in Sammy's love for Beatrice Ifor and his progress from Rotten Row to Paradise Hill. Sammy, adopted by Father Watts Watt, strives to find a bridge connecting the physical world to the realm of spirit, a conflict embodied in Sammy's teachers, Nick Shales, who teaches science, and Rowena Pringle, who teaches religion. Sammy is taken prisoner by the Germans and undergoes torture. Unlike Pincher Martin, he succumbs to terror and prays for help, and as a result he experiences a kind of revelation and redemption.

The most inspiring and convincing of Golding's explorations of the intersection of spirit with flesh, sacred with profane, and good with evil is *The Spire,* an imaginative recreation of the raising of the spire of Salisbury cathedral, in whose shadow Golding taught for 17 years. Rich in image and symbol, the story centers on Dean Jocelyn, who sacrifices his own physical and spiritual health and the lives of those dearest to him to erect the 404-foot spire that still miraculously crowns the cathedral to this day. *The Spire* is Golding's most poetic novel.

The decade from 1954 through 1964 was Golding's most fertile period. Between the mid-1960s and the end of his life, his most noteworthy novels were *Darkness Visible* (1979), about a prophet born out of the London blitz; and the sea trilogy, recently released under the overall title *To the Ends of the Earth.* This comprises *Rites of Passage* (1980), *Close Quarters* (1987), and *Fire Down Below* (1989). This final work is about the captain, crew, and passengers of a ship sailing from England to Australia after the Napoleonic wars.

Works about William Golding

Crompton, Don, and J. Briggs. *A View from the Spire: William Golding's Later Novels.* Oxford, England: Blackwell, 1985.

Dickson, L. L. *The Modern Allegories of William Golding.* Tampa: University of South Florida Press, 1990.

Gordon, James. *William Golding.* New York: Macmillan, 1988.

Johnson, Arnold. *Of Earth and Darkness: The Novels of William Golding.* Columbia: University of Missouri Press, 1980.

Gordimer, Nadine (1923–) *novelist, short story writer, essayist*

Nadine Gordimer published her first short story when she was 13, and she has not stopped writing since. Since that first publication in 1937, she has published eight collections of short stories and more than a dozen novels. She has also written extensively on political, literary, and cultural issues. In many ways, Gordimer has become a model for how writers can help to change the world by their involvement in it.

Gordimer was born in a small mining town outside of Johannesburg, South Africa, in late November 1923. Her father, Isidore Gordimer, a Jew, brought his jeweler's skills with him from Lithuania; her mother, Nan Myers Gordimer, helped him to become a shopkeeper in the conservative suburban town where Nadine was raised. Her first novel, *The Lying Days* (1953), evaluates the growth and development of a character not unlike young Gordimer herself as she confronts the conformity of a comfortable, middle-class existence. While still a young girl, Gordimer had an experience that was to forever change her life. Gordimer's mother removed the 11-year-old Gordimer from school. She was subsequently to have little contact with other children, and thus she felt isolated. Gordimer has been quoted as saying that she spent her "whole life, from eleven to sixteen, with older people, with the people of my mother's generation. . . . I simply lived her [her mother's] life." Scholar Rowland Smith connects this autobiographical detail with her greatest literary strength by saying that "reading and writing took the place of companionship with those of her own age." He also states that her constant attendance as a young outsider at older women's gatherings fostered the brilliant sense of dialogue and conversation that has characterized her writing throughout a tremendously productive public life.

Of more particular importance to students of literature, one of the novels Gordimer read during this long period of social isolation was Upton Sinclair's *The Jungle,* which recounts the horrible living conditions of those working in Chicago's meat-packing plants in the early 20th century. In a 1992 interview with Bill Moyers broadcast on PBS, Gordimer said that reading this book changed her life because she saw, clearly, that literature could change the world, that it could open people's eyes to inequity and foster change.

Many of Gordimer's stories and novels examine the status, and the responsibilities, of white, liberal intellectuals both in South Africa and abroad. Novels such as *The Late Bourgeois World* (1966), *A Guest of Honor* (1970), and *Burger's Daughter* (1979) all, in their various ways, call into question the need for political engagement with the world, and question whether smug self-assurance of one's choices is any more of a remove than direct withdrawal from involvement with the world. Perhaps in this way Gordimer has tried to more subtly approach the aloof remove she felt during those lonely teenage years at her mother's tea parties.

But it is tremendously inaccurate to suggest that Gordimer is one-dimensional. She has cast her eye on many issues of human relations and conduct, very often focusing on the awful effects of apartheid on all peoples in South Africa. In a collection of essays entitled *The Essential Gesture: Writing Politics and Places,* Gordimer makes it clear that we are who we are because of where we are. This willingness to examine the essential conditions of our existence is one reason for the international following that she has attracted over the years.

Nadine Gordimer has been one of South Africa's most important literary exports in the 20th century. She has been the recipient of many European, American, and South African literary awards; the capstone on her accomplishments was her 1991 Nobel Prize in literature.

Other Works by Nadine Gordimer

July's People. New York: Viking, 1981.
My Son's Story. New York: Farrar, Straus & Giroux, 1990.
A World of Strangers. London: Gollancz, 1958.

Works about Nadine Gordimer

Clingman, Stephen. *The Novels of Nadine Gordimer: History from the Inside.* Amherst: University of Massachusetts Press, 1992.
Smith, Rowland, ed. *Critical Essays on Nadine Gordimer.* Boston: G. K. Hall, 1990.

Graham, Winston Mawdsley (1910–)
novelist

Winston Graham was born in Manchester, England, to Albert Henry Graham, a chemist, and Anne Mawdsley Graham. Health problems forced him to leave school at age 16, but he continued his education with a private tutor. He began his literary career at age 21.

Graham first attained popular and critical recognition for his historical novels. *Ross Poldark* (1945), set in 18th-century Cornwall, describes the romantic life and social conflicts of a military captain as he rebuilds his estate after returning home from the Revolutionary War. The novel is the first in a popular series about Poldark and his descendants. Critics praised Graham's ability to convincingly depict the atmosphere and leisurely pace of a past era.

Six more Poldark novels would appear, the final, *The Angry Tide,* in 1977. Graham also wrote non-Poldark historicals and mysteries. When reviewing *The Grove of Eagles* (1963), a fictionalized account of the Elizabethan era, Robert Payne wrote that Graham "has soaked himself in local lore, knows his history, his towns, the shape of the vanished land . . . and he can follow his people through the daily round, hour by hour and minute by minute." Graham's historical novels were also popular because of his skill at drawing readers into the intrigues of his characters' lives. Near the end of *The Four Swans* (1977), Poldark's wife Demelza laments a series of unfortunate events in her life and seeks to return to her husband after an affair: "Now I weep tears, tears, tears, for so much youth and love buried into the ground. . . . They were internal—like blood. Now—now they stream down my face like rain—like rain that I cannot stop. Oh, Ross will you not hold me?"

Graham was also an accomplished mystery writer whom many critics credit with transforming the mystery and spy genre. He broke formulaic modes by probing the psychological and deep-seated historical motives that drive individuals. Graham's characters are usually ordinary people who must deal with past betrayals, inner demons, and moral dilemmas as they face increasingly complex situations. In his most popular thriller, *Marnie* (1961), he describes a woman caught in a cycle of criminal activity because of a psychoneurotic condition formed from a childhood trauma. Reviewer Anthony Bucher praised the author's "phenomenally successful use of a woman' viewpoint" and its "happy balance of psychoanalytic and novelistic method."

Graham's books have been made into two BBC television series and several movies, including Alfred Hitchcock's *Marnie* (1966). In 1983 Graham was made an Officer of the Order of the British Empire (OBE). Boucher observes that his mysteries are "long, meaty, serious and shrewdly calculated, with strong emphasis on story telling and surprise. Few men handle this have-it-both-ways form more skillfully. . . ."

Other Work by Winston Graham

A Green Flash. New York: Random House, 1987.

Grahame, Kenneth (1859–1932) *novelist, essayist, short story writer*

Kenneth Grahame was born in Edinburgh to James Cunningham Grahame and Bessie Ingles Grahame, who died of scarlet fever when her son was five. Shortly after her death, Grahame and his siblings were moved to their maternal grandmother's home in the Berkshire countryside, a place he loved and later incorporated into his stories.

From 1868 to 1875 Grahame excelled at St. Edward's School, Oxford, where he contributed anonymously to the school newspaper—the first evidence of his interest in writing. He aspired to academics, but instead began work as a clerk for an uncle, a parliamentary agent who controlled the family finances and refused to fund further education for his nephew. Soon Grahame left this job for the Bank of England, where he eventually became a senior executive before retiring in 1907 with the success of his classic children's novel, *The Wind in the Willows* (1908).

Grahame began his writing career contributing essays to such journals as the *St. James Gazette* and *The Yellow Book,* known for its stance against the literary and social establishment. William Ernest Henley, editor of *The National Observer,* was impressed with his essays and encouraged him to publish them as a collection. Grahame did so in *Pagan Papers* (1893), a book of personal essays and short stories for adults in which Grahame expresses a sentiment common among his contemporaries, that of a lost connection with the natural, animal world in a modern industrial society. In one essay, "The Lost Centaur," Grahame writes, "As we grow from our animal infancy and the threads snap one by one at each gallant wing-stroke of a soul poised for flight. . . . we have some forlorn sense of a vanished heritage."

Again encouraged by Henley, Grahame published two successful semiautobiographical works, *The Golden Age* (1895) and *Dream Days* (1898). In the stories of *The Golden Age,* five sibling orphans live with uncaring adult relatives who tend to everyday matters while the children use their imaginations to let the wind dictate their travels (as in the story "A Holiday") or become the knights of the Round Table (as in "Alarums and Excursions"). Grahame writes in the book's prologue that the adults "treated us, indeed, with kindness enough as to the needs of the flesh, but after that with indifference. . . . We *illuminati,* eating silently, our heads full of plans and conspiracies, could have told them what real life was. We had just left it outside, and were all on fire to get back to it."

Dream Days, the sequel to *The Golden Age,* includes the short story "The Reluctant Dragon," published separately as a children's picture book in 1938. A harbinger of Grahame's move toward animal stories, it tells of a young boy, Saint George, and a dragon staging a mock battle that fools villagers into accepting the dragon into their lives.

So well-received in both Britain and America were *The Golden Age* and *Dream Days* that Grahame's next and most enduring work, *The Wind in the Willows* (1908), at first disappointed readers. Grahame, who claimed to remember everything from age four to seven, had shifted the identification of the reader to the animal characters themselves, appealing more to children than adults.

Grahame began *The Wind in the Willows* as a series of letters to his son Alistair, whom he called "Mouse." The story of the friendship of four field and riverside animals—Mole, Rat, Badger, and Toad—begins one spring day when Mole breaks from cleaning his underground home to stroll along the river, where he meets Rat. Since Mole has never seen a river, Rat takes him on a picnic and boat ride, uttering the memorable line, "Believe

me, my young friend, there is nothing—absolutely nothing—half so much worth doing as simply messing about in boats." The two then meet the lovable but exasperating owner of the grand Toad Hall, Toad, on whose misadventures much of the book is based. When Toad buys and wrecks several cars and is later imprisoned for stealing another, Badger, a respected senior citizen, enlists Rat and Mole to help rescue Toad from his latest obsession. Critics have noted that *The Wind in the Willows* includes almost no female characters, but Grahame himself called it "free from the clash of sex."

Except for several essays and lectures and an editorship of *The Cambridge Book of Poetry for Children* (1916), Grahame stopped writing after *The Wind in the Willows.* In 1930 the book was dramatized by A. A. MILNE as "Toad of Toad Hall," and it has gone into more than 100 editions. Author Roger Sale writes, "Most writers and most people find that when they have tossed off adult tasks and human curses they have, left over, only a rather empty space. But Grahame could fill that space and invite us into the charmed circle he thereby created. He could make little sounds seem like bustle, make gestures of invitation seem like love, make food and fire feel like home."

A Work about Kenneth Grahame
Prince, Allison. *Kenneth Grahame: An Innocent in the Wood.* London: Allison & Busby, 1994.

Granville-Barker, Harley (1877–1946)
playwright, theater critic

Harley Granville-Barker was born in Kensington, London, to Albert James Barker, an architect, and Mary Elizabeth Bozzi-Granville Barker, who gave recitations and bird imitations on stage. Although his formal schooling was limited, his parents encouraged him to pursue a career in the theater and allowed him to attend numerous plays staged in London during his youth. In order to make himself sound more sophisticated, he added his mother's maiden name "Granville" to Barker soon after he started writing plays. He wrote a number of historical dramas that dealt with diverse topics, including personal relationships and politics.

Granville-Barker achieved his greatest success as a dramatist, actor, and director during the Edwardian era, just before World War I. His biographer, Eric Salmon, called Granville-Barker "in his day, the most famous and most respected director in the British theatre and his reputation as an actor stood only just short of his reputation as a director." Critics have compared his work to that of George Meredith and Henrik Ibsen. *The Marrying of Ann Leete*, written in 1899, traces the difficulties faced by the independent "New Woman" in a rigid patriarchal society. Another play, *Waste* (1907), found itself embroiled in controversy, and despite Bernard Shaw's calling the play "superb," it was banned by the British government for its treatment of themes such as abortion and political scandal.

After the war Granville-Barker came to be known largely for his critical writings on drama and the theater. His two-volume *Prefaces to Shakespeare*, written between 1927 and 1947, and a book he edited, *A Companion to Shakespeare Studies* (1934), established him as an expert in the field of Shakespearean dramatic interpretation. Critic J. L. Styan called "Prefaces to Shakespeare "remarkable" in that it attempted to create "a new descriptive dramatic criticism" that analyzed Shakespeare's plays as both literature and performance.

Today Granville-Barker's plays are seldom seen on stage. Though praised by critics of his day for his talented ability to deal with difficult and highly charged themes, others such as social reformer Beatrice Webb found his work "intellectual but dull." The scholar Allardyce Nicoll believed that this intellectuality made him "too inward-looking" and "aloof," preventing him from tapping into the more emotive elements of modern theater.

Works about Harley Granville-Barker

Purdom, C. B. *Harley Granville-Barker*. Cambridge, Mass.: Harvard University Press, 1955.
Salmon, Eric. *A Secret Life: Harley Granville-Barker*. London: Heinemann, 1984.

Graves, Robert (1895–1985) *poet, novelist, biographer, historian, nonfiction writer*

Robert Graves was a writer who spent much of his life in pursuit of the truth. As a poet, he wrote about love in an attempt to understand women and their power to inspire. Through his historical novels, including his most famous works, *I, Claudius* (1934) and *Claudius the God* (1934), he combed the pages of ancient history so that he and his readers might better understand life in the 20th century.

Graves was born in Wimbledon, England, to a middle-class Protestant family. He had a happy childhood, and from his parents he received two of the key interests that would serve him throughout his life. His father, Alfred Percival Graves, was a school inspector, and instilled in his son a love of Gaelic poetry. His mother, Amalie von Ranke Graves, nurtured Graves's interest in biblical literature. Graves attended Oxford University but did not graduate because of the outbreak of World War I, which would become a life-changing event for him.

At the age of 20, Graves joined the Royal Welsh Fusiliers, a regiment that was involved in some of the heaviest trench warfare on the western front. After nearly two years of witnessing the cruelty of war, the inequalities of Britain's class system within the army, and the slaughter of his friends, Graves was wounded by a nearby explosion, taken to a hospital tent, and left for dead. Miraculously, he survived the night and was taken to a military hospital, after which he was sent home on leave.

During the war, as he watched his friends die, Graves came to think of love as a trial and an ordeal. Witnessing the bravery of his close friend and fellow poet Siegfried SASSOON, Graves developed the idea that poets were a breed apart from other people, that they were people of daring and courage. Graves's poems are characterized by gracefulness and lucidity. Much of his poetry is concerned with his wartime experiences. His first collection of poetry, *Over the Brazier* (1917), was written while he was recovering from wounds. And with his next volume, *Fairies and Fusiliers* (1918), he became known as an accomplished war poet.

After his return from the war, Graves married the painter and feminist Nancy Nicholson in 1918. His friends and fellow writers E. M. FORSTER and Arnold BENNETT, helped get him a position as professor of English at the University of Cairo, and in 1926 he moved to Egypt with his wife and their two sons. The poet Laura Riding, a family friend, eventually joined them there.

The professorship was not a high-paying position, and money became tight for Graves. Again finding help from his friends, Graves was chosen by T. E. LAWRENCE, whom he had met at Oxford, to write Lawrence's biography, *Lawrence and the Arabs* (1927).

In 1929 Graves turned his biographical eye on himself and published his autobiography, *Good-bye to All That.* The book chronicled his early life, his war experiences, and the disillusioned postwar generation. Though the book was a success, it alienated several of Graves's friends, including Sassoon and the writer Edmund BLUNDEN, who felt that Graves had been too free with some details he shared with the public.

Good-bye to All That also detailed the end of Graves's marriage to Nicholson. While in Egypt, he had begun an affair with Riding, and in 1929 he moved with her to Deya, in Mallorca, which would be his home for much of the rest of his life.

It was during this time that Graves began work on *I, Claudius.* Described in his diary as an "interpretive biography," the novel is set during the height of the Roman Empire and tells the story of how Claudius, a club-footed and stammering member of the imperial family, thought of as an idiot by everyone around him, becomes emperor, almost by accident.

Although Graves was initially confused by why this subject matter had such a strong hold over him, he became deeply engrossed in the project until its publication in May 1934. *I, Claudius* met with immediate success, and in November that same year its sequel, *Claudius the God and his Wife Messalina,* was published to even greater success. In the following years, several film adaptations were attempted and Graves tackled the task of con-densing his two large books into one story. The film deals all fell through, but in 1976 the BBC (British Broadcasting Corporation) produced the 13-part miniseries *I, Claudius,* which boosted the sales of the books again.

Throughout the 1950s and 1960s, classical literature and mythology became a constant source of inspiration to Graves. With such books as *The Nazarene Gospel Restored* (1954), *The Greek Myths* (1955), and *Hebrew Myths: The Book of Genesis* (1964), he explored the foundations and formation of Western civilization.

In his exploration of the nature of poetry, Graves wrote that women and poets are natural allies. He argued that abstract reasoning is a predominantly male approach to thought and that rational schooling discourages intuitive thought. "Abstract reason," he wrote, "formerly the servant of practical human reasons, has everywhere become its master, and denies poetry any excuse for existence." Graves believed that reason could not prompt the writing of poetry, because reason shows no spark of humor or religious feeling. Similarly, he believed that philosophy is antipoetic: "Though philosophers like to define poetry as irrational fancy, for us it is a practical, humorous, reasonable way of being ourselves. Of never acquiescing in a fraud; of never accepting the second-rate in poetry, painting, music, love, friends. Of safeguarding our poetic institutions against the encroachments of mechanized, insensate, inhumane, abstract rationality."

Critical Analysis

Graves admitted to having no interest in historical fiction. It is only natural, therefore, that critics have made a close study of why *I, Claudius,* which some have called the only successful historical novel of the 20th century, captured Graves's imagination.

While very little is known about the character or personality of the real Claudius, one thing that historical texts specifically mention is that he was excessively devoted and submissive to his wife. In the novel, there are two concentrations of evil, both women: Claudius's grandmother Livia and his second wife Messalina, who uses her position as queen for her own conniving purposes while Claudius remains a fool in love, pathetically unaware of her treachery. Indeed, most of the evil deeds in the novel are carried out by women who are scheming to gain power by connecting themselves with men in powerful positions. In one powerful scene, Livia makes Claudius promise to make her a goddess after her death, so that she can escape punishment for all the crimes she has committed in what she sees as her service to Rome: "I have put the good of the Empire before all human considerations. To keep the Empire free from factions I have committed many crimes. . . . And what is the proper reward for a ruler who commits such crimes for the good of his subjects? The proper reward, obviously, is to be deified."

There is an ironic humor in this passage that can be found throughout the Claudius books, and this humor is another important part of the style Graves employed. It was the tradition of many authors at the time to treat historical characters as if they were more admirable, more villainous, or simply more elevated than people of the present. However, Graves chose to present his ancient Roman characters as recognizable contemporary people, as can be read in the sarcasm with which Claudius introduces himself to the reader in the opening of *I, Claudius*. "I, Tiberius Claudius Drusus Nero Germanicus This-that-and-the-other (for I shall not trouble you yet with all my titles) who was once, and not so long ago either, known to my friends and relatives and associates as 'Claudius the Idiot', or 'That Claudius', or 'Claudius the Stammerer', or 'Clau-Clau-Claudius' or at best as 'Poor Uncle Claudius', am now about to write this strange history of my life. . . ." As Graves scholar J. M. Cohen notes, touches like this "build up the impression that the Romans of the Empire were no more than twentieth-century people in period costume." Cohen goes on to explain that showing historical figures in this way stresses "the unchangingness of human motive and action."

Other Works by Robert Graves
King Jesus. New York: Creative Age Press, 1946.

The Poems of Robert Graves. New York: Doubleday, 1958.
The White Goddess. New York: Knopf, 1958.

Works about Robert Graves
Bloom, Harold, ed. *Robert Graves.* New York: Chelsea House, 1987.
Graves, Richard Perceval. *Robert Graves: The Assault Heroic 1895–1926.* New York: Viking, 1986.
Seymour, Miranda. *Robert Graves: Life on the Edge.* New York: Henry Holt, 1995.

Green, Henry (Henry Vincent Yorke)
(1905–1973) *novelist*

Born to a wealthy family near Tewkesbury in Gloucestershire, England, Henry Green, born Henry Vincent Yorke, grew up on a 2,500-acre country estate. His father ran the family engineering firm and was often away in London on business. His mother came from an aristocratic family. An avid sportswoman when young, she loved to hunt, read a great deal, and was a witty conversationalist.

Green attended the prestigious private school Eton. He did not enjoy it, saying later, "In my case it has been a long and in the end successful struggle to drive out what they taught me there." While at school, he and some friends formed a Society of Arts. Green described this as a watershed, recalling, "I determined to be a writer, the diary I began to keep with this end in view was full of loud shouts about it."

Green attended Oxford, where he studied English. He published his first novel while at the university. The protagonist of *Blindness* (1926) is a scholar who is blinded in an accident on the way home from boarding school. In the course of the book he struggles with his blindness and his first love affair. Many critics praised this gloomy novel, but Green himself was not particularly proud of it in later years.

Despite this literary success, Green did not excel at Oxford and left without a degree to join the family engineering firm in Birmingham. Meanwhile, he continued to write. *Living* (1929), his second novel, is set among factory workers in Birmingham and draws on much of Green's own work experience at the time. Christopher ISHERWOOD called *Living* "the best proletarian novel ever written," but Green himself was wary of the accolade, pointing out that only middle-class readers had praised it and that all the working-class people he had spoken to abhorred the book. Green also wrote novels about the upper and middle classes. His third novel, *Party Going* (1939), describes four hours in the aimless existence of several upperclass dilettantes in London.

In 1938 the almost certain approach of World War II disturbed Green deeply. He was well aware of the fatalities of the previous war, and he was sure that he—and many others—would be killed in the next. With this fear before him, he wrote the autobiography *Pack My Bag* (1940). While writing it, he was training as a volunteer fireman. His horrific experiences with the wartime fires in London enriched his Blitz novel *Caught* (1943). *Loving* (1945), his second war novel, is one of his best-known works. Set in an Irish castle during the war, it describes the intrigues among the British servants who steal, blackmail, and seduce. At the beginning of the book the mistress of the house declares, "We're really in enemy country here you know. We simply must keep things up." Self-contained though their world is, the foreign war frames their domestic conflicts. American author John Updike called the novel "a cosy anarchy of pilfering, gossip, giddiness, and love."

Green is famous for his unusual syntax. In his earlier novels he often uses run-on sentences, sometimes omits articles ("the" and "a"), and sometimes writes sentences without nouns. His sentences can become intensely lilting and poetic. After a small boy is kidnapped by a madwoman in *Caught*, for example, we hear how he is trapped in her living room: "She did not turn on the light, so that he could see her eyes only by their glitter, a sparkle by the fire, which, as it was disturbed to flame, sent her shadow reeling, gyrating round sprawling rosy walls." Green said he was influenced by the whimsical syntax of Charles DOUGHTY, a Victorian traveler who translated Arabic into English. John Updike notes that both Green and Doughty use "bold phrases roped together by a slack and flexible grammar." Some critics argue that this technique seems forced; Orville Prescott, for example, criticizes Green for "excessive concentration on method rather than matter." Many other critics, however, see Green's innovations as brilliant. Green's descriptive language becomes more sparse in his later novels, and his final novel, *Doting* (1952), is written almost entirely in dialogue.

Green wrote nine novels; he did not publish any more after 1952. The novelist Elizabeth BOWEN once said that Green's novels "reproduce, as so few English novels do, the actual sensations of living." Similarly, the critic Brooke Allen has written that Green "ardently mixes darkness and light, and his work must always appeal to those readers who, like him, do not fear life's inevitable contradictions."

Other Works by Henry Green

Back. 1946. Reprint, London: Havill Press, 1998.
Loving, Living, Party Going. 1978. Reprint, New York: Penguin, 1993.
Nothing. 1950. Reprint, Fairfield, N.J.: Augustus M. Kelley, 1970.
Surviving: The Uncollected Writings of Henry Green. Edited by Michael Yorke. New York: Viking, 1993.

A Work about Henry Green

North, Michael. *Henry Green and the Writing of His Generation.* Charlottesville: University Press of Virginia, 1984.

Greene, Graham (1904–1991) *novelist, short story writer, playwright, critic, poet, journalist, travel writer, screen writer, biographer*

Graham Greene was born Henry Graham Greene in Berkhamsted, Herefordshire, England, into a comfortable upper-middle-class family. His father was headmaster of the prestigious private school Berkhamsted.

A shy child, Greene loved to play with his many toy soldiers, imagining them doing daring deeds in faraway places. He enjoyed tales of adventure, and especially loved Rider Haggard's *King Solomon's Mines* (1886). He later wrote, "In childhood all books are books of divination . . . and like the fortune teller who sees a long journey in the cards or death by water they influence the future." Haggard's book stirred a wanderlust that affected Greene all his life.

At 14 Greene read Marjorie Bowen's novel *The Viper of Milan* (1906). The novel's protagonist is a villain, and its effect on Greene was dramatic: "From that moment I began to write. . . . It was as if I had been supplied once and for all with a subject." Evil was to fascinate him throughout his literary career.

At first Greene attended his father's school as a day student but at 13 he became a boarder. Greene hated boarding school, writing later that it was "a savage land of strange customs and inexplicable cruelties." He ran away, but his parents retrieved him and sent him to London for six months of psychoanalysis. Greene blossomed under the treatment and for the rest of his life respected the creative power of dreams.

Greene studied modern history at Oxford. In 1925 he published his first book, *Babbling April,* a volume of sentimental poetry about summer revels. After Greene graduated he worked as a journalist in Nottingham. There, he converted to Roman Catholicism in 1926, partly because of the influence of his fiancée, Vivien Dayrell-Browning.

Green's first novel was *The Man Within* (1929), which describes a criminal's flight from a smuggling gang for whom he used to work. The novel received glowing reviews, the *Sunday Times* (London) finding "no flaw in this strangely fascinating book." His publishers gave him a contract for two more books, and Greene left his journalism job.

Greene's next two novels were critical and commercial failures, and his fourth book (a biography of a minor poet) was rejected outright. Good fortune finally arrived when he became a respected book reviewer for the *Spectator.* Describing a 1952

book about explorers, for example, he wrote, "The imagination has its own geography that alters with the centuries. Each continent in turn looms up on the horizon like a great rock carved with unintelligible hieroglyphics and symbols catching at the unconscious." Film critic Dilys Powell said of Greene: "He was, he is, the best of critics." Reviewing honed Greene's critical ability and helped him completely transform his own style. He said that after the failed fourth book, "I had to begin again naked."

The result was the famous *Stamboul Train* (1932). This spy thriller describes interactions between various people sharing a train from the English Channel to Istanbul. Greene called this novel an "entertainment," which he defined as having the language and plot of a thriller but extra moral complexity. He classed several more of his novels as "entertainments" in this sense, and all were popular and later filmed. His second famous "entertainment" was *A Gun for Sale* (1936), a thriller whose protagonist is a hired killer.

In 1935 Greene traveled to the African country of Liberia, which he describes in his travelogue *Journey Without Maps* (1936). This book exults in the everyday details of the Liberian environment. The *Independent* described *Journey Without Maps* as "One of the best travel books this century." V. S. PRITCHETT has noted of Greene, "His originality lay in his gifts as a traveller. He had the foreign ear and eye for the strangeness of ordinary life and its ordinary crises."

Upon returning to England in 1935, Greene became film critic for the *Spectator,* and his own work acquired cinematic qualities. He was an acclaimed reviewer, alert to the new possibilities of the film as artistic medium. He tended to admire documentary films ("We are apt to forget, among the gangsters and the grand passions, that the cinema has other uses than fiction," he wrote), and to lose patience with historical dramas. His reviews were sometimes scathing, as when he described the 1935 film *Joan of Arc* as "very noisy, rather like the Zoo at feeding time." Greene had legal clashes with film producers over some of his critiques, and was sued when he described child actress Shirley Temple as precociously sexual: "Watch the way she measures a man with agile studio eyes, with dimpled depravity."

Brighton Rock (1938) is one of Greene's most famous novels. Set among the same Brighton racecourse gangs first seen in *A Gun for Sale,* this novel describes a marked man's flight from assassins. More than a thriller, it grapples with moral questions and the mystery of the "appalling . . . strangeness of the mercy of God." Author Marghanita Laski described the ending as "the most painful any novelist has ever written."

In 1937 Greene became a film reviewer for the short-lived magazine *Night and Day.* Soon after that he received a commission to travel to Mexico and report on the persecution of Catholics there. His ensuing travel book *The Lawless Roads* (1939) received lukewarm reviews. Greene used his Mexican experiences more successfully in *The Power and the Glory* (1940), a novel describing the flight of a Mexican priest during the persecutions. In 1936 he wrote a film review in which he lamented how glamorous artists made the church: "Alas! my poor Church, so picturesque, so noble, so superhumanly pious, so intensely dramatic. I really prefer the *New Statesman* view, shabby priests counting pesetas in their fingers in dingy cafés before blessing tanks." The priest of the *The Power and the Glory* does not have such a mercenary approach, but Greene does make him humanly weak instead of a traditional icon of glamour.

When World War II was declared, Greene longed to join the army but was too old to enlist. Instead, he worked briefly in the propaganda division of the Ministry of Information. His later short story "Men at Work" mocks the aimlessness of the Ministry. When the air raids began, he became a warden. His novel *The Ministry of Fear* (1943) is set during the Blitz and describes the bombing with phantasmagoric vividness: " . . . yet another raider came up from the south-east muttering . . . like a witch in a child's dream."

In autumn 1941 Greene joined the British Secret Service, and he spent 15 months in this capac-

ity in Sierra Leone. His experience there influenced his novel *The Heart of the Matter* (1948), which describes an English policeman working in West Africa during the Second World War.

Greene returned to London's Secret Service headquarters in 1943. His experiences with the Secret Service are featured in his mocking novel *Our Man in Havana* (1960), a comical treatment of inept spy service. A vacuum cleaner salesman, down on his luck, pretends to be a spy, and sends the service fictitious spy reports for six months, until they realize he is an impostor.

After the war Greene became a director of the publishing house Eyre and Spottiswode. He also began writing screenplays, including the successful *The Fallen Idol* (1948), a thriller told largely from a child's perspective. His most famous screenplay is *The Third Man* (1949), a film noir thriller set in a postwar Vienna made ominous by slanted camera angles and lens distortions. After the war, Greene also wrote a few children's books, all illustrated by his mistress Dorothy Glover.

Greene's passionate affair with Catherine Walston produced his masterpiece *The End of the Affair* (1951). The novel describes a rejected lover's anguished search for the reason his affair ended. The answer is a shocking surprise. American novelist William Faulkner called it "one of the most true and moving novels of my time, in anybody's language."

In 1950 and 1951 Greene traveled a great deal, including trips to Malaya and Vietnam. Vietnam, torn by civil war, inspired *The Quiet American* (1955), in which a well-meaning American begins funding a mysterious "Third Force" and giving them explosives, trusting them to fight the Vietminh. The consequences are ghastly: "He was seeing a real war for the first time: he had punted down into Phat Diem in a kind of schoolboy dream." The novel is narrated by a tough, lonely English reporter, who describes his deep love for a Vietnamese woman, his guilt at betraying his wife, and his pain at losing his lover to the naïve American: "The other kind of war is more innocent than this. One does less damage with a mortar."

Later in life, Greene wrote the lighthearted *Travels with My Aunt* (1969), "the only book I have written for the fun of it." Greene's biographer Norman Sherry calls this "a parody of his life and works," that affectionately satirizes Greene's thriller novels and adventurous travels. More serious is the novel *The Honorary Consul* (1973). Greene said this was "perhaps the novel I prefer to all the others." An alcoholic, unimportant honorary consul is kidnapped by a group of Argentinean revolutionaries, and all sides become corrupt in the ensuing drama.

In addition to his novels and travelogues, Greene published several collections of short stories, six plays, two biographies, and three autobiographies: *A Sort of Life* (1971), *Ways of Escape* (1980), and the posthumously published *A World of My Own: A Dream Diary* (1993). He once remarked, "Writing is a form of therapy; sometimes I wonder how all those who do not write, compose or paint can manage to escape the madness, the melancholia, the panic fear which is inherent in the human situation." The novelist William GOLDING declared, "Graham Greene was in a class by himself . . . He will be read and remembered as the ultimate chronicler of twentieth-century man's consciousness and anxiety."

Other Works by Graham Greene

Collected Essays. New York: Viking, 1993.
The Last Word and Other Stories. New York: Viking, 1991.
Mornings in the Dark: The Graham Greene Film Reader. Edited by David Parkinson. Manchester, England: Carcanet, 1993.

A Work about Graham Greene

Sherry, Norman. *The Life of Graham Greene.* New York: Viking, 1995.

Greer, Germaine (1939–) *nonfiction writer, essayist*

Born near Melbourne, Australia, to Erik and Margaret Lafrank Greer, Germaine Greer was educated at a local convent school. She took an undergraduate degree at the University of Melbourne, went to the University of Sydney for her M.A., and to Cambridge University in England for her Ph.D. in 1967. She was gifted in language study and exhibited intense interest in music and painting. As an educated woman of the '60s, she embraced the decade's excesses and enthusiasms—rock music, drugs, and sexual experimentation—and wrote articles on those topics for the underground magazine *Oz*.

Greer burst on the intellectual scene as a sexually liberated superfeminist with *The Female Eunuch* (1970). The book argues that the stereotypical feminine roles symbolically castrated women, and it called for freedom and emancipation: "I'm sick of the masquerade. I'm sick of pretending eternal youth. I'm sick of belying my own intelligence, my own will, my own sex. . . . I'm sick of being a transvestite. I refuse to be a female impersonator. I am a woman, not a castrate." The book was a worldwide best-seller and established Greer as "the feminist men like."

Greer acted out the liberation she called for by writing inflammatory articles for underground magazines, posing nude, having abortions, and espousing group sex. She extended her thesis with her book on women painters, *The Obstacle Race* (1979), wherein she contends that society's damage to women's egos prevents them from becoming the artistic equals of the great male painters. Always the contrarian, she provoked controversy with *Sex and Destiny: The Politics of Human Fertility* (1984) wherein she argued that western European ideas of population control are not applicable to the poor countries of the Third World.

Greer's latest book, *The Whole Woman* (1998), is sorrowfully colored by her personal failures with fertility experiments. In it, she repudiates her earlier work and attacks young American writers such as Kate Roiphe, Naomi Wolf, and Natasha Walter, who Greer feels have failed to grasp the essence of feminism. Her biographer Christine Wallace stresses Greer's achievement in popularizing feminist ideas: "Ask baby boomers and their elders in the English-speaking world to name a feminist, and more often than not they will name Germaine Greer and mention *The Female Eunuch.*"

Other Work by Germaine Greer

Suffragettes to She-Devils: Women's Liberation and Beyond. With Liz McQuiston. New York: Phaidon Press, 1997.

A Work about Germaine Greer

Wallace, Christine. *Germaine Greer: Untamed Shrew.* London: Faber & Faber, 1999.

Gregory, Lady (1852–1932) *folklorist, translator, playwright, biographer*

Lady Gregory was born Isabella Augusta Persse in Roxborough, Ireland, to Anglo-Irish parents Dudley Persse, a member of the landholding class in Ireland, and Frances Barry Persse. Her education took place on her family's large estate, Roxborough House, and during her travels with her brother to France and Italy. Lady Gregory taught herself four languages: French, German, Italian, and Gaelic. She married Sir William Gregory, a member of Parliament and governor of Ceylon in 1881, taking the title of Lady Gregory on her marriage. She had a notable career as a playwright and director, but she is best known for her work as an Irish folklorist and translator. In her writings, she expressed what she called her "passionate love of Ireland" by exploring the indigenous culture of the Irish and the highly political themes of colonialism and Irish nationalism.

Lady Gregory began her career as a folklorist by translating the legends and stories of the Gaelic-speaking people living in the Kiltartan district in Ireland. She published several major collections of folk tales, including *Cuculain of Muirthemne* in 1902 and *Gods and Fighting Men* in 1904.

Lady Gregory interpreted Irish mythology in order to express anticolonialism sentiment, a theme present in much of her work. Her 1907 play *The Rising of the Moon* describes the actions of early 20th-century Fenian nationalists who wanted the British to grant Ireland independence. Like her other works, this play relied heavily on replicating and interpreting Irish dialect for her audience. The following verse is sung by an anonymous man to torment an Irish policeman who himself is torn by his loyalty to the Crown and his mild Republican sympathies: "O, then, tell me, Shawn O'Farrell / Where the gathering is to be / In the old spot by the river / Right well known to you and me!"

Lady Gregory also edited her husband's and grandfather's letters for publication and wrote an autobiography, *Seventy Years,* published posthumously in 1976. In this work she proclaimed that, for her, "play-writing . . . came as if by accident. I think my preparation for it had been in great part that London life, that education in talking."

Despite the lasting impact of her work as a translator of myths and fables that are still read today, Lady Gregory is remembered primarily for her patronage of the Irish Literary Renaissance. Her friendship and support of Irish poet William Butler YEATS and his circle of writers remains an important part of her legacy. In *Our Irish Theatre* Gregory quotes Yeats's own reflections on her influence: "When our Irish dramatic movement took its present form, I say somebody must write a number of play[s] in prose if it was to have a good start. I did not know what do . . . You said I might dictate to you . . . and it was almost always you who gave the right turn to the phrase and gave it the ring of daily life." Lady Gregory made a career of encouraging writers to explore their Irish roots in order to spark a renewed interest in Irish culture and to support the cause of Irish independence. She has been called "the mother of folklore" by the Irish folklore commission. Contemporary critic Elizabeth Coxhead writes of Lady Gregory, "Hers is talent, not genius, but it is exquisitely satisfying of its kind, and her best things, notably her one-act plays, are minor classics."

Other Works by Lady Gregory

Selected Writings of Lady Gregory. New York: Penguin, 1996.
Irish Myths and Legends. Philadelphia: Running Press, 1998.

A Work about Lady Gregory

Saddlemyer, A., and C. Smythe, eds. *Lady Gregory, Fifty Years After.* Chester Springs, Pa.: Dufour Editions, 1987.

Grieve, Christopher Murray

See MACDIARMID, HUGH.

Griffiths, Trevor (1935–) *playwright, screenwriter*

Trevor Griffiths was born in Manchester, England, to Ernest Griffiths and Ann Connor. Growing up in a working-class family, he took advantage of the educational opportunities available to him in postwar Britain and spent his free time during his teens reading in the Manchester Central Library. He attended Manchester University, where he earned a bachelor's degree with honors in 1955 and later went on to study at the graduate level. Over the course of his long and prolific career, Griffiths made a reputation for himself in the British theater and literary world as a controversial writer whose work often dealt directly with radical political themes.

Griffiths's three best-known plays—*Occupations* (1970), *The Party* (1973), and *Comedians* (1975)—all address the possibility of social justice for the average citizen in modern Britain. A critic for the *Financial Times* claimed that even the humor in the *Comedians* was "a deadly serious business that also involved anger, pain, and truth." Of his more recent play, *Piano* (1990), which closely examines the lives of the guests who attend a weekend party in the Russian countryside in 1904, Griffiths claimed, "I suspect it may prove, like its illustrious forebears, to be about just this felt sense of breakdown and deadlock; and thus perhaps, in a nicely perverse irony, about what it's like to be living in our own post-capitalist, post-socialist, post-realist, post-modern time."

A left-leaning political agenda marks all aspects of Griffiths's work, as indicated by his decision to serve as editor the Labor Party newspaper, *North-ern Voice,* during the 1960s. More recently, he has turned his attention to writing for television and the movies, because he believes the theater remains "incapable . . . of reaching, let alone mobilising, large popular audiences." He achieved his greatest recognition in this medium for his 1981 screenplay *Reds,* a movie based on the life of socialist American journalist, John Reed, who wrote about the Russian Revolution. This work earned Griffiths a Writers Guild of America Award for Best Original Drama.

Today Griffiths continues to stir up controversy with his work. His recent television drama *Food for Ravens* (1997) boldly depicts the life of politician Aneurin Bevan, a Welsh politician known as the architect of the National Health Service in Britain. According to the *New Statesman,* Griffiths's commitment to a politics of social change enabled him to "redefine radical drama in the 1970s by making serious debate exciting to watch."

A Work about Trevor Griffiths

Garner, Stanton B. *Trevor Griffiths.* Ann Arbor: University of Michigan Press, 1999.

Gunn, Neil Miller (1891–1973) *novelist, playwright, essayist*

Neil Gunn was the son of a fishing boat skipper in Dunbeath, Caithness, which became the setting for some of his best-known novels. He entered the Customs and Excise Service in Scotland in 1911 and worked for various distilleries, leading to his publication of *Whisky and Scotland* in 1935. His first stories were published in 1923, and he became a full-time writer with the success of his novel *Highland River* (1937). This book, like his first novel, *Morning Tide* (1930), depicted a boy's growth into manhood in the Scottish Highlands.

Gunn wrote some plays that were generally less successful than his novels. He also wrote historical fiction. *Sun Circle* (1933) concerns the Viking invasion of Scotland. *The Silver Darlings* (1941), considered his best novel, is about the aftermath of the Clearances in Sunderland. During World War II, in answer to a friend's complaint that his pastoral *Young Art and Old Hector* (1942) was an insufficient response to the dangers of fascism, Gunn wrote *The Green Isle of the Great Deep* as a case against totalitarian rule. In this novel, the characters Art and Hector find themselves in a less-than-ideal world as the author critiques the workings of a materialist community. Gunn was a socialist and was involved in the politics of nationalism. While he was not himself a Gaelic speaker, he was concerned about the decline of Gaelic speech and culture. In his later life he wrote essays, short stories, travel writing, and autobiography in addition to the novels for which he was most well known. He is considered a leading figure of the Scottish Renaissance.

Other Work by Neil Gunn

The Serpent. 1944. Reprint, Edinburgh: Canongate, 1997.

A Work about Neil Gunn

Scott, Alexander, and Douglas Gifford, eds. *Neil M. Gunn, the Man and the Writer.* Edinburgh: Blackwood, 1973.

Gunn, Thomson William (1929–) *poet*

Thom Gunn was born in Gravesend, Kent, England, to Herbert Smith and Charlotte Thomson Gunn, who were both journalists. During World War II he lived in a boardinghouse safely distant from London, later served in the army, and earned B.A. (1953) and M.A. (1958) degrees in English from Cambridge.

While at Cambridge, Gunn attended numerous lectures by F. R. LEAVIS, whose passion for literature he greatly admired. He also began writing poetry. Gunn's first publication, *Fighting Terms* (1954) is a compilation of poetry he wrote at Cambridge. The opening poem, "The Wound," reveals his attention to poetic form and realism, using powerful images of soldiers and war that dominate the collection. Narrated by a soldier trying to overcome the psychological ravages of war, the poem begins with the lines, "The huge wound in my head began to

heal / About the beginning of the seventh week," which illustrates Gunn's realism and strong sense of rhythm.

Gunn's early interest in realism and formal verse structures (such as sonnets) caused him to be associated with the MOVEMENT, a group of authors including Donald DAVIE, with similar artistic preferences. Gunn resisted such grouping, however, and considered the Movement largely a journalistic construction. He quickly and permanently distanced himself, both geographically and philosophically, from the group by moving to California to study under the poet and critic Yvor Winters at Stanford in 1954.

Gunn continued writing highly structured poetry throughout the 1950s, but his work displayed a marked change in *My Sad Captains and Other Poems* (1961). Much less structured, it moves away from the images of war and soldiers and instead focuses on congenial interactions between living things. In "A Map of the City," for instance, Gunn presents the image of a man on a hill meditating on the physical place and the people surrounding him. In lines starkly different from those of "The Wound," Gunn writes, "I stand upon a hill and see / . . . Endless potentiality." His narrator, unlike the one in "The Wound," finds comfort and promise in the company of humanity.

Throughout the 1970s, Gunn continued writing poetry that expressed his comfort with humanity, but he broke new and important ground with *The Passages of Joy* (1982) and *The Man with Night Sweats* (1992). *The Passages of Joy,* which exhibits little of his early attention to structured poetic forms is, according to the scholar Blake Morrison, "the book in which Gunn 'comes out' as a homosexual and is confessional in the sense that he speaks candidly for the first time about his sexual experiences with, and attraction to, other men." In "Sweet Things," for instance, the poet matter-of-factly describes an encounter between two men, in which the narrator remarks, "How handsome he is in / his lust and energy."

With his sexual orientation no longer an issue, Gunn addressed the AIDS epidemic in *The Man with Night Sweats.* As Morrison has noted, "The first section of the book continues in the vein of *The Passages of Joy,* with reflections on the pleasures and hedonism of homosexual love. However, the concluding section consists of a sequence of elegies to the poet's friends who have died of AIDS." In *The Man with Night Sweats,* Gunn exhibits more human emotion than in any other collection of his poetry. In "A Sketch of the Great Dejection," for instance, his narrator ponders life and death while sitting on a gravestone in a dreary, neglected cemetery. He longs for passion, and wonders how he can live in a world that seems extremely bleak and lonely. In the poem's final lines, however, the narrator finds comfort in simply moving on: "I fared on and, though the landscape did not change, / it came to seem after a while like a place of recuperation." *The Man with Night Sweats* earned Gunn the first Forward Prize, Britain's highest recognition for poetry.

Gunn's critical reception has been positive throughout his career. His ability to shift between structured and unstructured verse, his position as a formally trained poet involved in the counterculture of the 1960s, and his status as an Englishman living in America make him something of a literary anomaly.

In addition to the Forward Prize, Gunn has also received the Levinson Prize, the Somerset Maugham Award, a Rockefeller Award, a Guggenheim Fellowship, the PEN/Los Angeles Prize for poetry, and the Sara Teasdale Prize. The scholar Jonathan Levin describes Gunn as "a poet of great sensuous responsiveness and rich intelligence" and considers *The Man with Night Sweats,* "a classic in the literature of AIDS," Gunn's greatest achievement.

Other Works by Thom Gunn

Collected Poems. New York: Farrar, Straus & Giroux, 1994.
Old Stories. New York: Sea Cliff, 1992.
Shelf Life: Essays, Memoirs, and an Interview. Ann Arbor: University of Michigan Press, 1993.

A Work about Thom Gunn

Dyson, A. E., ed. *Three Contemporary Poets: Thom Gunn, Ted Hughes and R. S. Thomas: A Casebook.* Basingstoke, England: Macmillan, 1990.

Gurney, Ivor Bertie (1890–1937) *poet, composer*

Born in Gloucester, England, Ivor Gurney attended the Royal College of Music from 1911 until the outbreak of World War I. Beginning in 1915, he served in the Gloucester Regiment on the western front as a private and was in active service in Flanders. Gassed and wounded at Passchendaele in September 1917, he was sent to a hospital in Edinburgh.

Gurney published two volumes of poetry: *Severn and Somme* (1917) and *War's Embers* (1919). Both collections were well received, though the latter less so, because of critics' reservations regarding Gurney's "colloquially direct diction." His early work tended to concern the Gloucestershire countryside and local incidents in the trenches, but his best war poems were written later as in the following lines from a quatrain entitled "Requiem," addressed to stars: "Pure and cold your radiance, pure and cold / My dead friend's face as well."

Because of the deterioration of his mental health, Gurney was committed in 1922 to the City of London Mental Hospital, where he continued to compose music (nearly 300 songs) and poetry until his death. The poems that he wrote in the mental hospital are uneven, but what they lack in control they often recover in vision and illumination.

Other Work by Ivor Gurney

Collected Poems: Ivor Gurney. Edited by Patrick J. Kavanagh. New York: Oxford University Press, 1992.

Works about Ivor Gurney

Hurd, Michael. *The Ordeal of Ivor Gurney.* New York: Oxford University Press, 1979.
Lucas, John. *Ivor Gurney.* Devon, England: Northcote House, 2001.

H

Hall, Radclyffe (1886–1943) *novelist, poet, short story writer*

Radclyffe Hall was christened Marguerite, but she was never comfortable with the name or the gender it denoted. She was raised primarily by her neglectful mother and stepfather. At age 17 she inherited her father's wealth, upon which she attended Cambridge and traveled throughout America and Europe. It was around this time that she took the name Radclyffe and began to wear male clothing.

Hall was only three when she wrote her first poem, and her earliest publications were poetry. She published five volumes of poetry from 1906 to 1915, including *'Twixt Earth and Stars* (1906) and *A Sheaf of Verses* (1900). Her poems are usually lyrics about nature's beauty and romantic love. One of her most accomplished poems is "Ode to Sappho": "Those love-burnt lips! Can death have quenched their fire? / Whose words oft stir our senses to unrest?"

Hall published her first novels in 1924: *The Forge,* a comedy about marriage; and *The Unlit Lamp,* which describes a mother and daughter relationship. In 1926 she published *Adam's Breed,* a psychological novel that has been compared to the work of Dorothy RICHARDSON and May SINCLAIR. It describes the struggle of an anguished orphan to find serenity. *Adam's Breed* was critically acclaimed, winning the Prix Femina and the James Tait Black prize.

Hall's next book, *The Well of Loneliness* (1928), is a semiautobiographical novel describing the painful life of a woman named Stephen who identifies as a man, has several romantic relationships with women, and suffers greatly from society's condemnation. The novel's only hint at sexual union is the famous line, "And that night they were not divided," but its lesbian theme caused it to be banned in Britain as obscene. A famous legal trial ensued, challenging the obscenity label, and many writers, among them Virginia WOOLF, Vera BRITTAIN, and Rebecca WEST, fought for the book's release.

Hall's next literary offerings were more cautious. A devout convert to Catholicism, she modernized the tale of Christ's nativity in her novel *The Master of the House* (1932), and in 1934 she published a collection of short stories, *Miss Ogilvie Finds Herself.* The title story was written in 1926 and was the first short story Hall wrote about lesbian identification. Her last novel was *The Sixth Beatitude* (1936), in which an unmarried mother struggles with social condemnation.

In a review of Sally Cline's biography of Hall, Andrea Dworkin summed up the author's influence: "Making lesbianism more visible, she helped destroy the protective cover of socially accepted romantic friendships between women. Ironically this increased clarity led to viewing homosexuality as a disease. Her vocabulary may have become archaic, but her stance was prescient and brave."

Other Work by Radclyffe Hall

Your John: The Love Letters of Radclyffe Hall. Edited by Joanne Glasgow. New York: New York University Press, 1997.

Works about Radclyffe Hall

Baker, Michael. *Our Three Selves: The Life of Radclyffe Hall.* New York: Morrow, 1985.

Cline, Sally. *Radclyffe Hall: A Woman Called John.* New York: Overlook Press, 1999.

Hamilton, Patrick (Anthony Walter Patrick Hamilton) (1904–1962)
playwright, novelist

Patrick Hamilton was born in Sussex, England, the youngest of three children. His parents were divorced and his home life was tumultuous; his wealthy solicitor father was an incorrigible womanizer who spent his inheritance on alcohol and revelry. Patrick was educated at various private schools, where he became interested in the theater. At age 17 he was briefly employed as an assistant stage manager and actor. He remained fascinated by the theater but gave up acting as too precarious. Instead, he became a stenographer.

Hamilton's first book was *Monday Morning* (1925), a witty novel about an upper-class young man who starts his first job in London and tries to write a book. Hamilton conveys the optimism and naïveté of youth in humorous terms: "The disillusionment phase did not run riot for much more than a week, being exorcised eventually by the sports-coat, which was all for an athletic phase." Hamilton's second novel, *Craven House* (1926), is a comical description of various small crises in the lives of residents at a boardinghouse. It was critically acclaimed in both England and America.

Hamilton is best known for his plays. *Rope* (1929) is about two undergraduates who kill a friend in order to prove they are superior to mundane people. Alfred Hitchcock made it into a film in 1948. The Victorian play *Gaslight* (1938) (also known as *Angel Street*) was similarly successful. It describes a man who tries to drive his wife mad in order to acquire her wealth.

Hamilton was a committed marxist, compassionate toward the many people crushed and neglected by capitalism's progress. He wrote several gritty novels about poor and marginalized Londoners, including his sequence *Twenty Thousand Streets under the Sky* (1935), which is composed of *The Midnight Bell* (1929) and *The Plains of Cement* (1934).

Hamilton's most famous novel is *Hangover Square* (1941), which describes the sad life of a kind but schizophrenic man obsessed with a cruel woman who torments him. His mental suffering sucks him deeper into insanity and alcoholism. Hamilton depicts his character's schizophrenia realistically, without any sensational prose: "It was a great relief, actually, to be dead and numbed like this . . . a great relief after all he had been suffering."

All of Hamilton's novels depict alcoholism and the weary hopelessness that accompanies it. He had personal experience with the disease, and he died of the associated liver and kidney failure. Poet John BETJEMAN called Hamilton "one of the best English novelists," and J. B. PRIESTLEY praised him for his ability to evoke "a kind of No-Man's-Land of shabby hotels, dingy boarding-houses and all those saloon bars where the homeless can meet."

Other Work by Patrick Hamilton

The West Pier. 1951. Reprint, New York: Penguin, 1996.

A Work about Patrick Hamilton

French, Sean. *Patrick Hamilton.* Winchester, Mass.: Faber & Faber, 1993.

Hare, David (1947–) *playwright*

David Hare was born in St. Leonard's, Sussex, England, to Clifford Theodore Hare, a sailor, and Agnes Gilmour Hare, a theater agent. He attended public schools throughout his childhood and earned B.A. and M.A. degrees in English from Cambridge.

Upon leaving Cambridge, Hare helped found the Portable Theater, a traveling troupe, and began a career in which he would distinguish himself as one of the most prominent left-wing political dramatists of his generation. As one of the loosely grouped "Fringe Playwrights," which also included Howard Brenton, Trevor GRIFFITHS, and David Edgar, Hare was pro-labor and socialist. He effectively presented his political messages through the subtlety of his writing and his well-developed characters.

Although Hare began writing much earlier, his serious work began with *Plenty* in 1978. This play is about a young woman, Susan, who has served as a secret agent behind enemy lines during World War II but becomes disillusioned after the war when the world does not become the prosperous place that she and others had hoped. With the war over, she has exchanged the exciting and important, albeit dangerous, life of a spy for that of an oppressed and sexually harassed office worker. Labeled by the critic Ted Whitehead as "a cry of disgust with Britain . . . and with the horror of sexual repression, the futility of sexual freedom, the corruption of wealth . . . the pettiness of life in the corporate bureaucracy," *Plenty* is considered by many to be Hare's finest play.

The Secret Rapture (1988) is another of Hare's major plays. It begins with the death of a wealthy man and then describes how his second wife, Katharine, and his elder daughter, Marion, rob the younger daughter, Isobel, of her inheritance. As is typical of many of Hare's dramas, the play is a political allegory: Marion, an ambitious middle-aged woman, represents Britain's then prime minister, Margaret Thatcher, and Isobel stands for a perfect citizen. Much of the play's success is a result of Hare's fair treatment of both characters, for while he vilifies Marion, he also makes Isobel so virtuous that her goodness becomes sickening.

Racing Demon (1990), the first and best-received of a trilogy that also includes *Murmuring Judges* (1991) and *The Absence of War* (1993), is a critical look at the Church of England. Its main characters are four priests: Lionel Espy, Tony Ferris, Donald Bacon (nicknamed "Streaky"), and Harry Henderson. While the priests are not wholly bad and faithfully serve their congregations as best they know how, each is flawed in some way: Lionel neglects his family but dotes on his parishioners, Tony is sexually involved with his girlfriend, Streaky refuses to admit his homosexuality, and Harry is an alcoholic. Moreover, the priests, when not struggling with their own flaws, bicker amongst themselves. The most important conflict is between Lionel and Tony. The former is more interested in the needs of his parishioners than in church doctrine, while the latter is a young, fiery evangelist whose sole mission is to increase the number of church members. In the end Lionel is the loser in this struggle and is removed from his parish (and therefore his home) by the Church.

The Judas Kiss (1998) is a speculative drama about the relationship between Oscar Wilde and his self-absorbed, treacherous lover, Lord Alfred Douglas. The reviews were mixed; Benedict Nightingale in the London *Times* characterized it as "a quiet celebration of a love, self-destructive but self-denying, for a person who merits contempt."

Hare continues to forge his literary reputation. In 1994 the scholar Kimball King placed him among the greats, commenting that the dramatist "follows in the footsteps of Shaw as a writer who can be immensely entertaining while he challenges the most intelligent audiences."

Other Work by David Hare
The Secret Rapture and Other Plays: The Secret Rapture; Fanshen; A Map of the World; Saigon; The Bay at Nice. New York: Grove Press, 1998.

Works about David Hare
Dean, Joan FitzPatrick. *David Hare.* Boston: Twayne, 1990.
Zeifman, Hersh. *David Hare: A Casebook.* New York: Garland, 1994.

Harris, John Benyon
See WYNDHAM, JOHN.

Harrison, Tony (1937–) *poet, translator, playwright*

Born in Leeds to Harry Harrison, a baker, and Florence Horner Harrison, a housewife, Tony Harrison studied classics at the University of Leeds and did postgraduate work in linguistics. From 1962 to 1966 he taught at Ahmadu Bello University in Nigeria and then spent a year lecturing at Charles University in Prague before returning to England to become the first Northern Arts Literary Fellow in 1967–68. He became an associate editor of *Stand* magazine in 1968, and among his many visiting appointments, he was resident dramatist at the National Theatre from 1977 to 1978.

Harrison's work, particularly that dealing with his English background and experiences of postcolonial Africa, combines "erotic candour, sardonic humour, and underlying political seriousness." His first poetry collection, *The Loiners* (1970), demonstrated his ability to adapt conventional forms to a fresh, colloquial tone. He is probably best known for his translation and adaptation of the ancient drama *The Oresteia* (1981) by Aeschylus. This play tells the story of the death of Agamemnon after his return from the Trojan War, and, like much of Harrison's work, was performed at the Royal National Theatre. His versatile command of a variety of speech idioms contributes much to the effectiveness of his verse-dramas, plays that are poetry rather than prose. A television version of his poem *V.* (1985) proved to be controversial because the language was considered obscene by many politicians and religious leaders. The scholar Robert Squillace writes that Harrison "may be the only important living poet who has never published a poem that does not rhyme," and maintains that he will be regarded as one of the leading poets of the late 20th century.

Other Works by Tony Harrison
A Cold Coming. Chester Springs, Pa.: Dufour Editions, 1991.

Selected Poems. New York: Random House, 1987.
The Shadow of Hiroshima. London: Faber & Faber, 1995.
Square Rounds. London: Faber & Faber, 1992.

A Work about Tony Harrison
Astley, Neil, ed. *Tony Harrison.* Chester Springs, Pa.: Dufour Editions, 1991.

Hartley, Leslie Poles (1895–1972) *novelist, short story writer*

Leslie Poles Hartley was born in Cambridgeshire, England, to Harry Bark Hartley, a country solicitor, and Mary Elizabeth Thompson Hartley. Educated by a private tutor until he was nearly 13 years old, he then attended Harrow School. His education was interrupted by World War I, during which he served as an officer in France. Graduating from Oxford in 1922, Hartley began reviewing fiction for a number of London publications, including *The Spectator* and the *Sunday Times*.

Nearly all the short stories in Hartley's first collection, *Night Fears* (1924), conjure up an aristocratic world. Eerie and mysterious, some of them suggest Edgar Allan Poe's tales. "The Island," for instance, brings to mind Poe's "The Fall of the House of Usher." The narrator is a guest in a remote island house: "In the library darkness was absolute. My host preceded me . . . I began to feel frightened . . . To add to my uneasiness my ears began to detect a sound, a small irregular sound; it might have been water dripping . . . it was more like an inhuman whisper." Other collections of stories include *The Killing Bottle* (1932), *The Travelling Grave* (1948), *The White Wand* (1954), and *Two for the River* (1961).

The novella *Simonetta Perkins* (1925) reflects the literary influence that would guide Hartley throughout most of his career: Henry James. The sophistication, the repressed tensions, the disappointment stewing beneath polished surfaces, the air of ambiguity, the paradoxical use of language to pinpoint this ambiguity, the line of dialogue left incomplete by the speaker's self-interruption or another character's interjection, the sheer suggestiveness of everything all echo James, although Hartley was just beginning to master these Jamesian qualities. In this early work one senses an author in search of a style rather than pursuing any substantial theme.

Style and theme would come together in Hartley's trio of novels called the "Eustace trilogy": *The Shrimp and the Anemone* (1944), *The Sixth Heaven* (1946), and *Eustace and Hilda* (1947). The first novel covers the childhood of a brother and sister, Eustace and Hilda Cherrington. Hilda dominates her younger brother, and this establishes the pattern of their relationship. Out of this grows, in the other two books, a study of the impact of the past on the present: the lingering influence of childhood, as in a contest, as the power seems to shift from one sibling to the other, only to be resolved by the reassertion of the original pattern. In the third novel, Hartley describes Eustace's ongoing waltz with defeat: "The past must be put in its place, and that place was a long way at the back of our . . . contemporary hero." Hartley combined this temporal theme with another: the attraction of an aristocratic world into which the siblings themselves were not born. Like the author, Eustace first touched the fringe of this world of position at Oxford.

Hartley's most famous novel is *The Go-Between* (1953). An outsider, 12-year-old Leo Colston, enters an aristocratic world: the mansion of a schoolmate, Marcus Maudsley, on holiday. Leo secretly carries letters between Marcus's older sister and her working class lover, a neighboring farmer, both of whom manipulate and emotionally blackmail him. On his 13th birthday Marcus's mother drags Leo in search of the place where her daughter and the farmer are making love. Hartley surely had James's *The Turn of the Screw* in mind when Leo explains: "I was more mystified than horrified; it was Mrs. Maudsley's repeated screams that frightened me."

Told more than 50 years later from the perspective of a loveless, empty Leo, a "foreigner in the world of the emotions, ignorant of their language but compelled to listen to it," *The Go-Between*

again explores the relationship between the past and the present. This theme is introduced with the novel's first sentence, one of the most often-quoted lines in 20th-century literature: "The past is a foreign country: they do things differently there." In 1954 *The Go-Between* won Hartley the Heinemann Award from the Royal Society of Literature.

Literary biographer and critic Lord David Cecil, Hartley's partner, described him as a "a keen and accurate observer of the processes of human thought and feeling" and "a sharp-eyed chronicler of the social scene." Cecil added: "But [Hartley's] picture of both is transformed by the light of a Gothic imagination that reveals itself now in a fanciful reverie, now in the mingled dark and gleam of a mysterious light and a mysterious darkness."

A Work about L. P. Hartley
Wright, Adrian. *Foreign Country: The Life of L. P. Hartley.* London: Andre Deutsch, 1996.

Haycraft, Anna Margaret
See ELLIS, ALICE THOMAS.

Heaney, Seamus (1939–) *poet*
Seamus Heaney was born at Mossbawn, his family's farm in County Derry, Northern Ireland, about 30 miles northwest of Belfast. The Heaney family had worked the farm for generations, and the landscape, history, and traditions of the region deeply influenced Heaney's later poetry, which was also shaped by the farm's proximity to Belfast. The violent conflict between Catholics and Protestants was then paralyzing the city, and its tensions spilled into the surrounding countryside.

In 1951 Heaney won a scholarship and attended St. Columb's College in Londonderry, where he studied Gaelic, the Irish language, and was first exposed to English literature. He eventually earned an honors degree in English language and literature from Queen's College in 1961.

While attending Queen's, Heaney became strongly influenced by the poets Patrick KAVANAGH, who dealt only with Irish subjects, and Ted HUGHES. Both the traditional forms and lyricism of Hughes's poetry appealed to Heaney, as did its use of natural images. The critic Michael Parker notes that both poets shared a "fascination for and ambiguous attitude towards the animal world. As young men both were keen hunters and fishers, which honed their powers of concentration and prepared them for 'capturing animals' in words." Heaney also studied under the writer and professor Philip Hobsbaum, a key literary influence and head of a literary circle that included Derek MAHON and Michael LONGLEY. This group provided a platform for Heaney's own poetical experimentation.

After graduating, Heaney briefly taught at a secondary school, but in 1963 he began lecturing at St. Joseph's College. While teaching, he married Marie Devlin. He also submitted his first poems for publication, and a number appeared in the *New Statesman.* In 1966 Heaney's first full collection, *Death of a Naturalist,* appeared. The poems draw heavily upon the natural scenes and images of his youth. He wistfully describes his childhood experiences even as he asserts his desire to be a poet. The poems also explore the process of growing up and confront questions of lost innocence, decay, and death.

Death of a Naturalist gained immediate praise. Heaney won the 1968 Somerset Maugham Award and was appointed as lecturer at Queen's University. His next volume of poetry, *Door into the Dark* (1969), combined his concern about rural traditions with the mythic legends of Irish history. Heaney uses the myths to seek patterns of meaning in both his life and Irish culture. This collection established his reputation in America, to which he had fled to escape the increasing Catholic-Protestant violence of Belfast. From 1970 to 1971, he served as a visiting professor at the University of California. In 1982 he accepted a position at Harvard, which he held until 1996.

In 1972 Heaney published *Wintering Out.* The poems in this collection confront the seemingly irreconcilable conflict in Northern Ireland. But Heaney does not solely rely on current events.

Drawing on myth, he distances himself from the raw emotions of the present and seeks the roots of the violence in Ireland's past. Heaney uses language to assuage the contemporary ills and to reassert the holiness of the land and nature. The critic Tony Curtis claims that "the body of the book acts almost as a counterpoint to that sense of present despair."

Critical Analysis

Heaney's 1987 collection *The Haw Lantern* illustrates his three primary poetical concerns. Throughout his career, he has remained spellbound by the land and nature, fascinated by Irish legends and myth, and disturbed by the fragmented, violent existence of Northern Ireland. While he was composing the volume, both of his parents died, and the poems thus trace the stages of life, confronting the terrors of loss and using myth to ease the poet's pain. The sonnet sequence "Clearances" commemorates Heaney's mother. He captures their relationship in a domestic image of their peeling potatoes together; the memory preserves his mother in time even as "the parish priest at her bedside / Went hammer and tongs at the prayers for the dying."

Yet Heaney struggles with her death, fearing that his memories are not enough to preserve her presence. When she dies, he reveals that "the space we stood around had been emptied." To ensure that his mother's spirit does not vanish, he invokes an image of his great-grandmother, a converted Protestant, as she runs to her first Mass. For Heaney, his great-grandmother embodies a spirit that is "mine to dispose with now she's gone." Therefore, he reasons, if his great-grandmother's presence still exists, it must also be possible to retain his mother's. Consequently, he embraces another domestic memory, of when he and his mother folded sheets. Although the memory is of a mundane chore, it also denotes an eternal permanence because Heaney and his mother repeat actions that have been performed for centuries. Therefore, by taking part in this unbroken sequence, they themselves assume a degree of immortality. In this sense, Heaney ensures that his mother is not completely gone. The sonnet sequence concludes with the memory of a chestnut tree which once stood in the family's yard. Although the tree is gone, and its former space is "utterly empty," Heaney remembers perfectly the sounds and sights of its falling. Similarly, his mother is physically gone, but his memory perfectly preserves her.

A more recent volume of poetry, *The Spirit Level* (1996), again invokes domestic images and the power of myth. The poems are Heaney's response to the 1994 cease-fire in Northern Ireland and its subsequent collapse. They embody the diverse emotions that the cease-fire and its failure evoked: joy, fear, anger, despair, hope, resignation.

The poem "Keeping Going," dedicated to Heaney's brother, embodies many of these emotions. The poet begins by describing the childhood act of whitewashing the family house. The memory is magical because of its innocent simplicity and lack of the violence that complicates their adult lives in Northern Ireland. The act of painting also reflects a spirit of renewal that Heaney links to the potential cease-fire.

But childhood memories also haunt Heaney. He recalls when his brother broke his arm and "a strange bird perched for days on the byre roof." In his childhood ignorance, Heaney believes a bird of death stalks his brother. His fear reveals his unease over the possible failure of the cease-fire, and the image of the whitewashed walls becomes associated with death when a contemporary wall is splattered with the blood of a man killed in a drive-by shooting. Thus, Heaney's childhood memory of innocence is erased as he views the murdered victim of the failed cease-fire.

But Heaney refuses to surrender hope. He applauds his brother, who has remained in Northern Ireland, and suggests that despair is an untenable response to the conflict. As the poem concludes, he wonders, "[I]s this all? As it was / In the beginning, is now and shall be?" The violence is so unnerving that he paraphrases the Nicene Creed to portray its seeming permanence. But the child-

hood memory of painting fortifies him. As the poem ends, Heaney declares that the only choice is "keeping going."

As a poet Heaney uses such traditional forms as the sonnet to seek some sense of unity among these disparate factors. Heaney enjoys widespread popularity in both Europe and America, and his poetry has received numerous awards, culminating with the 1995 Nobel Prize. The scholar Helen Vendler notes that his poetry allows readers to "recognize profound family affections, eloquent landscapes, and vigorous social concern."

Other Works by Seamus Heaney

Field Work. London: Faber & Faber, 1978.
North. London: Faber & Faber, 1975.
Seeing Things. London: Faber & Faber, 1991.
Station Island. London: Faber & Faber, 1984.
Sweeney Astray. London: Faber & Faber, 1984.

Works about Seamus Heaney

Corcoran, Neil. *The Poetry of Seamus Heaney: A Critical Study.* London: Faber & Faber, 1998.
Curtis, Tony, ed. *The Art of Seamus Heaney.* 4th ed. Bridgend, Wales: Seren, 2001.
Foster, John Wilson. *The Achievement of Seamus Heaney.* Chester Springs, Pa.: Dufour Editions, 1999.
Parker, Michael. *Seamus Heaney: The Making of the Poet.* Iowa City: University of Iowa Press, 1993.
Vendler, Helen. *Seamus Heaney.* Cambridge, Mass.: Harvard University Press, 1998.

Heath–Stubbs, John Francis Alexander
(1918–) *poet*

John Heath-Stubbs was born in London to Francis Heath-Stubbs, a nonpracticing lawyer, and Edith Heath-Stubbs, a professional pianist known as Edie Marr. He was awarded a B.A. and M.A. degrees from Oxford, where he attended lectures by Charles WILLIAMS, an Anglican poet and publisher whose love for romantic poets and the legends of King Arthur deeply affected him. Heath-Stubbs capitalized on both of these passions in his own

Arthurian epic, *Artorius* (1972), which employs all of the qualities of the neoclassical epic: a hero; an invocation to the muse; battles; a trip to the underworld; and discussions of religion, art, and government. In narrating one of the legend's most memorable moments, Arthur's death at the hands of his son, Mordred, Heath-Stubbs writes, "The rebel's thin and envenomed rapier / found a mark in the groin of Artorius." The scholar A. T. Tolley considers *Artorius* "one of the few impressive poems in the heroic manner by a modern poet."

Along with fellow poets Vernon WATKINS and David GASCOYNE, Heath-Stubbs contributed to the New Romanticism, a movement of the 1940s and 1950s in which poets focused on the individual, often using poems to closely examine the poet's own thoughts and emotions. Although he wrote prolifically while teaching at Leeds University in England, the University of Alexandria in Egypt, and the University of Michigan, Heath-Stubbs did not achieve popular success. Nonetheless, Tolley considers him "one of the best sustained and most impressive among British poets of his generation . . . [who] through a long and impressive career . . . brought to English poetry a voice distinctive and accomplished."

Other Works by John Heath-Stubbs

Collected Poems, 1943–1987. Manchester, England: Carcanet, 1988.
Hindsights: An Autobiography. London: Hodder, 1993.

A Work about John Heath-Stubbs

Van Domelen, John E. *The Haunted Heart*. Salzburg, Austria: University of Salzburg Press, 1993.

Hill, Geoffrey (1932–1999) *poet, critic, essayist*

Geoffrey Hill was born in Bromsgrove, Worcestershire, England, to William Hill, a village constable, and Hilda Hands Hill, whose family was in the nail-making business. He was educated at Keble College, Oxford, and taught at the University of Leeds from 1954 to 1980, when he became a lec-

turer in English at Cambridge. In 1988 he began teaching at Boston University.

Hill is known for giving a vivid voice to both distant and recent historical figures, and his poetry often deals with religious and moral themes, as well as music. Both *King Log* (1968), a study of the ironies of loss, and *Mercian Hymns* (1971), about the eighth-century King Offa, concern the disjunctions between power and morality. His work has been highly acclaimed: His second collection, *For the Unfallen 1952–1958* (1959), which explores the tensions surrounding the Creator and creation, earned him the Gregory Award. *King Log* won both the Hawthornden Prize and the Geoffrey Faber Memorial Award; *Mercian Hymns* won the Whitbread Award and the Alice Hunt Bartlett Award. Hill again won the latter with his *Somewhere in Such a Kingdom: Poems 1952–1971* (1975). *Tenebrae* (1978) won the Duff Cooper Memorial Prize and inspired scholar Terry Eagleton to comment on Hill's "grave contemplativeness."

In 1972 Hill became a Fellow of the Royal Society of Literature. His adaptation of Ibsen's *Brand* was produced in London in 1978, and he has also published criticism and essays.

Other Works by Geoffrey Hill

Collected Poems. New York: Oxford University Press, 1986.
The Enemy's Country: Words, Contextures, and Other Circumstances of Language. Stanford, Calif.: Stanford University Press, 1991.
Illuminating Shadows: The Mythic Power of Film. Boston: Shambala Publications, 1992.
Lords of Limit: Essays on Literature and Ideas. New York: Oxford University Press, 1984.
The Mystery of the Charity of Charles Peguy. New York: Oxford University Press, 1984.

Works about Geoffrey Hill

Bloom, Harold, ed. *Geoffrey Hill*. Broomall, Pa.: Chelsea House, 1986.
Sherry, Vincent. *The Uncommon Tongue: Poetry and Criticism of Geoffrey Hill*. Ann Arbor: University of Michigan Press, 1987.

Hill, James

See JAMESON, STORM.

Hill, Susan (1942–) *novelist, children's author, editor, scriptwriter*

Susan Hill was born in Yorkshire, England, in the seaside town of Scarborough. Her mother was a seamstress and designed dresses; her father died when she was young. Hill recalls that she had always wanted to be a writer: "I always wrote. I don't remember a time when I didn't." She attended a convent school until the family moved to Coventry in 1958, where she finished her schooling. At this time she began writing *The Enclosure* (1961), a novel about a married, middle-aged couple struggling with their marriage. It was accepted for publication before she finished high school.

Hill studied English at King's College, London, graduating in 1963. In the same year she published her second novel, *Do Me a Favour,* which received unenthusiastic reviews. Hill regards these early novels as apprentice works and considers *Gentlemen and Ladies* (1963) her first professional book. This novel was critically acclaimed.

Hill does not shrink from writing about violence and psychological pain. One of her most famous books is *I'm the King of the Castle* (1970), a chilling novel about childhood bullying and the damage it can do. This won the Somerset Maugham Award. Pain and despair also permeate her novel *Strange Meeting* (1971), which is set in the World War I trenches and takes its name from a famous poem by Wilfred OWEN.

Hill has written many books about the process of mourning. Her semiautobiographical novel *In the Springtime of the Year* (1974) is imbued with her own grief for a dead lover. Her memoir *Family* (1988) describes her desperate grief at watching the lingering death of her second daughter, who was born prematurely and survived for only five weeks. Her recent novel *The Service of Clouds* (1998) describes a doctor, mourning for his mother, who can find peace only in helping the dying to die. "Beside those who were dying, and

with them after death, his loss of her, the desolation of it and his absolute sense of abandonment, were eased. Nowhere else."

Hill has also written and edited books of ghost stories, most famously the novel *The Woman in Black* (1983). This novel describes a solicitor's visit to a lonely house on the east coast of England to deal with the funeral and will of an old woman. In the ensuing days, the calm, rational lawyer is driven nearly mad by haunting. In time he learns the horrible secret of a murderous ghost, and he does not escape her cruelty. *The Woman in Black* was adapted for the stage and has been a great theatrical success.

Hill's award-winning novel *The Bird of Night* (1972) describes the intense relationship between Francis Croft, a poet, and his friend Henry Lawson. Leafing through Croft's notebooks, the narrator reconstructs the intense friendship: "It is not an easy story, it is a most terrible story to write." The novel won the Whitbread Award and was shortlisted for the BOOKER PRIZE. In the same year, Hill was made a Fellow of the Royal Society of the Literature.

In 1975 Hill married Stanley Wells, a Shakespearean scholar. They have lived in Stratford-on-Avon, Oxfordshire, and the Cotswolds, and Hill has written books about these beautiful rural areas: *Shakespeare Country* (1987) and *The Magic Apple Tree* (1982).

Hill has also written several books for children, ranging from the practical to the whimsical. *Go Away Bad Dreams* (1984) was designed to help her daughter overcome her fear of nightmares by imagining throwing the dreams out of the window. *Can It Be True?* (1987) is a long poem set on Christmas Eve: a crowd of people and animals hear a rumor that something marvelous has happened in a nearby stable, and they all cease quarreling to go and see.

Hill admires and emulates Elizabeth BOWEN and Elizabeth TAYLOR. Like them, she often writes about bleak events that occur in seaside towns. Hill is also influenced by the Gothic romances of Daphne DU MAURIER. Hill's novel *Mrs. De Winter* (1993) is a sequel to du Maurier's *Rebecca* (1938).

Hill has written numerous novels, literary reviews, and plays for radio and television. She has also edited short-story compilations, edits a literary magazine called *Books and Company,* and has founded a publishing company, Long Barn Books.

Other Works by Susan Hill

Air and Angels. London: Sinclair-Stevenson, 1991.

A Bit of Singing and Dancing. London: Hamilton, 1973.

A Change for the Better. London: Hamilton, 1976.

The Cold Country and Other Plays for Radio. London: BBC, 1975.

Lanterns Across the Snow. London: Michael Joseph, 1987.

The Lighting of the Lamps. London: Hamilton, 1986.

Hillary, Richard (1919–1943) *memoirist*

Richard Chawner Hillary was born in Sydney, Australia, to Michael Hillary, a government employee, and Edwyna Hillary, but moved to England in his childhood. He attended Shrewsbury School and Oxford, where he was a member of the Oxford Royal Air Force Volunteer Reserve (RAFVR) when the war began. Though he lived only 24 years, Hillary wrote a powerful and enduring memoir of his role in Battle of Britain during World War II.

Hillary shot down five German planes in six days, but he was also one of the first British pilots to be downed by enemy fire in the Battle of Britain. While recovering from severe burns that he received in his plane crash, he wrote his memoir, *The Last Enemy* (1942), in which he narrates, in a matter-of-fact tone, his experience in war, from his first combat engagement to the painful rehabilitation that followed his crash. The memoir begins in an action-packed scene that is representative of the entire memoir:

> Down the loud-speaker came the emotionless voice of the controller: '603 Squadron take off and patrol base; you will receive further orders in air: 603 squadron take off as quickly as you can, please.' As I pressed the starter and the engine roared to life . . . I felt the usual sick feeling in the pit of the stomach, as though I were about to row a race, and then I was too busy getting into position to feel anything.

As soon as he regained the use of his hands, Hillary returned to the air and was killed in battle in January 1943. *The Last Enemy* was his only publication. In the words of Sebastian Faulks, this book "became, and has remained, a 'classic' in the sense that . . . it has something to say about flying, about the War and about people's attitudes to the War, that will always need to be read as long as interest in the subjects themselves continues."

A Work about Richard Hillary

Ross, David. *Richard Hillary: The Definitive Biography of a Battle of Britain Fighter Pilot and Author of The Last Enemy.* London: Grub Street, 2000.

Hilton, James (1900–1954) *novelist, screenwriter*

Born in Lancashire to schoolmaster parents, James Hilton was educated at Cambridge. His first novel, *Catherine Herself* (1920), was published when he was 20 and still an undergraduate. He became a journalist in both London and Dublin and contributed to many newspapers and journals.

Hilton is best known for the novel *Goodbye, Mr. Chips* (1934), which was serialized in *The British Weekly* the previous year. Based largely on Hilton's impressions of his father's teaching career, it is a sentimental tale of the life and death of a British public schoolmaster. According to a review in *Commonweal,* the novel managed to "hit almost every soft spot in the reading public." It was the fourth best-seller in 1934, and the fifth in 1935.

Hilton's other best-seller, *Lost Horizon* (1933), described "Shangri-La," an imaginary Himalayan paradise where the inhabitants are free from the anxieties of everyday life. The name has come to signify any idyllic retreat from the everyday. This novel won the Hawthornden Prize, awarded to the most imaginative work by a young British author.

In 1935 Hilton was invited to Hollywood to participate in the filming of some of his works, and he spent the rest of his life writing for the film industry. He received an Academy Award in 1942 for his work on the film *Mrs. Miniver.* Several of his novels were also adapted for the cinema.

Other Works by James Hilton

Random Harvest. Boston: Little Brown, 1941.
Time and Time Again. Boston: Little Brown, 1953.
Was It Murder? 1939. Reprint, New York: Garland, 1976.

Hodgson, Ralph (1871–1962) *poet*

Ralph Hodgson was born in Yorkshire, England, to Seth Hodgson, a dye works drier, and Ann Green Hodgson. His life is not well documented, particularly because of his reclusiveness in his later years. Hodgson worked as a journalist in London and became the editor of *Fry's Magazine.* He also worked as a scene-painter in New York and as an illustrator in London prior to the publication of his first collection of poetry, *The Last Blackbird* (1907). One estimate held that the first edition of this sold a modest 20 copies. His later works met with more success: *The Bull and the Song of Honour* (1914) earned the French literary award the Edmund de Polignac prize.

Hodgson became a publisher in 1913 and, with Holbrook Jackson and Lovat Fraser, under the imprint of "The Sign of the Flying Flame," produced editions known for their typographical individuality. His poem "Eve" from *Poems* (1917) was called "the most fascinating poem of our time" by the writer E. V. Lucas. It depicts temptation and the Fall with charming simplicity: "How the birds rated him, / How they all hated him! / How they all pitied / Poor motherless Eve!" Hodgson became known for his simple and mystical lyrics, and his work tends to express a love of nature and concern for the modern progressive alienation from it.

In 1924 Hodgson began 14 years of lecturing at Sendai University in Japan, and on finishing his work there he received the Order of the Rising Sun, a merit award bestowed upon military and civilian personnel. In 1938 he settled on a farm ("Owlacres") in Minerva, Ohio. He received the Annual Award of the National Institute of Arts and Letters from the United States in 1946 and England's Queen's Gold Medal for Poetry in 1954. He died in Minerva, survived by his third wife, whom he had met and married while in Japan. Poet and essayist George B. Saul has written that, sadly, the price of Hodgson's request for privacy was "a more limited popular knowledge of his human and sensitive poetry than its quality deserves," and that "there is no sweeter mind than Hodgson's discoverable in verse."

Other Works by Ralph Hodgson

Collected Poems. London: Macmillan, 1961.
The Skylark and Other Poems. New York: St. Martin's Press, 1959.

A Work about Ralph Hodgson

Saul, George B. "Merlin's Flight: An Essay on Ralph Hodgson." In *Withdrawn in Gold: Three Commentaries on Genius.* The Hague: Mouton, 1970.

Hoff, Harry Summerfield

See COOPER, WILLIAM.

Holden, Molly (1927–1981) *poet, children's author*

Molly Holden was born in London, the daughter of Conner Henry, a manager for the gas board, and Winifred Farrant Gilbert Henry. She graduated from Kings College, London, in 1948 with honors in English and went on to receive her M.A. from the same institution in 1951. She married Alan Holden, a schoolmaster, in 1949 and had two children. In 1964 she was diagnosed with multiple sclerosis, a permanently disabling disease that affects physical movement. That same year she published her first major work of poetry, which marked the beginning of a relatively short but illustrious career as a poet and novelist for children. Her work reflects her attempts to deal with her debilitating illness by nurturing her creative talents.

Holden's poetry was inspired by the time spent during her youth in the English countryside in Wiltshire. Images of nature full of life and movement fill her poetry, lending its rhyme a vivid lyrical quality. Her first major collected volume, *To Make Me Grieve*, was published in 1967 and contains poems that chronicle her battle with multiple sclerosis. In "Hospital," Holden confronts her deteriorating physical condition: "helpless indeed I lay, in that white bed, hands outspread / legs useless down the length before my eyes." Another poem from this collection, "Virtue in Necessity; from the parked car," opens with the lines "I tire / I tire" and describes the physical exhaustion that marked her struggle to perform everyday tasks.

Holden's subsequent volumes, *Air and Chill Earth* (1971) and *The Country Over* (1975), reflect lighter sensibilities and have been praised by critics for their "whimsical" quality. In "The Circle" the natural world lyrically comes alive: "Blackbirds are singing, the country over / each in his own bud-clotted plot of land."

Holden received several awards for her work during her lifetime, including the Cholmondeley Award in 1972, an Arts Council Award in 1970, and recognition from the Poetry Book Society. In addition to poetry, she wrote several widely acclaimed children's novels between 1970 and 1973, including *The Unfinished Feud* (1971), *A Tenancy of Flint* (1971), and *White Rose and Wanderer* (1972), all of which employ her characteristic power of observation.

Holden's illness influenced all of her writing. "Her power[s] of observation were always remarkably keen," according to her husband Alan Holden, who believed that this talent was "further sharpened by her enforced stillness." Described by the critic John Cotton as a writer whose work "steadily grows on you," Holden's poetry and novels reveal her mastery of the art of describing the trials and beauty of everyday life.

Holtby, Winifred (1898–1935) *novelist, poet, journalist*

Winifred Holtby's father was a farmer; her mother, Alice Winn Holtby, became the first female town councillor in the East Riding, Yorkshire. Alice encouraged her daughter to write, and when Holtby was 13 her mother surprised her with an inspiring gift: a privately printed collection of her own poetry. In 1928 Holtby recalled, "I could write before I could read with comfort, and before I could write, I told stories."

In 1917 Holtby entered Oxford University, but her distress at the casualties of World War I led her to join the Women's Auxiliary Army Corps in London and France. She returned to Oxford in 1919 to complete her history degree. There she started a close friendship with Vera BRITTAIN, and after they finished at Oxford the two lived together in London.

Holtby soon became a noted journalist on social issues. In 1926 she became editor of the feminist journal *Time and Tide*. A recognized leader in labor and feminist circles, she lectured before the League of Nations on women's rights, and she visited South Africa, where she worked tirelessly for the unionization of black workers. Some of her ensuing insights can be seen in her novel *Mandoa, Mandoa!* (1933), a satire of the British travel industry.

Holtby's novels often feature the haunting Yorkshire landscapes and strong women of her own childhood. Many of her female characters bravely challenge social expectations. In her first novel *Anderby Wold* (1923), a Yorkshire farmer's wife fights to keep her farm and to endure a monotonous marriage. The painfully shy heroine of *The Crowded Street* (1924) finds unexpected strength after working for a socialist group. Sarah, the main character in *South Riding* (1936), strives to transform a school in a small Yorkshire village. This novel, published posthumously, has been praised for its complex characters and evocative descriptions of Yorkshire.

After Holtby's death, Vera Brittain wrote, "Winifred was far too vital and radiant for a conventional memoir. . . . Her biography might be written as a poignant tragedy of exceptional artistic promise cut off by untimely death."

Other Works by Winifred Holtby

The Land of Green Ginger. 1927. Reprint, Chicago: Academy Press, 1978.

Poor Caroline. 1931. Reprint, New York: Penguin, 1985.

Virginia Woolf. 1932. Reprint, Chicago: Academy Press, 1978.

Women and a Changing Civilization. 1934. Reprint, Chicago: Academy Press, 1978.

Works about Winifred Holtby

Berry, Paul, and Alan Bishop, eds. *Testament of a Generation: The Journalism of Vera Brittain and Winifred Holtby.* London: Virago, 1985.

Brittain, Vera. *Testament of Friendship.* 1940. Reprint, London: Virago, 1985.

Shaw, Marion. *The Clear Stream: A Life of Winifred Holtby.* London: Virago, 1999.

Household, Geoffrey (1900–1988)

novelist, short story writer, children's author

Geoffrey Household was born in Bristol, the son of Beatrice and Horace W. Household, a lawyer, inspector of schools, and Secretary of Education for Gloucestershire. He was educated at Clifton and Magdalen College, Oxford. In the 1920s and 1930s he worked in international commerce; in the 1930s and 1940s became a writer of children's encyclopedias and also wrote historical radio plays for the Canadian Broadcast System. During World War II he was a member of British intelligence in the Middle East, decorated for his service.

Household wrote short stories and children's books, such as *The Spanish Cave* (1939) and *The Prisoner of the Indies* (1967), a much admired historical novel that follows the adventures of a boy sailor on one of Sir John Hawkins's ships. However, Household is best known for thrillers and adventure novels, written over 50 years. His most popular works are *Rogue Male* (1939), *Watcher in the Shadows* (1960), and *The Dance of the Dwarfs* (1968).

Gina Macdonald, an American critic, has praised the old-fashioned virtues of Household's adult thrillers, which display "charm and wit, an erudite appreciation of the historical and the literary, a sense of irony and humor, and a depth of feeling for nature." Household almost always uses a first-person narrator who is cosmopolitan, an Edwardian Etonian, and "a man of decency and honor," as Macdonald notes. Like Ernest Hemingway's characters, Household's heroes follow a code of behavior that includes grace under pressure.

Household's most famous novel is *Rogue Male,* which plunges the reader into immediate action. An unnamed British sportsman determines to shoot an anonymous Central European dictator, a character modeled on Adolf Hitler. The assassin wishes to avenge the death of his fiancée at the hands of the dictator's secret police. *Rogue Male* is prized for its thrilling depiction of a manhunt, its heady mixture of what Macdonald calls "the savage and the genteel," and its author's deep love for and knowledge of nature, exhibited when the hero goes underground.

These qualities also describe Household's *Watcher in the Shadows,* which follows Charles Dennim, an Austrian count and former British intelligence officer, stalked by a member of the French Resistance who mistakes him for a member of the Gestapo. In *The Dance of the Dwarfs* the hunter again becomes hunted, as research scientist Dr. Owen Dawnay is hounded to death by mysterious animals in the South American jungle. Household's best books involve manhunts, but these are hunts with a difference, for, as Gina Macdonald observes, they are infused with "chivalry and sportsmanship" and "the violence and savagery of life and death struggles . . . is played off against an assumption of sporting rules and civilized values."

Other Work by Geoffrey Household

Rogue Justice. New York: Viking, 1983.

Hoyle, Fred (1915–2001) *novelist, nonfiction writer*

Fred Hoyle was born in Bingley, Yorkshire, England, to the wool merchants Ben and Mabel Pickard Hoyle. As a student he distinguished himself at

Cambridge University, where he earned his B.A. and M.A. in mathematics with honors. He later received a Doctor of Science degree from the University of East Anglia.

Hoyle became known as one of Britain's foremost astronomers by developing and supporting the idea that the universe did not arise from an initial event, the Big Bang, but has always existed in what Hoyle called a steady state. This proposal earned him widespread fame in scientific circles, but he also developed a considerable reputation as a popularizer of science. He appeared regularly on BBC radio and published several books, such as *Man in the Universe* (1966), that presented complex scientific debates in language geared toward the general reading public.

Hoyle also wrote numerous science-fiction novels, the first of which, *The Black Cloud* (1957), is considered a classic of the genre. The novel focuses on the appearance of a tremendous celestial cloud that could possibly extinguish life on earth by blocking the rays of the sun. A lone scientist, Christ Kingsley, almost single-handedly saves the earth from disaster. One of the novel's trademarks is Hoyle's scientific expertise, which is particularly evident in a passage about the potential effects of "the Cloud":

> The heat rays from the Cloud would raise the temperature of the surface of the land more rapidly than the sea, and the air temperature would rise with the land while the moisture content of the air would rise more slowly with the sea. Hence the humidity would fall as the temperature rose, at any rate to begin with.

This authoritative scientific voice also permeates *Ossian's Ride* (1959), Hoyle's second novel, in which another scientist hero, Thomas Sherwood, goes to great lengths to ensure that technologies brought to earth by extraterrestrials do not fall into corrupt hands.

In all, Fred Hoyle published more than 50 nonfiction books about the nature of the universe and two dozen science fiction novels, many in collabo-

ration with his son, Geoffrey, and writer John Elliott. Hoyle's fiction is generally considered extremely entertaining and is vastly enhanced by his scientific fame. As the critic John Clute has observed, Hoyle's reputation often causes readers to feel that "what may seem simple—even simple-minded—on the surface of the text must . . . constitute a sly trap for the unwary." Hoyle was knighted for his work in mathematics and astronomy in 1972.

Other Works by Fred Hoyle
Comet Halley. New York: St. Martin's Press, 1985.
Rockets in Ursula Major. (With Geoffrey Hoyle.) Cutchogue, N.Y.: Buccaneer Books, 1991.

Hueffer, Ford Hermann
See FORD, FORD MADOX.

Hughes, Richard Arthur Warren
(1900–1976) *novelist, poet, short story writer, scriptwriter*

Richard Hughes was born in Surrey, England, to Louise Grace Warren and Arthur Hughes, a Public Record Office worker. By age five his father had died, and his mother began writing magazine fiction to support them. She often told Hughes stories of Jamaica, where she had lived as a child. Soon he began composing poetry, which his mother wrote down. Hughes attended Oxford, where he coedited the magazine *Oxford Poetry*; published *Gipsy Night and Other Poems* (1922), lyrical poems about nature's beauty and human suffering; and wrote the one-act play *The Sisters' Tragedy* (1922), about a young girl who commits a mercy killing to free her older sister to marry the man she loves.

After graduation Hughes cofounded the Welsh theatrical company Portmadoc Players and wrote his first radio play—the first play ever written specifically for radio, *Danger*, about three people trapped in a flooding coal mine. The play was aired by the BBC (British Broadcasting Company) in 1924. He also published the poetry collection *Con-*

fessio Juvenis (1925), containing poems he wrote at age 10 about human experience; and a volume of short stories, *A Moment in Time* (1926). In the latter, the story "A Steerage Passenger" recounts Hughes's experience sailing to America. He traveled extensively, including to Morocco and the Balkans; in his youth, he lived in Europe as a beggar and sidewalk artist, more for amusement than from necessity.

While in America, Hughes completed his first novel, for which he is best known: *A High Wind in Jamaica* (1929). Readers follow 10-year-old Emily on her journey to self-discovery in this story of a family of children captured by pirates while sailing to England. The work won the Femina Vie Heureuse prize, was adapted for the screen, and, with its portrayal of the children-turned-captors, is said to have ended the Victorian idea of sentimental childhood. Hughes writes: "How small the children all looked, on a ship, when you saw them beside the sailors! It was as if they were a different order of beings! Yet they were living creatures just the same, full of promise." Author Richard Poole writes, "The question Hughes poses is: Do the pirates possess the ruthlessness which in nature predators need to survive? It is not, perhaps, so easy to see children as predators, but Hughes sets out to seed the idea in the reader's mind from the very start."

Hughes published two works of short stories for children: *The Spider's Palace* (1932), including tales about living inside a whale and traveling into other people's homes via the telephone cord; and *Don't Blame Me* (1940), 13 stories with unpredictable plots, such as one in which a newly purchased bicycle turns into a crocodile. Hughes again addressed adults in *In Hazard: A Sea Story* (1938), which critics have often compared to Joseph CONRAD's *Typhoon* (1903). Both works recount the survival of a steamship during a storm at sea and the human response to grave danger.

Hughes's later work includes *The Human Predicament*, an unfinished trilogy of historical novels covering the period from the end of World War I through World War II; *The Fox in the Attic* (1961), winner of an Arts Council Award; and *The*

Wooden Shepherdess (1973). In 1956 he received an honorary doctorate in literature from the University of Wales. Critic Marcus Crouch comments, "Richard Hughes's understanding of the child mind is demonstrated most convincingly . . . in that remarkable novel on which his reputation was first based, *A High Wind in Jamaica*. . . . Hughes was always a craftsman, with respect for his medium whatever the prospective audience."

A Work about Richard Hughes

Morgan, Paul. *The Art of Richard Hughes: A Study of the Novels.* Cardiff: University of Wales Press, 1993.

Hughes, Ted (Edward James Hughes) (1930–1998) *poet, playwright, short story writer, editor, children's writer*

Ted Hughes was born Edward James Hughes in Mytholmroyd, a mill town in Yorkshire, England. He was the youngest child of William Henry Hughes, a veteran of World War I, and his wife Edith, a descendant of Nicholas Farrar, founder of the dissenting religious community of Little Gidding. Surrounded from infancy by wild moorland, Hughes developed a passion for animals, first expressed in hunting and then in capturing them on the page. For Hughes, animals embody the irrational life force and "the world under the world," as critic Keith Sagar expresses it.

In his teens Hughes began writing poetry at Mexborough Grammar School, and at age 18 he won a scholarship to Cambridge University. He studied English literature, but in his final year he switched to archaeology and anthropology, disciplines that served his mythic poetry. While doing his national service, Hughes was a wireless mechanic in the Royal Air Force. Posted to a radio station in East Yorkshire, Hughes at this time read Shakespeare voraciously and wrote several radio plays.

Early in 1956 Hughes met the American poet Sylvia Plath, who was also at Cambridge on a Fulbright. They married four months later and formed a close working partnership. They had two children. During the summer of 1962, however, the couple separated, and in February 1963 Sylvia Plath committed suicide. Hughes took over the care of their children and became his wife's literary executor. In 1970 he married Carol Orchard.

As man and poet, Hughes had ardent admirers and detractors. His bitterest critics are feminists who deplore the control he exerted over his first wife's works, the access he refused would-be critics and biographers to safeguard family privacy, and his decision to destroy one of Plath's journals in order to prevent his children from exploring the depth of their mother's clinical depression. Hughes was nevertheless a meticulous editor of Plath's and of others poets' work. These two poets' posthumous reputations will continue to be intertwined.

Hughes produced more than 30 volumes of poetry, as well as short stories, plays, translations, and works for children. In 1982 he was made an Officer of the Order of the British Empire (OBE), received the Order of Merit and in 1984 became poet laureate. From the first, he was a poet of nature. Among his influences are Anglo-Saxon verse with its strong beat, alliteration, and assonance. (Such verse uses heavily stressed syllables, four to the line, whose initial consonants sounds are repeated, or alliterate. Assonance entails repetition of vowel sounds in proximity to one another.) Also influential were the poetry of Gerard Manley Hopkins; D. H. LAWRENCE; W. B. YEATS, the American poets Walt Whitman and Robinson Jeffers, and the war poems of Wilfred OWEN.

Hughes's first volume, *The Hawk in the Rain* (1957), contains poetry of primal power and elemental violence at the furthest possible remove from the cool, urbane, domesticated verse of the 1950s' MOVEMENT in England, which included such poets as Donald DAVIE, D. J. ENRIGHT, and Philip LARKIN. This volume won the Guinness Poetry Award in 1957, which launched Hughes's career.

This strong first collection contains such poems as "The Thought-Fox" and "The Jaguar." "The Thought-Fox" deftly shows thought taking form, a poem being born as a hunter stalks a fox, a fox its prey. "The Jaguar" devotes only half its length to the presentation of the pacing animal, but Hughes's portrayal is as unforgettable as that in Rainer Maria Rilke's "The Panther" (1903).

Hughes's next volume was the quieter, more complex, and colloquial *Lupercal* (1961), which won the 1960 Hawthornden Prize. Its bestiary includes "Hawk Roosting," "An Otter," and "Pike." "Hawk Roosting" offers a predator personified, while the fluid lines of "An Otter" emulate the otter's agility. "Pike" is a poem about fishing for pike, cannibalistic fish that prove "killers from the egg." Beginning objectively in close physical observation, this poem moves into the realm of night and dream.

A five-year hiatus followed Plath's suicide before Hughes published *Wodwo* in 1967. (A "wodwo" is a wild man of the woods, a semihuman creature.) Hughes's verse loosens here, becoming freer. As critic Keith Sagar points out, several poems in *Wodwo* explore a no-man's-land between subhuman and human or human and superhuman. In this respect this volume looks forward to *Crow* (1970).

The *Crow* poems were written to illustrate a series of drawings of that bird by the American artist Leonard Baskin. The crow is a common bird, but also an embodiment of global folklore, an elemental life force, and a survivor of catastrophe. In giving voice to Crow, the poet said he had to compose "songs with no music whatsoever, in a super-simple and a super-ugly language." First published in 1970, *Crow* was revised and reissued in 1972.

Of all Hughes's volumes, this one is most open to the charge of repetitiveness or monotony. As reviewer Ian Hamilton remarks, initially Hughes's career appeared to some to consist of rewriting the same animal poem over and over again. Another way of viewing his work is suggested by the writer Robert Shaw, who describes Hughes's lifelong aim as approaching "ever more closely those things which enthralled his youthful imagination"—nature and its creatures.

Hughes's most assured and serene volume, though less unified than others, is *Moortown* (1979), which won the Heinemann Award in 1980.

The first of four separate sections is called "Moortown" after the Devonshire cattle and sheep farm Hughes worked with his father-in-law. Gentler and tenderer than his early nature poems, these poems are based on a diary Hughes kept and have an air of poetry-off-the-cuff, remarkable for their immediacy of perception and expression. There are some simple elegies, while other sections of the book reproduce poems from previously published collections. Also notable are the poems gathered in *River* (1983) and the simple poems for children in *Season Songs* (1985).

In 1998, the year he died of cancer, Hughes broke a long silence about his first marriage, publishing *Birthday Letters,* a sequence of prose poems about and addressed to Sylvia Plath. Composed over a period of over 30 years, Hughes said they were written to recall his wife to life. This last work of Hughes asks to be read alongside Plath's final collection, the posthumously published *Ariel* (1965) poems.

Works about Ted Hughes

Faas, Ekbert. *Ted Hughes: The Unaccommodated Universe.* Santa Barbara, Calif.: Black Sparrow Press, 1980.

Gifford, Terry, and Neil Roberts. *Ted Hughes: A Critical Study.* London: Faber & Faber, 1981.

Hirschberg, Stuart. *Myth in the Poetry of Ted Hughes: A Guide to the Poems.* New York: Barnes & Noble, 1981.

Sagar, Keith. *The Challenge of Ted Hughes.* New York: St. Martin's Press, 1995.

Scigaj, Leonard M. *Ted Hughes.* Boston: Twayne, 1991.

———, ed. *Critical Essays on Ted Hughes.* New York: G. K. Hall, 1992.

Uroff, Margaret Dickie. *Sylvia Plath & Ted Hughes.* Urbana: University of Illinois Press, 1979.

Hulme, Keri (1947–) *novelist, poet, short story writer*

Keri Hulme, born to John Hulme, a carpenter and businessman, and Mere Miller Hulme in Christchurch, New Zealand, attended public schools as a child and spent one year at the University of Canterbury, Christchurch. Until her writing career blossomed, Hulme worked as a television director, at fishing and tobacco picking, and as a mill worker.

Hulme's first novel, *The Bone People* (1984), won the New Zealand Book Award and the British BOOKER PRIZE. This novel, with an extremely fragmented, stream-of-consciousness narrative, is stylistically similar to the work of James JOYCE, Virginia WOOLF, and Lawrence Sterne. It tells the story of three characters: Kerewin Holmes, an amateur artist living in an isolated tower on the coast of New Zealand; Joe Gillayley, a factory worker; and Simon, a deaf boy whom Kerewin and Joe literally find washed ashore near Kerewin's home. Hulme begins the novel with a passage that suggests how tightly woven the lives of Joe and Kerewin will become:

> They would have been nothing more than people by themselves. But all together, they have become the heart and muscles and mind of something perilous and new, something strange and growing and great.
> Together, all together, they are the instruments of change.

On the surface, *The Bone People* is about the sometimes violent but ultimately resilient relationships of Joe, Kerewin, and Simon. However, the novel also deals with the issue of cultural identification. Joe, like Hulme, is one-eighth Maori (a tribe native to New Zealand) and struggles throughout the novel to accept his ethnic heritage. Many critics consider *The Bone People* a major landmark in the development of literature of New Zealand. The critic Bruce King, for instance, has remarked that "it reflects a change in New Zealand society, a shift from provincial, colonial . . . culture . . . to a post-sixties culture, open to new ideas, cosmopolitan, and with an increasingly prominent role for women and Maoris."

The success of *The Bone People* made Hulme somewhat of an ambassador for New Zealand and a champion of the Maori culture. So far this one book overshadows the rest of Hulme's work, which includes two volumes of poetry, a novella, and a collection of short stories. The critic Elaine Kendall has declared Hulme a "world-class writer who has taken it upon herself to acquaint international readers not only with the little-known and largely verbal Maori culture . . . a minority in an increasingly Europeanized society."

Other Work by Keri Hulme

Bait. 1979. Reprint, New York: Viking, 1999.

A Work about Keri Hulme

Heim, Otto. *Writing along Broken Lines: Violence and Ethnicity in Contemporary Maori Fiction.* Auckland, New Zealand: Auckland University Press, 1998.

Hulme, Thomas Ernest (1883–1917) *poet, essayist*

T. E. Hulme was born in the village of Endon in Staffordshire to Thomas Ernest Hulme, a farmer and manufacturer, and Mary Young Hulme. He studied formally at Cambridge University for two years until he was expelled for allegedly striking a police officer in a brawl, but even after the incident he continued to attend lectures in philosophy and foreign languages. He died in battle as a volunteer with Britain's Honourable Artillery Company during World War I.

Hulme's greatest literary accomplishment was the development of IMAGISM, which he introduced in his "School of Images" that began in Soho in 1909. He later articulated the concept of imagism in two posthumously published collections of essays: *Speculations: Essays on Humanism and the Philosophy of Art* (1924) and *Notes on Language and Style* (1929). Based heavily on Hulme's studies of philosophy and the idea that absolute truth no longer exists, imagism moved away from long, lyric, and especially epic poetry that attempted to tell elaborate and grandiose stories. Hulme argued that the mission of the modern poet should be, instead, to "fix an impression" in the reader's mind,

even if the impression is something as simple as the effect of "a London street at midnight, with its long rows of light." To create such a visual effect, he believed that "[e]ach *word* must be an image *seen.*" Hulme's ideas directly influenced two of the most important poets of the 20th century, T. S. ELIOT and the American Ezra Pound, whose two-line poem "In a Station of the Metro" may be one of the best examples of imagist poetry. Its visual images describe "faces in the crowd" as "petals on a wet, black bough."

In addition to his essays, Hulme wrote a number of poems embodying his belief that all poetry should be visually oriented. In the poem "Autumn" (1908), for instance, he writes that he "saw the ruddy moon lean over a hedge / Like a red-faced farmer," making nearly each word, like "ruddy," "moon," "lean," "hedge," "red-faced," and "farmer," a visual image that allows the reader to easily capture the "impression" of the moon that the poem describes.

Hulme is chiefly remembered for the effect he had on the poetry of Eliot and Pound. In 1924 Eliot gave an assessment that still rings true: "Hulme is classical, reactionary and revolutionary; he is the antipodes of the eclectic, tolerant, and democratic mind of the last century."

Other Work by T. E. Hulme

The Collected Writings of T. E. Hulme. Edited by Karen Csengeri. New York: Harvard University Press, 1994.

Works about T. E. Hulme

Rae, Patricia. *The Practical Muse: Pragmatist Poetics in Hulme, Pound, and Stevens.* Cranbury, N.J.: Bucknell University Press, 1997.

Roberts, Michael. *T. E. Hulme.* New York: Carcanet, 1982.

Hutchinson, Ray Coryton (1907–1975) *novelist*

R. C. Hutchinson was born in Finchley, Middlesex, a north London suburb, to Harry and Lucy

Mabel Coryton Hutchinson. At age 13 he enrolled in the Monkton Combe Boarding School in Bath, where he wrote an unpublished novel. In 1927 he earned his degree from Oxford.

Hutchinson's most successful novels chronicle the impact of wars and revolutions on individuals. His novel *The Unforgotten Prisoner* (1933), a vivid depiction of an orphan's struggle to survive the economic turmoil of post–World War I Germany, reportedly sold 15,000 copies one month after its release. *Shining Scabbard* (1936), which depicts a provincial French family seeking to overcome the dishonor of its patriarch losing his commission for cowardice during the Franco-Prussian War, was a Book-of-the-Month Club recommendation in the United States. It sold 78,000 copies in the United States the first two weeks after its release.

Hutchinson's best-known work is *Testament* (1938), an epic that describes the efforts of two former prisoners of war, Count Anton Schleffer and Captain Alexei Ostraveskov, to adjust to the changes brought about by the Russian Revolution. The breakdown of Russia's autocratic structure is mirrored in the dismantling of Ostraveskov's family structure. Although some reviewers objected to what they considered unnecessary plot complications, many critics praised Hutchinson's exploration of the spiritual implications of the Russian Revolution. Reviewer John Cournos noted Hutchinson's ability to create "human beings against a background of war and revolution, human beings who remain human entities, personalities to the end." The novel won the *Sunday Times* gold medal for fiction and has been translated into five other languages.

Hutchinson remained popular after World War II with the best-seller *Elephant and Castle: A Reconstruction* (1949), which describes the relationships of an upper-middle-class London woman between the wars. In *Johanna at Daybreak* (1969) he writes about a woman's struggle to remember and come to terms with her betrayal of her husband to the Nazis. She finally takes a step toward healing when she admits the magnitude of her past sins: "I realised I was back on the painful course I

could never finally escape from—itself my one escape from the despotism of the past; the only course which could lead towards an ultimate tranquility; the harsh, acceptable, exalting road."

Considered a meticulous craftsman for most of his career, Hutchinson's literary reputation declined after 1964. Scholar Robert Green explains that "his persistence in treating major issues of the century in novels that were serious, even moralistic, and always tinged with his belief in the possibility of salvation through endurance, may well have made him seem old-fashioned to a new generation."

Other Works by R. C. Hutchinson
Rising. London: Michael Joseph, 1976.
The Stepmother. New York: White Lion Publishers, 1973.

A Work about R. C. Hutchinson
Green, Robert. *R. C. Hutchinson: The Man and His Books.* Metuchen, N.J.: Scarecrow Press, 1985.

Huxley, Aldous (1894–1963) *novelist, short story writer, nonfiction writer*
Aldous Huxley was a member of one of England's most brilliant and distinguished families—one so famous that the *Encyclopaedia Britannica* devotes an individual entry to the family itself, in addition to separate entries for Aldous, his scientist brothers Sir Julian and Nobel laureate Andrew Fielding, and their grandfather Thomas Henry, friend and promoter of Charles Darwin.

Huxley was born in Godalming, Surrey, to Thomas Henry Huxley's third son, Leonard, and Julia Arnold Huxley. His mother was the granddaughter of the famous headmaster of Rugby School, Thomas Arnold, niece of the poet and essayist Matthew Arnold, and sister of the novelist Mary Ward. Huxley was intellectually precocious and would have distinguished himself more as a youth had he not been afflicted at 16 with a serious eye disease that almost blinded him. His education up to that point had been at the Hillside

School and Eton, which he had to leave because of his illness. He taught himself Braille, learned to play the piano and to use a typewriter and, with the aid of tutors, prepared himself for Oxford University in 1913. In the meantime he had, by age 17, written a novel, which he never published. Despite his near blindness he majored in English literature.

In 1915 Huxley was introduced to Phillip Morrell, a member of Parliament and a pacifist, and his wife Ottoline. The latter conducted a famous salon in the family home, Garsington Manor, where Huxley met many of the most creative young writers and artists of the day, among them D. H. LAWRENCE, Virginia WOOLF, and Bertrand Russell. He also met his future wife, Maria Nys. After graduation he taught school, began writing for the *Athenaeum*, and married in 1918. He and Maria had one child, Matthew, born in 1920.

Huxley's first major success was *Crome Yellow* (1921), a satirical novel drawn from his visits with fellow intellectuals and artists at Garsington. The "Crome" of the title is the name of the fictional mansion where young people gather and chat brilliantly, if superficially: "Mrs. Wimbush's question had been what the grammarians call rhetorical; it asked for no answer. It was a little conversational flourish, a gambit in the polite game." There is little in the way of plot in this highly conversational work, but it established Huxley as a keen observer of contemporary British upper-class society and its mores. Critic Guinevera Nance argues that the major theme of the novel is that "human beings are all 'parallel straight lines,' never really connecting."

In 1923 Huxley published *Antic Hay,* another satirical novel depicting more superficial young people, this time in London rather than the country. Again drawn from Huxley's own experience (the main character, Gumbril, is an Oxford graduate who teaches school), it delineates the emotional emptiness of upper-class life in postwar England. Gumbril attempts to bring meaning to his life by purchasing a false beard: "From melancholy and all too mild he saw himself transformed on the instant into a sort of jovial Henry the Eighth, into a massive Rabelaisian man, broad and powerful and

exuberant with vitality and hair." Huxley's admirer Evelyn WAUGH, claimed, "It was because he was then so near the essentials of the human condition that he could write a book that is frivolous and sentimental and perennially delightful."

Huxley gave up teaching to work exclusively as a writer in 1923. He published several collections of short stories: *Mortal Coils* (1922), *Little Mexican* (1924), and *Two or Three Graces* (1926). The book that earned him an international reputation, *Point Counterpoint* (1928), was influenced by the work of the French writer André Gide, which employs multiple points of view. Counterpoint in music is a form that simultaneously combines two or more distinct and independent melodic lines; the novel achieves the same effect by developing the plot through the conversations of the various characters. It also introduces passages from the notebooks of the fictional novelist Phillip Quarles, whose meditations on writing sound suspiciously like Huxley's own: "The chief defect about the novel of ideas is that you must write about people who have ideas to express." Critic Peter Firchow suggests that this novel marks the transition in Huxley's career from "the period of predominantly destructive satire [to] the period of predominantly constructive satire." *Point Counterpoint* was a huge success, allowing the Huxleys to purchase a house in France where they lived from 1930 to 1937.

The novel *Eyeless in Gaza* (1936) represents Huxley's searching for stable moral and spiritual values in an uncertain world. This search was to lead him through Eastern mysticism, hallucinogenic drugs (the nonfiction *The Doors of Perception* [1954]), and hypnotism. His intellectual, philosophical, and spiritual searches were reflected in the writing that he continued to produce after his move to California in 1938. One of the most important works of this period is the novel *The Devils of Loudon* (1952), which tells of the apparent possession by demons of a group of French nuns in the 17th century.

Huxley was much affected by his wife's death from cancer in 1955, although he married the Italian concert violinist Laura Archera a year later. He developed cancer in 1960, and in 1961 a fire totally destroyed his home and all his possessions. He died two years later. Critic Jerome Meckier writes of Huxley's achievement, "In one idea-laden novel after another, Huxley exposed the interrelated dilemmas of the modern age; he gave not just utterance but flesh and blood to life's perennial counterpoints and the modern era's cacophony of competing theories."

Critical Analysis

Huxley's most famous novel of ideas, *Brave New World* (1932), examines the problems of the present by projecting a frightening future world where technology has overtaken humanity. In the foreword, the author explains that the novel "is a book about the future and, whatever its artistic or philosophical qualities, a book about the future can interest us only if its prophecies look as though they might conceivably come true." Ever since Darwin's writings had come to be accepted by most people, there were those who proposed to help evolution along by controlling human breeding through the science of eugenics. The fearsome possible consequences of such ideas undergird the novel, where test-tube babies are produced en masse at the "Central London Hatchery and Conditioning Centre" to fill predetermined slots in an almost completely mechanically controlled society. Love, reading for pleasure, and being alone are discouraged, while the legal and universal drug "soma" keeps the citizens happy.

The true hero of the book is "the Savage," who questions the values of this "brave new world": "Don't you want to be free and men? Don't you even understand what manhood and freedom are?" He then throws the soma tablets out the window in an attempt to change society. In Huxley's dystopia, the citizens have names suggesting communism, such as Bernard Marx and Lenina Crowne, while they pray to the capitalistic god "Our Ford." Scholar James Sexton notes that "Huxley saw that the common denominator between Fordism and socialism was uncritical veneration of rationalization"—in other words, the attempt to regulate and standardize human behavior to the point that all humanity is lost.

Other Works by Aldous Huxley

After Many a Summer Dies the Swan. 1939. Reprint, Mattituck, N.Y.: American Reprint, 1976.
Ape and Essence. New York: Harper, 1948.

Works about Aldous Huxley

Meckier, Jerome, ed. *Critical Essays on Aldous Huxley.* New York: G. K. Hall, 1996.
Nance, Guinevera A. *Aldous Huxley.* New York: Continuum, 1988.

Huxley, Elspeth (1907–1997) *nonfiction writer, memoirist, novelist*

Born in Britain, Elspeth Huxley was raised in Africa. The Huxleys emigrated to Kenya in 1913, when Elspeth was six, and for the rest of her life she was to think and write about this land and its complexities. Her parents struggled to establish a coffee plantation, and Huxley grew up alongside their small triumphs and many setbacks. She was educated at home, and she particularly enjoyed drawing maps in geography lessons, as she later wrote: "I transferred the countries onto drawing-paper, put in rivers, towns, railways, and mountains, and painted everything in gay if blotchy colours, which was very satisfactory." She was sent away from the farm after World War I broke out: "To be torn up by the roots is a sad fate for any growing thing."

Huxley returned to England at age 18 and studied agriculture at Reading University. She then went to America to study agriculture at Cornell University and worked for several years as a farmer and a journalist. She became a respected writer with *White Man's Country* (1935), a biography of Lord Delamere, who was the primary mover behind colonizing Kenya. Commissioned by Delamere's widow, the biography is only mildly alert to his racism, primarily celebrating him as a rugged leader. One reviewer called it "the best apologia for white settlement that has been written."

Between 1935 and 1964 Huxley continually returned to the question of how nations were formed and how colonization had affected Africa. However, Huxley also defended colonization. In her novel *Back Street New Worlds* (1964) she mourns "the end of an imperial purpose that, right or wrong, sustained and magnified us in the nineteenth century."

Huxley's most famous book is her autobiography of her childhood in Kenya, *The Flame Trees of Thika* (1959). *The Mottled Lizard* (1962) describes her joyful return to Africa after years abroad: "I think that if one lived to be a hundred, and watched the dawn break and the sun rise over the highveld of Africa every morning, one would never tire of it." Both autobiographies were well received. In the 1980s they experienced a resurge in popularity, along with several other writers' books describing turn-of-the-century colonial life in Africa and India. In 1981 Huxley's books were turned into a British miniseries, *The Flame Trees of Thika*.

Huxley wrote more than 30 books, including the mystery novel *Murder at Government House* (1937). Her nonfiction was diverse, ranging from *Florence Nightingale* (1975) to a book about the naturalist Peter Scott. But she remains best known for her writing about Africa. As the anthropologist Laurens van der Post says, "No one who cares about the fate of Africa can possibly be ignorant of Mrs Huxley's distinguished role as an observer and interpreter of African events." Huxley was made a Commander of the Order of the British Empire (CBE) in 1962.

Other Works by Elspeth Huxley

Livingstone and His African Journeys. New York: Saturday Review, 1974.

Nine Faces of Kenya. New York: Viking, 1991.

imagism

Imagism was a literary movement whose impact and influence were greater and more lasting than the duration of the movement itself. It began in 1909 and continued through 1917, arising in reaction to what Ezra Pound called the "rather blurry, messy . . . sentimentalistic mannerish" poetry of early 20th-century England, notably the practitioners of GEORGIAN POETRY. Its leaders were poet-critic Pound and philosopher T. E. HULME. Later, the American poet Amy Lowell became a vocal supporter.

Pound traced the origins of imagism to Hulme's "School of Images" that began in Soho in spring 1909. He introduced poets H. D. (Hilda Doolittle) and Richard ALDINGTON as "Imagistes," and he persuaded Harriet Monroe, editor of *Poetry,* to publish a description of imagism in the first issue of her magazine. In March 1913 Pound issued three imagist principles: "1. Direct treatment of the 'thing,' whether subjective or objective. 2. To use absolutely no word that did not contribute to the presentation. 3. As regarding rhythm: to compose in sequence of the musical phrase, not in sequence of a metronome." To this he added a definition or doctrine of the image as "that which presents an intellectual and emotional complex in an instant of time," effecting a liberation from time and space limits.

Imagist poetry is direct, spare, economical, and focused. Pound's poem "In a Station of the Metro" shows how well imagists could translate a modern urban impression into an image as fresh and timeless as an exquisite oriental painting: "The apparition of these faces in the crowd; / Petals on a wet, black bough." Imagism had a positive effect on the poetry of the time, purging it of stale diction and imagery and rhetorical excesses. The movement flourished because it provided poets with practical advice; its greatest liability was that its tenets prevented the composition of long poems. It disappeared in a welter of other literary movements of the post–World War I era, but its principles continued to influence contemporary poetry.

A Work about Imagism

Gage, John T. *In the Arresting Eye: The Rhetoric of Imagism.* Baton Rouge: Louisiana State University Press, 1981.

Innes, Michael

See STEWART, JOHN INNES MACKINTOSH.

Isherwood, Christopher (1904–1986)

novelist, playwright, screenwriter, biographer

Christopher Isherwood, the son of Francis Edward and Kathleen Machell-Smith Isherwood, was born in Cheshire, England. His family was affluent, and he attended private as well as upper-class public schools as a boy; although he studied at Cambridge, he did not graduate. He was close friends with W. H. AUDEN and Stephen SPENDER and was heavily influenced by E. M. FORSTER, adopting what the scholar Stephen Wade has described as the author's "use of understatement and the power of ironies developing from apparently trivial, mundane events." Isherwood's long literary career was extremely diverse: He wrote novels, plays, screen adaptations, and a biography of his parents, engaging subjects as diverse as Nazi Germany, Eastern religion, and his own homosexuality.

Although Isherwood's first novel, *All the Conspirators* (1928), did not achieve commercial success, it is regarded as a worthy achievement. It focuses on the lives of three characters: Philip Lindsay; his widowed mother; and his sister Joan, whose relationship with her boyfriend, Victor Penge, sparks central interfamilial and intergenerational conflicts that Isherwood uses to indict traditional family structures as restrictive victimizers of youth. The novel's most interesting element is not its characters but instead the development of Isherwood's cinematic, or movielike, style, in which he often scans rooms and reveals, as a camera would, entire and elaborate scenes. In a typical passage, he writes, "Philip turned up his collar and stood for some minutes in the archway of a court. The place was full of children, swarming around in the gloom, dodging each other, falling over."

Two years after *All the Conspirators*, Isherwood moved to Berlin, where he published a group of novels collectively known as "the Berlin books." The most notable of these novels, *Goodbye to Berlin* (1939), is narrated matter-of-factly by a character named Christopher and is composed of a number of character sketches that paint Berlin as a soul-sick place where people never develop fulfilling personal relationships. Fritz, with a romantic history typical of the novel's characters, has never been able to sustain a relationship, remarking, "On the average . . . I'm having a big affair every two years." Isherwood adapted his "Berlin books" into a stage play, *I Am a Camera* (1951), then into a stage musical, *Cabaret* (1966), and finally he adapted it for the screen in 1972.

In the 1930s Isherwood also collaborated with W. H. Auden on several dramas: *The Dog Beneath the Skin* (1935), which centers on a character who has lived in a village for 10 years disguised as a dog and from that perspective has witnessed humanity's worst traits; *The Ascent of F6* (1936), about a man attempting to scale a previously unclimbed mountain; and *On the Frontier* (1938), a play that directly discusses political issues of the day, such as the end of the Spanish Revolution and Hitler's rise in Germany. Although the collaborations of Isherwood and Auden developed a cast of neurotic, introverted characters that would be emulated by Stephen Spender and Louis MACNEICE, they were generally not well received and were steadily criticized for their liberal political stance and support of communism.

Isherwood immigrated to the United States in 1939 and later wrote what some regard as his most enduring novel, *A Single Man* (1964). The story of George, a homosexual English professor, captures the essence of life in Los Angeles during the 1960s. Isherwood, in his characteristically matter-of-fact tone, narrates George's daily activities, which seem mundane at first but bloom into a highly textured and variegated story. Biographer C. J. Summers comments that the novel "alternates between poetic intensity and gentle irony" and assesses it as "a technical tour de force in which every nuance is perfectly controlled." This control and keen examination of every nuance is nowhere performed more skillfully than when Isherwood describes George encountering a line of ants moving toward "the closet where he keeps the jams and honeys" and moves away from the ants into a meditation on life, death, and evolution, before returning to the event taking place:

Doggedly he destroys them . . . and has a sudden glimpse of himself doing this: an obstinate, malevolent old thing imposing his will upon these instructive and admirable insects. Life destroying life before an audience of objects—pots and pans, knives and forks, cans and bottles—that have no part in the kingdom of evolution. Why? Why? . . . by the time George has thought all this, the ants are already dead.

Throughout Isherwood's career, some literary figures, such as Somerset MAUGHAM, predicted that he would achieve true literary greatness. His achievements never reached such a height, but, as the scholar Francis King has observed, his writing will endure because of his "marvelous ability . . . to produce one startling yet illuminating image after another" and "the . . . modest virtues of lucidity, simplicity, and an almost conversational relaxation."

Other Works by Christopher Isherwood

A Meeting by the River. 1967. Reprint, Minneapolis: University of Minnesota Press, 1999.
Where Joy Resides: A Christopher Isherwood Reader. Edited by Don Bachardy and James P. White. New York: Farrar, Straus & Giroux, 1989.
The World in the Evening. 1954. Reprint, Minneapolis: University of Minnesota Press, 1999.

Works about Christopher Isherwood

Berg, James, and Chris Freeman, eds. *The Isherwood Century: Essays on the Life and Work of Christopher Isherwood.* Madison: University of Wisconsin Press, 2000.
Ferres, Kay. *Christopher Isherwood: A World in Evening.* San Bernardino, Calif.: Borgo, 1994.

Ishiguro, Kazuo (1954–) *novelist, short story writer*

Kazuo Ishiguro was born in Nagasaki, Japan, the son of Shizuo Ishiguro, an oceanographer, and Shizuko Ishiguro. When the writer was five, his family emigrated to Britain, where his father was employed in the North Sea oil business. Ishiguro was educated in Surrey and later earned a bachelor's degree with honors from the University of Kent (1978), as well as an M.A. in creative writing from the University of East Anglia (1980). He studied under Malcolm BRADBURY and Angela CARTER. A social worker for several years, Ishiguro originally intended to become a musician, but turned to writing in his mid-20s.

Ishiguro's first publications were short stories in the anthology *Introduction 7: Stories by New Writers* (1981). On the strength of one of these—"A Strange and Sometimes Sadness"—he obtained a book contract, developing the story into his first novel. *A Pale View of Hills* (1982), about a Japanese widow revisiting her early life in Japan from the vantage point of life in England, won the Winifred Holtby Prize. Ishiguro's second novel, *An Artist of the Floating World* (1986), about an aging Japanese artist trying to arrange a marriage for his daughter, was named Whitbread Book of the Year. *The Remains of the Day* (1989) won the BOOKER PRIZE, launching his international reputation. This novel concerns Stevens, an elderly butler who, through a lifetime's unquestioning loyalty and obedience to a master who was a Nazi sympathizer, has sacrificed any possibility of living his own life.

All Ishiguro's fiction exhibits similar characteristics. His style is subtle and understated, superficially clear but with troubled depths, as remarkable for what it does not say as for what it does. Critic Gabriel Brownstein observes that, in the course of an Ishiguro novel, "the weight of the unsaid grows heavier and heavier." Fellow novelist Penelope LIVELY describes this style as "sparse, precise and plain."

Ishiguro's principal characters are fragile, marginal people with scant self-knowledge whose unwilling confessions, muddled memories, and dubious life stories are unreliable. A characteristic plot features such a protagonist-narrator looking back on life with regret and puzzlement, trying to discover where he or she took a wrong turn. The reader, confined to his or her point of view, must exercise the skills of a detective, assessing the narrator's credibility. In Ishiguro's recent novel, *When We Were Orphans* (2000), the protagonist is a detective trying to solve the mystery of his parents' disappearance.

Pervasive themes in Ishiguro's work include how individual memory relates to history; the intersecting of personal, social, and cultural identities; and how conformity stifles self-expression. The author continues to explore and expand these themes as he refines his techniques. Feeling hampered by British readers' adherence to the conventions of realism, in *The Unconsoled* (1995) he wrote a surreal novel that reads like being immersed in an anxiety dream.

Characters' backgrounds are also significant. *A Pale View of Hills* and *An Artist of the Floating World* both take place in postwar, post-Hiroshima Japan. Etsuko, the wraithlike woman in the former book, is haunted by the suicide of her elder daughter. A survivor of the atomic bomb dropped on her hometown, she seems to have a great, gaping hole at the center of her life. In *An Artist of the Floating World*, Ono, another survivor, looks back on the war that cost him wife, child, and profession, unable to understand how his promising youth resulted in such wreckage. Consciousness of a wasted or misspent life is as strong in *The Remains of the Day*, where the central character finally realizes he has sacrificed any possibility of happiness or fulfillment to his ideal of being the perfect servant. As Salman RUSHDIE commented in his review of this novel, Stevens and the whole race of butlers are extinct, a "tragicomic anachronism." Time passes Ishiguro's characters by, and they find themselves mourning lost worlds.

Ishiguro has remarked that his novels originally surface in his mind as dialogue, calling for a background or landscape against which to set this conversation. His narrators often look back from a postwar vantage point in the 1950s to events of the 1920s and 1930s that led to world conflict. The Japanese background of the first two novels, the English background in *The Remains of the Day*, a nightmarish Vienna in *The Unconsoled*, and turbulent Singapore in *When We Were Orphans* are integral to the action unfolding within them.

Critics disagree how Japanese Ishiguro is, although he places himself in the Western literary tradition, disclaiming knowledge of contemporary Japan. His fiction, however, bears the hallmarks of Japanese art in its delicacy, subtlety, and minimalism—a few well-placed objects evoke a world. Reviewer Gabriele Annan views his novels as concerned with "guilt and shame in the service of duty, loyalty, and tradition." The author's Japanese heritage may have been reinforced by residence in England, for the old insular societies of both England and Japan were devoted to tradition, hierarchy, understatement, and cultivation of self-control. Ishiguro's art resonates for the British. Before he was 30 he was hailed as one of England's 20 best novelists, and his works have been translated into 25 different languages.

A Work about Kazuo Ishiguro

Shaffer, Brian W. *Understanding Kazuo Ishiguro.* Columbia: University of South Carolina Press, 1997.

James, Montague Rhodes (1862–1936)
short story writer, memoirist

M. R. James was born in Goodnestone, Suffolk, England to Herbert James, an Anglican priest, and Mary Emily James. He studied medieval art and manuscripts, ancient Christian writings, linguistics, and paleography at Eton College and King's College, Cambridge, experiences that provided subject matter for his memoir *Eton and Kings: Recollections, Mostly Trivial, 1875–1925* (1926). He went on to become vice chancellor of Cambridge and Provost of Eton, and he was awarded the Order of Merit in 1930.

James is known for his ghost stories, chilling in their skillfully crafted suspense and plausibility of plot. What started as yearly ghost stories to entertain his friends on Christmas eventually turned into several volumes of stories, including *Ghost Stories of an Antiquary* (1904) and *Collected Ghost Stories* (1931). Critic Jacqueline Simpson explains why James's ghost stories are so effective:

One of the most striking features of James's style is the interplay between the leisurely, mildly pedantic phrasing of the preliminary narrative and descriptions, reflecting the persona of the donnish 'antiquary,' and the rapid glimpses of horrific concrete details at the climax, vividly but tersely expressed, and never over-explained.

"Oh, Whistle and I'll Come to You, My Lad," James's most popular ghost story, illustrates this observation beautifully. In the beginning of the story, a rational, scientific professor does not believe in ghosts, and in fact he tells his colleagues: "I hold that any semblance, any appearance of concession to the view that such things might exist is equivalent to the renunciation of all that I hold most sacred." While golfing on a haunted piece of land, he finds a whistle. Later that night, the whistle attracts the terrifying presence of a mysterious, faceless ghost who eventually forces the professor to change his beliefs about the supernatural.

Critic David Langford believes that "James's greatest strength is in inventiveness, an ability to unveil the unexpected horror in the unexpected place." A reviewer from the *New York Times* agrees: "No other ghost stories remotely approach the authentic James touch of actuality."

Other Work by M. R. James

The Ghost Stories of M. R. James. New York: Oxford University Press, 1987.

James, Phyllis Dorothy (1920–)
novelist

P. D. James was born in Oxford, England, to Sidney James, a civil servant, and his wife, Dorothy May Hone James, a former nurse. Lack of money forced her to leave school at 16. In 1941 she married Dr. Connor White, who was unable to support their two daughters after army service affected his mental health. James earned two degrees at night school and worked as a hospital administrator and in the Home Office criminal department before becoming a full-time writer in 1979, 17 years after the publication of her first novel.

In the 1950s James realized that she had to start writing or give up her dream of becoming a novelist. "It didn't occur to me . . . to begin with anything other than a detective story," she recalls. Like the classic writers she admires—Agatha CHRISTIE, Margery ALLINGHAM, and Dorothy L. SAYERS—James writes "old-fashioned" mysteries. In all her novels, she says, "You have a murder, which is a mystery. There is a closed circle of suspects. . . . [The detective] finds clues and information which, as he discovers them, are also available to the reader."

However, James's characters are more complex than those of her predecessors. She describes Adam Dalgliesh of Scotland Yard, introduced in her first novel, *Cover Her Face* (1962), as a "very private and detached man" whose personal tragedies lead him to use his job to protect himself from emotional involvement. Cordelia Gray—honest, independent, and compassionate—begins her practice as a private detective in *An Unsuitable Job for a Woman* (1972). Both detectives "are agents of justice who live according to a strict moral code," according to reviewer Marilyn Rye, while James's criminals "usually have complicated psychological motivations for their crimes."

James's works are also distinguished by their realism. She avoids stereotyped locations such as cozy English villages, preferring contemporary settings such as forensics laboratories and psychiatric clinics. She also notes that her detectives can always solve the crime, but they cannot restore lives "contaminated by murder."

Created a baroness in 1991, James has received several honorary degrees and the Crime Writers' Diamond Dagger Award for lifetime achievement. Carla Heffner of the *Washington Post* notes that James attracts two different audiences: "the lovers of a good 'whodunit' . . . and the literary world that admires the books for their character and motivation."

Other Works by P. D. James

Death of an Expert Witness. New York: Warner, 1992.
Shroud for a Nightingale. New York: Scribner, 2001.
Time to Be In Earnest: A Fragment of Autobiography. New York: Faber and Faber, 1999.

Works about P. D. James

Gidez, Richard. *P. D. James.* Boston: Twayne, 1986.
Siebenheller, Norma. *P. D. James.* New York: Ungar, 1981.

Jameson, Storm (Margaret Storm Jameson, James Hill, William Lamb) (1891–1986) *novelist, short story writer, critic, scriptwriter*

Storm Jameson was born to William Jameson, a sea captain, and Hannah Margaret Gallilee Jameson in Whitby, Yorkshire, England, where she endured an impoverished childhood. She earned a B.A. from Leeds University and an M.A. in modern drama from King's College, London. In her long life, Jameson wrote television scripts, short stories, criticism, an autobiography, and more than 40 novels, for which she is primarily remembered.

According to the critic Margaret McDowell, Jameson's "best books center on unresolved fragments of her own life and the lives of her parents and grandparents. The plots deal with families involved with shipbuilding or sailing, and they are set in Whitby or elsewhere in Yorkshire, the land

Jameson both hated and loved." Some of these "best books" make up the trilogy *The Triumph of Time*, which includes *The Lovely Ship* (1927), *The Voyage Home* (1930), and *A Richer Dust* (1930). All of these semiautobiographical novels focus on the life of Mary Hervey, the head of a shipbuilding company. The first volume takes Mary from her birth through a struggle to enter the shipping business despite prejudice against women in business; and it leaves her a successful businesswoman. *The Voyage Home* narrates Mary's intertwined business and family relationships, while the final novel, *A Richer Dust*, shows Mary, now a grandmother, confronting the need to pass her company on to an heir. Throughout the final two novels, Jameson focuses on Mary's increasing awareness of her old age and her process of coming to terms with her own mortality. The author establishes this dominant theme at the beginning of *The Voyage Home* when she writes, "If life would only stand still. If spring could renew itself forever while she watched. She felt now each year, with a more singular sharpness, the contrast between its recurring miracle and her shortening life."

Jameson's popularity peaked during the 1930s and 1940s, but the author's writing is of enduring quality.

Other Works by Storm Jameson

Autobiography of Storm Jameson: Journey from the North. London: Virago, 1986.

Women Against Men. New York: Viking, 1985.

Jenkins, Robin (John Robin Jenkins)
(1912–   ) *novelist*

Robin Jenkins was born in the Scottish village of Flemington, Lanarkshire. He was educated at Hamilton Academy and the University of Glasgow, where he received an honors degree in English in 1936. He then became a teacher, spending most of his career at Dunoon Grammar School in western Scotland.

Jenkins gained recognition for his novel *Happy for the Child* (1953), a study of innocence and cor-

ruptibility that describes the experiences of a Scottish boy who attends a local grammar school on a scholarship. In *Guests of War* (1956), he portrays the evacuation of a Scottish town during World War II. In recapping the life of the main character, Bell McShelvie, Jenkins reveals his concern about the degradation of modern Scotland: "It had been a tale of crudeness, ignorance, paganism, violence, hardship, selfishness and greed; unfolded in hovels in the country and grimy tenements in the city; without the alleviation of what was called culture. . . ."

Another recurring theme in Jenkins's works is the limitations and imperfections of love. When reviewing *The Changeling* (1958), a treatment of class distinctions in which a Glasgow teacher takes a poor but bright student on vacation with his family, the scholar Francis Russell Hart wrote that Jenkins teaches the lesson "to love people is to love a radical mixture of betrayal and corruption, innocence and evil." Jenkins explores the ambiguous nature of love in several other novels. In *A Very Scotch Affair* (1968), a story about an insurance supervisor who leaves his dying wife for a mistress who subsequently leaves him, Jenkins provides what is a recurring revelation in his works: "Maybe it's a miracle that love is able to exist here. But it does."

Although Jenkins was a prolific writer and won several awards, he was relatively unknown outside of Scotland. Many Scottish fiction writers, however, admired him for his sense of irony and sense of humor. Critic Francis Russell Hart writes of Jenkins that his "novels show a remarkable continuity of motif and theme, a cluster of situations and problems . . . without marked shifts in mode or method. His feelings for Scotland fluctuate widely between anger . . . and a marveling compassion for the sheer will to survive in those ground down by a life of Glasgow poverty."

Other Works by Robin Jenkins

Dust on the Paw. New York: Putnam, 1961.

The Expatriates. London: Gollancz, 1971.

Jennings, Elizabeth Joan Cecil (1926–   )
poet

Elizabeth Jennings was born in Boston, Lincolnshire, England. Her father, Henry Cecil Jennings, served as the medical officer for Oxford County. Jennings wrote her first poetry as a teenager when she began questioning her faith. She earned her degree in English at Oxford in 1949.

While she was a student at Oxford, Jennings mixed with a group of poets and writers, including Kingsley AMIS. Jennings's first book, *Poems* (1953), won an Arts Council Prize. It contains the well-known poem "Delay," which emphasizes the distance between lovers by comparing the speed of light to the speed of love: "Love that loves now may not reach me until / Its first desire is spent." Her early lyrics were short and simple, and often dealt with the themes of fear and loneliness.

Along with her college friends, Jennings was considered to be part of the MOVEMENT, a literary group formed in the 1950s as a reaction against the neoromanticism of earlier British writers. She was associated with the Movement because she combined traditional verse form, simple language, and rationality. However, Jennings differed from other Movement poets in that she often wrote about mystical and supernatural topics instead of popular issues and current events.

Jennings's second volume, *A Way of Looking* (1955), contains poems in which physical reality is used as a premise for self-understanding. After several more collections Jennings published *Collected Poems* (1967), reprinting much of her work from the previous 14 years. American scholar Sandra Gilbert wrote of Jennings's themes of personal, literary, and Christian history: "Her notion of history . . . is surely one to which we ought to attend, if only because its complex attention to enduring desires and ancient difficulties is so compelling."

Much of Jennings's best verse has a contemplative nature. Her poem "Madness" in *The Mind Has Mountains* (1966) reflects on those who suffer from mental illness. Jennings, who suffered a severe mental breakdown herself in the early 1960s, used poetry to gain peace. She believed "the act of writing a poem is itself an implicit affirmation of the possibility of order."

Jennings's later collections, such as *Consequently I Rejoice* (1977), contain meditations on prayer and her Catholic faith. Critic William Blissett has written that Jennings's work exhibits "the continuity of rhyme and reason, of syntax and stanza . . . the easy rhythms, the eschewing of decoration, the control of metaphor" as well as the special insights given to her by "the suffering of illness, by her librarian's nonacademic love of literature, and by her lifelong religious concern."

Other Work by Elizabeth Jennings
Familiar Spirits. Manchester, England: Carcanet, 1994.

A Work about Elizabeth Jennings
Gramang, Gerlinde. *Elizabeth Jennings.* Lewiston, N.Y.: Edwin Mellen Press, 1995.

Jesse, Fryniwyd Tennyson (1910–   )
novelist, short story writer, nonfiction writer

F. Tennyson Jesse was born in Chislehurst, Kent, England, to the Reverend Eustace Tennyson d'Eyncourt Jesse and Edith Louisa James Jesse. Although she was a grandniece of the poet Alfred, Lord Tennyson, Jesse's childhood was poverty-stricken due to her father's financial failures. At age 19 she studied painting at the Stanhope School in Cornwall. She later moved to London and worked as a journalist, book reviewer, and short story writer.

Jesse's first short story, "The Mask," was adapted into a successful stage drama, *The Black Mask* (1912). The story is about a Cornish woman, who, along with her lover, mistakenly believes that her repressive husband has been killed. "The Mask" culminates in murder and is the first of Jesse's many forays into criminology. In her influential study *Murder and Its Motives* (1924), she presents her theory that murderers fall into six distinct classifications. Jesse also edited several cases for the *Notable British Trials* series.

Jesse's most famous novel, *A Pin to See the Peepshow* (1934), was based on a real-life murder trial in London. The novel describes the life of Julia Almond, who is trapped in an unfulfilling marriage. As a middle-class woman, she is unable to find freedom because divorce would leave her penniless. She eventually has an affair with Leonard Carr. Although Carr kills Julia's husband without her knowledge, both are tried and convicted of murder. Since Julia was not guilty of anything more than adultery, her conviction is an indictment against the restrictive society that punished her for violating its accepted standards for women of her class. Julia is thus a tragic character who "never had a chance of anything she really wanted. That was why she always pretended." The novel remained popular for decades after its release, and in 1972 it was adapted for British television.

Jesse published several other works of fiction but never matched the success of *A Pin to See the Peepshow*. Her works nonetheless contain a social realism that set them apart from the writings of her contemporaries in the crime genre. As with her depiction of Julia, Jesse compassionately portrayed women struggling against social convention and discrimination in their efforts to escape unfulfilling lives.

Other Work by F. Tennyson Jesse
The Story of Burma. London: Macmillan, 1946.

A Work about F. Tennyson Jesse
Colenbrander, Joanna. *A Portrait of Fryn: A Biography of F. Tennyson Jesse.* London: Andre Deutsch, 1984.

Jhabvala, Ruth Prawer (1927–   )
novelist, short story writer, screenwriter
Born in Cologne to Polish parents, Ruth Prawer Jhabvala has a European (Jewish), British, Indian, and now American heritage, as she has made her home on three continents and absorbed several cultures. She was educated in England at Hendon County School and at the University of London's Queen Mary College, where she obtained an M.A. In 1951 she married Cyrus Jhabvala, a Parsi architect with whom she had three daughters; she lived with him in New Delhi from 1951 to 1975. In 1975 she emigrated to the United States, but she visits England frequently and spends winters in India.

In addition to a dozen novels and a half-dozen volumes of short stories, Jhabvala has written many film scripts. In 1962 she met the producer/director team of Ismail Merchant and James Ivory, and together the three of them are responsible for such films as *Shakespeare Wallah* (1965), *A Room with a View* (1986), *Howards End* (1992), and *The Remains of the Day* (1993). For *A Room with a View* Jhabvala won an Academy Award. Two of her own novels, *The Householder* (1960) and *Heat and Dust* (1975), have also been filmed.

Jhabvala's literary career spans 40 years and exhibits several phases. Often compared to Jane Austen and E. M. FORSTER because she writes comedies of manners, her influences include Charles Dickens, George Eliot, Thomas Hardy, Leo Tolstoy, Ivan Turgenev, and Marcel Proust. Her early novels are more narrowly focused than her later ones and often center on joint or extended Indian families and their problems. East/West conflict is another major theme and the chief reason for comparing her with Forster.

Esmond in India (1957) is about a philandering British civil servant with an Indian wife and a British mistress who befriends a number of middle-class Indian women and exhibits a love/hate relationship with the subcontinent. *The Householder* focuses on the marriage of Prem and Indu; Prem discovers he must defeat his mother-in-law and rise above himself to fulfill his marriage. *Heat and Dust,* which won the BOOKER PRIZE, is one of Jhabvala's most complex, sophisticated works, interweaving two love stories 50 years apart—that of Olivia, who runs off with an Indian prince, and that of her granddaughter. The novel raises the question "What is identity?" and probes the relations between history and reality, history and fiction, and fiction and reality. *A New Dominion* (1971) is experimental, employing omniscient narration (like Jhabvala's earlier fiction) but supplementing this by shifting from one character's viewpoint to another's. This novel and *Heat and Dust* are both reminiscent of Forster's *A Passage to India*.

Later Jhabvala novels, which are more complex in narration, more detached, and darker in mood, exhibit techniques learned from screenwriting. The first Jhabvala novel to be written in America, *In Search of Love and Beauty* (1983), is a quest novel exploring each part of its author's heritages—German, British, and Indian—against an American background. The later novels also address another favorite Jhabvala theme: the fraudulent guru or swami who cheats his devotees. In *Three Continents* (1987) American female twins turn over their lives and fortunes to sham gurus with disastrous results.

Jhabvala's fiction has received mixed reviews. Although she earns praise for her writing, some Indians are often annoyed by her outsider's "inside" view of them and the subcontinent, and they chafe at her detachment, which she claims is self-defense, as she discusses in the introduction to *Out of India* (1986). She admits that, while immersed in India, she was never of it. After reviewing differing oriental and occidental evaluations of Jhabvala, scholar Ralph Crane observes simply, "She is a writer whose work will stand the test of time."

Other Work by Ruth Prawer Jhabvala

East into Upper East: Plain Tales from New York and New Delhi. Washington, D.C.: Counterpoint Press, 2000.

Works about Ruth Prawer Jhabvala

Crane, Ralph J. *Ruth Prawer Jhabvala.* New York: Twayne, 1992.

Sucher, Laurie. *The Fiction of Ruth Prawer Jhabvala: The Politics of Passion.* New York: St. Martin's Press, 1989.

Johnson, Bryan Stanley (1933–1973)
novelist, poet

B. S. Johnson, the son of Emily Jane Johnson, a waitress, and Stanley Wilfred Johnson, a stores keeper (supply clerk), was born in London and grew up during World War II. His working-class roots influenced his bawdy, unpretentious writing style. Writer Chris Milton calls him "an unflinching

dissector of what it is to be human." Johnson published two volumes of poetry, the topics of which range from love poems to memories of a wartime childhood, but he is best known for his novels.

Johnson experimented constantly with new ways of constructing and telling his stories. Literary critic David John Davies explains: "In a genre not noted for its linguistic inventiveness, [Johnson] breathed new life into the English novel, making the novel itself a metaphor for the conditions it described." Each chapter of his first novel, *Travelling People* (1963), uses a different narrative device (a film script, a series of letters) to tell the story of Henry, a hitchhiker who unsuccessfully attempts to bond with people of both the working and middle classes. The book won the Gregory Award for Best First Novel.

Johnson's second novel, *Alberto Angelo* (1964), voices the frustrations of a man who wants to be an architect but is working instead as a substitute teacher. A hole cut into the pages of the book allows the reader to see future events in the story.

Johnson often wrote in long, conversational sentences. *Trawl* (1966), winner of the Somerset Maugham Prize, describes his experience on a fishing boat and employs this colloquial narrative style: "Ah! A ginnie, I must take special care of the ginnies, for her sake, for that is my name for her, I can't call you that, I said, when I first met her, I'll call you Ginnie."

Johnson continued to experiment in *The Unfortunates* (1969), which gathers recollections of a friend, who is dying of cancer, into a box of 27 separate booklets. The booklets can be read in any order as long as the one marked "First" is read first and the one marked "Last" is read last. James Marcus, in a review for the *New York Times,* credited Johnson with making "experimental writing seem not only natural but inevitable."

Other Works by B. S. Johnson

Christie Malry's Own Double Entry. New York: New Directions, 1973.

House Mother Normal. New York: New Directions, 1971.

A Work about B. S. Johnson

Tew, Philip. *B. S. Johnson: A Critical Reading*. Vancouver: University of British Columbia Press, 2001.

Johnson, Pamela Hansford (1912–1981)
novelist

Pamela Hansford Johnson was the daughter of Reginald Kenneth Johnson, a colonial administrator in Ghana, and his actress wife, Amy Clotilda Howson. Her father died when she was 11, and she and her mother moved to Clapham, London, the setting for several of her novels. She was educated at Clapham County Secondary School and became a shorthand-typist in a bank. She first married a historian and journalist; after they divorced, she married scientist and author C. P. SNOW in 1950.

A prolific and versatile author who published 30 novels, Johnson was not a literary experimenter or innovator, yet each of her works tackles different subject matter. Although she uses recurrent themes—notably the vagaries of love leading to all kinds of mismatches and misalliances—her characters, settings, and plots are diverse and display a wide-ranging mind, talent, and life experience. Her obituary in the London *Times* placed Johnson squarely in the English realistic tradition, commenting that some of her novels are "in their sad, lucid, honest acceptance of life in the direct line of descent from George Eliot's fiction . . ." Like Eliot, she was a stern moralist.

In Johnson's first novel, *This Bed Thy Centre* (1935), Elsie Cotton, the central character, is about to embark on marriage, although she knows little about men, sex, or life. Critic Isabel Quigley points out that Johnson's lovers are never ideal and rarely young, for this author is bent on showing how "people of many varied ages can love, depend on one another, desperately need one another; good people may need bad ones, worthy people be infatuated with wastrels . . . the decent person obsessed with the indecent . . ." Johnson's novels center on a moral crisis or dilemma, her plots often hinging on ill-conceived marriages. Their subplots pursue different strands of action in different social strata.

Several unremarkable novels followed the first, but Johnson found success with the publication of the first volume of the trilogy comprising *Too Dear for My Possessing* (1940), *An Avenue of Stone* (1947), and *A Summer to Decide* (1948). World War II had shaken up society and flung people of different classes and ways of life together, so that in *Too Dear*, as Quigley observes, life "is no longer envisaged in social layers, each separate . . . but as . . . lives jumbled together or criss-crossing" among the same set of people. The three novels range from the 1920s through the 1940s and may be read as a single work. The trilogy is a complex and perceptive sequence of novels offering fine portraits of its principals—Claud Pickering, the narrator; his father's mistress, Helena; and his half-sister, Charmian—and of the cities in which the action unfolds, notably Bruges and London.

The Unspeakable Skipton (1959) introduces a second, comic sequence of three novels, called the "Dorothy Merlin comedies." Johnson modeled the portrait of Skipton, a paranoid artist, on the writer Frederick Rolfe. The second Dorothy Merlin novel, *Night and Silence, Who is Here?* (1962), is a lightweight satire set in a New England college to which Matthew Pryar, one of Skipton's colleagues in Bruges, goes as a visiting fellow. Pryar is writing a monograph about Dorothy Merlin, a poet/playwright and doyenne of the Bruges group whose full awfulness is revealed in the third novel, *Cork Street, Next to the Hatters* (1965), which traces her decline and fall. This satire on British permissiveness denounces contemporary exploitations of violence and sexuality. In this work, a playwright creates a drama so vile that he expects the audience to be revolted. Instead, the attendees love it.

Critic Leonard R. N. Ashley points out that, whereas C. P. Snow was concerned with "might and right," his wife focused on individuals confronting dilemmas, which she handled with considerable psychological insight. The memorable novels *The Humbler Creation* (1959) and *An Error of Judgment* (1962) depict protagonists facing truly agonizing dilemmas.

A Work about Pamela Hansford Johnson

Lindblad, Ishrat. *Pamela Hansford Johnson*. Boston: Twayne, 1982.

Johnston, Denis (William Denis Johnston) (1901–1984) *playwright, biographer*

Denis Johnston was born in Dublin, Ireland, the son of Supreme Court judge William Johnston. He studied history and law at Cambridge in England, then attended Harvard Law School in the United States. In 1929 he submitted his first play, *Shadowdance,* to the Abbey Theater in Dublin, but Lady GREGORY, the theater's manager, rejected it. He retitled the play *The Old Lady Says 'No'!* in reference to the rejection that Lady Gregory wrote across the title page, and it was immediately accepted at a different theater.

The Old Lady Says 'No'! describes technology coming to the countryside, and expresses Johnston's disillusionment with the hypocrisy and low standards of Dublin politics and government. The tone of the play is sarcastic, as depicted in the following excerpt, which contains the Minister of Art's reply to an artist's request for funding: "... 'if he deserves it, mind you, only if he deserves it, under Section 15 of the Deserving Artists (Support) Act, number 65 of 1926. And there's no favouritism at all.' / Chorus: 'The State supports the Artist. And the Artist supports the State. Very satisfactory for everybody and no favouritism at all.'"

Johnston's experiences as a war correspondent for the BBC during World War II inspired *Nine Rivers to Jordan* (1953), the first of two autobiographical works. He wrote nine other plays in his lifetime and received a Guggenheim fellowship (1955) and an honorary doctorate from the New University of Ulster (1979). E. Martin Browne, editor of *Three Irish Plays,* calls Johnston "an author who was able to do for the modern Ireland, faced with the impact of science and invention upon its ancient way of life, what Yeats and Synge had done for the older Ireland."

Other Works by Denis Johnston

The Brazen Horn. 1976. Reprint, Buckinghamshire England: Colin Smythe, 1999.

John Millington Synge. New York: Columbia University Press, 1965.

Selected Plays of Denis Johnston (Irish Drama Selections 2). Washington, D.C.: Catholic University of America Press, 1984.

Jones, David Michael (1895–1974) *poet*

David Jones was born in Kent, England, the son of James Jones, a printer's manager, and Alice Jones, a sketch artist. After attending Camberwell Art School, he enlisted in the British army and spent three years fighting in World War I. A strong sense of visual imagery and his wartime experiences deeply influenced Jones's writing. After the war, he experimented with various forms of art in search of a way to express himself.

Jones's first book of poetry, *In Parenthesis* (1937), tells the story of a group of British troops during World War I. The poet Stephen SPENDER admired the book: "This work of a poet-painter has its every word chiseled out of experience, and it is probably the World War I monument most likely to survive." The following excerpt, in which the protagonist has just been hit in the legs by machine gun fire, gives an example of Jones' vivid and realistic imagery: "The warm fluid percolates between his toes and his left boot fills, as when you tread in a puddle—he crawled away in the opposite direction."

Jones's second book, the long poem *The Anathemata* (1952), is a complex, quasi-historical epic that weaves together several of his favorite themes: history, war, Catholicism, and mythology. W. H. AUDEN calls it "very probably the finest long poem written in English this century," but many readers find sentences like the following overly complex: "In the first month in the week of metamorphosis the fifth day past at about the sixth hour after the dusk of it towards the ebb time in the median silences for a second time again in the middle night-course he girds himself." Critic Brad Haas believes that there is brilliance in the many layers and references that Jones employs: "Jones sees possible explanations, if not solutions, in the juxtaposition of the present and the past. . . . He utilizes the mythic material in its own context, yet also lifts it and places it in the context of the modern age, and the symbols are shown to be relevant for both times."

A Work about David Jones

James, Merlin, et al. *David Jones 1895–1974: A Map of the Artist's Mind.* London: Lund Humphries, 1995.

Jones, Gwyn (1907–1999) *novelist, short story writer, nonfiction writer, translator*

Gwyn Jones was born in Blackwood, a mining town in south Wales. His father, George Henry Jones, was a miner; his mother, Lily Florence Nethercott Jones, was a teacher and a midwife. Jones attended the University of Wales at Cardiff, where he earned an M.A. in English. He taught at grammar schools in Wigan and Manchester before serving as an English lecturer and professor at his college alma mater.

Jones's first novel, *Richard Savage* (1935), describes the life of an 18th-century poet. The author displays a profound knowledge of England at that time as he chronicles Savage's interactions with the elite and the dregs of society. His skillful use of language to create atmosphere is evident in his description of a law officer who ventures into a crime district: "Strapping bravos would jostle him or splash mud upon him . . . from the sills above the wretched man could expect the peril of a dropped bucket or the nauseating drench of a tipped jordan [a Ruby play]."

Jones shifted to contemporary concerns in his second novel, *Times Like These* (1936), which depicts the hardships faced by a mining family during the 1926 Welsh miners strike. His novel *Garland of Bays* (1938) chronicles the life of poet and dramatist Robert Greene in Elizabethan England.

In the 1940s Jones published the short story collections *The Buttercup Field* (1945) and *The Still Waters* (1948). Many of the stories in these volumes depict the lives of farmers and miners in the Welsh industrial valleys. As with his novels, Jones displays compassion and sympathy, especially for his female characters. In "The Passionate People," the narrator describes looking at a picture of Mary Ellis, the object of his longing: "I often study that pretty portrait—imagine her older now, the rondeur and the bloom of her cheek contracted more than a shade, the mouth now sensitive to pain as well as joy, the lovely eyes drained of the candour, the ingenuousness of girlhood." A *Times Literary Supplement* critic wrote that "Jones has written stories in a variety of moods, and his eloquent prose has graced them all."

Jones attained his greatest fame for his nonfiction works. His translations of Icelandic sagas and medieval Welsh tales are noted for their accuracy. His prize-winning book *A History of the Vikings* (1968) made his reputation as an authority on the Norse voyages of discovery. When reviewing the volume, poet and critic Robert Conquest held that Jones's works elevated nonfiction literature: "All previous periods have taken history, and philosophy too, as at least equal, and often superior, components of the written culture. Professor Jones deserves to be treated in that light."

Other Work by Gwyn Jones

The Walk Home. New York: Norton, 1963.

A Work about Gwyn Jones

Price, Cecil. *Gwyn Jones.* Cardiff: University of Wales Press for the Welsh Arts Council, 1976.

Jordan, Neil Patrick (1950–   ) *screenwriter, novelist, playwright*

Neil Jordan was born in Sligo, Ireland. His father was a professor of education and his mother was a painter. Jordan studied at University College, Dublin. In 1974 he started his career as a writer and set up the Irish Writers' Cooperative. He is best known, however, for his accomplishments as a screenwriter and film director.

Jordan often writes about Ireland's politics and culture, but his trademark is to encourage a different way of thinking about such topics as violence, gender, sex, and race. To this end, he creates unconventional characters who have done something that goes against society. "The people in *Night in Tunisia* (1976) . . . are often 'suspended', suffering a kind of detachment from the world and, more significantly, from themselves," observed critic Terence Winch. *Night In Tunisia* is a collection of short stories set in Dublin that describe various rites of passage (the end of childhood, death, the end of a love affair).

Jordan published two more works that explore similar themes of passion and betrayal: the novels *The Past* (1979) and *The Dream of a Beast* (1983). *The Past,* the story of a man's search for the truth about his birth and his parents, is "a sensitive evocation of Irish people and places beyond Dublin, an elaborate literary jigsaw puzzle, a kind of love story and a kind of detective story, but above all, an exercise in imagination," according to critic Roger Dionne. *The Dream of A Beast* (1983) describes a disillusioned advertising executive's metamorphosis into a mysterious, imaginary creature.

Jordan has written and directed several award-winning films, including *The Crying Game* (1992), the story about an Irish Republican Army rebel, which won the Academy Award for best original screenplay. *Michael Collins* (1996), which is based on the life of the IRA commander, won the Golden Lion at the Cannes Film Festival. Jordan has also written for the stage and for Irish and British television and radio. Winch praises Jordan's writing as "poetic in the best sense of the word, which is to say that he manipulates certain images skillfully without using more words than necessary."

Other Works by Neil Jordan

Collected Fiction. New York: Vintage, 1997.
Michael Collins: Screenplay and Film Diary. New York: Plume, 1996.

A Work about Neil Jordan

Rockett, Kevin. *Neil Jordan.* Clarement, Calif.: Oak Tree Press, 2002.

Joyce, James (1882–1941) *novelist, short story writer, poet*

James Joyce was born in Dublin to John Joyce, a city official, and Mary Jane Murray Joyce, a devout Catholic. Joyce was extremely close to his brother Stanislaus, who was his faithful companion and later provided him with financial aid. First educated at Clongowes Wood College, Joyce later enrolled in the Jesuit Belvedere College and eventually attended University College, Dublin, where he took a degree in literature and set out to teach and write.

Joyce early came under the influence of the Irish poet William Butler YEATS and the Norwegian playwright Henrik Ibsen. Of the latter he wrote, "Ibsen has attained . . . such mastery over his art that, with apparently easy dialogue, he presents his men and women passing through different soul-crises." Joyce was also profoundly affected by the French Symbolists, who sought to explore the meaning of reality not only through images but also through the relationship between the sound and rhythms of words.

In general, unlike Yeats, Joyce had little fondness for Irish nationalism or culture, for he found Ireland to be narrow and conservative. In large part he blamed the Catholic Church for Ireland's problems and abandoned his faith in his late teens. From age 19 on, he lived in Paris, Trieste, Rome, and Zurich, visiting Dublin only a few times thereafter.

Called back to Dublin in 1903 because his mother was dying, Joyce sold several stories to George ("A. E.") RUSSELL's magazine *The Irish Homestead.* These stories later appeared in his collection *Dubliners* (1914). He also met and fell in love with Nora Barnacle, an uneducated chambermaid, with whom he eloped to Europe.

In 1907 Joyce's first book, *Chamber Music,* a collection of minor lyrical love poems, was published. Of more significance was his next work, *Dubliners,* a collection of stories that, as Joyce observed, "betray the soul of that . . . paralysis which many consider a city." In most of the stories Joyce's style is spare and his plots almost nonexistent as he reveals the paralysis of his Dubliners. In "Eveline," for example, the title character is unable to carry out her plans to flee Dublin by marrying a sailor: "He . . . called to her to follow. . . . She set her white face to him, passive, like a helpless animal. Her eyes gave him no love or farewell or recognition."

As the scholar William York Tindall notes, "The moral center of *Dubliners* . . . is not paralysis alone but the revelation of paralysis." In each story a character undergoes what Joyce labeled an epiphany, a sudden insight or moment of understanding brought about by a simple or commonplace event. In the final story, "The Dead," Gabriel Conroy, after hearing for the first time about a long-dead lover of his wife, realizes that, unlike that old flame, he is incapable of love because he is empty and dead inside. This epiphany comes as he gazes out on falling snow: "His soul swooned slowly as he heard the snow falling faintly through the universe."

Joyce's first novel, *A Portrait of the Artist as a Young Man,* was published in 1916 with the help of the American poet Ezra Pound. This semiautobiographical novel describes the early life and artistic awakening of writer-to-be Stephen Dedalus, who reappears in Joyce's second novel, *Ulysses* (1922). Again Pound, this time along with T. S. ELIOT, found a publisher for Joyce.

Banned in the United States until 1933, *Ulysses* takes place on June 16, 1904 (the day Joyce left for Europe with Nora and now known as Bloomsday). It follows the adventures of Leopold Bloom as he wanders through Dublin, consumed by worry about the faithfulness of his wife Molly. Loosely based on Homer's *The Odyssey,* the novel's chapters correspond to sections in the ancient Greek epic. However, the comparison is comic. Thus, where the hero Ulysses encounters the Sirens, whose song lures sailors to their deaths, Bloom meets three singing barmaids.

This novel is renowned for its use of language and imagery, as when Bloom is introduced:

> Mr. Leopold Bloom ate with relish the inner organs of beasts and fowls. He liked thick giblet soup, nutty gizzards, a stuffed roast heart, liver slices fried with crustcrumbs. . . . Most of all he liked grilled mutton kidneys which gave to his palate a fine tang of faintly scented urine.

In the "Oxen of the Sun" chapter, Joyce stylistically imitates the development of English literature, beginning with Old English poetry and ending with 20th-century prose.

Much of *Ulysses* is told through stream of consciousness—that is, writing that conveys the flow of a character's random, fragmented thoughts, feelings, and impressions. The entire last chapter, which inhabits the mind of Molly Bloom, reveals Joyce's mastery of this technique as he lays out Molly's earthy character and feelings in sentences, devoid of punctuation, that run pages long. At one point she thinks of her dead son:

> that disheartened me altogether I suppose I oughnt to have buried him in that little wooly jacket I knitted crying . . . but I knew well Id never have another . . . we were never the same since O Im not going to think myself into the glooms about that any more.

Joyce's final novel, *Finnegans Wake* (1939), takes place in the dreaming mind of Humphrey Chimpden Earwicker, whose initials, H. C. E., stand for "Here Comes Everybody." Earwicker's dream revolves around his family, but is a mythic retelling of every family's story. The language is extravagant and sometimes difficult, as in this description of Earwicker's wife, Anna Livia Plurabelle: "leaning with the sloothering slide of her giddygaddy, grannyma, gossipaceous Anna Livia." In this work history is cyclical, and thus the book opens in the middle of a sentence that begins at the very end of the novel.

Critical Analysis

A Portrait of the Artist as a Young Man depicts the early childhood, adolescence, and coming of age of Stephen Dedalus, a young Irishman who, not unlike Joyce, receives a Catholic education, loses his faith, despairs for Ireland, and sets off for Europe to become a writer. The novel opens when Stephen is a child trying to comprehend the structure of his family, as well as the passionate political loyalties he witnesses at family gatherings. Employing stream of consciousness, Joyce then portrays Stephen's experience at boarding school, where the boy undergoes the shame of being wrongly punished yet is able to summon the spirit to speak up for himself.

Chapter I reveals Stephen's sensitivity to language and his musical sensibility, characteristics of the artist, while Chapter II shows the budding of that artist:

> Words which he did not understand he said over and over to himself till he had learned them by heart; and through them he had glimpses of the real world about him. The hour when he too would take his part in the life of that world seemed drawing near and in secret he began to make ready for the great part which he felt awaited him the nature of which he only dimly apprehended.

During the several years telescoped into this second chapter, Stephen experiences his first sexual urges, recognizes his father's vanity, expresses his desire not to become like his father, and tastes independence when he wins a prize and has some money of his own.

In Chapter III Stephen becomes passionately religious as he participates in a Catholic retreat and confronts his sins. However, in the final two chapters he begins to doubt his faith and ends by rejecting the church. With this rejection comes the discovery and acceptance of his vocation as an artist.

The burgeoning artist is not entirely likeable in his judgments of others and his attitude of superiority. As his friend Davin tells him, "You're a terrible man, Stevie, ... Always alone." Indeed, Stephen is now separating himself from his friends and his family, declaring to his friend Cranly that he will go away and "try to express myself in some mode of life or art as freely as I can." In the final lines of the novel, a somewhat pretentious Stephen vows "to forge in the smithy of my soul the uncreated conscience of my race." He beseeches his namesake, the Ancient Greek inventor Daedalus, whom he considers his real father.

According to the scholar and biographer Richard Ellmann, "We are still learning to be James Joyce's contemporaries, to understand our interpreter." Ellmann adds, "he is a great experimentalist, a great city man." For the novelist Anthony BURGESS, Joyce's "need to tell the truth about man's daily mind necessitates the fracture of syntax, the fusion and truncation of words."

Other Work by James Joyce

Exiles. 1918. Reprint, New York: Dover, 2002.

Works about James Joyce

Attridge, Derek, ed. *The Cambridge Companion to James Joyce.* New York: Cambridge University Press, 1990.

Ellmann, Richard. *James Joyce.* Revised Edition. New York: Oxford University Press, 1983.

Fragnoli, A. Nicholas, and Michael Patrick Gillespie. *James Joyce A to Z: The Essential Reference to the Life and Work.* New York: Facts On File, 1995.

O'Brien, Edna. *James Joyce.* New York: Viking Penguin, 1999.

K

Kavanagh, Dan

See BARNES, JULIAN.

Kavanagh, Patrick Joseph Gregory

(1931–) *poet, memoirist*

P. J. Kavanagh was born in Worthing, Sussex, England, to H. E. Kavanagh, a radio scriptwriter, and Agnes O'Keefe Kavanagh. His education consisted of a prep school, a Catholic boarding school, a Swiss boarding school, and a drama school in Paris. After receiving an M.A. from Oxford University in 1954, Kavanagh worked as an assistant floor manager for BBC television.

Kavanagh's first volume of poetry, *One and One* (1959), contains verse written in the traditional poetic style. He uses rhyme, meter, and conventional forms such as sonnets and couplets. In this collection he is concerned with the uniting of opposing entities, such as war and art, and love and violence. His poem about Auschwitz, "Arbeit Macht Frei," concludes with the lines, "They learned the cruelty in passion, in a lover / was chaining them not only to each other." Kavanagh was devastated by the death of his wife, Sally, in 1958, and much of his verse explores the meaning and effects of death. He laments premature loss in his poem "Narrative," which closes with the lines

"Night picked him like a flower. I left him dead, / Still biting the hand that fed, that fed."

After writing *The Perfect Stranger* (1966), his award-winning autobiography, which describes the painful effects of his wife's death, Kavanagh resumed publishing poetry collections. In *Life before Death* (1979), he speculates on the possibility of making connections with the spiritual realm though experiences in the natural world. The poems, which convey Kavanagh's complex vision of life before and after death, are written in long lines and use off-rhymes within a rigid stanza form. In "The Dead" he asks, "Do this morning the dead, turned inwards towards brightness, / Over their shoulders feel pictures of living arrive?"

Kavanagh's poetry matured over time, exhibiting greater sensitivity for humanity and imaginative breadth as he looked to nature with its changing beauty to counteract the effects of loss. In "Nature Poet" in the *Presences* (1987) collection, he writes, "In wings of moths, in lists of patient Things he detected mercy / Wafting, like a smell. His voices had their say."

Kavanagh's *Selected Poems* (1982) was a Poetry Book Society recommendation, reflecting a greater recognition of his work. When reviewing *Collected Poems* (1992), critic Dick Davis wrote, "The poet appears to be wearily defeated by a multiplicity of experience, though he is able to record that defeat convincingly." Reviewer Frank Kermode added that Kavanagh is "a quiet-sounding poet, but he has more skills and far greater range than this description suggests," and that he occupies a "distinguished place among contemporary poets."

Other Work by P. J. Kavanagh
About Time. London: Chatto & Windus, 1970.

Keane, Molly (M. J. Farrell) (1904–1996)
novelist, playwright

Molly Keane was born Mary Nesta Skrine in County Kildare, Ireland, to Walter Clarmon and Nesta Shakespeare Skrine. Her father was a wealthy Anglo-Irish landowner; her mother was a well-known poet who wrote under the pseudonym Moira O'Neil. Keane was educated in traditional subjects at home by a governess. She also learned to hunt and ride horses. In 1938 she married director Robert Lumley Keane. Her long career as a writer earned her much praise for her ability to create believable characters who often faced difficult circumstances due to deprivations that came from losses of status and wealth.

Coming from a privileged background, Keane often wrote about the declining world of the landed elite that had surrounded her growing up in the early 20th century. She published her first novel, *The Knight of the Cheerful Countenance*, in 1928. Her first play, *Spring Meeting* was produced in 1938. Like her mother before her, Keane wanted to avoid publicity and wrote under the name M. J. Farrell, a name that she used until the late 1940s. Her novels and plays are often set in the Irish countryside and depict the decaying world of the landowning class in Ireland, as in the early novel *Taking Chances* (1929), the story of three sibling orphans whose lives are disrupted by the intrigues that accompany one sister's upcoming marriage. Other early novels include *Mad Puppetstown* (1931), a novel that introduced the highly politicized subject of the Anglo-Irish war to her writing about manners and morals; and *Devoted Ladies*

(1934), the story of a love triangle that the *New York Times Book Review* called "deliciously funny."

After her husband died in 1947, Keane stopped writing. At age 76, however, she broke her long silence and published her most critically acclaimed novel, *Good Behavior* (1980), under her own name. A finalist for the BOOKER PRIZE in 1981, *Good Behavior* uses Keane's favorite setting, the country estate, to tell the story of flawed characters who find themselves trapped in an aristocratic world that is slowly fading from existence. The main characters have had to face their fall from the world of the landed elite: "Our kitchen and dining room are on the lowest level of this small Gothic folly of a house. The stairs, with their skimpy iron banister, bring you up to the hall and the drawing room, where I put all of our mementos of Papa when we moved here from Temple Alice." In a review of the 2001 reprint of the novel, the *Sunday Times* called it "[a] fine novel, wickedly alive."

Keane's next work, *Time after Time* (1983), is a comic tale of the lives and adventures of four siblings living in a once beautiful but now run-down estate in Ireland. Compared to writers such as Noel COWARD and Iris MURDOCH for her witty style, Keane has been praised for her depiction of the manners and modes of a bygone era. As critic Polly Devlin observes, "Her novels deliver a remarkable and vivid social history, an impeccably observed, occasionally delinquent record, full of relevance and revelation of a way of life and a vanished world."

Other Work by Molly Keane
Molly Keane's Ireland: An Anthology. Edited by Sally Phipps. New York: HarperCollins, 1994.

Kell, Joseph
See BURGESS, ANTHONY.

Kelman, James (1946–) *novelist, short story writer*

James Kelman was born in Glasgow, Scotland, to a schoolteacher and a self-employed picture-frame maker. As a child he lived in a series of Glasgow tenements. He quit school at age 15 to embark on a series of odd jobs that included driving a bus and stocking store shelves. At age 29 he entered the University of Strathclyde and in two years of study developed a lasting disdain for classic English literature, with what he saw as its emphasis on empowered social classes.

Despite this, Kelman has become one of the most prominent Scottish writers and is part of a long tradition of working-class intellectuals that include Robert Burns, James Hogg, and Hugh MACDIARMID. Kelman writes about working-class characters who have little or no ambition beyond survival and lead extremely bleak lives.

Kelman's first major publication was a novel, *The Busconductor Hines* (1984), which he based on his own experience as a bus driver. Hines, a typical Kelman character, is incapable of rising above his circumstances. He has made no use of his education, and even when he knows that he will soon be fired because new technologies have reduced the number of drivers needed, he is unable to carry out any of the numerous plans that he concocts.

The Busconductor Hines earned Kelman public and critical attention, as did two later novels, *Disaffection* (1989) and *How Late It Was, How Late* (1994). *Disaffection,* which won the prestigious James Tait Black Memorial Prize, describes a week in the life of a Glasgow teacher. Patrick Doyle is depressed by his job and by a relationship with a married woman who, a constant flirt, refuses to become truly involved with him. The novel's tone of despair is established with its opening sentences: "Patrick Doyle was a teacher. Gradually he had become sickened by it." Doyle is trapped in an oppressive culture and is bitter because he knows that as a teacher he promotes that very culture.

How Late It Was, How Late won the BOOKER PRIZE. It is narrated by Sammy Stone, a petty criminal who goes on a drunken binge and, for reasons he cannot remember, finds himself in jail. He is horribly beaten by police until he becomes blind, and finally returns home to find that his girlfriend Helen has abandoned him. Sammy is such a pa-

thetic character that his mere survival seems heroic. In one of his more touching reveries, he wishes that he could have one more conversation with Helen, "just to let her know the score . . . to be honest, tell her the whole truth and nothing but. Cause that was the problem, he hadnay got the message across, he telt her a tale and it went wrong."

Kelman has also written numerous short stories. The title story of his collection *Greyhound for Breakfast* (1987) tells of an extremely poor man who uses the last of his money to buy a dog. The stories in *Busted Scotch: Selected Stories* (1997) display a small change in Kelman's writing; they contain characters who, if they cannot rise above their situations, become reconciled to them.

Although some critics have found Kelman's characters and plots repetitive, and others have found his work obscure because of his use of the Glasgow working-class dialect, he has secured a lasting position in Scottish literature. According to critic Todd Pruzan, "Kelman is a master at portraying the numb headaches afflicting morose, underwhelmed people. . . . [He] intimately documents times that are anxious, tedious, pointless—anything but good."

Other Works by James Kelman
The Good Times. New York: Random House, 1999.
Translated Accounts. New York: Doubleday, 2001.

Keneally, Thomas (1935–) *novelist, nonfiction writer*
Born in Sydney, Australia, Thomas Keneally is the descendant of Irish immigrants. As a child he was educated by the Christian Brothers while his father served in the Australian Air Force during World War II. In 1952 Keneally entered the seminary, but he withdrew eight years later, just before his scheduled ordination.

While working at various jobs during the early 1960s, Keneally began publishing short stories. His first novel, *The Place at Whitton,* appeared in 1964. His early novels examine Australian history and emphasize the cultural clashes between European settlers and Australian aborigines. In interviews, Keneally has frequently criticized the quality of his early novels, but he admits they show his interest in contrasting old and new worlds and in the declining influence of European imperial power.

This concern for cultures in conflict led Keneally to explore events beyond Australia and is central to his most famous novel, *Schindler's List* (1982), originally published as *Schindler's Ark*. Based on fact, the novel won the BOOKER PRIZE. Its protagonist, Oskar Schindler, rescues hundreds of Polish Jews from Nazi death camps by employing them in his factory. In his depiction of Nazism, Keneally portrays the last decadent stages of European cultural arrogance.

More recently, Keneally has turned to nonfiction to explore the theme of cultural conflict. *The Great Shame* (1999) studies Irish dissidents who were exiled to Australian penal colonies because they opposed British rule. Through narratives detailing the lives of historically minor figures, Keneally has created a sense of humanity and reality.

Keneally has been made a Fellow in the Royal Society of Literature, has been elected to the American Academy of Arts and Sciences, and has been made an Officer of the Order of Australia. The critic Peter Pierce notes that Keneally's fascination with cultural clashes arises out of a concern for "all that imperils the integrity of the self, and especially the means by which that self can be sustained."

Other Works by Thomas Keneally
A Dutiful Daughter. New York: Viking Press, 1971.
Family Madness. New York: Simon & Schuster, 1986.
Flying Hero Class. New York: Warner, 1991.

A Work about Thomas Keneally
Pierce, Peter. *Australian Melodramas: Thomas Keneally's Fiction*. St. Lucia, Australia: University of Queensland Press, 1995.

Kennedy, Alison Louise (1965–) *short story writer, novelist, screenwriter*
A. L. Kennedy was born in Dundee, Scotland, and attended the University of Warwick in England.

She is considered one of Scotland's most important contemporary writers and has received international acclaim for her fictional depiction of modern Scottish life.

Kennedy's first collection of stories, *Night Geometry and the Garscadden Train* (1990), won the Saltire First Book Award and the John Llewelyn Rhys Prize in 1991. The stories in this collection are set in Scotland and concern the lives of characters, mostly women, faced with difficult personal choices. The story "Night Geometry" describes the murderous desperation of the main character who has come home to find her husband in bed with another woman.

After her short story debut, Kennedy turned to dramatic fiction and wrote the screenplay for the 1996 movie *Stella Does Tricks*. More recently her work as a novelist has gained her international acclaim. *Looking for the Possible Dance* (1993) was her first novel. Paul Taylor, in a review in the *Sunday Independent*, praised the novel for its ability to bring "its quirky canniness to bear on a wide range of human relationships." The book traces the life of its despairing main character, Margaret, who has had a difficult time piecing together relationships. Born and raised in contemporary Scotland, Margaret must piece together her life in the midst of the trials and tribulations that characterize her own modern-day urban experience.

Another novel, *Original Bliss* (1997), deals with the theme of love and isolation by tracing the courtship of two deeply complicated characters. Helen Brindle feels trapped in an abusive marriage and seeks solace in the arms of a self-help guru, Edward Gluck, whom she first hears about while watching television. After going to the bookstore to find out more about this engaging figure, Helen is faced with a dilemma: "Having read Gluck as thoroughly as she could, Mrs. Brindle knew about obsession, its causes and signs. She was well equipped to consider whether she was currently obsessing over Gluck." Sylvia Brownrigg in her Salon.com review of the book, remarked that in this novel, "Kennedy has a beautiful way with the lonely and the bereft, and a keen sense of the pleasurable strangenesses of sexuality."

As an author, Kennedy believes in the transformative power of fiction. In a lecture given at the 2001 Edinburgh Book Festival she stated, "Fiction gives us dignity—why? Because it offers us what no other form fully does or can: the articulated potential, the spoken dreams, the unmistakable beauty and the possibilities of the immense, human interior reality inside that Other—inside all those human beings who are not myself, yourselves. It provides truth—the truth that we are all more than what we seem and that what each of us holds is irreplaceable."

Named in 1993 by the literary magazine *Granta* as one of the best new young writers, Kennedy, in the words of one reviewer for *Boldtype* literary magazine, "has established herself as a writer of startling originality and invention, who brings an element of surprise to themes of isolation, emotional destitution, passion, perversion and true love."

Other Works by A. L. Kennedy
Everything You Need. New York: Alfred A. Knopf, 2001.
On Bullfighting. New York: Anchor Books, 2001.

Kinsella, Thomas (1928–   ) *poet*
Thomas Kinsella was born in Dublin, Ireland, to John Paul and Agnes Casserly Kinsella. His father was a brewery worker, trade unionist, and member of the Labour Party. Kinsella attended University College in Dublin, where he earned a degree in public administration. He then spent two decades working for the Irish Civil Service. In 1965 he moved to the United States to teach English.

Among Kinsella's significant early volumes is *Another September* (1958), a collection of love poems and meditative poems. Much of the verse in this volume reflects Kinsella's use of poetry to pursue order in the midst of loss and waste.

Kinsella's critically acclaimed volume *Night-walker and Other Poems* (1968) contains "Night-walker," widely considered his most significant poem. It is a long poem of quest and a meditation on Ireland's past and present, as the narrator walks at night through the suburbs of Dublin. The poem broke new ground in Irish poetry by focusing on the decay in Ireland's art, religion, politics, and language. Influenced by T. S. ELIOT, Kinsella depicts Dublin as a lunar wasteland: "Rock needles stand up from the plain; the horizon / a ring of sharp mountains like broken spikes." Scholar Donatella Abbate Badin writes that the poem "is often marred by an excess of topicality, but Kinsella overcomes the narrowness of his grievances through the dominant theme of the poem: the quest for a pattern of order."

Kinsella continued writing significant poetry in the 1970s. He gained widespread exposure in the United States with *Collected Poems 1956–1973* (1980). In addition to his poems on Ireland, Kinsella also wrote verse that explores themes of life and death. In such poems as "Landscape and Figure" he accepts life as a form of death. He describes a man's existence as a journey toward returning to the earth: "The protecting flesh / When it falls will melt in a kind of mud."

Distinguished from his contemporaries by his original subject matter, Kinsella has been credited with revitalizing post-World War II Irish poetry. Scholar Maurice Harmon writes that Kinsella, "[r]ealizing that the chaos of modern life has emerged from human wills . . . has sought order and understanding through a complex and detailed exploration of the manifestations of chaos in the world at large, in the natural processes, in the life of his country, and in his own personal life."

Other Work by Thomas Kinsella
Fifteen Dead. Dublin: Dolman Press, 1979.

A Work about Thomas Kinsella
Abatte Badin, Donatella. *Thomas Kinsella.* Boston: Twayne, 1996.

Knowall, George
See O'BRIEN, FLANN.

Koestler, Arthur (1905–1983) *novelist, nonfiction writer*

The only child of a Jewish couple, Henrik and Adela Koestler, Arthur Koestler was born in Budapest. The family moved to Vienna when he was nine, and his education continued there until, without a degree, he left college after having studied science and modern languages. He left to immerse himself in the first of several causes through which he was to seek a kind of salvation: Zionism, the establishment of a Jewish national state in what was then Palestine.

Koestler became a Middle East correspondent for the powerful Ullstein publishing empire. In 1929 he was posted to Paris as a science writer, but he soon returned to headquarters in Berlin. There his horror at the sudden rise of Nazi power led him into communism. He was to remain a communist for seven years, during which time he was a fervid writer and organizer for this new cause—until he went to Russia and saw Josef Stalin's terrifying application of theoretical marxist principles. The trial of the great Russian revolutionary Nikolai Bukharin in 1938 led Koestler to resign from the party.

That same year Koestler published his first novel, *The Gladiators,* a story about the Roman slave Spartacus. Spartacus's failed revolution parallels similar failures in Russia. Early in the novel, Spartacus envisions a utopian "town of our own. Then, when the Romans come, they will break their heads against the walls of the town which belongs to us—a gladiators' town, a slaves' town." Koestler's good friend George ORWELL sums up the novel's message as expressing "the dreams of a just society which seems to haunt the human imagination . . . in all ages, whether it is called the Kingdom of Heaven or the classless society, or . . . a Golden Age."

While *The Gladiators* critiqued Soviet policies through historical analogy, Koestler's next and greatest novel delineated the failures of Soviet communism directly and in their starkest contemporary forms. *Darkness at Noon* (1941) is the story of a faithful and thoughtful revolutionary party member, Nikolai Rubashov (modeled on Nikolai

Bukharin), who must be sacrificed to the ends of his party, and who must participate in and agree to his own public trial and death. While in prison he reflects on the contradictions of revolution: "How can one change the world if one identifies oneself with everybody? How else can one change it?" V. S. PRITCHETT praised Koestler's "superb gift for the handling of argument in a living way," his abilities to turn political ideologies into compelling characters and incidents. The ideas contained in the novel were powerful enough, when it was published in France, to help turn the tide of political opinion away from communism.

Communism for Koestler was a "god that failed," but the scientist in him led him to seek answers through a kind of fusion of science (particularly psychology), art, and humanism and led to a trilogy of works devoted to theorizing in this area: *The Sleepwalkers* (1959), a study of the minds of the astronomers Kepler, Copernicus, and Galileo; *The Act of Creation* (1964), a study of the imagination and creativity; and *The Ghost in the Machine* (1967), a call for the invention of a pill that would change human psychology from its self-destructive character to one of universal benevolence.

In 1957 Koestler became a Fellow of the Royal Society of Literature; he later became a Fellow at the Center for the Advanced Study in the Behavioral Sciences at Stanford. He received an honorary doctorate from Queen's University, and in 1972 he was made a Commander of the Order of the British Empire (CBE). Afflicted with leukemia, he killed himself in 1983.

Koestler devoted his life to a search for a solution to the "human condition" that was sane, moral, and just, and that achieved a balance between idealized ends and the often cruel means by which the ends may be obtained. As critic David Astor said, "He was great in intellect and imagination, and great in moral courage. . . . Koestler will hold a place in the front rank of . . . those who have saved our century from disgrace."

Other Work by Arthur Koestler

The Call-Girls. New York: Macmillan, 1972.

Works about Arthur Koestler

Levene, Mark. *Arthur Koestler*. New York: Ungar, 1984.

Pearson, Sidney A. *Arthur Koestler*. Boston: Twayne, 1978.

Kops, Bernard (1926–) *playwright*

Bernard Kops was born in Stepney, London, England, to Joel and Ginny Kops. Both parents were Jewish and his father, a leather worker, struggled to support his large family. Kops attended Stepney Jewish School but left at the age of 13. He held many jobs, including cook, waiter, wandering actor, and book peddler. After establishing himself as a playwright, he was the resident dramatist at the Bristol Old Vic Theater.

Kops's first produced stage work, *The Hamlet of Stepney Green* (1958), adapted Shakespeare's *Hamlet* work to his own contemporary Jewish community in the Stepney slums. Kop's Hamlet is David, an aspiring crooner whose father, Sam, a neurotic pickled-herring peddler, is poisoned by his wife. The lighthearted play features characters that often burst into song. The key moment in the play comes when David asks his father's ghost "What is the purpose of life?" Sam replies, "The purpose of life is to be aware that that question exists." The play's happy ending provides a sentimental message that warmhearted simple people will ultimately prevail in life.

Kops's subsequent plays included *Change for the Angel* (1960), about a family in danger of losing its standards and identity in the modern city. The dreamer again wins out in the end when the young son, Paul, realizes his ambition to become a writer. The humor and sentimentality in Kops's plays drew mixed reactions from critics.

Kops shifted away from his sentimental optimism with pessimistic plays such as *The Lemmings* (1964), which depicts people who decide to fulfill their death wish by walking into the sea. Despite its apocalyptic pessimism, the play still contains the accurate portrayals of English working-class existence for which Kops is known. Mr. Lemming, a taxi driver, reflects on his life when asked what business he is in: "Made a living. Not wonderful but couldn't complain. I paid for everything out of that cab. Lovely house, fitted carpets, central heating, twenty-one inch screen, two indoor lavatories, holiday in Bournemouth, son's education, the lot."

Kops's play *Ezra* (1981) is a study of the life and mental breakdown of the poet Ezra Pound. His more recent dramas deal with such topics as Anne Frank's life, recluses, and suicide. Believing that Kops's best works are his simple, sentimental comedies, scholar John Russell Taylor writes: "Kops is not a thinker, even if possibly he would like to see himself as one, but just has a natural flair for the theatre which given the right material and the right form can produced a lively piece of theatrical fantasy."

Other Work by Bernard Kops

The World Is a Wedding. New York: Coward-McCann, 1963.

Lamb, William

See JAMESON, STORM.

Larkin, Philip (1922–1985) *poet, novelist, essayist*

Philip Larkin was born in Coventry, England, to Sydney Larkin, a city treasurer, and Eva Emily Larkin. Perpetually bored during his childhood, Larkin did not enjoy school, largely because he was nearsighted and stuttered. As he grew older, however, he became a better student and eventually earned his degree in English from Oxford.

Although Larkin was writing poetry before he went to Oxford, he found encouragement and intellectual stimulation from a group of close university friends that included Kingsley AMIS and John WAIN. While at Oxford, he came under the influence of the highly lyrical poetry of William Butler YEATS and W. H. AUDEN. Upon graduation, he became a librarian.

The influence of both Yeats and Auden is apparent in Larkin's first major collection of poetry, *The North Ship* (1945), which provides an important insight into the mind of a promising young poet. Dominated by themes of doom and despair, whose development lacks the concrete images that would lift them out of the abstract, this early poetry shows Larkin struggling to find his own voice. Shortly after *The North Ship,* he wrote two well-received novels, *Jill* (1945) and *A Girl in Winter* (1947), which were based, respectively, on his life at Oxford and his experiences as a librarian in a small town in Shropshire. Despite his success in prose, Larkin never wrote another novel. By chance, he rediscovered the poetry of Thomas Hardy and found in it the answer to his earlier problem of voice.

Larkin published *The Less Deceived,* the first of three major volumes of poetry, in 1955. This collection shows him as a confident poet finally satisfied with his own voice, and it sets the stage for the two volumes that earned Larkin his highest praise: *The Whitsun Weddings* (1964), which won the Queen's Gold Medal for Poetry; and *High Windows* (1974).

Larkin's final publication was a collection of essays, *Required Writing* (1983), which articulate the antimodernist stance he held throughout his career. As an antimodernist, he was recognized as a member of the MOVEMENT, a literary school that favored traditional verse forms and plain language instead of the often deliberately obscure imagery and language of such modernist poets as T. S. ELIOT.

The Less Deceived, aside from solidifying Larkin's voice, is an important text for the Movement. Even in his title Larkin distances himself from modernists (like Pablo Picasso in art and Eliot in literature) by suggesting that he is not deceived into believing that the modernists are more in tune with art because they have rejected realistic portrayals of the world. The very names of Larkin's poems in *The Less Deceived*—"Wires," "Spring," and "Strangers"—reflect his appreciation of realism and concrete images associated with the Movement. In "The Wires" he describes young, active cattle immediately losing the vigor and wanderlust of their youth after coming into contact with an electric fence. Larkin's poem, as the last lines reveal, is grounded in the reality of the world: "young steers become old cattle from that day, / Electric limits to their wildest senses."

The Whitsun Weddings, is Larkin's primary work. Unlike the verse in *The Less Deceived,* the poems in this volume all have the same narrator, traveling from the country to London, which he does not at all like and constantly criticizes. Set in spring and ostensibly about the weddings that the narrator witnesses along his way, the poetry covers a broad range of subjects including the rise of commercial culture in England. In "Sunny Prestatyn," for instance, Larkin's narrator describes a graffiti-covered billboard advertising a resort and featuring a bathing suit-clad girl with "huge tits and a fissured crotch." He detests such signs of commercial culture, but his faith in humanity is restored when he witnesses weddings and thinks about individuals rather than society as a whole. In *The Whitsun Weddings* he becomes so spellbound by the weddings taking place outside his railroad car that he sticks his head through a window so that he can better see "The fathers with broad belts under their suits / and seamy foreheads; mothers loud and fat."

In *High Windows* Larkin deals with loneliness and death, as well as how one ought to live. As "The Building," widely regarded as one of his best poems, unfolds, it becomes clear that the building is actually a hospital—a forbidding place, which Larkin describes as a very tall, sheer cliff where everyone must confront the reality of death: "All

know they are going to die. Not yet, perhaps not here, but in the end." Larkin also examines death in "The Old Fools," which is an honest and often harsh look at aging and senility. Although Larkin searches for answers throughout the poem, he never finds them. He cannot comprehend an enfeebled, dependent life and closes the poem suggesting that he will only understand old age when he reaches it himself.

Somewhat of a recluse his entire life, Larkin is one of the most important postwar British poets. According to Brownjohn, Larkin "produced the most technically brilliant and resonantly beautiful, profoundly disturbing yet appealing and approachable body of verse of any English poet in the last forty years." Moreover, according to Bruce Martin, Larkin has become "the center, if not the starting point, of most critical debate over postwar British verse."

Other Works by Philip Larkin

All What Jazz: A Record Diary, 1967–1971. New York: Farrar, Straus & Giroux, 1985.
Collected Poems. Edited by Anthony Thwaite. New York: Farrar, Straus & Giroux, 1988.
Selected Letters of Philip Larkin, 1940–1985. New York: Farrar, Straus & Giroux, 1999.

Works about Philip Larkin

Booth, James, ed. *New Larkins for Old: Critical Essays.* New York: St. Martin's Press, 1999.
Regan, Stephen. *Philip Larkin.* New York: St. Martin's Press, 1997.
Swarbrick, Andrew. *Out of Reach: The Poetry of Philip Larkin.* New York: St. Martin's Press, 1995.

Lavin, Mary (1912–1996) *short story writer, novelist*

Mary Lavin was born in Walpole, Massachusetts, and immigrated to Ireland at age nine with her parents, Thomas and Nora Mahon Lavin. Her father became an estate manager in Ireland, just north of Dublin. She received her B.A. from University College, Dublin, with honors, in 1934 and went on to receive her M.A. with honors. In the middle of writing her dissertation, Lavin quit her graduate studies in order to pursue a career as a writer. She is best known as a short story writer who captured the beauty of everyday life in contemporary Ireland by creating sympathetic characters placed in difficult circumstances.

Lavin first found success publishing stories in such literary periodicals as the *Atlantic Monthly, The New Yorker,* and *Southern Review.* Her first collection of short stories, *Tales from Bective Bridge* (1942), won the 1943 James Tait Black Memorial Prize, one of the oldest and most prestigious British literary prizes.

Lavin published her first novel, *Gabriel Galloway,* as a serialized story in the *Atlantic Monthly* during 1944 and 1945. The story follows the protagonist, Gabriel, through a series of complicated life decisions that lead him to discover his place in Irish society. Another novel, *Mary O'Grady* (1950), tells the tragic tale of a mother obsessed with the spiritual and physical well-being of her children. Author Anthony BURGESS praised Lavin's ability "to make much out of little, to compress an entire ethos into an apparently banal situation, she reminds us what literature is all about."

Lavin's talent for creating believable characters in real-life situations has contributed to her international acclaim as an author who has been translated into nine languages and has had her work adapted for film. As V. S. PRITCHETT writes, "I cannot think of any Irish writer who has gone so profoundly without fear into the Irish heart." Lavin's biographer, Zack Bowen, has written, "The verisimilitude of her stories and characters renders her work clear and at the same time significant to the reader . . . such clarity and craftsmanship in style and structure are the products of a writer of the first rank, a position which Mary Lavin had achieved in Ireland thirty years ago and has held every since."

Other Work by Mary Lavin
In a Café: Selected Stories. New York: Penguin, 1999.

Works about Mary Lavin
Bowen, Zack. *Mary Lavin.* Lewisburg, Pa.: Bucknell University Press, 1975.
Kelly, A. A. *Mary Lavin: Quiet Rebel.* New York: Irish American Book Company, 1997.

Lawrence, David Herbert (1885–1930)
novelist, short story writer, poet, playwright

D. H. Lawrence was born in the English mining village of Eastwood, Nottinghamshire, to John Arthur Lawrence, a coal miner, and Lydia Beardsall Lawrence, a schoolteacher. Lawrence's parents were locked in constant conflict throughout his childhood: his father was a simple, often rough, laborer, whereas his mother was better educated and aspired to rise out of the working class. Ultimately, Lawrence followed his mother's path, earning a scholarship to Nottingham High School and eventually earning a teaching certificate from Nottingham University College.

Beginning in 1910, with the first publication of his work in *The English Review,* Lawrence produced more than 10 collections of poetry, including *Amores* (1916), *Birds, Beasts, and Flowers* (1923), and *Fire and Other Poems* (1940), as well as eight plays that often made use of the gruff, working-class qualities that he observed in his father. Of those plays, only two, *The Widowing of Mrs. Holroyd* (1926) and *David* (1927), were produced during his lifetime.

It was as a novelist and writer of short stories, however, that Lawrence distinguished himself. He wrote more than 20 novels, six of which still attract large amounts of critical attention: *Sons and Lovers* (1913), a story about Paul Morel, his extremely close relationship with his mother, and his struggle to live on his own after her death; *The Plumed Serpent* (1926), a story laden with Aztec myths that focuses on Kate Leslie and her involvement in a religious cult striving for political control of Mexico; *The Rainbow* (1915) and *Women in Love* (1920), which tell an epic saga of the Brangwen family that stretches over two centuries and traces several generations' quests for love; and

Lady Chatterley's Lover (1928), which focuses on the romantic relationship of a married woman, Constance Chatterley, with her husband's gamekeeper, Oliver Mellors.

In addition to his novels, Lawrence published five collections of short stories, including *England, My England and Other Stories* (1922) and *The Woman Who Rode Away and Other Stories* (1928). "The Rocking Horse Winner" (1925), about a young boy who can predict the winners of horse races as he rides his rocking horse, has become one of the most anthologized short stories of the 20th century.

Throughout his career, D. H. Lawrence was the topic of debate in both public and literary spheres. The author single-handedly combated Victorian sexual prudishness, while pushing the limits of his craft. In all of his writing, Lawrence delved into the inner workings of human relationships and, through what the scholar Kinsley Widmer calls "his obsessive concern with exploring erotic themes, social angers, and religious perplexities" has achieved the "role of bedeviled prophet."

Critical Analysis

Lawrence's poetry was largely ignored throughout his lifetime and was even harshly attacked by the critic R. P. Blackmur, who once remarked that Lawrence "developed as little art as possible and left us the ruins of great intentions." Nevertheless, he produced a broad collection of poetry that engages such themes as youth, energy, and sexuality, and old age and death. The poem "Cherry Robbing" (1928) captures all of the qualities of Lawrence's early work as it describes a cherry-picking excursion that begins with lush descriptions of fruit-bearing branches but soon reveals a complex blending of blood and sexual images. Lawrence writes that the cherries remind him of "blood drops," but near the end of the poem he uses the same piece of fruit as a symbol of virginity when he writes that a girl "offers me her scarlet fruit."

Lawrence's late poetry presents an entirely different poet. In the posthumously published "The Ship of Death" (1932), for instance, he discusses

neither youth nor sexuality but his own death. In the poem he projects neither rage nor incredulity toward the idea that he must die but turns death into a metaphorical voyage, for which he urges his readers to prepare in the final lines: "Oh build your ship of death. O build it! . . . For the voyage of oblivion awaits you."

In his story "The Rocking-Horse Winner" Lawrence explores one of his favorite topics, mother-son relationships, and he does so in a clear, precise style typical of most of his short fiction. Both his dominant theme and his characteristic style are evident in the first paragraph of the story when he writes that Hester, the mother,

> had bonny children, yet she felt they had been thrust upon her, and she could not love them . . . only she herself knew that at the centre of her heart was a hard little place that could not feel love.

Hester's son Paul, almost by accident, realizes that he can predict the winners of horse races by riding on his rocking horse. He begins betting on races through his uncle and another adult friend in an effort to solve his mother's financial problems and win her adulation. His riding and gambling exhausts Paul and he dies, leaving his mother a tremendous sum of money. In the final lines of the book, Paul's uncle remarks, "My God, Hester, you're eight-odd thousand to the good, and a poor devil of a son to the bad," underscoring the price that she has paid for her greed.

Lawrence's novels *The Rainbow* and *Women in Love* together tell an epic saga about the Brangwen family, spanning both the 19th and 20th centuries. *The Rainbow* begins with Tom and Lydia Brangwen, whose initially very passionate marriage cools into a perpetual battle for dominance. This pattern of strong physical relationships that eventually dissipate into less-than-ideal partnerships repeats itself in the next generation of Brangwens, Anna and Will, and in the third, which is represented by Ursula. She has several affairs, including one with another woman, but she never marries, and at the end of the novel she is alone, pregnant, and still yearning for a fulfilling relationship. Illustrating Ursula's isolation, Lawrence writes that "in an ache of utter weariness she repeated: 'I have no father nor mother nor lover.'"

The power of *The Rainbow* lies in what the scholar Marianna Torgovnick has described as Lawrence's "innovation and courage" in broaching "views of sexuality rarely discussed in fiction before its time: sado-masochism, wild fluctuations in emotions within the love and sex relation, and the awareness and torment of bisexual longings which cannot speak their name," which appear throughout the novel, from the initial hot-and-cold marriage of Tom and Lydia to Ursula's experimentation with lesbianism.

Women in Love continues the story of Ursula Brangwen and her sister Gundrun. The novel covers one generation instead of three and devotes all of its attention to the attempts of Ursula and Rupert Birkin (Lawrence's persona in the novel) and Gundrun and Gerald Crich to transcend the problems of the world through love. Ultimately, the most marked difference between *The Rainbow* and *Women in Love* is their endings. While the first novel ends with an image of a rainbow in which Ursula sees "the world built up in a living fabric of Truth" and the promise of a better future, the latter novel offers no such closure. In the words of the scholar Alastair Niven, *Women in Love* "created a new form of fiction because it did not move toward a settled conclusion or seek to leave a comprehensive overview." Instead of such a conclusion, the novel ends with a series of questions passed between Ursula and Birkin in which he reveals that he felt romantically attached to Gerald, his deceased brother-in-law. After Ursula remarks, "You can't have two kinds of love," Lawrence ends the novel with Birkin's stark response, "I don't believe that," which hardly closes the discussion.

Other Works by D. H. Lawrence

The Collected Stories. New York: Everyman, 1994.
The Complete Plays of D. H. Lawrence. New York: Viking, 1966.
The Complete Poems. New York: Viking, 1994.
The Plumed Serpent. 1926. Reprint, Westminster, Md.: McKay, 1992.
Sons and Lovers. 1913. Reprint, New York: W. W. Norton, 1997.

Works about D. H. Lawrence

Fernihough, Anne, ed. *The Cambridge Companion to D. H. Lawrence.* New York: Cambridge University Press, 2001.
Marsh, Nicholas. *D. H. Lawrence: The Novels.* London: Macmillan, 2000.
Meyers, Jeffrey. *D. H. Lawrence: A Biography.* New York: Alfred A. Knopf, 1990.
Williams, Linda Ruth. *D. H. Lawrence.* Plymouth, England: Northcote, 1997.

Lawrence, Thomas Edward (1888–1935)
nonfiction writer, translator

Remembered more as the figure "Lawrence of Arabia" and for his remarkable exploits in guerrilla warfare than for his writing, T. E. Lawrence was born in Tremadoc, Caernarvonshire, Wales. From his parents, Thomas and Sarah Lawrence, came an interest in religion, and also from his father a love of outdoor activities and athletics. Lawrence was educated at Oxford, where he became fascinated by archaeology.

In the years just prior to World War I, Lawrence worked on archaeological digs in Turkey and Syria, a period he wrote about in *The Wilderness of Zin* (1915). During the war, because he knew Arabic, Lawrence organized Arab tribesmen in a revolt against Turkey, a German ally. The revolt helped to fragment and eventually destroy the ancient Ottoman Empire.

In the massive *Seven Pillars of Wisdom* (1926), Lawrence recounts the Arab military campaign and his travels in the Middle East. The book climaxes with the taking of Damascus from the Turks. Initially it was privately published and circulated among Lawrence's friends and colleagues, including Rudyard Kipling, Thomas Hardy, and Siegfried SASSOON.

Seven Pillars of Wisdom is full of philosophical observations and often conveys the sense that the author saw himself as much on a religious mission as on a mission of war. The philosophical and religious overtones have inspired some readers to hero-worship and others to doubts Lawrence's accuracy and emotional stability. For Lawrence there was a thin line between imagining oneself as a historically significant or messianic figure and becoming one. As he put it in his original introduction to *Seven Pillars,* "The dreamers of the day are dangerous men, for they may act their dreams with open eyes, to make it possible. This I did." Critic Flora Armitage says the book poetically captures Lawrence "and his moods, the awe and grandeur of the Arabian landscape, and the unpredictable, blood-stirring hazards of irregular warfare." On the other hand, the scholar Richard Aldington claims the book displays Lawrence's "pretentious egotism" and notes its self-conscious effort to be "literary," a result of Lawrence's desire to see the book stand alongside such classics as Herman Melville's *Moby-Dick,* Feodor Dostoevsky's *The Brothers Karamazov,* and Friedrich Nietzsche's *Thus Spake Zarathustra.*

In 1927 an abridged version of *Seven Pillars,* entitled *Revolt in the Desert,* which omitted much of Lawrence's philosophy, helped to turn him into a near-mythic figure and encouraged wild speculations about him, such as the claim that he was plotting to attack Russia from India during the 1920s. The British public enjoyed Lawrence's inspiring account of the war's eastern front, which contrasted with the many grim reports of the trench warfare that so many had suffered in the west.

Lawrence quickly became disillusioned with fame and with British foreign policy, which he felt had sacrificed Arab interests for those of Britain. Thus he adopted the name Ross and then Shaw, blending into the anonymous ranks of the British Royal Air Force. While partly hidden from the public eye in the RAF, Lawrence translated *The Odyssey of Homer* (1932), another tale of a soldier wandering through foreign lands. According to one critic this translation has been strongly criticized but its poor critical reception was partly due to Lawrence's refusal to translate the book into modern-sounding language, preferring an idiom more closely resembling the original Greek.

Lawrence also wrote a memoir of his RAF years, *The Mint* (1936), published a year after his retirement from the air force and his subsequent death in a motorcycle accident. Since then he has been the subject of biographies and a widely acclaimed film by director David Lean, *Lawrence of Arabia* (1962), a highly fictionalized account of the Arabian campaign. Critics continue to devote far more effort to understanding the man himself and his place in military history than to examining his skills as an author, although his grandiose writing style and what some consider his exaggerations in *Seven Pillars* about his importance in leading the Arab revolt contribute to the complexity of that effort. As biographer Michael Asher writes of his fellow Lawrence analysts and readers, "To his adulators, everything he said or wrote is held up as true, while his critics have gone to extraordinary lengths to prove the reverse."

Other Work by T. E. Lawrence

The Diary Kept by T. E. Lawrence While Travelling in Arabia During 1911. Reading, England: Garnet, 1997.

Works about T. E. Lawrence

Asher, Michael. *Lawrence: The Uncrowned King of Arabia.* Woodstock, N.Y.: Overlook Press, 1999.

Hart, B. H. Liddell. *Lawrence of Arabia.* New York: Da Capo Press, 1989.

Wilson, Jeremy. *Lawrence of Arabia: The Authorized Biography of T. E. Lawrence.* New York: Collier Books, 1992.

Leavis, Frank Raymond   (1895–1978)
literary critic, essayist

F. R. Leavis was born in Cambridge to Harry and Kate Sarah Moore Leavis. In 1924 he received a Ph.D. in English from Cambridge University, having written his dissertation on 18th-century periodical literature. During his education, Leavis was influenced by the literary criticism of Joseph Addison, George Santayana, and T. S. ELIOT, as well as Ford Maddox FORD's ideas about preserving high culture in a troubling new, industrial world.

The world that so concerned Ford was key in motivating much of Leavis's life work. As the scholar Ann Sampson puts it, Leavis viewed "the machine as the great enemy of human life" that disrupted traditional communities and economic systems and brought about "a hostile urban environment beset by rapid, disorienting change and stultifying production-line labour." As a remedy for this situation, Leavis promoted literature that contained preindustrial values, such as a sense of community and a close connection to work.

In promoting these values, Leavis became the chief proponent of the NEW CRITICISM, a movement that called for texts to be closely examined without any consideration of historical context or information about the author's life. Leavis first articulated this stance, largely the stance of all proponents of New Criticism, in *Mass Civilization and Minority Culture* (1930), in which, according to Ann Samson, he "maintained that literature . . . functioned as a storehouse of values, a living memory of what was best in the past, providing that continuity necessary for growth." However, literature, in Leavis's opinion, did not have a proper influence on society because those who knew "good" literature were a minority lacking any substantial influence over the rest of the reading public.

Leavis founded the journal *Scrutiny* in 1932 in an effort to guide the common reader toward high-quality literature. Most of the critic's longer works are extensions or collections of essays that first appeared in this journal. One such collection, *Revaluation: Tradition and Development in English Poetry* (1936), is solely concerned with evaluating canonical poets and their places in literary history. In the introduction to *Revaluation,* Leavis states that "in dealing with individual poets the critic, whether explicitly or not, is dealing with tradition, for they live in it. And it is in them that tradition lives." Moreover—and this is the point of Leavis's text—some poets are inherently more important to that tradition than others. Leavis, for instance, holds William Wordsworth, Percy Bysshe Shelley, and John Keats as intrinsically better and more important poets than many other notable figures of the 19th century, such as Alfred, Lord Tennyson.

Critical Analysis

Leavis performs the same type of historical, judgmental task with British novels in *The Great Tradition: George Eliot, Henry James, and Joseph Conrad* (1948). This text begins with a highly authoritative and contentious line, "The great English novelists are Jane Austen, George Eliot, Henry James and Joseph Conrad," which is indicative of his work as a whole. Leavis was compelled to hold texts to such high standards and levy harsh value judgments because to him, literature was an extremely important antidote to everything that he believed was wrong in the world.

Because his literary criticism was often harsh, many writers and scholars found his approach to literature repugnant, including J. B. PRIESTLEY, who described Leavis as "a sort of Calvinist" who "makes one feel that he hates books and authors . . . as if he had been frightened by a librarian in early childhood." He hated neither books nor authors, however, and in his criticism merely strove to make literature the curative social force that he felt it should be. Later in life, he received the accolades that his unconventionalities denied him in his youth. Before his death he received an appointment at Cambridge; visiting professorships at the University of York, the University of Wales, and the University of Bristol; and several honorary doctorates. In discussing Leavis's legacy, critic J. B. Bamborough has remarked, "It would be true to say that in the last thirty or more years hardly anyone seriously concerned with the study of English literature has not been influenced by him in some way."

Other Works by F. R. Leavis

D. H. Lawrence: Novelist. Chicago: University of Chicago Press, 1994.
Education and the University, a Sketch for an "English School". Manchester, England: Ayer, 1972.

Works about F. R. Leavis

Day, Gary. *Re-Reading Leavis: Culture and Literary Criticism*. New York: St. Martin's Press, 1996.

MacKillop, Ian. *F. R. Leavis: A Life in Criticism*. New York: St. Martin's Press, 1997.

le Carré, John (David John Moore Cornwell) (1931–   ) *novelist*

John le Carré was born David John Moore Cornwell in Poole, Dorset, England. His mother, Olive, left home when he was five, and his father, Ronnie, was in and out of prison for various business swindles.

In 1956 le Carré earned a degree in modern languages from Oxford University. Three years later he joined the British Foreign Office, where he did intelligence work in Germany, the setting for many of his early spy stories. For years he publicly denied that he had been a spy, but in fact he had worked for MI6, Britain's secret intelligence service during the height of the cold war and was in West Germany during the construction of the Berlin Wall. Later he came to admit his past, saying, "It would be terribly boring if people knew how boring my life had been in intelligence." Le Carré first used his pen name during this time because the Foreign Office required that people in his position use pseudonyms for their published work.

Le Carré's first novel, *Call for the Dead* (1961), was the first of his hugely successful spy thrillers. In this book the author introduced readers to a starkly realistic view of the world of spies and the intelligence community. While many spy novels are characterized by glamour, hi-tech gadgetry, and supervillains, le Carré's work explores the morality of patriotism and espionage through probing characterizations and tight plotting.

With *Call for the Dead* le Carré also introduced his most famous character: George Smiley, an aging, jaded, brilliant member of the British foreign service. In the opening chapter Smiley is described as a man who is detached from the humanity around him: "By the strength of his intellect, he forced himself to observe humanity with clinical objectivity. . . ." The novel applies many tra-ditions of detective fiction to the spy genre as he must find out why a man has taken his own life after Smiley performed a routine check to determine the man's political loyalty.

Le Carré secured his reputation as a master of the spy thriller with his third novel, *The Spy Who Came in from the Cold* (1963), which won the Somerset Maugham Award, and which the novelist Graham GREENE heralded as the best spy story he had ever read. Set during the cold war, the story tells of Alec Leamas, a British agent who is sent deep into communist territory to destroy the head of East German intelligence. In le Carré's hands, the "cold" of the title is both the isolation in which a spy lives while operating behind enemy lines and the cold detachment within him that lets him carry out his duty. In this novel, the author does away with the detective fiction formula and instead focuses tightly on the details of the workings of the world of espionage. Peter Lewis, a scholar of le Carré's work, attributes much of the novel's success to his ability to be "in tune with the times. The immediate success of *The Spy Who Came in from the Cold* suggests that at a period when the possibility of a third world war loomed larger than usual, there was a sizable audience for a more serious fiction about Cold War espionage."

Le Carré turned to writing full-time and eventually brought back George Smiley in *Tinker, Tailor, Soldier, Spy* (1974), in which Smiley must uncover the identity of a Soviet double agent. This book and le Carré's next two novels, *The Honourable Schoolboy* (1977) and *Smiley's People* (1979), comprise what is known as *The Quest for Karla* trilogy, as Smiley matches wits with the Soviet master spy Karla.

The Karla books, as well as le Carré's other cold war novels, express the author's conviction that there was "no virtue in the Cold War." These books raise the question of how far one can go to defend a society without betraying the values of that society. As Control tells Leamas in *The Spy Who Came in from the Cold,* "'I mean you can't be less ruthless than the opposition simply because your government's *policy* is benevolent, can you now?' He laughed quietly to himself: 'That would *never* do,' he said."

Le Carré's success has outlived the cold war itself, and his novels, including *The Tailor of Panama* (1996) and *Single and Single* (1999), continue to top the best-seller lists. Explaining le Carré's appeal, the critic Julian Symons writes that his work uses "the spy story as a means of conveying an attitude towards life and society."

Other Works by John le Carré

The Little Drummer Girl. New York: Alfred A. Knopf, 1983.

The Night Manager. New York: Alfred A. Knopf, 1990.

The Russia House. New York: Alfred A. Knopf, 1989.

Works about John le Carré

Bloom, Harold, ed. *John le Carré*. New York: Chelsea House Publishers, 1987.

Lewis, Peter. *John le Carré*. New York: Frederick Ungar, 1985.

Lee, Laurie (1914–1997) *poet, memoirist*

Laurie Lee was born in Stroud, Gloucestershire, England, the 11th of 12 children in a working-class family. He was educated at a local school and left home for London at age 19. There he attempted to earn his living as a writer and street musician. During World War II he worked for the Ministry of Information in London as a scriptwriter for wartime movies funded by the British government. In 1950 he married Catherine Francesca Polge. As a writer, Lee avoided political themes in favor of more intimate and personal themes that drew on his experiences growing up in the English countryside.

Lee focused his writing career on poetry and published his first collection of poems, *The Sun my Monument*, in 1944. He won the William Foyle Poetry Prize in 1955 for his collection entitled *My Many-Coated Man*. These poems celebrate the realization of adult selfhood by using the natural rhythms of the seasons as a metaphor for rebirth. The final lines from "The Long Summer" read, "I cannot doubt the cold is dead, / The gold earth turned to good—forever." Another poem in this collection, "The Abandoned Shade" explores the difficulty of recapturing lost youth: "but the voice of the boy, the boy I seem, within my mouth is dumb."

Lee also wrote a critically acclaimed memoir about his life growing up in rural England called *Cider with Rosie* (1959; published in the United States in 1960 as *The Edge of Day: A Boyhood in the West of England*). In describing this work, Lee claimed, "Autobiography is too fancy and too solemn a name for it. It is a love story, of an uncommon kind: a love story about life." The book was an immediate success and earned him much critical acclaim in England and the United States. His editor, Norman P. Ross, believed that the book's appeal rested in the author's ability to draw believable and intimate portraits of his characters: "What Lee writes about so compassionately in *The Edge of Day* is his family and their neighbors. He gives life an entire cast of characters. Like an artist who can paint lace with a few simple strokes, he captures people in half a sentence." Lee went on to write two other well-received autobiographical books based on his later life experiences: *As I Walked Out One Midsummer Morning* (1969) and *A Moment of War* (1991).

Lee wanted to be remembered not for his autobiographical prose but for his lyric poetry. However, some critics believe that he achieved his greatest success in his memoirs. As a writer, he has been praised for his ability to artfully use language in both his prose and poetry. Ross claimed that "Stylistically, Laurie Lee is a master; the technique of the poet shows in every line." According to Albert Hoxie of the *Los Angeles Times Book Review*, Lee "writes with the care of a poet who must weigh each word to find the precise one that will be the most telling and the most true."

Other Work by Laurie Lee

A Moment of War: A Memoir of the Spanish Civil War. New York: New Press, 1991.

A Work about Laurie Lee

Grove, Valerie. *Laurie Lee: The Well-Loved Stranger*. North Pomfret, Vt.: Trafalgar Square, 2001.

Lehmann, Rosamond (1901–1990)
novelist, short story writer

Rosamond Lehmann was born in Buckinghamshire, England, to a gifted family. Her father, Rudolph Lehmann, was a Liberal politician who also edited and wrote for the magazine *Punch*. Her older brother John became a critic and poet and founded the magazine *New Writing*, while her younger sister became an actress. Lehman too was encouraged to develop her talents, and from 1919 to 1922 she studied modern languages at Cambridge University.

Many of Lehmann's most successful works are sympathetic depictions of young women about to enter adulthood. Her first novel, *Dusty Answer* (1927), was controversial because of its depiction of teenage lesbian infatuation. The book ends with the heroine traveling alone on a train. Though she has lost all her ties through the course of the novel, she finds this isolation energizing and seems poised to dive into a world of possibility: "Soon she must begin to think: What next?"

This theme recurs in *Invitation to the Waltz* (1932), which opens with a young woman excited at the prospect of her first dance. The same character, 10 years older, appears in the somber *The Weather in the Streets* (1936), which startled critics with its portrayal of a clandestine love affair.

During World War II Lehmann wrote several short stories for the new magazine *New Writing*, edited by her brother. These were collected as *The Gipsy's Baby and Other Stories* (1946). The story "The Red-Haired Miss Daintreys" has a strange but interesting narrator who describes herself with a detached melancholy as "a kind of preserving jar in which float fragments of people and landscapes, snatches of sound."

Several of the stories hint at the tension that mounted in the early years of the war. "A Dream of Winter" describes a young woman staying in the country during the war, caring for her children and recovering from illness. One day a workman comes to remove a swarm of bees from the house, and she is filled with a disproportionate horror at the sight of the raided honeycomb: "The papery transparent aspect of these ethereal growths meant a world extinct. She shivered violently, her spirit overwhelmed by symbols of frustration."

Lehmann's most famous novel is *The Ballad and the Source* (1945), which describes a young girl's fascination with Sybil Jardine, a strange, domineering elderly woman. Sybil gradually unfolds her intricate and passionate history, and the reader gradually realizes that her eloquence and charm conceal horrific acts of cruelty. The narrator admits, "As time went on I grew more sad, uneasy, suspect in Mrs. Jardine's house. I could not get rid of a vision of her . . . savage, distraught, unearthly: Enchantress Queen in an antique ballad of revenge." Novelist Raymond Mortimer called *The Ballad and the Source* Lehmann's "best and most permanent book." The young girl of *Ballad* appears again, much older, in *The Echoing Grove* (1953), where she learns how to endure the pain of romantic betrayal.

In 1958 Lehmann's daughter Sally died unexpectedly, and Lehmann was desolated. She found some solace in mysticism, which features in her spiritualist autobiography *The Swan in the Evening* (1967). She was made a Commander of the Order of the British Empire in 1982 (CBE). Author Marghanita Laski wrote, "No English writer has told of the pains of women in love more truly or more movingly than Rosamond Lehmann."

Other Works by Rosamond Lehmann
A Note in Music. New York: Doubleday, 1983.
Rosamond Lehmann's Album. London: Chatto & Windus, 1986.
A Sea-Grape Tree. London: Collins, 1976.

Works about Rosamond Lehmann
Simons, Judy. *Rosamond Lehmann.* New York: Palgrave Macmillan, 1992.
Tindall, Gillian. *Rosamond Lehmann: An Appreciation.* London: Chatto & Windus, 1986.

Lessing, Doris (1919–) *novelist, short story writer, playwright, nonfiction writer*

Doris Lessing was born Doris May Taylor in Kermanshah, Persia (now Iran), to Alfred Cook Taylor, a bank clerk who lost a leg during World War I, and Emily Maude McVeagh Taylor, a former nun, who served as her father's nurse. According to Lessing, hearing her father's war experiences gave her a political awareness that found its way into her later work. When she was six, Lessing and her family moved to a farm in Rhodesia. There she attended a Catholic school until she was 14, at which time she left, frustrated by school restrictions, and became self-educated.

In 1937 Lessing moved to Salisbury, Rhodesia, where she began writing short stories. During the 1940s she was attracted to communism, and in 1948 married fellow communist Gottfried Lessing. A year later, the marriage ended. By 1949 she was living in London, where she published her first novel, *The Grass Is Singing* (1950), about a young wife's hard adjustment to life on an African farm. She has continued to make her home in London, with occasional trips to Zimbabwe, which she chronicles in *African Laughter: Four Visits to Zimbabwe* (1992).

Considered by many critics to be a leading feminist writer, although she herself tends to avoid labels, Lessing employs the various lenses of psychological and political analyses, ethics, feminism, social criticism, and Sufism (a mystical branch of Islam) to examine the world. *Martha Quest* (1952) and *A Proper Marriage* (1954) are the first of five autobiographical novels that comprise the *Children of Violence* series. These novels about a woman named Martha Quest come out of Lessing's life in southern Africa and her awareness of the injustices experienced by native Africans. In the third and fourth novels of the series, *A Ripple From the Storm* (1958) and *Landlocked* (1965), Lessing addresses what it is to be a member of the Communist Party and to be a young woman struggling to forge her own identity.

In her ground-breaking novel *The Golden Notebook* (1962), as well as in *The Four-Gated City* (1969), the final *Children of Violence* novel, Lessing breaks away from realism and explores the landscape of madness as a means of transformation. Now considered classics of feminist writing, these two works, along with the short story "To Room Nineteen," reveal her concern with the way a woman experiences the psychological descent that strips away her illusions about her place in the world before she can be regenerated and transformed—although such regeneration may not always be possible.

Disenchanted with the Communist Party and its jargon and still dissatisfied in her search for a means of personal and societal transformation, in 1964 Lessing discovered Sufism, which played a role in her series of science fiction novels, *Canopus in Argus: Archives,* which she began publishing in 1979. Lessing regards these works as inner-space fiction, not really science fiction, as vehicles for Sufism, and as a means of exploring stereotypical images of women and men. For example, in the second novel of the series, *The Marriages of Zones Three, Four, and Five* (1980), the gentle queen Al·Ith of Zone Three marries the soldier king Ben Ata of Zone Four. While Zone Three inhabitants are kind, compassionate, nonviolent, Zone Four is a patriarchal world of war and hierarchy. The marriage of the two rulers teaches Ben Ata and his people love and acceptance, and it encourages positive changes in both Zones. Ben Ata, in turn, is commanded to marry Queen Vahshi of Zone Five in order to teach her and her kingdom how to give up their own savage ways. In the words of critic John Leonard, this novel "is wise about men and women at a time when almost everybody else is stupid."

Lessing's novel *The Good Terrorist* (1986), the story of a group of middle-class terrorists, was followed by another fable, *The Fifth Child* (1988), the story of an upper middle-class British family who refuse to concern themselves with overpopulation as their offspring grow in number. When their freakish fifth child, Ben, is born, he disrupts the calm of the entire household and alienates the other children. He also forces a wedge between his parents because his mother cannot forsake him, despite the danger he brings and the damage he causes. Lessing uses this tale to offer a scathing portrait of contemporary society.

In 1995 the first volume of Lessing's unflinchingly honest autobiography, *Under My Skin:*

Volume One of My Autobiography, to 1949 appeared; the second, *Walking in the Shade: Volume Two of My Autobiography, to 1962,* was published in 1997. Of the latter critic Frank Kermode writes, "Volume 2 has plenty to say about the famous and the great, about friends, lovers, and comrades. . . . [and] it is excellent on the London of 1949, bleak, bombed and rationed." Lessing decided not to write further volumes, claiming she would be forced to reveal too much about others whose privacy should be respected. Instead, she chose Michael Holroyd, husband of Margaret DRABBLE, as her official biographer.

Lessing has continued to write novels. *Love, Again* (1996) is about the unexpected romances of Sarah Durham, a 65-year-old widow working in the London theater, and shows that the potential for romantic love is not limited to youth or middle age. Although *Mara and Dann: An Adventure* (1999) is set thousands of years in the future, it is based on Lessing's relationship with her younger brother, Harry Taylor. Her next novel, *Ben, In the World* (2000), the sequel to *The Fifth Child,* depicts the trials of Ben Lovatt as he reaches adulthood and must find ways to survive a world he can barely understand. Most recently, Lessing has returned to the autobiographical mode in *The Sweetest Dream* (2002), a fictional portrayal of the last 40 years.

Lessing is also noted for her many short stories, collected in several volumes; and her plays, including *Play with a Tiger* (1962), about a mismatched couple whose love fails to overcome their different temperaments. In 1997 she collaborated with the American composer Philip Glass on an opera based on *The Marriages of Zones Three, Four, and Five.* She has received many prizes, including the French Prix Medicis for Foreigners (1976), the W. H. Smith Literary Award (1986), and the James Tait Black prize for best biography (1995).

Critical Analysis

The Golden Notebook is considered one of Lessing's most important novels. As the scholar Carolyn G. Heilbrun wrote in 1973, "*The Golden Notebook* has been of overwhelming importance to women in the past decade precisely because it is almost the only contemporary novel in which an intellectual woman can recognize some of her own experience." It is the story of writer Anna Wulf's search for wholeness at a time when her life is fragmented, as symbolized by the different notebooks she keeps. Each of the four color-coded notebooks concerns a different part of her life: black for her previous life in Africa; blue for her personal diary; red for her political life and criticism of communism; and yellow for her current novel, whose protagonist, Ella, resembles Anna. Anna attempts to weave together the threads of these notebooks into one book, "the golden notebook." At the center of the novel is Anna's breakdown, but in this case madness becomes a means of healing, rebirth, and transformation rather than a sign of disintegration.

Ultimately, *The Golden Notebook* succeeds in conveying a portrait of a multifaceted, intelligent woman struggling with her writing, her relationships with men and women, her motherhood, and her place in society. Her writing and her reflections on what she has written aid her quest for wholeness, for as Anna recognizes, "Literature is analysis after the fact."

As the scholar Mona Knapp writes of *The Golden Notebook,* "A feminist critique of this novel is . . . inevitable," for "[n]o work of fiction has had more of an impact on the women's movement of the 60's and 70's." As with all of Lessing's work, this novel, with its concern for politics and novel-writing, is no simple tract and appeals to no single group of people. The American novelist Joyce Carol Oates observes that Lessing's work has "traced an evolutionary progress of the soul, which to some extent transforms the reader as he reads. . . . Doris Lessing possesses a unique sensitivity, writing out of her own intense experience, . . . but at the same time writing out of the spirit of the times."

Other Work by Doris Lessing
Stories. New York: Knopf, 1980.

Works about Doris Lessing

Greene, Gayle. *Doris Lessing.* Ann Arbor: University of Michigan Press, 1997.

Perrakis, Phyllis Sternberg, ed. *Spiritual Exploration in the Works of Doris Lessing.* Westport, Conn.: Greenwood Publishing, 1999.

Lewis, Alun (1915–1944) *poet, short story writer*

Born as World War I was under way, Alun Lewis died a year before the end of World War II. He was born and raised in Wales, the son of schoolteachers, and educated at the University College of Aberystwyth, Wales, and Manchester University in England. He worked as a teacher for a year, writing and publishing stories in periodicals, before joining the army in 1940.

While Lewis was in the service, he published two books that established his reputation. *Raider's Dawn* (1942), a collection of 47 poems, deals with the problems of identity and environment in the industrial life of Wales. "Bequest," for example, celebrates memories of his forebears: "My uncle trudging coal-black from the pit/With such transcendent music in his head . . ."

The Last Inspection (1943) is a collection of short stories, a few rooted in Lewis's Welsh background. His "Author's Note" states that most of the stories "are concerned with the Army in England during the two years' attented since the disaster of June 1940 [the German invasion of France]. . . . The main motif is the rootless life of soldiers having no enemy, and always, somehow, under a shadow." This rootless life is also captured in many of Lewis's poems, such as "All Day It Has Rained . . ." which describes humdrum life of soldiers in training, waiting: " . . . And we talked of girls, and dropping bombs on Rome,/And thought of the quiet dead and the loud celebrities."

In 1942 Lewis was shipped with his regiment to the war in India, and many poems and stories grew from his experience there. He died in Burma of a gunshot wound that may have been accidental, although many of his comrades believed that the pressures of military life had led him to suicide. The literary world of Britain united to mourn him. Dylan THOMAS spoke of him in a radio tribute as "a healer and an illuminator, humble before his own confessions."

After the war, in 1945, Lewis's poetry collection *Ha! Ha! Among the Trumpets* was published, with a foreword by Robert GRAVES. His Indian short stories and some letters were published in *In the Green Tree* (1948). "The Orange Grove," which Cary Archard, editor of a uniform edition of Lewis's work regards as Lewis's masterpiece, is about a British reconnaissance officer in India who gets lost. His driver is killed and his truck abandoned in a river. Alone and unsupported, he is driven to seek help from a band of gypsies and reaches a new sense of identity: "Stumbling up the track in the half-light among the ragged garish gipsies he gradually left the stiff self-consciousness with which he had first approached them. . . ." As Cary Archard writes, the officer "puts his trust in a simple humanity whose life has an instinctive integrity which was unavailable to the British Officer."

Other Works by Alun Lewis

Alun Lewis: Collected Stories. Edited by Cary Archard. Bridgend, Wales: Seren Books, 1990.

Selected Poems of Alun Lewis. Edited by Jeremy Hooker and Gweno Lewis. London: Unwin Paperbacks, 1981.

A Work about Alun Lewis

Pikoulls, John. *Alun Lewis: A Life.* Bridgend, Wales: Seren Books, 1990.

Lewis, Clive Staples (1898–1963) *novelist, nonfiction writer, children's writer*

C. S. Lewis was born in Belfast, Ireland, to Albert Lewis, a solicitor and partner in a boiler-making and shipbuilding firm who loved books and humor, and Florence Hamilton, daughter of an intensely religious clergyman. Lewis later recalled that at a young age he was fascinated by Beatrix POTTER's books and by his mother's religious stories.

After serving in France during World War I, Lewis attended Oxford University, then stayed on as a Fellow at Magdalen College from 1925 to 1954. He joined with J. R. R. TOLKIEN and Charles WILLIAMS to form the Inklings, a literary group whose members critiqued one another's writing. In 1954 Lewis became a professor of medieval and Renaissance English at Cambridge.

In 1965 Lewis married American poet Joy Davidmon. Four years later, Davidmon died of cancer, and Lewis recorded his struggle with his grief in *A Grief Observed* (1961).

Lewis was an advocate for Christianity, explaining and defending the religion in such studies as *Mere Christianity* (1952). He also wrote novels that were religious allegories. In his nonfiction and fiction alike, Lewis depicted the conflict between God and Satan as a universal war in which the planet Earth was territory seized by the villain.

The scenario of that metaphysical conflict plays out in Lewis's science-fiction sequence *Out of the Silent Planet* (1938), *Perelandra* (1944), and *That Hideous Strength* (1946), in which angels and demons are portrayed as beings from a higher plane of reality intersecting our own. In *Perelandra,* the narrator "Lewis" sees an eldil, a Martian angel, and is frightened by its power even though he knows it is good: "Here at last was a bit of that world beyond the world . . . breaking through and appearing to my senses: and I didn't like it, I wanted it to go away." These novels place less emphasis on plot developments than on the main characters' efforts to understand the supernatural elements of the world.

In Lewis's novel *The Screwtape Letters* (1940), the battle between good and evil is glimpsed from behind enemy lines as an elder demon instructs a younger in the latter's efforts to corrupt a human. The elder, Screwtape, warns his nephew Wormwood about God's love of humans: "Remember always that He really likes the little vermin and sets an absurd value on the distinctness of every one of them." The human must resist corruption not simply by feeling love instead of hatred but by rejecting false arguments against God. "Lewis holds up

the life of rational orderliness as superior to reactions based on feelings," says scholar Clyde S. Kilby, and Lewis believed "our age, in spite of its claims to the contrary, is not one that reasons well."

Lewis's most popular work is the seven children's novels making up the *Chronicles of Narnia* (1950–56). Beginning with *The Lion, the Witch, and the Wardrobe* (1950), the Chronicles show children from Earth entering a wardrobe and traveling to the magical land of Narnia, which is initially in the clutches of an evil witch. As one of her subjects laments, "It's she that makes it always winter. Always winter and never Christmas: think of that!" Manlove says Lewis contrasts the static, dead quality of the Witch's evil with "the dancing variety that is goodness" in the form of individual human personalities and the diverse works of magic and nature, including the talking lion Aslan. At one point, Aslan dies and comes back to life, describing his resurrection in terms that echo the New Testament: "When a willing victim who had committed no treachery was killed in a traitor's stead . . . Death itself would start working backwards." The Narnia novels culminate in *The Last Battle* (1956), in which a talking donkey is disguised as Aslan and becomes an unwitting anti-Christ figure while an evil talking ape becomes his false prophet.

In Lewis's autobiography *Surprised by Joy* (1955) he describes his spiritual odyssey and his struggle to reconcile religion and rationality. Before his conversion to Catholicism, he writes, "all that I loved I believed to be imaginary; nearly all that I believed to be real I thought grim and meaningless." Lewis came to see the imagination as providing a partial and imperfect but deeply satisfying glimpse of the divine realm. He strongly believed that religious truths were so overwhelming that only allegories could begin to capture them. As theologian Gilbert Meilaender says, Lewis's extremely popular stories were intended as "a temporal net to capture what is eternal." Lewis's fantasy work is nonetheless popular among many who are unfamiliar with its religious underpinnings. Critic Thomas Howard predicts "that it will be on the basis of his works of imagination as much as on his essays and apologetics that Lewis's lasting reputation will rest."

Other Works by C. S. Lewis

The Great Divorce. New York: Simon & Schuster, 1946.
The Problem of Pain. New York: Simon & Schuster, 1940.

Works about C. S. Lewis

Como, James T. *Branches to Heaven: The Geniuses of C. S. Lewis.* Dallas, Tex.: Spence Publishing, 1998.
Wilson, A. N. *C. S. Lewis: A Biography.* New York: W. W. Norton, 1990.

Lewis, Wyndham (Percy Wyndham Lewis) (1884–1957) *novelist, literary critic, nonfiction writer*

Wyndham Lewis was born on a yacht moored at Amherst, Nova Scotia, Canada, to Charles Lewis, who had fought in the American Civil War, and Anne Prickett Lewis. In 1888 his parents moved to England, where Charles abandoned the family. Lewis attended a variety of public schools, including Rugby, as well as London's Slade School of Art. Rather than going to college, he toured Europe for nearly eight years before returning to London, where he became a noteworthy critic, novelist, and artist.

In 1914, with the American poet Ezra Pound, Lewis founded the magazine *Blast,* in which he published controversial criticism and promoted VORTICISM. This was a movement among painters (which Pound attempted to translate into literature) based on bold lines and strong angular forms. *Blast,* which was never financially profitable and published only two issues, dissolved at the outset of World War I.

In 1926 and 1927, respectively, Lewis produced two important nonfiction works: *The Art of Being Ruled* and *Time and Western Man.* In *The Art of Being Ruled* he promotes his conservative political views. He laments feminism, jazz, and parliamentary government and suggests that the fragmentation of the world may be remedied by more authoritarian governments. In *Time and Western Man* he looks at the role of art in the modern worlds and attacks advertising and the rise of commercial culture. He also specifically attacks the theories and work of Pound and James JOYCE.

During the next few years Lewis's popularity sagged because he was seen as a fascist sympathizer. His reputation rebounded, however, with the publication of his autobiography, *Blasting and Bombardiering* (1937). Different in tone from his earlier writing, the autobiography focuses on his contributions to vorticism and his war experiences, and it describes his friendships with Pound, Joyce, and T. S. ELIOT. In the book's final paragraph, the frequently pretentious and prickly critic humbly states, "I hope I may have entertained you, here and there, for it is amazing the number of different sorts of things I have done. And I hope that . . . some portion of my experience may have passed over into you."

Of Lewis's novels the three most important are *Tarr* (1918), *The Apes of God* (1930), and *Self-Condemned* (1954). *Tarr,* his first novel, tells the story of two artists: the title character, an Englishman, and Kreisler, a German, both struggling toward artistic success while living bohemian lives in France. In the end Tarr becomes successful and Kreisler fails, committing suicide. The major difference between the two is that, unlike Tarr, Kreisler yearns for praise and popular success.

Although *The Apes of God* was judged a failure by many critics, it conveys Lewis's anger toward London's literary establishment. The central character, a young man involved in numerous sexual exploits, is little more than a thin screen from behind which Lewis stages a number of literary attacks. While exploring another of his favorite themes—the artist who is not a true creator but only an imitator—Lewis harshly satirizes and attacks one literary figure after another, pouring particular venom upon the highly influential BLOOMSBURY GROUP, which included Virginia WOOLF and members of the SITWELL family.

Self-Condemned, a semiautobiographical novel widely considered to be Lewis's best, tells the story of René Harding, an English history professor living in Canada. Like Lewis, Harding goes into a self-imposed exile and struggles to remain true to his ideals, but ultimately he acquiesces to the pressures of society. The novel shows that Lewis was aware of the price he paid for his earlier work, which cost him friendships and, to an extent, his reputation.

Lewis is generally regarded as a talented writer who never fully lived up to his potential. He was always torn between the visual and literary arts, and his constant need to make money through his work contributed greatly to his overall sense of anger and frustration. Nonetheless, the scholar Jeffrey Meyers writes, "Lewis was one of the most lively and stimulating forces in modern English literature, an independent, courageous artist and brilliant social observer."

Other Works by Wyndham Lewis

The Enemy: A Review of Art and Literature. Edited by David P. Corbett. Santa Rosa, Calif.: Black Sparrow, 1994.
Rude Assignment. 1950. Reprint, Santa Rosa, Calif.: Black Sparrow, 1984.
The Vulgar Streak. 1941. Reprint, Santa Rosa, Calif.: Black Sparrow, 1985.

Works about Wyndham Lewis

Ayers, David. *Wyndham Lewis and Western Man.* New York: St. Martin's Press, 1992.
Normand, Tom. *Wyndham Lewis the Artist: Holding the Mirror up to Politics.* New York: Cambridge University Press, 1992.

Liddell, Robert (John Robert Liddell)

(1908–1992) *literary critic, novelist*
Robert Liddell was born in Tunbridge Wells, England, the son of John Liddell, an engineer for the British military, and Anna Liddell. He earned his degree at Oxford University and went on to teach in Finland, Egypt, and Greece. He wrote about Oxford in several of his novels, including *The Last En-*

chantments (1948), his best known work, which uses dark comedy to reveal the gossip and hypocrisy that the main character, Mrs. Foyle, a widow, endures when her daughter Miranda marries a well-known local actor.

Of Liddell's autobiographical works, two novels stand out. *Kind Relations* (1939) tells the story of two boys, Andrew and Stephen, whose father leaves them to be brought up by aunts after their mother dies. The boys' experience is rendered with an unusual vividness and freedom from adult interpretations. *Stepsons* (1969) continues Andrew and Stephen's story, introducing readers to a cruel stepmother who torments and ridicules the boys.

Liddell also wrote literary criticism, including *The Novels of Ivy Compton-Burnett* (1955), *The Novels of Jane Austen* (1963), and *The Novels of George Eliot* (1977). A critic from *Publisher's Weekly* admired "Liddell's restraint and sly wit (not for nothing was he compared to Jane Austen)."

Other Works by Robert Liddell

Cavafy: A Critical Biography. 1974. Reprint, London: Duckworth, 2001.
The Deep End. London: Peter Owen, 1994.
Unreal City. 1952. Reprint, Chester Springs, Pa.: Dufour Editions, 1993.

Lindholm, Anna Margaret

See ELLIS, ALICE THOMAS.

Linklater, Eric Robert Russell

(1899–1974) *novelist, short story writer, nonfiction writer, children's writer*
Eric Linklater was born in Penarth, South Wales, Australia, to Robert Baikie Linklater, a master mariner, and Mary Elizabeth Young Linklater. His family moved to the Orkney Islands when Linklater was young. He served in the British army during World War I before studying medicine and English literature at Aberdeen University, where he earned an M.A. in 1925.

Linklater maintained a lifelong interest in verse and wrote his first best-seller, the novel *Poet's Pub* (1929), about the life of a Scottish poet named Saturday Keith. After visiting the United States on a fellowship, Linklater chronicled the adventures of a foreigner traveling in that country in *Juan in America* (1931). The novel enjoyed great popularity, remaining in print for more than 30 years. Critic Andrew Rutherford considers it a masterpiece that "engages very directly with 'the realities of life' in its affectionate, amused, at times almost anthropological scrutiny of the American way of life. . . . The novel is a *tour de force* of comedy. . . ." In addition to its humorous commentary, the book also includes philosophical insights about America. When Juan observes the lives of the descendants of slaves in South Carolina, he reflects: "Their laughter too was a pleasant thing to hear. It had much in common with their songs, being rich and mellow in sound uncontrollable as hunger, natural as thirst. . . ."

After World War II, Linklater published *Private Angelo* (1946), an antiwar novel that many critics consider to be his finest work. Its central character is an Italian soldier who, although lacking in courage, successfully copes with the difficulties of a war being fought in his homeland. The novel is noted for its wit and irony, which are evident when Angelo describes the liberation of a village: "[t]hough the Allied soldiers do not loot, of course, they will find a number of things such as geese and hens and wine, that apparently belong to no one . . . and to prevent the wine and geese from being wasted, the soldiers will naturally take care of them."

Linklater, a Scottish nationalist, also wrote several works about his country's history. *The Lion and the Unicorn* (1935) explores the historical relationship between England and Scotland and makes a case for Scottish autonomy. In addition to his novels and historical works, Linklater also wrote three children's books, three autobiographies, and seven short story collections. Writer George Mackay Brown pays tribute to him by stating "Eric Linklater is one of Scotland's best storytellers ever. . . . he is such a consummate artist. . . . He has a marvelous lyricism, a delight in the land and shifting seas and skies of the north."

Other Work by Eric Linklater
A Spell for Old Bones. New York: Arno, 1949, reprinted 1978.

A Work about Eric Linklater
Parnell, Michael. *Eric Linklater: A Critical Biography.* London: John Murray, 1984.

Lively, Penelope Margaret (1933–)
novelist, children's author, nonfiction writer
Penelope Lively, born Penelope Margaret Low, was the daughter of Roger Low, who worked for the National Bank of Egypt, and Vera Greer Low. Born in Cairo, she was educated at home. Her childhood reading included the Bible, Greek and Norse mythology, the *Arabian Nights,* and the novels of Charles Dickens. In 1954 she graduated from Oxford with a degree in history, and three years later she married a professor of politics, Jack Lively; they had a son and daughter.

Lively is a popular, prolific author whose work has been split between children's and adult fiction. She began with a children's book, *Astercotec* (1970), about a village destroyed by plague. It was followed by more than a dozen other children's books, including *The Ghost of Thomas Kempe* (1973), about a Jacobean poltergeist; and *A Stitch in Time* (1976), about a girl who becomes obsessed with a previous occupant of the house she is staying in. (The former novel won the Carnegie Medal and the latter, the Whitbread Prize.) Both her children's and adult fiction demonstrate Lively's preoccupation with time, connecting past with the present.

A nonfiction work, *The Presence of the Past: An Introduction to Landscape History* (1976), shows that Lively's interest in the past is balanced by a strong sense of place. She writes that she felt privileged to grow up in an ancient civilization whose past was physically present. In an interview with critic Mary Moran, Lively observed that Egypt surrounds one with "Pharaonic and Mameluke and

Turkish ruins and Greek and Roman all coexisting, so that there seems to be no sequence of time."

Lively is a historian and author who reads a landscape or cityscape as a palimpsest, a parchment or tablet containing multilayered inscriptions and erasures. She says places are like clocks, "full of all the time there's ever been in them, and all the people, and all the things that have happened, like the ammonites in the stones." All her work is rooted in "the permanence of place and the strong feeling of continuity that haunts the English countryside."

In Lively's adult novels, death is a vantage point for reviewing life, bringing change and rearranging the pattern of one or many lives. This happens in her first adult novel, *The Road to Lichfield* (1977), and in *Perfect Happiness* (1983), *Moon Tiger* (1987), and *Passing On* (1989). In the first book, Anne Linton discovers, while setting her dying father's affairs in order, that he had an extramarital affair—just as she is doing. In *Perfect Happiness* and *Passing On*, a widow and bereaved children gain new leases on life after the deaths of husband and mother, respectively. In *Moon Tiger*, winner of the Booker-McConnell Prize (*see* BOOKER PRIZE) and National Book Awards, war correspondent/historian Claudia Hampton reviews her life on the brink of death, recalling complex relationships with brother, lover, and daughter. Through points of view that shift from present to past, various characters offer different perspectives on the same events.

Winter Ann Thwaite regards Lively as "one of the most intelligent and rewarding" of children's writers, and her adult fiction has been acclaimed as the work of a "gifted novelist with . . . independence of mind."

Other Works by Penelope Lively

According to Mark. New York: Beaufort Books, 1985.
City of the Mind. New York: HarperCollins, 1991.
Cleopatra's Sister. New York: HarperCollins, 1993.
Oleander, Jacaranda: A Childhood Perceived. New York: HarperPerennial, 1995.

Work about Penelope Lively

Moran, Mary. *Penelope Lively.* Boston: Twayne, 1993.

Lodge, David (1935–) *novelist, literary critic, essayist*

David Lodge was born in South London, England, to the lower-middle-class family of William Lodge, a musician, and Rosalie Murphy Lodge. He represents the post–World War II phenomenon of the provincial university intellectual, having been educated at the Universities of London and Birmingham, instead of Oxford or Cambridge.

For more than 25 years Lodge taught English at the University of Birmingham, writing scholarly essays and influential books of literary criticism. Many of his novels have academic settings. Reviewer Brooke Allen says of him, "David Lodge, the extraordinarily clever and accomplished author of comic masterpieces . . . has always been a deft anatomist of intellectual trends."

Lodge's first three books were novels: *The Picturegoers* (1960), about suburban London cinemagoers; *Ginger, You're Barmy* (1962), about the different reactions of a pair of friends to mandatory military service; and *The British Museum Is Falling Down* (1965), a comic novel about a Catholic family. He then produced a scholarly work, *The Language of Fiction* (1966), which used the insights of American NEW CRITICISM to argue that readers should pay as much attention to the way novelists use language as they do poets. A coming-of-age novel, *Out of the Shelter* (1970), is Lodge's most autobiographical work, about a Catholic family in the London suburbs. Another scholarly work, *The Novelist at the Crossroads* (1971), contains essays on 20th-century authors such as Graham GREENE, William Burroughs, and John Updike.

With *Changing Places* (1975), Lodge came into his own as a comic novelist. Subtitled "A Tale of Two Universities," it uses a parallel structure to follow two English professors and their families. Philip Swallow, professor at Rummidge University, participates in an exchange program with the American Morris Zapp of Euphoric State University. Zapp successfully brings his experience with student unrest to bear on problems at Rummidge, while Swallow successfully becomes a part of the unrest at

Euphoric State. Each man seduces the other's wife. Throughout the novel Lodge displays an academic self-consciousness about writing a novel, including the book's last lines, "PHILIP shrugs. The camera stops, freezing him in mid-gesture."

The same cast of characters resurfaces nine years later in *Small World* (1984) in an even more elaborate and complicated plot. Included this time is the lovely and chaste Angelica who, true to Lodge's sense of symmetry, has a twin sister who is a stripper. Lodge fills the novel with references to other works of literature, particularly those of the romance tradition. Angelica is writing a thesis on the history of the romance, and the plot of the novel is an updating of the Arthurian quest romance. The pure young hero Persse (i.e., Percival) seeks the chaste Angelica, and as Percival is in Arthurian legend a "wise fool," so is the unsophisticated and relatively unlettered Persse when he confounds all the learned scholars who are supposedly his intellectual superiors when he asks, "What do you do if everybody agrees with you?" He does not win Angelica but instead embarks on a new quest as the novel ends, this time pursuing a naïve airline attendant, Cheryl Summerbee.

Lodge's next novel, *Nice Work* (1988), also involves place changing; only this time a young single woman, again a professor of English, has an affair with an unintellectual married businessman. Swallow and Zapp make cameo appearances. As in almost all Lodge's comic novels, adultery figures prominently in *Nice Work*. As a female creative-writing professor says in Lodge's recent novel *Thinks* (2001), "There's not a great deal of narrative mileage in the stable monogamous marriage."

All of Lodge's comic novels are filled with characters whose speech and behavior are sometimes silly and absurd, as are the situations in which they find themselves. As a *Chicago Tribune* reviewer said, "David Lodge seems to have the heritage of the British intellectuals and the Keystone Kops," but there is none of the malice in his work that one finds in Evelyn WAUGH, with whom he is frequently compared. Critics find him gentle in his humor; as a reviewer for the *Christian Science Monitor* said,

"Whether he is speaking of city types pushing paper for fun, the academics indulging in psychobabble, or the measurement of corporate success, he mocks these absurdities without resorting to cynicism."

A Work about David Lodge
Martin, Bruce K. *David Lodge.* New York: Twayne, 1999.

Longley, Michael (1939–) *poet*
Longley was born in Belfast, Ireland, to English Protestant parents. He studied Classics at Trinity College in Dublin. His poetic subjects range from nature to his father. Influenced by the violence and politics in Northern Ireland in the 1970s, he has also explored the realities and consequences of war. Critic Fran Brearton commends Longley for his work on this topic: "[Longley] has written as intelligently, movingly, and consistently about the Northern Irish Troubles as have any of his contemporaries, probably more so." The following lines from the three-poem sequence "Wreaths" from *The Echo Gate* (1979) demonstrate how Longley uses details to make a political murder personal: "There fell on the road beside them spectacles, / Wallets, small change, and a set of dentures."

Longley won the 1991 Whitbread Poetry Prize for his collection *Gorse Fires* (1991), which concentrates on his love of the natural world. *The Ghost Orchid* (1996) continues to explore this theme.

His recent work *The Weather in Japan* (2000) received the 2001 Irish Times Irish Literature Prize for Poetry, among other awards. The poems in this collection cover the familiar themes of war, the poet's dead father, and nature, and they continue to demonstrate his trademark listing of simple details to evoke an environment: "Begin the invocation: rice cakes, say, buckwheat / Flowers or temple bells, bamboo, a caged cricket". Literary critic Fran Brearton writes of Longley's accomplishments: "It is the gradual merging of all three categories—nature, love, war—into the individual poem, allied with a growing confidence in his lyric voice that makes Longley one of the foremost poets writing in Britain and Ireland today."

Other Works by Michael Longley

No Continuing City. Chester Springs, Pa.: Dufour Editions, 1969.

Poems 1963–1983. Winston-Salem, N.C.: Wake Forest University Press, 1987.

Selected Poems. Winston-Salem, N.C.: Wake Forest University Press, 1999.

Works About Michael Longley

Brearton, Fran. *The Great War in Irish Poetry: W. B. Yeats to Michael Longley.* New York: Oxford University Press, 2000.

Peacock, Alan J., and Kathleen Devine, eds. *The Poetry of Michael Longley (Ulster Editions and Monographs, 10).* New York: Oxford University Press, 2001.

Lowndes, Marie Belloc

See BELLOC LOWNDES, MARIE.

Lowry, Malcolm (1909–1957) *novelist*

Malcolm Lowry was born in New Brighton to upper-middle-class parents Arthur Osborne Lowry, a cotton broker, and Evelyn Boden Lowry. According to the scholar Tony Bareham, Lowry "was never easy to handle, and . . . was a constant source of anxiety and financial strain." A mediocre student, he did not plan to attend college and entered Cambridge only after his father allowed him to ship out as a cabin boy on an Asian voyage. This trip would later serve as a major source for the novel *Ultramarine* (1933), and Lowry returned from it determined to be a writer. During his university years he met the American novelist Conrad Aiken, whose complex, multilayered, and nonlinear style Lowry adopted.

Upon earning his degree at Cambridge, Lowry lived off an allowance from his father and Aiken's hospitality and managed to publish *Ultramarine*. Dana Hilliot, Lowry's protagonist, joins a ship's crew but is despised because he is socially superior to his shipmates. After being cruelly treated, Hilliot

wins the respect of those on the ship and becomes an accepted member of the crew. Critics reviewed the novel poorly, its sales floundered, and Lowry came to view *Ultramarine* as a failure.

Shortly after his first novel was published, Lowry met and married the American actress and writer Jan Gabrial and moved to Mexico, where he began writing the novel on which his reputation rests: *Under the Volcano.* The novel was published in 1947 after more than 10 years of drafting and revision. Often compared to James JOYCE's *Ulysses* because of its complexity, innovations, and stream of consciousness, *Under the Volcano* describes 12 momentous hours in the life of Geoffrey Firmin. Largely an autobiographical representation of Lowry himself, the alcoholic Firmin is a former British consul recently abandoned by his wife and rendered unemployed by diplomatic problems between his own nation and Mexico. During the day in which the novel is set, Firmin's estranged wife Yvonne returns to him in an attempt to repair their ruined marriage, but her efforts are thwarted by Firmin's constant drinking and the reappearance of several of her former lovers. At the novel's end Firmin, while drinking in a bar and reviewing the problems of his life, is mistaken for someone else and killed by a Mexican fascist; his body is dumped into a ravine. With the final line of his novel Lowry sums up the Firmin's life and accomplishments when he writes that "somebody threw a dead dog after him down the ravine."

Lowry exhausted himself in writing *Under the Volcano.* He spent the final 10 years of his life beginning and abandoning one literary project after another and descending further into alcoholism, finally dying after mixing alcohol and sleeping pills.

Lowry's lasting place in British literature is a subject of much debate. While some scholars, such as Ronald Binns, argue that "Lowry's dense and difficult prose style, together with the narrow range of his fictional interests, make it unlikely that his appeal will ever be wide," others, such as David Galef, expect him to be remembered as an author who "worked belatedly in the high modernist mode in the tradition" of Joyce and T. S. ELIOT.

Other Works by Malcolm Lowry

Hear Us O Lord from Heaven Thy Dwelling Place. 1961. Reprint, New York: Carroll & Graf, 1986

Malcolm Lowry's La Mordida. Edited by Patrick Mc-Carthy. Athens: University of Georgia Press, 1996.

Works about Malcolm Lowry

Bareham, Tony. *Malcolm Lowry.* New York: St. Martin's Press, 1989

Bowker, Gordon. *Pursued by Furies: A Life of Malcolm Lowry.* New York: St. Martin's Press, 1995.

M

Macaulay, Rose (1881–1958) *novelist, poet, nonfiction writer*

Born in Rugby, Rose Macaulay later wrote that she was "descended on both sides from long lines of eloquent and well-informed clergymen, few of whom had denied themselves the indulgence of breaking into print." Her mother had been a schoolteacher; her father had a Cambridge degree in Classics and taught at private schools. One of seven children, Macaulay could read before she was four, and when she learned to write she expressed her glee by writing "I CAN WRITE" over everything she could reach. From 1887 to 1894 the family lived in a village in Italy, where the Macaulay children were educated at home by their parents. Macaulay also spent much time playing on the seashore. She was an enthusiastic tomboy and wanted to be a sailor when she grew up.

Macaulay's early years were mostly happy. Her mother, however, was violently cruel to one of her sisters. Macaulay's first novel, *Abbots Verney* (1906), and several of her later books feature a helpless victim being tormented and excluded.

At age 17 Macaulay had her first work published, a poem in the school magazine. In 1900 she enrolled at Oxford to study modern history, completing her degree in 1903. After graduating, she published several poems and *Abbots Verney,* the

name of a fictional family house in Cumberland. The Ruth family has lived there for decades in stolid respectability, but their youngest son, Verney, is too adventurous to fit in with the predictable routine. The book describes Verney's adventures and misfortunes. Ultimately he loses the family home but gains a cosmopolitan confidence in the world: "He had lost Abbot's Verney; but Rome and the cities of the world were his, a wide heritage. The adventurer's spirit stirred in his blood as he looked down over the great sea of roofs to the purple sunset."

Macaulay's next novel was the critically acclaimed *The Lee Shore* (1912), which describes the difficult life of a gentle boy, from his days at public school and Cambridge University to years of poverty, a failed marriage, and homelessness. Yet the novel ends optimistically. Peter becomes a wanderer, walking around the Mediterranean with his small son and relishing the peace and simplicity of that life: "the merry, shifting life of the roads, the passing friendships, lightly made, lightly loosed, the olive hills, silver like ghostly armies in the moonlight, . . . the cities, like many-coloured nosegays on a pale chain."

During World War I Macaulay published her first book of poems, *The Two Blind Countries* (1914). These poems are sad lyrics about the vulnerability of Arcadian village life in a newly violent world. In the poem "Keyless," she muses: "Like a lost child my strayed soul drifted / Back from the lit intelligible ways." Macaulay worked as a nurse during the war, and from 1916 she was a civil servant in the department concerning conscientious objectors. Her insights here bore fruit in her pacifist *Noncombatants and Others* (1916), one of the first novels to describe the effect of trench warfare on soldiers.

In 1918 Macaulay was transferred to the Ministry of Information, and there she met the man with whom she was to remain secretly involved for over 20 years: Gerald O'Donovan, a married novelist. The situation caused her great suffering, for it obliged her to stop taking communion in the Catholic Church.

In 1920 Macaulay published *Potterism: A Tragifarcical Tract,* a satire mocking the tabloid press. Over the next 20 years she wrote 11 more novels and several books on literature and history.

World War II was painful for Macaulay. In 1941 her apartment was bombed and she lost almost all her possessions, and in 1942 her longtime lover O'Donovan died. Her novel, *The World My Wilderness* (1950) describes a grief-stricken young woman gravely distressed by the war. After years of running free without supervision, she suddenly finds herself in a conventional English home. Miserably unable to make sense of the contrast, she begins to roam London for solace. She finds comfort in the ruins around St. Peter's Cathedral. In this wasteland of rubble covered with flowers, she feels "it made a lunatic sense, as the unshattered streets and squares did not; it was the country that one's soul recognized and knew."

Macaulay's most famous book is *The Towers of Trebizond* (1956), a witty novel describing the adventures of the eccentric English "Aunt Dot" and her niece, who go to Turkey to investigate establishing an Anglican Mission station there. The book's beginning sets the tone for the rest of the romp through the desert: "'Take my camel, dear,' said Aunt Dot, as she climbed down from this animal on her return from High Mass." The book also draws on Macaulay's own spiritual return to Christianity. The book was an enormous success, and won the James Tait Black Memorial Prize.

In 1958 Macaulay was made a Dame Commander of the Order of the British Empire (DBE). She died unexpectedly of a heart attack seven months later. Up to the morning of her death she was composing a new novel and fully involved in London's intellectual life. She was never happy about the prospect of eternal rest after death: "Rest is *not* what we want surely, but more scope for work and new knowledge."

Other Works by Rose Macaulay

Crewe Train. 1926. Reprint, London: Virago, 2000.
Fabled Shore: From the Pyrenees to Portugal. 1949. Reprint, New York: Oxford University Press, 1987.
They Went to Portugal. 1946. Reprint, Manchester, England: Carcanet, 1991.
Told by an Idiot. 1923. Reprint, New York: Doubleday, 1983.

Work about Rose Macaulay

Emery, Jane. *Rose Macaulay: A Writer's Life.* London: John Murray, 1992.

MacDiarmid, Hugh (Christopher Murray Grieve) (1892–1978) *poet*

Critically acclaimed as the best Scots poet since Robert Burns, Hugh MacDiarmid wrote in both Scots dialect and standard English. Like Burns, MacDiarmid also was a maverick. Although he was content to use the English language, he was otherwise hostile to all things English, including literature, particularly English poetry and poets, and forms of government. MacDiarmid forged an expressive language based on Lallans, a revised Scots dialect in which he wrote his best poetry.

He was born Christopher Murray Grieve in Langholm, Scotland, near the Scottish-English border, to James Grieve, a postal worker, and Elizabeth Graham Grieve. He was educated at Langholm Academy, and read voraciously as a child—his family lived in the same building as the town library.

After returning from World War I, having been wounded in action, in 1918 he resumed the itinerant journalistic career that he had begun in 1910, and he married Margaret Skinner. He subsequently founded *The Scottish Chapbook* in 1922, a periodical that contained his first Scots dialect experiments. The journal's motto was, significantly, "Not Traditions—Precedents." In this periodical the writer in English, Christopher Grieve, became Hugh MacDiarmid, the Scots poet. Although his first published book, *Annals of the Five Senses* (1923), was in English, as MacDiarmid he subsequently produced *Sangschaw* (1925), *Pennywheep* (1926), and his masterpiece, *A Drunk Man Looks at a Thistle* (1926), all in his own version of Lallans.

MacDiarmid was also a political activist and wrote poems promoting the socialist cause, such as "First Hymn to Lenin" (1931) and "Second Hymn to Lenin" (1932). All of his strongest characteristics are displayed in *A Drunk Man,* which, as the scholar David Daiches comments, came upon "a startled and incredulous Scotland with all the shock of a childbirth in church." According to Daiches, the poem's texture, a soliloquy interrupted by incidental lyrics, is "[g]rotesque, passionate, meditative, violent, plangent and reminiscent by turns, [and] moves with a fine assurance and a rich vitality." MacDiarmid begins with the drunken man complaining that he suffers from fatigue as much as from drink:

> It's gey and hard work coupin gless for gless
> Wi' Cruvie and Gilsanquhar and the like.

And later on:

> I ken what I am in Life and Daith
> But Life and Daith for nae man are enough.

The drunk man comes to no conclusion regarding eternal questions but asserts the centrality of Scotland in regenerating his world, a world that still rejoices in the thrills and feelings of his physical senses as they apprehend the natural world about him.

MacDiarmid lived and wrote for another 50 years and produced, mostly in English, biographies; descriptive works about Scotland and its political future, the Scottish islands, and his eccentric countrymen; and essays on numbers of subjects. His two autobiographical works, *Lucky Poet* (1943) and *The Company I've Kept* (1966), are rich sources of information about the mind of the man who, as critic Ian Gordon said in 1933, "brought back thought to Scottish poetry."

A Work about Hugh MacDiarmid
Bold, Alan Norman. *MacDiarmid: Christopher Murray Grieve, a Critical Biography.* London: John Murray, 1988.

Mackenzie, Compton Edward Montague (1883–1972) *novelist, memoirist*

Compton Mackenzie was born in West Hartlepool, England. His parents, Edward Compton and Virginia Bateman Mackenzie, were famous actors. Mackenzie attended Oxford University, where he earned a B.A. in history with honors. He served in the Royal Marines during World War I and later cofounded the Scottish National Party.

Mackenzie's first novel, *The Passionate Elopement* (1911), describes events at an 18th-century spa. His next novel, *Carnival* (1912), is about Jenny Pearl, a teenage ballerina who tries to retain her morals while part of a chorus line in a London production. *Carnival* was a popular success, a reviewer in *The Spectator* wrote that the book deserved notice for its "occasional brilliancy of presentation, for its frank disregard of the conventional canons of taste, and for the curious hostility toward the male sex betrayed by the author." The following year Mackenzie published *Sinister Street* (1913), describing a young man's experiences at Oxford and his eventual moral ruin in London's East End. Banned by many librarians for its graphic descriptions of urban low life, the novel was a major commercial success.

Mackenzie's literary reputation flagged in the 1920s but was revived with the *Four Winds of Love* series, which includes the novels *The East Wind of Love* (1937), *The South Wind of Love* (1937), *The West Wind of Love* (1940), *West to North* (1940), and *The North Wind of Love* (two volumes, 1944–45). The sweeping series portrays the private and professional life of John Pendarves Ogilvie, a dramatist and British Secret Service agent, from 1900 through the 1930s. Sympathetic to Scots who "feel lost in the vastness of a modern imperialistic State," Ogilvie eventually becomes a Scottish nationalist. Noting the importance of this cause to the author, the scholar D. J. Dooley concludes: "The *Four Winds* is a protest against depersonalization; Mackenzie wants a political community small enough for the individual to feel that he has some voice in its affairs."

The most notable of Mackenzie's later works is the entertaining 10-volume autobiography *My Life and Times* (1963–71). Throughout his six-decade literary career, Mackenzie promoted his belief that modern progress had gone awry and that standardization and urbanization were destroying the identity of the individual. Dooley concludes that "Mackenzie's writing eloquently defended the soul of man against the various threats against it brought by successive decades of the twentieth century."

Other Work by Compton Mackenzie
Thin Ice. New York: Putnam, 1957.

A Work about Compton Mackenzie
Linklater, Andro. *Compton Mackenzie: A Life.* London: Chatto & Windus, 1987.

Mackintosh, Elizabeth
See TEY, JOSEPHINE.

MacNeice, Louis (Frederick Louis MacNeice) (1907–1963) *poet, scriptwriter*
Louis MacNeice was born to John Frederick MacNeice, a Protestant bishop, and Elizabeth Margaret Clesham MacNeice in Belfast, Ireland. After a lonely childhood, during which his mother died

and he adopted the responsibility of overseeing the family's often abusive servants, MacNeice went to college at Oxford University. There he became an avid reader of the German philosopher Friedrich Nietzsche, became friends with the poet Stephen SPENDER, and graduated with honors in 1930.

MacNeice later met W. H. AUDEN and became associated with the "Auden Group" (also known as the Oxford Poets), which included Auden, Spender, and C. DAY LEWIS. Unlike the rest of this group, however, MacNeice was never a socialist but instead maintained a steady political skepticism.

After his graduation from Oxford, MacNeice taught at Birmingham University for five years before publishing *Poems* (1935), one of his most important collections of poetry. These poems rely heavily on urban imagery and often examine various scenes with what the scholar Robert Canary calls "detached but sympathetic irony." One poem, "Sunday Morning," captures the events of a typical Sunday morning, describing the sounds of someone in a nearby house practicing scales on a piano and a man joyfully working on his car. MacNeice adds irony to the poem's simple observations when, in the final four lines, church bells ring and remind both characters and readers of their own mortality and the day's religious meaning.

Many critics consider *Autumn Journal* (1939) MacNeice's greatest poetic achievement. This is a journal, written in verse, about the events of 1938. It reveals the everyday life of the poet—his commute to work and his memories—but is constantly interrupted by images of Hitler in the form of "posters flapping on the railings" that "tell the fluttered world that Hitler speaks, that Hitler speaks" and a voice blasting from a radio. The poem is a superb technical achievement with an unwavering tone and rhythm. Some scholars have argued, however, that it lacks an ideological center and relies on a calendar for motion and conclusion instead of on a larger, more ambitious system of thought.

MacNeice obtained a position with the BBC (British Broadcasting Corporation) writing scripts for radio plays in 1940. According to the scholar Michael Sidnell, MacNeice's radio plays are particularly notable for his ability to "blend fantasy and parable." An example of this is *The Dark Tower* (1946), the story of a boy named Roland who embarks on a quest that all of his male ancestors have pursued. The quest takes him to a dark tower where he faces a dragon that killed all of his forebears. As the story progresses, it becomes apparent that the journey is a metaphor for humanity's constant search for a better way of life, which often ends in disappointment. In Sidnell's words, the radio play is "a dense, mysterious allegory of life's quest, indefinite in terms of action and location but very concrete in its poetic imagery and rich in psychological suggestion."

MacNeice is remembered primarily as a poet. According to the scholar Robert Canary, because of his subtle ironies, understatements, and technical mastery, MacNeice's "reputation is certainly as high as that of any British poet of the 1930s other than Auden." John Press, another scholar, concurs, adding that "he deserves to be honored as a man of letters who practiced his craft with devotion, as a pioneer of radio drama, and as a poet whose sardonic gaiety, brooding sadness, and integrity of mind are reflected in the lyrics . . . that are his surest title to remembrance."

Other Works by Louis MacNeice

Collected Poems. Edited by E. R. Dodds. London: Faber & Faber, 1968.
Selected Prose of Louis MacNeice. Edited by Alan Heuser. New York: Oxford University Press, 1990.

Works about Louis MacNeice

McDonald, Peter. *Louis MacNeice: The Poet in His Contexts.* London: Oxford University Press, 1991.
Stallworthy, Jon. *Louis MacNeice.* New York: W. W. Norton, 1995.

Mahon, Derek (1941–) *poet, translator*

Derek Mahon was born in Belfast, Ireland, and made his name as one of the "Northern Poets" along with Seamus HEANEY and Michael LONGLEY. After studying French at Trinity College in Dublin,

Mahon left Ireland to live abroad. His poetry explores themes of loss and alienation, with lonely, isolated characters who live on the periphery of society. His talent lies in making ordinary aspects of everyday life seem remarkable.

Mahon has published four major books of poems, the most critically acclaimed of which is *The Snow Party* (1975). In "A Refusal to Mourn," a selection from *The Snow Party,* he describes the lonely existence of an old man who lives and dies on the fringe of society. "A Disused Shed in Co. Wexford," the best-known poem in *The Snow Party,* deals with similar themes of loneliness and exile. The poem conveys the emotions of a group of mushrooms locked in an abandoned shed, and in so doing creates a powerful metaphor representing all those people who have been persecuted and forgotten. The isolated mushrooms "crowd to a keyhole. . . . / They are begging us, you see, in their wordless way . . ."

An accomplished translator, Mahon also published his own interpretation of Gerard de Nerval's *The Chimeras* (1982), a series of poems about yearning, desire, and the loss of a lover. The speaker in "El Desdichado," the first poem in this collection, "expresses his sense of loss and isolation with a precision and control that mask passion and evoke a detached pathos," according to critic Brian Donnelly. Donnelly believes that "Mahon is restoring to English poetry qualities which are rare at the present time—conversational narrative combined with wit, intelligence and humour capable of realising a deep seriousness."

Other Works by Derek Mahon

Collected Poems. Chester Springs, Pa.: Dufour Editions, 2000.
The Hudson Letter. Winston-Salem, N.C.: Wake Forest University Press, 1996.
Hunt By Night. Winston-Salem, N.C.: Wake Forest University Press, 1983.

Man Booker Prize

See BOOKER PRIZE.

Manning, Olivia (ca. 1908–1980) *novelist, short story writer, journalist*

Olivia Manning was born in Portsmouth, England, in either 1908 or 1911 (sources vary). Her father was a naval commander. Little is known of her childhood, but she recalled that living in Ireland, where she spent much of her early years, gave her "the usual Anglo-Irish sense of belonging nowhere." As an adult Manning lived in London, where she became close friends with the poet Stevie SMITH.

In 1938 Manning published her first novel, *The Wind Changes*. Set during the Irish conflicts of 1921, it is less about the social complexities of that time than it is about the interior lives of the novel's protagonists.

Manning spent much time overseas, and her travels gave her material for her famous *Balkan Trilogy*, made up of *The Great Fortune* (1960), *The Spoilt City* (1962), and *Friends and Heroes* (1965). Set in the Balkans, these three novels describe the relationship of a married couple, Guy and Harriet Pringle. Posted to Bucharest because of Guy's work as a British cultural representative, the two learn to know each other as husband and wife as they come to terms with the war and the impending threat of an invasion of Britain. When Paris falls, they gaze in horror at the map outside the German bureau, "the dot of Paris hidden by a swastika that squatted like a spider, black on the heart of the country." Throughout the trilogy, the Pringles' complex relationship plays out in the tumultuous Balkans of World War II. The novels have been praised for the vivid way they make history intersect with characters' lives.

Manning returned to the Pringles' saga a decade later in her *Levant Trilogy: The Danger Tree* (1977), *The Battle Lost and Won* (1978) and *The Sum of Things* (1980). This trilogy describes the Pringles' flight from the German army to Cairo, where their marriage eventually grows stronger despite the trials of the war. Author Anthony BURGESS praised the sequence as "the finest fictional record of the war produced by a British writer. . . . Guy Pringle certainly is one of the major characters in modern fic-

tion." The Balkan and Levant Trilogies became a television series called *The Fortunes of War* (1987).

Manning wrote numerous other novels and two volumes of short stories. She was also a journalist and a respected landscape painter. In 1976 the multitalented Manning was made a Commander of the Order of the British Empire (CBE).

Other Works by Olivia Manning

The Doves of Venus. 1955. Reprint, London: Virago, 1984.

A Romantic Hero and Other Stories. 1967. Reprint, London: Arrow, 2001.

Mansfield, Katherine (Kathleen Mansfield Beauchamp) (1888–1923) *short story writer, poet*

Katherine Mansfield was born Kathleen Mansfield Beauchamp in Wellington, New Zealand, to a middle-class family, but in 1909 she left for London to pursue a career as a writer. There she met and married George Bowdon, a music teacher, but left him a few days after the wedding. Her first complete volume of short stories was published in 1911 under the title *In a German Pension*. These stories were based on Mansfield's stay at a Bavarian health resort, where she lived for a time after she left her husband and where she suffered a miscarriage.

Shortly after her return to London, she met John Middleton Murry, a critic, poet, and editor whom she married in 1918. In the same year she was diagnosed with tuberculosis. In London she met a number of artists and writers, including D. H. LAWRENCE and Virginia WOOLF. Lawrence modeled one of his characters in his novel *Women in Love* after Mansfield and described her as "so *charming,* so infinitely charming. . . ." But she could also be vicious, especially toward people she considered slow-witted. The painter Dorothy Brett described Mansfield as having "a sort of ironic ruthlessness toward the small minds and less agile brains. . . . Katherine had a tongue like a knife, she could cut the very heart of one with it." In fiction writing, Virginia Woolf treated Mansfield as such a serious rival that, after her death, Woolf said there was "no point in writing. Katherine won't read it."

When her brother Leslie was killed during World War I, Mansfield began to write stories about her family. Some of her best stories are set in New Zealand at the turn of the century.

Although *Poems* (1923) and *The Letters of Katherine Mansfield* (1928) were published posthumously, Mansfield is primarily remembered for her seven books of short stories, and she has exerted a lasting influence on modern short-story writers. She crafted her stories carefully, writing and rewriting, striving to make every word perfect, setting a standard that has been often imitated but seldom equaled. Her stories depend less on plot and character development than on a single moment or event that seems to sum up the life of a character. Her writing is always subtle and often ironic and witty. As she defied conventions in her life, so her stories question conventional ideas about social class, family life, and marriage.

Katherine Mansfield died of tuberculosis in 1923 near Fontainebleau, France. Her last words were, "I love the rain. I want the feeling of it on my face."

Critical Analysis

One of Mansfield's most famous stories, "The Garden Party," published in 1922, deals with both social class and the awakening of an artist's sensibility. Laura Sheridan's family is hosting an elaborate garden party when a delivery man brings the news that Mr. Scott, a lower-class worker who lived in one of the little cottages near the Sheridan house, has been killed in an accident. Laura immediately assumes that the party will be canceled, but no one else in her family agrees. Mrs. Sheridan's only concern is whether or not the man actually died in her garden, and when she is reassured that he did not, she insists that the party go on. She tells her daughter, "People like that don't expect sacrifices from us." Later, Mrs. Sheridan sends Laura to the Scott house with the leftovers from the party. On the way, Laura cannot make herself realize that someone has really died because, Mansfield tells the reader with razor sharp

insight and poetic specificity, "it seemed to her that kisses, voices, tinkling spoons, laughter, the smell of crushed grass, were somehow inside her. She had no room for anything else." When she arrives at the "pokey little hole . . .," she accidentally enters the room where the body is laid out. Gazing at the dead man, she thinks, "He was given up to his dream. What did garden parties . . . matter to him?" She finds his serenity to be moving and very beautiful, not at all frightening as she feared. On her way home she meets her brother Laurie. He notices that she is crying and asks, "Was it awful?" She replies, "No. . . . It was simply marvelous." She struggles to say something about her experience, but all she can manage is "Isn't life—." The story ends with Laurie's response: "*Isn't* it, darling?" This story exemplifies Mansfield's delicate, poetic style, her tendency to focus on a life-changing moment, and her habit of ending on a note of ambiguity.

"The Fly," published in 1923, is another well-known story that showcases Mansfield's ability to create powerful symbols. A successful businessman is reminded by a visitor of the death of his son six years earlier in World War I. Like Laura Sheridan in "The Garden Party," he can't quite summon up the grief he wants to feel, so he picks up an old photograph of his son. At this moment, he notices a fly that has fallen into the inkpot. He rescues the fly and watches as it begins the tedious process of cleaning itself off. Just as it is "ready for life again," the man drops more ink on it. He repeats the process, amazed at the fly's courage and resilience, until the final blot of ink kills the fly, at which point the man is seized by "a grinding feeling of wretchedness." He calls for fresh blotting paper but cannot remember what he had been thinking about before he began to torment the fly. Although the man cannot remember, the reader knows that the fly stands for all those who are helpless victims of a cruel fate.

Other Works by Katherine Mansfield

Bliss and Other Stories. 1920. Reprint, London: Wordsworth, 1996.
Something Childish. 1924. Reprint, North Pomfret, Vt.: Trafalgar Square, 2000.

Works about Katherine Mansfield

Kobler, J. F. *Katherine Mansfield: A Study of the Short Fiction.* Boston: Twayne, 1990.

Tomalin, Claire. *Katherine Mansfield: A Secret Life.* New York: Alfred A. Knopf, 1988.

March, Maxwell

See ALLINGHAM, MARGERY.

Markham, Robert

See AMIS, KINGSLEY.

Marsh, Ngaio (Edith Ngaio Marsh)
(1899–1982) *novelist*

Ngaio Marsh was born in Christchurch, New Zealand. Her name, pronounced NY-o, is a Maori word meaning cleverness. Her father, Henry, was a tea broker and her mother, Rose, a talented amateur actress. After graduating from art school, Marsh became an actress and theatrical producer. She eventually divided her time between England and New Zealand, and her energies among painting, plays, and writing.

Although Marsh's first love was the theater, in which she worked as an actress and producer, she is far better known as a mystery writer and is ranked with Margery ALLINGHAM, Agatha CHRISTIE, and Dorothy L. SAYERS among the "Golden Age" mystery writers who wrote during the 1920s to 1940s. Marsh began the first of her 32 mysteries, *A Man Lay Dead* (1934) "as much to amuse my mother as anything else," she recalled. While the plot, in which a party murder game turns deadly, is ordinary, her detective, Inspector Roderick Alleyn, is one of Marsh's most significant contributions to the genre. The elegant Alleyn is a brilliant detective who manages to be both aristocratic and likeable. Yet, unlike his Golden Age predecessors, he is a professional who scrupulously follows police procedures.

Marsh is also known for her use of theatrical settings. In *Killer Dolphin* (1966), the characters are actors who are superstitious about staging Shakespeare's *Macbeth*. Critic Jane Hipolito suggests that Marsh uses this play-within-a-play construction in many novels, with the characters' interaction mirroring the unfolding of the mystery. Jennifer Smith describes Marsh's murders as theatrical, featuring "bizarrely clever murderers who bludgeon their victims with jeroboams of champagne, decapitate them with ancient weapons, [and] shoot them by means of booby traps in pianos."

While critics praise Marsh's well-constructed plots, engaging characters, and vivid settings, she has been faulted for not probing the depths of evil or human emotion. She herself considered *Colour Scheme* (1943), a World War II spy thriller and her first book to feature the Maori culture, her best-written work.

Marsh was made a Dame Commander of the Order of the British Empire (DBE) in 1966 for her contributions to the New Zealand theater. In 1977 the Mystery Writers of America named her a Grand Master.

Other Work by Ngaio Marsh

Death in a White Tie. 1938. Reprint, New York: St. Martin's Press, 1997.

Works About Ngaio Marsh

Lewis, Margaret. *Ngaio Marsh: A Life.* London: Chatto & Windus, 1991.

McDorman, Kathryne Slate. *Ngaio Marsh.* Boston: Twayne, 1991.

Mars-Jones, Adam (1954–) *novelist, short story writer, essayist*

Adam Mars-Jones was born in London, the son of William Lloyd Mars-Jones, a judge, and Sheila Mars-Jones, an attorney. He studied Classics and American literature at Cambridge University, then obtained a master's degree from the University of Virginia, studying William Faulkner.

In his writings Mars-Jones blends fact with fiction, writing mostly about some aspects of families and relationships. His first collection of stories,

Lantern Lecture (1981), which was republished as *Fabrications* in the United States, won the Somerset Maugham Award. Exploring the line between fact and fiction, *Lantern Lecture* tells the tale of a fictional English eccentric, Philip Yorke, but integrates into the story real people such as the Queen of England and the criminal Donald Neilson. Critic Galen Strawson found that "[t]here is something punk, in the modern sense of the word, about this extremely clever and original collection of stories. It's to do with the emotionally dead-panned style of delivery, the technical impassivity of the allusive, cloisonné construction."

The goal of Mars-Jones's next two works was to explore AIDS from the perspectives of both sick and well people in relationships with people afflicted with AIDS. He wrote two collections of short stories on this topic: *The Darker Proof: Stories from a Crisis* (1987) and *Monopolies of Loss: Stories from the Crisis* (1992). These stories deal "less with the disease and its case-histories than with the effect it has had on the consciousness of people who are living in close proximity to it," according to the writer Anne Billson. Mars-Jones followed these short stories with another work: *The Waters of Thirst* (1993), a novel about a gay couple who make every effort to avoid AIDS. When one of the men (William) contracts kidney disease, "he ends up in exactly the same place as somebody with AIDS even though all his choices seem to have taken him in the other direction," according to the author. William makes his own ironic observation of this situation: "After such a long time of going my own way I rejoined my generation in its place of special suffering."

Mars-Jones also writes about father and mother figures as part of his interest in family relationships. His essay "Venus Envy: On the Womb and the Bomb" (1990) explores the complicated and conflicting persona of the father. "Blind Bitter Happiness" (1996), an essay about his mother, blends fact and fiction. Critic Richard McCann believes that Mars-Jones is unique because he "devotes his considerable intelligence and compassion to the exploration of smaller moments in which characters renegotiate their daily lives."

Martin, Violet Florence

See SOMERVILLE, EDITH ANNA OENONE AND MARTIN ROSS.

Mascott, R D

See CALDER-MARSHALL, ARTHUR.

Masefield, John (1878–1967) *poet, novelist*

John Masefield was born in Ledbury, Herefordshire, England. His mother, Caroline Louisa Parker, died in 1884 after the birth of her sixth child, and his father, William, a solicitor, died when John was 13. After a stint at boarding school, Masefield spent two and a half years aboard a school ship, where he developed a lifelong love of sailing.

On his second trip to sea, Masefield deserted in New York and wandered around America, eventually ending up in a carpet mill. He wrote about his American experiences in his autobiography *In the Mill* (1941). During his two years at the carpet mill, he began to write.

In 1897 Masefield returned to England, settling in London and devoting his life to writing. His love of the sea is expressed in many of his poems and stories, such as his best-known poem, "Sea-Fever." Appearing in his first collection of poetry, *Salt-Water Ballads* (1902), "Sea-Fever" opens with a sailor's need: "I must go down to the seas again, to the lonely sea and the sky, / And all I ask is a tall ship and a star to steer her by."

Masefield's first long narrative poem, *The Everlasting Mercy* (1911), made him notorious. Of this tale of Saul Kane—who, like the biblical St. Paul, rejects sin and finds salvation—critic Frank SWINNERTON write that hard-to-please readers found themselves "compelled to read it the better to ridicule it." Masefield's later poem *Reynard the Fox* (1919) was described by critic Sanford Sternlicht as "vigorous, vital, precise . . . dramatic . . . and . . . a masterpiece of English poetry."

Masefield's popularity was at its height between 1923 and 1930. Critics hailed his novel *Sard*

Harker (1924), a tale of an Englishman's adventures in a Central American republic, as comparable to works by Joseph CONRAD and Thomas Hardy. This popularity led to Masefield's appointment as poet laureate of England in 1930. His appeal waned, however, as later scholars and readers grew dissatisfied with his frequent sentimentality. Nonetheless, Masefield contributed exceptional examples of English lyrical and narrative forms. Critic Newman I. White wrote that "it is hard to see how the future can reject [Masefield] as one of the foremost English poets of the first half of the twentieth century."

Other Work by John Masefield

Collected Poems and Plays. New York: Classic Books, 2000.

A Work about John Masefield

Sternlicht, Sanford. *John Masefield.* Boston: Twayne, 1977.

Masters, John (1914–1983) *novelist, memoirist*

John Masters was born to English parents in Calcutta, India. His father, John Masters, was an officer in the Indian army. After attending the Royal Military College, he followed in a family tradition and served in India, commanding a brigade in Burma. He then settled in the United States.

Masters began writing after he left the army. When his works first appeared in the 1950s, he was praised for his knowledge of India. John Barkham, in the *New York Times,* wrote that Masters "knows India, its people and its landscapes like his own right hand." His first book, *Nightrunners of Bengal,* about the Indian Mutiny of 1857, was published in 1951 and attracted a great deal of attention. *New York Times* critic Orville Prescott wrote that it was unusual for a first novel to be "greeted by such a blare of trumpets," but he complained about "violence for its own sake" and questioned the necessity of vehemently loading on "horrible details of rape and murder." John Raymond in the *New Statesman* said that the novel was "the best historical novel about the Indian Mutiny." John Barkham praised *Bhowani Junction* (1954), Master's fourth book, as "far and away his best book" and the "best novel of India since E. M. Forster's *Passage to India.*" The novel follows the "self-exploration" of an Anglo-Indian woman in her late 20s and explores how the lives of Anglo-Indians were thrown into confusion after the departure of the British. It was made into a film starring Ava Gardner in 1955, which increased Masters's literary popularity.

Masters's autobiographical account, *Bugles and a Tiger* (1956), tells "the story of how a schoolboy became a professional soldier of the old Indian Army . . . and what India was like in those last twilit days of the Indian Empire." The book received generally good reviews, but Bernard Fergusson of *The London Sunday Times,* while praising Masters for his "superbly written, remarkably vivid" works, also criticized them as being "marred . . . by a lurid vein of savagery." *Bugles and a Tiger* created a popular stir on both sides of the Atlantic; Masters received more fan mail on its publication than from any of his previous books.

On beginning his career, Masters set out to write 35 novels based on a combination of Indian history during 300 years of British rule and his own experiences. He completed 12 books (nine novels and three autobiographies). He wanted to write about India as an insider and took great pride in noting that the author and critic Khushwant Singh wrote, "Both Kipling and Masters understand India, but only Masters understands Indians."

Other Works by John Masters

Coromandel. New York: Viking Press, 1955.
The Ravi Lancers. Garden City, N.Y.: Doubleday, 1972.

A Work about John Masters

Clay, John. *John Masters: A Regimented Life.* London: Michael Joseph, 1992.

Maugham, William Somerset

(1874–1965) *novelist, playwright, travel writer, memoirist*

W. Somerset Maugham was born in Paris, the son of Robert Ormund Maugham, a lawyer with the British embassy, and Edith Mary Shell Maugham. The boy was frustrated by a persistent stammer. By the time he was 10, his father had died of cancer, and his mother died in childbirth shortly thereafter. He was then raised by a minister uncle, Henry Macdonald Maugham.

Maugham trained to be a doctor, and in the process spent time in the London slums. This experience, along with reading novels of realism, such as those by George Moore, influenced Maugham's first novel, *Liza of Lambeth* (1897), which describes the hardships of poverty.

Remembered today primarily for his fiction, Maugham first found fame through the theater with the play *Lady Frederick* (1907), a comedy about money troubles and marriage. Several successful plays, such as *A Man of Honor* (1903), followed, often comedies rooted in the disappointments and minor tragedies of everyday life.

In 1917 Maugham married Syrie Wellcome, with whom he had a daughter. At the same time he began frequent trips to exotic destinations with his friend, secretary, and male lover, Gerald Haxton, the two of them gathering information about people and locations. This research provided background for Maugham's fiction, such as the novel *The Moon and Sixpence* (1919), set in Tahiti (where the protagonist Charles Strickland abandons his family and career for a life as an artist); and the short story "Rain" (1921), set in tropical Samoa (where prostitute Sadie Thompson encounters a zealous but conflicted missionary who tries to reform her). Maugham also wrote travel memoirs, such as *The Explorer* (1909) and *The Gentleman in the Parlor: A Record of a Journey from Rangoon to Haiphong* (1930). Maugham's marriage ended in divorce in 1928, and he and Haxton eventually made their home in Southern France, where they threw lavish parties and hosted many famous people, including Winston CHURCHILL.

Maugham's fiction and plays often feature travel to other countries, medical problems such as stillbirths, an orphan's sense of abandonment and loss, and the occasional appearance of kind, maternal female figures. Throughout his career he showed a willingness to depict failure, weakness, physical imperfection, and embarrassment even in his most likable characters.

Maugham's best-known novel is *Of Human Bondage* (1915), which closely parallels his own life. Maugham's stammer is replaced by the protagonist's club foot, and place names are slightly altered, but the story is still one of loneliness and a search for quasi-maternal companionship. The protagonist, Carey, is greatly influenced by a free-thinking artist mentor who helps introduce him to more bohemian and cosmopolitan living, chipping away at Carey's morals and forcing him to confront life more honestly. The conflict between reality and comforting illusions is apparent in lines such as "[p]eople ask for your criticism, but they only want praise." Carey finds solace in the form of a motherly waitress and potential girlfriend. Maugham often leaves the reader with the impression that life is full of sad circumstances, regardless of whether one is in Paris, a London slum, or the tropics. A person's best hope is to accept disappointments and loss as part of the human condition.

Maugham's awareness of human suffering no doubt contributed to his strong opposition to war, reflected in his war memoir *Strictly Personal* (1941) and in the antiwar play *For Services Rendered* (1932), in which the callous protagonist Ardsley dismisses the problems of a debt-saddled ex-soldier, telling him, "The country was up against it and had to economize and if a certain number of individuals had to suffer it can't be helped."

Maugham's dissatisfaction with the world combines with his love of travel in the novel *The Razor's Edge* (1944), which tells the story of an American who grows tired of the pettiness and violence of life in the West and travels to India to stay at an ashram, a small community for religious study and meditation. Spirituality apparently offers an escape from the various physical and emotional ailments that compose Maugham's world.

Though *The Razor's Edge* is generally regarded as Maugham's last important novel, he went on to publish the insightful nonfiction volume *A Writer's Notebook* (1949). Compiled from years' worth of his notes, the book reveals his concern for realism. Of older authors he writes, "[t]hings were easier for the old novelists who saw people all of a piece. Speaking generally, their heroes were good through and through, their villains wholly bad." By contrast, Maugham's characters are a mix. Even his best are prone to suicide and depression and guilty of social climbing and neglect of duty. These characters operate in a world of doomed romance, divorce, and prostitution.

Critics have often been hard on Maugham, many believing that he had failed to live up to the promise of *Of Human Bondage*, that he never again reached the same thematic depth or richness of character. As the critic Stanley Archer writes, although Maugham was "one of the most popular writers who ever lived," he would "produce a largely negative reaction from serious critics." Still, Archer concludes that Maugham had "one of the most varied productive literary careers in history."

Other Works by W. Somerset Maugham

Cakes and Ale. 1930. Reprint, New York: Viking, 1993.
The Great Exotic Novels and Short Stories of Somerset Maugham. New York: Carroll & Graf, 2001.
Up at the Villa. 1941. Reprint, New York: Viking, 2000.

Works about W. Somerset Maugham

Archer, Stanley. *W. Somerset Maugham: A Study of the Short Fiction.* Boston: Twayne, 1993.
Curtis, Anthony, and John Whitehead, eds. *W. Somerset Maugham: The Critical Heritage.* New York: Routledge, 1987.
Rogal, Samuel J. *A William Somerset Maugham Encyclopedia.* Westport, Conn.: Greenwood Press, 1997.

Mavor, Osborne Henry

See BRIDIE, JAMES.

McEwan, Ian (1948–   ) *novelist, short story writer, playwright, screen writer*

Ian McEwan was born in Aldershot, Hampshire, England, to David and Rose Lilian Violet McEwan. Because his father was a British army officer, McEwan spent portions of his childhood in Singapore and North Africa, but he returned to England for school. He eventually earned a B.A. in English from the University of Sussex and an M.A. from the University of East Anglia, where he took courses with the author Angus WILSON.

At the outset of McEwan's career, as the scholar Kiernan Ryan writes, "The secret of his appeal lay in his stylish morbidity, in the elegant detachment with which he chronicled acts of sexual abuse, sadistic torment and pure insanity." These qualities define the stories in McEwan's first book, *First Love, Last Rites* (1975). One story, "Cocker at the Theatre," for instance, describes a rehearsal for a pornographic play in which two of the actors, against the wishes of a director who believes he is creating art, actually have intercourse. The discomfort that many experience in reading this story is mirrored somewhat by the characters themselves as they wait naked backstage for the rehearsal to begin. "How do naked strangers begin a conversation?" McEwan writes, "No one knew. The professional men—for professional reasons—glanced at each other's parts, while the others . . . regarded the women without appearing to."

Such dark and unsettling themes also dominate McEwan's first novel, *The Cement Garden* (1978), in which a group of children, fearing that they will be separated, hide the body of their dead mother and descend into an animal-like state of existence. Much like William GOLDING's *Lord of the Flies*, the novel examines what happens when adult supervision and the social norms such supervision usually enforces disappear. According to the scholar David Malcolm, McEwan's final message is that people "indifferent to normally accepted standards . . . would be capable of anything under the right circumstances."

In the 1980s McEwan turned to political themes. In the screenplays *The Imitation Game* (1980) and *The Ploughman's Lunch* (1983), he bitterly attacks Margaret Thatcher's political conservatism. He continued his campaign against Thatcher in his play *Or Shall We Die* (1983), which also examines the threat of nuclear war.

Two recent novels, *Enduring Love* (1997) and *Amsterdam* (1998), have earned critical praise. The former centers on a character named Joe, who tries to prevent a fatal hot-air balloon accident. One of those involved in the accident, Jed, develops a complex religious and psychotic fixation on Joe.

Amsterdam, which won the BOOKER PRIZE, opens as two friends, Clive and Vernon, contemplate the death of a woman with whom each has been lovers. The sudden death of fortyish Molly from an unspecified disease confounds everyone she has known, and in response Vernon and Clive each agree to kill the other if either develops an incurable illness. *Atonement* (2002), McEwan's ninth novel, is an ambitious work about a 13-year-old girl growing up in 1935. It presents a morality tale set against the English countryside.

For some critics McEwan is an author who, particularly in his early work, relies on shock value and obscenity for effect. Others disagree. In the scholar Merritt Moseley's estimation, McEwan is "above all a serious novelist—serious about his craft, about life and politics, about the important things in life such as love and marriage—he stands among the most important of contemporary British fiction writers."

Other Works by Ian McEwan

Atonement. New York: Doubleday, 2002.
The Innocent. New York: Doubleday, 1990.

Works about Ian McEwan

Malcolm, David. *Understanding Ian McEwan.* Columbia: University of South Carolina Press, 2002.
Slay, Jack, Jr. *Ian McEwan.* Boston: Twayne, 1996.

McGahern, John (1934–) *novelist, short story writer, scriptwriter*

John McGahern was born in Dublin to John McGahern, a police officer, and Susan McManus McGahern, a schoolteacher. When his mother died of cancer, McGahern and his five sisters went to live with their father in a police barracks. After graduating from St. Patrick's Teacher Training College, Dublin, McGahern began teaching while attending night school at University College, earning his B.A. in 1957. That year he began a novel, *The End and the Beginning of Love,* which remains unpublished except for an extract in *X: A Literary Magazine* (1961).

McGahern's first published novel, *The Barracks* (1963), about the final months of a cancer-stricken police officer's wife, won him an A. E. Memorial Award and the Macauley Fellowship to write full time in London. But upon his return, he was fired from teaching for publishing *The Dark* (1965), a novel about a Catholic adolescent and his abusive father. Critics outside Ireland praised the book, but in Ireland it was banned until 1972. McGahern's marriage to Finnish theatrical producer Annikki Laaksi also ended in 1965. Reflecting the author's experience, the Irish protagonist in *The Leavetaking* (1975) loses both his marriage and his teaching job at a Catholic school, but he gains self-knowledge.

The novel *Amongst Women* (1990)—about Michael Moran, an embittered IRA leader turned farmer whose weakening state of health has left him in the care of his second wife and three daughters—addresses the role and power of women in the household, the broader role of women in Irish society, and how the Morans became the way they are. The work was nominated for the BOOKER PRIZE, won the *Irish Times* Literary Award, and was broadcast by the BBC (British Broadcasting Corporation) in 1998.

McGahern's desire to perfect his prose in part accounts for the long gaps between his novels. A *Guardian* profile of McGahern reported that when the BBC dramatized *Amongst Women* for television and complained of a shortage of sex and violence in the story, McGahern said he could give them plenty more from all the material he had discarded.

That They May Face the Rising Sun (2002), Mc-Gahern's first novel since 1990, focuses on a year in the life of a close-knit community in rural Ireland. *The Scotsman* reviewer Tom Adair writes, "In his latest novel, it's business as usual: the weighing and sifting with scrupulous scrutiny, the taste, the cadence, the process of melting words slowly into meaning. . . ."

McGahern's novels, story collections (*Nightlines*, 1970, and *High Ground*, 1985), and television and radio plays have earned him 14 awards, an honorary doctorate from Dublin University, and fellowships and visiting professorships at British and American universities. Author Denis Sampson writes, "As in the case of other major artists, McGahern's ability to develop and adjust the literary medium as a refined instrument for reflecting the self in its constancy and its change, is rooted in the energy that makes his writing urgent and vital."

A Work about John McGahern

Sampson, Denis. *Outstaring Nature's Eye: The Fiction of John McGahern*. Washington, D.C.: Catholic University of America Press, 1993.

McGrath, John (1935–2002) *playwright, screenwriter, nonfiction writer*

John McGrath was born in Birkenhead, Cheshire, England, the son of Francis and Margaret McCann McGrath. At St. John's College, Oxford, he became interested in theater. One of his first plays of note was *Events While Guarding the Bofors Gun* (1966), which is based on his observations of class structure within the military. Taking place in the early 1950s, it dramatizes the conflict between six working-class soldiers in a British army camp in Germany and their immediate supervisor, an ambitious petty-bourgeois officer. This play was later made into the film *The Bofors Gun* (1968).

In the 1970s, McGrath became interested in the intertwined histories of Scotland and England. *Random Happenings in the Hebrides; or The Social Democrat and the Stormy Sea* (1970) was the first of his plays on the subject. A young man, attempting to save the local fishing industry on the northwest coast of Scotland, tries and fails to organize a union, but is elected as a Labor Party candidate to the British Parliament. Critic Helen Dawson found McGrath to be a playwright "bursting with ideas."

McGrath founded his own theatrical production company, 7:84, in 1971. Its name refers to the claim that 7 percent of the British population owned 84 percent of the national wealth. The company's objective was to entertain and bring radical ideas to a working-class audience. The first production was *Trees in the Wind* (1971), in which one man in a group of four revolutionaries denounces his former Maoist principles and sells out. A reviewer called the play a "beautifully balanced piece of writing."

McGrath gained recognition with his company and through screenplays on television. His most notable success as a screenwriter came with *The Dressmaker* (1989) an adaptation of the Beryl Bainbridge novel, starring Joan Plowright, that focuses on an extremely dysfunctional family. Critic Vincent Canby lauded the film for "its short, intense narrative focus."

In a series of lectures given at Cambridge University, published as *A Good Night Out: Popular Theatre; Audience, Class, and Form* (1981), McGrath criticized the condition of contemporary theater in Britain and explained that his most successful plays have components of the popular and political, combining a riveting plot, contemporary music, and political ideas that challenge audiences to question accepted norms.

The passionately political McGrath was forced to give up his post as director of the 7:84 by the Scottish Arts Council in 1988. Critic Randall Stevenson observed that McGrath's post-7:84 plays, such as *Border Warfare* (1989), a four-hour musical play about one thousand years of Scottish history, marked a new direction for the author. Stevenson refers to McGrath's book on the theater *The Bone Won't Break* (1990) as "with luck, a guarantee that his and other voices proclaiming that co-operation rather than individual possessiveness is the better principle for the future happiness of humanity. . . ."

Other Works by John McGrath

Fish in the Sea. London: Pluto Press, 1977.

Six-Pack: Plays for Scotland. Edinburgh: Polygon, 1996.

McGuckian, Medbh (1950–) *poet*

Medbh McGuckian was born in Belfast, Northern Ireland, to Catholic parents, Hugh Albert and Margaret McCaughan. Her father was a teacher and farmer in Ireland. McGuckian inherited her mother's love of art and music. She received her B.A. from Queen's University in Belfast in 1972 and her M.A. from the same university in 1974. In 1977 she married John McGuckian, a schoolteacher. During her years at Queen's University, one of her teachers was the renowned poet Seamus HEANEY. Her originality and lyrical use of language have earned her accolades as one of Ireland's greatest female poets. Critics have compared McGuckian to Emily Dickinson for her self-reflexive and introverted style.

Taking the themes of her poetry from the home and from nature, McGuckian uses rhythmic language to convey what she calls "the intensity of images to shadow-paint the inner life of the soul": "No living woman / was more alive in her sleep," the poet writes in "Killing the Muse." One of her first poems, "The Flitting," records her feelings upon moving to a new house. Her attempt to find her sense of place in the midst of this change is revealed in the line "I am well earthed here as the digital clock." The poem won the National Poetry Competition in 1979.

Despite the difficulty some readers have in interpreting her poetry, McGuckian's subsequent works have continued to win critical acclaim. Her book of verse *Shelmalier* (1998) explores the complexities of Irish identity by focusing on the conflict in Northern Ireland. In her preface to the collection she describes her reasons for exploring this difficult topic:

The theme is less the experienced despair of a noble struggle brutally quenched than the dawn of my own enlightenment after the medieval ignorance, my being suddenly able to welcome into consciousness the figures of an integrity I had never learned to be proud of.

In "Shannon's Recovery" she attempts to reclaim a long suppressed Irish identity: "And welcome back ourselves, our own almost."

McGuckian's other collections of poetry include *Single Ladies* (1980) and *Selected Poems, 1978–1994* (1997). Although she is recognized as an important poet, Clair Wills in the *Times Literary Supplement* remarks that the "widespread recognition of the beauty and power of [McGuckian's] poetry has been matched by a similarly widespread uncertainty with regard to its meaning."

Other Work by Medbh McGuckian

Horsepower Pass By! Coleraine, Northern Ireland: University of Ulster Press, 1999.

Menen, Aubrey (Salvator Aubrey Clarence Menen) (1912–1989) *novelist, essayist, nonfiction writer*

Aubrey Menen was born in London, England, to Kali Narain and Alice Everett Menen. He was educated at the University of London and worked as a drama critic, theater director, and script editor before dedicating himself to freelance writing from 1948 until his death.

Menen worked in wide variety of genres, but he is best known for his satirical work. His first novel, *The Prevalence of Witches* (1948), is set in a remote part of India and satirizes modern culture. Critic J. M. Lalley praised Menen for having created "a novel of remarkable wit and originality . . . full of philosophic implications." Several of Menen's works are autobiographical, such as *Dead Man in the Silver Market: An Autobiographical Essay on National Pride* (1953), which J. A. May called "perhaps the wittiest and funniest essay in autobiography and philosophy" of its era.

Menen's nonfiction account of a Neapolitan uprising against the Nazis in *Four Days of Naples* (1979) attracted both criticism (critic Tom Buckley called it "vague on important details") and praise: Reviewer John Barkham called the narrative "vivid, exciting, and unsentimental" as it brought a historical episode out of obscurity.

The Space within the Heart (1970), Menen's unusual autobiography, is described by critic Phoebe Adams as "odd [and] witty," and she equates Menen's choices of what to reveal about himself with one who manipulates a "shell game." Menen's philosophical ideals are exemplified in *Speaking the Language Like a Native* (1962), which was exalted as a "brilliant collection of essays" presented by an "urbane and witty author [who] explodes popular myths . . ., shatters stereotypes . . . and creates a brand new portrait that will tempt the most seasoned traveler to return pronto."

About the art of writing Menen once said that it could be likened to "physical exercise." His "exercise" consisted of writing "from 5 P.M. to 7 P.M. six days a week" and throwing "things at people who interrupted [him]."

Other Works by Aubrey Menen

Art and Money: An Irreverent History. New York: McGraw Hill, 1980.

The Ramayana as Told by Aubrey Menen. New York: Scribner, 1954.

Milne, Alan Alexander (1882–1956)
novelist, poet, essayist, playwright, children's writer

A. A. Milne was born in London to John and Maria Milne. At the age of seven he attended Henley House, a private school owned by his father where his science teacher was a man who would later become world-famous as a science-fiction writer, H. G. WELLS. Milne went on to attend Cambridge University, where he studied mathematics and edited the undergraduate magazine *Granta*. After graduating, he wrote essays and poems for the *St. James' Gazette* and the satirical magazine *Punch*, which hired him as a staff member in 1906.

Milne worked in many genres and forms of writing during his career, including plays, detective novels, and humorous verse. He is best known, however, as a children's writer and as the creator of Winnie-the-Pooh.

Milne's first novel, *Lovers in London* (1905), was based on a collection of short romantic pieces about a young American girl in London, which he had written for *St. James' Gazette*. His next four books, including *The Day's Play* (1910) and *Once a Week* (1914) were collections of his humorous *Punch* pieces.

In 1913 Milne married Dorothy de Sêlincourt and the couple had a son, Christopher Robin Milne, in 1920. In 1922 Milne published a detective story, *The Red House Mystery*, which was written almost as a parody of the Sherlock Holmes mysteries. In the novel, the guests at Red House, a residence in the English countryside, must play detective to solve the mystery of their host's disappearance. Although the novel was Milne's greatest success to date, the detective novelist Raymond Chandler later criticized it for the unrealistic methods used by the story's hero, Anthony Gillingman.

During World War I Milne served in the army, and he credited his jarring experiences on the battlefield with steering his writing toward the safety of childhood. *When We Were Very Young* (1924) is a collection of poetry for children, some of which features Milne's son Christopher Robin: "They're changing the guard at Buckingham Palace— / Christopher Robin went down with Alice."

Two years later, Milne published *Winnie-the-Pooh* (1926). The stories and verse that make up the book were again inspired by his son Christopher as well as Christopher's toys, including Piglet; the donkey Eeyore; and Pooh himself, Christopher Robin's teddy bear. The stories are set in the Hundred Acre Wood, in which Pooh deals with such problems as getting honey from honeybees, and getting stuck in a friend's doorway after eating too much. Pooh's adventures continue in *The House at Pooh Corner* (1928).

Readers delighted in the charm of the books' silly, simple dialogue. Some critics disliked the simplicity of Pooh's world, arguing that it was too familiar and not steeped enough in fantasy, as so much other children's literature is. But as children's literature scholar Jackie Wullschläger writes, "Everyone can laugh at Pooh because everyone knows him, and the very security and middle-class complacency and parochial Englishness of the Pooh world . . . are precisely the qualities which continue to endear the books to children and adults more than half a century after they were written."

Works about A. A. Milne

Melrose, A. R., ed. *Beyond the World of Pooh.* New York: Dutton, 1998.

Thwaite, Ann. *A. A. Milne: The Man Behind Winnie-the-Pooh.* New York: Random House, 1990.

Mitchison, Naomi Margaret
(1897–1999) *novelist*

Naomi Mitchison was born Naomi Mary Margaret Haldane in Edinburgh, Scotland, to Kathleen Louise Trotter and John Scott Haldane. Her mother was a suffragist and her father was a physiologist. Her brother was the well-known scientist and writer J. B. S. Haldane. Mitchison started a home-study degree program in science at Oxford University but quit to work as a voluntary aid detachment nurse in World War I. In 1916 she married Gordon Richard Mitchison, a barrister and Labour member of Parliament.

Mitchison is best known for her historical novels, which attracted critical praise for their compelling characters. Her first, *The Conquered* (1923), describes the lives of two young Celts in Gaul during the years of Julius Caesar's occupation. In what many critics consider her masterpiece, *The Corn King and the Spring Queen* (1931), Mitchison depicts a three-way war among Sparta, several Greek city-states, and the mythical country of Marob.

Caught in the middle of the conflict is Erif Der, the Marob Spring Queen, who falls in love with the king she is supposed to topple. Similar to many of Mitchison's female characters, Erif Der is powerful and independent. At a festival, she displays her magical powers for a group of Greek women: "She cut off the hair of one of them and then made it long again; and at last she made the room turn red for a moment as though they were in the light of a bonfire." A *New Statesman* critic wrote that Mitchison's "descriptions of ritual and magic are superb; no less lovely are her accounts of simple, natural things. . . . To read her is like looking down into deep warm water, through which the smallest pebble and the most radiant weed shine and are seen most clearly."

Mitchison switched to contemporary issues with the novel *We Have Been Warned* (1935). A radical portrayal of modern sexual behavior, the book includes depictions of rape, seduction, and abortion. This novel, like many of Mitchison's writings, promotes birth control and sex outside of marriage to provide greater independence for women. Later in her career, Mitchison wrote science-fiction works such as *Memoirs of a Spacewoman* (1962), which describes a human connection with extraterrestrial life forms. Continuing to challenge traditional sexual and social norms, the author used this work to promote expanded roles for women in society.

Mitchison wrote her last novel while in her 90s. In 1997 the University of Scotland held an exhibition to celebrate her 100th birthday. Critic Alex Clark writes that Mitchison "found expression in a lifetime of writing . . . and appears to evince a near obsessional drive both to amass experience in order to write about it, and to make sense of the experience through writing it."

Other Work by Naomi Mitchison
Not by Bread Alone. New York: Miriam Boyars, 1983.

A Work about Naomi Mitchison
Calder, Jenni. *The Nine Lives of Naomi Mitchison.* London: Virago, 1997.

Mitford, Nancy (1904–1973) *novelist, biographer, journalist*

Nancy Mitford was born in London to David Bertram Ogilvy Mitford, the second Baron Redesdale, and Sydney Bowles Mitford. As the eldest child of an aristocratic family, she was raised in the countryside in the Cotswold district of England and educated at home by private tutors. She later attended a finishing school, where she learned French and horseback riding. Of her five sisters, one, Unity, was an enthusiastic admirer of Hitler, while another, Diana, married a leading British fascist, Oswald Mosley. Mitford's sister Jessica moved to the United States, where she became a writer.

Some have compared Mitford to a modern-day Jane Austen in style and sensibility. Many of her novels, such as *Highland Fling* (1931) and *Christmas Pudding* (1932), portray upper-class life in England with sensitivity and wit. In *Love in a Cold Climate* (1949), Mitford offers the following description of one of the upper-class characters, Lady Montdore: "When her worldly greed and snobbishness, her terrible relentless rudeness had become proverbial and formed the subject of many a legendary tale, people were inclined to suppose that her origins must have been low . . . but, in fact, she was perfectly well born and had been decently brought up, what used to be called 'a lady', so that there were no mitigating circumstances, and she ought to have known better."

Mitford also demonstrated this ability to satirize the upper classes in her journalism. Concerned about the potential response of the subject of one of her biting reviews, Mitford wrote to her sister the Duchess of Devonshire in 1956, "I've toned it down a bit—one must remember she won't be here for ever. Even so, she may not like it, she only likes *total* praise."

Much of Mitford's work draws on her experiences growing up in a privileged family during the years between the two world wars. Her 1940 novel, *Pigeon Pie: A Wartime Receipt,* satirizes the ideologies and ambitions during the "phony" war, the period from 1939 to 1940 before Hitler's invasion of France. The novel soon disappeared after the real threat of Hitler to mainland Britain became clear in the subsequent months.

After World War II Mitford moved to Paris, and her subsequent novels reflect her new French surroundings. *The Pursuit of Love,* first published in 1945, has a French hero who is embroiled in the politics of occupied France. Mitford describes the dilemma of her English heroine while in Paris: "How could one, how could she, Linda, with the horror and contempt she had always felt for casual affairs, allow herself to be picked up by any stray foreigner? . . . She was profoundly shocked, and, at the same, intensely excited." Another novel set in France, *The Blessing* (1951), takes up a similar theme, telling the story of an Englishwoman's tempestuous romance with a mysterious Frenchman.

Mitford also wrote biographies of famous historical figures such as Frederick the Great and Madame de Pompadour. She has been praised by book editor Charlotte Mosley for "her sharp sense of personalities and their idiosyncrasies."

Mitford is remembered primarily for her comic studies of the aristocracy in her novels. These depictions of the social class that she came from, however, did not always earn her praise from her own family. In a letter to Evelyn WAUGH in 1962, she wrote, "My mother is displeased with what I shall say about her in the *Sunday Times*. . . . It comes from seeing one's own life and all ones relations as a tremendous joke which one expects them to share." Despite such difficulties, her wit and lighthearted manner as a writer has earned her much acclaim. For others, such as critic Anne Fremantle, Mitford's talents run much deeper: "She is . . . is a serious writer, an artist who senses and sees the quirks and quiddities of the human condition."

A Work about Nancy Mitford

Lovell, Mary. *The Sisters: The Saga of the Mitford Family.* New York: W. W. Norton, 2002.

Modernism

See INTRODUCTION.

Monsarrat, Nicholas John Turney

(1910–1979) *novelist, playwright, memoirist*

Nicholas Monsarrat, born in Liverpool, was the son of Keith Waldegrave, a surgeon, and Marguerite Turney Waldegrave. Monsarrat began writing short stories while at Cambridge. His first novel, *Think of Tomorrow*, was published in 1934 and a play, *The Visitor*, appeared briefly in London's West End.

The most important experience of Monsarrat's life was serving in the Royal Navy during World War II as a lieutenant commander escorting convoys across the Atlantic. He kept a sea journal on which he drew for three novels. The most important of these is *The Cruel Sea* (1951), which follows the exploits of the corvette (a small warship) *The Compass Rose*. The novel became a best-seller, established Monsarrat's reputation, and won the Heinemann Award for Literature in 1952 for its exciting battle scenes and authentic portrayal of the Battle for the Atlantic.

Other Monsarrat novels were less successful. *The Story of Esther Costello* (1953), though a commercial success, suffers from shallow characterization, as did *The Cruel Sea*. It is the story of a young Irish girl, injured in an accident and befriended by a wealthy American woman and her husband; their assistance turns into exploitation.

J. Jaffe writes of Monsarrat's exotic adventure novels *The Tribe That Lost Its Head* (1956), *The White Rajah* (1961), and *Richer Than All His Tribe* (1968); "The narrators of these stories are drawn into the web of violence and bestiality that characterizes life in . . . primitive cultures."

Monsarrat published his autobiography in two volumes: *Breaking In* (1966) and *Breaking Out* (1970). He died before completing what he considered his major work: a three-volume novel about British seafaring life from the time of the Spanish Armada to the present. The first volume, *The Master Mariner: Running Proud,* and an incomplete second volume were published posthumously.

Other Works by Nicholas Monsarrat

Three Corvettes. London: Cassell Academic, 2001.
The Kapillan of Malta. 1973. Reprint, London: Cassell Academic, 2001.

Montgomery, Robert Bruce

See CRISPIN, EDMUND.

Moorcock, Michael (1939–) *novelist, short story writer, editor*

Michael Moorcock, son of draftsman Arthur and June Taylor Moorcock, was born in Mitcham, Surrey, England. By the time he was 17, he was editing the magazine *Tarzan Adventures*. In 1964 he became editor of the popular British science-fiction magazine *New Worlds*. As part of the British "New Wave" of science fiction, he helped introduce greater psychological depth, sociological commentary, and sexual content to the genre.

As a writer, especially in the late 1960s and early 1970s, Moorcock introduced numerous interlocking fantasy and science-fiction series, including the Elric Saga, the Eternal Champion novels, the two Hawkmoon trilogies, the Corum sequence, and the adventures of Oswald Bastable. Of his many characters, Moorcock's most popular is Elric of Melniboné, whose first appearance was in the story "The Dreaming City" (1961) and whose most recent is in the novel *The Dreamthief's Daughter* (2000). Elric is a sword-wielding albino warrior in a quasi-medieval world where good and evil struggle for control. His own allegiances are not always clear, for although he battles on the side of good, he derives his physical strength from the souls that his demon-possessed sword, Stormbringer, pulls from dying foes.

Although much of Moorcock's fiction is heroic fantasy or adventure science fiction, he has also produced more ambitious work. *The Final Program* (1968) introduced the amoral, street-smart Jerry Cornelius, who seeks riches and women amidst the wreckage of a catastrophe-prone future. Jerry's adventures fill three more novels and a dozen short stories.

In Moorcock's *Behold the Man* (1969), whose shorter magazine version won a Nebula Award in 1967, time traveler Karl Glogauer, a Christian, is shocked to discover that the real Jesus was a slobbering imbecile: "The Face [of Jesus] was vacant. . . .

There was a little spittle on its lips." Glogauer's fate is to become Christ: he preaches, gathers followers, and is finally crucified. In *Gloriana* (1978), which received a Campbell Award and the World Fantasy Award, the queen of a British empire stretching from America to Asia is frustrated by her duties and her inability to have an orgasm, making her ripe for corruption by a member of her court. *Mother London* (1988), which was nominated for the Whitbread Prize, is a realistic depiction of life in World War II London. Iain Sinclair says this novel "pivots on the Blitz, on psychic damage, small urban miracles worked by human affection" in the midst of terror. As critic John Clute observes, Moorcock, as writer and editor, "proved that literate SF and fantasy could be written."

Other Works by Michael Moorcock
Byzantium Endures. London: Orion, 1981.
Cornelius Quartet. New York: Four Walls Eight Windows, 1979.

A Work about Michael Moorcock
Greenland, Colin. *The Entropy Exhibition.* London: Routledge & Kegan Paul, 1983.

Moore, Brian (1921–1999) *novelist*
Brian Moore was born in Belfast, Northern Ireland, to James Brian Moore, a surgeon, and Eileen McFadden Moore, and attended St. Malachy's College. He emigrated to Canada in 1948 after serving with the British Ministry of War Transport during World War II in Africa, Italy, and France.

Moore's first, most widely known, and best novel, *The Lonely Passion of Judith Hearne* (1956), is about woman's effort to discover her identity as her life begins to fall apart. The main character, an unmarried middle-aged woman, desperately seeks love from a deceitful suitor. Moore's early works, in the words of critic Kerry McSweeney, "are studies of losers, whose fates are determined by the claustrophobic gentility of Belfast and the suffocating weight of Irish Catholicism." The literary critic Hallvard Dahlie proposes that in this as in the others of Moore's first four novels, the author "exploited the constituents of failure so skillfully and sensitively that the characters achieve much more stature than many triumphant heroes of less gifted writers."

Moore referred to himself as a person who was not religious but who was influenced by his religious background: "I've wondered what if all this stuff was true and you didn't want it to be true and it was happening in the worst possible way?" An exploration of Catholicism appears in much of his work. Critic Paul Gray sees in *Cold Heaven* (1983) and *Black Robe* (1985), as well as other works, a common theme: "When beliefs can no longer comfort, they turn destructive."

Moore also explores the supernatural. Critic David MacFarlane has praised his "ability to make tangible the unbelievable and the miraculous." For example, in *The Great Victorian Collection* (1975), a professor dreams about a display of Victoriana, which then materializes in a hotel parking lot. Literary critic Paul Binding suggests that these works are an attempt by the author to examine the intricacies of American life while unraveling his Irish past.

Bruce Cook in *New Republic* wrote that Moore built "a body of work that is . . . about as good as that of any novelist writing today in English." He called Moore "a writer's writer," adding that "his special virtues—his deft presentation of characters . . . and the limpid simplicity of his style—are those that other writers most admire." Hallvard Dahlie has commented that Moore's fiction "constitutes a rich and varied aesthetic accomplishment matched by relatively few contemporary writers of the three nations which have shaped him: North Ireland, Canada and the United States."

Other Works by Brian Moore
The Color of Blood. New York: Dutton, 1987.
The Emperor of Ice Cream. New York: Viking Press, 1965.
The Temptation of Eileen Hughes. New York: Farrar, Straus & Giroux, 1981.

Works about Brian Moore

O'Donoghue, Jo. *Brian Moore: A Critical Study*. Montreal, Que.: McGill University Press, 1991.

Sampson, Denis. *Brian Moore: The Chameleon Novelist*. Toronto: Doubleday, 1998.

Morris, Jan (1926–) *journalist, travel writer, biographer*

Jan Morris was born James Humphrey Morris in Clevedon, Somerset, England, to Walter and Enid Payne Morris. Born a man, he changed his name to Jan after a sex-change operation in 1972. Before this, he served as an intelligence officer in the British army and worked in Italy and Palestine. He then attended Oxford University, receiving his degree in 1951. During the 1950s he made a name for himself as a journalist after covering Sir Edmund Hillary's famous Mt. Everest expedition for the London *Times*.

Both before and after her sex change, Morris built a reputation writing about famous people. Her recent book *Lincoln: A Foreigner's Journey* (2000) discusses American attitudes toward Abraham Lincoln. In addition, she is known for insightful travel books about regions that made up the former British Empire. She has written general works on the empire, such as *The Spectacle of Empire* (1982); as well as books on more specific locations, such as *Hong Kong: Epilogue to an Empire* (1997), which recounts her observations of changes in the former British colony as it passed to Chinese control. The book opens with a portrait of China as a vast, diverse region with a long history: "The traveler in China sees many marvels. From Harbin in the bitter north to Urumqi among the deserts of Xinjiang, from the frontiers of the Soviet Union to the marches of India, the way is marked everywhere by spectacle and anomaly."

Morris has also written more personal works. Her autobiography *Conundrum* explores the difficult transition she faced during the time preceding her sex-change operation. Another autobiographical book, *Pleasure of a Tangled Life* (1989), is more reflective and speaks more generally about her life experiences.

Morris continues to publish travel books on such places as Venice, Ireland, and Wales, and articles for the British and American press. As Anatole Broyard of the *New York Times* remarked of her writing, "Her travel books are oddly reassuring, showing us that there are more ways of experiencing cultures than most of us supposed."

Other Works by Jan Morris

Heaven's Command: An Imperial Progress. 1974. Reprint, San Francisco: Harvest Books, 2002.

Hong Kong: Epilogue to an Empire. New York: Vintage, 1997.

Mortimer, John Clifford (1923–) *novelist, short story writer, playwright*

John Mortimer was born to Clifford Mortimer, a barrister, and Kathleen May Smith Mortimer in London, England. In 1949 he married Penelope Fletcher, who wrote as Penelope MORTIMER.

He is best known in America for his *Rumpole of the Bailey* (1978) stories and for his television adaptation of Evelyn WAUGH's novel *Brideshead Revisited*.

The character Rumpole, a barrister, grew out of Mortimer's years as a defense attorney in which he came to know people accused of murder and other crimes. Rumpole's adventures fill 12 books; crime appears in Mortimer's other writings, such as his play *The Dock Brief* (1970), in which Morgenhall, a small-time barrister, has the chance to defend a murder suspect and improve his failing career. Morgenhall spends more time fantasizing about success than dealing with the realities of the case and the accused; the critic George Wellwarth refers to such characterizations in Mortimer's work as "the glorification of the failure." "Mortimer's failures," according to Wellwarth, "are the antithesis of the organization men" and the "survival-of-the-fittest doctrine."

Mortimer achieved his greatest commercial success in the 1970s and 1980s. At about the same time as his "Rumpole" television series, Mortimer published his autobiography *Clinging to the Wreckage: A Part of Life* (1982), as well as an autobiographical play *A Voyage Round My Father* (1970). The play, adapted for television in 1980, revealed "bonds so deep that words cannot begin to express them," according to columnist Tom Shales. However, critic Clive Barnes called the character of Mortimer's father "a caricature blandly begging for kindness."

Mortimer's 1980 novel *Paradise Postponed*, about a minister who leaves a fortune to a local young man instead of his own family, was touted by critic Stuart Evans as a "witty chronicle of rural English life as it reflects national fads and preoccupations from 1945 to the present day." Mortimer was a prolific writer throughout the 1980s and 1990s. Both *Titmuss Regained* and *Summer's Lease* were published in 1991. The former focuses on the conflict "between liberals and conservatives when [they] ascend on the English countryside"; the latter pokes fun at British vacationers in Tuscany and includes a murder mystery.

Mortimer's short story collections, including *Rumpole's Last Case* (1988), have received critical acclaim. Although the Rumpole stories are formulaic, they attract a wide audience for their humor and well-drawn characters.

Other Works by John Mortimer

Felix in the Underworld. New York: Viking, 1997.
In Character. New York: Allan Lane, 1983.
Like Men Betrayed. New York: Viking, 1953.

Mortimer, Penelope Fletcher
(1918–1999) *novelist*

Penelope Mortimer was born Penelope Ruth Fletcher in Rhyl, Wales. Because her father, A. F. G. Fletcher, was an itinerant minister, she attended a number of schools before finally enrolling at London University, which she left after only one year. In 1937 she married her first husband, with whom she had four daughters. She began to work as a freelance writer, producing articles for the *New Statesman.* In 1947 she wrote her first novel, *Johanna,* under the pseudonym Penelope Dimont. Mortimer divorced her first husband and married John MORTIMER, the playwright and novelist, in 1949.

Mortimer's first widely recognized novel, *A Villa in Summer* (1955), explores the bitter end of a marriage, a theme that would dominate her future novels. She frequently reverses the standard pattern of the Victorian novel: Instead of depicting women who are searching for marriage and social position, she describes destructive marital conflicts and presents heroines who are unable to act.

Mortimer's most successful novel, *The Pumpkin Eater* (1962), features a protagonist who has been married three times and has six children. She believes she has finally found happiness in her fourth marriage, but her new husband is unwilling to have children. When the protagonist becomes pregnant, she unwillingly has an abortion to preserve her marriage. Significantly, the main character is nameless and functions as a symbol for all women who feel emotionally isolated. As the critic Roberta Rubenstein notes, "Mortimer's novels are about loss: of love and sexual fidelity; of parents, children, and spouses; of self."

Other Work by Penelope Mortimer

My Friend Says It's Bullet-Proof. New York: Penguin Books, 1991.

A Work about Penelope Mortimer

Rubenstein, Roberta. *Boundaries of the Self.* Urbana: University of Illinois Press, 1987.

Motion, Andrew Peter (1952–) *poet, biographer*

Andrew Motion was born in London, England, to Andrew Richard and Catherine Gillian Bakewell Motion. His father was a brewer. He earned a first-class degree in English with honors at Oxford. Motion's professional career included serving as editorial director for the publishing house Chatto & Windus and teaching creative writing at the University of East Anglia.

Motion's first poetry collection, *The Pleasure Steamers* (1978), contains his award-winning poem "Inland." Like much of his verse, this poem reflects feelings of insecurity and isolation as it depicts a narrator who is forced to abandon his village after a flood. In a review of the volume, the scholar Blake Morrison observed that Motion is influenced by poets Philip LARKIN and Edward THOMAS: "From them he has learnt the power of negatives . . . to create feelings of nostalgia, sadness and loss." The poem "Anniversaries," about a loved one lying comatose in a hospital, captures the poet's somber style: "What I remember is not / your leaving, but your not / coming back."

Motion continued to write about loss in his *Independence* (1981) collection. The lengthy title poem, set in India the year it gained independence, describes a man whose wife dies during a miscarriage. The narrator's sense of political freedom is overwhelmed by his personal grief.

In 1984 Motion won the John Llewelyn Rhys Memorial Prize for *Dangerous Play: Poems, 1974–1984* (1984), which contains a handful of new poems about loss and loneliness, Motion's recurring themes. In "Dangerous Play," for example, the narrator and a companion discover a man murdered in a car. The companion leaves the narrator alone at the grisly scene: "When you say / *I'll go for some help; stay put*, you've already gone."

Motion's other works include critically acclaimed biographies of the poet Philip Larkin and Australian painter George Lambert. He has received numerous honors, including the Cholmondeley Award, and was named England's poet laureate in 1999. Critic Dick Davis writes that "Motion's verse is extremely fastidiously written, the pathos presented through understatement; almost all of his poems have a lonely, unfulfilled character at their centre, and he writes of such people with sympathy and insight, if a little monotonously."

Other Works by Andrew Motion
Love in a Life. London: Faber & Faber, 1991.
Salt Water. London: Faber & Faber, 1997.

Movement, the
"The Movement" is the term coined in 1954 by J. D. Scott, then literary editor of London's periodical *The Spectator*, to describe a group of influential British writers. Members of the group included Kingsley AMIS, D. J. ENRIGHT, Phillip LARKIN, John WAIN, and Donald DAVIE. These writers had in common a reaction against modernism and neoromanticism, and valued in their work, according to the scholars William Harmon and C. Hugh Holman, "normality, regularity, practicality, stoicism, traditionalism, and solid middle-class virtues rather than flamboyant heroics in substance or style."

In 1954 Robert CONQUEST anthologized work from most of these writers in *New Lines* and in so doing helped identify the group. By 1957, though, most of the members sought to distance themselves from the term.

Works about The Movement
Bradley, Jerry. *The Movement: British Poets of the 1950s*. New York: Macmillan, 1993.
Morrison, Blake. *The Movement: English Poetry and Fiction of the 1950s*. New York: Oxford University Press, 1980.

Muggeridge, Malcolm (1903–1990)
journalist, novelist, nonfiction writer
Malcolm Muggeridge was born in the village of Sanderstead, near London, into a relatively poor family. His father, Henry Thomas Muggeridge, was a clerk in a shirt factory; his mother, Annie Booler, came from a working-class background. Educated in state-supported schools as a youth, Muggeridge attended Cambridge University, where he studied science and English literature. At Cambridge he

also turned for a time to religion, which led him to take a teaching position at a missionary school in India.

While in India Muggeridge became a correspondent for *The Calcutta Express*. Intellectually he inherited his socialist father's suspicion of politicians, leading him to mock and debunk high-profile figures. In 1927 he married Kitty Dobbs, and the two moved to Egypt. His stories about Egyptian politics, published in various English newspapers, attracted the attention of the *Manchester Guardian*, and he returned to England to work for that newspaper.

Assigned to Moscow in 1932, Muggeridge's experiences there turned him from a Soviet sympathizer into Russia's most formidable British critic. He became convinced that no persons or groups who sought and obtained absolute power could be trusted. His novel *Winter in Moscow* (1934) details the disillusion of the journalist Wraithby: "He had observed from afar the Dictatorship of the Proletariat and had felt it to be substantial. He knew that it was brutal and intolerant and ruthless. He had no illusions about its consequences to individuals and to classes. Only, he thought, it offered a way of escape from himself."

Muggeridge attained a certain notoriety with his book-length biography and attack on the English writer Samuel Butler in *Earnest Atheist* (1936), which would today be labeled fiercely homophobic. In 1940 he published what is widely considered to be his best work, *The Thirties*, a political memoir of that turbulent decade.

Even while turning out books, Muggeridge continued his newspaper work. After World War II he began writing for BBC radio, which led to television, for which he became a lecturer, panelist, host of documentaries, and gadfly. He also became a vocal advocate of Christianity, to which he returned when he and his wife converted to Catholicism in 1982. His biographer Gregory Wolfe writes of Muggeridge's achievement: "Though his best writing is scattered through six decades of journalistic production, Malcolm's prose style is among the finest of his generation."

Works about Malcolm Muggeridge

Ingrams, Richard. *Malcolm Muggeridge: The Biography*. New York: HarperCollins, 1995.
Wolfe, Gregory. *Malcolm Muggeridge: A Biography*. Grand Rapids, Mich.: Eerdrans, 1997.

Muir, Edwin (1887–1959) *poet, literary critic, essayist, novelist, translator*

Edwin Muir was born on the Orkney Islands, Scotland, to tenant farmer parents. Largely self-taught, he was not formally educated beyond grammar school. His marriage in 1919 to Wilhelmina "Willa" Anderson proved to be an important turning point. On her urging they moved to London, where he began working as a journalist.

Although Muir wrote several fictional works, including autobiographical novels, he is best known for his poetry and literary criticism. During the 1920s he gained renown for his works, including *Latitudes* (1924), his first collection of essays on literary subjects as well as aesthetics, morals, and psychology. Also from this period, *The Structure of the Novel* (1928) is arguably the most read and influential of all of Muir's critical writings. It argues that the novel, once considered unworthy of serious study, "has a valid, independent life" and "is a form of art, or it is nothing." During this period Muir and his wife also began a long and successful collaboration translating works of German writers, such as Franz Kafka's novel *The Castle*.

Muir's poetry during the 1920s is collected in *First Poems* and *Chorus of the Newly Dead*. These works include his first efforts at dealing with his central themes, including an idyllic childhood until his move to Glasgow and the early deaths of family members. Early criticism praised Muir's poems for their "simplicity and peace" and "originality." By the 1930s his poetry had improved. Poet Stephen SPENDER, in his review of *Journeys and Places* (1937), wrote that the collection "contains the best poems Muir has written and some of the most serious, interesting, and individual poems of our time."

Near the time of his death, Muir was beginning to be recognized as a major poet. The scholar Horace Gregory, summing up Muir's literary contributions, called his *Collected Poems* (1957) "the most important of all" his works. "In retrospect," Gregory wrote, "it is now clear that his singular . . . dream-haunted imagination was of the first order." The critic Joseph H. Summers asserts that Muir's accomplishment in poetry and prose is "larger than merely literary. . . . Implicit in all of his works is the recognition that there are things more important than literature—life and love, the physical world, the individual spirit within its body."

Other Work by Edwin Muir

The Complete Poems of Edwin Muir. Edited by Peter Butter. London: Association for Scottish Literary Studies, 1991.

Works about Edwin Muir

Aitchison, James. *The Golden Harvester: The Vision of Edwin Muir.* Aberdeen, Scotland: Aberdeen University Press, 1988.

Mellown, Elgin. *Edwin Muir.* Boston: Twayne, 1979.

Muldoon, Paul (1951–) *poet*

Paul Muldoon was born in Portadown, Northern Ireland, to Roman Catholic parents Patrick Muldoon, a laborer and mushroom farmer, and Brigid Muldoon, a teacher. As a child he studied both Gaelic and English languages and literatures, and he began writing poetry in both languages. He attended Queens University, Belfast, and there entered an important literary circle that included Seamus HEANEY and Michael LONGLEY. Heaney tutored the young poet, but Muldoon was also influenced by the work of Louis MACNIECE and William Butler YEATS. After he earned his B.A., he went to work for the BBC (British Broadcasting Corporation) in Northern Ireland as a radio and television producer until he moved to America in 1980 to teach at Princeton University.

Even in his first collections of poetry, *New Weather* (1973) and *Mules* (1977), Muldoon displayed imagination and technical skill, but it was *Why Brownlee Left* (1980), which won the Faber Memorial Prize, that established his reputation. In the title poem, a sonnet, Muldoon plays with one of the classic images from Irish literature, the farmer with his plow. "Why Brownlee Left," however, contains not a farmer and plow, but a plow mysteriously abandoned: "Why Brownlee left, and where he went / Is a mystery even now." Instead of solving the mystery, the poem focuses on the things Brownlee abandoned: his farm and team of horses who stand listlessly without knowing what to do.

"Immram," another poem in *Why Brownlee Left,* is also grounded in Irish traditions, based on a medieval tale about a hero attempting to avenge his father's death until a hermit tells him to forgive and forget. Muldoon's version takes place in New York and contains a staggering number of images of the modern world: pool halls, Cadillacs, Buicks, King Kong, and Baskin-Robbins ice cream.

Muldoon's next collection of poetry, *Quoof* (1983), received mixed reviews. Some critics found it too light and playful. The poems are fraught with ambiguity and revel in word play. His next volume, *The Annals of Chile* (1994), won the T. S. Eliot Prize, awarded for the best new collection of poetry. The poems of *The Annals of Chile* contain references to a diverse array of people, from the ancient Roman poet Ovid to the popular newspaper columnist Emily Post, and an equally broad range of settings. In the poem "Milkweed and Monarch" the poet describes a visit to his parents' grave. His mind darts away from the tombstones to fasten on various smells and their associations, a former lover, and butterflies before finally returning to the graves.

Many critics admire the collection *Hay* (1998) as Muldoon's most technically advanced work. The volume ends with "The Bangle (Slight Return)," which tells a whimsical tale of the classical Roman poet Virgil rollicking through England and Ireland in another of Muldoon's characteristically dizzying montages of images. This long poem is actually a sequence of 30 sonnets; the final 15 sonnets perfectly invert the rhyme schemes of the first 15.

Although some readers consider Muldoon's poetry artificial or overly playful, he has achieved a substantial literary reputation. His latest collection, *Moy Sand and Gravel* (2002), won the Pulitzer Prize in 2003. Critic Lester I. Connor writes that Muldoon, along with Heaney and Longley, represent "an outbreak of rich and varied talent . . . [that] has not been seen in Ireland since Yeats and the Celtic Renaissance."

Other Works by Paul Muldoon

Madoc: A Mystery. New York: Farrar, Straus & Giroux, 1991.

Poems, 1968–1998. New York: Farrar, Straus & Giroux, 2001.

To Ireland, I. New York: Oxford University Press, 2001.

A Work about Paul Muldoon

Kendall, Tim. *Paul Muldoon.* Chester Springs, Pa.: Dufour Editions, 1996.

Munro, Alice (1931–   ) *novelist, short story writer*

Alice Munro was born Alice Laidlaw in Wingham, Ontario, to Robert Laidlaw and Ann Chamney. During the Great Depression, her father bred silver foxes. She began college at the University of Western Ontario, but left in 1951 to marry James Munro.

During the 1950s and 1960s, Munro privately wrote short stories. Her first collection, *Dance of the Happy Shades,* was published in 1968 and drew on her own experiences. For example, the story "Boys and Girls" begins, "My father was a fox farmer. That is, he raised silver foxes, in pens; and in the fall and early winter . . ."

After the success of her first work, Munro continued publishing stories and novels. She writes realistic, domestic fiction about ordinary people grounded in a particular region. Her second work, *Lives of Girls and Women* (1971), is an episodic novel set in Jubilee, Ontario, exploring the emotional and imaginative development of the protagonist Del Jordan. Geoffrey Wolff of *Time* magazine remarked on the homespun realism of the work: "The book is a fiction for people who like to read brittle, yellow clips from newspapers published in towns where they never lived, who like to look through the snapshot albums of imperfect strangers."

Who Do You Think You Are? (1978), which some critics consider Munro's best work, is a collection of interrelated stories following the life of a character named Rose through childhood, college, marriage, and back to her childhood home. It explores the dark secrets underneath the surface of small-town life, such as incest and abuse: "He shakes her and hits her against the wall, he kicks her legs. She is incoherent, insane, shrieking. *Forgive me! Oh please, forgive me!*"

One of Munro's hallmarks is the coherence of her short story collections, as critic Ildiko de Papp Carrington notes: "Although eight of the ten stories in *Who Do You Think You Are?* were originally published separately, the collection constitutes an organic whole." The collection was short-listed for the BOOKER PRIZE. Munro's latest collection of short stories, the acclaimed volume, *Hateship, Friendship, Courtship, Loveship, Marriage* (2002), continues her exploration of life in rural Ontario. Critic Beverly Rasporich contends that "the fictional world that Munro creates is an expanding, visionary location but at the same time always recognizably hers."

Other Work by Alice Munro

Selected Stories. New York: Alfred A. Knopf, 1996.

A Work about Alice Munro

Howells, Coral Ann. *Alice Munro.* New York: St. Martin's Press, 1998.

Munro, Hector Hugh

See SAKI.

Murdoch, Iris (1919–1999) *novelist, nonfiction writer, playwright*

Iris Murdoch was born in Dublin, Ireland, the daughter of Irene Alice Richardson Murdoch, who had trained as an opera singer, and Willis John Hughes Murdoch, an Irish cavalry officer in World War I and later a British civil servant. (Many of Murdoch's characters would share her mother's love of music and her father's love of books.) She lived in England for most of her life. Educated at Oxford, she lectured in philosophy in Oxford and London.

Murdoch's first of 26 novels was *Under the Net* (1954), which examines how difficult it is to know other people and thus how difficult communication is. She went on to produce novels that bring groups of strange characters into conflict with each other and themselves. She published a novel almost every year between 1956 and 1976, from *The Flight from the Enchanter* (1956) to *Henry and Cato* (1976). Thereafter she produced a novel about every other year. Her last was *Jackson's Dilemma* (1995). A friend reportedly asked Murdoch how much time she took off between writing novels, and she replied, "About half an hour." She also found time to write two plays, *The Three Arrows* (1973) and *The Servants and the Snow* (1973).

Although Murdoch's acute mind began to falter because of Alzheimer's disease in her final years, she remained productive almost to the end. Her husband John Bayley wrote two memoirs about that anguished period.

Ethics, religion, sex, and guilt are recurring themes in Murdoch's work, and like many intellectuals after World War II, she was fascinated by the existentialists' treatment of these topics. To the existentialists, people possess free will and are therefore fully capable of defying moral conventions, but in doing so they must also be held strictly accountable for their actions. Murdoch's first nonfiction book, *Sartre, Romantic Rationalist* (1953), examines these ideas.

Murdoch observed that her novels often contrasted a "saint" character with an "artist" character. The saint possesses philosophical insight and the artist the power to articulate ideas, but neither personality is complete in itself. According to the scholar Frank Baldanza, to some extent Murdoch's fiction reflects her own reality: "As philosopher turned novelist, the very tension in Miss Murdoch's career . . . between time-consuming work in philosophy and novel-writing actually casts a saint-artist dichotomy."

Many of Murdoch's novels feature characters who embody her favorite religious and ethical themes, from the schizophrenic monk in *The Bell* (1958) to the evil priest in *The Black Prince* (1973). Critic Elizabeth Dipple writes that *The Black Prince*, which received great critical praise and won the James Tait Black Memorial Prize, depicts the erotic impulse as a means of fusing artistic and spiritual ways of seeing: "In the disciplined activity of the serious artist, this creative Eros connects to the ethical demands of truth-telling."

In *The Sea, the Sea* (1978), which won the BOOKER PRIZE, narrator Charles Arrowby, a Shakespearean actor, director, and playwright who confesses to self-absorption, uses and discards lovers. He is jealous of his more successful cousin, James, who uses his psychic powers to locate the lost child of one of Charles's former lovers. Charles even kidnaps his ex-girlfriend in an effort to win her back, confessing to himself that his manipulation and abuse of others is a perverse form of his theatrical instincts: "Of course actors regard audiences as enemies, to be deceived, drugged, incarcerated, stupefied." Critic Cheryl Bove notes that James, on the other hand, is a "spiritually good character."

On a few occasions, Murdoch departed from the novel to write philosophy, most famously in *The Sovereignty of Good* (1970) and *Metaphysics as a Guide to Morals* (1992). Like the more recent philosopher Martha Nussbaum, Murdoch argued that philosophy and novels can be seen as related in that both help us look at life more attentively. Murdoch viewed close attention to life as a morally significant act, arguably the starting point of ethics. As she writes in *Metaphysics as a Guide to Morals:* "How we see our situation is itself, already, a moral activity."

In order to achieve an accurate picture of life Murdoch sought to avoid the false sterility and mathematical quality of much of contemporary philosophy. She also rejected the view of many early 20th-century philosophers such as G. E. Moore that goodness and other important attributes of the universe were mere conventions of language, labels that could be shifted around depending on the beliefs of the observer.

Murdoch was conscious of the power of art and literature to shape moral perceptions. She wrote of Plato's concerns about that power in *The Fire and the Sun: Why Plato Banished the Artists* (1977). Critics are divided, however, about whether she used that power to full effect. Some think her philosophical concerns got in the way of her art, making her novels humorless and formalistic. Murdoch argued that just as she was striving to avoid sterility and shallowness in philosophy, she was attempting to write fiction that was neither too realistic nor too artful.

Murdoch's later novels display an increased clarity about what she came to view as one of her most important ideas: that God is essentially a metaphor for the more permanent thing called the Good, which Murdoch, like Plato, viewed as a metaphysical but real part of the world. Philosophy is the process of striving to perceive that Good correctly, while art is in part the ability to depict it convincingly, and evil then is misperception of the Good.

In 1993 Cheryl Bove called Murdoch "Britain's most critically acclaimed living writer," noting that she was the recipient of the Black Memorial Prize, Whitbread Literary Award, BOOKER PRIZE, and the National Arts Club's Medal of Honor, and had been designated a Dame Commander of the Order of the British Empire (DBE) and a Companion of Literature. Shortly before Murdoch's death, English professor Alan Jacobs of Wheaton College called her novels "one of the more impressive bodies of fiction produced in English in this century."

Other Works by Iris Murdoch

Existentialists and Mystics: Writings on Philosophy and Literature. London: Chatto & Windus, 1997.
The Green Knight. New York: Viking, 1993.
Nuns and Soldiers. New York: Penguin, 1980.
A Severed Head. New York: Penguin, 1961.

Works about Iris Murdoch

Antonaccio, Maria. *Picturing the Human: The Moral Thought of Iris Murdoch.* Oxford, England: Oxford University Press, 2000.
Bayley, John. *Elegy for Iris.* New York: St. Martin's, 1999.
Gordon, David J. *Iris Murdoch's Fables of Unselfing.* Columbia: University of Missouri Press, 1995.
Heusel, Barbara Stevens. *Patterned Aimlessness: Iris Murdoch's Novels of the 1970s and 1980s.* Athens: University of Georgia Press, 1995.

Murphy, Richard (1927–) *poet, memoirist*

Richard Murphy was born in County Galway, Ireland, to William and Elizabeth Ormsby Murphy. During the 1930s, his father served as the last British colonial mayor of Colombo, Ceylon, so Murphy spent part of his childhood there. He was educated at Magdalen College, Oxford, where he studied with C. S. LEWIS, and attended the Sorbonne, University of Paris. His memoir *The Kick* (2002) draws on 50 years of diaries to evoke the varied scenes of his life, from Connemara to London to Ceylon; his love of the west coast of Ireland; and the literary personalities he has known, among them W. H. AUDEN, J. R. ACKERLEY, and Ted HUGHES.

Critic Chad Walsh praises Murphy's "strong sense of history, and the rootedness of the present in the past" in his work. This unique vision is revealed in such poems as "The Cleggan Disaster," from his 1963 collection *Sailing to an Island,* which mourns the death of 25 men in a storm off Connemara. Part of the inspiration for this poem came from a night the poet spent on the water in an open sailboat. Murphy's long poem *The Battle of Aughrim* (1968) is about a decisive battle fought between the English and Irish in 1691. Critic Daniel Hoffman sees this poem as "surely one of the most deeply felt and successfully rendered interpretations of history in modern Irish verse, and in poetry in English in our generation." In this ambitious poem Murphy, whose ancestors fought on both sides during the struggle, reflects on the history of even a stone slab in his garden:

> *"To quarry it men had to row/*
> *Five miles, twelve centuries ago."*

As an Anglo-Irish poet, Murphy explores both sides of his inheritance. He is characterized as one of the last of his kind, who in the tradition of William Butler YEATS dwells on his heritage, but he searches deeper into his legacy by seeking out the "Ireland of hovels, famine and disaster." His best poetry combines his interest in understanding both his personal and cultural identity.

Hoffman has viewed Murphy's greatest strength in "the lyrical loveliness and narrative movement of his long, sustained poems." Writing in the 1960s, Hoffman referred to Murphy as "the most important Irish poet now coming along, and very possibly a major figure in the entire English-speaking world."

Other Works by Richard Murphy
High Island. New York: Harper & Row, 1975.
The Mirror Wall. Winston-Salem, N.C.: Wake Forest University Press, 1989.
Richard Murphy: Collected Poems, 1952–2000. Winston-Salem, N.C.: Wake Forest University Press, 2001.

A Work about Richard Murphy
Harmon, Maurice. *Richard Murphy: Poet of Two Traditions.* Dublin: Wolfhound Press, 1978.

Murray, Leslie Allan (1938–) *poet*
Les Murray was born to dairy farmers Cecil Allan and Miriam Pauline Arnall Murray, in New South Wales, Australia, and attended the University of Sydney. He has said that the "Australian landscape, folklore, history, war, technology, deserts" inspire him to express the previously "unexpressed elements of [the] Australian mind and character." These elements are apparent in *The Boys Who Stole the Funeral: A Novel Sequence* (1980), a collection of 140 sonnets that tell the story of two boys who take the body of one boy's great-uncle to the outback he came from for burial. Their mission has unexpected consequences, some tragic. Murray incorporates aboriginal wisdom and his political point of view—for example, in the battle between the government and farmers—in what he sees as "a struggle between simple heroism and the modern bureaucracy that seeks to erase it."

The poet and critic William Logan describes Murray's writing as "hard to categorize, like a platypus." However, Fleur ADCOCK, in her review of *The Vernacular Republic: Poems, 1961–1981* (1982), writes, "Of all the poets now writing in Australia Les A. Murray is probably the most Australian and probably the best." Critic Clive James, in his review of the same collection, declares that Murray is calling for "the Australian poets of his generation" to take on the mission of giving voice to Australian culture.

Murray's *Freddy Neptune: A Novel in Verse* (1999), the story of an Australian sailor who travels throughout the globe from World War I to the end of World War II, is "the best long poem in English for some time," according to scholar Stephen Burt. The protagonist experiences strange and diverse adventures, from contracting leprosy to fighting in the Holy Land to working as a circus strongman, lion tamer, and more, including meeting Marlene Dietrich and the German poet Rainer Maria Rilke—all in easy, colloquial, eight-line stanzas. In a review of Murray's *Collected Poems* (1998), Burt sums up his work as "prodigious and frustrating, welcoming and cantankerous . . . a body of work [that] has made him both Australia's best-known poet and its most powerful."

Murray explains his attraction to poetry "as a way of battling my inarticulacy; I love the state in which it is done, for the unemployment it causes, for how it constrains one to work always beyond one's own intelligence, for its not requiring one to rise socially and betray the poor, and for its bringing only a non-devouring fame."

Other Works by Les Murray

The Ilex Tree. Canberra: Australian National University, 1965.

Learning Human: Selected Poems. New York: Farrar, Straus & Giroux, 2000.

Lunch and Counter Lunch. Sydney: Angus and Robertson, 1974.

Works about Les Murray

Alexander, Peter. *Les Murray: A Life In Progress.* New York: Oxford University Press, 2000.

Matthews, Steven. *Les Murray.* Manchester, England: Manchester University Press, 2001.

Murry, John Middleton, Jr.

See COWPER, RICHARD.

Na Gopaleen, Myles

See O'BRIEN, FLANN.

Naipaul, Vidiadhar Surajprasad

(1932–) *novelist, travel writer, essayist*
Born in Chaguanas, Trinidad, V. S. Naipaul is de-
scended from Indian Hindus. His grandfather
worked on a sugarcane plantation, and his father,
Seepersad, was a journalist and short story writer.
As a child, Naipaul spent most of his time in the
matriarchal Tiwari clan house in Chaguanas or on
the streets of Port of Spain. He attended Queen's
Royal College, Trinidad, and University College,
Oxford, where he studied English literature.

After graduation, Naipaul stayed in England
and worked as a freelance writer with the BBC's
Caribbean Voices and with the *New Statesman,* a
literary journal. Inspired by his father, Naipaul
began to write about his childhood experiences.
Multiple publications followed, and selections of
his published reviews and essays appear in *The
Overcrowded Barracoon* (1972) and *The Return of
Eva Peron with The Killings in Trinidad* (1980).

Western critics gave positive reviews to
Naipaul's first novels, but others, especially those
from the Caribbean and developing countries, vehemently criticized the treatment of colonial people in his writings. His first three novels—*The
Mystic Masseur* (1957); *The Suffrage of Elvira*
(1958); and *Miguel Street* (1957), which Naipaul
wrote first but published last—ironically and
satirically portray the absurdities of Trinidadian
life while exploring the lives of East Indian community members.

A House for Mr. Biswas (1961), Naipaul's fourth
work, earned substantially more recognition than
his earlier novels. It focuses on Biswas, a sensitive
man loosely modeled after Naipaul's father, who
struggles with displacement, disorder, and alienation to establish his own identity. The hierarchical
relations in Biswas's house symbolize and comment on colonial relationships. Many of Naipaul's
subsequent novels also explore themes of alienation as his characters strive to integrate cultural
tensions, especially the tensions between native
and Western-colonial traditions and influences.

The same year Naipaul published *A House for
Mr. Biswas,* he received a grant from the Trinidad
government to travel in the Caribbean. In the 1960s
and early 1970s, his excursions to many countries,
including Uganda, Argentina, Iran, Pakistan,
Malaysia, and the United States, enhanced his writing. *Mr. Stone and the Knight's Companion* (1963),
which takes place in England, was Naipaul's first
novel not set in a West Indian context.

More serious place-specific cultural studies replaced the more comedic aspects of Naipaul's earlier novels. The three short stories in *In a Free State* (1971), which won the BOOKER PRIZE, take place in different countries. Naipaul uses a novella as well as travel diary excerpts to explore individual and universal freedom. The novel *Guerillas* (1975) follows an uprising in the Caribbean, and *A Bend in the River* (1979), which has been compared to Joseph CONRAD's *Heart of Darkness,* examines the future of a newly independent state in central Africa. The introspective *The Enigma of Arrival* (1979) juxtaposes autobiography and fiction to construct an almost anthropological exploration of the life of a writer of Caribbean origin living in rural England.

While some praised Naipaul's complex and sometimes scathing cultural analyses of his journeys as honest and visionary, others criticized them as pessimistic portrayals of the developing world, as seen in two of his travel books on India: *An Area of Darkness* (1964) and *India: A Wounded Civilisation* (1977). Other nonfiction works include the more widely accepted *India: A Million Mutinies Now* (1990); *The Middle Passage: Impressions of Five Societies—British, French, and Dutch—in the West Indies* (1963); and *Among the Believers: An Islamic Journey* (1989), which critically assesses Muslim fundamentalists in non-Arab countries.

The Mimic Men (1967), one of Naipaul's best novels, traces the life of Ralph Singh, a politician in early retirement, who explains his own position: "The career of the colonial politician is short and ends brutally. We lack order. Above all, we lack power, and we do not understand that we lack power." Set in the Caribbean island of Isabella and in England, the novel raises many questions about authenticity, politics, and psychology.

After the publication of *The Loss of El Dorado* (1970), which describes Trinidad's colonial history, Naipaul returned to Trinidad. Dissatisfied, he went to live in England and began to publish works that blurred fictional boundaries. He wrote, "Fiction, which had once liberated me and enlightened me, now seemed to be pushing me toward being simpler than I was." He explained this concept further in *Reading and Writing: A Personal Account* (2000): "So, as my world widened, beyond the immediate personal circumstances that bred fiction, and as my comprehension widened, the literary forms I practiced flowed together and supported one another; and I couldn't say that one form was higher than another." The multivocal *A Way in the World* (1994), for instance, is a mix of history, fiction, memoir, and documentary. Its nine thematically linked but segmented narratives address personal, historical, and sociopolitical issues.

Naipaul's distinctive incorporation of multiple genres in literary works has earned him a reputation as an innovator. Themes of alienation, mistrust, and self-deception run through many of his works, but his later works tend to embrace more than criticize. Naipaul received the Nobel Prize in literature in 2001. The Nobel Prize press release called him "a modern *philosophe,* carrying on the tradition that started originally with *Lettres persanes* and *Candide.* In a vigilant style, which has been deservedly admired, he transforms rage into precision and allows events to speak with their own inherent irony."

Other Works by V. S. Naipaul

Between Father and Son: Family Letters. New York: Vintage Books, 2001.
Half a Life. New York: Alfred A. Knopf, 2001.
"To a Young Writer." *New Yorker,* June 26–July 3, 1995: pp. 144–53.

Works about V. S. Naipaul

Feder, Lillian. *Naipaul's Truth: The Making of a Writer.* Lanham, Md.: Rowman & Littlefield, 2000.
Gorra, Michael. *After Empire: Scott, Naipaul, Rushdie.* Chicago: University of Chicago Press, 1997.
Gupta, Suman. *V. S. Naipaul.* Jackson: University Press of Mississippi, 2001.

Naughton, Bill (William John Francis Naughton) (1910–1992) *playwright, memoirist, novelist*

Bill Naughton was born in Ballyhaunis, Ireland, and raised in Bolton, Lancashire, England. His parents were Thomas Naughton, a coal miner, and Maria Fleming Naughton. Naughton received his education at the primary school St. Peter and St. Paul School. He held numerous jobs, including truck driver, weaver, coal-bagger, and bleacher. During World War II he was a civil defense driver.

Naughton is remembered for three plays that he wrote for the stage in the 1960s, all good-natured portrayals of English working-class life. *Alfie* (1963) is a comedy about a Cockney Don Juan. Although selfish and sometimes cruel as he moves from girl to girl, Alfie occasionally displays a tender side. Near the end of the play, after a woman he loves rejects him, Alfie shows a newfound maturity as he reflects: "After all, it's 'ow your 'eart 'ungers for summink as makes it beautiful. It ain't in the eyes you feel beauty—it's in the hunger of the poor bleedin' 'eart." The play was a hit in Britain, where critics praised Naughton's humor and ability to portray Alfie's inner loneliness, but it drew mixed reviews in the United States. A *Newsweek* critic wrote that the play "is simply a mildly appealing little comedy with a large structural weakness and a tendency to soften its humor in the interests of commercial viability." Michael Caine played Alfie in the movie version of the play.

Naughton's comedy *All in Good Time* (1963) depicts the wedding-night tensions and early marital difficulties of a young Lancashire couple. Despite his humorous treatment of the subject matter, Naughton is sympathetic toward the characters, who happily adjust to married life by the end of the play. His next play, *Spring and Port Wine* (1964), depicts tensions in a patriarchal northern family during a spring weekend. The central characters include the father, who learns to respect his wife, and the family's young daughter, who has a weakness for port wine. After these three successes, Naughton's later plays attracted little attention.

Later in his career, Naughton focused on writing autobiographical volumes. *On the Pig's Back* (1987) describes his childhood and World War II experience as a conscientious objector. *Saintly Billy* (1988) covers his early life from ages 10 to 13, while *Neither Use Nor Ornament* (1995) chronicles a single month when he was 14 and began his transition to manhood. In 1969 scholar John Russell Taylor described Naughton as "an older man who has graduated from manual labor to professional writing" best known for his "subtly evocative studies of working-class life in London and the North."

Other Works by Bill Naughton
A Dog Called Nelson. London: Dent, 1976.
A Roof over Your Head. London: Pilot Press, 1945.

Newby, Percy Howard (1918–1997)
novelist, short story writer
P. H. Newby was born in Crowborough, Sussex, England, to Percy Newby, a baker, and Isabel Bryant Newby. He attended St. Paul's College in Cheltenham before serving in the British army's medical corps during World War II. He taught English literature at Fouad I University in Cairo and had a three-decade career working as a controller and managing director for the BBC (British Broadcasting Corporation).

Newby's first novel, *A Journey to the Interior* (1945), is set in a Near Eastern desert sultanate. It describes an English scholar, Robert Winter, who, after his wife's death, embarks on a spiritual quest for self-discovery in the desert. The novel provides an example of Newby's noted skill at character descriptions when Winter observes his neighbor's wife: "He saw round, red cheeks, well fed and shiny, moist lips and dancing eyes. They were the eyes of a girl who has just come in from playing hockey in the frost."

In *A Season in England* (1951) Newby returns to his recurring theme of personal growth. In this novel, Tom Passmore, an English academic, travels from Egypt to England to tell the parents of a colleague, Guy Nash, that their son has died. Tom overcomes his resentment of their smugness and grows to truly love Guy's parents, who themselves develop a greater understanding for their late rebellious son. Critic Harold Watts writes that the book "offers us benefits over and above the pleasures that are generally available in Newby: sharp phrasing, economy in selection and detail, penetration as he renders one emotional phase and then another."

Picnic at Sakkara (1955) describes the domestic and cultural complications faced by an English professor, Edgar Perry, teaching at Cairo University. As with many of his works, Newby uses comedy to cover serious subjects. One example of this comes with Perry's wife's announcement that she is leaving him for another man: "When Perry asked her why she had bothered to come all the way to Egypt, at his expense, to give him news of this kind she said she liked him and could not bear to think of him suffering."

Newby's critically acclaimed novel *Something to Answer For* (1968), which received the first BOOKER PRIZE, is about an Englishman who travels to Egypt during the turbulent Suez Canal crisis. After he is robbed in Port Said, he begins to question who he is and what he believes in, as well as the foreign policy of his government. When assessing Newby's body of work, the critic Stanley Poss wrote that his novels contain "an original and resourceful imagination pursuing its vision in deceptively traditional forms, chiefly that of the comedy of manners."

Other Work by P. H. Newby
Feelings Have Changed. London: Faber & Faber, 1981.

A Work about P. H. Newby
Bufkin, E. C. *P. H. Newby.* Boston: Twayne, 1975.

New Criticism
New Criticism is a collection of similar ideas about the nature of literature that arose after World War I and was given a name with the appearance of John Crowe Ransom's book *The New Criticism* (1941). It was, most of all, a rejection of the previous ways of looking at literature. The New Critics formulated tenets to explain how to interpret literature. According to what Ransom called the "heresy of paraphrase," a poem is not reducible to a single, stable meaning. Instead, New Critics celebrated the ironies and ambiguities of lyric poetry. The "intentional fallacy" stated that the intentions of the author are ultimately irrecoverable and irrelevant. Equally irrelevant were the social, historical, cultural, political, or geographical circumstances under which the poem was brought into being. According to the "affective fallacy," the emotional response of the reader was also to be set aside. In place of all these previous elements was substituted "close reading": a careful attention to the language of a work of literature, treating each work as a self-contained, internally consistent entity.

New Criticism was strongly influenced by the careful attention to poetic form in the critical works of T. S. ELIOT. It gained impetus with the publication in 1924 of I. A. Richards's *The Principles of Literary Criticism.* Following and commenting on this work was the highly influential *Seven Types of Ambiguity* by William Empson in 1930. In the United States leaders of the movement were, in addition to Ransom, Allen Tate, Robert Penn Warren, Cleanth Brooks, and R. P. Blackmur, a group of southern critics who originally met at Vanderbilt University. Brooks and Warren popularized the New Critical approach with their influential anthologies, *Understanding Poetry* (1938) and *Understanding Fiction* (1943), which were widely adopted in American high schools and colleges. Ultimately, the New Critical emphasis on form—looking at poetic devices, structure, patterns of imagery, figures of speech, and the like—has been replaced by new approaches that return to an interest in the content and context of literary works, such as feminism, cultural studies, and psychoanalytic criticism.

Works about New Criticism
Winchell, Mark Royden. *Cleanth Brooks and the Rise of Modern Criticism.* Charlottesville: University of Virginia Press, 1996.
Jones, James T. *Wayward Skeptic: The Theories of R. P. Blackmur.* Urbana: University of Illinois Press, 1986.

Ni Dhomhnaill, Nuala (1952–) *poet*

Born in Lancashire, England, to Irish physicians, Nuala Ni Dhomhnaill was sent to live with relatives in the Kerry Gaeltacht (an Irish-speaking region of Ireland) at the age of five. She studied both English and Irish at University College, Cork, and became one of the young poets associated with the radical periodical *Innti* and the movement to reclaim the Irish language. She then lived in the Netherlands and taught English in Turkey before returning to Ireland with her husband and four children. Ni Dhomhnaill was the artist-in-residence for Cork University in 1991–92, and the recipient of an honorary degree from Dublin City University in 1995.

While rooted in the Gaelic tradition, Ni Dhomhnaill's Irish-language poetry combines mythology and folklore with modern concerns and issues, including those of political and social matters. Her first collection, *An Dealg Droighin* (1981), contains a series of poems about the Munster fertility goddess. Ni Dhomhnaill's commitment to the Irish Gaeltacht and to reshaping Irish legend and tradition in a feminist manner has made her followers eager to make her work better known. She has received numerous prizes, including the American Ireland Fund Literary Award.

Ni Dhomhnaill's work has been translated into English and other languages by many prominent Irish writers, including Nobel Prize–winning poet Seamus HEANEY. She is one of the most prominent contemporary Irish-language poets.

Other Works by Nuala Ni Dhomhnaill

The Astrakhan Cloak. Winston-Salem. N.C.: Wake Forest University Press, 1992.

Pharoah's Daughter. Winston-Salem. N.C.: Wake Forest University Press, 1990.

Selected Poems: Rogha Danta. Dublin: Raven Arts Press, 1988.

Norris, Leslie (1921–) *poet, short story writer*

Leslie Norris was born to George William and Janie Norris in Merthyr Tydfil, Glamorganshire, a poor area of Wales, where his father supported the family by working as a milkman and a farmer. Although his education was cut short due to financial concerns, Norris described his home as a place where "reading was going on all the time." Norris escaped the sometimes dangerous and rough realities of his youth by exploring the beautiful countryside that surrounded his small city. He attended college in England and trained to be a teacher. To support his writing, Norris worked as a teacher in schools throughout England. He was employed as a lecturer at several universities in the United States and England.

Norris's writings tell the story of man's attempts to find his place in an often cruel world, a journey that requires both perseverance and understanding. His first collection of poetry, a small volume entitled *Tongue of Beauty* (1942), drew upon his early experiences growing up in Wales. Deeply influenced by Welsh writer Dylan THOMAS, Norris began to find his own voice as a poet in subsequent works that have been published individually in magazines and in collections and have been read on the radio. He started to become widely known as a poet in the late 1960s and recently has been compared to the Welsh poet Vernon WATKINS.

Many critics believe that Norris's finest poems are in *Finding Gold* (1967). After his success with this collection, *Atlantic Monthly* began publishing his poetry regularly. In 1970 Norris won the Alice Hunt Bartlett Prize for his collection entitled *Ransoms*. In poems such as "Water" and "Stones" he uses images of everyday life to convey his interest in the timeless world that he associates with his time growing up in Wales. Poet and critic Ted Walker claims Norris's genius as a poet rests in his "humanity, generosity, wisdom, a sure ear, a true voice and craftsmanship."

Norris's fame as a poet, however, has in recent years been overshadowed by his success as a short story writer. He has published stories in *The New Yorker* and *Atlantic Monthly* and in the collection *Sliding and Other Stories* (1976). "Waxwings" won him the Katherine Mansfield Triennial Award in

1981. Many of these stories use first-person narrative to look at youth from the vantage point of adulthood. "A Flight of Geese" describes the world of an anonymous schoolboy and his relationship with his uncle, the main character of the story, who refuses to spend his life in "senseless toil." According to the narrator, "he never did."

Equally comfortable writing both prose and poetry, Norris describes himself as a writer who enjoys "the art of telling the story." He continues to elicit praise for his ability to clearly convey his ideas through his writing. *The Los Angeles Times Book Review* described Norris's poetry as reflecting "extraordinarily refreshing clarity whose magic lies not in symbolist indirection, nor solely in its lovely musicality, but . . . in the absolute realism of its vision."

A Work about Leslie Norris

England, Eugene, and Peter Makuck, eds. *An Open World: Essays on Leslie Norris.* Columbia, S.C.: Camden House, 1994.

Noyes, Alfred (1880–1958) *poet*

Alfred Noyes was born in Wolverhampton, England, to Alfred and Amelia Adams Rawley Noyes. His father was a teacher in Wales, where Noyes drew his early inspiration from the coast and mountains. He was educated at Exeter College, Oxford, but did not finish his degree, concentrating instead on the publication of his first volume of poems, *The Loom of Years* (1902). In 1907 he married an American, Garnett Daniels, and he subsequently spent many years living in the United States.

Noyes was extremely prolific, and by the age of 30 he was the most commercially popular and successful poet of his era. He had an early success with *Drake: An English Epic* (1906–08), a two-volume saga in blank verse about the 16th-century naval hero and explorer Sir Francis Drake. The work most often remembered today is "The Highwayman," which appeared in *Forty Singing Seamen and Other Poems* (1907). It tells of an innkeeper's daughter who gives up her life in order to save her lover, who is wanted by the law. Held hostage by the police, with a gun to her chest, she fires the gun to warn him away. "The Highwayman" is one of Noyes's most quoted pieces, a rhyming, rhythmic ballad, filled with alliteration and metaphor:

> The wind was a torrent of darkness among
>   the gusty trees,
> The moon was a ghostly galleon tossed
>   upon cloudy seas,
> The road was a ribbon of moonlight, over
>   the purple moor,
> And the highwayman came riding—
> Riding—riding—
> The highwayman came riding, up to the old
>   inn-door.

The poem is both atypical in its violence and solemnity and typical in its romanticism: "Bowed with her head o'er the musket drenched with her own red blood!"

Noyes's most ambitious work is the trilogy *The Torch-Bearers*, which consists of *Watchers of the Sky* (1922), *The Book of Earth* (1925), and *The Last Voyage* (1930). In this trilogy he explores the development of scientific discoveries and their connections to Christianity. After the death of his wife in 1926, Noyes converted to Catholicism, and this event is reflected in *The Last Voyage*.

Writing in 1918, William Lyon Phelps referred to Noyes as "one of the most melodious of modern writers, with a witchery in words that at its best is irresistible. . . ." Though Noyes continued to write until his death, this romantic traditionalist, not surprisingly, was out of step with the modernist movement of the 20th century, which he detested for its "haphazardness and comparative literary disrespect," and for which he was rebuked by critics for "his resistance to change and literary evolution."

Other Works by Alfred Noyes

Collected Poems in One Volume. Port Washington, N.Y.: McCutcheon, 1966.

A Letter to Lucian and Other Poems. London: John Murray, 1956.

A Work about Alfred Noyes

Jerrold, Walter. *Alfred Noyes.* Darby, Pa.: Arden Library, 1970.

O'Brien, Edna (1932–) *novelist, short story writer*

Edna O'Brien's fiction repeatedly presents heroines who are trapped in smothering marriages, who struggle to fulfill their sexual drives, and who possess an unappeased desire for love. A standard cast of characters appears in most of her works, including an abusive, alcoholic father, ineffective mother, cruel husband, isolated wife, and children who repeat their parents' mistakes. O'Brien depicts their stories in a lyrical, detailed, confessional narrative voice that reveals their sensibilities.

O'Brien's tone is often confessional because her novels reflect her own experiences. In numerous interviews, she has acknowledged that her stories are fantasies derived from her life. Born in Taumgraney, County Clare, Ireland she has claimed that her father was irresponsible and her mother was overly submissive. As a child, she attended the National School in Scariff. In 1944 she entered the Convent of Mercy at Loughrea, but she left two years later with the desire to be a movie star.

At age 14, O'Brien moved to Dublin, where she worked in a pharmacy. She also discovered the fiction of James JOYCE, whose novels inspired her to begin writing. In 1948 she submitted her first stories to the *Irish Press*. Four years later she married the writer Ernest Gabler. The couple had two sons,

but their union eventually failed, and the marriage was annulled in 1964. Prior to the annulment, O'Brien and her two sons moved to London.

O'Brien's first novel, *The Country Girls,* was published in 1960, and although she completed it in three weeks, many critics still consider it her best novel. The book is the first in a trilogy that includes *The Lonely Girls* (1962) and *Girls in their Married Bliss* (1964). Two primary characters—the brash, partially manic Baba and the quiet, naive Kate—dominate the trilogy. In *The Country Girls* Kate flees her family because her father is a violent alcoholic, and her mother, after abandoning the family, dies in an accident. She and Baba move to Dublin, where they live in a boardinghouse. They soon adopt a lifestyle filled with parties and affaires, but these activities are interrupted when Baba contracts tuberculosis and Kate's lover, Mr. Gentleman, returns to his wife.

The first novel establishes the pattern for the trilogy and much of O'Brien's fiction. Kate and Baba experience repeated disappointments in love but are trapped in what the critic Patricia Boyle Haberstroh describes as "a fictional world of women destroyed by their dependence on men." The trilogy conveys a tragic sense of time wasted in pursuit of the ideal relationship. But it balances this loss with humorous jabs at the two heroines. Baba is especially comical because she creates wild stories to extricate herself from uncomfortable situations.

After the success of *The Country Girls*, O'Brien established herself permanently in London to pursue a literary career. In 1970 her novel *A Pagan Place* won the Yorkshire Post Book Award. Set in rural Ireland, the novel depicts a village whose pagan traditions clash with its Catholic present. The protagonist is a young woman whose older sister experiences an illegitimate pregnancy. Disturbed by her sister's pregnancy and her own sexuality, she has a brief affair with the village priest. The novel concludes with the woman's rejection by her family. *A Pagan Place* lacks the humor of O'Brien's earlier novels. Instead, by portraying the village's repressed natural sexual desires, she suggests that the emotional satisfaction that her previous characters sought is unattainable.

In 1978 O'Brien published a short story collection entitled *Mrs. Reinhardt and Other Stories*. These stories are often praised as her best work, because they contain a wide range of fully developed characters. For the first time, O'Brien offers men who are not merely one-dimensional foils for the frustrations of her heroines. She also reintroduces the humor that had characterized her earlier novels and creates a number of heroines who are ultimately content with their lives. The stories contained in *Mrs. Reinhardt* and in O'Brien's next collection, *Returning* (1982), refined her ability to present realistic situations, and she has successfully incorporated this realism in her later fiction. Describing this maturity in her fiction, the critic Michael Gillespie claims that "a both/and incorporating impulse rather than an either/or exclusivity stands as the feature distinguishing O'Brien's humor."

Other Works by Edna O'Brien

House of Splendid Isolation. New York: Farrar, Straus & Giroux, 1994.
Johnny I Hardly Knew You. Garden City, N.Y.: Doubleday, 1978.
Night. New York: Knopf, 1973.
Wild Decembers. Boston: Houghton Mifflin, 2000.

Works about Edna O'Brien

Eckley, Grace. *Edna O'Brien.* Lewisburg, Pa.: Bucknell University Press, 1974.
O'Connor, Theresa, ed. *The Comic Tradition in Irish Women Writers.* Gainesville: University Press of Florida, 1996.

O'Brien, Flann (Brian O'Nolan, Myles Na Gopaleen, George Knowall, John James Doe) (1911–1966) *novelist, columnist, playwright*

Flann O'Brien was born Brian O'Nolan, but as a novelist he used the name O'Brien. For 25 years as a columnist for the *Irish Times* he wrote as Myles Na Gopaleen, while for the *Nationalist* and *Leinster Times* he was George Knowall and for the *Southern Star* John James Doe. These various pseudonyms masked a careful craftsman and a deeply private man.

O'Brien was born in Strabane, County Tyrone, Ireland, into a middle-class household where only Gaelic was spoken by his parents, Michael and Agnes O'Nolan. Initially educated at home, he eventually attended University College, Dublin. While there, he wrote comedic pieces for the student newspaper, *Comhthrom Feinne*, and in 1934 helped launch a humor magazine called *Blather*. In 1935 he became an Irish civil servant, which he remained for 18 years.

At Swim-Two-Birds, a novel begun in college, was published in 1939. It was highly praised by novelist Graham GREENE in a reader's report to the publisher, Longman. "We have had books inside books before," wrote Greene, saying that O'Brien "takes it a long way further . . . here we have a) a book about a man called Trellis who is b) writing a book about certain characters who c) are turning the tables on Trellis by writing about him." He praised the book's "humorous vigor" and compared it to Laurence Sterne's *Tristram Shandy* and James JOYCE's *Ulysses*. In fact, Joyce had read the book and told the writer Niall Sheridan, "That's a real writer, with the true comic spirit. A really funny book." As one character notes, "Trellis's dominion over his characters, I explained, is impaired by his addiction to sleep. There is a moral in that."

However, the book sold poorly, and in 1940, during an air raid in London, the remaining copies were destroyed. With the exception of a short book in Gaelic, called *An Beal Bocht* (The Poor Mouth, 1941) a satiric look at a poverty-stricken Irishman in the midst of the beauty of western Ireland, O'Brien was not to publish another novel for two decades.

During this period he poured his creative energies into his columns for the *Irish Times*. O'Brien took his pseudonym Myles Na Gopaleen, which in Gaelic means Myles of the Little Ponies, from a 19th-century novel by Gerald Griffin called *The Collegians*. His column attacked all manner of hypocrisy and pomposity in Irish life, ranging from an exaggerated sense of patriotism to an equally exaggerated pride in handball abilities. He kept a list of printed and overheard absurdities in his Catechism of Clichés. He referred to the English language as "a delusion and a snare." In 1943 he wrote a play for the Abbey Theatre called *Faustus Kelly*, about a politician who sells his soul for a seat in the Irish parliament.

O'Brien returned to novel writing in 1961 with *The Hard Life*, a dark comedy about a Dublin family falling apart. He followed this with *The Dalkey Archive* (1964), in which James Joyce appears as one of the characters. It is the story of how two Irishmen prevent a lunatic, time-traveling philosopher from destroying the world.

A final novel, *The Third Policeman*, was published posthumously in 1967. Considered his best work, along with *At Swim-Two-Birds*, it tells of a nameless murdered man who thinks he is trying to find his way back home, but who, unbeknownst to himself, is dead and lost in hell. He runs into a series of demented policemen who waylay him with theories about how people may be absorbing the atoms of their bicycles to the point where they are becoming half human and half bicycle. Fatigued and confused by these confrontations, the narrator falls into a bed in the police station and passes out. He says, "Compared with this sleep, death is a restive thing, peace is a clamour, and darkness a burst of light." Novelist John Updike wrote of O'Brien in *The New Yorker* that "there is a brilliant ease in his prose, a poignant grace glimmering off of every page. . . . O'Brien has the gift of the perfect sentence . . . of tuning plain language to a perfect pitch. Humor . . . remained his muse, and writing became, under his magical pen, a sort of fooling away."

Other Work by Flann O'Brien

The Best of Myles. Edited by Kevin O'Nolan. 1975. Reprint, Normal, Ill.: Dalkey Archive Press, 1999.

Works about Flann O'Brien

Asbee, Sue. *Flann O'Brien.* Boston: Twayne, 1991.
Costello, Peter, and Peter Van De Kamp. *Flann O'Brien: An Illustrated Biography.* London: Grafton Books, 1989.
Updike, John. "Flann O'Brien." In *Hugging the Shore: Essays and Criticism.* New York: Alfred A. Knopf, 1983.

O'Casey, Sean (1880–1946) *playwright*

Sean O'Casey was born John Casey to Michael Casey, a clerk, and Susan Archer Casey in Dublin, Ireland. His family was working class and constantly struggled financially, which became even more difficult after his father died when O'Casey was six. He educated himself by reading Shakespeare and the British classics and began working at the age of 14; he would eventually hold positions as an ironmonger, a clerk, and a railway worker. In his 20s O'Casey became politically active as a member of the Gaelic League, a group of Irish intellectuals; a member of the Irish Republican Brotherhood, a group fighting for Irish independence; and a member of the Irish labor movement, to which he was so attached that he became a socialist.

In his 30s, however, O'Casey turned all of his attention toward drama and established a reputation as a serious playwright with the production of *The Shadow of a Gunman* in 1923. The central characters of the play—Seumas Shields, a peddler, and

Donal Davoren, a struggling poet—are typical of all of O'Casey's characters in that they are both lower-class figures generally down on their luck. As the play develops, Shields and Davoren are mistaken for a pair of fugitive gunmen and are taken by surprise when British soldiers besiege their apartment in an attempt to arrest them. Although they survive the raid, the play displays O'Casey's concern for innocent civilians who find themselves, by no fault of their own, involved in the violence of the Irish revolution.

O'Casey's next successful production was *Juno and the Paycock* (1924), which also explores the effects of the war on innocent civilians and features two of the most interesting characters in all of his work: Mrs. Juno Boyle and her husband, Captain Jack, a shiftless man known as the "paycock." The main action of the play concerns Mrs. Boyle's ultimately futile efforts at holding together her family, which consists of not only her lazy husband but also an equally useless son, Johnny, and an unwed pregnant daughter, Mary. After the family finally falls apart and Mrs. Boyle has gone to live in an apartment with her daughter, she refuses to become pessimistic; near the end of the play she even attempts to buoy Mary's faith in God after the girl denounces His existence: "Mary, Mary, you musn't say them things. We'll want all the help we can get from God an' His Blessed Mother now! These things have nothin' to do with the Will o' God. Ah, what can God go agen the stupidity o' men!" The scholar James Scrimgeour has attributed much of the play's success to the appeal of Mrs. Boyle's character, whom he describes as "a saint who has won salvation through good deeds as well as through faith, a saint with dirty hands."

The Plough and the Stars (1926), deeply satiric and critical of war, focuses on another female figure, the newly married and pregnant Nora Clitheroe, who, despite her desperate pleas, is abandoned by her husband when he joins the Irish Republican Army. As the play progresses, the tenements where Nora lives descend into rioting, Jack dies in battle, and Nora loses her child. In its first presentations, audiences recoiled from *The Plough and the Stars* because it did not depict Irish fighters as heroes but focused instead on the horrible impact of war on noncombatants. One of the most disgusted of the playgoers was a Mrs. Sheehy-Skeffington, who organized a protest at one of the performances and remarked that because of its negative depiction of the war, the *The Plough and the Stars* represented "not art, but morbid perversity" and made "a mockery and a byword of a revolutionary movement" crucial to the Irish state.

O'Casey broke new ground for Irish theater by helping change it from an institution focused on a historical, "jolly old Ireland" to a more socially conscious entity that was not afraid to confront even the ugliest aspects of lower-class Irish life. According to the Irish poet Seamus HEANEY, O'Casey's work is memorable because it captures "the swim of Dublin culture and politics during an era of revolutionary change," and because it "urbanized and demythologized" Irish theater with characters who "came in from the pub round the corner, whiskey on their breath, rags on their back and realism written all over them."

Other Works by Sean O'Casey

Niall: A Lament. New York: Calder, 1991.
Sean O'Casey: Plays. 2 vols. London: Faber & Faber, 1998.

Works about Sean O'Casey

Murray, Christopher. *A Faber Critical Guide: Sean O'Casey.* New York: Faber & Faber, 2000.
O'Casey, Eileen. *Cheerio, Titan: The Friendship between George Bernard Shaw and Sean O'Casey.* New York: Scribner, 1989.

O'Connor, Frank (Michael John O'Donovan) (1903–1966) *short story writer*

Frank O'Connor was born Michael John O'Donovan in Cork, Ireland, to Michael O'Donovan, a laborer, and Mary O'Donovan, a maid. His father was an alcoholic who abused his mother throughout his childhood. Because the family was poor,

O'Connor received hardly any education. Later in life, the author remarked, "I had to content myself with a make-believe education, and the curious thing is that it was the make-believe that succeeded." Despite his lack of formal education, O'-Connor had a keen mind and at the age of 12 was already writing poetry, autobiographies, and essays.

O'Connor fought in the Irish Republican Army during the Irish Civil War, but when the war ended, he met the Irish dramatist Lennox ROBINSON, who secured him a job as a librarian that allowed him time to hone his literary skills and work his way into literary circles. In the following years, he became friends with the influential editor George RUSSELL and the writers Sean O'CASEY and Sean O'FAOLAIN. From 1935 to 1939 he also codirected Dublin's Abbey Theatre Company with W. B. YEATS.

All of O'Connor's short stories are set in Ireland and attempt to accurately capture the voice and spirit of Irish people. *Guests of the Nation* (1931) is his first collection of these stories. In this volume, the author draws heavily on his experiences in the civil war, especially in the title piece, the story of a group of young Irish soldiers holding two British hostages. Captives and captors become friends, but in a heart-wrenching moment, the Irish soldiers are forced to kill the hostages. According to the scholar Michael Steinman, O'Connor described the story as "a small group of characters passing through a transfiguring experience with lasting emotional repercussions." At the end of the story, the narrator remarks, "With me it was as if the patch of bog where the Englishmen were was a million miles away . . . and I was somehow very small and very lost and lonely like a child astray in the snow. And anything that happened to me afterwards, I never felt the same about again."

Some of O'Connor's most critically acclaimed short stories appear in *Traveller's Samples: Stories and Tales* (1951). The stories in this collection are drawn from O'Connor's childhood and present, in Steinman's words, "a boy's-eye view of the universe in which the boy and his affectionate but often puzzled mother are allied against an ominous world most often personified by an unsympathetic father." In one of these stories, "The Drunkard," O'-Connor writes about a boy who drinks his father's liquor while his parents are out of the house. He becomes drunk and ill and embarrasses his father, who later returns uncharacteristically sober.

O'Connor primarily wrote short stories, and never fit into a well-defined literary movement. Despite this, his work accurately portrays the Irish countryside and the lives and voices of Irish people. In the words of his biographer, O'Connor "saw life through keyholes and windows, catching glimpses of the whole in the parts, and he tried to seize it as quickly as possible. He wrote as he lived, impatient for the next adventure, the next cause, impatient for the next flash of clarity, and always on the prowl for a story to light up the darkness."

Other Works by Frank O'Connor

The Collar: Stories of Irish Priests. Belfast, Northern Ireland: Blackstaff, 1993.

A Frank O'Connor Reader. Edited by Michael Steinman. Syracuse, N.Y.: Syracuse University Press, 1994.

Works about Frank O'Connor

Evans, Robert C., and Richard Harp. *Frank O'Connor: New Perspectives.* West Cornwall, Conn.: Locust Hill, 1998.

McKeon, Jim. *Frank O'Connor: A Life.* London: Mainstream, 1998.

O'Donovan, Michael John

See O'CONNOR, FRANK.

O'Faolain, Julia (1932–) *novelist, short story writer*

Julia O'Faolain was born in London, the daughter of two writers, Sean O'FAOLAIN and Eileen Gould, to whom she is often compared. She received both a bachelor's and a master's degree in the arts from University College, Dublin. Graduate studies in Italy and France influenced her writing and distinguish her from other Irish writers who focus mainly on Ireland and Irish culture. O'Faolain's writing explores cultural attitudes, male-female relationships, and sexuality, especially in the context of Catholicism and politics. Her characters are often women who are trying to establish their identities.

O'Faolain's first short story collection, *We Might See Sights! and Other Stories* (1968), delves into cultural attitudes in relation to young females discovering their sexuality in both Italy and Ireland. Her second collection, *Man in the Cellar* (1974), takes these themes one step further to examine the power struggles between men and women. The main character in the title story chains her husband in the cellar and tries to point out how their roles are not equal.

O'Faolain also wrote several novels about sexuality in a variety of cultural and historical contexts. *Women in the Wall* (1975) embellishes history with fiction to tell the story of Queen Radegund, who founded the monastery of the Holy Cross in the sixth century as a result of her desire to escape both her husband (she believes that "sexual love is linked with death") and the political problems of medieval society. Critic Doris Grumbach admired the novel's "subtle and entirely successful recreation by means of the spirit as well as the events of Gallic life 13 centuries ago."

No Country for Young Men (1980), a finalist for the BOOKER PRIZE, follows three generations of a politically involved Irish family in the context of their relationship with a visiting American. The novel explores how tradition, politics, and patriotism affect the role of women in Ireland. Judith, one of the characters in *No Country for Young Men*, laments, "The men in this country would never let women have a say." Critic Sally Beauman praised O'Faolain's "well planned, intelligent, concise" style, finding her writing "more pointed than that of [her father] with a cold female eye for the egocentricities of masculine behavior."

Other Works by Julia O'Faolain

The Irish Signorina. London: Viking, 1984.
The Judas Cloth. London: Sinclair-Stevenson, 1992.

O'Faolain, Sean (1900–1991) *novelist, short story writer, biographer, editor, literary critic, travel writer*

Born John Whelan in County Cork, Ireland, Sean O'Faolain was the son of Denis Whelan, an officer in the Royal Irish Constabulary, and Bridget Whelan. He had a strict religious upbringing with emphasis on prayer and study. In his autobiography, *Vive Moi* (1964), he wrote that he came from the "lowest possible social level," but discovered, while visiting country relatives in County Limerick, that life could be more open and free.

Until the 1916 uprising in Ireland, O'Faolain had shared his father's politics, which were pro-British and antirebel. But the executions that followed in the wake of the rebellion changed his feelings completely. He became fluent in Gaelic and adopted the Gaelic version of his name. While attending University College, Cork, he joined the Irish Volunteers, an early precursor to the Irish Republican Army (IRA).

During the Civil War of 1922–23 O'Faolain spent several months in hiding and on the run. He was placed in charge of publicity for the republican movement, but he became disillusioned with republicanism, feeling that the new Ireland, dominated by the bourgeoisie and the Roman Catholic Church, was as stultifying as British rule.

After the war O'Faolain returned to school and won a Commonwealth Fellowship to Harvard University in 1926. It was there that he began to write. He was teaching in a school in England when his first book, *Midsummer Night Madness* (1932), a collection of short stories about Irish rural life, was published to great acclaim. With the money he made from the book's success, he and his wife, children's writer Eileen O'Faolain, moved back to Ireland, only to find that his book had been banned there.

O'Faolain's first novel, *A Nest of Simple Folk* (1934), is a largely autobiographical tale that shows the effects of his political education on his relationship with his family. He continued to explore the effects of the Irish Rebellion on the lives of the people who lived through it in his next two novels, *Bird*

Alone (1936) and *Come Back to Erin* (1940). In all three books the lead characters find great difficulty in living useful lives in the "new Ireland." Both his novels and his short stories show a deep sympathy with those who fight against the oppressive elements of Irish political and religious life of that time.

In 1940 O'Faolain started a magazine called *The Bell*. It published many of Ireland's leading writers, including Patrick KAVANAGH, Flann O'BRIEN, and Frank O'CONNOR. O'Faolain was the first to publish Brendan BEHAN, while Behan was still in prison for participating in IRA activities.

O'Faolain was also a biographer who wrote accounts of Irish patriots in *Wolf Tone* (1937) and *Daniel O'Connell: King of the Beggars* (1938). Throughout both books, the author reveals ambivalence about Ireland, which became more pronounced in his negative biography of Ireland's first president, *Eamon de Valera* (1939).

O'Faolain ceased editing *The Bell* in 1946. Afterward he concentrated on short stories and literary criticism. He also traveled in Italy and the United States, and wrote two travel books about Italy. His later work became less and less political. Like many participants of the civil war, O'Faolain did not so much turn his back on his earlier ideals as simply let them fade. The critic Pierce Butler remarks on the relationship of O'Faolain's stories to Ireland's oral tradition of story-telling: "In his later work, one hears quite clearly the voice of the story teller drawing the reader into an intimate relationship. It is an urbane and knowing voice, to be sure, but it observes conventions analogous to the oral practitioner's confidential manner and verbal flourishes. Above all, O'Faolain wants to tell a good story—and to do so in an intimate and engaging manner."

Other Work by Sean O'Faolain

The Collected Stories of Sean O'Faolain. Boston: Little, Brown, 1983.

Works about Sean O'Faolain

Arndt, Eva Marie. *A Critical Study of Sean O'Faolain's Life and Work.* Lewiston, N.Y.: Edwin Mellen Press, 2001.

Bonaccorso, Richard. *Sean O'Faolain's Irish Vision.* Albany: State University of New York Press, 1987.

Butler, Pierce. *Sean O'Faolain: A Study of the Short Fiction.* Boston: Twayne, 1993.

O'Flaherty, Liam (1896–1984) *novelist, short story writer*

Liam O'Flaherty was born in the village of Gort na gCapall, Inishmore, on the Irish Aran Islands to Michael Flaherty, a farmer, and Margaret Ganly Flaherty. The island's raw weather, rough farming, and geographical isolation would indelibly shape his future writing. Because of his family's poverty, O'Flaherty entered Dublin seminary to gain an education, but he left in 1914 to enroll briefly at University College. The next nine years were tempestuous. He joined the Irish Republican rebels but then abruptly enlisted in the British army. He was wounded in World War I and, after recovering, traveled extensively and briefly considered joining the Communist Party.

In 1922 O'Flaherty moved to London and started writing, dividing his career between novels and short stories. His early novels explore the lonely, often sordid lives of the working class. But his finest novel, *Famine* (1937), is a fictional portrayal of the Great Potato Famine. O'Flaherty uses the Kilmartin family to depict the decay of rural Irish customs in the 19th century. Instead of resisting these changes, the Kilmartins passively accept them. The novel was praised for its realistic style, authentic dialogue, and objective viewpoint.

O'Flaherty's short stories deal primarily with life on the Aran Islands and fall into three general categories. Initially, he wrote lyrical and detailed sketches of local animals in *Spring Sowing* (1924). In subsequent story collections he created fables of human and animal interaction that stress elemental principles, such as love defeating hatred and the concern for the common good. His later stories examine the Aran Islands inhabitants, portraying the demanding lives of the farmers and fishers and following the timeless progression of youth to death and the relationship of people to the earth.

After the 1950s, O'Flaherty largely abandoned writing and lived on the royalties of his works. Many critics contend that he is second only to James JOYCE as Ireland's greatest short story writer. The critic James Cahalan credits his stories' dualism for their success, noting that O'Flaherty portrays "life and death every day among the animals and people of the island and the ocean in which they are perched."

Other Work by Liam O'Flaherty
The Collected Stories. Dublin: Wolfhound Press, 1999.

A Work about Liam O'Flaherty
Cahalan, James M. *Liam O'Flaherty: A Study the Short Fiction.* Boston: Twayne, 1991.

Okri, Ben (1959–   ) *novelist, poet, essayist*

Ben Okri was born in Minna, Nigeria, to Grace and Silver Oghekeneshineeke Loloje Okri. He spent part of his early childhood in England, where his father had earned a law degree. Okri eventually settled in England, earning a B.A. in comparative literature from Essex University, writing, working for the BBC (British Broadcasting Corporation), and editing several periodicals. From the beginning of his career he has garnered international acclaim for his novels, poetry, and essays, which are almost exclusively about the corruption and civil war that rocked Nigeria after the end of British colonial rule.

While he gained critical attention for his first novel, *Flowers and Shadows* (1980), which describes the horrors of the Nigerian civil war, Okri's most successful novels make up what the author himself regards as *The Famished Road* trilogy. Set in Nigeria and beginning with the BOOKER PRIZE-winning *The Famished Road* (1991), all of the books are works of magical realism, containing elements of the fantastic or supernatural from traditional Nigerian myths. The protagonist of the series, for instance, is Azaro, an *abiku,* a mythic "spirit-child," who is equally in touch with the physical and spirit worlds and who is born only to die and be reborn in an endless cycle. He becomes attached to the physical world, however, and bitterly resists his cyclical fate.

Songs of Enchantment (1993) continues the story begun in *The Famished Road.* At the end of the first paragraph, in a lyrical style indicative of his work, Okri writes, "[T]his is the song of a circling spirit. This is a story for all of us who never see the seven mountains of our secret destiny, who never see that beyond the chaos there can always be new sunlight." In this novel Azaro is capable of entering other characters' dreams and is thus able to explore a range of intricate problems that have developed between his mother and father.

The series concludes with *Infinite Riches* (1998), which works on two different levels. On the personal level, Azaro's father commits murder, while on the public, white imperialism in Nigeria is about to end. A cautious sense of hope runs throughout the novel. Okri writes the final chapter in verse, capturing the sense of change and uncertainty in the lines: "Old ways are dying. / . . . We do not know the things to come."

As the end of *Infinite Riches* suggests, Okri has also written poetry. *An African Elegy* (1992) is at times harsh and extremely political, as the poet depicts the chaos and barbarism of the Nigerian civil war. Okri vividly captures this turmoil in "Darkening City: Lagos, 83," in which Nigeria's capital is shown as a place where the innocent are executed along with the guilty, where mere survival is the highest goal of the people, and where "politicians disgorge our lives / in vomitoriums of power." In his latest collection, *Mental Flight* (1999), Okri has tempered the roughness of his verse, but remains very concerned with social issues. In the sixth section of the chapter, "Time to Be Real," he writes, "Everyone loves a Spring cleaning. Let's have a humanity cleaning," and goes on to wish that the world could be cleaned of racism, genocide, and hatred in general.

In 1997 Okri published a collection of essays, *A Way of Being Free,* that articulate his views on art and the potential of literature as a tool for social change. He also includes three essays as tributes to authors he holds in the highest esteem: "The Human Race is Not Yet Free" is dedicated to the novelist Salman RUSHDIE; "Fables are Made of This" is for the Nigerian writer Ken Saro-Wiwa; and "Redreaming the World" honors of the renowned Nigerian author Chinua Achebe.

Okri established a solid literary reputation with *The Famished Road,* and his work appeals to an audience both within and outside of Africa. According to the scholar Ato Quayson, Okri is "a major new voice in African and world literature . . . in the same league with the most innovative African writers, and . . . such cosmopolitan postcolonial writers as Gabriel García Márquez and Salman Rushdie."

Other Works by Ben Okri

Astonishing the Gods. London: Phoenix, 1995.
Birds of Heaven. London: Phoenix, 1996.

A Work about Ben Okri

Quayson, Ato. *Strategic Transformations in Nigerian Writing: Orality and History in the Work of Rev. Samuel Johnson, Amos Tutuola, Wole Soyinka, and Ben Okri.* Bloomington: University of Indiana Press, 1997.

Ondaatje, Michael (1943–) *poet, novelist*

Born in Colombo, Ceylon (now Sri Lanka), of Dutch, English, Sinhalese, and Tamil descent, Philip Michael Ondaatje is the youngest child of Mervyn Ondaatje, a tea and rubber plantation superintendent, and Enid Doris Ondaatje, who ran a dance and theater school. In 1962 he emigrated to Canada, where he studied English and history at Bishop's University in Quebec; he has baccalaureate and master's degrees.

Ondaatje is one of an increasing number of Canadian writers also published in the United States and Britain and known internationally. His early poems appeared in *New Wave Canada: The New Explosion in Canadian Poetry* (1967). His poetry collection *Secular Love* (1984) explores the pain of the failure of his first marriage and celebrates his second.

In his first foray into fiction, *The Collected Works of Billy the Kid* (1970), Ondaatje retells the story of the outlaw William H. Bonney through a mixture of poetry, prose, photographs, and other illustrations. In *Coming through Slaughter* (1976) he interweaves biography, history, and fiction to relate the story of jazz cornetist Buddy Bolden, who went insane. *In the Skin of the Lion* retells the story of the building of Toronto's Prince Edward Viaduct.

In 1978, after a 24-year absence, Ondaatje returned to his homeland. In journals he recorded family anecdotes and stories that developed into his "fictional memoir" *Running in the Family* (1982), composed of vivid, rhapsodic reminiscences.

In many of his novels Ondaatje uses his central characters to explore a violent reality, mixing the ordinary and the fantastic to create a surreal montage, as in *The English Patient* (1993). Here a quartet of characters—Hana Lewis, a Canadian nurse; the "English patient," burned beyond recognition, who is in fact a Hungarian count; thief and double agent David Caravaggio; and a British soldier, Kip Singh, who has been sent to clear the area of enemy mines—during the last days of World War II take shelter in a dilapidated Italian villa. Ondaatje biographer Douglas Barbour writes, "As the complexly ordered fragments of the novel accumulate, their pasts, their presents, and their possible futures intertwine in an intricate collage," creating in the process, as critic Lorna Sage observes, "an improbable civilization of their own, a zone of fragile intimacy and understanding . . ."

Fascinated by history, documentation, and biography, Ondaatje reinvents history through imagination. The dominant features of his style are a dynamic beauty and a scarcely contained violence. He has won many awards, including the Governor General's Award three times, the BOOKER PRIZE, and the Toronto Book Award.

Other Works by Michael Ondaatje

Anil's Ghost. New York: Random House, 2001.
Handwriting. New York: Alfred A. Knopf, 1999.

A Work about Michael Ondaatje

Barbour, Douglas. *Michael Ondaatje.* Boston: Twayne, 1993.

O'Nolan, Brian

See O'BRIEN, FLANN.

Orczy, Baroness (1865–1947) *novelist, children's writer*

Baroness Orczy was born Emmuska Orczy in Hungary to aristocratic parents. Her father was Baron Felix Orczy, a famous musical composer. She was educated in Brussels and Paris, and when she was 15 her family moved to London, where she studied art and met her future husband, the book illustrator Montagu Barstow. Orczy spoke no English before going to Britain, but she learned the new language quickly and wrote all of her books in English.

Orczy began her writing career in the 1890s, writing for magazines. She then turned her hand to children's fiction. Her first foray into historical fiction was *The Emperor's Candlesticks* (1899), a historical thriller involving 19th-century Russian and Viennese aristocracy.

Orczy eventually excelled in historical fiction. Always intrigued by the French Revolution, she wrote a novel about a dashing English lord who rescues French aristocrats from bloodthirsty revolutionaries. Every single publisher rejected it, but Orczy refused to give up, and she and her husband rewrote the novel into a play. It was extremely successful, and this eventually persuaded a publisher to give it a chance. The novel was *The Scarlet Pimpernel* (1905), Orczy's most famous book.

The Scarlet Pimpernel hinges on the activities of Sir Percy Blakeney, a cool, collected and charming master of disguise whose ability to whisk away prisoners is regarded as almost supernatural by the awed French: "There was no doubt that this band of meddlesome Englishmen did exist; moreover, they seemed to be under the leadership of a man whose pluck and audacity were almost fabulous." The novel was followed by several Pimpernel sequels, including *The Elusive Pimpernel* (1908), *Eldorado: A Story of the Scarlet Pimpernel* (1913), and *Triumph of the Scarlet Pimpernel* (1922), in which the Pimpernel becomes increasingly romantically involved. Orczy also wrote detective novels, including *Unravelled Knots* (1925) and *Lady Molly of Scotland Yard* (1910).

Other Works by Baroness Orczy

Nicolette: A Tale of Old Provence. Leipzig, Germany: Tauschnitz, 1923.
A True Woman. London: Hutchinson, 1911.

Orton, Joe (John Kingsley Orton) (1933–1967) *playwright, novelist, screenwriter*

Joe Orton was born John Kingsley Orton in Leicester, England, to William Orton, a municipal gardener, and Elsie Orton, a housecleaner. From 1945 to 1947, he attended Clark's College, a preparatory, commercial school for clerks and secretaries. After graduation he worked as a clerk in various offices throughout Leicester. He had other plans, however, as his diary entry from 1949 shows: "I suddenly knew that my ambition is and has always been to act and act. . . . I know now I shall always want to act and I can no more sit in an office all my life than fly." Orton participated in various dramatic societies in Leicester, and in 1950 he successfully auditioned for the Royal Academy of Dramatic Art in London.

In 1953 Orton worked briefly as an assistant stage manager for Ipswich Repertory Company. He abandoned his theatrical career to write fiction in collaboration with Kenneth Halliwell, his roommate and lover. Although the novels ultimately proved unsuccessful—the only published novel of this collaborative effort, *Head to Toe* (1971), appeared posthumously—they provided ideas for plots and characters that would later appear in Orton's plays.

Orton's various experiences were reflected time and time again in the antisocial themes of his plays. In many ways he toyed with the ideas of polite society both in his life and in his work. From 1959 to

1962, Orton and Halliwell stole books from public libraries, modifying the dust jackets and the inside flaps to make them appear obscene and absurd. They also created a massive floor to ceiling collage, using more than 1,600 prints from art books borrowed from the library and later defaced to make the collage. The couple was eventually discovered and sentenced to six months in prison.

Orton's career as a playwright truly began when the BBC (British Broadcasting Company) purchased his one-act play *The Ruffian on the Stair* (1963). Based on one of the unpublished novels written with Halliwell, this farcical play demonstrated the great influence of Harold PINTER on Orton's work in terms of themes that emphasized the absurdity of modern life. The play revealed his skill in composing dialogue and was well received by the critics.

Orton's first successful stage play, *Entertaining Mr. Sloane* (1964), premiered in the New Arts Theatre Club in London. The play, largely an allegorical commentary on mass media and entertainment, contains explicit dialogue and deals with the anesthetized sensibility of the contemporary environment. The dialogue artfully mimics the established clichés of mass media, particularly television. In this portrayal of mass media, even the father's murder is processed by other characters with the detachment of television viewers. The subtle allusions to homosexuality in the play shocked some viewers; some critics even called it obscene and immoral. Amused and enchanted by the play's originality, general audiences thought otherwise. Alan Schneider, the famous and influential American director, praised *Entertaining Mr. Sloane* and staged it on Broadway in 1965.

Biographer Maurice Charney describes *The Good and Faithful Servant* (1967), Orton's second major play, as his "tenderest and most moving play, more a bitter satire on the deadening, dehumanizing factory system than a farce." The play presents the retirement of Buchanan, a man who devoted his entire life to the company that has employed him. Buchanan is completely alone and alienated within the corporate system. In a futile gesture, he smashes his retirement gifts, a clock and a toaster that do not work. Buchanan ultimately discovers that he cannot live outside this system.

What the Butler Saw (1969) is considered Orton's comic masterpiece. A candid parody of Oscar Wilde's *The Importance of Being Earnest*, the play is an explicit sexual farce. Mrs. Prentice, "born with her legs apart," has an illusion that "The world is full of naked men running in all directions!" Another character, Geraldine, carries about a mysterious box that contains the phallus of Sir Winston Churchill, as is revealed at the end. *What the Butler Saw* is a play about sexual anarchy and madness. Between the lines of sexual humor, Orton makes a number of interesting observations about the nature of one's sexual identity. As a caricature of heterosexuality, the play clearly attacks the traditional values, morals, and sensibilities of the English gentry and middle class. Frank Marcus, a fellow playwright, notes, "I think the play will survive and tell people more about what it felt to be alive in the Sixties than almost anything else of the period."

Joe Orton's death was perhaps as histrionic as one of his plays: He was brutally murdered by his jealous lover, Kenneth Halliwell. His reputation as a playwright and screenwriter for *Funeral Games* (1968), among others, seem to have increased after his death, as the plays continue to be released posthumously. Many critics today consider Orton's plays poignant social commentaries, instrumental in the development of modern social drama: "The plays of Orton are not as merry as their plots would suggest; in fact, they leave us with an unpleasant sense of a world gone awry," writes Orton's biographer Maurice Charney.

Other Work by Joe Orton

Joe Orton: The Complete Plays. New York: Grove Press, 1990.

Works about Joe Orton

Charney, Maurice. *Joe Orton.* New York: Grove Press, 1984.
Lahr, John. *Prick Up Your Ears: The Biography of Joe Orton.* New York: Alfred A. Knopf, 1978.

Orwell, George (Eric Arthur Blair)

(1903–1950) *novelist, essayist, nonfiction writer*
George Orwell was born Eric Arthur Blair in
Mother, Bengal, India, but raised in England. He
was the son of Ida Amble Limousine and Richard
Wellesley Blair, an administrator in the Opium Department of the Indian government. Educated at
Eton, Orwell chose service with the Indian Imperial Police in Burma instead of attending a university. His Burmese experience taught him the evils
of institutionalized force, and his writing reflects
his mission to oppose all forms of oppression.

Orwell's early days as a writer were marked by
poverty, his meager writing income being supplemented with earnings from occasional teaching
jobs. He recounts those days in his first nonfiction
book, *Down and Out in Paris and London* (1933),
which displays his growing socialist convictions.

Orwell attacked imperialistic abuse of the sort
he had witnessed in Burma in his first novel,
Burmese Days (1934). His next novel, *The Clergyman's Daughter* (1935), was about an amnesiac
hobo. It was followed by *Keep the Aspidistra Flying*
(1936), which tells the misadventures of a bookstore clerk who discovers the pitfalls of domestic
conformity and middle-class competition. In *The
Road to Wigan Pier* (1937) Orwell focused on the
plight of the poor in northern England.

Orwell always thought of himself as a socialist,
but he increasingly became a critic of the left's totalitarian tendencies and was seen as a traitor by
many of his fellow leftists. In *Homage to Catalonia*
(1939), which critic Lionel Trilling called "one of
the important documents of our time," Orwell describes the courageous efforts of communists and
Republicans against Franco's fascist revolutionary
forces. However, his descriptions of the fighting
were not as vividly remembered by some on the
left as were his harsh criticisms of the hard-line
communists who sought to purge all Trotskyites
and anarchists from the Republican side. Orwell
writes that for those sitting comfortably in England, the politics of the war seemed "so beautifully simple," but he was convinced that evil was
spreading in Europe while England was in a stu-
por. He writes that "we shall never wake till we are
jerked out of it by bombs." Critic Ruth Ann Life
observes, "Decree as the alternative to law and violence as the internal and international alternative
to policy had become the rule, Orwell realized, in
three European countries other than Spain."

Orwell opposed political dogmatism, as reflected in many of the articles he wrote for the
London *Tribune* and other British papers during
World War II. No matter how critical he might become, he retained his faith in socialism and urged
the British to adopt it in *The Lion and the Unicorn:
Socialism and the English Genius* (1941).

After World War II, on the eve of the cold war,
Orwell found a receptive popular audience for his
antitotalitarian fable *Animal Farm* (1945), in
which talking animals revolt against farmers, allowing pigs to become their leaders. Unfortunately,
one tyranny has been exchanged for another, led
by a pig named Napoleon. The maxims of the revolution are soon corrupted: "All animals are equal"
soon becomes "All animals are equal, but some animals are more equal than others."

Unfortunately, the suffering animals do not understand what is happening to them. The work-
horse Boxer, for instance, reassures himself, "If
Napoleon says it, it must be right." Scholar Robert
A. Lee says that in *Animal Farm*, "So long as the animals cannot remember the past, because it is continually altered, they have no control over the
present and hence over the future."

Orwell made his antitotalitarian views clear in
newspaper essays throughout this period, his most
famous being "Politics and the English Language"
(1946). Considered by some the best political essay
ever written, it was an early condemnation of the
distortion and misuse of words so as to hide the
true nature of political activity. "Orthodoxy, of
whatever colour," said Orwell, "seems to demand a
lifeless, imitative style." Critic William Steinhoff
noted that since Orwell "believed that political
speech and writing were largely 'the defense of the
indefensible' . . . they were bound to be couched in
false and evasive language." Condemning eu-
phemisms such as "pacification," "transfer of popu-

lation," and "elimination of undesirable elements," Orwell said political language "is designed to make lies sound truthful and murder respectable."

The close tie between totalitarianism and abuse of language would be a central theme of Orwell's *Nineteen Eighty-four* (1949), set in a then-futuristic totalitarian society, with a Stalinesque ruler called Big Brother. Orwell died of tuberculosis, from which he had long suffered, shortly after writing this book.

Critical Analysis

Nineteen Eighty-four shows how, with sufficient political control, a regime can condition its citizens so that even their thoughts are not free. The protagonist, Winston Smith, works in a censorship office in charge of discarding old articles that do not conform to the regime's official version of history. He and his fellow citizens must employ a legally enforced dialect called Newspeak, in which many words are forbidden. As one character says, "In the end we shall make thoughtcrime literally impossible, because there will be no words in which to express it."

Like Aldous HUXLEY's novel *Brave New World* (1932), *Nineteen Eighty-four* was influenced by Russian author Yevgeny Zamyatin's 1924 dystopian novel *We,* in which citizens of a future police state are forbidden to have proper names, only serial numbers, and must live in transparent buildings, under observation at all times. In Orwell's police state, video cameras monitor citizens' every move, unauthorized sex is a crime, and posters simultaneously reassure and threaten that "Big Brother is watching you." Everyone has been trained to believe the state's lies, no matter how obvious they are. Thus, while citizens suffer shortages of all sorts and live in dismal conditions, the state tells them that life is getting better: "The fabulous statistics continued to pour out of the telescreen. As compared with last year, there was more food, more clothes, more houses, more furniture . . ."

In the final chapters, Winston Smith is tortured by an agent of the state who is so confident of the state's power to reshape minds he vows that he will make Smith believe that two plus two equals five if the state commands it. Scholar Philip Rahv notes that in the novel, "one of the major themes is the psychology of capitulation." What also gives the novel a tone of dread, notes critic Irving Howe, "is the sickening awareness that . . . Orwell has seized upon those elements of our public life that, given courage and intelligence, were avoidable."

Nineteen Eighty-four had a profound impact on the popular imagination, enough so that in magazine and TV pieces the actual year 1984 was often judged by comparison to Orwell's dismal prediction, as was the computer revolution that followed shortly thereafter, with its potential for new forms of control and new forms of escape. When deceptive jargon is criticized as "Orwellian," surveillance systems are likened to those in *Nineteen Eighty-four,* or an intrusive government is disparagingly called "Big Brother," the echoes of Orwell's novel are heard. As early as 1949, the year of the book's publication, the *New York Times* wrote of *Nineteen Eighty-four* that "it is probable that no other work of this generation has made us desire freedom more earnestly or loathe tyranny with such fullness." Historian Isaac Deutscher notes that "few novels written in this generation have obtained a popularity as great. . . . Few, if any, have made a similar impact on politics."

Other Works by George Orwell
The English People. 1944. Reprint, New York: Hastel House, 1974.
Shooting an Elephant, and Other Essays. New York: Harcourt, Brace, 1950.
Such, Such Were the Joys. New York: Harcourt, Brace, 1953.

Works about George Orwell
Agathocleous, Tanya. *George Orwell: Battling Big Brother.* New York: Oxford University Press, 2000.
Newsinger, John. *Orwell's Politics.* New York: St. Martin's Press, 1999.
Shelden, Michael. *Orwell: The Authorized Biography.* New York: HarperCollins, 1991.
Stansky, Peter, and William Abrahams. *The Unknown Orwell and Orwell: The Transformation.* Stanford, Calif.: Stanford University Press, 1994.

Osborne, John (1929–1994) *playwright, screenwriter, essayist*

John Osborne was born in Fulham, a London suburb, to Thomas Osborne, a commercial artist, and Nellie Grove Osborne, a barmaid. He briefly attended boarding school but was expelled when he was 16 for striking the headmaster. He worked as a journalist for various commercial and trade journals, then developed an interest in theater and became an acting stage manager with a touring company in 1948. For the next eight years he directed and performed at various resort towns along the English coast.

Osborne began his prolific career as a playwright with the performance of *The Devil Inside Him* (1950), a play about a romantic Welsh youth who is seen as an idiot by the fellow villagers and as obsessed with sex by his family because he writes poetry. The play was well received in the local papers, and Osborne decided to concentrate on writing plays rather than on acting. In 1956 he joined the prestigious English Stage Company at the Royal Court Theater, where he staged his first major play, *Look Back in Anger* (1956). The protagonist of the play, Jimmy, is socially, politically, and emotionally frustrated. Raised in the working class, Jimmy "rises" socially and intellectually. The play also introduces several nuances about Jimmy's sexuality, which complicate his relationships with his mother and with his future wife, Allison. The production received mixed reviews; however, Osborne's talent and name became nationally recognized. The renowned playwright Arthur Miller described *Look Back in Anger* as "the only modern English play." It illuminated several conflicts present in contemporary society, such as conflicts of class and of sexual identity. Osborne wanted viewers to consider whether the conditions of society are responsible for Jimmy's attitudes and behaviors: "You see, I learnt at an early age what it was to be angry—angry and helpless. And I can never forget it," explains Jimmy.

Because of the anger in Osborne's play, the journalist J. B. PRIESTLEY labeled him an "angry young man." Along with other writers, such as Kingsley AMIS, Malcolm BRADBURY, and John BRAINE, who despised middle-class materialism and concern for social status. Osborne would for years be one of the ANGRY YOUNG MEN.

In 1957 Osborne produced *The Entertainer*, which focused on the social problems of contemporary society. *The Entertainer* combined vaudeville performances with realistic scenes. Archie, a struggling comedian, patronizes his family and consistently displays an arrogant attitude. The play was praised by critics who applauded its histrionic innovations and social sensibility.

Osborne's next major play, *Luther* (1961), is "about religious experience and various other things," according to the playwright. The play itself demonstrates his ambivalent feelings toward organized religion. He presents Martin Luther, the originator of the Reformation movement, not as a founder of an institution but rather as a person fed up with religious institutions. The major psychological conflict in the play is between Luther and his father, Hans. Hans, as Osborne's biographer Arnold Hinchliffe keenly observes, "cannot understand why Martin should give up fame, fortune, and domestic bliss to become a monk," nor can the audience as they gaze on Luther in the confession scene, "wracked by doubts compounded of sex, violence, and inadequacy, while his fellow monks speak of minor faults of ritual and sloth." Furthermore, the psychological conflict between Hans and Luther translates into a deeper spiritual conflict between Luther and God the Father in the later acts of the play. The play was performed in the major theaters of London, Paris, and New York, and was accorded the prestigious New York Drama Critics Award and the Tony Award for Best Play in 1963. It was made into a film in 1971.

Many critics believe that *Inadmissible Evidence* (1965) was Osborne's last truly great play. Maitland, an unsuccessful attorney at a law firm, deteriorates as a result of a series of terrible events: divorce, arrest, and imprisonment. Osborne portrays Maitland as an utterly independent figure, void of emotions and lacking significant personal relationships. Dispossessed, bitter, disillusioned, Maitland testifies to the emergence of a new kind of individual, one tethered to a social landscape grown ungovernably hostile. Maitland questions contemporary notions about the premises and relationships of the modern society.

Throughout the rest of his writing career, Osborne continued to produce plays and screenplays as he battled the critics in the later stages of his career. As a screenwriter he achieved recognition for his film adaptation of Henry Fielding's *Tom Jones* (1963), which won him an Oscar. In the 1970s and 1980s, he wrote a number of plays and screenplays for the British television. He also published a number of critical essays on theater, short works of fiction, and an autobiography, *A Better Class of Person* (1981). Ironically, Osborne's autobiography received much more positive critical attention than his later plays. As Arnold Hinchliffe puts it, *A Better Class of Person* is "quite the best thing he has written since *Inadmissible Evidence*" because "it shows admirable control over words, tone, and feelings."

Osborne's life was at times as dramatic and unpredictable as his plays; it included five marriages and four divorces. He worked under the assumption that words are "our last link with God," and therefore he was able to reach wide audiences. Osborne was capable of integrating personal drama with a profound social statement. His early plays are still admired by audiences in England and the United States.

Other Works by John Osborne

Damn You England: Collected Prose. Winchester, Mass.: Faber and Faber, 1994.
Plays for England: The Blood of the Bambergs, Under Plain Cover, Watch It Come Down. New York: Theatre Communications Group, 2000.
Plays: Look Back in Anger, Epitaph for George Dillon, the World of Paul Slickey and Dejavu. Winchester, Mass.: Faber and Faber, 1996.

Works about John Osborne

Goldstone, Herbert. *Coping with Vulnerability: the Achievement of John Osborne.* Lanham, Md.: University Press of America, 1982.
Hinchliffe, Arnold. *John Osborne.* Boston: Twayne, 1984.

Owen, Wilfred Edward Salter
(1893–1918) *poet*

Wilfred Owen was born in Oswestry, near the Welsh border of Shropshire, England, to Thomas Owen, a railway stationmaster, and Susan Owen. After graduating from Shrewsbury Technical School, he failed to gain acceptance to London University and instead entered a period of religious study as an assistant to an Anglican vicar. Owen is chiefly known as one of the "trench poets" who, like Rupert BROOKE and his friend Siegfried SASSOON, served on the western front during World War I and wrote poetry about the experience. He died in battle one week before the Armistice.

Before the war, especially during his years as a religious apprentice, Owen was already writing poetry, usually imitating the rhyme schemes and intense introspection of his romantic idols, Percy Bysshe Shelley, John Keats, and Alfred Lord Tennyson. All the while, however, as the scholar Merryn Williams has aptly put it, his poetry suffered because "he had nothing important to say." With the onslaught of war, however, Owen found his subject. He wrote the majority of his poems during a 14-month treatment for shell shock, a nervous condition brought about by combat experience, at the Craiglockhart War Hospital in Edinburgh with the encouragement of Sassoon, also a patient. His most famous poems, "Anthem for Doomed Youth" (1917), "Dulce et Decorum Est" (1917) (Latin for "sweet and fitting it is"), and "Strange Meeting" (1917) all come from this period.

The first of these poems, "Anthem for Doomed Youth," represented a marked change from poetry written near the beginning of the war, such as Rupert Brooke's patriotic and prowar poem "The Soldier." Owen's poem, which reveals the early influence of poets such as Shelley, with its sonnet form, speaks of neither glory nor honor, but with lines such as "What passing-bells for these who die as cattle? / Only the monstrous anger of the guns" confronts fear, horror, and death while clearly voicing the poet's bitterness toward the war. "Dulce et Decorum Est" paints a similarly bleak picture of the war as it describes a gas attack on a group of young British soldiers whom Owen describes as young men "Bent double, like old beggars under sacks, / Knock-kneed, coughing like hags," and walking behind a cart carrying a wounded man dying a painful death.

All of Owen's war poetry was well received by critics such as C. Day LEWIS and Stephen SPENDER, but no other poem received such high praise as "Strange Meeting," which, in an intricate, mournful rhythm, describes a soldier's descent into Hell, where he meets a man who says, "I am the enemy you killed . . . / I parried; but my hands were loath and cold." In underscoring the horrors of war, the two become friends and rejoice that they no longer have to hear the incessant roar of guns. T. S. ELIOT praised its rhythm as a "technical achievement of great originality" and called the poem "one of the most moving pieces of verse inspired by the war."

Although Owen's career was extremely short, he made lasting impressions on many of the prominent poets of the 20th century, such as Eliot and W. H. AUDEN, with his method of blending new subjects, particularly social protest, into classic poetic forms such as the sonnet. In his assessment of Owen's ultimate contribution to British literature, the scholar John Purkis has remarked that the poet "established a norm for the concept of 'war poetry' and permanently coloured the view of the Great War for later generations." Another scholar, Margaret McDowell, argues that "the best of Owen's 1917–1918 poems are great by any standard."

Other Work by Wilfred Owen
The Poems of Wilfred Owen, 2 vols. Edited by John Stallworthy. London: Chatto, 1985.

Works about Wilfred Owen
Kerr, Douglas. *Wilfred Owen's Voices: Language and Community.* New York: Oxford University Press, 1993.
Stallworthy, John. *Wilfred Owen: A Biography.* London: Oxford University Press, 1979.

Peake, Mervyn (1911–1968) *novelist, poet*

Mervyn Peake was born in China, the second son of Amanda Elizabeth Powell and Ernest Cromwell Peake, a medical missionary. His family was plagued by hereditary insanity, a theme that would appear in his "Gormenghast" novels. At age 11 Peake moved to England, where he later became an art teacher, writer, and illustrator. Although he was in the army during World War II, he was discharged after suffering a nervous breakdown. In 1945 the *Leader* newspaper sent him to visit the Belsen concentration camp upon its liberation. The images he sketched of victims there haunted him for years afterward.

During the war and immediately after, Peake also illustrated new editions of works by classic authors, including Samuel Taylor Coleridge's *Rime of the Ancient Mariner* (1943), Lewis Carroll's *The Hunting of the Snark* (1948), and Robert Louis Stevenson's *Treasure Island* (1949). His macabre illustrations and sense of humor have been likened to those of cartoonist Edward Gorey. He later wrote and illustrated volumes of his own poetry, including *The Rhyme of the Flying Bomb* (1962), which describes the tension caused by German "buzzbombs" used to attack England during World War II.

In 1946 *Titus Groan,* the first of Peake's novels about the gloomy and conspiracy-filled castle called Gormenghast, was published. Highly atmospheric and filled with Peake's illustrations, the book depicts an ancient, city-sized castle, full of dank, gloomy hallways and mean-spirited characters with bizarre names such as Flay and Prunesquallor. The central characters are the members of the insanity-prone royal family, including Titus, the newborn 77th Earl of Groan. Titus is envied by both his scheming aunts and a rebellious kitchen servant boy, Steerpike, who together plot to burn down the library of Titus's father, Lord Sepulchrave. This act hastens Lord Sepulchrave's descent into madness.

Most of those living in Gormenghast have an air of futility and decrepitude about them. Thus, Flay, Lord Sepulchrave's servant, "took a step forward . . . his knee joints cracking as he did so. . . . [H]is passage through life . . . was accompanied by these cracking sounds."

Although *Titus Groan* received mixed responses, reviewer Elizabeth BOWEN correctly forecast, "I predict for Titus a smallish but fervent public," which will "renew itself, and probably enlarge, with each generation." Indeed, reception of the second novel, *Gormenghast* (1950), was better. This book earned Peake the Heinemann Prize for Literature, in combination with his volume of poetry *The Glassblowers* (1950).

In *Gormenghast* various members of the royal family and their associates are murdered, leading to a final battle with Steerpike. In the end young Titus, tired of Gormenghast's intrigues, sets out on his own to explore the world.

Peake wrote a third Gormenghast novel, *Titus Alone* (1959), about the young earl's adventures in the wider world, where sadism and conflict turn out to be almost as common as in Gormenghast and where Titus is pursued by zombielike policemen: "He remembered how it was always the same—the sudden appearance, the leap of evasion, and the strange following silence as his would-be captors dwindled away into the distance, to vanish—but not forever." Titus also witnesses evil rituals at the Black House: "It had an atmosphere about it that was unutterably mournful . . . a darkness that owed nothing to the night and seemed to dye the day." Worst of all, Titus witnesses all-out war. Critics found the book was clever but eccentric. The *Times Literary Supplement* called it "a piece of fine writing—if you can take it."

Peake was troubled by mental illness during the writing of the final Gormenghast novel, and years later he died as a result of Parkinson's disease. He is remembered more by his devoted readers than by critics in general, and his work has inspired fan clubs around the world. According to critic John Clute, the Gormenghast trilogy "is perhaps the most intensely visual fantasy every written. . . . [Peake is a] most potent visionary."

Other Work by Mervyn Peake

Peake's Progress: Selected Writings and Drawings by Mervyn Peake. La Vergne, Tenn.: Lightning Source, 1981.

Works about Mervyn Peake

Gardiner-Scott, Tanya J. *Mervyn Peake: The Evolution of a Dark Romantic.* New York: Peter Lang, 1998.

Winnington, Peter G. *Vast Alchemies.* Chester Springs, Pa.: Dufour Editions, 2000.

Percy, Charles Henry

See SMITH, DODIE.

Phillips, Caryl (1958–) *novelist, playwright, essayist, screenwriter*

Caryl Phillips was born in St. Kitts, West Indies, to Lillian and Malcolm Phillips. The family soon moved to England, and he grew up primarily in Leeds and Birmingham. During these years Phillips could never escape his blackness; he attended primarily white schools but even into his university years at Oxford he felt that he was treated as a second-class citizen.

Phillips graduated from Oxford with a degree in English in 1979, and he immediately embarked on a writing career. His first works were plays—*Strange Fruit* (1980), *Where There Is Darkness* (1982), and *The Shelter* (1983)—which contained several themes that run throughout most of his work: forced and voluntary immigration, cultural displacement, and a nostalgia for a mythic homeland.

Despite the financial success of his early plays, it was his 1985 novel *The Final Passage* that established Phillips as an important literary figure. The novel focuses on Leila Preston, who along with her young son Calvin emigrates from the Caribbean to England in order to join her mother and no-good husband, Michael. For Leila, England is a harsh land. Her mother dies in a hospital, and her marriage finally disintegrates. At the novel's end Leila, impoverished and nearly broken (at one point having to burn furniture for warmth), plans to return to her native island, where she knows that she can find at least "safety and two friends."

In 1987 Phillips published a collection of essays, *The European Tribe,* which features several travel narratives and essays about his interactions with other prominent black artists such as jazz musician Miles Davis and the American novelist James Baldwin. Following this he published his most highly acclaimed novel, *Crossing the River* (1994). A finalist for the BOOKER PRIZE and the winner of the James Tait Black Memorial Prize, this novel is composed of the three separate narratives of siblings Nash, Martha, and Travis, each unknown to the other, who were sold into slavery as children in Africa and then transported to America. In the opening section Nash, the oldest of the three, a freed slave and a Christian missionary, returns to his native country in 1830 to convert Africans but slowly blends back into the culture of his homeland. The second narrative, which takes place before and after the U.S. Civil War, tells the story of aged Martha, who is physically and emotionally scarred by her experiences as a slave and who finds freedom in the American West near the end of the 19th century. The last section focuses on Travis, the son of the original Travis and an American soldier stationed in a small British town during World War II, where he enjoys an acceptance that he never felt in the United States and that he knows his half-English son will never experience when they return home after the war.

These individual stories of hardship are united by the novel's opening and ending, in which a father despairs over his decision to sell his children into slavery. This figure, the father of Nash, Martha, and Travis, also functions symbolically as a voice for the entire continent of Africa mourning the irreparable loss of generations of children sold into slavery.

Most recently, Phillips has turned to screenwriting, producing the script for *The Mystic Masseur* (2002), based on the V. S. NAIPAUL novel about the rise of a Trinidadian politician. Since the mid-1980s he has lectured and held temporary professorships at several universities and is currently a tenured professor at Amherst College in Massachusetts. According to the scholar Reinhard Sander, Phillips's writings have "become part of the new postcolonial 'canon' taught in colleges in North America, Britain, the Caribbean, and elsewhere."

Other Works by Caryl Phillips

Cambridge. New York: Alfred A. Knopf, 1992.
The Nature of Blood. New York: Alfred A. Knopf, 1997.

Pinter, Harold (1930–) *playwright, screenwriter, poet, novelist*

Pinter was born in Hackney, a working-class district of London, to Jewish parents Hyman Pinter, a tailor, and Frances Mann Pinter. He was educated at Hackney Downs Grammar School and, briefly, at the Royal Academy of Dramatic Art. He began writing poetry at the age of 13 and in high school was attracted to drama. From 1949 until 1959 he was a professional actor touring Britain and Ireland under the stage name David Baron. From 1973 to 1983 he was an associate director of Britain's National Theatre. In 1966 Pinter was made a Commander of the Order of the British Empire (CBE). He has been twice married, to actress Vivien Merchant (1956–80) and since then to historical novelist Lady Antonia FRASER.

When Pinter's plays were staged in London in the early 1960s, they were hailed as THEATER OF THE ABSURD. Pinter has been influenced by Samuel BECKETT, Franz Kafka, and Feodor Dostoevsky. His drama shares with theater of the absurd an uneasy commingling of farce and tragedy; similar to other absurdist plays, his are about being rather than acting and reveal patterns rather than tell stories. However, Pinter's seedy characters and squalid settings have nothing to do with realism. His plays are well-knit and observe the unities of time and space, but in their multidimensionality they are mysterious, slightly surreal. He is essentially a poetic dramatist.

Pinter is probably the most important and influential British dramatist of the second half of the 20th century. His original, distinctive plays could never be mistaken for anyone else's. As drama critic John Russell Taylor remarks, they differ from most drama in lacking exposition—Pinter characters do not confide their concerns to an audience—and in offering neither explanation nor conventional dénouement. Nor, above all, are motives given for any action. The playwright has acknowledged that his plays begin as images or scenes, glimpsed or imagined, retaining an aura of mystery. As Taylor also observes, Pinter's plays resemble poetry and music in lending themselves to analysis through imagery and theme rather than dissection of ideas. One of the most distinctive aspects of this drama is the inimitable Pinteresque dialogue. Pinter has an uncanny ear that faithfully reproduces everyday conversation in all its banality, yet it is somehow heightened or enhanced; as he transcribes it, speech becomes both more lucid and opaque. Pinter distrusts language because he finds it a smokescreen designed to conceal rather than to reveal. His plays also make use of pauses and silences that speak volumes.

The archetypal Pinter plot appears in his first one-act play, significantly entitled *The Room* (1957). Many of Pinter's plays take place in womb-like rooms where the central character or characters huddle in hiding from the world until an intruder enters. In *The Room* Rose and Bert Hudd are thus holed up when their uneasy peace is disturbed by visitors. The elderly Rose endlessly mothers and fusses over her silent, lumpish mate, Bert. The Hudds are visited first by their landlord, Mr. Kidd, and then by a young couple, the Sands, who are looking for a flat and have been told by someone in the basement that this one is vacant. This makes Rose uneasy, but she becomes positively alarmed when Kidd again enters (Bert having gone out) and informs her that a man is lurking in the basement waiting to see her. When this man, Riley, enters, he is discovered to be old, black, and blind. He addresses Rose as "Sal," telling her, "Your father wants you to come home." At first fending off the stranger, Rose finally caresses him, but Bert returns and begins punching and kicking the old man. As he does so, Rose cries out she can no longer see—she, too, is now blind. The ending is startling but has an air of rightness and inevitability about it. The implication is that Rose and/or Bert have violated some taboo and Rose pays for this with her sight. The play, like many of Pinter's, is susceptible of Freudian interpretation: The man hiding in the basement seems to be a projection of Rose's subconscious.

The plots of Pinter's other plays of this period—*The Birthday Party* (1958/1965), *A Slight Ache* (1959/1961), and *The Dumb Waiter* (1960)—resemble *The Room* with variations and additional complexities. Some critics call them "comedies of menace," for they are both funny and frightening. *The Birthday Party* was Pinter's first full-length play.

When it was first produced in 1958, it was not a success because the audience could not make sense of it. Yet the critic Harold Hobson recognized its power and hailed its author as "the most original, disturbing, and arresting talent in theatrical London." In this play, the Hudds are replaced by Stanley Webber and Meg, who are in a seaside boardinghouse invaded by two killers: Goldberg, a Jew, and McCann, an Irishman. Just as Rose becomes blind, Stanley, who is celebrating his birthday and who is interrogated and tormented by the two gangsters, at the end becomes mute. Critics have interpreted the play as centering on Stanley Webber's "crime and punishment" for an unspecified sin.

In *The Dumb Waiter,* two hit men wait in a Birmingham basement for orders to carry out a contract killing. The intruder this time is the dumbwaiter of the title, which also functions as a deus ex machina. Through a speaking tube, Ben and Gus are given more and more outrageous orders to fill and place on the dumbwaiter, which mysteriously travels up and down. The play resembles a comic version of Ernest Hemingway's short story "The Killers" transported on stage and filled with the hilarious but sinister repartee between Ben and Gus. The pair resembles a vaudeville turn; their characters are subtly differentiated, too.

A Slight Ache, which was written for radio—Pinter has written many scripts for radio and television, as well as for film—resembles *The Room* in presenting what appears to be a primal scene. Here Edward and Flora occupy a room, while outside stands a blind and mute matchseller, making the couple vaguely uneasy. By the play's end the matchseller has literally changed places with Edward; Flora sends Edward out to sell matches and makes much of the beggar. The archetypal Pinter plot bears strongly on territorial imperatives and entails someone's displacement and dispossession.

Critic Martin Esslin upholds *The Birthday Party, The Caretaker* (1960), and *The Homecoming* (1965) as "classics of our time." *The Caretaker* and *The Homecoming* are more complex and fully developed versions of the earlier plays. In the former play, a shifty and shiftless tramp, Davies, forms a triangle with two neurotic brothers, Aston and Mick, when he comes to share their room. Davies upsets the fragile balance the brothers have achieved—Aston has undergone shock therapy as a mental patient and his brother is solicitous and protective of him. In Davies's efforts to establish and ingratiate himself, first with one brother, then with the other, he plays them off against each other but ends by rousing both against him, so that he is evicted. The play ends as it began, with the brothers together in retreat from the world. Pinter has said this drama pitting an intruder against a vestigial family concerns "a particular human situation" and "three particular people . . . not, incidentally, symbols."

The Homecoming centers on a married son bringing home his new wife to meet his family. Teddy, a university teacher who has settled in America, introduces his bride Ruth to his family: his father Max, his brothers Lenny and Joey, and his uncle Sam. The woman's entrance into this all-male household upsets the balance of power and rouses confused, primal passions. In the end, she gives up on her husband, deciding to remain with this brutish clan, despite the sexual overtures her new relatives make to her.

Pinter's three short plays *Landscape* (1967), *Silence* (1969), and *Night* (1969) represent a change of direction. As Lois Gordon observes, the dramatist is here moving from plays externalizing the deepest drives, desires, and fears to meditations exploring ever-shifting borders between reality and fantasy, imagination and memory. In this regard, it is interesting to ponder Pinter's own observation: "There can be no hard distinction between what is real and what is unreal, nor between what is true and what is false. A thing is not necessarily either true or false; it can be both . . ." Such themes carry through *Old Times* (1971), *No Man's Land* (1975), and *Betrayal* (1978).

During the 1980s and 1990s, Pinter wrote more overtly political plays. *One for the Road* (1984/85) explores the symbiotic relationship between a torturer and his victim; *Mountain Language* (1988) is about the willful extinction of an ethnic minority's

tongue; and the brief *New World Order* (1991) is about political torture that is all the more terrifying for remaining inexplicit.

Pinter scholar Steven H. Gale detects a progression in Pinter from the physical to the more psychic or abstract. He shows a tendency to "examine a problem in a series of plays," gathering all his thoughts and intuitions on that subject, then to move on and write "another set of plays which is a logical extension of the previous set." Pinter has written more than two dozen plays, of which at least half a dozen are contemporary classics. His drama fascinates through its psychological penetration and masterly dialogue. He has also published two volumes of poetry, *Poems* (1966, 1971) and *I Know the Place* (1979), and a novel, *The Dwarfs* (1990).

Works about Harold Pinter
Esslin, Martin. *Pinter the Playwright.* London: Methuen, 1982.
———. *Pinter: A Study of His Plays.* New York: W. W. Norton, 1976.
Gale, Steven H., ed. *Harold Pinter: Critical Approaches.* Boston: G. K. Hall, 1990.
Regal, Martin S. *Harold Pinter: A Question of Timing.* New York: St. Martin's Press, 1995.

Pitter, Ruth (1897–1992) *poet*
Ruth Pitter was born in Ilford, Essex, England, to George and Louisa R. Pitter. Both of her parents were schoolteachers in a working-class area of London and had a love of art and poetry. She attended a girls' charity school in London, where she learned cooking and art. Pitter took a job as a clerk in the War Office after World War I broke out. She spent her youth in the countryside of England, and this experience shaped much of her writing about rural life, religious themes, and the importance of nature.

Pitter earned a reputation as a poet at a young age, publishing her first poem, "Field Glasses," in *New Age* magazine when she was only 13 years old. *First Poems* (1920) was her initial collection of poetry and reveals the author's attempt to find her voice as a poet. One of her early admirers, writer

Hilaire BELLOC, disappointed in the poor reception given to the work, decided to help Pitter's career by writing a preface for her next collection, *First and Second Poems*. In these poems she begins to develop what would become two key connected themes in her later poetry: nature and spirituality. As David Cecil has written in *Ruth Pitter: Homage to a Poet*, "Ruth Pitter is a Christian mystic of nature, seeing natural beauty as an image, an incarnation of a Divine reality."

Pitter's best-known work of poetry was *A Trophy of Arms* (1936). The collection, which earned the prestigious Hawthornden Prize in 1937 for its imaginative poetic qualities and spiritual symbolism, included poems such as "The Beautiful Negress" and "Elegy to Mary." Another poem, "The Strawberry Plant," describes the yet-unrealized potential locked within the essence of the fruit itself, "one greenish berry spangling into yellow where the light touched the seed." This use of concrete imagery and highly visual language inspired the critic Edmund Blunden to count Pitter "among the true poets of the period." Pitter also appeared on British television and wrote for a popular women's magazine.

Although Pitter was not well known during her lifetime, she was recognized by Queen Elizabeth in 1955 with the Queen's Gold Medal for Poetry—the first woman to receive this award. Critic Derek Stafford wrote of Pitter's talent as a poet, "Miss Pitter is melodious and eloquacious—a mystically-minded writer with a healthy respect for the hard facts . . . (she has) a lovely earthy humor."

A Work about Ruth Pitter

Russell, Arthur, ed. *Ruth Pitter: Homage to a Poet.* Chester Springs, Pa.: Dufour Editions, 1969.

Plomer, William (1903–1973) *novelist, short story writer, poet, playwright*

William Plomer was born in Pietersburg, South Africa, to Charles Campbell Plomer, a civil servant in the Department of Native Affairs, and Edythe Waite-Browne Plomer. He attended preparatory school in England and spent much of his life out-side of his native country. Plomer finished his education at St. John's College in Johannesburg, South Africa, during which he became sure that he wanted to be a writer. Between farming in South Africa, teaching in Tokyo, and traveling the world, he achieved his goal. His fair treatment of peoples exploited or oppressed by European imperialism earned him a reputation as one of South Africa's finest postcolonial writers.

Plomer's first and best-known novel, *Turbotte Wolfe* (1925), is one of the earliest works of fiction to address the social and political problems arising from South Africa's racism. It tells the tale of Turbotte Wolfe, who runs a trading post in Africa. Wolfe is fully aware of the wrongs committed by European colonization and exploitation, but he is far from being free of racism; he bristles, for example, at the idea of interracial marriage. The novel ends when the trading post is sold and a new and sinister man named Bloodfield comes to replace Wolfe.

Plomer examines Japanese culture in his collection of short stories, *Paper Houses* (1929), one of the first pieces of European writing to avoid portraying Japan and Asia as romantic and exotic. While the collection confronts the problems of Western imperialism and exploitation, it also examines subservience on an individual and personal level. In "Nakamura," for instance, the title character, a taxi driver, is forced to serve a woman with whom he had previously had a sexual relationship and her new wrestler boyfriend. The woman never acknowledges that she knows Nakamura and, in Plomer's words, relegates him to servanthood:

> The girl turned her head the other way, and on her face there was a look of hard, cruel, shallow, primitive sexual pride, for she could see in front of her the back of the rejected Nakamura, who was now going to drive her—as if he were servant, she thought.

Plomer's final novel, *Museum Pieces* (1954), is a tribute to his close friend Anthony Butts, who was mentally and morally devastated by World War II and committed suicide in 1941. In the novel Toby

D'Arfey is shocked by the horrors of the 20th century, and after witnessing drug users and German bombing, he eventually dies in a nursing home. As Plomer's narrator observes, "Toby was a civilized man. He was always on the side of creators against destroyers, he was an enemy of the banal . . . he always knew and always returned towards what was enduring and vigorous and best."

While Plomer is best known as a novelist and writer of short stories, he also wrote poetry and drama. *The Dorking Thigh and Other Satires* (1945), *Celebrations* (1972), and *Collected Poems* (1973) contain a mixture of poems about Africa and address the same problems found in *Turbotte Wolfe*. Other verses are biting satires of the middle class. While his poetry can be refreshingly direct when dealing with political issues, it can also seem, at times, cold and unemotional.

In collaboration with the composer Benjamin Britten Plomer produced several musicals, most important *Gloriana: Opera in Three Acts* (1953) and *Curlew River: A Parable for Church Performance* (1964). *Gloriana* is a modernized version of a masque, a 15th- and 16th-century form of drama featuring elaborately costumed dancing and singing characters. Plomer's masque celebrates the crowning of Queen Elizabeth II in 1952. *Curlew River* is based on the medieval Japanese opera *Sumidagawa* about a woman whose son dies only to reappear to her as a spirit.

Plomer was a writer of remarkable range, as comfortable in verse as in prose, who is remembered largely for his vehement opposition to South African racism. According to the scholar Robert Martin, "His anger and his simultaneous belief in the future of South Africa, the land itself and its peoples, should make him one of the most distinguished [writers] to have arisen out of that tormented history."

Other Works by William Plomer

At Home: Memoirs. 1958. Reprint, Manchester, N.H.: Ayer, 1988.

Double Lives: An Autobiography. 1943. Reprint, Manchester, N.H.: Ayer, 1977.

A Work about William Plomer

Alexander, Peter F. *William Plomer: A Biography.* New York: Oxford University Press, 1989.

Pollock, Mary

See BLYTON, ENID.

Potter, Beatrix (1866–1943) *children's writer*

Beatrix Potter was born in Kensington, England, to Rupert and Helen Leech Potter, both heirs to family fortunes. She was educated by private tutors and spent most of her time with small pets such as mice, snails, and rabbits, of which she was extremely fond. Her family had a summer home in northern England's Lake District, and she used the summers to satisfy her curiosity about animals. According to the scholar Ruth K. MacDonald, while roaming the English countryside, "Potter and her brother skinned and boiled dead animals until only the skeletons remained to be examined." She also had more conventional means of learning about animals—she often went to museums and spent time drawing pictures of the skeletons she saw there.

Potter developed into one of the world's best-known authors of children's books, writing more than 20 books featuring the small animals with which she became so well acquainted during her childhood. The most famous of these books is *The Tale of Peter Rabbit* (1901). Begun as an effort to entertain the sick child of a former governess, *Peter Rabbit* is the story of four rabbits, Flopsy, Mopsy, Cottontail, and Peter. The central character, Peter, ventures into Farmer MacDonald's garden and eats his vegetables before the farmer finds Peter and chases him from the garden back into his mother's warm burrow. When he finally returns home, Potter writes, "His mother put him to bed, and made him some chamomile tea; and she gave a dose of it to Peter" while the good rabbits, "Flopsy, Mopsy, and Cotton-tail had bread and milk and blackberries for supper." The book has been praised for its realism—Peter faces a real, mortal danger in the farmer, and humans are accurately depicted as menacing to animals. Ruth MacDonald recognizes this realism and argues that the existence of "pain and death" in *Peter Rabbit* and Potter's work in general reflects the author's "unwillingness to compromise the truth in order to shelter young readers" and has the effect of inviting "the reader . . . into the fantasy with a sense that he is not being patronized, and that life is not being edited for his benefit and protection."

Potter's second book, *The Tailor of Gloucester* (1902), is considered her greatest achievement. The story is based on the Grimm Brothers' fairy tale "The Shoemaker and the Elves," but in Potter's version, mice replace the elves. Living near a tailor, the mice observe his inability to finish a waistcoat for the Lord Mayor before his wedding on Christmas day. On Christmas Eve the mice finish the coat for the tailor with such skill that he becomes renowned throughout the village, until, in Potter's words, "he grew quite stout, and . . . quite rich. He made the most wonderful waistcoats for all the rich merchants of Gloucester, and for all the fine gentlemen of the country round." *The Tailor of Gloucester* is remarkable because it is more of a fairy tale than any of Potter's other work, and it places animals in direct, peaceful contact with humans.

Most of Potter's books have never gone out of print, and many have been translated into other languages. The scholar Margaret Lane acknowledges the author's unique realism and intriguing animal characters, but explains that her work has endured because there is "nothing namby-pamby about it. It is completely free from any touch of sentimentality. An unstressed faintly ironical humor is alive on every page, and running below the surface of the narrative is a seam of something which can only be described as *toughness*."

Other Works by Beatrix Potter

Beatrix Potter's Nursery Rhyme Book. New York: Penguin, 1984, 1999.
The Tale of Squirrel Nutkin. 1903. Reprint, New York: Penguin, 1992.
The World of Peter Rabbit. New York: Penguin, 1986, 1993.

A Work about Beatrix Potter

Taylor, Judy. *Beatrix Potter: Artist, Storyteller, and Countrywoman.* New York: Warne Frederick, 1996.

Powell, Anthony (1905–2000) *novelist, memoirist*

Anthony Powell was born in London to an aristocratic family. His father, Philip Lionel William Powell, was an officer in the British army and his mother, Maude Mary Powell, was a member of the Dymoke family, which extends back to the days of William the Conqueror. Powell always thought that he would follow in his father's footsteps as a career soldier, but after an early education at various private prep schools and a degree in history from Oxford, he embarked on a long and successful writing career.

Powell's first novel, *Afternoon Men* (1931), tells the story of William Atwater, who works in a museum, and his search for deep and engaging love with a series of shallow and flighty women. Although the novel contains several funny characters, it also has overtones of sadness. After one of his failed relationships, Atwater restlessly walks the streets of London thinking,

> And so she was gone, ridiculous, lovely creature, absurdly hopeless and impossible love who was and had always been so far away. Absurdly lovely, hopeless creature who was gone away so that he would never see her again and would only remember as an absurdly hopeless love.

The novel contains tight, terse dialogue that reveals the influence of the American novelist Ernest Hemingway. Because of its keenly developed characters, *Afternoon Men* drew praise from some of England's most prestigious literary figures, including Edith SITWELL.

Powell is chiefly known for a 12-volume sequence of novels, *A Dance to the Music of Time*, which he wrote over a 25-year span, from 1951 to 1976. The series is inspired by a painting of the same title by Nicolas Poussin, which shows a group of young people dancing to music being played by Father Time. Powell uses the image of the dance in his novels as a metaphor for the delicate social interactions that lie at his work's center.

All of the volumes of *A Dance to the Music of Time* are narrated by Nicholas Jenkins, who generally remains an objective, outside observer of the events that take place around him. Beginning during Jenkins's teenage years and progressing through his old age, the series has been described as a roman-fleuve—literally, a river novel. Long and slow-moving, it has a broad scope: the social history of England over seven decades.

With the first volume, *A Question of Upbringing* (1951), Powell abandons his use of sparse dialogue; indeed, he hardly uses dialogue at all (he considered it the weakest aspect of his writing). This book introduces Jenkins and the other important figures of the entire series—Charles Stringham, Peter Templer, and Kenneth Widmerpool—as schoolboys. It also reveals Jenkins's fondness for keen observation and his vivid imagination. Near the beginning of the book he sees a group of men working in the snow warming themselves by a fire and remarks:

> For some reason, the sight of snow descending on fire always makes me think of the ancient world—legionaires in sheepskin warming themselves at a brazier: mountain altars where offerings glow between wintry pillars; centaurs with torches cantering beside a frozen sea-scattered, uncoordinated shapes from a fabulous past, infinitely removed from life.

Throughout the rest of the volumes, Jenkins works his way into London's varied social circles, embarks on a literary career, marries Lady Isobel Tolland, serves in World War II, and in the final novel, *Hearing Secret Harmonies* (1976), enters old age. Much of the final volume focuses on Widmerpool, who has been a dominating and sinister influence in the earlier novels. Here he becomes involved with a younger set of people, dab-bles in the occult, and dies. In the final pages it becomes apparent that the complications of the middle books have smoothed away with the arrival of old age, and Powell leaves the reader with an image of Jenkins standing beside a bonfire, completing a circle that began with an image of fire in the first book.

Powell has since published several books, including *O, How the Wheel Becomes It!* (1983), a novel about a second-rate writer who makes the rounds of TV talk shows posing as a literary expert; *The Fisher King* (1986), a tale of a wounded World War II veteran on an archaeological holiday cruise; and a series of memoirs. His reputation, however, lies primarily with *A Dance to the Music of Time*. As the scholar Neil McEwan asserts, Powell is considered one of the preeminent British writers of the 20th century: "Anthony Powell gained his reputation . . . more slowly than his near contemporaries Evelyn WAUGH and Graham GREENE, but he is today equally regarded by many readers and increasingly widely known."

Other Works by Anthony Powell
Miscellaneous Verdicts: Writings on Writers, 1946–1989. Chicago: University of Chicago Press, 1992.
To Keep the Ball Rolling: The Memoirs of Anthony Powell. Edited by Ferdinand Mount. Chicago: University of Chicago Press, 2001.

Works about Anthony Powell
Brennan, Neil. *Anthony Powell.* Revised ed. Boston: Twayne, 1995.
Joyau, Isabelle. *Investigating Powell's "A Dance to the Music of Time."* New York: St. Martin's Press, 1994.
McEwan, Neil. *Anthony Powell.* New York: St. Martin's Press, 1991.

Powys, John Cowper (1872–1963)
novelist, essayist
The eldest in a trio of literary brothers (Llewelyn and T. F. POWYS were both also novelists), John Cowper Powys was born in Dorset to the Reverend C. F. Powys, and his wife Mary Cowper Powys.

There were eight other children in the family, and for all of them their sense of family connection was a vital part of their lives. Powys received his education at Sherborne School and Cambridge University. For a number of years he worked as a lecturer in the United States, although he continued to write novels set in England. When he was in his 60s, he returned to Great Britain and lived the remainder of his long life in north Wales.

Powys began his career writing poems and essays. In 1899 he published a verse collection, *Poems*. His first novel, a rambling romance, was called *Wood and Stone* (1915). Its characters include an unscrupulous quarry owner, who represents power and pride, or Stone; and a young woman who intends to become a nun, representing sacrifice and love, or the Wood of Christ's cross. However, it was not until the publication in 1929 of *Wolf Solent* that Powys became known. Wolf Solent is a 35-year-old teacher who has lost his London job and returns to his native Dorset, where he embarks on a journey of self-discovery. The novel set the pattern of Powys's production: idiosyncratic and exceptionally long stories involving elements of folklore and the supernatural.

Powys's next novel, *A Glastonbury Romance* (1932), has proved to be his most enduring. It concerns a performance of the Passion Play (a dramatization of the story of Christ's crucifixion) by a group of locals in the town of Glastonbury. The company of performers is varied and eccentric, and by the end of the novel it is clear that a strong pagan undercurrent still flows in this Christian world. Toward the end Powys writes:

[T]he great goddess Cybele, whose forehead is crowned with the Turrets of the Impossible, moves through the generations from one twilight to another; and of her long journeying from cult to cult, from shrine to shrine, from revelation to revelation, there is no end. . . . The powers of reason and science gather in the strong light of the Sun to beat her down. But evermore she rises again. . . .

A Glastonbury Romance is a difficult book, but highly valued for its intense conveyance of the wide range of feelings of its characters. Like all of Powys's best work, it rewards serious reading with the depth and power of its writing.

Powys followed the book with *Maiden Castle* (1936), which focuses on a prehistoric fort site outside Dorchester. Its main character has the odd name of Dud No-Man, which may reflect the author's depressed feelings at the time of writing. The other main character, Uryen Quirm, believes that the relics at Maiden Castle belong to an ancient civilization, far older than that of Rome and far superior to it, and that the power inherent in them can be brought to life.

In 1937 Powys wrote *Morwyn: Or the Vengeance of God*, a fantasy that reflects his passionate championship of animals' rights. The main characters are an elderly captain and his dog, Black Peter (modeled on Powys's own dog, "The Black"), and its villain is known only as "the vivisector." Part of the novel takes place in Hell, where the hero meets such characters as Socrates and Merlin.

Powys followed these novels with several historical romances, the most popular of which is *Owen Glendower* (1940), about a medieval Welsh hero. Other novels include *The Inmates* (1952), about people who are treated and work in an asylum; and *Atlantis* (1956), a fantasy tale in which the author has Odysseus, from Homer's *Odyssey*, discover America. In his book of essays *In Defence of Sensuality* (1930), Powys argues for a fuller use of all the senses to make one aware of beauty in an ugly world.

Critics have mixed reactions to Powys's literary merits. The most passionate in his defense are undaunted by, but keenly aware of, his sometimes knotted, humorless prose. Novelist Robertson DAVIES, writing in the Toronto *Daily Star,* observed: "John Cowper Powys is a writer of our times who has asked extraordinary things from his readers. He is like nobody else, and has no imitators. . . . He is obstinately great . . . [and] deeply loved by those readers who know him. . . . He must be numbered among those rare authors who add to our range of understanding."

A Work about John Cowper Powys

Graves, Richard Perceval. *The Brothers Powys*. London: Routledge & Kegan Paul, 1983.

Powys, Theodore Francis (1875–1953)
novelist, short story writer

T. F. Powys was born and raised in Dorset, England. He was the brother of the writers John Cowper POWYS and Llewelyn Powys; and the son of Charles Powys, an Anglican clergyman, and Mary Cowper Johnson Powys. Unlike his two brothers, Powys did not attend college and chose a career in farming. Although he failed as a farmer, his writing, which explored a conflict between Christian morality and a negative vision of the human race, was always set in the pastoral English countryside in which he lived.

Powys's first major work, *The Soliloquy of a Hermit* (1916), attracted the attention of critics. Unusual characters were introduced in his early fiction, in which he turned the mythology of the ideal countryside upside down. In *The Left Leg* (1923), God is embodied in a character called Tinker Jar, and the Virgin Mary is represented by a character called Mary Gillet. These characters signify good or evil in a symbolic distortion of a biblical account.

In *Mr. Weston's Good Wine* (1927), Powys explores who is responsible for evil in the world. God is represented by Mr. Weston, a wine salesman who comes to the village of Folly Down to sell light and dark wines, symbolizing love and death. The novel explores the effects of the wines on the village's many inhabitants, notably including Mrs. Vosper, the madam, and the unhappy clergyman Nicholas Grobe (who, in the wake of his wife's death, has lost his faith). Critic Richard Graves has noted that the central question of evil is never satisfactorily answered: "Mr. Weston's pity for mankind leads him to do everything he can to ease man's burden; and this he achieves by selling him some of his 'good wine'. But since drinking wine blurs our sense of reality . . . illusion rather than illumination is seen to be at the centre of God's plans for us."

Fables (1929) is regarded as Powys's finest collection of short stories, the genre in which many critics believe he is most proficient. In this book unlikely and inanimate objects, such as a flea, a spittoon, darkness, seaweed, a bucket, and a rope, engage in conversations that espouse Powys's tragic world view.

In *Unclay* (1931), Powys's last novel, the allegorical visitor to a village (here called Dodder) is not God but Death. Death has come to the village with instructions from God to "unclay" (a term Powys invented to describe the action of Death) two of its inhabitants, but he has a bad memory; he loses his instructions, forgets his orders, and falls in love with one of the village girls. The village's eccentric and colorful inhabitants include Daisy Huddy, a prostitute; the master of the hunt; and Mr. Solly, whose technique for avoiding the pitfalls of love involves visualizing women as vegetables. God appears as Tinker Jar, weeping over the trouble he has brought to the world.

Powys published some short stories after *Unclay*, but by 1947 he had stopped writing, retreating into rustic solitude in Dorset. Richard Graves places *Unclay* with *Mr. Weston's Good Wine* at "the summit of Powys's achievement as a novelist."

Other Works by T. F. Powys

Father Adam. New York: Hyperion, 1990.
Robinson, Ian, ed. *The Market Bell*. New York: Hyperion, 1992.

Works about T. F. Powys

Churchill, R. C. *The Powys Brothers*. London: Longman's, Green & Co., 1962.
Graves, Richard. *The Brothers Powys*. London: Routledge & Kegan Paul, 1983.

Pratt, Dennis Charles
See CRISP, QUENTIN.

Prescott, Hilda Frances Margaret
(1896–1972) *novelist, biographer*

Born in Latchford, Cheshire, England, and a graduate of Manchester University, H. F. M. Prescott was primarily a historical novelist. Known for her solid scholarship, she imparted precise background details in her works. The action of *The Unhurrying Chase* (1925), for example, takes place in late 12th-century France, with its knightly codes of honor, amid the brutal realities of the feudal world and the destruction of southwestern France by mercenary armies. Its main fictional character is a former feudal lord resentful of other overlords, in particular Richard I of England, because the protagonist has been driven out of his own fiefdom.

All three of Prescott's earliest novels, including *The Unhurrying Chase; The Lost Fight* (1928), which takes place in 13th-century Lorraine and Cyprus; and *Son of Dust* (1932), set in 11th-century Normandy, are primarily love stories with a similar theme: the conflict between the imposition of strict Church sanctions on sexual activity and the reality of human needs and desires.

Prescott's scholarly acumen also appears in her nonfiction work, especially her biography of Mary Tudor, *Spanish Tudor: The Life of Bloody Mary* (1940), and in *Friar Felix Fabri: A Fifteenth-Century Pilgrimage to the Holy Land* (1950). But her greatest success is the critically acclaimed historical novel *The Man on a Donkey* (1952). Considered to be one of the most notable and believable English historical novels of the 20th century, the plot covers the years from 1509 to 1539, during a rebellion of English Catholics against Henry VIII's closure of the monasteries. Parallel stories of five principal characters—an Abbey prioress, a loyal Catholic noble, a Protestant malcontent, a squire who is the leader of the revolt, and the married woman who is in love with him—are brought together through the narrative. Secondary nonfictional characters such as King Henry VIII, Catherine of Aragon, Princess Mary, Anne Boleyn, Thomas Cromwell, Cardinal Wolsey, and Sir Thomas More also appear throughout the novel and charge it with historical reality. Prescott's historical precision and descriptive clarity draws readers into everyday life of the early 16th century, with, as one reader put it, "images as clear and easily intelligible as landscape photographs."

Priestley, John Boynton (1894–1984)
novelist, short story writer, playwright, nonfiction writer

J. B. Priestley was born in Bradford, Yorkshire, England, to working-class parents: Jonathan Priestley, a schoolmaster, and a mother about whom little is known, except that she was Irish, probably a factory worker, and died during Priestley's infancy. He attended Bradford Grammar School, where he published essays in London newspapers and magazines. At 16 he quit school to work as a clerk, but after World War I he entered Cambridge University and earned a B.A. in English literature, modern history, and political science. In the writing career that ensued, Priestley wrote more than 150 books, both fiction and nonfiction, ranging from biographies to literary criticism. He also wrote short stories and plays and became one of the most prominent figures of 20th-century British letters.

It was Priestley's fourth novel, *The Good Companions* (1929; awarded the James Tait Black prize in 1930), that initially caught the interest of the literary world. Critics drew comparisons between Priestley and 19th-century novelists Charles Dickens and William Thackeray, because of the book's length (over 600 pages) and its sprawling, often sentimental plot. The novel describes the rise of an initially rag-tag band of entertainers who transform themselves into a successful traveling theater troupe called the Good Companions. As successful as the Good Companions are, at the end of the novel they disband, each having achieved happiness in his or her own way. Priestley was a Christian socialist, and as with much of his writing he made the human collective, here represented by the Good Companions, an instrument for hope and positive change.

Priestley's many novels cover a variety of subjects and are written in varied styles. He produced lighthearted romps with country settings, such as *The Good Companions;* novels of intrigue and espionage such as *Doomsday Men* (1938) and *Saturn Over the Water* (1961); and serious works such as *Bright Day* (1946), which delves into the protagonist's psychology and personal history.

Priestley's work in drama began with a 1931 adaptation of *The Good Companions* for the stage and continued with *Dangerous Corner* (1932), his most popular play. The comedy's small cast of characters embark on a truth-telling binge. In the end each realizes that pure truth is seldom desirable:

Stanton: I think telling the truth's about as healthy as skidding round a corner at sixty.
Olwen: I agree with you. I think telling everything is dangerous. What most people mean by telling the truth is only half the truth.

For *The Linden Tree* (1947), Priestley received the Ellen Terry Award for best play. Ostensibly about middle-class people coping with change, the play features an aging Professor Linden who, while fighting a forced retirement, refuses to become bitter or disillusioned and instead maintains an optimistic outlook.

Priestley also established a reputation as a literary biographer with close examinations of the lives and work of two 19th-century British writers, *George Meredith* (1926) and *Thomas Love Peacock* (1927). He also wrote several nonfiction accounts of his travels. The first, *English Journey* (1934), details a trip through English backwaters and in a relaxed, down-to-earth tone describes many of the economic hardships facing the British lower and middle classes during the 1930s. *Russian Journey* (1946) is about Priestley's travels in the Soviet Union and *Journey down a Rainbow* (1955) centers on a trip to the American Southwest.

Priestley's literary reputation has been somewhat weakened by the sheer volume of his writing, and, as scholar Bes Stark Spangler notes, by "critics' assumption that to be a versatile writer is to be a mediocre writer." Nevertheless, Priestley's biographers A. A. DeVitis and Albert E. Kalson have called him "one of England's national treasures." The scholar Kenneth Young, considering the reading public the mightiest critic, finds Priestley a tremendous success who has "stimulated political, sociological, and literary thought; entertained us mightily with his . . . novels; [and] made us laugh and cry and

wonder with his plays, some of which . . . have earned the right to the title of modern classics."

Other Works by J. B. Priestley

Bright Day. Chicago: University of Chicago Press, 1983.
The Magicians. 1954. Reprint, Savannah, Ga.: Beil, 1996.

A Work about J. B. Priestley

DeVitis, A. A., and Albert E. Kalson. *J. B. Priestley.* Boston: Twayne, 1980.

Pritchett, V. S. (Victor Sawdon Pritchett) (1900–1997) *short story writer, novelist, nonfiction writer, literary critic, essayist, memoirist*

V. S. Pritchett was born in Ipswich to Sawdon Pritchett, an unsuccessful businessman, and Beatrice Pritchett. During his childhood, which became the subject of his memoir *A Cab at the Door* (1968), his family moved 18 times in 12 years. Pritchett's education ended at age 16 when his father apprenticed him to a leather trader in London, but that city soon became a source of inspiration for the young man, putting him in close contact with the lower- and middle-class people who would become the focus of his fiction.

Pritchett produced a large body of work that included travel narratives, literary criticism, biography, autobiography, novels, and short stories, but it was for his short stories that he would become best known. His reputation as a storyteller grew steadily from his first collection, *The Spanish Virgin and Other Stories* (1930), through more than 14 additional volumes, which include *When My Girl Comes Home* (1961) and *Blind Love and Other Stories* (1969). His *Complete Collected Stories* (1991) brought him a wave of critical acclaim and introduced him to a new generation of readers.

Pritchett's stories typically contain eccentric lower-middle-class characters, promote tolerance and understanding, substitute a montage of scenes critically important to his characters in place of conventional plots, and are written in clear and simple prose. Pritchett himself considered the title story of *When My Girl Comes Home* his best tale. It describes the homecoming of Hilda, a woman who left for Bombay with her husband before World War II and who then went missing throughout the war years. When Hilda returns, "her tinted brown hair . . . was done in a tight high style and still unloosened . . . her breasts were full in her green, flowered dress . . . [and] her eyebrows seemed to be lacquered. How Oriental she looked on that first day!" As the story unfolds, it becomes apparent that Hilda's "Oriental" nature is no coincidence, for her first husband had died in Bombay, and circumstances took her to Tokyo, were she married a Japanese soldier and remained during the war. Eventually she was imprisoned, not by the Japanese but by the Americans. Immediately labeled abnormal, Hilda spends several weeks in London, where she is viewed alternately as a friend of the former enemy, the Japanese, and, as a result of her Oriental qualities, an exotic, sexual figure on whom several male characters fixate.

In addition to short stories Pritchett wrote five novels that never received the acclaim of his shorter pieces. Of the novels, *Nothing like Leather* (1935) and *Mr. Beluncle* (1951) are the most memorable. *Nothing Like Leather* tells the story of Mathew Burkle, a workaholic leather merchant who rises to prominence only to die by falling into a tanning vat. Burkle's end is a heavy-handed warning against the dangers of becoming obsessed with work. More mature, but still considered unsatisfactory even by Pritchett himself, *Mr. Beluncle* is about a family impoverished by a father who chooses a life of intellectual pursuit that leads to poverty. The novel, narrated by Mr. Beluncle's son, focuses on the conflicts that arise between the son and the father and remains funny even while describing the sad frustrations of every family member except the father.

While Pritchett was never satisfied with his efforts as a novelist, he was as comfortable writing nonfiction as he was writing short stories. His first nonfiction work, *Marching Spain* (1928), a travel narrative, was also his first publication. He would eventually write six additional travelogues, three biographies, three memoirs, and nine books of criticism. *Complete Collected Essays* (1992), with more than 200 essays from over 50 years of writing, captures the essence of Pritchett as a literary critic who constantly shies away from academic criticism in favor of analyses that would be accessible to the same common people who inhabit his fiction. He won the PEN Award for biography for *Balzac* (1974), about the famous 19th-century French novelist, and wrote late into his life, publishing another highly acclaimed biography, *Chekhov: A Spirit Set Free* (1988), at the age of 88.

Before his death Pritchett was named Commander of the Order of the British Empire (CBE), knighted, and granted honorary degrees from several universities including Harvard and Columbia. In the words of the novelist William TREVOR, Pritchett "has done more for the short story in his lifetime than anyone since Joyce or Chekhov. He has probably done more for the English short story than anyone has ever done."

Other Work by V. S. Pritchett
London Perceived. 1962. Reprint, Boston: David R. Godine, 2001.

A Work about V. S. Pritchett
Stinson, John J. *V. S. Pritchett: A Study of the Short Fiction.* Boston: Twayne, 1992.

Pudney, John (1909–1977) *novelist, poet, journalist, biographer, literary critic*
John Pudney was born in Langley, Buckinghamshire, to Harry William and Mabel Pudney. He served as an intelligence officer for the Royal Air Force before beginning his long career as a writer for the BBC (British Broadcasting Corporation) and the London *News Chronicle* and as a literary editor and critic for the *Daily Express* and the *News Review*.

A successful journalist, editor, and critic, Pudney was also a prolific writer of novels and poetry, the most popular of which target young people. In the "Hartwarp" series, for instance, which contains seven novels such as *The Hartwarp Balloon* (1963) and *The Hartwarp Bakehouse* (1964), Pudney provided tightly woven and action-packed stories set in the quirky village of Hartwarp.

In his more serious and adult-oriented writing, Pudney often wrote about his experiences in the Royal Air Force. In his best-known poem, "For Johnny," a tribute to the British airmen who died during World War II, Pudney writes, "keep your tears / For him in after years," and counsels England to resist undue mourning for men who died in the cause of freedom.

One of Pudney's final works, which shows his range as a writer, was *Lewis Carroll and His World* (1976). The biography of Carroll, according to the reviewer Charles Bishop, is a "serviceable short biography . . . useful as a general introduction" and appealing "to the specialist and the general reader alike." Pudney will be best remembered, though, as a World War II poet and a writer of literature for children and young adults.

Pym, Barbara (1913–1980) *novelist, editor*

Born in Shropshire, England, to a middle-class family, Barbara Pym spent her early life in the town of Oswestry. She had a happy childhood, and one reason for her happiness was the pleasure she took in writing. She was sent to boarding school, where she excelled at English; she was especially inspired by Aldous HUXLEY's satire *Crome Yellow* (1921). She earned her degree in English literature at Oxford, where she was influenced by the writing of Stevie SMITH; Ivy COMPTON-BURNETT; and John BETJEMAN, whom she especially admired for his ability to cherish ordinary things. At Oxford Pym playfully wrote a story about her sister and herself as 50-year-old spinsters, and years later this became her first novel, *Some Tame Gazelle* (1950).

Although Pym began writing in the 1930s, her work did not make it into print until 1950. But writing nonetheless became increasingly important to her as her heady university days receded.

She wrote in her diary, "I honestly don't believe I can be happy unless I am writing. It seems to be the only thing I really want to do."

Pym spent the first part of World War II back in Oswestry, where she found wartime provincial isolation boring. She wrote copiously through this time, working on several novels at once. After the war she began working for the International Africa Institute, becoming assistant editor for the academic journal *Africa*. She continued with this job until 1974 and wrote in the evenings and on weekends.

Some Tame Gazelle, published in 1950, is a gently comical book about two middle-aged, unmarried women whose lives center on their parish church. The novel's title comes from a poem by Thomas Bealy and serves as the epigraph to the book: "Some tame gazelle, or some gentle dove: / Something to love, oh, something to love!" These two wistful lines sum up the plight of almost all Pym's female characters: without husbands, children, or pets, it is natural and imperative for them to lavish their love on other things—institutions, libraries, curates, the local church—even if that love is not returned.

Pym produced five more novels by 1961, but in 1962 her next novel was rejected for publication. For more than 20 years she continued to write without publication. Throughout these years she was greatly comforted by the encouraging letters of her friend Philip LARKIN. In 1974, after a mild stroke, she retired from editing and moved to a village in Oxfordshire with her sister.

Pym's retirement from literary life was suddenly reversed when she was in her mid-60s. In January 1977 the *Times Literary Supplement* invited famous authors to choose the most underrated writers of the 20th century; both Lord David Cecil, who taught at Oxford, and Philip Larkin listed her name. Larkin wrote, "She has a unique eye and ear for the small poignancies and comedies of everyday life." This recognition had a dramatic effect on Pym's life. Macmillan immediately published her previously rejected work *Quartet in Autumn* (1977), and all her earlier books were reprinted.

Quartet in Autumn is an unsentimental depiction of four lonely people growing old. They have nothing to love: "In the past both Letty and Marcia might have loved and been loved, but now the feeling that should have been directed towards husband, lover, child or even grandchild, had no natural outlet; no cat, dog, no bird, even, shared their lives." In this loneliness, Pym's characters are often brave but never melodramatic.

Quartet in Autumn was short-listed for the BOOKER PRIZE, and in 1978 Pym was made a Fellow of the Royal Society of Literature. In the last two years of her life she continued working despite illness, and was deeply gratified by the new appreciation of her novels. To quote a *Newsweek* review, "Her books work; they are taut with art."

Other Works by Barbara Pym

Civil to Strangers and Other Writings. New York: Plume, 1988.

Excellent Women. 1952. Reprint, New York: Plume, 1988.

A Glass of Blessings. 1958. Reprint, New York: Harper-Collins, 1987.

Jane and Prudence. 1953. Reprint, London: Moyer Bell, 1999.

Less Than Angels. 1955. Reprint, New York: Dutton, 1980.

No Fond Return of Love. 1961. Reprint, London: Moyer Bell, 2002.

The Sweet Dove Died. 1968. Reprint, London: Moyer Bell, 2002.

A Very Private Eye: An Autobiography in Diaries and Letters. Edited by Hazel Holt and Hilary Pym. New York: Dutton, 1984.

A Work about Barbara Pym

Holt, Hazel. *A Lot to Ask: A Life of Barbara Pym.* New York: Dutton, 1991.

Raine, Craig (1944–) poet

Craig Raine was born in Bishop Auckland, England, the son of Norman Edward and Olive Marie Cheeseborough Raine. He was educated at Exeter College, Oxford.

Reviewer Andrew MOTION describes Raine's early work in *The Onion, Memory* (1978) as "lacking the human element," but perceives a new willingness in the poet's later work to show emotion. Raine's best-known work is *A Martian Sends a Postcard Home* (1979), in which an alien describes Earth to his fellow Martians. The imagery and metaphors ("mist is when the sky is tired of flight") that represent an alien perspective have led to his being known as the founder of "the Martian School of poets."

The narrative style that begins to emerge in *A Martian Sends a Postcard Home* is further developed in *Rich* (1984), a collection that includes poems from an earlier publication, *A Free Translation* (1981). Reviewer Dick Davis praised Raine for writing "a marvelously responsive poetry of childhood," particularly the prose memoir of the poet's father, an amateur boxer. Raine's most monumental poem, the 600-page *History: The Home Movie* (1994) chronicling the history of his and his wife's families in the 20th century, took 10 years to complete.

An account of a long-past love affair, *A la Recherche du Temps Perdu* (2000) received contrasting reactions. "The book's avowed purpose to 'remember' the lost love, rings hollow against the prevailing evidence of covert revenge," wrote Gerald Mangan in the *Times Literary Supplement*, while reviewer Sam Leith commended the poem as "purposive, a project to revive and reconcile."

The prolific Raine has received both high praise and harsh criticism since his debut as a writer in the late 1970s. As critic Sean French observed, he "can be infuriating in his rudenesses . . . but he always has the engagement of the practitioner, of the man for whom poetry is an activity and a craft as well as an elevated art form."

Other Work by Craig Raine

Collected Poems, 1978–1999. London: Picador, 2000.

Raine, Kathleen (1908–) poet, literary critic, translator, memoirist

Kathleen Raine was born in London to George and Jessie Raine, both schoolteachers. She received her M.A. from Girton College, Cambridge, in 1929. Raine was remarked that "Nature is the common, universal language, understood by all," and incorporates themes from both mythology and nature in her poems to express a greater understanding of the human condition.

Raine's numerous poetry collections include *The Collected Poems of Kathleen Raine* (1956), which established her reputation as a talented poet with an ability to use language to express feeling and a sense of intimacy in her work. A more recent collection, *Selected Poems* (1988), draws from some of her earliest work, starting in 1943, and traces her career through the subsequent decades. New and previously uncollected poems conclude this work.

Early poems such as "The Hyacinth" and "Vegetation" (1956) reveal Raine's deep respect for the natural world. Her fascination with the dreamlike quality of things found in nature continued in her later work as well. "A Dream of Roses," first published in 1969, begins, "So many roses in the garden / Of last night's dream, and all were golden." Raine has compared the act of writing itself to an innate response: "In writing poems I have but obeyed an inner impulse, as does the bird when it sings."

Raine has also written scholarly works on famous writers. *Blake and Tradition* is a critical work about the visionary writer William Blake. She has translated two works by the 19th-century French writer Honoré de Balzac: *Cousin Bette* (1948) and *Lost Illusions* (1951; reissued 1985).

Raine's other writings include a three-volume autobiography that chronicles her intellectual life, from her pre-Cambridge years to her success as a poet and critic. Written over a period of many years, the three volumes were published individually at first. They were issued together for the first time as *Autobiographies* in 1992.

Despite high critical acclaim for her poetry, criticism, and autobiographical writing, Raine remains virtually unknown as a writer in the United States. Her reflective and imaginative style, which draws deeply on ideas of the past, led the critic Howard Nemerov to claim that "Kathleen Raine's poems are unfashionable on purpose, unworldly, traditional, meditative, belonging to memory and dream, to solitude and silence."

A Work by Kathleen Raine

The Collected Poems of Kathleen Raine. New York: Counterpoint Press, 2001.

Rattigan, Terence Mervyn (1911–1977)
playwright, screenwriter

Terence Rattigan's father, William Rattigan, was a diplomat; his mother, Vera, hailed from Dublin, Ireland. Rattigan attended Trinity College, Cambridge, where he was expected to study history in preparation for his diplomatic career, but he was more interested in the theater than in his studies. While still an undergraduate, he cowrote a play, *First Episode* (1933), the story of a student who falls in love with an older woman. Produced in both London and New York, the play was a failure, but it led Rattigan to leave school and work full-time at becoming a successful playwright. He managed to talk his father into giving him two years to succeed, agreeing that if he did not, he would prepare for a career in diplomacy.

Over the next two years Rattigan wrote five unsuccessful plays, but his luck changed in 1936 with the production of *French Without Tears,* an immediate hit. This play is a witty romantic comedy with a bit of French farce thrown in. The story focuses on a beautiful young woman who enjoys having several men in love with her at the same time. The first act ends with broken hearts all around. In the second act the men band together to turn the tables on the young siren, and the characters trade lovers and roles.

French Without Tears is a good example of the "well-made" play that Rattigan became famous for. Its theme is often slight, but its structure is perfectly balanced, and the characters and their dilemmas are well-developed and always interesting. Rattigan once said he wrote for an imaginary theatergoer whom he called "Aunt Edna." She was a "nice, respectable, middle-class, middle-aged maiden lady, with time on her hands and money to help her pass it, who resides in a West Kensington hotel."

Rattigan wrote many serious dramas as well, including *The Deep Blue Sea* (1952), which portrays a woman's obsession with a drunken womanizer; *The Browning Version* (1949), about a failed classics teacher who must retire because of poor health; and *The Winslow Boy* (1946), a play loosely based on the true story of a boy expelled from the British Naval Academy for theft.

Rattigan wrote more than two dozen plays and nearly as many screenplays, in addition to seven original television scripts. *French Without Tears* was filmed in 1939, *The Winslow Boy* in 1948 and again in 2000. His original screenplays include *The Prince and the Showgirl* (1957), which starred Laurence Olivier and Marilyn Monroe. He also wrote the screenplay for the 1969 version of James HILTON's *Goodbye Mr. Chips,* starring Peter O'Toole.

The kind of play that Rattigan wrote went out of fashion in the years following the production of John OSBORNE's *Look Back in Anger* (1956). Osborne and other ANGRY YOUNG MEN took the British theater by storm, questioning the values and ideas of British society before World War II, and by implication many of the values inherent in Rattigan's plays. But Rattigan held firm, saying he preferred the "play that unashamedly says nothing—except possibly that human beings are strange creatures, and worth putting on the stage where they can be laughed at or cried over, as our pleasure takes us." He was knighted by Queen Elizabeth II in 1971.

Works about Terence Rattigan

Darlow, Michael. *Terence Rattigan: The Man and His Work.* London: Quartet Books, 1983.

Young, B. A. *The Rattigan Version: Sir Terence Rattigan and the Theatre of Character.* New York: Atheneum, 1988.

Raven, Simon (1927–2001) *novelist*

Simon Raven was born in London, England, to Arthur Godart and Esther Kate Christmas Raven. His father was a man of independent means who enjoyed golfing. Raven rose to the rank of captain in the British army but had to resign his commission because of unpaid gambling debts. He at-

tended King's College, Cambridge, where he received B.A. and M.A. degrees.

Raven's first novel *The Feathers of Death* (1959) describes homosexuality and scandal in the army. A few years later he started his 10-novel series entitled *Alms for Oblivion* (1964–75). Raven has explained that the theme for the series is "that human effort and goodwill are persistently vulnerable to the malice of time, chance, and the rest of the human race." The series focuses on 10 main characters and humorously depicts upper-class society in postwar Britain. Raven's characters are worldly, lacking in morality, and often involved in scandals and love affairs. In the series opener, *The Rich Pay Later* (1965), Carton Weir, a member of Parliament, discusses women with his friends: "If you just say, 'Let's have a bit of fun,' they look shocked. But if you say something portentous, like 'Darling, I'm so unhappy,' they'll drop flat on the nearest bed. . . . Too tedious. Which is why . . . I prefer boys."

The *Arms for Oblivion* novels received qualified praise from critics. When reviewing *The Rich Pay Later* along with *Friends in Low Places* (1965), critic Kerry McSweeney wrote, "Raven handles most skillfully a large and variegated cast of characters and implicates them in the novels' main actions without becoming forced or contrived." When describing the first six novels in the series, McSweeney wrote that "they are uneven in quality, occasionally repetitious and forced, and sometimes no more than entertaining." In 1984 Raven started a second series, *The First Born of Egypt.* These novels trace the stories of people related to the main characters in the *Arms for Oblivion* series.

Raven is known for his imaginative descriptions of bad behavior ranging from corruption in high places to childish pranks. In *The Roses of Picardie* (1980), a novel about the search for an ancient ruby necklace, Raven describes the friendship and antics of a French boy and an English boy: "[T]hey often climbed into each other's beds to play games which combined violence with endearment. . . . It was more fun to hit, squeeze and gouge, and then to go under the bedclothes together to see who farted the fouler smell." Critic Peter Ackroyd describes Raven as "a master craftsman, who can change scenes and characters without overt discomfort; his prose is always amusing, elegant, intelligent and never below the belt."

Other Work by Simon Raven

The Islands of Sorrow. London: Winged Lion, 1994.

A Work about Simon Raven.

Barber, Michael. *The Captain: The Life and Times of Simon Raven.* London: Duckworth, 1996.

Raworth, Thomas Moore (1938–   ) *poet*

Tom Raworth was born in Bexleyheath, Kent, England, to Catholic parents. His father served in the British army during World War II as a radio operator. Raworth attended St. Joseph's Academy in London but became bored and dropped out at the age of 16. He then held a variety of jobs including insurance clerk, costume jewelry packager, construction worker, and international telephone operator. Raworth attended the University of Grenada in Spain and the University of Essex in Colchester, where he received an M.A. in 1971. He founded the Matrix and Goliard Presses and has worked at several British and American universities as a poet-in-residence.

Raworth's first poetry collection, *The Relation Ship* (1966), contains poems that make disquieting observations of domestic life and daily routine. As with his later verse, the poems in *The Relation Ship* have isolated points of view and record momentary distractions and sudden memories. In another common Raworth trait, the poems are detailed and have quick shifts of attention, as in "Not Under Holly or Green Boughs": "aircraft's trail dispersed into Cloud / he entered the car at the lights and gave me an apple."

Drawing on his studies of Latin American literature and experiences in Spain, Raworth published *Lion Lion* (1970), a volume of witty, fast moving verses reflecting his radical political views of the revolutionary sentiments that were gaining strength in Spain at the time. Although critically acclaimed, he remained a relatively obscure poet until the publication of *Tottering State: Selected Poems 1963–1987* (1988) brought him a greater popular acceptance. Critic Robert Sheppard, noting the many long poems of short lines in the volume, writes, "Like subliminal messages on film, the lines flicker past the reading eye: the sudden jumps in point of view and discourse are alarmingly unpredictable."

From 1966 to 1989, Raworth published more than 30 collections of poems. He won the Alice Hunt Bartlett Prize in 1969 and the Cholmondeley Award in 1972. When describing Raworth's work, the critic Alan Brownjohn wrote, "The method by which he thinks his way into the essence of a situation (usually a personal, domestic situation, but the implications are wider) seems altogether original—catching up minute, very clear images into coherent, meaningful structures which vibrate with tension and suggestiveness."

Other Works by Tom Raworth

Blue Screen. Cambridge, Mass.: Equipage, 1992.
Muted Hawks. Berkeley, Calif.: Poltroon Press, 1995.

A Work about Tom Raworth

Barrell, John. *The Flight of Syntax: Percy Bysshe Shelley and Tom Raworth.* London: Ruddock, 1990.

Rayner, Elizabeth

See BELLOC LOWNDES, MARIE ADELAIDE.

Read, Herbert Edward (1893–1968) *poet, literary critic, nonfiction writer, novelist, memoirist*

Herbert Read was born in North Yorkshire, England, to a farming couple, Herbert and Eliza Strickland Read, and studied economics at the University of Leeds. After serving in World War I, he published his first major volume of poetry, *Naked Warriors* (1919), which explored the themes of war and lost childhood. Read's early work reflects his rural background and his admiration for William Wordsworth. The American poet James Dickey observed, "The poems I think of most persuasively as Read's . . . are about land, and its relationship to those who live on it. These poems have more of the . . . sense of *belonging* to the land than any I know since Wordsworth's." Other critics, however, regard Read's poetry as cerebral, citing the influence of IMAGISM and of T. S. ELIOT, his close friend.

After the war, Read married and began working in the government treasury office, but he left that bureaucratic job for one that better fitted his artistic inclinations, assistant keeper in the Victoria and Albert Museum in London. He worked there from 1922 to 1931. At the same time, he published prose works on a variety of subjects, especially the literary and visual arts. He published seven books of criticism in the last half of the 1920s alone. His works of literary criticism include *English Prose Style* (1928), a rhetorical handbook; and *Phases of English Poetry* (1928), a history of English poetry published by Leonard and Virginia WOOLF. In numerous critical works, he championed romantic poets such as Wordsworth and Percy Bysshe Shelley. He also promoted the works of younger poets, such as Henry TREECE and J. F. Hendry, who published *The New Apocalypse* in 1939.

In 1932 Read published one of his most important works, *Form in Modern Poetry*, wherein he explains the important distinction, still associated with his name, between organic and abstract form. According to Read, while an artist imposes abstract form on a work of art, organic form grows out of the artistic impulse. In 1933 he became editor of Britain's most important art periodical, the *Burlington Magazine*. While editing this journal, he continued to write criticism. His *Art Now* (1933) promoted avant-garde artistic movements such as SURREALISM and constructivism and became immensely popular, going through five editions by the time of his death.

Read's one novel, *The Green Child* (1935), is a surrealistic tale of an Englishman, Oliver, who becomes Olivero, president of a South American country. Read scholar George Woodcock calls it a "small and unique classic:" "It has been called a parable, a romance, a fairy tale, a Utopian fantasy, an allegory, and it contains elements of all these in its intricate symbolic suggestiveness."

In *Education through Art* (1943) Read wrote about the liberating effect of art on the development of young minds and personalities: "It follows that in any ideal system of education we should educate the senses, and to this end each of the arts should have its place in the curriculum." It was his most influential work, helping to bring the teaching of art to British schoolchildren.

Read also published two autobiographical works, *The Innocent Eye* (1933) and *The Contrary Experience* (1963). He was knighted in 1953. His accomplishment as a critic and philosopher is perhaps best summed up by George Woodcock: "He went beyond the contemplation of actual works of art and literature to seek the sources of artistic creativity and to establish the relationship between the work of art and the percipient mind."

Other Works by Herbert Read

A Concise History of Modern Painting. 1959. Reprint, London: Thames and Hudson, 1988.
Modern Sculpture: A Concise History. 1964. Reprint, London: Thames and Hudson, 1996.

Works about Herbert Read

Goodway, David. *Herbert Read Reassessed,* Liverpool, England: Liverpool University Press, 1998.
King, James. *The Last Modern: A Life of Herbert Read.* New York: St. Martin's Press, 1990.

Reed, Eliot
See AMBLER, ERIC.

Reed, Henry (1914–1986) *poet, playwright*
Henry Reed was born in Birmingham, England. His father worked long hours as a foreman in a brick factory; his mother was illiterate. Encouraged by his older sister, Reed developed a love for learning.

He graduated from the prestigious King Edward VI Grammar School and the University of Birmingham, then began working as a freelance writer, journalist, and teacher.

After World War II Reed published *A Map of Verona* (1946), a book of poetry in five sections. The section called "Lessons of the War" contains poems based on his brief and unsatisfying experience in the army. One of these poems, "Naming of Parts," became widely anthologized and so well known as an antiwar poem that it made Reed famous as a one-poem poet and overshadowed his other work. (On being introduced to him, a person would usually say, "Oh, Mr. Reed, I've read your poem.")

After the war, Reed worked as a translator and as a broadcaster and playwright for the BBC (British Broadcasting Corporation) and its "Third Programme," which featured high culture and classical music. He also wrote plays that made fun of opera, and his poem "Chard Whitlow" (1941), a *New Statesman* prize-winning parody of T. S. Eliot, opens with the sententious line "As we get older we do not get any younger." Eliot told Reed it was the best parody of his style that he had seen. The critic David Cecil characterized Reed's poems as being "made personal and delightful by his sense of decorative elegance and the play of his neat and graceful wit."

Other Works by Henry Reed

Hilda Tablet and Others: Four Pieces for Radio. London: British Broadcasting Corporation, 1971.

Collected Poems. Edited by J. Stallworthy. Oxford, England: Oxford University Press, 1991.

Renault, Mary (Eileen Mary Challans)
(1905–1983) *novelist*

Mary Renault was born Eileen Mary Challans in London to Frank Challans, a doctor, and Clementine Baxter Challans. She went to Oxford University at a time when very few women went to college at all, and she refused to become a schoolteacher, the traditional career for college-educated women.

Instead, she became a nurse in 1937 and worked in the medical profession for about 10 years, including World War II.

Renault's first novel, *Purpose of Love* (1939), is a love story set at a hospital and draws on the author's experiences as a nurse. *The Friendly Young Ladies* (1944), also based on personal experience, includes a lesbian relationship between two of the characters. Some years earlier Renault had begun a lifelong relationship with Julie Mullard.

Renault's next novel, *Return to Night* (1946), tells the story of the romance between Hilary Mansell, a brain surgeon, and Julian Fleming, a man 10 years her junior. It brought the author financial success when she won a £40,000 award from the movie studio Metro-Goldwyn Mayer (MGM). This money enabled Renault to give up nursing and become a full-time writer. In 1948 she moved to South Africa, where she became an early protester against apartheid. Her next novel was *The Charioteer* (1953), concerning gay servicemen in wartime England.

The Last of the Wine (1956) was the first of a series of novels Renault set in the ancient Mediterranean world, a culture that accepted homosexuality more freely than 20th-century Britain and thus allowed her more freedom to depict homosexual relationships. The story takes place in Athens in the fifth century B.C., during the Third Peloponnesian War. The friendship magnified into love between Alexias, the narrator, and Lysis, a soldier, allows Alexias to attain personal and philosophical maturity. The power of this novel arises, according to the critic Landon Burns, Jr., out of Renault's ability "to make us believe in a world remote from ours, but one in which we recognize problems and people who reflect our own society."

Renault's most famous work, *The King Must Die* (1958), is the first of two novels concerning the life and adventures of the mythological Greek hero Theseus. The sections concerning Theseus's training in Crete to become a bull dancer are particularly vivid and memorable: "We would dance and sway out of the way, while Aktor shouted, 'No! No! Move as if he was your lover! You lead him on, you give him the slip, you make him sweat for you; but it's a love affair and the whole world knows it.'" Critic Dudley Fitts wrote that in this novel, "an act of scholarship and art combined to give us a novel that was at once ancient and contemporary, as beautifully and horribly moving as the wild legends on which it was based." Renault's next novel, *The Bull from the Sea* (1962), picks up the story of Theseus from his leaving Crete until his death.

Renault's interest in Greek drama informed her next work, *The Mask of Apollo* (1966), whose first-person narrator is Nikeratos, a professional actor during the fourth century B.C. The novel provides firsthand accounts of the Greek theater: "By the time I was twenty-six, I was not quite unknown in Athens. I had played first roles at Piraeus, and at the City Theatre done second in some winning plays."

Beginning in 1969 Renault occupied herself with three novels about Alexander the Great: *Fire from Heaven* (1969), *The Persian Boy* (1972), and *Funeral Games* (1981). The first of these novels deals with Alexander's youth; his conflicts with his parents; his ambition; and his hero-worship of Achilles, the great warrior of the *Iliad*. Alexander's later youth and early young manhood form the subject of *The Persian Boy*, and *Funeral Games* details his death. Renault also wrote a nonfiction study of the Macedonian conqueror, *The Nature of Alexander* (1975). Her final, non-Alexander novel was *The Praise Singer* (1978) about Simonides, a Greek poet of the sixth century B.C. Renault's biographer David Sweetman notes, "She told a good story, with enough adventure to satisfy the common reader, and her fastidious attention to historical detail made classical scholars some of her greatest fans, but it was also true that several of her leading characters were unashamedly homosexual at a time when many of those same readers would, under other circumstances, have considered the subject repellent."

A Work about Mary Renault
Zilboorg, Caroline. *The Masks of Mary Renault: A Literary Biography.* Columbia: University of Missouri Press, 2001.

Rendell, Ruth (Barbara Vine) (1930–)
novelist

Ruth Rendell was born in London to Arthur Grasemann and Ebba Kruse Grasemann, both school-teachers. She graduated from Loughton High School in Essex, England, and started her writing career as a journalist. In 1950 she married journalist Don Rendell. As a novelist she has earned a reputation as a master of the psychological mystery.

Rendell is primarily known as a writer of murder mysteries set in Britain, and her work is often compared in style and tone to that of Agatha CHRISTIE. Her first novel, *From Doon with Death* (1964), introduces the characters of Wexford and Burden, two detectives whom Rendell writes about repeatedly in subsequent novels. The novel tells the story of Margaret Parsons, who has disappeared and is subsequently found murdered. Wexford and Burden are left to solve her violent and mysterious death and to comfort Parson's distraught husband, who has the dark secrets of his home life revealed during the course of the police investigation.

In *A New Lease of Death* and *Wolf to the Slaughter* (both 1967), Rendell develops her two main characters more fully by tracing their attempts to solve extraordinary crimes. In *Wolf to the Slaughter* the heroes have to solve a mystery involving a missing corpse that has disappeared from a pay-by-the-hour hotel and a beautiful promiscuous woman who has also vanished. In the more recent novel, *Harm Done* (1999), Wexford has to solve the mystery of the disappearance and then reappearance of two Sussex teenagers, Rachel and Lizzie. Wexford himself is presented as a sympathetic father who cares deeply about children. Remarking that "some childhoods are unhappier than others" in the opening scene, Wexford tries to unravel the mystery of Lizzie's earlier unknown whereabouts through careful interviews.

Rendell has also published novels under the pseudonym Barbara Vine, allowing her to experiment with a new mystery genre without disappointing dedicated readers of her Wexford series books. The novels published under this name include *A Dark Eye Adapted* (1985), which tells the story of a murder caused by a domineering mother's attempt to control the lives of her son and daughter. In 1986 the novel won the Edgar Award for best murder mystery. In this book, as in others in the Barbara Vine series, the murder remains secondary to the exploration of deeper psychological elements such as madness and emotional deceit.

As a mystery writer, Rendell has found success in creating both sympathetic and believable characters who are sometimes deeply psychologically disturbed. As one critic for the *New York Times Book Review* described Rendell in a review of her book *A Demon in My View* (1976), "Nothing much seems to happen, but a bit here, a bit there, a telling thrust, and suddenly we are in a sustained mood of horror. Rendell is awfully good at this kind of psycho-suspense." In assessing her contribution as writer, the *Los Angeles Times* called her "[u]ndoubtedly one of the best writers of English mysteries and chiller-killer plots."

Other Work by Ruth Rendell

A Sight for Sore Eyes. New York: Crown, 1999.

Rhys, Jean (Ella Gwendolyn Rees Williams) (1890–1979) *novelist, short story writer*

The daughter of Minna Lockhart Rhys, a Creole mother, and Dr. William Rees Williams, a Welsh doctor, Jean Rhys was born in Roseau, Dominica, into a life of poverty. At age 16 she went to London, where she made a precarious living working in a chorus line. In 1919 she married Jean Lenglet, a Dutch journalist, and moved to Paris, where she began writing. Lenglet was imprisoned for violating currency regulations, and the couple divorced in 1932. Rhys then married Leslie Tilden Smith, a publisher's reader. After he died in 1945, she married his cousin, Max Hamer, who was also imprisoned for misappropriation of funds. The Hamers lived in poverty in Cornwall.

While in Paris, Rhys began writing, encouraged by the British writer Ford Madox FORD. Her literary career is sharply divided in two. An elegant and economical stylist, she wrote half a dozen novels and several collections of short stories. By 1945 she had stopped writing and lost her literary friends and contacts; her own work had gone out of print. Thirty years separated the fiction she wrote in the late 1920s and early 1930s from the publication in England of her final, most successful novel, *Wide Sargasso Sea* in 1966. In old age Rhys also published two collections of short stories, *Tigers Are Better-Looking* (1968) and *Sleep It Off, Lady* (1976). An unfinished autobiography, *Smile, Please,* was published posthumously in 1979.

For Rhys, point of view was much more than a literary device: It was a painful, inescapable fact of the human condition. Her marginal perspective as an outsider and the alienation and rejection that are at the core of all her fiction stem from her racial, religious, and colonial background. As Jean d'Costa observes in *Fifty Caribbean Writers,* Rhys's pervasive theme of exile and insight "into placelessness and loss of identity derives from her Dominican origins," being part of the "paradox of belonging without owning, or of owning without belonging. . . ."

In her introduction to a volume containing all of Rhys's novels (*Voyage in the Dark* [1934, but actually written first], *Quartet* [1928], *After Leaving Mr. Mackenzie* [1930], and *Good Morning, Midnight* [1939]), the scholar Diana Athill shows how Rhys creates progressively more mature female protagonists and also achieves a more detached point of view. This detached and refined perspective culminates in the haunting loveliness of *Wide Sargasso Sea,* Rhys's prequel to Charlotte Brontë's *Jane Eyre.*

Athill observes, "Nowhere else did [Rhys] write with more poignancy about what it is like to be rejected, and nowhere else did she go so deeply into . . . what it is like to be driven . . . mad." Antoinette Cosgrave, Creole heiress to a plantation in Jamaica, is affianced to Edward Fairfax Mason (Brontë's Rochester), an Englishman in need of a fortune. After a blissful Caribbean honeymoon, he turns against her, suspecting her of infidelity, and transports her to England, where he imprisons her in the attic of his country home. In a fateful reenactment of the fire set to Coulibri, her own home, which drove her mother mad, Antoinette plans to set fire to Thornfield Hall, her husband's estate.

Rediscovered and acclaimed on publication of *Wide Sargasso Sea*, Rhys at last received recognition, and in 1978 she was made a Companion of the Order of the British Empire (CBE). In 1974 British critic A. ALVAREZ observed of her, "Although her range is narrow, sometimes to the point of obsession, there is no one else now writing who combines such emotional penetration and formal artistry or approaches her unemphatic, unblinking truthfulness."

Works about Jean Rhys

Angier, Carole. *Jean Rhys: Life and Work*. Boston: Little, Brown, 1990.

Howells, Coral Ann. *Jean Rhys*. New York: St. Martin's Press, 1991.

Sternlicht, Sanford. *Jean Rhys*. Boston: Twayne, 1997.

Richardson, Dorothy Miller
(1873–1957) *novelist, nonfiction writer, translator*

Dorothy Richardson was born in the town of Abington in Berkshire, England, a rural area that she later described as "a vast garden, flowers, bees and sunlight." Richardson's family seemed more conventional than it was. Although her father Charles was prosperous, he was secretly tormented about his class position because he had begun life as a grocer. Richardson's mother Mary was extremely depressed, and in 1895 she committed suicide when she and Richardson went on vacation together.

Richardson was educated at home by a governess and then at a private school in London. When she was 20 her father went bankrupt, and she was obliged to leave her studies and become a governess in Germany. She taught for four years and then returned to London, where she made a number of literary friends, particularly H. G. WELLS. She spent many years translating and writing journalism and reviews.

In 1912 Richardson began writing her famous epic novel sequence, *Pilgrimage*, whose 13 volumes she considered to be one novel, with each volume being one chapter. The first volume, *Pointed Roofs*, appeared in 1915 and the 12th in 1938. The 13th and final volume, *March Moonlight*, was published in 1967, 10 years after the author's death.

In *Pilgrimage* Richardson invented a new narrative style. Instead of setting down objective statements about her heroine Miriam's experiences, Richardson wanted to set down Miriam's thoughts as they occurred to her. Thus Miriam's acquaintances and environment are seen through her own awareness; as Richardson said in a 1921 letter, readers "share her impressions such as they are." This new narrative style of a character's flowing, continuous thoughts was famously named "stream of consciousness" by the critic May SINCLAIR, who took the term from the work of psychologist William James. (Richardson herself was not impressed by the label.) Other authors, notably Virginia WOOLF, the French writer Marcel Proust, and the Irish writer James JOYCE, are also acclaimed as writers of stream-of-consciousness prose.

This stream-of-consciousness style had political significance to Richardson. She was suspicious of the conventional realistic novel form, which relied on objective statements about characters and events. Richardson believed that such realism often led to blindness toward a female point of view; she noticed that the seemingly neutral objective statements in novels were in fact frequently written from a male perspective. She therefore wanted to produce "a feminine equivalent of the current masculine realism." As the critic Gillian Hanscombe writes, *Pilgrimage* is feminist "not in the sense of arguing for equal rights and votes for women, but in the more radical sense of insisting on the authority of a woman's experience and world view."

Because Richardson wanted to make her prose more subjective than objective, she was careful to make sure that her language did not slide into the conventional, third-person reportage that characterized most novels. In her books she jumps between first-person and third-person narration constantly. She also often ignores conventional grammar, for example by using ellipsis dots to string together several phrases to make a long paragraph simulating reverie: "Marriage . . . the new house . . . the red brick wall at the end of the garden where young peach-trees were planted . . . running up and downstairs and singing . . ."

Pilgrimage explores the struggles of Miriam Henderson to become a financially and emotionally independent woman. Much of the work is semiautobiographical: The first two volumes, *Pointed Roofs* and *Backwater* (1916), draw on Richardson's experiences as a young governess in Germany. Volume four of *Pilgrimage, The Tunnel* (1919), begins her thorough examination of Miriam's relationship with London. Miriam does not draw her window blinds, instead welcoming the city into her home at all hours: "London, just outside all the time, coming in with the light, coming in with the darkness, always present in the depths of the air in the room." Even the street is cherished: "The street had lost its first terrifying impression and had become part of her home." Richardson later wrote that "what London can mean as a companion, I have tried to set down in *Pilgrimage*."

Richardson also wrote nonfiction, including *The Quakers Past and Present* (1914), in which she explored her longstanding fascination with and admiration for this sect. Her other nonfiction includes the illustrated book *John Austen and the Inseparables* (1930), which discusses the work of the illustrator John Austen. Richardson argues that pictures and stories are inseparable: "All literature is in some degree pictorial." She also translated numerous books, including Léon Pierre-Quint's *André Gide: His Life and Work* (1934), a biography of the French writer.

Although Richardson has been admired by many writers, her work is surprisingly little read. Some readers become uneasy with her lack of an objective narrator and her linguistic innovations. Yet *Pilgrimage* is acclaimed as an innovative feminist work. As Gillian Hanscombe says, "Richard-son's very original vision of female experience, together with her uncompromising experimental style, make the novel an extraordinary testament to the validity of female individuality."

Other Work by Dorothy Miller Richardson
Windows on Modernism: Selected Letters of Dorothy Richardson, Edited by Gloria G. Fromm. Athens: University of Georgia Press, 1995.

A Work about Dorothy Miller Richardson
Redford, Jean. *Dorothy Richardson.* New York: Hamester Wheatsheaf, 1991.

Robinson, Lennox (Esmé Stuart Lennox Robinson) (1886–1958) *playwright*
Lennox Robinson was born in Douglas, Ireland, to Andrew Craig Robinson, a stockbroker and minister, and Emily Jones Robinson. A sickly child, he was educated at home by private tutors. During his years of forced rest, however, he read voraciously and even wrote, developed, and published a family magazine, *Contributions*. In 1907 he saw performances of William Butler YEATS's *Kathleen ni Houlihan* and Lady GREGORY's *Rising of the Moon*, which inspired him to pursue a career in the theater.

A year later Yeats and Gregory staged Robinson's first play, *The Clancy Name* (1908), which immediately earned the young playwright a prominent place among Irish dramatists. With this and other realistic plays about common Irish people, Robinson ushered in, according to biographer Michael J. O'Neill, "a . . . breed of Irish playwrights. . . interested in baring the harsher aspects, the sterner realities of Irish life." *The Clancy Name* so impressed Yeats and Gregory that in 1909 they hired the 23-year-old poet and producer for Dublin's Abbey Theatre.

Although Robinson was successful from the beginning, several years elapsed before he fully realized his potential in the critically acclaimed and enduring comedies, *The Whiteheaded Boy* (1916) and *Crabbed Youth and Age* (1922). The more subtle and kindhearted of the two, *The Whiteheaded Boy* tells the story of the lower-middle-class Geoghegan family, whose mother favors her youngest son Denis, whom she dubs "the whiteheaded boy." Mrs. Geoghegan forces the rest of her children to make constant sacrifices so that Denis can pursue what she considers his destiny: going to college and becoming a doctor. Denis, however, who cares little for his mother's dreams, spends his time playing instead of studying and fails his medical examinations three times. Eventually, by threatening to become a manual laborer, he manipulates a wealthy aunt into providing him a store to manage, which saves the family's reputation and allows him to marry his sweetheart Delia. Even at the end, with all of his siblings absolutely exasperated by his continued success, he is still Mrs. Geoghegan's "whiteheaded boy":

> What sort of unnatural children have I got at all? Would you grudge your brother the one little bit of luck he's had in all his life? Look at him sitting there with the girl he loves . . . and not one of you would as much as wish him joy.

Crabbed Youth and Age, a satirical one-act comedy of manners, is the story of Mrs. Swan and her attempt, which fails miserably, to introduce her three daughters to eligible bachelors. Tommy, Gerald, and Charlie, the three men whom she invites to her home, are not attracted to the young, awkward daughters but rather to Mrs. Swan herself, who is older and more experienced in social situations. In the final lines of the play Gerald and Charlie stand thunderstruck as they watch Mrs. Swan dance with Tommy, and when one of the daughters approaches with drinks, Gerald, with his eye on the girl's mother, remarks, "Hush: Don't break the spell . . . wonderful . . . wonderful."

Only one of Robinson's later plays, *The Far-Off Hills* (1928), ever approached the popularity of *The Whiteheaded Boy.* Another comedy dealing with marriage-making, *The Far-Off Hills* tells of the Clancy family, which is headed by a temporarily blind father and the pious eldest daughter, Mar-

ian, who plans to become a nun. Marian's two younger sisters writhe beneath her strict gaze and long for the moment when she will leave for the convent. When a man named Pierce arrives at their home, the younger girls egg him on as he woos and wins Marian, who now gives up her earlier religious plans.

Although he attempted to find dramatic subjects outside of Ireland, Robinson was most successful when he wrote about his homeland. In his assessment of Robinson's achievement, Michael J. O'Neill writes that the playwright remains "best known today . . . as a . . . sympathetic observer and critic of the imperfections of Irish family life . . . who well merits a place among the most entertaining and versatile of his kind in the English-speaking theatre of modern times."

Other Works by Lennox Robinson
Selected Play of Lennox Robinson. Washington, D.C.: Catholic University of America Press, 1982.
Towards an Appreciation of the Theatre. New York: Haskell House, 1974.

Rohmer, Sax (Arthur Henry Sarsfield Ward) (1883–1959) *novelist, short story writer*

Sax Rohmer, born Arthur Henry Ward (he later changed his middle name to Sarsfield), was the son of Irish parents who had immigrated to England. As a child he reportedly led a life rich in fantasy. After failing at a series of jobs, including bank clerk and gas company clerk, he turned to writing. His first stories were accepted for publication in 1903. Rohmer spent the next decade writing for the English music hall in various forms before returning to fiction. His stories began to appear serially in *Cassell's Magazine* in June 1912; at the time he was also working on the stories that would make his name.

Beginning in October 1912 *Cassell's* published a series of stories titled *Fu-Manchu.* The book *The Mystery of Dr. Fu-Manchu,* composed of the serialized stories and the first book to appear under the pen name Sax Rohmer, appeared in 1913. Fu Manchu, head of Si-Fan, a sinister and insidious secret organization, is an evil genius who aims at world domination. Rohmer's reputation would henceforth rest primarily on Fu Manchu and the 15 novels in which the villain appeared, although Rohmer produced other works that explored his interest in the exotic, the occult, and the "Mysterious East," such as *The Romance of Sorcery* (1914) and *Brood of the Witch Queen* (1918).

Rohmer excelled at neither plotting nor prose. His popular Fu Manchu character is of interest, however, as a racist stereotype that embodied the anxieties of a far-flung empire attempting to control "restless" and "inscrutable" natives: a powerful and threatening rival rising up from a despised, powerless, and colonized people. Critic Robert Bickers has written, "As a thriller writer Ward is of little importance . . . However, Ward was an entrepreneur with a knack for identifying what might sell, and where his market lay."

A Work about Sax Rohmer

Van Ash, Cay, and Elizabeth Sax Rohmer. *Master of Villainy: A Biography of Sax Rohmer*. Edited by Robert E. Briney. Bowling Green, Ohio: Bowling Green University Popular Press, 1972.

Rosenberg, Isaac (1890–1918) *poet, painter*

Isaac Rosenberg was born in Bristol, England, to immigrant Jewish parents. The family moved to Whitechapel, in London's East End, in 1897 in an unsuccessful effort to escape poverty, which dogged Rosenberg the rest of his life. In school he began to sketch and to write under the headmaster's encouragement. In 1904 Rosenberg was compelled to leave school, and he began an apprenticeship with an engraver. He worked at his poetry on lunch hours, and in 1907 he sought solace in evening drawing classes at Birkbeck College.

In 1911 Rosenberg quit his job and began to study painting at the Slade School of Art. While there, he had printed 50 copies of a pamphlet containing nine of his romantic poems, *Night and Day*. By spring 1914, however, he had become plagued by a respiratory ailment and had also exhausted the sources of financial support for his studies.

In 1914, in search of employment and respite from ill health, Rosenberg set off for South Africa, where a sister lived. While there he lectured, painted, and worked on a verse drama, *Moses*. World War I broke out in Europe while he was in Africa, and he returned to England in February 1915. Still sickly and unable to find employment, he enlisted in the army in October 1915 in hopes of financially improving his mother's lot. Despite the rigors of life in the ranks, he persisted in writing poetry. In May 1916 he shipped to France, where he was killed two years later.

Rosenberg is often grouped today with the "trench poets" such as Wilfred OWEN. "Break of Day in the Trenches" is among his best-known works. The narrator, reaching up from the trench for a poppy, touches a rat, whom he addresses, observing that the rat touches German and English hands alike: "Droll rat, they would shoot you if they knew / Your cosmopolitan sympathies."

Steeped in the irony of a world turned upside down, the poem is nevertheless naturalistic and realistic in tone; the critic Paul Fussell called it "the greatest poem of the war." Rosenberg has come to be regarded as a major figure. According to the scholar Fred Crawford, Rosenberg was "less a war poet than a poet at war."

Other Work by Isaac Rosenberg

Parsons, Ian, ed. *Collected Works of Isaac Rosenberg*. London: Chatto & Windus, 1979.

Works about Isaac Rosenberg

Graham, Desmond. *The Truth of War: Owen, Blunden, Rosenberg*. Manchester, England: Carcanet Press, 1984.
Liddiard, Jean. *Isaac Rosenberg: The Half Used Life*. London: Victor Gollancz, 1975.

Ross, Martin

See SOMERVILLE, EDITH ANNA OENONE AND MARTIN ROSS.

Rowling, Joanne Kathleen (1966–   )
novelist

To explain her love of strange names, J. K. Rowling likes to say that she was born in Chipping Sodbury, England. Although this town was nearby, Rowling was actually born in Yate to Peter Rowling and Anne Volant Rowling. She was educated at the Tutshill Church of England primary school and later at the Wydean Comprehensive School. Several of the teachers in Rowling's fictional school for wizards, Hogwarts, are based on teachers she encountered during these years. She then attended the University of Exeter, where she took a degree in French. When she graduated, she took a series of office jobs.

On a train ride from Manchester to London in June 1990, Rowling suddenly had an idea for a novel. She imagined a train carrying a boy to a boarding school where he would study wizardry. Though she had neither pen nor paper with her, she began to think about characters and plot elements.

In 1992 Rowling moved to Portugal and married a journalist, Jorge Arantes. Their daughter Jessica was born in 1993. Soon afterward, Rowling left her husband and moved to Edinburgh, Scotland, where she completed the first Harry Potter novel, *Harry Potter and the Philosopher's Stone* (1997; published as *Harry Potter and the Sorcerer's Stone* in the United States). Because her apartment was unheated, Rowling would take long walks with Jessica in a stroller, stopping at a local coffeehouse. While Jessica slept, Rowling would write. When the novel became a huge success, the story of how it was written became almost legendary.

No one predicted the incredible success of Rowling's first Harry Potter novel, which was quickly followed by two more, *Harry Potter and the Chamber of Secrets* (1998) and *Harry Potter and the Prisoner of Askaban* (1999). By the time the third novel was published, Rowling's three books held the top three spots on the *New York Times* bestseller list. As a result, the *Times* established a separate list for best-selling children's books. *Harry Potter and the Sorcerer's Stone* won many awards, including Britain's most prestigious for children's books, the Whitbread, in 1999. A fourth volume— of seven planned—was published in 2000: *Harry Potter and the Goblet of Fire.*

An orphan, Harry Potter lives with his dreadful relatives, the Dursleys. While his ill-tempered, hugely fat cousin Dudley is doted on and thoroughly spoiled, poor Harry suffers all manner of abuse, including having to live in a tiny cupboard under the stairs. But on his 11th birthday he discovers that his parents, who he thought were killed in an automobile accident, were actually wizards. Harry too has magical powers and is invited to study magic at the Hogwarts school for wizards. Hogwarts is an amazing place, part English boarding school, part fairy tale. Instead of algebra and world history, Harry and his friends take classes in casting spells, making potions, and wielding a magic wand.

Readers respond to Rowling's sense of humor, which is evident in characters' names, situations, and word play. Rowling invented a wizard candy, for example, called Bertie Botts Everyflavor Beans—and they really do come in every flavor, including "vomit" and "booger." In typical British understatement, the huge, snarling, three-headed dog that guards the sorcerer's stone is named Fluffy. When Harry makes the mistake of using magic in the world of the "muggles" (non-wizards) and fears he will be punished, Minister of Magic Cornelius Fudge comforts him: "Oh, my dear. . . . It was an accident! We don't send people to Azkaban just for blowing up their aunts!"

Each of the four novels published as of 2002 has a similar structure. Each begins with Harry in the clutches of his awful muggle relatives. Then, as the school year begins, Harry escapes back to the world of Hogwarts, where he is something of a celebrity. Harry and his best friends, Hermione Granger and Ron Weasley, get into a variety of minor scrapes—but the larger threat of the evil Lord Voldemort, who had killed Harry's parents, is always present.

One of Rowling's many fans is the American novelist Stephen King, who wrote in the *New York Times,* "Harry is the kid most children feel themselves to be, adrift in a world of unimaginative and often unpleasant adults . . . who neither understand them nor care to. Harry is, in fact, a male Cinderella, waiting for someone to invite him to the ball."

A Work about J. K. Rowling

Kirk, Connie Ann. *J. K. Rowling: A Biography.* Westport, Conn.: Greenwood Publishing, 2003.

Rubens, Bernice (1923–) *novelist*

Bernice Rubens was born in Cardiff, Wales, to Eli Rubens, an orthodox Jew who had fled Russia, and Dorothy Cohen Rubens. She attended public schools and earned a B.A. in English from the University College of South Wales in 1947. Rubens spent nearly a decade teaching and working on documentary films before she published her first novel, *Set on Edge* (1960), in which she established herself as an author who looks closely at Jewish life and whose primary theme is loneliness.

Set on Edge centers on the Sperber family, a tight-knit unit surrounded by a larger Jewish community. Throughout the novel, characters attempt to break away from the family, but all eventually return. As the novel develops, its focus narrows to Gladys, the family's eldest daughter, who remains single until her 60s, having resisted family pressure to marry. On her honeymoon, Gladys's husband dies, and she returns home alone to experience another profound abandonment when her parents die. She is left bewildered, lonely, and lacking the family community that surrounded her all her life.

Rubens received the BOOKER PRIZE for her novel *Chosen People* (1969). This novel, too, is about a Jewish family struggling to meet cultural expectations and to survive the stifling closeness of family and community. Set in the present with flashbacks to and the past, the novel tells of Norman Zweck, initially a child prodigy, who becomes a successful lawyer before crumpling under the strain of meeting his family's expectations. Until his breakdown Norman's success allows the family to present itself as happy and nearly perfect, even in the face of such shameful events as the elopement of one of his sisters with a gentile. After Norman collapses into drug use and

mental illness, however, he becomes a source of shame to his father, a rabbi, and his sister Bella. As Norman's attempts at recovery fail, the shame Rabbi Zweck and Bella feel turns to anger. Deciding that he is using drugs out of spite, they make him the scapegoat for all of the family's problem.

While Jewishness plays a central role in much of her work, Rubens has set her novels in a wide range of places, including Southeast Asia and Asia Minor, and has addressed subjects as varied as history and aging. Her novels *Brothers* (1983) and *Mother Russia* (1992) are set in Russia. The first is the story of a Jewish family struggling to survive in czarist Russia, while the second traces the fates of two Russian families of vastly different social classes, linked by romance through the Russian Revolution, World War I, and World War II.

In one of Ruben's recent novels, *The Waiting Game* (1997), set in a retirement home, the author examines with wit and irony the psychology of aging. While all of her characters are awaiting death, they are a comical cast: Lady Celia runs a quiet blackmailing business, Mr. Cross asks each morning whom he will outlive that day, and Mrs. Green hides a mysterious past.

Rubens is a keen observer of human nature, and her tender, compassionate treatment of her characters has earned her a wide readership. In the words of the critic David Haworth, Rubens is "one of our finest Jewish writers. She has a large compassion, and an intelligence which makes her compulsively readable. She is deeply committed, yet objectively truthful, about the Jewish world and people she describes."

Other Works by Bernice Rubens

I, Dreyfus. London: Little, Brown UK, 1999.
Milwaukee. London: Little, Brown UK, 2001.
A Solitary Grief. London: Little, Brown UK, 2001.

Rushdie, Ahmed Salman (1947–)
novelist, short story writer, essayist

Salman Rushdie was born to wealthy, liberal, secularized Muslim parents, Anis Ahmed Rushdie and

Negin Rushdie, in Bombay, India, but has lived much of his life in England. He describes himself as an agnostic Muslim and feels torn between different cultures. Referring to his short-story collection *East, West* (1994), Rushdie told the *Daily Telegraph,* "The most important part of the title is the comma. Because it seems to me that I am that comma."

Rushdie's first three novels, *Grimus* (1975), *Midnight's Children* (1980), and *Shame* (1983) won critical approval. *Midnight's Children* was a multiple award winner: the BOOKER PRIZE, an award from the English Speaking Union, the James Tait Black prize, and a special "Booker of Bookers" award as the best novel in the first 25 years of the Booker Prize.

Rushdie gained international fame with his novel *The Satanic Verses* (1988), which rewrote the story of the Islamic prophet Mohammed, depicting him as a skeptic and a man driven by sexual desire. The prophet's scribe "Salman" is initially faithful, but then, faced with religious hypocrisy, he says, "I began to get a bad smell in my nose."

Satanic Verses enraged Islamic fundamentalists, leading Iran's spiritual leader at the time, the Ayatollah Ruhollah Khomeini, to issue a death sentence against Rushdie for offending God. After Khomeini's pronouncement, some bookstores believed to be carrying Rushdie's book were bombed, and riots occurred in places the author was believed to be staying. One translator of the book was stabbed to death. Many writers publicly announced their support for Rushdie, and politicians around the world condemned the death sentence. Critic Amir Mufti wrote, "The violence of the novel's reception . . . is an accurate indicator of the anger generated by its insistence on a sweeping rearrangement and rethinking of the terms of Muslim public culture."

Despite the death threat, which eventually was lifted, Rushdie continued to write. After publishing a nonfiction account of travels in Nicaragua, *The Jaguar Smile* (1997), Rushdie took a sympathetic interest in the United States, setting his novel *Fury* (2001) there. It is the story of Malik Solanka, professor and dollmaker, who tries to lose himself in New York City but discovers that one's deeds take on a life of their own as he watches his dolls become extremely popular. Solanka sees parallels between God's strange relationship to the humans he created, who have free will and his own relationship to his dolls: "Nowadays, they started out as clay figurines. Clay, of which God, who didn't exist, made man, who did."

Solanka also struggles to control his own anger, often amplified by the chaos of the city: "He was never out of earshot of a siren, an alarm, a large vehicle's reverse-gear bleeps, the beat of some unbearable music." Rushdie argued in newspaper editorials in the years prior to *Fury* that America has generated hostility from both left-wing and right-wing groups around the globe precisely because it is an embodiment of freedom and change. In America's ability to constantly reinvent itself, Rushdie sees parallels to the dangerous power of fiction-making and to his own status as a cultural nomad, a theme that arises repeatedly in his collection *Imaginary Homelands: Essays and Criticism 1981–1991* (1991).

Critical Analysis

Much of Rushdie's work can be classified as "magic realism," which combines realistic, even weighty or political issues and events, with elements of magic or mythology. *Grimus,* for instance, sends its Native American protagonist, Flapping Eagle, in search of his sister and involves him with magicians, intelligent stone frogs, extraterrestrials, and a host of other fantastic devices.

In *Midnight's Children* political satire mixes with Hindu fantasy and psychic abilities, as it is revealed that 1,001 children born at the stroke of midnight on August 15, 1947, the day of Indian independence from Britain, gained such superpowers as telepathy and telekinesis. Two of those children, one wealthy and one poor, are switched at birth, leading to political complications.

The Muslim Indian narrator, Saleem Sinai, says he is "handcuffed to history," the events of his life "indissolubly chained to those of my country." Sinai's psychic powers, says critic Dubravka Juraga, enable him "to empathize with members of all segments of India's complex, multilayered society," from a starving man to a rich man bullying serfs and even real-life political figures such as Prime Minister Nehru. Throughout the novel Saleem struggles to retain his own identity. Scholar Michael Reder remarks, "as Saleem's story demonstrates, individuals can fall victim to a discourse—such as a national myth—in which they themselves are denied a role." Individual identity is constrained by historical circumstances.

Shame, patterned after Gabriel Garcia Marquez's *One Hundred Years of Solitude,* combines the Pakistan civil war with the fairy tale-like story of a little girl so wracked by shame that her blushes can set objects on fire. An accusatory narrative voice sometimes interrupts Rushdie's main narration, demanding to know whether Rushdie is close enough to Indian and Pakistani culture to tell this tale: "We know you, with your foreign language wrapped around you like a flag: speaking about us in your forked tongue, what can you tell but lies?" Critic Timothy Brennan calls this "Rushdie's most fully realized and densely crafted novel."

In *Haroun and the Sea of Stories* (1990) Rushdie artfully blends references to *The Thousand and One Arabian Nights,* Rushdie's philosophy that reality is open to many interpretations, and his love of fiction as a playground of the mind where countless ideas, even heretical ones, can be displayed. It is the story of a boy who hopes to rescue his father by returning to him the gift of storytelling: "And because the stories were held here in liquid form, they retained the ability to change, to become new versions of themselves." Rushdie and his characters savor the ability to rework old tales and old beliefs.

Rushdie's blending of different cultural influences has been a chief interest of his critics, who have seen in him both a testament to the relevance of tradition and folklore and a reminder that the entire idea of nationhood is in some sense a fiction, maintained by common beliefs and touchstone stories. Further, as critic Timothy Brennan observes, by rewriting sacred stories with the imagination and freedom of a fiction writer rather than the ferocity of a heretic or adherent of a rival religion, Rushdie "unravels the religion from within." Scholar M. Keith Booker, in his introduction to a collection of essays on Rushdie, writes that "Rushdie has undoubtedly been one of the most important writers in world literature in the past quarter century. . . [and] a major commentator on Indian and other postcolonial cultures."

Other Works by Salman Rushdie

The Ground Beneath Her Feet. New York: Holt, 1999.
The Moor's Last Sigh. Thorndike, Me.: Chivers, 1995.

Works about Salman Rushdie

Booker, M. Keith, ed. *Critical Essays on Salman Rushdie.* Boston: G. K. Hall, 1999.
Cundy, Catherine. *Salman Rushdie.* Manchester, England: Manchester University Press, 1996.
Harrison, James. *Salman Rushdie.* Boston: Twayne, 1992.

Russell, George William (A.E.)
(1867–1935) *poet, essayist*

Born in Ulster, Ireland, to Thomas and Marianne Russell, George William Russell became part of the Irish Literary Renaissance that occurred in the late 19th and early 20th centuries. In 1878 his family moved to Dublin, where his father worked as an accountant. Russell began taking courses at the Metropolitan School of Art in 1880. At Rathmines College, from 1882 to 1884, he decided to reject the religion of his parents, both of whom were Church of Ireland members.

In 1884 Russell began to have visions—vivid waking dreams that gave him access, he believed, to "supernature," the spiritual world. He described these visions in his highly poetic autobiography, *The Candle of Vision* (1918): "Once I lay on the sand dunes by the western sea. . . . Then there was an intensity of light before my eyes. . . . [,] and I saw the light was streaming from the heart of a glowing figure. Its body was pervaded with light as if sunfire rather than blood ran through its limbs."

Also in 1884 Russell met William Butler YEATS, another budding mystic. The two established a friendship that lasted nearly a quarter-century. Yeats infected Russell with his cause of creating a national Irish literature separate from England's literature. Russell also joined the Dublin Hermetic Society, which Yeats helped found. He was drawn to Eastern religion and thought; theosophy, the search for life's meaning through mysticism and philosophical inquiry; and otherworldly Celtic legends.

In 1897, representing the Irish Agricultural Organization Society, Russell toured every Irish county explaining to farmers the benefits of farming cooperatives; he also started creameries throughout Ireland. As editor of the periodicals *The Irish Homestead* (1904–23) and *The Irish Statesman* (1923–30), he effectively influenced Irish economic reform.

In 1888 an aural "vision" gave Russell the title for his series of paintings on the theme of humanity's divinity—human life, that is, as beginning in the mind of God and achieving completion on earth. A voice told him to "Call it 'The Birth of Æon,'" and he did. (In Greek mythology Æon means "the new year,") Russell also adopted the word as his pen name. However, a printer's mistake reduced the word to A.E. The pseudonym variously appears as Æ, æ, A.E., and ae.

Russell's essays had begun to appear in the journal *Irish Theosophist* in 1892. Among the most famous is "The Hero in Man" (1897), in which he draws kinship between humanity and gods, or spirits, the contemplation of whose "giant sorrows . . . awakens what is noblest in [human] nature." Russell writes, "[O]ur deepest comprehension of the seemingly apart divine is also our furthest inroad to self-knowledge; Prometheus and Christ are in every heart. The story of one is the story of all." Russell's style drew critical fire from some quarters; Sean O'CASEY, for instance, described A.E.'s prose as "a mass of congested nonsense."

Russell's first poems appeared in the Hermetic Society's journal, and in his first volume of poetry, *Homeward: Songs of the Way* (1894). This volume contained many of his most famous poems, such as "The Unknown God"; "Sacrifice"; "Unity"; and "By the Margin of the Great Deep," which begins "When the breath of twilight blows to flame the misty skies / . . . I am one with the twilight's dream." Many critics belittled Russell's verse because of its nebulous spirituality and "twilit" imagery. However, in an assessment that could also cover Russell's philosophical essays, the scholar Ernest Boyd writes, "A.E.'s verse is not so much the utterance of a poet as the song of a prophet."

Other Work by George William Russell (A.E.)

Song and Its Fountains. 1932. Reprint, Burdett, N.Y.: Larson Publications, 1991.

Russell, William Martin (1947–)
playwright, screenwriter

Willy Russell was born in Whiston, near Liverpool, England, to a shopkeeper and a warehouse worker. He left school at age 15 knowing he wanted to be a writer—a realization he recalled as "wonderful" but "terrible because how could I . . . a piece of factory fodder, ever change the course that my life was already set upon?" Russell worked in a warehouse and, at his mother's suggestion, as a women's hairdresser until deciding at age 20 to become a teacher. In 1969 he enrolled at Childwall College of Further Education, and from 1970 to 1973 he trained as a drama teacher at St. Katherine's College of Higher Education, Liverpool. Here he wrote his first play, *Keep Your Eyes Down* (1971), which was performed by St. Katherine's College at the 1971 Edinburgh Fringe Festival.

Russell had decided to become a playwright after seeing John MCGRATH's *Unruly Elements* performed in 1971 at Liverpool's Everyman Theatre. Several of his own plays were commissioned by the theater after McGrath saw *Blind Scouse* (1972), his trilogy of *Keep Your Eyes Down, Playground,* and *Sam O'Shanker,* performed at the 1972 Edinburgh Fringe Festival. Russell wrote several one-act plays before winning the *Evening Standard*'s and London Theatre Critics' award for Best Musical for *John, Paul, George, Ringo . . . and Bert* (1974), a story of the Beatles' ups and downs by a loyal fan named Bert. In one scene, a group of wheelchair-bound fans wait to be healed by the Beatles.

In *Breezeblock Park* (1975), about a young woman desperate to escape a meaningless life, Russell explores the theme of escape. He continues this theme in *Educating Rita* (1980), about a 26-year-old hairdresser who turns to her Open University tutor to help her improve her life through literature. *Educating Rita* was made into an award-winning film starring Michael Caine and Julie Waters, for which Russell wrote the screenplay.

In *Shirley Valentine* (1986), another stage and screen hit, the 42-year-old title character escapes from her life as a Liverpool wife and mother to an extended vacation in Greece. Shirley, who dreams of drinking wine "in a country where the grape is grown," speaks to her kitchen wall: "I hate a life of talkin' to the wall. But I've been talkin' to the wall for more years than I care to remember now. An' I'm frightened. I'm frightened of life beyond the wall."

Besides plays for stage, screen, and television, Russell has written musical scores for several films (including his own) and the musical *Blood Brothers* (1983), about twin brothers separated at birth and raised in different social classes. A member since 1965 of the musical group the Kirbytown Three, Russell is also founding director of Quintet Films (London). He has been a writer-in-residence and a fellow in creative writing at colleges in Liverpool and Manchester, respectively, and in 1983 he was awarded an honorary M.A. by the Open University. Critic Edward Pearce writes that Russell uses ". . . a popular medium for a grave end. It is his genius to straddle two cultures and talk brilliant sense to both."

Other Work by Willy Russell
Plays: 1. London: Methuen, 1996.

Sabatini, Rafael (1875–1950) *novelist, short story writer, playwright, nonfiction writer*

Rafael Sabatini was born in Jesi, Italy, to the opera singers Anna Trafford and Vincenzo Sabatini, both well known in their time. Fluent in the Italian of his father and the English of his mother, he was sent to school in Switzerland, where he learned French and German. He began his working life in his mother's hometown of Liverpool as a translator, mainly of Portuguese.

Sabatini became a full-time writer and married in 1905. By the end of his life he had published 31 novels, eight volumes of short stories and short novels, a play, and six books of nonfiction. *The Sea-Hawk* (1915) tells the story of Sir Oliver Tressilian, a nobleman who becomes a slave, then a pirate. Sabatini's most popular work, *Scaramouche* (1921), begins with his most famous line, which also served as his epitaph: "He was born with a gift of laughter and a sense that the world was mad." Set during the French Revolution, the novel follows the adventures of an aristocrat who is banished from the estate of his foster father and becomes an actor and hero of the Revolution. That work was followed shortly by another swashbuckler, *Captain Blood* (1922), based on the true story of Henry Pitman, an English surgeon who was sold into slavery in Barbados.

Sabatini's nonfiction works include *The Life of Cesare Borgia* (1912) and *Torquemada and the Spanish Inquisition* (1913). During his lifetime his historical novels were immensely popular, and several were made into movies. Several of his novels remain in print. The scholar Larry Landrum explains, "Sabatini's period novels and romances have not lost their charm over time for those readers willing to suspend disbelief in their romantic premises."

Other Work by Rafael Sabatini

The Fortune of Casanova and Other Stories. Edited by Jack Adrian. Oxford, England: Oxford University Press, 1994.

Sackville-West, Vita (Victoria Mary Sackville-West) (1892–1962) *poet, novelist, memoirist*

Vita Sackville-West was the daughter of the British aristocrat Lionel Edward Sackville-West, Baron Sackville, and Josephine Victoria Sackville-West. She was born in Paris and lived in southwest France during her early years, but moved to her father's estate, Knole Castle in Kent (given to the family in 1556 by Queen Elizabeth), after her mother's death. Educated by private tutors, she was writing poetry by the age of 11. In 1913 she married Harold Nicholson.

Although she published several early volumes of poetry, including *Constantinople* (1915), at her own expense, Sackville-West established her reputation, and several of her dominant themes, with the Hawthornden Prize–winning poem *The Land* in 1926. The long poem (nearly 2,500 lines) is written in the traditional pastoral mode—that is, it is narrated by a shepherd figure who meditates on the virtues of the countryside—and in a manner indicative of all Sackville-West's writing, paying close attention to the details of rural British landscapes. The poet glorifies the place and the rustic figures who inhabit it, as she does with a shepherd's occupation in the lines, "Only the shepherd watching by his flock / Sees the moon wax and wane." In 1946 she wrote another, similar long poem, *The Garden,* which turns its attention to cultivated land rather than the partially wild countryside.

In addition to her poetry, Sackville-West published several novels, including three best-sellers: *The Edwardians* (1930), *All Passion Spent* (1931), and *Family History* (1932), all of which explore themes of British social relationships, heredity, and women's independence from men. These novels demonstrate Sackville-West's resistance to modernism's fragmentation and experimentation by telling fairly straightforward, linear stories.

The Edwardians is the story of two aristocratic siblings, Sebastian and Viola, who eventually have their entire way of life called into question by the arrival of a house guest, an adventurer named Leonard Anquetil. Faced with Anquetil's stark disregard for the social constraints and traditions of the aristocracy, Sebastian and Viola consequently realize some of the absurdities of their own way of life and, while the novel ends with the matter unresolved, consider drastically changing the way they live.

All Passion Spent, the most popular of Sackville-West's novels because of its feminism, is the story of an elderly female aristocrat, Lady Slane, who rediscovers her artistic spirit after the death of her hus-

band and years of meeting family obligations. Near the end of the novel, after Lady Slane has told her friend Mr. FitzGeorge that her marriage "had everything that most women would covet," Mr. Fitz-George, in one of the most feminist passages of the novel, remarks, "Face it, Lady Slane. Your children, your husband, your splendour, were nothing but obstacles that kept you from yourself. They were what you chose to substitute for your real vocation."

Family History, drawing the three novels into somewhat of an informal trilogy, also contains an aristocratic female protagonist, Evelyn Jarrod, who meets social resistance for her relationship with a much younger man. This book features the reappearance of Leonard Anquetil, now happily though unconventionally married to Viola of *The Edwardians.*

Sackville-West is best remembered for her poems and novels, but she also penned a number of memoirs. After her death, her son Nigel Nicholson found one of these, which turned out to be an almost complete autobiography up to 1920. The memoir, which reveals the author's lesbian relationships with Rosamund Grosvenor and Violet Keppel, other members of the British aristocracy, was published by Nicholson as *Portrait of a Marriage* in 1973. Sackville-West was also intimately involved with Virginia WOOLF, another prominent British author and the most famous member of one of London's premier literary circles, the BLOOMSBURY GROUP.

In writing pastoral poetry and novels with conventional narratives focusing most closely on characters and social situations, Sackville-West constantly resisted modernism's experimental impulse. In such traditional modes, she nonetheless created work that endures because of its close critiques of English high society and the restrictions that society as a whole places on women. According to one critic, "When placed in the tradition of twentieth-century British women novelists, her writings contribute to the history of women's thought during the turbulent years after emancipation when British women were seeking a new identity."

Other Work by Vita Sackville-West

No Signposts in the Sea. 1961. Reprint, London: Virago, 2001.

Works about Vita Sackville-West

Glendinning, Victoria. *Vita: The Life of Vita Sackville-West.* New York: Alfred A. Knopf, 1983.
Raitt, Suzanne. *Vita and Virginia: The Work and Friendship of V. Sackville-West and Virginia Woolf.* New York: Oxford University Press, 1993.

Saki (Hector Hugh Munro) (1870–1916)
short story writer, novelist, nonfiction writer

Saki was born Hector Hugh Munro in Akyab, Burma, to Charles Munro, a British civil servant, and Mary Frances Mercer Munro. His mother died not long after his birth, and he was sent to England to be raised by two aunts. Saki began writing satire for the *Westminster Gazette* in 1896, taking his pen name from a character in the *Rubaiyat of Omar Khayyam,* translated by Edward Fitzgerald. Over the next 20 years he wrote 135 short stories, two novels, three plays, and a book on Russian history. He was killed by a sniper's bullet in France during World War I.

Saki's tales are witty, macabre, and feature surprise endings. One of his best-known short stories, "Sredni Vishtar" (1911), is about a vicious ferret, Sredni Vishtar (given the characteristics and name of an eastern god) to whom his young master, Conradin, a helpless boy being raised by an overbearing maiden aunt, prays for salvation. His salvation comes after the aunt gives away the boy's pet hen and then decides to go after whatever is in the other pen the boy keeps. The ferret murders the aunt, and the boy's prayers are answered.

In "Tobermory" (1911), the title character, a cat that is taught to speak and write English, overhears malicious remarks about people at a house party. Later, he repeats these remarks verbatim to the victims in the presence of the person who made them. Tobermory is eventually killed by another cat, and his teacher is killed by an elephant in a Dresden zoo. A former guest at the house party, upon hearing of the event, says, "If he was trying German ir-regular verbs on the poor beast, he deserved all he got." Critic Charles Gillen has noted that Saki's greatest accomplishment "was to recognize the potential of the story material in the denizens and in the trappings of the upper classes."

Other Work by Saki

The Complete Saki. New York: Penguin, 1998.

Sansom, William (1912–1976) *novelist, short story writer, biographer, travel writer*

William Sansom was born in London to a wealthy family. His father was a businessman in London and an amateur painter. One of Sansom's earliest memories was running away from home at age two, not out of distress at home life but because the view outdoors was so fascinating: "I remember very clearly," he wrote, "getting on a chair and opening the front door—on to a short path of bright red geraniums, bright sunshine, and all the brightness of liberty."

Sansom was educated at the prestigious private school of Uppingham, then worked in advertising and banking. He later wrote that advertising was excellent training for writing economical prose, for "every word is calculated to count, space is money."

When World War II broke out, Sansom became a volunteer fireman in London. Firefighting during the blitz was extraordinarily dangerous, and he expected to be dead in a week. He began jotting down notes on his experiences, recalling, "In view of my coming decease, I was in no way concerned with possible publication. I simply wanted to put down the truth for myself." The truth produced the short story "The Wall," which describes how a huge wall from a burning building crashed down on a group of firefighters. Several months later, a friend secretly submitted the story to *Horizon* magazine, and it became Sansom's first published story. His stories about firefighting were collected in *Fireman Flower* (1944).

Sansom continued to write after the war, producing several short story collections, including *Something Terrible, Something Lovely* (1948) and

The Marmalade Bird (1973). He also wrote many novels. One of his best known is *The Body* (1949), a critically acclaimed and poignant story narrated by a middle-aged man who is sliding into jealous madness: "The full disaster fell again on me; but magnified, magnified. And overpoweringly then, an immediate whim that flooded up huge, I found I had to tell them. I had to have my illness recognized. I had to strip myself." American writer Eudora Welty wrote, "Mr. Sansom's descriptive power is a steady firework."

Sansom's other novels include *A Bed of Roses* (1954) and *The Loving Eye* (1956). Sansom also wrote a biography of the French modernist writer Marcel Proust, as well as travel books about visits to Europe. Some of his travel essays are collected in *Blue Skies, Brown Studies* (1961).

Sansom once declared, "A writer lives, at best, in a state of astonishment. Beneath any feeling he has of the good or the evil of the world lies a deeper one of wonder at it all. To transmit that feeling, he writes." In 1951 he was elected a Fellow of the Royal Society of Literature.

Other Works by William Sansom

Icicle and the Sun. London: Hogarth, 1958.
Pleasures Strange and Simple. London: Hogarth, 1953.

A Work About William Sansom

Chalpin, Lila. *William Sansom.* Boston: Twayne, 1980.

Sassoon, Siegfried (1886–1967) *poet, novelist, memoirist*

Siegfried Lorraine Sassoon was born in Brenchley, Kent. He came from a background of wealth: His father, Alfred Ezra Sassoon, was from a prominent Jewish merchant family; his mother, Theresa Thornycroft Sassoon, was from a landowning family in which there was substantial artistic talent. He was educated first at home, then at Marlborough School, attending Cambridge University for two years.

In 1913 Sassoon privately published a small volume of poetry. With the start of World War I, he became an army officer but continued to write poetry. Along with Rupert BROOKE and Wilfred OWEN, Sassoon became one of the "trench poets" of the Great War with the publication of his *The Old Huntsman and Other Poems* (1917) and *Counterattack and Other Poems* (1918). Despite his living another 50 years and writing scores of other poems and several prose works, in the public mind he remained a "soldier poet."

Early in the war Sassoon wrote poems romanticizing combat and death in battle, including the following lines from "To My Brother" (1915) on his brother Hamo's death: "Your lot is with the ghosts of soldiers dead, / . . . And through your victory I shall win the light." But mechanized warfare and a few months in the trenches changed his outlook forever. Embittered at the carnage he witnessed and at what he saw as a false patriotism, or jingoism, on the civilian and political fronts, he began turning out antiwar poetry, as with "They" (1917). Other of Sassoon's war poems explore the grim effects of the war on veterans, such as "Repression of War Experience" (1917): "I'm going stark, staring mad because of the guns."

Because of his antiwar stance, Sassoon was given psychiatric treatment before being returned to combat. As critic Marguerite Wilkinson writes, "Sassoon's poetry unites an intellectual poise and rectitude that belong to idealism. That, I believe, is why his presentation of the facts and emotions of warfare can be made with such acrid irony."

After the war and the publications of his war poetry, Sassoon tried his hand at journalism, editing *The Daily Herald* for a short while, but he soon retired to his family's estate to take up the life of a country gentleman. Although he continued to write poetry for the next 30 years, none of it rose to the level of feeling and intensity of that of 1917–19. At the same time he mined his own life for a series of autobiographical and semiautobiographical works. *Memoirs of a Fox-Hunting Man* (1928) is a novel whose main character, George Sherston, closely resembles Sassoon. The book follows Sherston from his carefree country youth to his early army life.

Two more Sherston volumes followed: *Memoirs of an Infantry Officer* (1930); set during the war, and *Sherston's Progress* (1936), which follows Sherston through the end of the war and traces his gradual recovery from that experience. These volumes share the bleak and satirical outlook of Sassoon's poetry. In *Memoirs of an Infantry Officer* George Sherston says, "I was only beginning to learn that life, for the majority of the population, is an unlovely struggle against unfair odds, culminating in a cheap funeral."

Sassoon returned to his own life story, but this time as straight autobiography, in *The Old Country and Seven More Years* (1938), *Siegfried's Journey, 1916–1920* (1940), and *The Weald of Youth* (1942). Critic Paul Fussell notes: "What is unique in Sassoon is the brilliance with which he exploits the dichotomies forced to his attention by his wartime experience and refines them until they become the very fiber of his superb memoir of the war."

A Work about Siegfried Sassoon

Moyes, Paul. *Siegfried Sassoon: Scorched Glory.* New York: St. Martin's Press, 1997.

Sayers, Dorothy L. (1893–1957) *novelist, playwright, nonfiction writer, translator*

Dorothy L. Sayers was born in Oxford, England, to the Reverend Henry Sayers and Helen May Leigh Sayers. Her education began early, with her father and private tutors instructing her in Latin, French, and German before she went to a boarding school in Salisbury at the age of 15. She eventually earned her degree in modern languages from Oxford, where she was one of the university's first female graduates.

After her graduation, Sayers supported herself as a teacher and a reader for Blackwell's, an Oxford publisher. She found time to write, however, and in 1923 she published *Whose Body*, the first of her 12 mystery novels to focus on Lord Peter Wimsey. An aristocratic and witty detective, Wimsey, much like Arthur Conan Doyle's Sherlock Holmes, solves crimes casually while traditional detectives fret about the details.

Murder Must Advertise (1933) is generally regarded as one of Sayers's best mystery novels. The novel is set in Pym's, a London advertising agency, where a copywriter, Victor Dean, has recently and mysteriously died on a rickety staircase. The owner of the agency, Mr. Pym, hires Wimsey to fill Dean's writing post while secretly investigating the death. Wimsey, known as Death Bredon at work, discovers that the office is filled with infighting, that it is involved in a complex drug-smuggling ring, and that Victor Dean was murdered by one of his coworkers. More than any of Sayers's other detective stories, this novel, in the words of the scholar Mary Brian Durkin, comes closest to "fusing the novel of manners with the detective novel," and "makes trenchant observations on current problems of society." In a conversation between Wimsey and his sister, Sayers masterfully blends the elements of the novel of manners—close detail to character interactions—with a criticism of the less-than-ethical advertising industry. After Wimsey has returned home from Pym's office from a day of writing advertisements, Lady Mary poses the question, "How about truth in advertising?" to which Wimsey responds in his typically sophisticated, metaphor-laden language:

> "Truth in advertising," announced Lord Peter sententiously, "is like leaven, which a woman hid in three measure of meal. It provides a suitable quantity of gas, with which to blow out a mass of crude misrepresentation into a form that the public can swallow."

Sayers's mystery novels, and particularly Peter Wimsey, her central character, were wildly popular and threatened to overwhelm the author's own personality. According to the scholar Nancy M. Tischler, by 1937 Sayers "was weary of writing about Lord Peter Wimsey and was eager to develop her scholarly abilities and to write about her religious beliefs." The author first turned to drama as a new artistic medium and a forum for her Christianity. From 1937 into the 1950s Sayers wrote several religious dramas, but she reached her highest level of dramatic achievement with *The Man Born to Be King* (1943), a series of radio plays written for the BBC. This cycle of 12 plays tells the entire story of Christ's life and draws parallels between modern people, like Nazi supporters, and historical figures involved in Christ's death, like influential Romans. The critics David Glover and Cora Kaplan assert that in the plays "political themes are frequently emphasized, and Sayers would sometimes draw disturbing parallels in her stage notes between those who collaborated with the occupying Roman forces and the Nazi sympathizers of her own day."

When Sayers was writing neither detective novels nor drama, she wrote nonfiction books. In 1928 she published *Great Short Stories of Detection, Mystery and Horror,* which evaluated the history of the detective story. Although this book became an instant classic, her most widely acclaimed nonfiction publication is *Mind of the Maker* (1941), which examines Christian aesthetics. According to the scholar R. D. Stock, the book-length essay was Sayers's attempt "to give guidance to a dismayed, demoralized generation." Near the end of her life, she translated the first two books of Dante's *Divine Comedy,* which was completed after her death by Barbara Reynolds and published in three volumes as *The "Comedy" of Dante Alighieri the Florentine: Hell, Purgatory, and Paradise* between 1949 and 1962.

Sayers's body of work alone—broad enough to include formula detective fiction, drama, and book-length theological tracts—is worthy of admiration.

Other Works by Dorothy Sayers

Busman's Honeymoon. 1937. Reprint, New York: HarperCollins, 1995.
Gaudy Night. 1935. Reprint, New York: Random House, 1992.

Works about Dorothy Sayers

Lewis, Terrance L. *Dorothy L. Sayers' Wimsey and Interwar British Society.* Lewiston, N.Y.: Edwin Mellen Press, 1994.
Reynolds, Barbara. *Dorothy L. Sayers: Her Life and Soul.* New York: St. Martin's Press, 1993.

Scannell, Vernon (1922–) *poet*

Vernon Scannell was born in Spilsby, Lincolnshire, England, and attended the University of Leeds. Early critics had mixed opinions of his earliest works. In his review of *A Mortal Pitch* (1957), poet Alan Brownjohn cites Scannell's "no-nonsense standpoint" and "marvelously clean and clear accuracy." However, another reviewer, Donald Hall, accuses the author of being "unaware that he is using metaphor" and calls his meter "sloppy"; charges Scannell with writing "poem-length thoughts" rather than poems.

Scannell's second collection, *The Masks of Love* (1960), was greeted with some enthusiasm by a *Times Literary Supplement* reviewer as having the "ability to speak through images." The reviewer praised Scannell's writing as the type "that really stops one short," as exemplified in "The Lynching," where a hanged man and his wives are compared: "fastened at the neck / And neat at feet." Scannell's next collection, *The Winter Man* (1973), is considered his best. One reviewer cited the poet's "delicate judgment and dramatizing skill."

Scannell's desertion from the army after recovering from a severe wound during World War II, his time spent in a mental institution, his experience as a professional boxer, and other diverse life experiences have influenced the form and content of his writing. Although some say his style is reminiscent of the late 19th-century poets in its formality, it is firmly rooted in familiar, everyday human experiences of the 20th century, and it clearly scrutinizes the disenchantment, dreams, and underlying violence of that century.

Though Scannell has met with severe criticism, over time he has won the admiration of numerous critics, many citing "The Walking Wounded" as one of the best poems to emerge from the experience of World War II. Critic David McDuff refers to Scannell as one of those poets who work for years and live without looking for or gaining much attention, "but who on reaching later years turn out to have amassed an oeuvre that unquestionably merits it. The poetry of Vernon Scannell is such a body of work."

Other Work by Vernon Scannell

The Black and White Days: Poems. London: Robson Books, 1996.

Scott, Paul Mark (1920–1978) *novelist*

Paul Scott was born in Southgate, London, England, the younger son of Tom and Frances Scott, both commercial artists. On leaving Winchmore Hill Collegiate School, he trained as an accountant but later became a literary agent. In June 1943 Scott was sent to India as an air-supply officer. India cast an immediate spell over him, and during the war years he traveled widely throughout India, Burma, and Malaya. Scott revisited India three times after the war, gathering literary material for *The Raj Quartet* (1966–76) and *Staying On* (1977), a brief, free-standing sequel to *Quartet*.

Scott's first novel, *Johnnie Sahib* (1952), was published by Eyre & Spottiswood, receiving that publisher's literary prize. The protagonist is a charismatic, devil-may-care leader of a company of soldiers in the Burmese jungle who is in conflict with his superiors and is eventually posted elsewhere. *The Alien Sky* (1953) examines India on the eve of independence through its memsahibs, the wives of the British rulers, and is suffused with an emotion many characters in Scott's fiction share—the feeling of "almost tragic alienation" affecting those who have dedicated their lives to India and Indians, only to be rejected when India becomes independent. *The Mark of the Warrior* (1958) is about jungle warfare in Burma.

In *The Chinese Love-Pavilion* (1960), the last of Scott's novels about British soldiers in India and Malaya in World War II, critic Margaret B. Lewis observes that Scott develops a "sensuous, poetic prose" and the kind of nonsequential narrative that culminates in *The Raj Quartet*. *The Birds of Paradise* (1962) is an intricate symbolic novel about Bill Conway's attempt to recapture his Indian past. Perhaps Scott's most uncharacteristic work, set in London, is *The Bender: Pictures from an Exhibition of Middle-Class Portraits* (1963). It concerns two brothers of opposite character:

George Spruce is a gifted, handsome charmer, while Tim, a respectable citizen and responsible family man, is a plodding dullard. *The Corrida at San Feliu* (1964), with an intricate, mosaic-like structure, focuses on a successful author who is nevertheless riddled with self-doubt and discontent and who precipitates a fatal accident.

Scott's greatest achievement was *The Raj Quartet*, comprised of *The Jewel in the Crown* (1966), *The Day of the Scorpion* (1968), *The Towers of Silence* (1971), and *A Division of the Spoils* (1976). This tetralogy describes the decline and fall of the British raj, or rule in India. The four books focus on the period 1942–47, from the Ghandi Resolution stipulating that the British leave India to the subcontinent's partition by the British into India and Pakistan.

In *The Raj Quartet* Scott presents an extraordinary range of vision and sweep of action, creating believable and often unforgettable characters of many races, both sexes, all ages, and from many different walks of life. Ronald Merrick, the district superintendent of Mayapore, is the evil genius presiding over the entire *Quartet*. He is a masterly creation, presented so that his admirable qualities are as plain as his detestable ones. Many of Scott's women are equally memorable— Daphne Manners for her innocence, Sarah Layton for her humaneness and rationality—as are such complex male characters as Mohammed Ali Kasim, Count Bronowsky, and Ahmed. The epilogue to the epic *Quartet* is the tightly focused, almost domestic novel *Staying On,* in which the Smalleys, minor characters from *The Towers of Silence,* remain in India after independence, eking out a shabby living.

Paul Scott was recognized only belatedly for his literary accomplishments: A year before his death he received the BOOKER PRIZE for *Staying On*. The recognition and sales he aspired to all his life came posthumously. In 1979 the BBC produced *Staying On* for television and, five years later, made the quartet into the miniseries *The Jewel in the Crown* (1984). In critic Francine S. Weinbaum's judgment, Scott's works are among "the most comprehensive and searching treatments of British colonialism in contemporary literature."

A Work about Paul Scott
Spurling, Hilary. *Paul Scott: A Life of the Author of The Raj Quartet.* New York: W. W. Norton, 1991.

Self, Will (1961–   ) short story writer, novelist

Will Self was born in London and received his degree from Oxford University. He is the son of Peter Self, a college professor, and Elaine Rosenbloom Self, a publisher.

A socially aware satirist of the postmodern world, Self addresses such themes as gender and mental illness in his short stories, novellas, and novels. "Ward 9," a short story in the collection *The Quantity of Theory* (1991), presents a character who suffers a nervous breakdown and enters a mental hospital. In "Cock," one of two novellas in *Cock and Bull* (1992), a woman grows a penis, develops traditionally masculine traits, and starts to dominate her husband. In "Bull," a man discovers a vagina has grown behind his knees and his doctor attempts to seduce him. *New York Times* critic Michiko Kakutani, in her review of "Cock," accuses Self of "blatant sexism," seeing the story as one in which a woman who asserts herself, surrenders her femininity, and literally becomes a man. However, critic Julie Wheelright sees the stories as "satirical metaphors of liberation." Self proclaims that he wrote both novellas to declare his "anger at the way gender-based sexuality is so predetermined, the way we fit into our sex roles as surely as if we had cut them off the back of a cereal packet and pasted them onto ourselves."

Self's first novel, *My Idea of Fun: A Cautionary Tale* (1994) pulls the reader into the world of a psychotic who randomly kills and mutilates his victims. One critic called the book an "extraordinary novel [that] is an allegory of diseased consciousness, a parable for a decade when what trickled down was not money but scorn for those without it." It is *Great Apes* (1997), however, that Gary Krist of the *New York Times Book Review* deems Self's

"most satisfying book so far." In this bizarre tale, the protagonist finds himself in a world populated by chimpanzees. He finds that he is turning into a chimpanzee himself, but goes into denial and is sent to a mental institution, from where his therapist takes him on talk shows. One critic exclaimed that the novel "hypnotizes with its comic romps, existential posturings, and Shakespearean intrigues," while another, Barbara Hoffert, asserts that though the book is funny at times, its profanity and focus on sex takes away from its credibility.

Self, a difficult but capable social critic, is obviously unique. As Nick Hornby has said in the *Times Literary Supplement*, Self's work is "full of dreary but threatening institutions," and "though you wouldn't want to live in the Self universe . . . in the end, you are grateful that he has gone through the agonies necessary for its creation."

Other Works by Will Self
Grey Area and Other Stories. New York: Atlantic Monthly Press, 1994.
How the Dead Live. New York: Grove Press, 2000.

Shackleton, Ernest Henry (1874–1922) nonfiction writer

Born to Henrietta Letitia Sophia Gavan and Henry Shackleton, a farmer, in County Kildare, Ireland, Sir Ernest Shackleton had a lifelong interest in the sea. At age 16 he made his first voyage, which involved a stormy passage around Cape Horn. He joined Robert Scott's 1901 expedition to the Antarctic, but became ill and was ordered home. About this time he married and ran unsuccessfully for political office.

From 1907 to 1909 Shackleton led a scientific exploratory expedition near the South Pole using the ship *Nimrod*. Upon his return in 1909, he was knighted. From expedition notes he wrote *The Heart of the Antarctic: The Farthest South Expedition* (1909). Ever since being sent home, Shackleton had felt a sense of rivalry with Scott, so he observed with pride that he and his crew surpassed Robert Scott's "furthest south" record set in 1902.

Indeed, Shackleton almost reached the South Pole, coming within 97 miles of his goal before weather forced him back.

More disastrous but more famous was Shackleton's 1913–17 expedition, in which his aim was to cross the entire continent of Antarctica. In January 1915, however, the expedition ship *Endurance* became frozen in place, a common danger in winter Antarctic waters and one that could easily prove fatal. With no means of escape, in an era before helicopter rescues, the crew waited for months and hoped for a shift in the ice to free the ship. Instead, in November 1915, the *Endurance* sank after being crushed by masses of ice, and the crew was forced to move their supplies and their dogs onto a nearby ice floe.

For almost two years the men survived, sometimes in the lifeboats they had rescued from the *Endurance,* sometimes on ice floes, and eventually on more hospitable islands. Finally, in a tiny boat, Shackleton and two volunteers braved the fierce southern seas, where waves 70 to 90 feet high are the norm, and reached the island of South Georgia. After a difficult crossing of the island, the castaways made contact with a whaling station. It took four attempts, but Shackleton managed to rescue the remainder of the expedition. Throughout the entire ordeal, from the loss of the *Endurance* to the rescue, not a single life was lost.

Shackleton's notes from the journey have been collected and re-edited in several editions, including his own *South: The Story of Shackleton's Lost Expedition* (1919). Critic Apsley Cherry-Garrard said that after reading *South* one is haunted by a picture "of three boats, crammed with frost-bitten, wet, and dreadfully thirsty men" clinging to life.

Shackleton's *South* combined matter-of-fact reporting with a gripping sense of barely repressed dread, as when he noted a change in the weather one day in 1915: "The seals were disappearing and the birds were leaving us. The land showed still in fair weather on the distant horizon, but it was beyond our reach now, and regrets for havens that lay beneath us were in vain." In the end Shackleton saw their narrow survival as a testament to the presence of a divine protector: "I have no doubt that Providence guided us, not only across the snowfields, but across the storm-white sea that separated Elephant Island from our landing-place on South Georgia. I know that during that long and racking march of thirty-six hours over the unnamed mountains and glaciers of South Georgia it seemed to me often that we were four, not three."

Shackleton returned to England and died of a heart attack a few years later as he was setting out once more for the Antarctic. His fellow explorer, the Norwegian Ronald Amundsen, said, "Shackleton's name will forevermore be engraved with letters of fire in the history of Antarctic exploration." Shackleton's accomplishments and his accounts of them have inspired later travel writers and have resulted in several biographies of the explorer. Biographer Roland Huntford notes that people were accustomed to explorers chronicling their own adventures in the early 20th century, but Shackleton's made a special impact: "Shackleton was more than a polar explorer; he was a hero, and a popular hero, of his own times."

Works about Ernest Shackleton

Alexander, Caroline. *The Endurance: Shackleton's Legendary Antarctic Expedition.* New York: Alfred A. Knopf, 1998.

Heacox, Kim. *Shackleton: The Antarctic Challenge.* Washington, D.C.: National Geographic Society, 1999.

Kimmel, Elizabeth Cody. *Ice Story: Shackleton's Lost Expedition.* New York: Clarion Books, 1999.

Shaffer, Peter (1926–) *playwright, screenwriter, novelist*

Peter Shaffer was born in Liverpool, England, to Jack and Reka Shaffer. His father worked in real estate and was able to provide a comfortable living for the Shaffer family, who moved all over England. In 1942 Shaffer enrolled in St. Paul's School. That same year he was conscripted as a coal miner, which continued until 1947. He was a brilliant student and received a full scholarship to Trinity College,

Cambridge University, where he received a B.A. degree in history in 1950. During his years at Cambridge, he wrote for a university journal and decided to seek a career in publishing.

Because careers in publishing were scarce in London, Shaffer moved to New York, where he worked as a salesperson for Doubleday bookshops and as a manager of the acquisitions department of the New York Public Library. He did not enjoy his career as a librarian and in 1954 returned to London, where he became a literary critic for *Truth* magazine and a music critic for *Time and Tide.* Between 1951 and 1956, Shaffer also cowrote three detective novels with his brother Anthony and also began experimenting with dramatic pieces, writing three short radio plays that were produced by the BBC (British Broadcasting Corporation).

Shaffer's successful debut as a dramatist for the stage came in 1958 with the production of *Five Finger Exercise,* a play about the individual and family crises of the Harrington family. Particularly interesting is the relationship between Mrs. Harrington and her son Clive, who breaks away from her rigid control and asserts himself as an individual. There is also an underlying conflict between Clive and his father, Stanley, who disapproves of his son's "frivolous" literary pursuits. Another trauma that emerges in the play is an intimate relationship between Mrs. Harrington and Walter, her daughters' tutor. The play, which won the Evening Standard Award for the best new playwright, moved to New York the following year, where it received the New York Drama Critics' Circle Award for the best foreign play.

During the 1960s there was hardly a time when Shaffer's work did not appear on the stages of New York and London. He produced two comic one-act plays, *The Private Ear* (1962) and *The Public Eye* (1962), and staged another minor play, *The Merry Roosters' Panto* (1963), in London. He also collaborated with Peter Brook on the film script of William Golding's *Lord of the Flies.*

The Royal Hunt of the Sun (1964) became one of the best-known masterpieces of contemporary drama. The play presents Pizarro's conquest of the Inca Empire in Peru. Shaffer vividly described his intentions in the play: "The 'totality' of it was in my head for ages: not just the words, but jungle cries and ululations; metals and masks; the fantastic apparition of the pre-Columbian world. . . . I did deeply want to create, by means both austere and rich . . . an experience that was entirely and only theatrical." This epic play is divided into two major acts: The Hunt and The Kill. The narration is presented through the voice of Martin, a grizzled old man who was a soldier in Pizarro's army. Instead of demonizing Pizarro, Shaffer portrays him as completely human: hubristic, spiritually weak, and vulnerable to suffering the pain of others. Pizarro attempts to transcend his humble, peasant origin and enter into the annals of history. But this spiritual quest is not without a price, as Pizarro finds out: "To save my own soul I must kill another man!" As Shaffer himself puts it, "Ultimately, the play is about a man's search for immortality."

Many critics consider *Equus* (1973) Shaffer's crowning achievement. The play is performed throughout the world and made theatrical history in Spain by ending a taboo on nudity. The substantial part of the plot is presented through a series of flashbacks. Alan Strang, a stableboy, is confined to a psychiatric hospital for blinding six horses. Martin Dysart, a children's psychiatrist, develops a close relationship with the boy, whose childhood trauma illuminates the source of personal problems in Dysart's own life: "Essentially I cannot know what I do—yet I do essential things. Irreversible, terminal things. I stand in the dark with a pick in my hand, striking at heads!" As a psychological drama, *Equus* presents disturbing graphic images to reveal the dark labyrinth of Alan's mind and to allow the audience to discover the full circumstances of his mental breakdown. There were more than 1,000 performances on Broadway, and the play was made into a film in 1977.

In another exceptional drama, *Amadeus* (1979), Shaffer portrays the musical genius and eccentricity of Wolfgang Amadeus Mozart. In this play set in Vienna, Mozart is surreptitiously undermined by his jealous archrival, Antonio Salieri, the court composer, who sets out to destroy Mozart and his reputation at the court. *Amadeus* received a Tony Award for Best Play in 1981 and ran for more than 1,000 performances. The play was made into a film, *Amadeus* (1984), which received eight Academy Awards, including Best Picture.

Peter Shaffer continues to write and is one of the most widely recognized playwrights in the world. As his biographer Dennis Klein writes, "Shaffer probes questions as intimate as identity crises and sexual self-doubt and as far-reaching as loneliness and man's need for worship."

Other Works by Peter Shaffer

Lettice and Lovage: A Comedy. New York: Harper-Collins, 1990.
Whom Do I Have the Honor of Addressing? London: André Deutsch, 1990.

Works about Peter Shaffer

Eberle, Thomas. *Peter Shaffer: An Annotated Bibliography.* New York: Garland, 1991.
Klein, Dennis. *Peter Shaffer.* Boston: Twayne, 1993.

Sharp, Margery (1905–1991) *novelist, short story writer, essayist, children's author*

Born in Wiltshire, England, to J. H. Sharp Margery Sharp spent much of her childhood in Malta. She loved the sunny island and was reluctant to return to Britain in 1914. She studied French at London University, where she wrote articles for campus journals, then spent a year at Westminster Art School.

The magazine *Punch* began publishing Sharp's work when she was 21. In the following years she published witty essays and stories in numerous magazines, from *Good Housekeeping* to *Strand*. Her first novel was *Rhododendron Pie* (1930), a comical story about a young woman in a sophisticated, intellectual family who prefers humble, conventional pleasures. In the course of the novel the heroine finds the courage to be conventional. Like many of Sharp's books, this novel celebrates finding delight in everyday things.

Sharp's heroines are frequently young women who do not quite fit in with their immediate surroundings and unwittingly introduce delightful chaos. Her heroes, too, are deftly drawn: She often writes about amusingly prosaic men who are bemused by unusual women. The cheerful, unconventional heroine of *Cluny Brown* (1944) exemplifies Sharp's characters: She is a plumber's niece, but somehow eludes all class constraints and bewilders all the humdrum people around her. Although Sharp's works are often classified as romantic, she uses understated prose instead of sentimental language. When *Cluny Brown* ends with Cluny finding a surprising soulmate, the two characters gaze at each other and simply feel a calm, happy connection: "Beneath the surface constraint a deep current of ease and understanding had begun to flow between them, a sense of naturalness as strong as sweet."

Sharp also wrote many children's books. She began the most famous of these in the 1960s with *The Rescuers* (1959), featuring the heroic efforts of an international brigade of heroic mice, the Rescue Aid Society. These brave mice are led by the glamorous mouse Miss Bianca and her stalwart secretary Bernard. Walt Disney made some films from the books.

Sharp's novels are so lighthearted and elegant they seem to belie the discipline and effort she put into her work as she revised meticulously. She once said, "I absolutely believe it is fatal ever to write below your best, even if what you write may never be published."

Other Works by Margery Sharp

The Nutmeg Tree. New York: HarperCollins, 1982.
The Sun in Scorpio. New York: HarperCollins, 1982.

Sherriff, Robert Cedric (1896–1975) *playwright, novelist, screenwriter*

R. C. Sherriff was born in Kingston-on-Thames near London, England, to Herbert Hankin Sherriff, an employee of an insurance company, and Constance Winder Sherriff. After graduating from Kingston Grammar School, he followed in his father's footsteps, becoming a clerk for the Sun Insurance Company until the outbreak of World War I.

Sherriff achieved his first literary success with a play about his experiences in the trenches of World War I. *Journey's End* was produced for the stage in 1928 and opened to rave reviews. It was later translated into several languages and performed all over the world. The play describes the friendship of men fighting in trenches and the trauma of their wartime experiences with striking realism. In the opening scene Hardy, one of the main characters, reports, "They simply blew us to bits yesterday. Minnies, enormous ones; about twenty. Three bang in the trench. I really am glad you've come; I'm not simply being polite." (Minnies are German mortars.) Hannen Swaffer of the *Daily Express* wrote after seeing the play in 1928, "This is English theater at its best."

After this promising start, Sherriff wrote a series of novels and plays on a wide range of themes with varying degrees of success. *Badgers Green,* his second play, turns away from the theme of war to tell the story of an English village's battle to maintain the traditional way of life in the face of encroaching development. It first appeared in London in 1930 and was a disappointment. In 1936 Sherriff wrote a historical play about Napoléon called *St. Helena.* The play had a difficult start until Winston CHURCHILL endorsed it in a letter to the London *Times.* However, even this much-needed publicity was not enough to attract an audience for long.

Sherriff had greater success in the theater with comedies and murder mysteries. *Home at Seven* (1950) and *A Shred of Evidence* (1960), both murder mysteries, revealed his ability to write suspense plays that had a strong comic element.

During the 1950s the field of archeology began to fascinate Sherriff. In 1955 he wrote *The Long Sunset,* a play about a family trying to protect their way of life in Roman Britain during its period of decline. The play was based loosely on the playwright's own archeological work at a Roman ruins found in the south of England.

Sherriff's novel *The Fortnight in September* (1931) employs what he called a "down-to-earth style of writing" and tells the story of a family whose members discover what drives their individual desires while on vacation at an English resort.

Sherriff also cowrote screenplays, including an adaptation of H. G. WELLS'S *The Invisible Man* in 1933. Though some critics have called his initial success as a playwright a fluke, the literary critic Peter Raby asserts in a review of Sherriff's writing that "[h]is body of work . . . adds up to something substantial, not least for its insight into the way many people lived in England in the first half of the twentieth century."

Silkin, Jon (1930–1997) *poet*

Jon Silkin, the son of Joseph Silkin, a solicitor, and Dora Rubenstein Silkin, was born in London and attended the University of Leeds. His early poetry collection, *The Peaceable Kingdom* (1969), raised issues that he expounded on throughout his career: the beauty and innocence of animals, fear in the face of cruelty in nature and humankind, the struggle to find love and to know oneself, and the desire to understand a world full of loss. He often addresses the issue of poetry as a "civilizing agent" in a world that engineered the Holocaust and other inhumane abuses,

Pronouncing himself a "mixture of rationalist agnosticism and dilute Orthodox Judaism," in *The Little Time-Keeper* (1977) Silkin calls on his Jewish and Northumbrian identities in the cause of "moral commentary," To further promote poetry he cofounded and edited the literary magazine *Stand,* which encouraged social responsibility.

In the poem "Killhope Wheel" from *Amana Grass* (1971), Silkin tells the story of striking County Durham miners brutally attacked by soldiers to protect the interest of the mine owners, while in several other collections he scrutinizes Jewish history and his own Jewishness. He relates the story of the massacre of the Jews of York in 1190 in "The Malabestia," from *The Principles of Water* (1974); and in "Trying to Hide Treblinka" and other poems in *The Lens-Breakers* (1992), he seeks to convey the "moral urgency" that "requires an accounting from men" for their unimaginable cruelty.

"Death of a Son," Silkin's most celebrated poem, is a thinly veiled autobiographical elegy for his brain damaged son who died at the age of one in a mental institution: "He turned over as if he could be sorry for this / And out of his eyes two great tears rolled, like stones, and he died." "The People" recounts what lies behind "Death of a Son": the deep strain on the parents' relationship and how their neighbor, a Holocaust survivor, helps "two unloving animals / [to] find mercy's image: love."

Critics describe Silkin's poetry as sometimes difficult to read and suggest that it can be best appreciated if read aloud. But as one critic says, "At his best . . . he has written some of the most moving poems of the century. By any standard he is one of the best poets [of contemporary England]."

Other Works by Jon Silkin

The Psalms with Their Spoils. New York: Routledge, 1980.

Watersmeet. Whitley Bay, England: Bay Press, 1994.

Sillitoe, Alan (1928–) *novelist, short story writer, poet, playwright*

Alan Sillitoe was born in Nottingham, England, to Christopher Sillitoe, a laborer, and Sabina Burton Sillitoe. At age 14, after an abbreviated formal education, he began working as a laborer in a bicycle plant; he pursued an odd assortment of jobs before embarking on a literary career. Despite working from an early age, he read constantly, especially during a period of time, near the end of his military service, when he was recovering from tuberculosis.

Sillitoe quickly emerged as an author of the working class. Most of his work, set in Nottingham, the industrial town of his youth, examines the lives of—and is often narrated by—factory workers and shop girls who live lonely lives controlled by social and economic factors beyond their control. Although Sillitoe has written prolifi-

cally since their publication, his reputation rests almost entirely on his first two publications: *Saturday Night and Sunday Morning* (1958), a novel; and *The Loneliness of the Long-Distance Runner* (1959), a collection of short stories.

In *Saturday Night and Sunday Morning*, factory worker Arthur Seaton has a number of problems. He has trouble with his factory supervisors, hates his long hours of monotonous work, and is involved in complicated and simultaneous romantic relationships with two married sisters. His life revolves around raucous Saturday nights and peaceful Sunday mornings. The novel begins with Arthur horribly drunk in a bar on a Saturday night and ends on a Sunday morning with the much wiser Arthur revealing that, although he fully understands the bleak realities of his life, he will make the best of it: "Well, it's a good life and a good world, all said and done, if you don't weaken, and if you know that the big wide world hasn't heard from you yet, no, not by a long way, though it won't be long now."

In the title story of *The Loneliness of the Long-Distance Runner*, a 17-year-old antisocial boy named Smith feels every bit as downtrodden and abused by the system as Arthur does in *Saturday Night and Sunday Morning*. The story begins with Smith recounting his first days at reform school and mockingly recalling that "they made me a long-distance cross-country runner." Smith has natural talent as a runner, but he is intensely frustrated and angered at the idea of being "made" a runner by the school's authorities. The entire story builds toward a climactic race, which Smith ultimately decides to lose, and in so doing he gains the only victory possible over those who control him. In his triumphant moment, approaching the finish line in first place, Smith suddenly stops and in a frozen moment

could hear the lords and ladies . . . from the grandstand, and could see them standing to wave me in: 'Run!' they were shouting in their posh voices. 'Run!' But I was deaf, daft, and blind, and stood where I was.

Smith finally feels the exhilaration of controlling his own destiny and considers himself a success.

Since *The Loneliness of the Long-Distance Runner,* Sillitoe has published more than 50 books—novels, collections of poetry, and plays. His poetry, most of which can be found in *Collected Poems* (1993), also deals with the British working class and industrial cities. His plays, such as *The Slot Machine* (1970), *The Interview* (1977), and *Pit Strike* (1978), are largely responsible for making the lower classes a popular subject for British theatre. Of his recent work, *Life Without Armour* (1995), an autobiography that ends in the 1960s, and *Birthday* (2001), a sequel to *Saturday Night and Sunday Morning,* have been well received but have left critics longing for the power of Sillitoe's early writing. Despite critics' ambivalence toward his later work, for nearly 50 years Sillitoe has entertained a wide audience in Great Britain and abroad. His chief "triumph," according to the scholar David Gerard, "is to have revealed lives that had scarcely been noticed because by their nature they were unlikely to produce a literary spokesman. Such a spokesman appeared with Alan Sillitoe, able to render their condition without falsifying or condescension because he saw and felt as one of them gifted with prophecy."

Other Works by Alan Sillitoe

Collected Stories. New York: HarperCollins, 1996.
The German Numbers Woman. North Pomfret, Vt.: Trafalgar Square, 1999.

A Work about Alan Sillitoe

Hanson, Gillian Mary. *Understanding Alan Sillitoe.* Columbia: University of South Carolina Press, 1997.

Sinclair, Andrew (1935–) *novelist, screenwriter, biographer*

Andrew Sinclair was born in Oxford, England, the son of Stanley Charles Sinclair, who was in the British Colonial Service and Hilary Nash-Webber Sinclair, a writer, as was his second wife, Sonia

Melchett, whom he married in 1984 and with whom he had another son. Sinclair received his Ph.D. from Cambridge University. Besides his work as a teacher, founding fellow and director of historical studies at Churchill College, Cambridge, England, he was the managing director of Lorimar Publishing in London from 1967 to 1991. His diverse career also included film directing and screenwriting.

Sinclair's best-known novels are the trilogy *Gog* (1967), *Magog* (1972) and *King Ludd* (1988). The first two works allude to giants of British legend. In *Gog,* a naked giant with amnesia washes ashore in Scotland seeking to reclaim his memory. Some reviewers found it an unsuccessful satire, but others called it "ambitious" and imaginative. In the trilogy's second book, Gog's half-brother Magog is a corrupt civil servant who goes through a transformation in which he realizes "that his material success is hollow. . . ." The *Times Literary Supplement* review called Sinclair "always interesting and convincing," but critic Anthony Thwaite, among others, attacked it as "a febrile, self-indulgent, opinionated and finally rather squalidly boring fling at the picaresque." *King Ludd,* appearing many years after the first two books, begins with the Luddites, 19th-century British workers who, after being thrown out of work with the advent of mechanization, smash machines in protest. The writer Robert Nye asserts that the entire trilogy, a mixture of Celtic and druidic mythology and British history, is a success in "engaging and holding our attention," and that "these books are important, and they'll last."

Sinclair shows his prowess as a scholar, social historian, and biographer in such works as *Francis Bacon: His Life and Violent Times* (1993), the biography of the painter, which Alan Ross calls a "social [history] rather than . . . art [criticism]"; and in *Death by Fame: A Life of Elisabeth of Austria* (1999) in which Sinclair parallels the lives of the empress and Diana, Princess of Wales. Writing for more than 40 years, Sinclair is distinguished for his examination of notable historical figures, epochs, and places from a modern viewpoint, whether it is in allegorical and historical fiction or biography.

Other Works by Andrew Sinclair

The Discovery of the Grail. London: Century, 1998.
The Emancipation of the American Woman. New York: Harper & Row, 1975.

Sinclair, Clive (1948–) *novelist, short story writer, biographer*

Clive Sinclair, one of England's 20 best novelists of 1983, was born in London and educated at the University of East Anglia. The son of David Sinclair, a director, and Betty Jacobs Sinclair, he is best known for his groundbreaking short stories. Often compared to authors such as Martin AMIS, Vladimir Nabokov, and Isaac Bashevis Singer, Sinclair's stories are known for their wit mixed with sexual suggestiveness, cynicism, unusual narrators, and Jewish history and culture.

Bibliosexuality (1973), Sinclair's first novel, is about a strange disorder that causes a desire for an aberrant relationship with a book. *Hearts of Gold* (1979), a collection of short stories that included an array of strange narrators, such as vampires, a Jewish giraffe, and a second-rate private eye, fulfilled the first book's promise.

Generally a fiction writer, Sinclair made one attempt at biography in *The Brothers Singer* (1983) about Nobel Prize–winning author Isaac Bashevis Singer, who wrote in Yiddish about the trials of interpersonal relationships, and his brother, Joshua, who wrote anti-Stalinist novels. It was criticized for its brevity and attending too much to Joshua and not enough to Isaac. Nonetheless, critic Anthony Quinton praised Sinclair for instructing readers about the nature of the problems Jews experienced in Europe long before the Holocaust.

Interested in exploring his Jewishness, Sinclair said of himself, "My subject matter remains a mixture of the personal and historical, the history being that of the Jews. Being English I look at the Holocaust and Israel as an inside-outsider." This view is reflected in *Diaspora Blues: A View of Israel* (1987), which expresses the ambivalence of Jews living outside of Israel toward the politics of Israel and their relationship to the Jewish people who live there.

After the death of his wife in 1994, Sinclair feared that he would never write again, but during a trip to the Middle East with his son, as he boarded a ferry on the Nile River, he recalled *The Lady with the Lapdog* by Anton Chekhov, which was set in Yalta. His literary imagination and spirit rekindled, Sinclair reread the story and began to write his own version, with the action set in Egypt. This led to his short story collection *The Lady with the Laptop* (1996).

Linda Taylor noted in her review of *Blood Libels* (1985) that "the plot and counter-plots crackle with violent lusts and macabre accidents." As in his earlier work, editor Art Seidenbaum has pointed out, Clive Sinclair is a writer for whom "[n]othing is too raw to risk."

Other Works by Clive Sinclair

Augustus Rex. London: André Deutsch, 1992.
For Good or Evil. New York: Penguin, 1991.

Sinclair, May (Sinclair; Mary Amelia St. Clair) (1863–1946) *novelist, short story writer, biographer, nonfiction writer*

May Sinclair was born Mary Amelia St. Clair Sinclair in Cheshire, England. Her mother was a devout Christian who raised the children strictly. Her father owned a shipping business, but when this went bankrupt he became an alcoholic. His wife left him, and Sinclair looked after her mother until she died in 1901. Her semiautobiographical novel *Mary Olivier* (1919) examines a woman's intense relationship with her mother.

For two years Sinclair attended Cheltenham Ladies' College, where she became increasingly interested in philosophy. The famous educator and suffragette Dorothea Beale was teaching there and encouraged Sinclair to write. She began by writing scholarly articles about philosophy for journals in the 1880s, covering philosophers from Plato to Hegel. She also wrote long, philosophical poems that often explored Platonic idealism.

Sinclair's first successful novel, *The Divine Fire* (1904), describes how writers can be exploited by critics. From 1908 onward she was involved with the women's suffrage movement. In 1912 she published *The Three Brontës*, a biography of Anne, Charlotte, and Emily Brontë; and a novel, *The Three Sisters* (1914), based on the Brontës' lives. Charlotte Brontë was her favorite novelist.

In World War I Sinclair worked on the front line with the ambulance service in Belgium. She explored both the horror of the war and the spiritual uplift it could bring in her novel *The Tree of Heaven* (1917).

In 1918 Sinclair became the first person to use "stream of consciousness" as a literary term, describing Dorothy RICHARDSON's sprawling novel sequence *Pilgrimage* (1915) as "life going on and on. It is Miriam Henderson's stream of consciousness going on and on." This technique, Sinclair said, could seize "reality alive." The psychologist William James had coined the term earlier to describe the flow of a person's thoughts from moment to moment. Sinclair was the first to use the term to describe the way modernist literature was representing the psyche.

Sinclair was fascinated by psychology, particularly psychoanalysis. She was psychoanalysed herself, and she discusses what effect this had on her writing in *The Judgement of Eve and Other Stories* (1914). She was also interested in mysticism and particularly the prolific Indian poet and novelist Rabindranath Tagore. She touches on spiritualism in *Uncanny Stories* (1923), in which several characters are able to communicate with a spirit world.

Sinclair wrote 24 novels, two books of philosophy, and many articles and short stories. She was also a mentor to many younger writers.

Other Work by May Sinclair

Life and Death of Harriet Frean. 1921. Reprint, London: Virago, 1980.

A Work about May Sinclair

Raitt, Suzanne. *May Sinclair: A Modern Victorian.* New York: Oxford University Press, 2000.

Sitwell, Edith Louisa (1887–1964) *poet*

Dame Edith Sitwell was born in Scarborough, Yorkshire, England, to an eccentric aristocrat, Sir George Reresby Sitwell, and Lady Ida Emily Augusta Denison Sitwell. She was the sister of Osbert SITWELL and Sacheverell SITWELL, who also became important writers. Educated by private tutors, she cultivated interests in art and music despite the discouragement of her mother, who preferred that she spend her time in more social pursuits.

Sitwell began working her way into literary circles as an editor and contributor to the poetry anthology *Wheels* (1916–21), where she was responsible for the publication of seven poems by the famous World War I "trench poet" Wilfred OWEN. After her involvement with *Wheels* ended, she gained national attention with *Façade* (1922), a collection of poems designed to be read aloud to audiences in London. The poems are remarkable because, as the scholar Robert K. Martin has written, they reveal that "it was Edith Sitwell more than anyone else who realized the importance of sound and texture in modern poetry." The poem "Scotch Rhapsody," which describes an old hunter whose bagpipe music is "boring the ptarmigan and grouse for fun—/ Boring them worse than a nine-bore gun," displays the internal rhythms and rhyming lines that make the collection's plays well suited to oral presentation. Because the poems in *Façade* were more concerned with sound and rhythm than with "meaning," they aligned Sitwell with modernism—an experimental movement in literature lead primarily by T. S. ELIOT, and necessarily against GEORGIAN POETRY, an older tradition that focused on rural, rustic settings and more romantic themes, such as truth and love.

Sitwell's most enduring poem, "Still Falls the Rain" (included in *Street Songs*, 1942), made her the leading poet of World War II. Subtitled "The Raids, 1940. Night and Dawn," the poem is set during the Battle of Britain and is filled with images of blood, human blindness, and greed. Despite its attention to human flaws, however, the poem remains hopeful for regeneration after the war, and it reminds readers that God "bears in

His heart all wounds." It ends, moreover, with words Sitwell imagines coming from the mouth of God: "Still do I love, still shed my innocent light . . . for thee."

After the nuclear attacks on Japan, Sitwell returned again to the issues of destruction and regeneration in the poem "The Shadow of Cain" (1947). Although it describes the fragmentation of humanity and greed as a central source of all human conflict, it ends with an image of a judgmental Christ in the lines "He walks again on the Seas of Blood, He comes in the / terrible Rain." The presence of God in this poem is not as forgiving as in "Still Falls the Rain," but Sitwell's use of Christian imagery reflects a belief that life will continue and order will be restored even after the appearance of nuclear war. In his interpretation of the poem, the scholar John Lehmann remarks that Sitwell's "instinct was not to despair but to call upon the most powerful symbols of love she knew, the symbols of Christianity."

Sitwell was awarded an honorary doctorate from Oxford in 1951 and was made a Dame Commander of the Order of the British Empire (DBE) in 1954. Robert K. Martin has commented that "inadequate attention has been paid to her development as a social poet, as a religious poet, and as a visionary. Her career traces the development of English poetry from the immediate post-World War I period of brightness and jazzy rhythms through the political involvements of the 1930s and the return to spiritual values after World War II."

Other Works by Edith Sitwell

Collected Poems. New York: Vanguard, 1954.
Selected Letters of Edith Sitwell. Edited by Richard Greene. London: Virago, 2001.

Works about Edith Sitwell

Brophy, James. *Edith Sitwell: The Symbolist Order.* Carbondale: Southern Illinois University Press, 1968.
Bradford, Sarah. *The Sitwells and the Arts of the 1920s and 1930s.* Austin: University of Texas Press, 1996.
Cevasco, G. A. *The Sitwells: Edith, Osbert, and Sacheverell.* Boston: Twayne, 1987.
Glendinning, Victoria. *Edith Sitwell: A Unicorn Among Lions.* London: Weidenfeld & Nicolson, 1981.

Sitwell, Osbert (Francis Osbert Sacheverell Sitwell) (1892–1969)
nonfiction writer, memoirist, novelist, poet, essayist, playwright, journalist

Osbert Sitwell was born in London to Sir George Reresby and Lady Ida Denison Sitwell. He was the younger brother of Edith SITWELL and older brother of Sacheverell SITWELL. While attending Eton, he developed a lifelong hatred not only for such schools but particularly for games and sports. He was sent to Eton by his strong-willed father, whom he succeeded in 1943 as fifth baronet of Renishaw Hall. Sitwell said of his father's many attempts to direct his eldest son's life, "Though . . . my father was determined to prevent it, as far as it lay within his power, I was resolved to devote my future, my whole life, to writing."

Though Sitwell would have preferred an Oxford education, his father forced him to go to a school that prepared young men for Sandhurst (the English equivalent of West Point). In defiance of Sir George's ambitions, Sitwell deliberately failed his entrance exams. Undaunted, his father got him commissioned anyway. Sitwell saw combat in World War I, was injured and invalided out in 1916, and developed a lifelong aversion to war and its effects.

Sitwell's main interest was in the arts, and he numbered among his friends and acquaintances the composers Claude Debussy, Frederick Delius, and Richard Strauss; the dancer Nijinsky; the ballet impresario Diaghilev; and writers such as Ezra Pound, T. S. ELIOT, and Evelyn WAUGH. In 1916 he published *Twentieth Century Harlequinade and Other Poems,* a collection of satirical verse. Over the next 50 years he wrote four novels, scores of poems, three plays, four volumes of travel essays, several biographies, essays on literature, and dozens of introductions to other author's works.

He also acted as editor and journalist for several periodicals.

Sitwell's most lasting works have proved to be his five volumes of autobiography: *Left Hand! Right Hand!* (1944); *The Scarlet Tree* (1946); *Great Morning!* (1947); *Laughter in the Next Room* (1948); and *Noble Essences* (1950), which critic Thomas Kuhlman has compared to Marcel Proust's *Remembrance of Things Past* "as a compendium of the author's detailed impressions of a fashionable milieu." In these volumes, as in two important collections of essays, *Penny Foolish* (1935) and *Pound Wise* (1963), Sitwell displays an attitude that has been described as that of "the self-aware imperialist." He concludes his essay "America Before the Fall" (1935), for example, "Yet no one knows the sheer joy of *being* in Europe or being European until he has visited America." Sitwell biographer Philip Ziegler defends Sitwell's apparent elitism: "So accurate is the skewering of contemporary folly among all social classes, and so genuine is his passionate approval of the truly creative, honest, and beautiful that Sitwell ultimately must be judged innocent of snobbery."

Other Work by Osbert Sitwell

Before the Bombardment. 1926. Reprint, Oxford, England: Oxford University Press, 1986.

A Work about Osbert Sitwell

Ziegler, Philip. *Osbert Sitwell.* New York: Alfred A. Knopf, 1998.

Sitwell, Sacheverell (1897–1988) *art critic, travel writer, poet, journalist*

Sacheverell Sitwell was born in Scarborough, England, to Sir George Reresby Sitwell, a baronet, and Lady Ida Denison Sitwell, the youngest child in a family of well-known writers. He attended Eton College, followed by Balliol College, Oxford University. His sister Edith SITWELL and brother Osbert SITWELL had notable writing careers during the 1920s and 1930s. Some critics believe that Sitwell's writings have been unfairly neglected in comparison to his older siblings. However, perhaps due to their fame, Sitwell had the opportunity to develop his talent as an author early in life. His sister Edith was the first to encourage him to write poetry during his teens; his early poems were collected in *The Cyder Feast* (1927). He is known for his historical and travel writings as well as his work as a poet and art critic. He also had a notable career as a journalist and publisher.

Critics have praised Sitwell's "imaginative" style and the sense of enthusiasm that he brought to his work. He did not have immediate success as an independent writer, however. His privileged position as the son of an aristocrat provided him with the necessary income and connections to start his literary career. He had to pay around $80 to have his first book, *Southern Baroque Art,* published in 1923. The book highlights the work of forgotten master artists of the baroque period. Drawing on his own extensive travels to Italy and his early experiences writing poetry, Sitwell claimed that his "poetical diet had fitted me for such expeditions, preparing and intoxicating my imagination." *Southern Baroque Art* was soon recognized as an innovative approach to art history, and it shifted Sitwell's focus from poetry to art criticism. His attempt to bring a better understanding to the baroque and rococo periods led critic Cyril CONNOLLY to call the book "a milestone in the development of our modern sensibility."

Sitwell is probably best known for his writings on art and travel; he wrote extensively on Europe and the Far East. Books such as *Gothick North: A Study of Medieval Life, Art, and Thought* (1929) and *Baroque Revisited* (1967) emphasize both the aesthetic and historical significance of early modern art movements. As critic Michael Borrie remarked in a review of *Gothic Europe* (1969), "The range of Sir Sacheverell's visual experience is truly vast, and his enthusiasm and affection for his subject are unbounded. Everything he sees conjures up a host of other images, memories and associations, the harvest of a long lifetime's looking, which pour from his pen in an almost Joycean flood."

A Work about Sacheverell Sitwell

Bradford, Sarah. *Splendours and Miseries: A Life of Sacheverell Sitwell.* New York: Farrar, Straus, & Giroux, 1993.

Smart, Elizabeth (1913–1986) *novelist, poet, journalist*

Elizabeth Smart was born into a wealthy family in Ottawa, Canada. Fascinated by writing, she published her first poem when she was 10. She was educated at private schools, and at 19 she went to London to study music at King's College.

One day, browsing through a London bookshop, she found a volume of poems by the poet George BARKER. She fell in love with him simply by reading his poems and eventually met him through mutual friends. Barker was married, but he and Smart nonetheless began a tragic affair. Smart had four children by him, but they never married.

Smart's first novel was *By Grand Central Station I Sat Down and Wept* (1945). Still her most famous book, it draws on the exhilaration and anguish of her affair. The narrator laments, "O lucky Daphne, motionless and green to avoid the touch of a God! Lucky Syrinx, who chose a legend instead of too much blood. For me there was no choice. There were no crossroads at all." The *Spectator* said of the book, "Constructed as a single, sustained climax, it is like a cry of ecstasy which, without changing volume or pitch, becomes a cry of agony. Author Michael ONDAATJE has said, "At some point every good reader comes across *By Grand Central Station I Sat Down and Wept.* And he or she recognizes an emotion essential and permanent to us."

After the war, Smart supported her family by working as a journalist and advertising writer. In 1963 she became literary editor of *Queen,* but three years later she retired from full-time commercial writing and moved to a cottage in Suffolk. In the late 1970s she published a book of poetry, *A Bonus* (1977), and her second novel, *The Assumption of the Rogues and Rascals* (1977), a blend of prose and poetry describing a writer's struggles.

She returned briefly to Canada in 1982–83 as writer-in-residence at the University of Alberta, then returned to live her last years in her secluded, wooded cottage.

Other Works by Elizabeth Smart

Collected Poems of Elizabeth Smart. London: Palladin, 1992.
Necessary Secrets: The Journals of Elizabeth Smart. Edited by Alice Van Wart. Toronto: Deneau, 1986.
On the Side of the Angels: Second Volume of the Journals of Elizabeth Smart. Edited by Alice Van Wart. New York: HarperCollins, 1994.

A Work about Elizabeth Smart

Sullivan, Rosemary. *By Heart: Elizabeth Smart, A Life.* New York: Viking, 1991.

Smith, Dodie (Dorothy Gladys Smith, C. L. Anthony, Charles Henry Percy) (1896–1990) *playwright, novelist, children's author, memoirist*

Dodie Smith was born Dorothy Gladys Smith in Lancashire, England. Her father died when she was 18 months old, and she and her mother went to live with her mother's parents and brothers. All the family members were enthusiastic about books, music, and theater, and Smith herself was an excellent storyteller. She later recalled, "Almost anything could get my imagination going, the pattern on wallpapers and carpets, cracks on the ceiling, flowers, leaves and even blades of grass."

Smith trained briefly at drama school in London, but she was unsuccessful on the stage. Seven years after her first stage appearance, she wrote her first play, *Autumn Crocus* (1931), a moving romance set in the Tyrol. The play was so profitable that she could begin writing full-time.

Smith's greatest theatrical success was *Dear Octopus* (1938), a widely praised West End play about her vibrant Manchester family. But she did not stay in Britain to receive the accolades. She and her pacifist husband Alec Beesley moved to California for the duration of World War II. There she wrote her acclaimed first novel, *I Capture the Castle* (1948). This book is narrated by Cassandra, a 17-year old girl who lives with her family in a ramshackle castle. She wants to be a writer, and the novel comprises her diary. The book opens, "I write this sitting in the kitchen sink. That is, my feet are in it; the rest of me is on the draining-board, which I have padded with the dog's blanket and the tea-cosy." With the same delightfully eccentric candor, Cassandra describes her family's romantic and economic struggles and records her own joy and grief at first love. The novelist Erica Jong describes *I Capture the Castle* as "[a] delicious, compulsively readable novel about young love and its vicissitudes." Enormously successful, the novel is still popular today.

Smith returned to England in 1950. There she felt out of touch with gloomy, gritty, postwar theater, so she tried children's fiction instead. Her first children's book was inspired by her Dalmatian dog Pongo: *The Hundred and One Dalmatians* (1956) features the villainous Cruella de Vil, who intends to make a fur coat out of Dalmatian puppies whose parents, two heroic Dalmatians, set out to rescue them. This witty book is written from the perspective of the dogs, who regard their human owners as *their* pets (the humans are "gentle, obedient and unusually intelligent—almost canine at times").

Smith wrote many novels, plays, and volumes of autobiography. She had scintillating literary successes in three different genres. Right to the end of her life she retained her vivacity, once asking in wonder if she were "the only woman in the world who at my age—and after a lifetime of quite rampant independence—still did not feel quite grown up?"

Other Work by Dodie Smith

Look Back with Love: A Manchester Childhood. London: Heinemann, 1974.

A Work about Dodie Smith

Grove, Valerie. *Dear Dodie: The Life of Dodie Smith.* London: Chatto & Windus, 1997.

Smith, Iain Crichton (1928–1998) *poet, novelist, short story writer*

Iain Crichton Smith is well known for his poetry, though he was a prolific novelist and short story writer as well. The son of John Smith, a sailor, and Christina Campbell Smith, he was born in Glasgow, Scotland, brought up in the Hebrides, and educated at the University of Aberdeen. His Gaelic roots, history, and culture play an important role in both his poetry and prose.

Smith's antiauthoritarian, anticlerical attitudes are seen in much of his writing, such as in his novel *Consider the Lilies* (1968). In this book he writes about the Clearances, when Highland Scots were forced off their land to make room for sheep in the 19th century, and Gaelic culture went into decline. The main character, a widow whose husband died in a battle under the command of the duke of Sutherland, awaits her pension but instead is evicted by the same duke. The author shows the hypocrisies and collusion of the established church and demonstrates that new understanding about the realities of life are possible no matter what one's age. Though *Consider the Lilies* is generally considered his best novel, Smith was criticized for historical inaccuracies, to which he responded that he realized the "history was a bit haphazard" but he "was more concerned with the old woman's mind."

Smith further investigates the contradictions and conflicts inherent when living in two worlds, in *The Dream* (1990). In this book a lecturer in Gaelic working in Glasgow wishes to return to his Gaelic island community, but he is at odds with his wife, also from that community; she hates Gaelic and desires a life of international travel.

Smith also indicts his country for its "hypocritical culture" in his poetry. He criticizes Scotland for failing to strive for excellence, as in such poems as "The White Air of March":

> *There shall not be excellence there shall be average.*
> *We shall be the intrepid hunters of golf balls.*

Smith's poems are wide-ranging, hard-hitting and unapologetic, whether he is talking about death, as in "World War One" ("If you are about to die now / there is nothing I can write for you") or myriad experiences of exile in *The Exiles* (1984). Though he is a poet concerned with and rooted in his own culture, Smith offers "a global vision in a writing of international stature."

Other Works by Iain Crichton Smith
The Black Halo: The Complete English Stories, 1977–98. Edinburgh: Birlinn, 2002.
Collected Poems. Manchester, England: Carcanet, 1996.
The Red Door: The Complete English Stories, 1946–76. Edinburgh: Birlinn, 2002.

Works about Iain Crichton Smith
Gow, Carol. *Mirror and Marble: The Poetry of Iain Crichton Smith.* New York: Hyperion Books, 1993.
Nicholson, Colin. *Iain Crichton Smith: Critical Essays.* Edinburgh: Edinburgh University Press, 1992.

Smith, Stevie (Florence Margaret Smith)
(1902–1971) *poet, novelist, essayist*
Born Florence Margaret Smith in Hull, Yorkshire, Stevie Smith was called Peggy by her parents, Ethel Spear and Charles Ward Smith. She did not acquire her famous nickname until she was past her teens.

Smith's childhood was clouded. Her health was fragile from birth; she contracted tubercular peritonitis at the age of five and was in and out of a convalescent home for three years. Her mother had heart trouble, and Smith was three years old when her father abandoned the family. Unable to afford their home, Spear moved with her two daughters and her unmarried sister to a London suburb. In 1919 Ethel Spear died. Smith herself never married, continuing to live with "the Lion of Hull," as she affectionately called her aunt. Her adult home life was the subject of Hugh Whitemore's *Stevie: A Play from the Life and Work of Stevie Smith* (1977), which became a film starring Glenda Jackson the following year.

Smith worked as a secretary at a publishing firm for 30 years. The year after she began this job she began writing poems, but it took 11 years before any of them appeared in print. The popularity of her public readings of her poems exceeded their critical acceptance.

Smith's first volume of verse, *A Good Time Was Had by All* (1936), displayed her dry, witty, satirical, sometimes whimsical style. The deliciously titled "Lord Mope," who, a young man, is described as "Sitting at the feet of the old men because they are old/Warming his shivering behind at their gutted flame," justifies reviewer George Stonier's contemporary assessment that Smith's style allows her to be "brilliantly funny and intimate at the same time."

Smith often wrote about children and about death. Some of her poems, like "Infant" and "Little Boy Lost," show the influence of William Blake, as does "Death Bereaves our Common Mother, Nature Grieves for my Dead Brother," which begins, "Lamb dead, dead lamb, / He was, I am." "Death Came to Me" culminates in the speaker's suicide by gunshot.

Smith's next three volumes of poetry were *Tender Only to One* (1938), *Mother, What Is Man?* (1942), and *Harold's Leap* (1950). *Some Are More Human Than Others: A Sketchbook* (1958) was what the title declares; scribbled captions accompany the sketches, or drawings.

Smith's poems, with their streak of morbidity, did not suit the fashion of the day. As a result, she had enormous difficulty finding a publisher for her best volume, *Not Waving but Drowning* (1957). The title poem is her most famous, with its kinship between "the dead man" whom "[n]obody heard," and the speaker who, herself drowning, could not save him. One line, "I was much too far out all my life," encapsulates Smith's keen sense of alienation and self-alienation. "In the course of [this book]," novelist Muriel SPARK wrote, Smith "has created a poetic *persona* which she presents as a fantastic, somewhat blighted, observant and irrepressible soul, not so cheerful as you think, and 'not waving but drowning.'"

Smith's persona in "The Hostage" is a man waiting to be hanged the next morning for no other crime than *wishing* to be dead. His companion is "Father Whatshisname," who will "look after [him] well"—a reminder of how Smith's poetry can sting. The poem also demonstrates her abiding contest with religious faith.

Two volumes, *Scorpion and Other Poems* (1972) and *Me Again: Uncollected Writings of Stevie Smith* (1981), appeared posthumously.

Smith was also a novelist. *Novel on Yellow Paper* (1935) was autobiographical. The first person narrator chattily addresses the reader regarding a romance, platonic relationships, and her ideas about literature and life. Because the book was perceived as anti-Semitic in its sometimes stereotypic portrayal of Jews, it cost Smith Jewish friends. Her anti-fascist novel *Over the Frontier* (1938) addresses this issue when Smith's surrogate, Pompey, confesses hatred of Jews despite cherishing Jewish friends—a painful disclosure. The *Times Literary Supplement* reviewer praised the book while noting that it is not really a novel: "It has no plot . . . It is rather a . . . record of Pompey's spasmodic thoughts and emotions."

In 1980 historian Jean Liddiard wrote of Pompey's "living out fantasies of glamorous daring and strength." This provides an index of how psychoanalytic and feminist strains in literary criticism have enhanced Smith's reputation over time. Smith herself rejected the label "feminist;" but in noting the first novel's "aware[ness] of the ideology of domesticity and its potentially dangerous effect on women," scholar Laura Severin reflects a recent trend to regard Smith as a social critic.

Smith's work remains distinctive for its intensely personal quality. Journalist Richard Church has described it as "a garment worn with courage by a tragic spirit." "The tragedy is there," he explains, because "in almost every phrase she utters, not excepting the many witty and hilarious ones, her purpose is to explore the cavities of pain and to find a way out of their horror and darkness."

Works about Stevie Smith

Civello, Catherine A. *Patterns of Ambivalence: The Fiction and Poetry of Stevie Smith*. Columbia, S.C.: Camden House, 1997.

Severin, Laura. *Stevie Smith's Resistant Antics*. Madison: University of Wisconsin Press, 1997.

Spalding, Frances. *Stevie Smith: A Critical Biography*. New York: W. W. Norton, 1988.

Smith, Zadie (1975–) *novelist*

Zadie Smith was born in the North London suburb of Willesden to an English father and Jamaican mother. She loved reading, and was especially fond of the Narnia books by C. S. LEWIS. Although she wrote a little when young, her original passion was for dancing.

Smith attended Cambridge University and graduated with a degree in English. She began writing her first novel at the university. Soon after graduating, she made news when a publisher gave her a six-figure advance after reading only 80 pages of her novel-in-progress. *White Teeth* was published in 2001 to great critical acclaim. Set in London, the novel opens with a character, Archie, attempting suicide. He tries to gas himself in his car: In his fists, "he held his army service medals (left) and his marriage license (right), for he had decided to take his mistakes with him." He survives when an annoyed butcher objects to him dying in his parking lot. Rescued by chance, Archie then staggers into a party where he meets his future wife, Clara, a 19-year-old Jamaican woman. They marry, have a daughter, and the reader plunges into a satirical, fast-paced story.

The novel's characters come from Bangladesh, Jamaica, Ireland, and England. Salman RUSHDIE has said that *White Teeth* is "about how we all got here—from the Caribbean, from the Indian subcontinent . . . and about what 'here' turned out to be." Smith herself has said, "I just wanted to show that there are communities that function well. There's sadness for the way tradition is fading away but I wanted to show people making an effort to understand each other, despite their cultural differences." However, she also emphasizes that racism is not dead.

Smith has edited a handful of short story collections. Her second novel, *The Autograph Man* (2002) is set in the London suburb of Golders Green.

Snow, Charles Percy (1905–1980)
novelist, nonfiction writer

C. P. Snow was born in Leicester, England, to Ada Sophia Robinson Snow and William Edward Snow, a shoe factory worker. Though born into a lower-middle-class family, he went on to become a physics instructor at Cambridge, a science expert for the military, a member of the civil service, the editor of the science magazine *Discovery,* and in 1966 an undersecretary in the ministry of technology.

Snow had a distinguished career in government: technical director of the ministry of labor (1940–1944), civil service commissioner (1945–1960), and official in the ministry of technology (1960–1964). In 1943 he was made a Commander of the Order of the British Empire (CBE), knighted in 1957, and elevated to the peerage as a baron in 1964.

Snow's career as a novelist began with the crime thriller *Death Under Sail* (1932). The themes that would be central to most of his fiction emerged in *The Search* (1934), which depicts the life of a scientist.

Snow's series of 11 novels, known collectively as "Strangers and Brothers," reflects some of the tensions in his own life, depicting characters who go from humble origins to positions of great scientific or political influence and who must cope with the ethical crises caused by the relationship between science and government funding of scientific research. The series begins with *Strangers and Brothers* (1940) and concludes with *Last Things* (1970). Snow unintentionally added a phrase to political discourse with the title of the ninth book in the series, *Corridors of Power* (1963).

Snow also addressed ethical issues in the nonfiction *Science and Government* (1961). His most influential work, however, and the one that has inspired the most debate and critical analysis, is the nonfiction *The Two Cultures and the Scientific Revolution* (1959). This book is based on a Cambridge lecture in which the author said the arts and sciences had become distanced from one another: "Literary intellectuals at one pole—at the other scientists, and as the most representative, the physical scientists. Between the two a gulf of mutual incomprehension." While few critics think Snow's novels bridged that gap, his lecture is remembered for drawing attention to the problem. Biographer David Shusterman notes that "Snow's influence has, in the main, been not artistic but intellectual and moral."

A Work about C. P. Snow
Shusterman, David. *C. P. Snow.* Boston: Twayne, 1991.

Somerville, Edith Anna Oenone (1858–1949) and **Martin Ross** (Violet Florence Martin) (1862–1915)
novelists, short story writers

Edith Somerville and Violet Martin, who wrote as Somerville and Ross, were born into the Ascendancy, the Anglo-Irish Protestant gentry that dominated rural Ireland. This group was caught between the larger tensions that divided England and Ireland; viewed as foreign and Protestant by the Irish Catholics and as alien and Irish by the English, the Ascendancy was never entirely sure of itself. This uncertainty informed Somerville and Ross's collaborative work, for their carefully observed and unsentimental novels of social manners explored both the pleasures and the anxieties of what it meant to live in their world.

An Irish Cousin (1889), Somerville and Ross's first published novel, has as its heroine a Canadian cousin who comes to visit her Irish family for the first time. Her situation provides the opportunity for observation of both her relatives and the local servants, in language that ranges from the formal to dialect; neither master nor servant is condescended to.

Somerville and Ross's best, if not best-known, novel was *The Real Charlotte* (1894). In this book the Dysarts, an amiably idiosyncratic aristocratic family teetering into decline, are contrasted with Charlotte Mullen, a grasping and unscrupulous lower-middle-class social climber. The novel often depicts social hierarchy effectively in the dialogue, where characters speak in the voice of their classes and dialect is revealing: "T' was last Tuesday . . . an' he came thunderin' round the house, and every big rock of English he had he called it to her, . . . sure she's hardly able to lave the bed . . . an owld woman that's not four stone weight!"

Somerville and Ross were, in a sense, waylaid by success. In 1899 they published *Some Experiences of an Irish R.M.*, humorous stories that first appeared in magazines, about a rural judge (Resident Magistrate). The book proved both popular and lucrative. Somerville and Ross were encouraged by their publisher to concentrate on similar work, which they did, though not exclusively, and they mined the same vein in two other works, *Further Experiences of an Irish R.M.* and *In Mr. Knox's Country. Dan Russell the Fox*, a light and humorous hunting novel, was the only other book on which they collaborated before Ross's death. Somerville continued to publish under the name "Somerville and Ross," but the works were not up to the standard set collaboratively.

Feminist critics have found much in Somerville and Ross to admire. James M. Cahalan has argued that "intermixed in the R. M. stories with a nostalgia for a dying way of life was a subversively gendered portrait of strong, vital women."

Works about Somerville and Ross

Lewis, Gifford. *Somerville and Ross: The World of the Irish R.M.* New York: Viking, 1985.
Robinson, Hilary. *Somerville and Ross: A Critical Appreciation.* New York: St. Martin's Press, 1980.

Sorley, Charles Hamilton (1895–1915)
poet

Charles Sorley was born in Aberdeen, Scotland. His father, William Ritchie Sorly, was a professor of moral philosophy at the University of Aberdeen. His mother, Janetta Sorley, stayed home to educate her children. Sorley attended Marlborough College, where the Wiltshire countryside inspired him to write poetry about nature. *The Marlburian* published a dozen of his poems. He was vacationing in Germany when World War I broke out. He immediately returned home and enlisted in the British army; while serving in France, he wrote poetry.

Sorley criticized the "trench poets" of the time such as Rupert BROOKE and Julian Grenfell, who glorified war and the romantic notion of dying for your country in newspapers that were produced by soldiers on the battlefield. He chose instead to emphasize the death, horror, and loss that the war created. One of his more famous poems, "All the Hills and Vales Along," begins in the same way many of the poems of the time begin, with confident soldiers singing as they march through a beautiful countryside. The third and fourth lines of the opening stanza, however, reveal the darker side of war: "And the singers are the chaps / Who are going to die perhaps." The rest of the poem continues with this sarcastic tone, driving home the pointlessness of war and asking the reader not to honor the "millions of mouthless dead."

Sorley's poetry was discovered in his effects after he was shot and killed by a sniper in the battle of Loos. His family published 37 of his poems in 1916 in *Marlborough and Other Poems*. Writer Hazel Powell observes that Sorley is of particular interest because he was writing at the beginning of the war, yet his poems show a maturity of outlook and a realism which was out of step with most of the other poets writing at that time."

Other Work by Charles Sorley

The Poems and Selected Letters of Charles Hamilton Sorley. Edited by Hilda D. Spear. Dundee, Scotland: Blackness Press, 1978.

Spark, Muriel (1918–) *novelist*

Muriel Spark, one of the 20th century's best, although underappreciated, novelists, was born Muriel Camberg in Edinburgh, Scotland, to Bernard Camberg, an engineer, and Sarah Elizabeth Maud Camberg. She was educated in religious and public schools and graduated from James Gillespie's High School for Girls in Edinburgh. After her graduation, she married S. O.

Spark and traveled to South Africa, where she lived until the marriage ended eight years later. She returned to London in 1944 and supported herself with a series of odd jobs before writing several scholarly books on Mary Shelley, William Wordsworth, and Emily Brontë (the latter two with Derek Stanford).

This portion of Spark's life came to a close in the 1950s through several life-changing events. In 1954, after a sustained struggle with religion (her father was Jewish, her mother Presbyterian), Spark converted to Roman Catholicism, which gave her a new sense of focus and a source for the religious and moral themes that would infuse her work throughout the rest of her career. The second turning point in Spark's life came in 1957 when, after writing poetry since grade school, she published her first novel, *The Comforters*, about a heroine named Caroline who, like Spark herself, is attempting to write a novel. Evelyn WAUGH praised the novel as a "complicated, subtle . . . and intensely interesting first novel." But Spark achieved even greater success with two later novels, *The Prime of Miss Jean Brodie* (1961), about the interactions of an influential teacher and her students, and the James Tait Black Memorial Prize–winning *The Mandelbaum Gate* (1965), about a British woman traveling in the Holy Land during years of political unrest.

Throughout her career, Muriel Spark has received high praise from many literary critics and fellow novelists. One of these, John Updike, has written that Spark "is one of the few writers of the language on either side of the Atlantic with enough resources, daring, and stamina to be altering, as well as feeding, the fiction machine." To this assessment, the scholar and critic Norman Page has added that Spark is "a novelist who sets out to 'make it new' in the long-established . . . genre of the novel," and whose use of language and "subtlety of style are a constant source of surprise and delight." Spark has received honorary degrees from the University of Edinburgh and Oxford University, and the PEN International Gold Pen Award (1998).

Critical Analysis

Nearly all of Spark's novels exhibit the influence of her religious beliefs and possess a starkly economical style. According to the scholar Ruth Whittaker, "throughout her work Spark economically exploits the connection she sees between God and the novelist, both omniscient authors, creators of worlds in which everything, however contingent and trivial, is shown finally to be causal and significant."

The Prime of Miss Jean Brodie is widely considered Spark's masterpiece for its masterfully developed title character and its powerful theme of betrayal. Brodie revels in manipulating her young students, and the main action of the story concerns her use of two students, Sandy Stranger and Rose Stanley, to carry out a vicarious affair with the school's married art teacher, Teddy Lloyd. While she wishes Rose to have the affair with Lloyd, it is Sandy who does so. After her involvement with Lloyd has ended, Sandy learns of Brodie's previous and ill-fated attempts at manipulation and betrays her to the school's administration, which, in turn, dismisses the teacher.

From the beginning of the novel, Spark develops Brodie as a devious and conniving character. In the opening scene, for instance, Spark writes that "Miss Brodie never discussed her affairs with the other members of the staff, but only with those former pupils whom she had trained up in her confidence." From that point forward, Brodie becomes an increasingly despicable character. When she is not directly guiding her students, she spends her time discussing the virtues of fascism and going to church. "She was not in any doubt" of her virtue, writes Spark, and "she let everyone know she was in no doubt, that God was on her side whatever her course, and so she experienced no difficulty or hypocrisy in worship while at the same time she went to bed with the singing master."

The Mandelbaum Gate (1965), yet another novel that explores religious issues, is set in the Middle East in 1961, when Israel was at war with Jordan. The story's protagonist, Barbara Vaughan, is similar to Spark herself in that she is a Jewish woman and a Catholic convert. She is in Israel planning to combine a tour of the region with a visit to her fiancé, Harry Clegg, a British archaeologist who is investigating the Dead Sea Scrolls in Jordan. As Barbara defies the orders of the British consulate and endangers her life by venturing into Jordan to find Harry, Spark introduces themes of the categorization and division of people, as well as personal identity, while narrating the story with a godlike omniscient narrator that is typical of nearly all her work.

Nearly every figure in the novel is categorized along national and geographical lines—British, Israeli, Arabic, or Western—just as the region itself is visually divided by a series of walls. The title of Spark's book, *The Mandelbaum Gate,* refers to an actual gate that separates Israel from Jordan, and even the landscape itself is divided. But the most divided place in the book is Jerusalem, the region's most holy city. In the final page of her novel, Spark writes that Barbara walked through Jerusalem's streets, passing beneath "the Zion Gate, Dung Gate, Jaffa Gate, New Gate. Then St. Stephens Gate opened within the Old City to another medieval maze of streets—Damascus Gate," constantly underscoring the division and fragmentation of the place.

Barbara's identity as a Christian Jew contains divisions that metaphorically mirror Jerusalem's physical fragmentation, and Spark spends a great deal of time illustrating her character's internal conflicts. From the moment of her arrival in the Middle East, Barbara is forced to come to terms with her Jewish heritage as she never has before, and the conflict reaches its peak during a conversation with a tour guide. The guide asks Barbara why she considers herself a "half Jew," and Barbara begins an intense period of soul-searching:

> Barbara knew then that the essential thing about herself remained unspoken, uncategorized and unlocated. She was agitated, and felt a compelling need to find some definition that would accurately explain herself.

Spark does not offer a solution to this conflict, but its mere presence in *The Mandelbaum Gate* marks a distinct shift in her writing. While her early novels pay close attention to her religious conversion, this one examines the other side of her religious makeup. In the words of the scholar Bryan Cheyette, *The Mandelbaum Gate* is Spark's exploration of the "unconverted self" and is consequently her "most Jewish book."

If *The Mandelbaum Gate* is the "most Jewish" of Spark's novels, it is also, as the scholar D. J. Enright wrote upon its publication, "much more concrete and solidly rooted in a very detailed setting" than her earlier work. In a passage that establishes a sense of place more than any other, as Barbara stands upon the summit of Mount Tabor, Spark surveys the entire region:

> To the east, from the top of Tabor was the valley of Jordan and the very blue waters of Galilee with the mountains of Syria, a different blue, on the far side. On the west, far across Palestine, the Carmel range rose from the Mediterranean. There seemed no mental difficulty about the miracles, here on the spot. They seemed to be very historic and factual, considered from this standpoint.

Other Works by Muriel Spark

Aiding and Abetting. New York: Doubleday, 2001.
The Novels of Muriel Spark (2 vols.). Boston: Houghton Mifflin, 1995.
Reality and Dreams. London: Constable, 1996.

Works about Muriel Spark

Cheyette, Bryan. *Muriel Spark.* Hordon, England: Northcote, 2000.
Edgecombe, Rodney Stenning. *Vocation and Identity in the Fiction of Muriel Spark.* Columbia: University of Missouri Press, 1990.
Page, Norman. *Muriel Spark.* New York: St. Martin's Press, 1990.
Sproxton, Judy. *The Women of Muriel Spark.* London: Constable, 1992.

Spender, Stephen (1909–1995) *poet, literary critic*

Stephen Spender was born in London, England, to Edward Harold Spender, a political journalist, and Violet Hilda Schuster Spender. Educated in boarding schools, he suffered from terrible bouts of homesickness. For two years he studied at Oxford, although he did not graduate. However, he became friends with W. H. AUDEN and was known as a member of the "Oxford Poets" or "the Auden group," which also included C. DAY LEWIS and Louis MACNEICE. From MacNeice Spender learned that he could find poetic material in the world around him, and he later said he discovered that "unpoetic-seeming things were material for poetry" and "modern life could be material for art."

In 1933 Spender published *Poems*, a communist reaction against fascism that also, as the scholar David Leeming asserts, battles the "technology, the agony, the fragmentation, and the material tyranny of his time." The opening lines of "The Express," a poem from this collection, illustrate this technological tyranny by describing the train's whistle as a "powerful plain manifesto" and further developing the train as an object possessing "restrained unconcern" for humanity. The collection also includes "The Funeral," which clearly yearns for a communist state while discussing figures who "walk home remembering the straining red flags" and "speak of the world state." According to the scholar Stanford Sternlicht, *Poems* was a success because, with its criticism of the machine age and its consideration of other types of government, it captured the interest "of a British public still exhausted by World War I, still grieving over the decimation of the brightest of a generation, and continually disappointed by its leadership."

In 1949 Spender published another noteworthy volume of poetry, *The Edge of Being*, which presents poems that realistically confront the horrors of World War II. One poem, "Rejoice in the Abyss," narrates the shock experienced by the victims of a London Bridge bombing. It begins, "The great pulsation passed. Glass lay around me," and follows its narrator as he views the aftermath through "an acrid cloud of dust."

Spender was a formidable poet, but he was also an influential literary critic. One of his most important pieces of criticism is *Destructive Element* (1935). Primarily a study of Henry James, this book also explores the belief systems of a range of modern authors. Spender was particularly interested in how authors encounter the external world, internalize it, and then transform it into their new works of fiction. He strongly believed that authors should not be criticized for writing ideologically or politically laden texts instead of what he called "art for art's sake" or "pure art" that attempts to put aside all references to the real world. Spender believed, as he put it, that "having a particular moral or political axe to grind" does not necessarily "destroy art."

Spender established a formidable reputation as a critic and held teaching positions at a number of universities in Britain and the United States, including professorships at Cambridge, the University of London, and Vanderbilt University. The scholar Doris Elder has described Spender as "a visionary with an acute sense of his world and times, who has dedicated himself to the difficult integration of self with society," whose "poetry and prose fuse the concrete and the abstract vividly, unifying flesh and the spirit, inner and outer existence."

Other Works by Stephen Spender

Collected Poems, 1928–1985. New York: Random House, 1986.
World Within World: The Autobiography of Stephen Spender. Westminster, Md.: Modern Library, 2001.

Works about Stephen Spender

Leeming, David. *Stephen Spender*. New York: St. Martin's Press, 2000.
O'Neill, Michael, and Gareth Reeves. *Auden, MacNeice, Spender: The Thirties Poetry*. London: Macmillan, 1992.

Squire, John Collings (Solomon Eagle)

(1884–1958) *poet, literary critic, editor*

J. C. Squire was born in Plymouth, England, and attended Cambridge University. He was known for writing humorous parodies and poetry, as shown in the following lines in which he responds to the claim of both sides in World War I that God was on their side:

> God heard the embattled nations shout
>   and sing,
> "Gott strafe England!" *and* "God save
>   the King!"
> God this, God that, and God the other
>   thing—
> "Good God!" *said God,* "I've got my work
>   cut out."

Squire, along with Rupert BROOKE and Edmund BLUNDEN, was a poet of the GEORGIAN POETRY school, which was extremely popular in the early 20th century. The Georgians, named after King George V of England, wrote about nature in a way that was accessible to the general public. *Steps to Parnassus* (1913) and *Tricks of the Trade* (1917) are two representative collections of Squire's Georgian poetry. His poems are simple but technically interesting for their fluent and variable rhythms. The following lines from "Mr. Belloc's Fancy" in *Tricks of the Trade* show the frivolous and light-hearted nature of this musically rhythmic poetry: "And they brew at the "Chequers" on Chanctonbury Green / The very best beer that ever was seen."

Founder and editor of *The London Mercury,* a journal of original poems, stories, illustrations, bibliographies, and critical evaluations, for several years, as Solomon Eagle, he wrote a weekly literary column for a number of publications. These pieces were collected in *Books in General* (1919). He edited a collection of essays that propose "what-if" situations from influential periods in history: *Or, If, History Rewritten* (1931), republished as *If It Had Happened Otherwise* (1972). The collection includes such essays as Philip Guedalla's "If the Moors in Spain had won" and

Sir Winston CHURCHILL's "If Lee Had Not Won the Battle of Gettysburg." Squire also edited several collections of poetry. His best-known quote today is probably this line from the "Ballade of Soporific Absorption" (1931): "But I'm not so think as you drunk I am."

Stapledon, Olaf (William Olaf Stapledon)

(1886–1950) *novelist, nonfiction writer*

Olaf Stapledon was born in Cheshire, England, to William Stapledon, the manager of a shipping agency, and Emmeline Stapledon. He spent part of his childhood in Egypt, but at the age of eight he returned to England to begin his education at Abbotsholme School. He went on to Oxford, where he earned his degree in modern history. Stapledon drove an ambulance at the front during World War I, after which he eventually returned to school, earning a Ph.D. in philosophy at the University of Liverpool in 1925.

In his first book, *A Modern Theory of Ethics* (1929), Stapledon investigated the relations between ethics and psychology. He argued that the "moods" of "moral zeal," "disillusion," and "ecstasy" are ones "which the mind may experience with regard to good and evil." He furthermore posited that we move from the indignation of moral zeal and a desire to change the world to disillusion and then to the ecstasy of discovering "a hitherto unappreciated excellence of the familiar world itself"; the ecstatic in particular implies what amounts to an aesthetic view of the world and an acceptance of it on a cosmic level. Stapledon thought spiritual values of the utmost importance. He explored the implications of his theories in his best-known fiction.

In *Last and First Men* (1930), "an essay in myth creation," one of the Last Men recounts the history of the human species over a 2 billion-year period, through 18 mutations, cataclysms, renewals, and finally to the verge of extinction. The author roots his story in natural science and is concerned to discover the place of humans in an impersonal universe.

In *Star Maker*, (1937) Stapledon continued his mythmaking as a way to explore the place of humanity in the universe, but on a broader scale, encompassing a hundred billion years of evolution, with the narrator on a pilgrimage to discover ultimate purposes. *Odd John: A Story between Jest and Earnest* (1935) is a utopian novel in which the protagonist establishes a colony of beings who, like him, are of a superior order and who aspire to spiritual ends, to be realized within this community. Community is an important theme in Stapledon's fictional, ethical, and political lives. From his youth he remained committed to progressive political positions that included antifascism and world peace.

Stapledon was a seminal figure in science fiction. The scholar James L. Campbell said of him that he was "a writer and thinker of the first magnitude whose influence and readership will continue to widen in the future."

Other Work by Olaf Stapledon

An Olaf Stapledon Reader. Edited by Robert Crossley. Syracuse, N.Y.: Syracuse University Press, 1997.

A Work about Olaf Stapledon

Crossley, Robert. *Olaf Stapledon: Speaking for the Future*. Liverpool, England: Liverpool University Press, 1994.

Stark, Freya (1893–1993) *travel writer, journalist, memoirist*

Freya Madeline Stark was born in Paris to nomadic artist parents Robert and Flora Stark. Educated at her grandmother's home in Italy, she became fluent in Italian, French, German, and English. After studying history and literature at Bedford College, London, she served as a battlefield nurse in Bologna during World War I.

Having studied Arabic at London's School of Oriental and African Studies, Stark set out for the Middle East, where few Westerners—male or female—had ever been. Along the way she encountered storms and bandits, and she almost died from malaria and dengue fever. Yet she not only survived but eventually produced more than two dozen works about her experiences, beginning with *Baghdad Sketches* (1932). This was a collection of news reports from a year Stark spent writing for *Baghdad Times* at the request of its editor.

In *The Valleys of the Assassins and Other Persian Travels* (1934), Stark—who preferred to wear Arab dress while traveling—combines travel tips with observations of Iran's land, history, and people. Having bluffed her way into Luristan before Persian police find her and escort her back to the Iraqi border, she observes: "The great and almost only comfort in being a woman is that one can always pretend to be more stupid than one is and no one is surprised."

In 1942 Stark won the Founder's Medal, the Royal Geographical Society's highest honor. During World War II, while working for the British Ministry of Information in Aden, Baghdad, and Cairo, Stark established the secret anti-Nazi society Brothers and Sisters of Freedom. She describes her experiences in *East Is West* (1945):

> "The Brothers of Freedom gave me a number of happy days. Their small centres sprang up spontaneously in unexpected places. . . . One of our members was a typographer, and ran a little business of his own in two dark rooms off the long dull street that runs to the mosque of Muhammad Ali; . . . and I sat meeting with them . . . and in that Rembrandt setting listened to what the Egyptian craftsman thinks on freedom."

Stark's extensive travels, which she continued into her 80s, inspired four autobiographies, beginning with *Traveller's Prelude* (1950), an account of her journey to Beirut after learning Arabic. Also in 1950, she learned yet another language by reading the Bible and detective stories in Turkish. *Riding to the Tigris* (1959), Stark's account of her travels in Turkey's interior, and *The Minaret of Djam: An Excursion to Afghanistan* (1970) are among the works that reveal her unending fascination with the history and archaeology of the East.

Stark was also a noted photographer and pro-lific letter writer, and in 1988 she published a volume of selected letters, *Over the Rim of the World*. She was made a Dame Commander of the Order of the British Empire (DBE) in 1972 and died a centenarian at her home in Asola, Italy. Reviewer Paul T. Hornak wrote in 1984, "Freya Stark travels as travel writers should: with mind open, receptive to nuance, tolerant of squalor, prepared to admit the unlikely to the realm of the treasured."

A Work about Freya Stark

Geniesse, Jane. *Passionate Nomad: The Life of Freya Stark*. New York: Random House, 1999.

Stephens, James (ca. 1882–1950) *poet, novelist, essayist*

Born in Dublin, James Stephens was always vague about his origins and was known to entertain others with such unlikely tales of boyhood as his having worked as a circus acrobat. In fact, he apparently spent his childhood at the Meath Protestant Industrial School for poor or homeless boys. He left in 1896 to clerk at several Dublin solicitors' offices before being discovered in 1907 when the poet George RUSSELL read his Irish nationalistic contributions to the newspaper *Sinn Féin*.

Fluent in Gaelic (an Irish language), Stephens was a leading figure of the Irish Literary Renaissance, a late-19th- and early 20th-century movement to revive ancient Irish folklore, legend, and traditions in new literary works, for which he drew upon his own broad knowledge. In 1909 he published his first poetry collection, *Insurrections*, about life in Dublin slums.

Stephens's most celebrated work is *The Crock of Gold* (1912). A fantasy novel written in English with an Irish flavor, this book contains leprechauns and spirits and makes fun of stuffy professionals and differences between men and women in Irish society. "You would have a good time with us," says a leprechaun to the philosopher, "travelling on moonlit nights and seeing strange things. . . ." The work won the 1912 Polignac Prize for fiction by a promising young writer.

Along with the success of the novel *The Charwoman's Daughter* (1912), about a young woman's growing independence, *The Crock of Gold* allowed Stephens to quit his hated clerical work to write full-time. He produced many volumes of poetry essays, and fiction in his lifetime, including *Deirdre* (1923), winner of the Tailteann Gold Medal for fiction, about a young woman ordered to marry an older king. Although Stephens remains faithful to Irish characters and settings, William Blake's influence can be found in imagery and inspirations in his poetry collection *The Hill of Vision* (1912), which uses plain language and simple rhyme schemes to portray rural Irish people. Stephens himself influenced other writers, including James JOYCE, who said that if he died before completing *Finnegan's Wake*, Stephens was the only person he would trust to finish it.

Shaken by the accidental death of his 28-year-old son and the deaths of close friends Stephen MacKenna and George Russell—and his own recurring health problems resulting from malnutrition in his youth—Stephens turned from writing to broadcasting. From 1941 until his death he gave more than 70 BBC radio talks on such subjects as poetry, poets, and old friends. In 1947 he received an honorary doctorate from Trinity College, Dublin. Author Patricia McFate writes, "Stephens' works reveal a personality like that of Ireland: brooding, highly comic, and bold."

A Work about James Stephens

McFate, Patricia. *The Writings of James Stephens: Variations on a Theme of Love*. New York: St. Martin's Press, 1979.

Stewart, John Innes Mackintosh (Michael Innes) (1906–1994) *novelist, biographer*

J. I. M. Stewart was born in Edinburgh, Scotland, to John and Eliza Jane Stewart. His father was a lawyer and director of education in Edinburgh.

Stewart wrote more than 50 novels over the course of his career, most of which were set at his alma mater, Oxford University. He also wrote several biographies, including books about Thomas Hardy, Joseph CONRAD, and Rudyard Kipling. He was best known, however, for his mysteries written under the pseudonym Michael Innes. Many of these novels feature Inspector John Appleby, a resourceful crime solver who eventually becomes chief police commissioner of London, as well as one of Innes's most popular characters.

Critics often praise Stewart's writing style for its mannered sophistication, humor, and educated tone, and he has been compared to the American novelist Henry James. Critic George L. Scheper, in a review of *Myself and Michael Innes: A Memoir* (1987), calls Stewart's mysteries "highly literate, witty and, as they say, 'donnish,'" (a reference to Oxford educators). Scheper also states that the best of the mystery novels "give us the privileged sense of having been invited to a common-room tea or Oxford High Table to hear an exceptionally witty and entertaining raconteur," as in the following passage from *A Comedy of Terrors* (1940):

> It has always been possible to make a gentleman in three generations; nowadays—when families are smaller and the upper class has to be recruited hastily—the thing is done in two. Nevertheless remote ancestors continue to be prized; the remoter they are the more proudly we regard them.

Stewart's autobiographical "Staircase in Surrey" series—which includes *The Gaudy* (1974), *Young Pattullo* (1975), *A Memorial Service* (1976), *The Madonna of the Astrolabe* (1976), and *Full Term* (1978)—describes the life experiences of Duncan Pattullo, a teacher at Oxford, and his colleagues. Critic A. N. Wilson admires Stewart as "one of the most accomplished authors of detective stories in our language. . . . [He] has no difficulty in concocting improbable and exciting twists of plot whenever he picks up his pen."

Other Works by J. I. M. Stewart
Myself and Michael Innes: A Memoir. New York: W. W. Norton 1988.
A Use of Riches. Chicago: University of Chicago Press, 1983.

Other Works by Michael Innes
Appleby's Answer. New York: Viking, 1995.
The Gay Phoenix. New York: Viking, 1981.

Stoppard, Tom (1937–) *playwright, novelist*
Tom Stoppard was born Tom Strausser in Zlin, Czechoslovakia (now Gottwaldov in the Czech Republic). His father, a doctor for the Bata shoe company, emigrated to Singapore in 1939. When the Japanese invaded that country, Dr. Strausser was killed, but his wife and two sons were evacuated to India. In 1945 Martha Strausser married British major Kenneth Stoppard, and her sons took his name.

Stoppard was educated at a multilingual boarding school in Darjeeling, then emigrated with his mother and brother to England, where he attended schools in Nottinghamshire and Yorkshire. In the 1950s he was a reporter for Bristol's *Western Daily Press* and the *Bristol Evening World*, for which he also wrote drama reviews. In the early 1960s he reviewed plays for the short-lived magazine *Scene* under the pseudonym William Boot. He has been married twice—to Jose Ingle, a nurse (1965–72), and to the doctor and television personality Miriam Moore-Robinson (1972–1992). He has four sons.

Stoppard is an intensely intellectual playwright. His belief that "truth is a matter of perspective" may well be the product of a youth spent in many parts of the world. The London premiere of *Rosencrantz and Guildenstern Are Dead* in 1967 catapulted him to fame at age 29. (The play had been performed the year before at the Edinburgh Fringe Festival.) Stoppard's production was hailed as "the most brilliant debut by a young playwright since John Arden's." Though his work has changed as it has evolved over nearly four decades, all his characteristic hallmarks as a dramatist are evident in *Rosencrantz and Guildenstern Are Dead.* He writes plays of ideas that are witty, parodic, and allusive, erudite but playful, artfully constructed, and full of brilliant flights of fancy. According to the scholar Thomas Whitaker, Stoppard has the "ability to shape intellectual debate into a dazzling three-ring circus."

Rosencrantz and Guildenstern Are Dead originated as a one-act verse play Stoppard wrote while on a Ford Foundation grant in Berlin with other young playwrights in 1964. The first draft was called *Rosencrantz and Guildenstern Meet King Lear,* but King Lear was soon dropped. The central idea stemmed from Stoppard's realization that in Shakespeare's *Hamlet,* the marginal characters Rosencrantz and Guildenstern are "the most expendable people," and that "the fact that they die without ever really understanding why they lived makes them somehow cosmic." This absurdist drama echoes Samuel BECKETT's *Waiting for Godot* with its two central characters who flip coins and play verbal games as they ponder their identities and destiny. In Stoppard's play, the melancholy Hamlet and the royal house of Denmark are relegated to the sidelines as Rosencrantz and Guildenstern take center stage.

In 1966 Stoppard wrote a novel, *Lord Malquist and Mr. Moon,* followed by two short plays, *The Real Inspector Hound* (1968) and *After Magritte* (1971), which are often produced together. The first draws on the author's experience as a drama critic and contrasts two different critics who are drawn into the play they are reviewing, a spoof of an Agatha Christie whodunit. When the curtain rises on *After Magritte,* an audience may think it is facing a René Magritte painting come to life. People and objects are wrenched out of their normal settings or contexts, creating absurd effects. A policeman looks through a window into a room where a woman is lying upended on an ironing board, draped in a white sheet, with a bowler hat on her stomach; while another well-coiffed lady, dressed in a full-length ball gown, crawls along the floor, and a man (her husband), clad in evening dress and fishing boots, blows into a lamp shade. It is the play's task to "explain" this scene.

Stoppard's next major success was *Jumpers* (1972), whose complex, many-stranded plot is difficult to unravel. It was inspired by the first moon landing, about which Stoppard commented, "You can't just land on the moon. It's much more than a location, it's a whole heritage of associations, poetic and religious." In *Jumpers* George Moore, a professor of ethics, tries to prove the existence of God and thus of moral absolutes while competing for the chair of logic at his university. George's rival for the chair is Duncan McFee, one of a pyramid of acrobats—the "jumpers" of the title—who are, in fact, professors of philosophy. Sir Archibald Jumpers—vice chancellor of the university, a modern Renaissance man and, unlike George, a moral relativist—takes McFee's place in debate. (Here Stoppard parodies the rival philosophical views of George Moore and Sir Alfred Ayer.) George's wife, Dotty, is a retired musical comedy singer who suffers a breakdown because she finds her repertoire of romantic songs about the moon has been wholly undercut by the recent British moon landing. McFee is shot—possibly by Dotty—and an Inspector Bones investigates the case. Throughout the play Stoppard makes use of different dramatic modes: The opening scene with the jumpers and a secretary doing a striptease on a trapeze is truly a three-ring circus; Dotty's performance is cabaret or revue; the interplay between the three principals resembles a Noël COWARD–like comedy of manners.

Two years after *Jumpers,* Stoppard produced *Travesties* (1974), which juggles as many ideas and interweaves more strands of action than *Jumpers.* The germ of the play was Stoppard's realization that the cultural movements Dadaism and Leninism emerged at about the same time in the same place—Zurich in 1918—as James JOYCE's composition of *Ulysses,* which revolutionized the novel. *Travesties* is a debate on the nature and purpose of art, particularly the relation of art to politics. Joyce, Tristan Tzara, founder of Dadaism, and Vladimir

Lenin, oddly assorted expatriates, become spokesmen for antithetical points of view on art. It appears the playwright was wrestling at this time with the question of whether art needs to be "committed," whether an artist is required to justify his art through political commitment. As is Stoppard's custom, the play gives no definitive answer. Stoppard filters the drama through the mind of a minor consular official, Henry Carr. Carr is an unreliable narrator with an erratic memory. In a Stoppardian shift of context, he remarks, "To be an artist *at all* is like living in Switzerland during a world war."

In the 1970s, after a visit Stoppard paid to Eastern Europe with a member of Amnesty International, his plays, including *Dogg's Hamlet, Cahoot's Macbeth* (1979) and *Squaring the Circle* (1985), began to engage political issues. In his career as a dramatist, Stoppard has evolved from writing what he terms "nuts-and-bolts comedies" or farces to creating complex plays of ideas in which high comedy becomes more metaphysical. Among his most successful later plays are *The Real Thing* (1982), *Arcadia* (1993), and the recent *The Invention of Love* (1997).

The Real Thing explores the nature of love through its protagonist, a playwright who is educated in love by his second wife and teenage daughter. Another theme is the contrasting views of art of playwrights Henry and Brodie, which carries over from *Travesties*. The well-wrought *Arcadia* spans successive generations of a family in the early 19th and late 20th centuries and is a meditation, among other things, on mathematics, chaos theory, literature, landscape, and death. As Mel Gussow observed in his *New York Times Magazine* profile of the playwright, "Stoppard's distinction is his linguistic and conceptual virtuosity." The recent *The Invention of Love* (1997) explores the contrary gifts of the classicist and poet A. E. Housman, portraying his life and times from a vantage point beyond the grave.

For more than a quarter century, Stoppard has intrigued the theater world with clever wordplay melded with fantastic ideas. According to one reviewer, "Stoppard questions everything from the nature of love to the nature of the universe, from the compulsion to act to the compulsion to act out, from the impulse to create to the impulse to procreate. And while absolutes are scant in Stoppard's work, interrogatives and insights abound."

Works about Tom Stoppard

Cahn, Victor L. *Beyond Absurdity: The Plays of Tom Stoppard*. Rutherford, N.J.: Fairleigh Dickinson University Press, 1979.

Rusinko, Susan. *Tom Stoppard*. Boston: G. K. Hall, 1986.

Whitaker, Thomas R. *Tom Stoppard*. New York: Grove Press, 1983.

Storey, David (1933–) *playwright, novelist, screenwriter*

David Storey was born in the industrial town of Wakefield to Frank Richmond Storey, a coal miner, and Lily Cartwright Storey. At the age of 18, much to the chagrin of his working-class father who wanted him to become a businessman, he enrolled in the Wakefield School of Art and from there went on to the Slade School of Fine Art in London. Storey funded his later education as a professional rugby player, and before his writing career took off he worked a number of jobs that would become important subjects for his writing: a tent erector, a bus driver, a postman, a farmhand, and a teacher.

With the appearance of *This Sporting Life* (1960), Storey quickly became known as a writer of realistic novels that often portray conflicts between working-class parents and their educated children. Many of Storey's protagonists are isolated, moody, and attempting to balance their physical and spiritual lives. *This Sporting Life,* which is drawn directly from Storey's rugby experience, features Arthur Machin, who is physically powerful but emotionally sensitive and somewhat of an outcast amongst his less intellectual teammates. Sandwiched between intense descriptions of rugby matches is the story of Machin's relationship with his widowed landlady, Mrs. Hammond, with whom he eventually falls in love. Mrs. Hammond, despite all Machin's efforts, refuses to return her tenant's feelings, and at the end of the novel she dies with the devoted young man standing beside her hospital bed. In the final chapter Storey offers no closure: Instead of giving Machin the physical and emotional balance for which he has searched throughout the novel, he simply shows the now-aging rugby player involved in another violent match. Storey successfully adapted *This Sporting Life* (1963) into a screenplay.

Storey's BOOKER PRIZE–winning novel *Saville* (1976) follows the life of Colin Saville from childhood through early manhood, when he tries to escape the oppressive poverty of industrial northern England and the stifling expectations of his family. Colin's father, initially an admirable figure who wishes for his son to have a life better than his own, rejoices when Colin earns an academic scholarship and goes to school, only to become scornful and abusive when Colin becomes a teacher and poet rather than a business owner or industrial manager. To his working-class family and neighbors, Colin's intellectual lifestyle seems lazy, even decadent, and eventually he has to flee to London in hopes of finding freedom, living a better life, and perhaps even fulfilling the artistic potential that he senses within himself. After deciding to depart for London, Colin feels

> a cloud had lifted: the town, even the village when he finally arrived there, no longer held him. There was nothing to detain him. The shell had cracked.

Storey is also an exceptional playwright. Indicative of all his plays, *The Contractor* (1969) centers on a single event: setting up and eventually taking down a tent, which is performed on stage. In the process, through choppy dialogue and snippets of conversation, the workers create a portrait of their world. Storey's play *Home* (1970) is set in a mental institution and captures the loss and fragmented lives of four patients. *Changing Room* (1971) takes place in a locker room, where audiences gain intimate access to the gritty, often bawdy conversations of amateur rugby players before, during, and after a game.

While Storey received high praise for his novels early in his career, his dramatic work has earned him an enduring place in the tradition of British literature. As the scholar Herbert Liebman remarks, "Even if David Storey writes nothing else—and this is quite unlikely . . . his reputation as a major and inventive twentieth century British dramatist is secure. He clearly deserves our respect and admiration."

Other Works by David Storey

A Serious Man. London: Cape, 1998.
Storey: Plays One. London: Methuen, 1992.
Storey: Plays Two. London: Methuen, 1994.

Works about David Storey

Hutchings, William, ed. *David Storey: A Casebook.* New York: Garland, 1992.
Liebman, Herbert. *The Dramatic Art of David Storey: The Journey of a Playwright.* Westport, Conn.: Greenwood, 1996.

Strachey, Lytton (Giles Lytton Strachey)
(1880–1932) *biographer, essayist, journalist*

Lytton Strachey was born in London to Sir Richard and Jane Maria Grant Strachey. His father had a distinguished career in the British army and went on to develop a wide range of interests in the arts and sciences, serving as the president of the Royal Geographical Society. Strachey attended Liverpool University College and later studied at Cambridge, where he failed after three years to win a scholarship.

After leaving Cambridge in 1905, Strachey began to build a successful career as a writer. His essays and journalism earned him a reputation as a witty and engaging critic. He published articles in well-known periodicals such as *New Statesman, Independent Review, Nation,* and *New Quarterly.* As a journalist, Strachey was probably best known for his work as drama critic for the *Spectator,* for which he wrote more than 90 reviews.

Strachey was an important member of the BLOOMSBURY GROUP, an assemblage of young intellectuals that included such notable figures as Virginia and Leonard WOOLF, Clive BELL, and Roger FRY. The Bloomsbury Group represented a rejection of Victorian morality and traditions, particularly those having to do with literary conventions. Its members met once a week to discuss literature, art, history, and philosophy.

In 1918 Strachey earned widespread literary acclaim with the publication of his book *Eminent Victorians.* In this work he experiments with biographical writing in order to offer a critique of what he viewed as the hypocrisy of Victorian society. His decision to write short character studies of such figures as Florence Nightingale and Cardinal Manning was a reaction to long hagiographical biographies popular in the Victorian period. Strachey himself claimed to seek in his writing "a brevity which excludes everything that is redundant and nothing that is significant." According to the editor of the Modern Library edition of *Eminent Victorians,* Strachey's method brought fresh life into a genre that "had declined to a journeyman's task of compiling fat volumes commemorating the dead." In contrast to other biographers, he possessed an "acute sense of the past, a scholarship both profound and spirited and a crystalline style." Written during World War I, the book functions as both history and biography and expresses the author's profound disillusionment with a post-Victorian world that gave birth to a devastating war. Strachey himself was a conscientious objector during the war.

Another famous Strachey biography is *Queen Victoria* (1921), a sympathetic look at the life of the monarch under whom he grew up; it was awarded the James Tait Black Memorial Prize. With wit, but also with compassion, Strachey follows Victoria from her sheltered childhood and through her final years. In his assessment of the person and career of Victoria, the author writes, "The girl, the wife, the aged women, were the same: vitality, conscientiousness, pride and simplicity were hers to the latest hour."

After the publication of *Queen Victoria* Strachey's reputation began a steady decline. His last major work, *Elizabeth and Essex: A Tragic History* (1928), about Queen Elizabeth I's reign, received mixed reviews. One of his biographers, R. A. Scott-James, wrote of the author's reputation, "To make history, and especially biography, interesting—that is the essence of Strachey's work. Every one of his biographies, long and short, reads like a novel or short story, with this difference, that unlike the majority of novels and short stories, it is usually done with sensitive art, and in the manner which gives full scope to irony and wit."

Other Works by Lytton Strachey
Landmarks in French Literature. 1912. Reprint, New York: Oxford University Press, 1969.
Literary Essays. San Diego, Calif.: Harcourt Brace Jovanovich, 1985.

Works about Lytton Strachey
Holroyd, Michael. *Lytton Strachey.* New York: Farrar, Straus, & Giroux, 1995.
Johnstone, John Keith. *The Bloomsbury Group: A Study of E. M. Forster, Lytton Strachey, Virginia Woolf, and Their Circle.* London: Octagon Books, 1978.

surrealism
The surrealist movement began in France in the 1920s. The poet André Breton, one of its major shapers, published his *Manifesto of Surrealism* in 1924. Breton's ideas were strongly influenced by Sigmund Freud's theories. The literary and artistic movement that was built on the *Manifesto* has its roots primarily in French poetry and Italian art.

The surrealist's aim is to produce literature and art based on the imagination, with a particular interest in dreams and hallucinations. The source for all of these, according to Breton's reading of Freud, is the unconscious. The surrealists therefore attempted to present the workings of the unconscious mind and to mesh that with the conscious in a "quest" for "psychic forces." For Breton and other surrealists, genius was the ability to tap the unconscious reservoir, and they believed that poets and painters had the readiest access.

The writers of surrealism explore the semiconscious as well, delving into the border of sleeping and waking to find and expose the mind's internal chaos. Surrealists' writing, which sometimes uses stream of consciousness (the random flow of thoughts, emotions, memories, and associations of characters), intends to reveal a freedom from convention and the conscious control of reason. The critic Herbert Read argues that surrealism was the logical and inevitable end product of ROMANTICISM. Surrealist writers were more interested in the associations and implications of words than in the literal meaning of the language, which can make their work difficult to understand.

Although surrealism never became the major literary movement in Great Britain that it was in France, it found advocates in such writers as the poet David GASCOYNE. Elements of surrealism also can be found in the work of many 20th-century British writers, such as James JOYCE and Virginia WOOLF. Surrealism became less popular after World War II, but its long-term influence all over the world has been substantial, affecting poetry, the novel, film, theater, painting, and sculpture.

See also THEATER OF THE ABSURD; VORTICISM.

Swift, Graham (1949–   ) *novelist*

Graham Swift was born in London to Allan Stanley Swift, a civil servant, and Sheila Irene Bourne Swift. He was educated in public schools and eventually earned B.A. and M.A. degrees in English from Cambridge. Choosing not to pursue a career as an academic, Swift taught high school English for several years before establishing himself as a writer.

Beginning with his first novel, *The Sweet-Shop Owner* (1980), Swift has compellingly explored themes of loss, bereavement, history, identity, and faith. *The Sweet-Shop Owner* is about the last day in the life of Willy Chapman, the title character. It

was remarkable for a first effort, but Swift earned more critical acclaim with his second novel, *Shuttlecock* (1981). This novel is narrated by Prentice, who works for the department of London's police bureau that reviews and preserves old police records. From the beginning Prentice is obsessed with his father's history as a hero of the French resistance during World War II. The son becomes even more engrossed after discovering files suggesting that his father may have cracked during a Gestapo interrogation, giving up information that led to the deaths of British agents. Eventually Prentice's supervisor reveals that he possesses files that will establish the father either as a hero or as a coward who cost several men their lives. Offering Prentice the file, the supervisor says, "The file's here, in the flat . . . it's up to you whether we destroy it, now. And it's up to you whether you want to look at it before it's destroyed."

Waterland (1984), Swift's next novel, tells the story of a history teacher, Tom Crick, whose world is collapsing around him. With his marriage quickly disintegrating and his school planning to phase history out of its curriculum, Crick begins lecturing his classes about the fenlands of his childhood home, along with his personal and ancestral history. His stories range from ancient tales of familial abuse and incest to much more intimate and haunting ones, such as his father's discovery of a mysterious dead body that only Crick himself, through some harrowing detective work of his own, knows to be the victim of his mentally retarded brother.

As he does in both *Shuttlecock* and *Waterland*, Swift also explores history and loss in his most highly acclaimed novel, the BOOKER PRIZE–winning *Last Orders* (1996). The novel follows four elderly friends—Vince, Ray, Lenny, and Vick—as they journey from London to the coast of England in order to scatter the ashes of a fifth friend, Jack, into the ocean. Told in the vernacular of four ordinary men whose heyday, the World War II years, is long past, the book presents conversations about those glory days, the various adventures the men have since had, and the subject of mortality.

Swift's work has been translated into more than 20 languages. Writing for the *New York Review of Books*, critic John Banville observed, "Swift has involved . . . [the reader] in real, lived lives. . . . Quietly, but with conviction, he seeks to affirm the values of decency, loyalty, love."

Other Works by Graham Swift

Ever After. New York: Alfred A. Knopf, 1992.
Out of This World. New York: Poseidon, 1988.

A Work about Graham Swift

Cooper, Pamela. *Graham Swift's Last Orders: A Reader's Guide*. New York: Continuum, 2002.

Swinnerton, Frank Arthur   (1884–1982)
novelist, nonfiction writer

Frank Swinnerton was born in Wood Green, a suburb of London, England, the son of Charles Swinnerton, a copperplate engraver, and Rose Swinnerton. Although he wrote some nonfiction, including *The Georgian Scene: A Literary Panorama* (1934) and *Swinnerton: An Autobiography* (1936), he was best known for his novels, of which he wrote more than 60. Themes of the anxiety of youth, the conflict between family loyalties and personal identity, and attitudes toward class distinctions are prevalent in these works.

Swinnerton's most famous novel, *Nocturne* (1917), takes place during a single night. Two sisters, Jenny and Emmy, are torn between the loyalty they feel for one another and for their invalid father and the guilt-ridden hope for a better life. An accident that occurs when Jenny abandons her invalid father to be with her lover only increases her guilt and frustration. *Shops and Houses* (1918) examines attitudes toward class differences in two related families as a small grocer moves to a new town with his family, not knowing that his distant cousins are the richest family in town. When one of the poor family's sons seeks contact with his high-society cousins, tempers flare on both sides. Critic H. W. Boynton said of Swinnerton's novels: "Mr. Swinnerton is

after, not a slice of life, but a distilled and golden drop of life. . . . As for the meaning or moral of the story, it is inherent, not appended."

Other Works by Frank Swinnerton

Figures in the Foreground : Literary Reminiscences, 1917–1940. North Stratford, N.H.: Ayer Company Publishers, 1963.
A Galaxy of Fathers. North Stratford, N.H.: Ayer Company Publishers, 1966.

Symons, Julian Gustave   (1912–1994)
literary critic, novelist, biographer

Julian Symons was born in London to an English mother and an immigrant Jewish father. He attended school until age 14, then worked as a secretary until 1937, when he founded and edited the literary magazine *Twentieth Century Verse*. After World War II he succeeded George ORWELL as a writer for the *Manchester Evening News*, and began to write full-time.

As a literary critic, Symons wrote and reviewed widely, establishing a reputation for insight, meticulousness, and keen judgment. As a biographer he wrote about Charles Dickens; Thomas Carlyle; and the American authors Edgar Allan Poe and Dashiell Hammett. He also established himself as a detective and crime novelist.

In 1945 Symons published *The Immaterial Murder Case*, his first detective novel, an elaborate confection that included parodies of contemporary art. In *Bloody Murder; From the Detective Story to the Crime Novel: A History* (1972), Symons wrote that "a crime story can have the depth and subtlety of characterization, the moral and social point of what is generally called a 'straight' novel." In his own novels, such as *The Thirty-first of February* (1950), set in an advertising agency, or *The End of Solomon Grundy* (1964), with an advertising man as protagonist, he did not follow the narrow conventions that centered a story only on a crime and its solution. Instead, he used crime as an opportunity to develop characters of some depth and to engage in social criticism.

The novelist Patricia Highsmith wrote of Symons that "as a critic [he] can be counted on for fair and intelligent reviews, which are given substance by his thorough knowledge of crime novel history. His own novels attest to his interest in and dedication to this genre."

Other Works by Julian Symons

The Narrowing Circle. 1954. Reprint, Thirsk, North Yorkshire, England: The House of Stratus, 2001.

The Progress of a Crime. 1960. Reprint, Thirsk, North Yorkshire, England: The House of Stratus, 2001.

A Work about Julian Symons

Walsdorf, John J., and Bonnie J. Allen. *Julian Symons: A Bibliography.* New Castle, Del.: Oak Knoll Press, 1996.

Synge, John Millington (1871–1909)
playwright, nonfiction writer, poet

J. M. Synge was born in Rathfarnham, a suburb of Dublin, Ireland, into a Protestant Anglo-Irish family. His ancestors were bitter anti-Catholics, and his grandfather and uncle, both Protestant ministers, spent their lives attempting to convert Irish Catholics to Protestantism. His brother Edward worked as a land agent and was notorious for his brutal methods of eviction. Synge's early education was frequently interrupted by illness, and he found little comfort in the religious strictness of his family. At age 14 he read the works of Charles Darwin, which led him to reject Christianity just two years later.

Like many young people of his day, Synge supported the nationalist cause of Ireland's independence from England. In 1889 he entered Trinity College, Dublin, to study Gaelic, which was taught in the Divinity School for the sole purpose of helping the Protestant missionaries convert Catholics in the west of Ireland. While studying at Trinity, Synge became a student at the Royal Irish Academy of Music, where he studied counterpoint and harmony, the essential elements of classical chamber music. After graduating, he moved to Germany to study music; however, after only six months, he decided to dedicate his life to literature.

In 1895 Synge moved to Paris, where he studied languages and literature at the Sorbonne. He tutored in English, wrote poetry, and attended lectures on philosophy, ethics, politics, and Breton culture. In 1896, after meeting W. B. YEATS and Maud Gonne, an Irish nationalist who had fled to France to avoid arrest, he joined the Irish League, an organization dedicated to liberation of Ireland from the British rule. Yeats also influenced his views on Irish liberation and nationalism. In 1898, as advised by Gonne, Synge visited the Aran Islands off the western coast of Ireland, which were inhabited by Gaelic-speaking Catholics. The experience helped nurture the imagination of the young writer.

After visiting the Aran Islands, Synge dedicated his time to writing reviews of contemporary French and Irish literature, as well as to writing *The Aran Islands* (1907). The book, divided into four parts corresponding to each visit he made, poetically captures the islanders' culture and customs, as well as the dreary, desolate environment of the islands: "Grey floods of water were sweeping everywhere upon the limestone, making at times a wild torrent of the road, which twined continually over low hills and cavities in the rock or passed between a few small fields of potatoes or grass hidden away in corners that had shelter." *The Aran Islands* describes a traditional culture beginning to sense the intrusion of the modern life.

Synge's first play, *Riders to the Sea* (1902), is an exceptionally mature and intricate work of art. It depicts the plight of Maurya, an old woman who has lost all the men in her family to the sea, as she waits for nine days for the body of her son to be washed ashore. Many of the motifs in the play are drawn from Synge's own experiences among the fishermen of the Aran Islands. The play embodies the symbols and archetypes of the Gaelic culture almost mystically, while detailing the common, everyday lives of the villagers. As Synge scholar Eugene Benson writes, "Synge secures in his audience a willing suspension of disbelief because he roots his theme of multiple death and terrifying presence in a meticulous faithfulness to the details of everyday peasant life."

The Shadow of the Glen (1902) is notably different from the epic quality of *Riders to the Sea*. Set in the County Wicklow, a few miles outside of Dublin, the play deals with everyday concerns of peasant life. Seemingly farcical, it is disturbing in its thematic concentration on death and mutilation. A husband pretends to be dead in order to confront his adulterous wife. As the young lover sneaks into her bedroom, the husband is suddenly "resurrected" and unleashes physical force on both of them. The ironic twist in the play, however, is that the audience's sympathies are directed toward the lover instead of toward the respectable farmer. Similarly, *The Tinker's Wedding* (1902) presents a humorous story of a young couple who attempt to trick a priest into marrying them. Synge's portrayal of the priest is less than kind: He is a drinker, gambler, and a womanizer. The natural wildness of the tinker is contrasted with the immorality of the priest.

The Playboy of the Western World (1907) was Synge's best and the most controversial play. At the premiere in Dublin, the play's violence and the unsympathetic image of Ireland that it presented caused the audience to riot. This play, too, emphasizes contrasts. The dream world of Christy Mahon, the playboy protagonist, is contrasted against the brutal reality of life in Ireland. The play explores the Oedipal themes of patricide and incest, as Christy Mahon considers killing his father. When he finally carries out the deed, Christy is rewarded with the approval of the villagers, the admiration of the local girls, and the courtship of two rich women. He is eventually betrayed by two fellow Irish villagers and handed over to the British authorities for trial. The play infuriated many people in Ireland, including W. B. Yeats.

Synge left the Irish League to show his contempt for his unruly critics.

In his final major play, *Deirdre of the Sorrows* (1910), Synge dramatizes a well-known folktale of a young woman who is promised as a bride to an old, senile king. She elopes with a young man but is tragically forced by circumstances to return home. With this play, Synge returns to his earlier epic conventions. The play dramatizes such conflicts as society versus nature, youthfulness versus age, and power versus love. The lovers' passion forces them to make heroic sacrifices for each other.

Synge's talent as a playwright was widely recognized throughout his lifetime. He found supporters for his work among the remote villages of Ireland and the sophisticated literary circles that included Yeats and James JOYCE. Synge produced his plays at a time when Ireland was engulfed in fervent nationalism and political upheaval. His plays remain popular today not only in Ireland but also in England and the United States. As Eugene Benson writes, "To say that Synge's work is contemporary is to recognize that while his plays are a priceless portion of the Irish dramatic movement, they belong also to the wider patria of twentieth-century drama."

Other Works by J. M. Synge

Collected Works Volume 1: Poems. Washington, D.C: Catholic University of America Press, 1998.
Collected Works Volume 2: Prose. Washington, D.C. Catholic University of America Press, 1998.
"The Playboy of the Western World" and Other Plays. Oxford, England: Oxford University Press, 1998.

Works about J. M. Synge

Benson, Eugene. *J. M. Synge*. New York: Grove Press, 1980.
McCormack, W. J. *Fool of the Family: The Life of J. M. Synge*. London: Weidenfeld, 2000.

Taylor, Elizabeth (1912–1975) *novelist, short story writer*

Born Elizabeth Coles to Oliver Coles, an insurance inspector, and Elsie Fewtrell Coles in Reading, England, Elizabeth Taylor determined to become a novelist early in her childhood. She attended the Abbey School in Reading and worked as both a teacher and a librarian there until her marriage to John William Kendall Taylor, a confectionery manufacturer, in 1936. They had a daughter and a son and lived in the village of Penn, in Buckinghamshire, which appealed to Taylor's sensibilities: "Village-life . . . seems a better background for a woman novelist and certainly more congenial to me," she wrote. This prosperous, rural environment would provide the kind of setting found in her novels.

Many of Taylor's novels, including *At Mrs. Lippincote's* (1946) and *Palladian* (1947), depict bourgeois life and manners and were written with the shrewd observation and precision for which she became known. Angus WILSON described Taylor as having a "warm heart and sharp claws." Many of her works examine the collapse of order (usually depicted in the breakdown of marital or sexual relationships) and show the tensions and hidden drama of the superficially comfortable and respectable world of the bourgeoisie.

Taylor wrote 11 novels and five volumes of short stories, but because of her subject matter, the English middle classes, her work was neglected. However, most of her books have recently been reprinted. Her combination of elegance, subtlety, and ironic wit has led to comparisons with Jane Austen. In 1984 her novel *Angel* (1957), about a popular romantic novelist, was named by the British Book Marketing Council one of the "Best Novels of Our Time." *Mrs. Palfrey at Claremont* (1971), a study of old age, was adapted for television and short-listed for the BOOKER PRIZE in 1971. Taylor also published stories in the *New Yorker*, *Harper's Magazine*, and *Harper's Bazaar*, winning her a large American following.

Other Works by Elizabeth Taylor

In a Summer Season. 1961. Reprint, New York: Carroll & Groft, 1990.

The Wedding Group. 1968. Reprint, London: Virago, 1968.

A Wreath of Roses. 1949. Reprint, London: Virago, 1994.

A Work about Elizabeth Taylor

Leclerq, Florence. *Elizabeth Taylor.* Boston: Twayne, 1985.

Tennant, Emma (Catherine Aydy)

(1937–   ) *novelist, memoirist*

Born into an aristocratic family in London, Emma Tennant was the daughter of Christopher Grey Tennant, Second Baron Glenconner, and Elizabeth Lady Glenconner. She spent the first nine years of her life in Scotland, where she attended a small village school. She then attended a private girls' school in London and a finishing school in Oxford. There she became extremely interested in fine art. She went to the Louvre in Paris to study art history when she was 15, then returned to London, became a debutante, and was presented at court in 1956.

Tennant has been married three times. One of her fathers-in-law was the novelist Henry GREEN, and his work heavily influenced her first book. Published under the name Catherine Aydy, *The Colour of Rain* (1964) is a comic novel set in the early 1960s that features wealthy young Londoners living rather aimless lives. Although it received generally positive one reviewer denounced it as decadent; Tennant was so distressed she did not publish anything else for nine years. When she returned, she published under her own name. After this she turned to science fiction for a while, with *The Time of the Crack* (1973), a witty novella imagining a London thrown into chaos when the Thames runs dry. Reviewer Gavin Ewart wrote, "As a comic apocalypse this novel could hardly be bettered." In the 1970s Tennant also founded and edited the magazine *Bananas*, which featured such promising new writers as Angela CARTER, Elaine FEINSTEIN, and Sara Maitland.

Many of Tennant's novels grapple with the idea that truth is colored by our perceptions and imagination. Her novel *Queen of Stones* (1982), for example, is an "imaginative reconstruction" of a strange event that happened in October 1981 at the Isle of Portland. A young girl dies violently while out among her friends, and yet somehow, despite witnesses and spectators, no sure facts can be unearthed about how she met her death. Tennant demonstrates the way in which multiple perspectives make the truth even harder to grasp.

Strangers: A Family Romance (1998) raises similar questions. A fictional autobiography, this book demonstrates some of Tennant's own "family romances"—her term for the stories one invents as a child about a more romantic parentage than one actually has. The postscript is written in the first person, and the speaker muses, "How much of what I thought then is truth, and how much fantasy? As with the dreams and documents that fed my obsession with the past, there is no way of saying that what is true to me is not also history." Author Gore Vidal said of *Strangers* that it "reads like the account of a young girl's dream—a castle, secret rooms, overheard conversations . . . as well as an entire generation of prince charmings alive, one moment, on old lawns, and next gone in the First World War."

Tennant has written numerous novels that flirt with the fantastic. *Faustine* (1992) is a modern rewriting of the myth of Faust. The devil tempts a middle-aged woman to sell her soul in return for restored youth and beauty. The novel is written from multiple points of view.

Tennant has written several sequels to novels by Jane Austen. Inspired by *Pride and Prejudice,* she wrote *Pemberley* (1993) and *An Unequal Marriage* (1994), describing Elizabeth and Mr. Darcy's conflicts and dilemmas; while *Elinor and Marianne* (1996) is a sequel to Austen's *Sense and Sensibility.* Tennant's *Emma in Love,* (1996) a sequel to Austen's *Emma,* startled some reviewers by giving Emma a lesbian attachment. In all her sequels, Tennant strikingly replicates Austen's elegant prose, as in the following extract from *Emma in Love.*

> Emma Knightley, handsome, married and rich, with a comfortable home and a doting husband, seemed to unite some of the best blessings of existence, and had lived nearly four years since her marriage with very little to distress or vex her.

Tennant has written several books taken from her own experiences with the aristocracy, including *Wild Nights* (1979), a fictional autobiography about her childhood home in Scotland. The author J. G. BALLARD said this novel was "as exhilarating as racing with rapids in a glass gondola with a white witch at the helm." Another playful autobiography is *The Adventures of Robina by Herself, being the Memoirs of a Debutante at the Court of Queen Elizabeth II* (1986). Recently Tennant has written the memoirs *Girlitude: A Memoir of the 50s and 60s* (1999) and *Burnt Diaries,* which describes an affair with the poet Ted HUGHES. Her novel *Sylvia and Ted* (2001) is a fictional account from three perspectives, depicting the doomed love triangle of Sylvia Plath, Hughes, and Hughes's mistress Assia Wevill. Tennant was also general editor of the Penguin Lives of Modern Women series.

Other Works by Emma Tennant

The ABC of Writing. Winchester, Mass.: Faber & Faber, 1992.
The Half-Mother. Boston: Little, Brown, 1983.
The House of Hospitalities. New York: Viking, 1987.
Tess. London: Flamingo, 1993.
Two Women of London: The Strange Case of Ms. Jekyll and Mrs. Hyde. Winchester, Mass.: Faber & Faber, 1989.

Tey, Josephine (Elizabeth Mackintosh, Gordon Daviot) (ca. 1896–1952) *novelist*

Born Elizabeth Mackintosh in Inverness, Scotland, Josephine Tey was the oldest daughter of Colin Mackintosh, a greengrocer, and Josephine Horne Mackintosh, a former teacher. She completed her studies at Anstey Physical Training College in Birmingham, England, in 1917. She never published under her own name but instead wrote plays as Gordon Daviot and novels as Josephine Tey.

During Tey's lifetime, she was best known for her plays under the Daviot pseudonym. *Richard of Bordeaux* (1932), a study of England's King Richard II, provides an alternate view to that of Shakespeare's *The Tragedy of King Richard II.* With John Gielgud in the lead, the production had a successful run. In all, Tey wrote 30 plays, including

six full-length dramas that were produced in London and several radio plays. The most successful were based on English or biblical history.

Today Tey's reputation rests on her mysteries, which she once dismissed as her "yearly knitting." She introduced Scotland Yard Inspector Alan Grant in *The Man in the Queue* (1929), which won the Dutton Mystery Prize. Murder "bored" Tey's unconventional detective, whom she described as more interested in "the possible play of mind on mind, of emotion on emotion" than in the hard facts of a case.

Although Tey was reluctant to talk about herself, several of her eight mysteries give hints about her life. In *Miss Pym Disposes* (1946), a murder victim dies from an injury similar to one Tey suffered as a physical education teacher. *Brat Farrar* (1949) reflects the author's enthusiasm for the English countryside and for horses and racing.

Although Tey's early works were criticized for not providing enough clues for the reader to determine the villain, her later novels include deft characterization and plentiful clues. *The Daughter of Time* (1951), in which a bedridden Inspector Grant investigates the historical question of whether Richard III really murdered his two young nephews, "remains her most famous book," according to mystery scholar Martha Hailey DuBose, "loved or hated by readers, but rarely failing to hold the interest of anyone who gets into it."

Dubose credits Tey with "forcing" the mystery novel to grow by creating "people who do wrong but are not outside the circle of human understanding and sympathy." Alexandra Von Malokttke Roy believes Tey's "focus on the conscience of the detective, the doubts, the anxieties, and the wrong conclusions" has caused her writing to grow in influence even after her death.

Other Works by Josephine Tey

A Shilling for Candles. 1936. Reprint, New York: Scribner, 1998.
To Love and Be Wise. 1950. Reprint, New York: Scribner, 1998.

Works about Josephine Tey

DuBose, Martha Hailey. *Women of Mystery: The Lives and Works of Notable Women Crime Novelists.* New York: St. Martin's Press, 2000.
Roy, Sandra. *Josephine Tey.* Boston: Twayne, 1980.

Theater of the Absurd

The Theater of the Absurd describes the work of several playwrights, primarily in the 1950s and 1960s, who dealt with what they saw as the absurdity of human existence. The term *Theater of the Absurd* is attributed to the critic Martin Esslin and is derived from an essay by the French novelist Albert Camus. In his 1942 *Myth of Sisyphus,* Camus defined the human situation as basically meaningless and absurd. Theater of the Absurd grew out of the avant-garde artistic experiments of the 1920s and 1930s. World War II also contributed to the growth of the movement as it exposed people to a sense of the impermanence of their values and beliefs.

Plays by such dramatists as Samuel BECKETT, Arthur Adamov, Eugene Ionesco, and Harold PINTER present the view that human beings inhabit a universe with which they are out of step. These plays focus on the difference between human intent and the chaos that results. One benchmark of absurdist theater was Beckett's *Waiting for Godot* (1953). The play consists of two men standing by a tree, waiting for a man named Godot. Godot never arrives, and the two men repeat their monotonous, meaningless, and Godless existence day after day.

It is one of the missions of absurdist theater to shake the audience out of its complacency. As a result, plays in the Theater of the Absurd style tend to be innovative, creatively unusual, and often very funny.

Thomas, Donald Michael (1935–)
novelist, poet, translator

Born into a working-class family in Cornwall, England, D. M. Thomas attended Oxford University upon completing his National Service and graduated with a degree in English literature in 1958. During his undergraduate years he began to write poetry as well as to cultivate his interest in Russian literature, since he had learned Russian during his National Service. He became a schoolteacher, but during a period of British economizing that culminated in his school's closure, Thomas wrote to supplement his income.

Much of Thomas's fiction is represented by the title of his autobiographical piece *Memories and Hallucinations,* (1988) and by a chapter within it, "The Nightmare of History." Psychoanalytically symbolic and significant dreamscapes often appear in his fiction, suffused with eroticism and populated by the victims of the historical catastrophes of the 20th century. His first published novel, *The Flute-Player,* (1979) was inspired by the life of Anna Akhmatova, the great Russian poet who both witnessed and bore witness against the tyranny of Stalinism. His second novel, *The White Hotel,* (1981) for which he is best known, relies on one of Sigmund FREUD's case histories, *Frau Anna G.* It includes quotations from the protagonist's prescient dreams within an atmosphere of historical tragedy and violence, and it concludes in the metaphorical conjunction of the two great Freudian themes of eros and thanatos, love and death. In a later novel, *Ararat,* (1983) Thomas treats the Turkish slaughter of Armenians in 1915.

Ararat is the first of five novels, making up the *Russian Nights* sequence, the other titles being *Swallow* (1984), *Sphinx* (1986), *Summit* (1987), and *Lying Together* (1990). This series reflects his interest in Russian literature. Thomas has translated works by Akhmatova, Pushkin, and Yevtushenko. He has also used excerpts from Pushkin, improvisations, and stories within stories told by various narrators to create *Russian Nights.*

Thomas's reliance on borrowed texts, his use of pastiche and the way in which his narratives turn in on themselves place him clearly within the postmodern camp. Although his more recent work has met with mixed responses, reviewer Rosemary

Dinnage said of Thomas in the *Times Literary Supplement,* that he is "exceptional . . . in understanding and feeling such themes [Freudian opposites] directly through fantasy, rather than imposing them intellectually."

Other Works by D. M. Thomas

Eating Pavlova. New York: Carroll and Graf, 1994.

Pictures at an Exhibition. New York: Carroll and Graf, 1993.

Selected Poems. New York: Penguin, 1983.

Thomas, Dylan Marlais (1914–1953)
poet, short story writer

Dylan Thomas was born in Swansea, Wales, to David John and Florence Williams Thomas. His father, an English teacher at Swansea Grammar School, had a love of literature and a fine library, both of which were strong influences on the young Dylan, who developed an immense knowledge of English poems. Thomas later claimed to have no interest in poetry but only in poems. He began writing seriously shortly after entering his father's school in 1925. At age 12 he published his first poem, "His Requiem," in the Cardiff *Western Mail.* In 1971, however, this poem was discovered to be plagiarized from Lilian Gard in *Boy's Own Magazine.* In 1929 Thomas left school and became a reporter at a local newspaper. The next year he joined the Swansea Little Theatre, where he appeared in several productions.

In 1934 Thomas published his first volume of poetry (all original), *Eighteen Poems,* followed in 1936 by *Twenty-Five Poems* and in 1939 by *The Map of Love.* Among these early poems were two of his most famous, "The Force That Through the Green Fuse Drives the Flower," an exploration of the creative and destructive powers of nature; and "After the Funeral," about the death of his aunt. In her review of the former, Edith SITWELL wrote in the London *Sunday Times,* "I could not name one poet of this, the younger generation, who shows so great a promise, and even so great an achievement."

In the year following *Twenty-Five Poems* Thomas married a young dancer, Caitlin Macnamara; the marriage would prove to be stormy because of financial problems and Thomas's drinking. Over the next 18 months he composed only one poem, "Poem to Caitlin," but wrote several semiautobiographical short stories that made up his 1940 collection *Portrait of the Artist as a Young Dog.* He would mine his Welsh past again when he wrote one of his most popular short stories, "A Child's Christmas in Wales," published in 1954, a year after his death.

Because of poor financial management and the drying up of several sources of income after World War II broke out in 1939, Thomas sought aid from fellow poet Stephen SPENDER. Other contributions came from writer Herbert READ, poet T. S. ELIOT, and artist Henry Moore. Thomas also moved to London and wrote scripts for the BBC (British Broadcasting Corporation), performed in BBC radio plays, and gave poetry readings, drawing on his previous theatrical experience.

In 1944, in the face of increasingly destructive German bombings of London, Thomas left the city and returned to Wales. This return to his homeland led to the most productive period of his life. The poems Thomas wrote during this period, together with those written earlier in the war, were published in 1946 as *Deaths and Entrances,* considered his finest and most mature volume of poetry. Of this work, poet and novelist Vita SACKVILLE-WEST wrote, "These verses are no careless expression of exuberance . . . [but] they are carefully wrought, in a combination of rare vigour and virtuosity."

As a result of *Deaths and Entrances,* Thomas became a radio star. He read both his poetry and his short stories, which were often reminiscences of his boyhood in Wales. With spreading fame came an invitation to read his work in New York; he was to make two other trips to the United States. In 1952 he published *Collected Poems,* which contained his most famous poem, "Do Not Go Gentle into That Good Night," an anguished cry over the death of his father. A year later, on his third American tour, he died of alcohol poisoning in New

York. At the time, his popularity had been growing, but his early death promoted him to the status of a cultural icon, especially in the 1960s and 1970s. Critic George Gaston explains, "So much sensational notoriety was attached to Thomas that decades after his death the distorting influence of the 'legend' continues to cast a shadow over his accomplishments."

Critical Analysis

One of Thomas's best early poems is "The Force That Through the Green Fuse Drives the Flower" (1933), which explores themes of the interrelation of life and death and the role of the poet, important motifs throughout his career. The poem describes how the forces of life and death in nature are also present in the poet: "The force that drives the water through the rocks Drives my red blood." The poem's refrain, "And I am dumb to tell," encapsulates a central paradox of the poem. The poet feels deprived of his own creative powers before the violent forces of nature, yet he expresses his powerlessness through the same creative impulse of which he feels deprived.

Another of Thomas's most celebrated poems, "Fern Hill" (1945), continues his explorations of the connections between life and death, as suggested by the title of the collection in which it first appeared, *Deaths and Entrances*. Most of the poem evokes an idealized memory of Thomas's youth in Wales in the style of William Wordsworth's "Tintern Abbey" or "Ode: Intimations of Immortality." The poem, which begins, "Now as I was young and easy under the apple boughs," suggests Adam in the Garden of Eden. There are no other humans in this world, just the boy and nature. With the last lines of the poem, however, Thomas interjects the present, postwar reality of death: "Time held me green and dying." Critic James A. Davies describes "Fern Hill" as "the view of an adult who knows all too well that childhood is fleeting and that time conquers."

One of Thomas's best-loved poems, "Do Not Go Gentle into That Good Night" (1951), is a villanelle, a French verse form with an elaborate structure of repeated lines. The poem starts with an injunction to resist death: "Rage, rage against the dying of the light." The next four stanzas then illustrate this command through the examples of "wise men," "good men," "wild men," and "grave men." The last stanza, however, reveals that the poem has been an address to Thomas's father, who has recently died. The repeated lines of the villanelle thus take on a new, ironic meaning: the angry grief of a son who is helpless before the forces of nature.

Other Work by Dylan Thomas
Under Milkwood. 1954. Reprint, New York: W. W. Norton, 1984.

Works about Dylan Thomas
Davies, James A. *A Reference Companion to Dylan Thomas.* Westport, Conn.: Greenwood Press, 1998.
Goodby, John, and Chris Wigginton, eds. *Dylan Thomas.* New York: Palgrave, 2001.

Thomas, Edward (Philip Edward Thomas, Edward Eastaway) (1878–1917)
poet, essayist, nonfiction writer

Edward Thomas was born in London to parents of Welsh descent. He spent most of his summers in south Wales, where he enjoyed taking long nature walks. His first book, *The Woodland Life* (1897), a collection of nature essays, was published when he was just 18. He graduated from Oxford in 1900.

Although his father did not approve, Thomas determined to make his living as a writer. To make enough money to live even frugally, he had to turn out a huge amount of material in a short period of time. Between 1910 and 1912, he published 12 books, which included biographical-critical studies of Richard Jefferies, Algernon Charles Swinburne, and Walter Pater. Yet Thomas was unhappy with his situation; he found the writing he was doing unfulfilling, and he was weighed down by financial problems. An addiction to opium increased his depression.

In 1914, however, Thomas met the American poet Robert Frost, who had read some of his prose and felt that his true talent might lie in poetry. This inspired Thomas, and he began to write about nature as a metaphor for speculation about the human condition, much like Frost. One of his friends said that when he began to write poems, it was as if "a living stream was undammed." In the next two years, Thomas wrote 143 poems. Most were composed after the outbreak of World War I, and after he had enlisted in the army.

To some extent Thomas's poetry fits into the tradition of English pastoral poetry. Although he was living in the age of GEORGIAN POETRY, his work was more casual and conversational than that of the Georgian poets. In "Roads," for example, he writes that roads "go on" while people forget and "are / Forgotten like a star / That shoots and is gone." While his poetry is clearly influenced by the war, it is not conventional war poetry. He refers to the conflict, but the insights and feelings he attributes to his solitary individual characters concern the condition of being mortal humans in a natural world that will go on nonetheless, not with any particular feelings that result from war. Literary critic Martin Seymour Smith writes that Thomas's work seeks "to define a rural concept of beauty that was finally invalidated by the First World War."

"Adlestrop" is a short poem that has a Frost-like simplicity and depth. The speaker recalls riding on a train on a hot summer day when the train, for no apparent reason, stops at the village of Adlestrop. As the speaker looks out the window, he sees nothing but the name of the village; "No one left and no one came / On the bare platform." In just a few words, Thomas conveys a profound sense of loneliness and isolation. But if human life is not present, the speaker says, the landscape is beautiful. He sees the trees and the sky and hears the song of blackbirds. The poem hovers uneasily between melancholy and joy. The loneliness of the place and the isolation of the speaker are painful, alleviated momentarily by the echoing sound of the birds.

Even more profoundly melancholy is "Rain," in which the rain beating on the speaker's hut seems to highlight his profound solitude. Nature is as beautiful to him as it was to the romantics, but the link between nature and humanity is gone. Humankind is not *of* nature, but apart from it; an observer is a momentary creature whose time in nature is all too brief.

Thomas was killed in World War I less than an hour into his first battle, in France. Although some of his poems were published between 1915 and 1917 under the pseudonym of Edward Eastaway, the rest were published posthumously under his own name.

Other Work by Edward Thomas
Edward Thomas: Everyman's Poetry Library. New York: Everyman's Poetry Classics, 1997.

Works about Edward Thomas
Smith, Stan. *Edward Thomas.* Winchester, Mass.: Faber & Faber, 1986.
Thomas, R. George. *Edward Thomas: A Portrait.* New York: Oxford University Press, 1985.

Thwaite, Anthony Simon (1930–) *poet*
Anthony Thwaite was born in Chester, England, the son of a banker. After traveling with his family throughout Britain and the United States as a child, he attended Oxford University. He continued to travel after graduating, taking a teaching assignment in Tokyo for his first job. His poetry recounts his many experiences living abroad and reflects on domestic themes and the details of everyday life.

The poems in the collection *The Owl in the Tree* (1963) represent Thwaite's interest in specific incidents and settings from everyday experiences. *New Confessions* (1974), on the other hand, takes place far from the familiar, in North Africa. This collection of meditations and reflection combines poetry and prose to reinterpret St. Augustine's life and thoughts. In *A Portion for Foxes* (1977), Thwaite travels to different time periods as well as different countries, integrating a lifelong interest in archeology into a collection of poems about historical objects (such as Victorian stereoscopes and Romano-British altars) and ancient places, including the Balkans and the Arabian Gulf.

Victorian Voices (1980) presents monologues by 14 prominent Victorian figures who represent literature, social reform, colonial administration, and the clergy. Critic Roy Fuller sums up Thwaite's mastery as "a poet who cares about interesting (and, often, amusing) his readers, as well as delineating the poignant histories of cultures, creatures and human beings."

Other Works by Anthony Thwaite

Poems 1953–1983. Devon, England: David & Charles, 1984.
Selected Poems 1956–1996. Chester Springs, Pa.: Dufour Editions, 1997.

Tolkien, John Ronald Reuel (1892–1973)
novelist

J. R. R. Tolkien was born to Arthur Reuel Tolkien, British civil servant, and Mabel Suffield Tolkien in South Africa. Upon the death of his father in 1896, he moved with his mother to England. Tolkien was influenced by the rural environment of his childhood, his mother's Catholicism, his youthful study of the classics and Norse legend, and his experiences in World War I, including the Battle of the Somme, in which two of his closest friends were killed. He eventually became the Merton Professor of English language and literature at Oxford. He joined with C. S. LEWIS and Charles WILLIAMS to form the Inklings, a literary group whose members discussed and evaluated one another's writing.

Tolkien's interest in language led him to create his own, which he called Elvish. Wanting to make use of his creation, he constructed an elaborate fantasy world, Middle-Earth, where elves and other mythological beings lived side by side with humans. The first novel set in Middle-Earth is *The Hobbit, or There and Back Again* (1937), a story originally written for Tolkien's own children. In this book Bilbo Baggins, a member of the dwarf-like race called hobbits, is tricked by the wizard Gandalf into traveling to a distant land, where Bilbo defeats the dragon Smaug.

Along his journey, Bilbo meets a repellent creature, Gollum, whose prized possession, a ring, the hobbit acquires. This ring becomes central to *The Lord of the Rings*, set several decades after *The Hobbit*. Often called a trilogy because it was published in three volumes—*The Fellowship of the Ring* (1954), *The Two Towers* (1954), and *The Return of the King* (1955)—*The Lord of the Rings* is actually a single, large novel, darker in tone than its predecessor and meant for adults.

Bilbo's ring turns out to be desired not only by its former owner, Gollum, but also by the Dark Lord Sauron because it will grant its possessor absolute power over Middle-Earth. It falls to Frodo Baggins, Bilbo's nephew, to carry the ring to Sauron's home, Mordor, and cast it into the volcano Mount Doom, the site of the ring's forging. Only in this way will the ring be destroyed and Middle-Earth saved.

Frodo must resist both the servants of Sauron and the intoxicating power of the Ring itself, sometimes doubting his worthiness to be its bearer, as when he asks Gandalf, "Why did you let me keep it? Why didn't you make me throw it away?" Gandalf tells Frodo, as well as their Elvish and dwarfish allies, that "it is not our part here to take thought only for a season, or for a few lives of Men, or for a passing age of the world. We should seek a final end of this menace, even if we do not hope to make one."

Tolkien also wrote several lighter tales, some in verse, aimed at young readers. He translated Old and Middle English poetry as well. After his death, his voluminous background materials for *The Lord of the Rings*, including guides to imaginary languages and elaborate histories for imaginary peoples, were collected and edited for publication in several volumes by his son Christopher.

Tolkien's writing has influenced other works of fantasy, many of which are filled with dark lords, quests, magic objects, and warring tribes of dwarfs, elves, and goblins. Even the popular *Star Wars* owes a debt to *Lord of the Rings*.

The political journal *American Prospect* noted in 2001 that through sheer force of popularity Tolkien had become a much-studied author in academia despite his complete rejection of a major premise of "serious" 20th-century literature: the idea that subtle psychological changes in characters are more important than broad plot developments. Tolkien reached back to mythology and folklore for inspiration, telling epic stories of a sort that had long seemed out of fashion. Such a practice led the American critic Edmund Wilson to call *The Lord of the Rings* "juvenile trash" in the pages of *The Nation*. However, the British poet W. H. AUDEN lavishly praised Tolkien's work in his essay "The Quest Hero" (1962), saying the work captures the human dilemma of existing between a mythic past and an uncertain future, especially in wartime: "If there is any Quest Tale which . . . manages to do more justice to our experience of social-historical realities than *Lord of the Rings*, I should be glad to hear of it."

Other Works by J. R. R. Tolkien

The Silmarillion. Edited by Christopher Tolkien. Boston: Houghton Mifflin, 1977.

Smith of Wootton Major; and, Farmer Giles of Ham. New York: Ballantine Books, 1988.

Works about J. R. R. Tolkien

Bloom, Harold, ed. *J. R. R. Tolkien.* Philadelphia: Chelsea House Publishers, 2000.

Flieger, Verlyn. *A Question of Time: J. R. R. Tolkien's Road to Faerie.* Kent, Ohio: Kent State University Press, 1997.

Neimark, Anne E. *Myth Maker: J. R. R. Tolkien.* San Diego, Calif.: Harcourt Brace, 1996.

Toynbee, Arnold Joseph (1889–1975)
historian

Arnold Toynbee was born in London. His father was a social reformer and his mother, a historian, used to put him to sleep as a child by reciting to him episodes from English history. At Oxford University he majored in classics, and after gradua-

tion he studied at the British Archaeological School in Athens. After teaching at Oxford and serving in British intelligence during World War I, he became a professor at the University of London.

In the early 1920s Toynbee conceived the idea of writing a history of the world and most of its civilizations preceding those of the 20th century. The result was the 12-volume *A Study of History* (1934–61). Describing his intention for this massive work, Toynbee said, "My conscious and deliberate aim has been to be a student of human affairs studied as a whole, [not] . . . partitioned into the so-called 'disciplines.'" In other words, instead of writing a history of politics, religion, art, or literature, he attempted to integrate all those pursuits under the concept of "civilization." He divided up world history into civilizations such as Egyptian, Hellenic, Islamic, and Christian, describing each entity as a unified whole springing from a central religious concept. He then tried to analyze the cycles of growth and decline for each civilization to deduce general principles and thereby to predict the future decline of the West.

The final volume of *A Study of History,* entitled *Reconsiderations,* was Toynbee's answer to the many criticisms of his work. Objections were raised on two grounds. First, some historians felt he had put too much emphasis on religions as motivating forces in shaping civilizations. Second, others questioned his view that knowledge of the past was the key to the knowledge of the future, or that civilizations progress based on universal laws. Toynbee's answer to his critics was to cite yet more evidence for his basic conclusions. He was quoted as saying, "I feel confident that the tradition of the past is also 'the wave of the future.'" Although his all-encompassing vision of the history of the world's civilizations sacrificed individual details to his overarching pattern, the scholars C. T. McIntire and Marvin Perry praise his ambition: "Toynbee's global vision of the history of all the peoples, cultures, and religions of the world moves us beyond our self-centredness and our numberless parochialisms and overspecializations."

Other Works by Arnold Toynbee

Change and Habit. 1966. Reprint, Oxford, England: One World Publications, 1966.

Hellenism: The History of a Civilization. 1959. Reprint, Westport, Conn.: Greenwood Publishing, 1981.

A Work about Arnold Toynbee

McIntire, C. T., and Marvin Perry, eds. *Toynbee: Reappraisals.* Toronto: University of Toronto Press, 1989.

Travers, Benjamin (1886–1980)
playwright, novelist, screenwriter

Ben Travers was born in Hendon, England, the son of Walter Francis Travers, a director of a London wholesale grocery firm, and Margaret Travers. He left school at age 17 to join his father's grocery business, and started writing plays after a stint in the Royal Naval Air Service. Writer Barbara J. Small describes Travers's plays as "farces of suspense in which the characters go through extraordinary machinations to cover up improprieties that did not take place." Critic R. W. Strang believes that "an overall playful approach to language gives his farces a particularly English tone."

Travers's first real success as a playwright came with his second play, *A Cuckoo in the Nest* (1925), in which a young man finds himself sharing a hotel room with a woman who is not his wife. The man professes his innocence in the face of highly suspicious circumstances to first his mother-in-law and then his wife, and after a series of comic misunderstandings, all is finally explained. This play, adapted from his 1922 novel, marked the beginning of Travers's relationship with the Aldwych Theatre, for whose company he wrote eight more plays. These plays ran for nearly 2,700 performances, and established Travers's reputation as a masterful writer of farces.

Rookery Nook (1926), in which a husband is surprised at his country house by a beautiful woman clad only in pajamas, was the next of Travers's successes. *Plunder* (1928), in which two men are accused of having committed murder, and *Mischief* (1928), about a middle-aged businessman who suspects his wife of adultery, also contributed to Travers's success at the Aldwych.

In the 1930s, Travers began writing screenplays, adapting several of his plays for television and film. His London *Times* obituary said of his contribution to literature, "[Farce] . . . can be of the happiest of theatrical forms. It is also among the most difficult to write. Ben Travers, undeniably, was the twentieth century's chief practitioner."

Other Work by Ben Travers

A-sitting on a Gate: Autobiography. London: W. N. Allen, 1978.

Travers, Pamela Lyndon (Helen Lyndon Goff) (1899–1996) *children's writer*

P. L. Travers was an extremely private person who deliberately told conflicting stories about her life. Even some of the most basic facts about her life, therefore, are not certain. She was born Helen Lyndon Goff in Queensland, Australia, to Robert and Margaret Goff. In her late teens or early 20s she traveled to England, where she worked as a dancer and actor and wrote both fiction and nonfiction. Eventually she ended her acting career and began to write full-time.

Now best known for her books about Mary Poppins, Travers never set out to be a writer for children. She published the first volume of Mary Poppins stories, entitled simply *Mary Poppins,* in 1934, followed by *Mary Poppins Comes Back* (1935), *Mary Poppins Opens the Door* (1943), and *Mary Poppins in the Park* (1952). The stories were immediate best-sellers and have been in print ever since.

Mary Poppins is a prim and proper nanny who arrives at the Banks household on the east wind, carrying her carpetbag and umbrella, and is hired to take care of the four Banks children. Unlike Julie Andrews in the 1964 Disney movie of the same name, the original Mary Poppins has as many negative characteristics as positive ones. She can be unfair, egotistical, grouchy, impatient, and sarcastic. For example, after the children's encounter with Mary's uncle, who becomes weightless when he laughs, Michael Banks asks "Does he often go rolling and bobbing about on the ceiling?" Mary gives "an offended sniff" and responds, "I'll have you know that my uncle is a sober, honest, hardworking man, and you'll be kind enough to speak of him respectfully." She is also extremely vain, constantly checking her appearance in mirrors and shop windows. But she offers her young charges comfort and security in the real world, along with the possibility of escape to a magical world.

Travers wrote a few non-Poppins children novels, such as the fable *Happy Ever After* (1940) and the Christmas fantasy *The Fox at the Manger* (1962), in which a fox gives Christ the gift of cunning. Still, it is as the creator of Mary Poppins that Travers is remembered. A critic for the *Times Literary Supplement* wrote that Mary Poppins is the "embodiment of authority, protection, and cynical common sense; her powers are magical. Basically she is the Good Fairy, whom we are all seeking, but in priggish human guise."

Works about P. L. Travers

Demers, Patricia, *P. L. Travers*. Twayne's English Author's Series. Boston: Twayne, 1991.

Draper, Ellen Dooling, and Jenny Koralek, eds. *A Lively Oracle: A Centennial Celebration of P. L. Travers, Creator of Mary Poppins*. Burdett, N.Y.: Larson Publications, 1999.

Treece, Henry (ca. 1911–1966) *poet, novelist, playwright, nonfiction writer, children's writer*

Henry Treece was born and raised in the town of Wednesbury in Staffordshire, England. He attended a local school and won a scholarship to Birmingham University, graduating with an English degree in 1933. He then became a schoolteacher and remained one for most of the next 25 years.

Treece started writing poetry in the late 1930s. Inspired by the romantic tradition, he and J. F. Hendry founded the New Apocalypse movement in poetry, which reacted against W. H. AUDEN's restrained verse and instead used turbulent language and numerous metaphors. Treece's poem "The Sons of Peace," for example, describes a nightingale's song as "Opalescent arabesques to the moon's dead world." He published poetry in the movement's various anthologies, beginning with *The New Apocalypse* (1939). In 1945 he published his verse collection *The Black Seasons* (1945), featuring many passionate romantic poems about the beauty of the world despite World War II.

In the 1950s Treece began writing stark historical novels, among which the most famous is his Celtic tetralogy. This begins with *The Dark Island* (1952), which relates the Roman invasion of Britain. The novel focuses on Gwyndoc, a brave and loving Celtic warrior. *The Golden Strangers* (1956) describes a young Celtic prince's efforts to fight off the Vikings, and *Red Queen, White Queen* (1958) depicts the rise of the Celtic warrior queen Boadicea. *The Great Captains* (1956) offers a gritty version of King Arthur. Treece called this "the story of 'King' Arthur as I think it might have happened." All these novels use unsentimental and often bleak language, in contrast to his earlier poetry. The reviewer John Harrison writes that, paradoxically, "Through a stark and unmitigated realism Henry Treece conveys what it must have been like to believe in magic."

Treece is most famous for his many historical novels for children. His first were *Legions of the Eagle* (1954) and *The Eagles Have Flown* (1954), realistic versions of the Roman invasion and Arthurian story, respectively. Treece wrote 25 novels for children, all of them focusing on moments in history when society and culture changed dramatically because of external pressures. He frequently uses a boy protagonist, so that the world-shaking events are glimpsed through a child's perspective.

Treece was a prolific writer whose work also included nonfiction histories, plays, and literary lectures. He worked right up to his death to complete his last work, *The Dream-Time* (1967), which describes the plight of a Stone Age boy who does not wish to be a warrior. Treece once said, "The act of writing a novel is, for me, the slow, and lonely, and infinitely tiring process of finding how to make magic happen."

Other Works by Henry Treece

The Magic Wood, a Poem. 1945. Reprint, Illustrated by Barry Moser. New York: HarperCollins, 1992.

Man with a Sword. 1964. Reprint, New York: Oxford University Press, 1979.

Tremain, Rose (1943–   ) novelist

Rose Tremain was born in London to Keith Nicholas Home and Viola Thomson Home. Her father was a writer. She received a degree in literature from the University of Paris at the Sorbonne in 1963 and graduated with honors from the University of East Anglia.

Tremain is known for her sympathetic portrayal of deeply flawed characters who often feel trapped by external circumstance. Her first novel, *Sadler's Birthday,* published in 1976, chronicles the life of a lonely English butler living on a country estate. *Letter to Sister Benedicta* (1978) portrays the life of a woman who, after a series of personal disasters linked to her family, attempts to put the pieces of her life back together by writing letters to her former teacher Sister Benedicta. *The Way I Found Her* (1998) opens darkly with the main character, Lewis Little, sitting motionless in the cold: "I like lying in the dark listening to the wind. I've begun to believe, anyway, that the cold comes from inside me, not from outside." Clarie Messud of the *The New York Times Book Review* described the novel as "at once a mystery story, a psychological exploration and a novel of ideas."

Tremain's choice of subject and time period has varied dramatically. In the novel *Restoration* (1989) she abandons contemporary society and takes the reader to 17th-century England during the reign of Charles II. This highly successful work earned the author a BOOKER PRIZE nomination. The eccentric main character, Robert Merivel, in describing himself to the reader, weaves the story of his circumstances with minute details about his appearance. In the middle of one of his digressions he declares, "So, to me again—whither my thoughts are extremely fond of returning." A more recent work, *Sacred Country* (1992), explores themes of identity and selfhood through a protagonist who becomes a transsexual.

Tremain has also written works for radio and television. Critics describe her as an important creative voice in contemporary British literary culture. At the beginning of her career she was named one of the "Twenty Best Young British Novelists" by the literary magazine *Granta.* Critic John Mellors writes, "She has the knack of using humour, especially in dialogue, to hold the reader's sympathy with her characters in their predicament."

Other Work by Rose Tremain

Music and Silence. New York: Pocket Books, 2001.

Trevor, William (William Trevor Cox)
(1928–   ) novelist, short story writer, scriptwriter, essayist, memoirist

William Trevor is one of the most prolific writers in English—a dozen novels, 10 collections of short stories, radio plays, literary essays, a memoir, and a novel for children. He is also one of the most distinguished prose stylists in the language.

Born William Trevor Cox in Mitchelstown, County of Cork, Ireland, Trevor was the second child and eldest son of James William and Gertrude Davidson Cox, both bank clerks and members of the Protestant middle class. He attended Trinity College, Dublin, and worked as a sculptor, teacher, and a writer of advertising copy. He moved to Devon, England, in 1953 and dropped the Cox from his name when his first published novel, *The Old Boys* (1964), appeared.

Trevor writes as he lives, the attentive outsider, the man at the margin, looking at England from Ireland and Ireland from England. His novels provide a comprehensive view of life in England and Ireland. *The Old Boys* established him as a wry and acute observer of English public schools and their consequences for adult life. Other novels—*The Boarding House* (1965), *Mrs. Eckdorf in O'Neill's Hotel* (1969), and *Miss Gomez and the Brethren* (1971)—are what Thomas Hardy (one of Trevor's influences, the others being Chekhov, Turgenev, and James JOYCE) called satires of circumstance. They are studies of the messiness, comedy, despair, and occasional joy of ordinary domestic life and social and sexual relationships, with a particular focus on religious and romantic intensities. Others, such as *The Children of Dynmouth* (1976), *Other People's Worlds* (1980), and *Felicia's Journey* (1994), turn Gothic and become ghost stories and murder mysteries. The novels set in Ireland, *Fools of Fortune* (1983) and *The Silence in the Garden* (1988), concern themselves with the colonial and postcolonial life, Anglo-Irish antagonisms, religious sensibility and conflict, and poverty and provinciality and their consequences.

Trevor's short stories, his field of complete mastery, involve the same range of topics and themes. Since 1970 and the start of the contemporary, violent "Troubles" in Northern Ireland, he has written a series of painful and powerful stories exploring the matter of England and Ireland once again: "Beyond the Pale," "Attracta," and "The News from Ireland" are representative achievements in this difficult genre.

Trevor has received many literary awards, including the Royal Society of Literature (1975) prize and the Heinemann (1976) and Whitbread (1983) awards. In 1977 he was named a Commander of the Order of the British Empire (CBE), and he has received several honorary doctor of letters degrees from, among others, Exeter University (1984) and Trinity College, Dublin (1986).

In a prose of extraordinary restraint, control and beauty, Trevor has explored the relationships between the ordinary and the extraordinary, the surface and the depths as thoroughly and movingly as any modern writer of fiction. He is a prose poet of the quietly heroic and silently desperate, the explorer of the face of human evil and the fact of human goodness. As novelist V.S. PRITCHETT

wrote in the *New York Review of Books*, "In nearly all Trevor's stories we are led on at first by plain unpretending words about things done to prosaic people; then comes the explosion of conscience, the assertion of will which in some cases may lead to hallucination and madness."

Other Works by William Trevor

The Collected Stories. New York: Viking, 1992.
Death in Summer. New York: Viking, 1998.
The Hill Bachelors. New York: Viking, 2000.
Three Early Novels: The Old Boys, The Boarding House, The Love Department. New York: Penguin, 2000.

Works about William Trevor

MacKenna, Dolores. *William Trevor: The Man and His Work.* Chester Springs, Pa.: Dufour Editions, 2000.
Paulson, Susan Morrow. *William Trevor: A Study of the Short Fiction.* Boston: Twayne, 1993.

Tynan, Katharine (1861–1931) *poet, novelist, short story writer*

Katharine Tynan was born in Dublin, the fourth of 11 children. She was very close to her father, a wealthy farmer, and they often talked about poetry. Tynan was educated at a convent, which she later described as "a green garden-place of quiet restfulness." Many of her poems are devout meditations on Catholic subjects. Her mother died in 1874, and Tynan left school to care for her many siblings. Her father then took over her education, giving her challenging books and introducing her to Irish nationalist writing.

Tynan's first book was *Louise de la Vallière and Other Poems* (1885). Many of these poems describe her love for her father, her religious devotion, and her appreciation of nature. The lyric "A Day of Frost," for example, describes how "Every bare bough's a-glitter. Hush! I hear / From yon stark tree a gush of melody." Tynan also included three poems that referred to Irish history and legends. This particular interest became more pronounced in her later anthology *Ballads and Lyrics* (1891), which opens with "The Children of Lir," a verse version of the Irish legend of the aristocratic children turned into swans by a jealous stepmother. Tynan unites her religious and her Celtic interests in "The Charity of the Countess Kathleen," a West Irish folk tale about a woman who sells her soul to save others. Other poems describe Tynan's quiet life in Ireland, and she called the collection "The quiet thoughts of one whose feet / Have scarcely left her green retreat."

Early in her literary career Tynan became friends with William Butler YEATS. Both were interested in enriching Irish literature with traditional Celtic folklore. Tynan, Yeats, and other Irish poets collaborated on the famous anthology *Poems and Ballads of Young Ireland* (1888), which aimed to revitalize Irish writing by rooting work in Ireland's own landscapes, history, and legends.

A Cluster of Nuts (1894) was Tynan's first collection of short stories, all set in Irish villages. Her first novel, *The Way of a Maid* (1895), is also set in Ireland, and describes a young woman's courtship. Tynan herself had married Henry Albert Hinkson in 1893. She wrote many more novels in the first two decades of the century. Ann Fallon notes, "Her plots are intriguingly complicated, and move with lightning speed, the impetus always being the union of star-crossed lovers."

Tynan wrote poetry about World War I, collected in *Herb o' Grace* (1918) and *The Holy War* (1916). Many of the poems in these collections are religious and maintain that the war has not produced lasting trauma to those who fought. In *The Holy War*, for example, the poem "The Broken Soldier" describes a half-blind, maimed soldier whose soul "goes singing like the lark, / Like the incarnate Joy that will not be confined."

After her husband died in 1919, Tynan lived for some time in France. There she wrote novels and a memoir, *Life in the Occupied Area* (1925). Tynan was an extraordinarily prolific writer, publishing hundreds of stories, anthologies, and novels. She herself described her novels as somewhat formulaic, tending to depict a quest for love that ends neatly in marriage. Her earlier poetry, however, is still acclaimed.

A Work about Katharine Tynan

Fallon, Ann Connerton. *Katharine Tynan.* Boston: Twayne, 1979.

Vine, Barbara

See RENDELL, RUTH.

vorticism

Vorticism was first an artistic and then, shortly thereafter, a literary movement of the early 20th century that grew out of several other artistic movements including IMAGISM. Imagism argued that the modern poets should not strive to create long, lyrical, and romantic poems exploring themes of truth or the glory of the individual, but instead shorter, more compact poems that communicate visual impressions. Vorticism was a similar reaction against romanticism and, according to the scholar Chris Baldick, "celebrated the dynamic energies of the machine age . . . [calling] for an end to all sentimentality, and for a new abstraction that would, paradoxically, be both dynamic and static."

Wyndham LEWIS, the British writer and painter, promoted vorticism in *Blast* (1914), a magazine he founded and edited with the American poet Ezra Pound. According to Pound, the vortex was the source of all energy in poetry, and it was the job of the poet to transform that energy into a poem. It was this conception of the vortex as the source of all poetic inspiration that prompted Lewis to name the ensuing literary movement "vorticism."

Works about Vorticism

Dasenbrouck, Reed Way. *The Literary Vorticism of Ezra Pound and Wyndham Lewis: Towards the Condition of Painting.* Baltimore: Johns Hopkins University Press, 1985.

Edwards, Paul, ed. *Blast: Vorticism 1914–1918.* Burlington, Vt.: Lund Humphries, 2001.

Wain, John Barrington (1925–1994)

poet, novelist, critic

John Wain was born in Stoke-on-Trent, England, to Arnold A. Wain, a dentist, and Anne Turner Wain. After high school in Newcastle-under-Lyme, he earned his degree from Oxford. He was a lecturer in English literature at Reading University from 1947 until 1955, when he resigned to write full-time.

Wain's first novel, *Hurry On Down* (1953), describes the adventures of Charles Lumley, who upon leaving the university rejects the middle-class life expected of him. Just after causing a disturbance at a working-class bar, "a new clarity came to him as a series of cleanly etched visions and a rapid re-living of all the major emotions of his life in a series of sharp bursts." In his vision, Lumley sees that unless he escapes the university he will be reshaped by the demands of his middle-class colleagues until he is exactly like them.

The work established Wain among such writers as Kingsley AMIS and John BRAINE as one of the ANGRY YOUNG MEN, a group of 1950s British playwrights and novelists whose heroes share rebellious, critical attitudes toward established society. Through the novels *The Contenders* (1958), about two boys' competitiveness in school, and *A Travelling Woman* (1959), about a man who turns to adultery to end his boredom, Wain criticizes such social values as the rigid class lines and competitive capitalism he believed stifled individualism in postwar Great Britain, particularly London. In *Strike the Father Dead* (1962) a rebellious young man runs away from school and from his father's expectations so he can become a jazz pianist.

Wain also edited literary magazines and wrote magazine pieces and plays, but he expressed a preference for poetry. In 1953 he directed "First Readings," a BBC (British Broadcasting Corporation) radio show featuring new poetry. He is perhaps best known for his long poems, such as *Feng* (1975), a sequence of meditations on power and isolation by Feng, the central character, based on Hamlet; and *Letters to Five Artists* (1969), an introductory poem and five separate epistles to artist friends of Wain's.

Wain also wrote a highly acclaimed biography for the general reader, *Samuel Johnson* (1974). Author Dale Salwak writes that although Wain lived in the 20th century, "he is very much an eighteenth-century man who defends—as did his 'moral hero' Samuel Johnson—the value of reason, moderation, common sense, moral courage, and intellectual self-respect."

Wain received several honorary degrees and fellowships, holding the first creative arts fellowship from Oxford, where he was also elected to the prestigious Professor of Poetry chair. He won the 1958 W. Somerset Maugham Award for the criticism *Preliminary Essays* (1957). Salwak calls Wain an all-around man of letters: "Not only has he written fiction and poetry which deserve a place of reckoning among his contemporaries, but he has published criticism which communicates a sensitive and scholarly appreciation of good books."

Works about John Wain

Hatziolou, Elizabeth. *John Wain: A Man of Letters*. London: Pisces Press, 1997.
Salwak, Dale. *John Wain*. Boston: Twayne, 1981.

Walcott, Derek Alton (1930–) *poet, playwright, essayist, journalist*

Derek Walcott was born in Castries, St. Lucia, a former British colony. His grandmothers were descended from slaves, and his grandfathers were English and Dutch. Both his father, Warwick, a bohemian poet and artist, and his mother, Alix, who ran Castries's Methodist school and recited Shakespeare at home, influenced the pursuits of Derek and his twin brother, Roderick, who later became a distinguished playwright. Harold Simmons, a painter, folklorist, and family friend, gave the young Derek Walcott painting and drawing lessons as well as access to his library of poetry and art books and his collection of classical records. By the age of eight, Walcott had decided he wanted to become a poet.

Educated at St. Mary's College, a high school for boys in Castries, Walcott published his first poem at age 14 in *The Voice of St. Lucia*. As an 18-year-old he published his first volume of poetry, *Twenty-Five Poems* (1948). His long poem *Epitaph for the Young* (1949) appeared the same year the Barbadian writer Frank Collymore called *Twenty-Five Poems* "the work of an accomplished poet." Collymore added, "there are [those] . . . who are poets from birth: to them poetry is all in all, the very breath of life; and I do not think I am mistaken when I make this high claim for Derek Walcott." Looking back at his earlier verse writing in "What

the Twilight Says," a 1970 autobiographical essay, Walcott wrote that he strove to "legitimately [prolong] the mighty line of Marlow and Milton."

In 1950 Walcott went to the University College of the West Indies in Jamaica. He graduated in three years with a B.A. in English, French, and Latin, and did graduate work in education. Before graduating, he designed and directed the student drama society's presentation of *Henri Christophe*, his first and best-known play, previously produced in 1950 by the St. Lucia Arts Guild, which he had founded.

From 1953 to 1957 Walcott worked as a teacher at the Grenada Boys' School, St. Mary's College, and Jamaica College. In 1956 he became a feature writer for *Public Opinion*, a Jamaican weekly in Kingston, and then a feature writer and drama critic for the Trinidad *Guardian*. Sponsored by a Rockefeller Foundation theater fellowship, Walcott went to New York in 1958 and studied directing and set design, but returned to Trinidad one year later. In 1960 he founded the Little Carib Theatre Workshop (which later became the Trinidad Theatre Workshop). There he trained actors and produced a number of his own plays, many based on the myths and rituals of West Indian folk life.

Walcott's plays examine Caribbean identity and life using verse, prose, and elements of pantomime, realism, fable, and fantasy. In his essay "What the Twilight Says," (1998) he wrote that in his play he strove to use "a language that went beyond mimicry" and one that "begins to create an oral culture, of chants, jokes, folk-songs, and fables." Of his many plays, *Dream on Monkey Mountain* (1967), an allegorical study of the rootless condition of black people in the postcolonial world, is considered his most impressive. It won an Obie Award as the best foreign play of 1971 after being staged in New York.

In addition to playwriting, Walcott has worked with the American composer Galt MacDermott, best known for the musical *Hair*; and has written musicals, including *O Babylon!* (first performed in 1976), a portrayal of Rastafarians in Jamaica that examines capitalism. Drawing on varied literary and dramatic traditions—classical and contemporary, African, Asiatic, and European—Walcott writes in standard English and West Indian dialect. His work uses imagery and traditional literary techniques to explore themes of exile, injustice, oppression, and identity formation while reconstructing history.

In a Green Night (1962), Walcott's first widely distributed and commercially published volume of poetry, fuses traditional verse with examinations of Caribbean experiences. Two years later he published *Selected Poems* (1964). Soon after, Robert GRAVES asserted, "Derek Walcott handles English with a closer understanding of its inner magic than most (if not any) of his English-born contemporaries."

Since the 1970s Walcott has periodically lived and worked in the United States, serving as a visiting lecturer at many universities, including Columbia, Rutgers, Yale, Princeton, and Harvard. He has taught creative writing and literature at Boston University since 1982, and he continues to write prolifically. He has published essays on literary culture and several volumes of poetry. The epic poem *Omeros* (1992) is considered his most ambitious work. The title is the Greek version of Homer's name, and the poem is among other things a modern, Caribbean response to Homer's *Odyssey*. The poem uses terza rima, a series of interlocking tercets—a form notably used by Dante in *The Divine Comedy*—and Creole to explore the histories of common people with Greek names—Helen, Achille, and Hector.

In 1992, two years after the publication of *Omeros,* Walcott received the Nobel Prize for literature. Critic D. S. Izevbaye has said that "his skill in creating new meanings out of old, that is, the creation of a new language based on his commitment to standard English and a mythohistoric interpretation of West Indian identity, is a central part of Walcott's achievement."

Other Works by Derek Walcott

The Bounty. New York: Farrar, Straus & Giroux, 1997.
Tiepolo's Hound. New York: Farrar, Straus & Giroux, 2000.
What the Twilight Says: Essays. New York: Farrar, Straus & Giroux 1999.

Works about Derek Walcott

Breslin, Paul. *Nobody's Nation: Reading Derek Walcott.* Chicago: University of Chicago Press, 2001.
Burnett, Paula. *Derek Walcott: Politics and Poetics.* Gainesville: University Press of Florida, 2000.
King, Bruce. *Derek Walcott: A Caribbean Life.* New York: Oxford University Press, 2000.

Wallace, Richard Horatio Edgar

(1875–1932) *novelist, playwright, journalist*
Edgar Wallace was born in Greenwich, England, to two actors, Richard Horatio Wallace and Mary Jane (Polly) Richards. He dropped out of school at the age of 12 and worked at various jobs before enlisting in the army at age 18. Until his unflattering reports about an influential British field marshal got him banned, Wallace worked as a war reporter in Africa for several years. Known as the "King of Thrillers," he wrote nearly 175 books, most of which are plot-driven crime and mystery novels. In addition to his novels, he wrote 17 plays.

Wallace's first novel, *The Four Just Men* (1905), about a plot against the English foreign secretary, distinguishes itself from other literature of the genre with its "precise, realistic details which lend credibility to a series of events which would not have been believable if written in a more flamboyant style," according to writer J. Randolph Cox. Succinct descriptions of two of the "Just Men" demonstrate the author's descriptive skills: Poiccart is "heavy, saturnine, and suspicious," while Manfred is "cynical, smiling, and sarcastic."

Sanders of the River (1911), about a British commissioner in West Africa, established Wallace's fame as a writer and introduced a popular character who was to appear in many more of his novels: Commissioner Sanders. Sanders's stories are based on Wallace's own experiences in Africa. *Sanders of the River* marks the first use of Wallace's trademark format: He describes a series of events to a specific point, then stops to begin an apparently unrelated story. Eventually the stories merge and their relationship becomes apparent.

The Green Archer (1923), about a man who is murdered after a quarrel with the owner of a haunted castle, is one of Wallace's most famous novels. This and others of his stories inspired hundreds of films, including *King Kong*. Wallace's rhythmic, descriptive writing style made for an easy transition to the screen. Unfortunately he died just after completing *King Kong* and never saw the classic film version. J. Randolph Cox recognized Wallace's ability as a storyteller: "He was not a great writer, for all of his flashes of genius and inspiration. . . . He was a great storyteller who appealed mainly to his own generation."

Other Works by Edgar Wallace
Black Abbot. 1926. Reprint, London: House of Stratus, 2001.
Crimson Circle. 1936. Reprint, London: House of Stratus, 2001.
Red Aces. 1932. Reprint, London: House of Stratus, 2001.

Walpole, Hugh Seymour (1884–1941)
novelist, playwright, essayist
Hugh Walpole was born in Auckland, New Zealand, to George Henry Somerset, a minister, and Mildred Barham Walpole. He attended a series of English public schools before going to Cambridge University, where he studied for a career in the church. It soon became apparent to him, though, that he was not cut out for church work, and he took up writing instead.

While Walpole wrote a number of plays and essays, he is primarily remembered as one of the most popular British novelists of the pre–World War II period, with more than 70 novels to his credit. His writing rejects modernism, the dominant literary movement of the early 20th century that valued experimentation with form, and instead emulates the work of 19th-century writers like Thomas Hardy and Sir Walter Scott.

Walpole gained popular and critical attention with the novel *Fortitude* (1913), a bildungsroman, or coming-of-age story. At the beginning of the story, Peter Wescott is a public school student faced daily with bullies and various other trials. At one of the novel's low points, when Peter is caught outdoors during a storm, he shouts into the wind and rain, "Make of me a man—to be afraid of nothing . . . to be ready for everything—love, friendship, success . . . to take if it comes . . . to care nothing if these things are not for me—Make me brave! Make me brave!" As the novel progresses, Peter's wish comes true—he eventually triumphs over his adversaries and becomes a successful writer. Immediately upon the novel's publication, the critic Rupert Hart-Davis declared Walpole among "the front rank of contemporary novelists."

Fortitude quietly resists modernism with a conventional chronological plot, but in *Wintersmoon* (1928), Walpole directly attacks it with a plot that pits two characters representative of modernism, Roselind and Ravage, against another pair, Janet Grandison and Wildherne Poole, who defend traditionalism and whose relationship outlasts that of their competitors.

Walpole wrote nearly a novel a year during his writing career, enjoyed widespread popular appeal, and was knighted in 1937. His popularity flagged after his death, but he is still regarded, as the scholar Elizabeth Steele has pointed out, as "the most prolific and . . . the widest known" of "the many traditional writers of his generation."

Other Work by Hugh Walpole
The Secret City. 1919. Reprint, Stroud, England: Sutton, 1998.

A Work about Hugh Walpole
Hart-Davis, Rupert. *Hugh Walpole.* North Pomfret, Vt.: Trafalgar Square, 1985.

Ward, Arthur Henry Sarsfield
See ROHMER, SAX.

Warner, Rex Ernest (1905–1986) *novelist, translator, poet*
Rex Warner was born in Birmingham, England, the son of Frederick Warner, a clergyman, and

Kathleen Warner, a schoolteacher. He studied classics, philosophy, and English at Oxford University. Franz Kafka greatly influenced his writing, in that Warner's stories, like Kafka's, often incorporate a surreal element of fantasy. Critic Joseph Cary observes that "the recurrent theme of Warner's various novels is the tension obtaining between private freedom and public authority, between innovation and tradition, between the individual and the polis" (city-state).

In Warner's first novel, *The Wild Goose Chase: An Allegory* (1937), three brothers search a bucolic, poverty-stricken countryside and a bureaucracy-ridden town for a wild goose that represents the hope of humanity. Critic Thomas Churchill wrote that *The Wild Goose Chase* "is a case study of the good-Many against the totalitarian state, established on power, violence, and fear." One of the brothers' final lines reflects the political themes of the novel: "What our old leaders most respected we chiefly despise—the frantic assertion of an ego, do-nothings, . . . money, the police; and to what they used to despise we attach great value—to comradeship, and to profane love, to hard work, honesty, the sight of the sun, reverence for those who have helped us, flesh and blood . . . Long live the Revolution!" *The Aerodrome: a Love Story* (1941) also explores the familiar themes of tension between the individual and government, this time through the relationship between a group of neo-fascist military leaders and the citizens of a rural town.

In addition to his own novels, Warner also wrote poetry, translated Greek classics, and combined the two styles of writing in the form of historical novels such as *Pericles the Athenian* (1963) and *Imperial Caesar* (1960). His best-known historical novel is *The Converts* (1967), which tells the story of St. Augustine's life in fourth-century Africa and Italy. "By evoking the total environment—including intellectual ferment, social change, and political activity of the age—Rex Warner makes ancient history come alive," wrote the scholar Clara M. Siggins. Critic Joseph Cary believes that in all of his works "it is Warner's own developing theme of the elusiveness of genuine po-litical authority coupled with his early fondness for poetic fantasy which best explains his qualities."

Other Work by Rex Warner
Poems and Contradictions. New York: AMS Press, 1945.

Works about Rex Warner
Reeve, N. H. *The Novels of Rex Warner: An Introduction.* New York: Palgrave, 1990.

Tabachnick, Stephen Ely. *Fiercer Than Tigers: The Life and Work of Rex Warner.* East Lansing: Michigan State University Press, 2002.

Warner, Sylvia Townsend (1893–1978)
poet, novelist, short story writer, biographer, librettist, diarist

Born in Devon, England, Sylvia Townsend Warner was the daughter of George Townsend and Nora Huddleston Warner. She received no formal education but, following her father's example as a learned man—he taught history at Harrow—she fully developed her native talents and imagination. Her first career was as a musicologist; she was the only female editor to work on the 10-volume edition of *Tudor Church Music* in the 1920s.

In 1917 Warner had moved to London and soon after began writing poetry. Literary friends such as T. F. POWYS and David Garnett helped foster her literary career. Through Powys in 1930 she met Valentine Ackland, who became her life companion; the two women lived together for 39 years. In 1935 they joined the Communist Party and in 1936, during the Spanish Civil War, they worked in Barcelona for the Red Cross.

A gifted and prolific writer, Warner is only now becoming the subject of critical review, particularly as a lesbian writer. Her literary output over 50 years included seven novels, eight volumes of verse, 18 collections of short stories, and several biographies (including a charming one of T. H. WHITE), as well as the libretto for an opera based on the life of Percy Bysshe Shelley and a translation of Proust.

Warner's first published volume of poems was *The Espalier* (1925). Her *Selected Poems* were published in 1982 and her *Collected Poem* in 1985. As a poet, she knew the importance of every word and had a gift for metaphor and nuance. Her poetic models were the English writers Emily Brontë and Christina Rossetti and the American poet Emily Dickinson. However, her poetry is most often compared with Thomas Hardy's because of its Dorset setting, feeling for nature, understated themes and tones, and melancholy, as in the following lines from "The Staring Traveller":

> *I saw the ghosts throng to your lighted door,*
> *Indulged and confident as heretofore,*
> *And you upon them like a hostess wait.*
> *And only I too late?*

Warner's style, whether in poetry or prose, is remarkable for simplicity, clarity, and immediacy, as in this description from the story "Oxenhope": "He had lain so still in his happiness that after a while an adder elongated itself from the heather roots, lowered the poised head with its delicate, tranquil features, and basked on the rock beside him."

Warner's first novel, *Lolly Willowes* (1926), was inspired by its author's realization that, as Lolly tells the devil, "Women have such vivid imaginations, and lead such dull lives." Lolly, tired of being taken for granted by her brother's dull family, opts for independence and goes to live in Great Mop, where she becomes a witch. This sly feminist attack on the lot of a spinster both made and, in a sense, fixed Warner's reputation; it was the first novel chosen for the American Book-of-the-Month Club.

Mr. Fortune's Maggot followed in 1927. This novel, inspired by a dream, contrasts religious zealotry with tolerance. (A "maggot" in this context is a whimsical or perverse fantasy.) Fortune is a middle-aged missionary who believes his vocation is to convert the natives of the South Sea Island of Fanua. Once there, however, the only convert he makes is a charming native boy by whom he is seduced, in the process losing his own faith. In this work the scholar Glen Cavaliero detects a persistent theme of Warner's: the tragic tug-of-war "between romantic adventurousness that has nowhere to go, and acceptance of one's lot which ends up in stagnation." *The True Heart* (1929), described as "the tale of Cupid and Psyche transposed to the Essex marshes," is the funny but sad story of an orphan girl who falls in love with a village idiot.

Warner also wrote historical novels. Her first, *Summer Will Show* (1936), is about the French Revolution. Her own favorite work was *The Corner That Held Them* (1948), a vivid portrayal of medieval religious life. It focuses on a group of nuns in a 14th-century convent and takes place between the coming of the Black Plague and the Peasants' Uprising. Warner's final novel, *The Flint Anchor* (1954), is a family chronicle set in East Anglia about a Victorian tyrant.

The best known of Warner's works are short stories published in the *New Yorker*—144 of them. These are subversive, fantastic fables peopled by eccentrics, full of wit and irony; they have been gathered in the volume *Kingdom of Elfin* (1977). Warner's *Selected Stories* (1988) contains four dozen stories, including English "slice-of-life" tales and some from *Kingdom of Elfin*.

In 1927 the author began keeping a diary that she maintained till her death. *The Diaries of Sylvia Townsend Warner* (1992), together with her *Scenes of Childhood* (1982), offers a valuable portrait of the author.

Works about Sylvia Townsend Warner

Ackland, Valentine. *For Sylvia: An Honest Account.* New York: W. W. Norton, 1985.

Harman, Claire. *Sylvia Townsend Warner: A Biography.* London: Chatto & Windus, 1989.

Mulford, Wendy. *This Narrow Place: Sylvia Townsend Warner and Valentine Ackland, Life, Letters, Politics, 1930–1951.* London: Pandora Press, 1988.

Wachman, Gay. *Lesbian Empire: Radical Cross-writing in the Twenties.* New Brunswick, N.J.: Rutgers University Press, 2001.

Waterhouse, Keith (1929–) *novelist, playwright, journalist*

Keith Waterhouse was born in Leeds, England, to Ernest and Elsie Waterhouse. When he was three, his father, a grocer, died and left little behind to help his widow and five children. Waterhouse was educated at several local primary schools until age 15 and then went on to study at the Leeds College of Commerce on scholarship.

Beginning as a freelance journalist, Waterhouse came to have a respected place as a writer in both the local and national press. *City Lights: A Street Life,* published in 1994, chronicles his difficult life growing up in Leeds and describes the beginning years of his success as a writer.

Waterhouse's work portrays the experiences of outcasts and characters stuck on the margins of society. Whether writing plays, novels, or reviews, he remains famous for his witty and satirical style. His most famous novel, *Billy Liar,* was published in 1959 and later adapted for the theater. The book is a coming-of-age story set in postwar London, and it quickly established the author's reputation as a writer of exceptional talent. The *Saturday Review* called the book "a brilliant novel, in language fresh and sweet, with characters vivid and singular in an inventive and dynamic story." In the opening passage, Billy attempts to gain control over his surroundings "by going 'Da da da da da' aloud to drive the thinking out of my head. It was a day for big decisions."

Waterhouse turned to more political themes in his later work. *All Things Bright and Beautiful,* published in 1962, depicts the hardships of contemporary working class life in England. He has also written extensively for the theatre, television, radio, and film. His 1965 play *Say Who You Are,* which he wrote with Willis Hall, "brought the 'drawing-room comedy' up to date," according to director Shirley Butler. While dealing with difficult themes of adultery and deception, the play manages to both keep the audience guessing and maintain its comic edge. "I'd rather not talk about it," remarks one of the play's main characters, Sarah. "After all, when one has been married to an adulterous sex maniac, what is there to say." In his review of *Say Who You Are,* W. A. Darlington of the *Daily Telegraph* called it "good unclean fun."

Today Waterhouse continues his work as a writer and makes regular contributions to major British newspapers. Though he is criticized by more conservative critics for his left-leaning political views, intellectuals such as Richard Hoggart call him "very talented and witty, quirky, and outspoken." Others such as Burling Lowrey have remarked "He is himself an original with a talent for exposing hypocrisy, stupidity, and corruption with comic detachment."

Other Work by Keith Waterhouse

City Lights: A Street Life. London: Hodder and Stoughton, 1994.

Watkins, Vernon (1906–1967) *poet, translator*

Vernon Watkins was born in Maestag, Wales, to William and Sarah Phillips Watkins. He enjoyed books and poetry from a young age and showed little interest in following in his father's footsteps as a banker. He attended Cambridge University, where he studied French and German from 1924 to 1925, but decided not to finish his degree, believing that his formal education got in the way of his creative instincts. Although financial necessity forced him to take a position at his father's bank in 1925, he continued to pursue a career as a poet while working as a clerk.

In 1927 Watkins fell victim to a mental collapse that changed the subsequent course of his career as a poet. Destroying his early poetry, Watkins resolved to start again and try to better articulate his creative vision through his verse. Still employed at the bank, he wrote every evening after work. After traveling to Dublin to meet the eminent poet William Butler YEATS in 1938, he composed "Yeats in Dublin." The poem, which was eventually published in 1945, describes Watkins's meeting with the poet: "After the waves of silence/I look him in the eyes."

In addition to Yeats, Watkins was deeply influenced by Dylan THOMAS, who encouraged him to publish his poetry in the magazine *Wales.* Thomas's and Watkins's relationship was described by his biographer Gwen Watkins as "one of the great literary friendships, and one of the most productive." Watkins's poem "Griefs of the Sea," which first appeared in *Wales,* describes his sometimes difficult relationship with Thomas: "Yet in that gesture of anger we must admit/We were quarrelling with a phantom unawares."

Dylan valued his friendship with Watkins and admired his work as a poet, saying, "I think him to be the most profound and greatly accomplished Welshman writing poems in English."

Watkins was also known for his work as a translator. In 1951 he collected and translated the poetry of German poet Heinrich Heine under the title of *The North Sea.*

Although he is not widely read today, Watkins's artistry has been recognized by numerous literary critics and reviewers. His poetry has been described by Kathleen RAINE as both "moving and beautiful"; she considers Watkins "the greatest lyric poet of my generation."

Other Work by Vernon Watkins
Fidelities. 1968. Reprint, New York: W. W. Norton, 1996.

Waugh, Auberon (1939–2001) *journalist, novelist*

Auberon Waugh was born in Dulverton, Somerset, to the writer Evelyn WAUGH and Laura Herbert Waugh. Describing himself as a member of the bourgeois cultural elite, Waugh adopted early on many of his father's prejudices against Americans, popular culture, and the lower classes. He was educated first at Catholic schools and then at Oxford University. When his first novel, *The Foxglove Saga* (1960), was published by his father's publishers, he gave up Oxford for the literary life. The novel follows two boys—the attractive and privileged Martin Foxglove and the ugly and less well-off Kenneth Stoat—from childhood to maturity.

Although Waugh was to publish four more novels over the next 10 years, his literary reputation rests on the satirical columns that he wrote for such periodicals as *Private Eye,* a satire and gossip magazine, and the *Spectator,* a political and literary journal. His gift, as he put it, was "for making the comment, at any given time, which people least wish to hear," such as "Bill Clinton's sexual recklessness is [his] only likeable characteristic."

In 1972 Waugh began writing for *Private Eye* "Auberon Waugh's Diary," a series which continued through 1986. These columns were collected in two volumes, *Four Crowded Years* (1976) and *A Turbulent Decade* (1985). In his "Diary" Waugh frequently wrote of contemporary events as if he had attended them, exaggerating the foibles and behavior (and occasionally making them up) of those who really did. He claimed, for example, that Prince Andrew did not know how to speak and that Marshall Tito was actually a woman seen "breast-feeding a seal pup on the Island of Vis." Many, if not most, of those written about were not amused.

In 1991 Waugh published an autobiography entitled *Will This Do?* His work, according to writer Geoffrey Wheatcroft, made him "the most violently controversial English journalist of his age."

Other Work by Auberon Waugh
Closing the Circle: The Best of the Way of the World. London: Macmillan, 2001.

Waugh, Evelyn (Arthur Evelyn St. John Waugh) (1903–1966) *novelist, travel writer, biographer*

Evelyn Waugh was born in London to a successful publisher, Arthur Waugh, and Catherine Raban Waugh. Educated at Lancing College and Oxford University, his pre–World War II upper-middle-class attitudes form the psychological backbone of most of his novels.

Waugh left Oxford without a degree after only two years, and began to teach school, a career for which he was ill suited. However, his experiences served him well in his first novel, *Decline and Fall*

(1928), which details the misadventures of Paul Pennyfeather, expelled from Oxford and forced to teach school for a living. In the course of the novel Pennyfeather, though innocent, is convicted of pandering and imprisoned; he escapes only by faking his own death. Waugh's dark humor was enormously popular with critics and the public. A critic for the *Observer* called *Decline and Fall* "richly and roaringly funny."

Over the next 30 years Waugh turned out a series of novels, travel writings about the Mediterranean, journalism, and biographies of Ronald Knox and Dante Gabriel Rossetti. A misanthrope who was violently opposed to almost everything modern, he embraced the ritual of the Catholic Church, old-fashioned decorum, and realistic novelists such as Charles Dickens and William Thackeray. In a letter to John BETJEMAN, Waugh summed up his views on literary modernism: "I am reading Proust for the first time. Very poor stuff. I think he was mentally defective."

Vile Bodies (1930) portrays a group of "Bright Young Things" who move from one decadent party to the next: "It was called a Savage party, that is to say that Johnnie Hoop had written in the invitation that they were to come dressed as savages. Numbers of them had done so; Johnnie himself in a mask and black gloves represented the Maharanee of Pukkapore, somewhat to the annoyance of the Maharajah, who happened to drop in."

A Handful of Dust (1934) concerns an aristocratic couple, Tony and Brenda Last, and illustrates people's indifference to human suffering in the death of the Lasts' son, John Andrew, and Brenda's abandonment of Tony for the utterly contemptible John Beaver. The novel ends with Tony's expedition to South America, where he is held prisoner by a demented man who forces him to read the works of Dickens to him for the rest of his life. An editorial in the *Tablet* called it "sedulously and diabolically cruel."

Scoop (1938) is a satirical look at the newspaper world, and *Put Out More Flags* (1942) is a send-up of pre–World War II Britain. Several years previously, in 1930, Waugh had become a Roman

Catholic. His new religion figured prominently in his later, more serious novels, especially *Brideshead Revisited* (1945) and *The Sword of Honor* trilogy (1952–61).

The advent of World War II changed Waugh's life; its aftermath changed and began to destroy his way of life and that of his class. His army service forms the frame story and background to the wildly successful *Brideshead Revisited*. The novel opens as Captain Charles Ryder and his unit are billeted early in the war at Brideshead, the ancestral home of the noble Roman Catholic Marchmain family. Ryder thinks back to happier times, between the wars, when he had been a house guest there, first as a friend of Sebastian Flyte, youngest son of Lord Brideshead, and then as the prospective bridegroom of Sebastian's sister Julia, when they both attended the dying days of her father.

While at Oxford, Ryder had formed an intense friendship with Sebastian and fallen in love with Julia. The war turned Ryder into a soldier. As Lord Brideshead dies, he makes a gesture that can be interpreted as a return to the rites of the church, and this convinces Julia that she cannot marry Charles; such a union would be a sin in the eyes of the church because she is divorced. But with Lord Brideshead's death comes the death of the old prewar aristocratic order. Not many months later, distinctly unaristocratic British enlisted soldiers, with no respect for rank or privilege and its trappings, soil and deface the castle, except the chapel. In reviewing *Brideshead Revisited*, one commentator referred to its ". . . almost overwhelming sense of loss (the loss of love, friendship, youth and faith). . . . Brideshead dies right before the war breaks out, while Charles is negotiating for a commission in the Special Reserve. War comes, and with it the turmoil within the British social order that changed it forever." Waugh described the novel as "steeped in theology."

The Loved One (1948), one of Waugh's best and best-known satires, grew out of his experience in Hollywood, where he traveled to discuss a movie version of *Brideshead Revisited* that was never made. In this book he returns to the darkly absurdist satire of his earliest works but continues his exploration of the horrors of modernity in a set of related satirical targets: America, Hollywood, and the funeral industry. The novel traces the career of Dennis Barlow, an English poet who has come to Hollywood to work in the movies but ends up taking a job at a pet cemetery. Barlow comes from "a generation which enjoys a vicarious intimacy with death." After his host, Sir Francis Hinsley, commits suicide, Barlow must arrange the funeral at Whispering Glades, a parody of Los Angeles's Forest Lawn cemetery. There he falls in love with Aimee Thanatogenos (whose name means "child of death"), a mortuary cosmetician. He attempts to use his poetic powers to seduce her but discovers that they, too, have died in the American climate. Even his attempt to write a funeral elegy for Sir Francis fails: "They told me, Francis Hinsley, they told me you were hung / With red protruding eye-balls and black protruding tongue." Instead, Barlow passes off famous English poems as his own to the ignorant Aimee: "Once he came near to exposure when she remarked that *Shall I compare thee to a summer's day* reminded her of something she had learned at school." Scholar Douglas Patey commented on the significance of death in the novel: "[D]eath, judgment and the afterlife alone give meaning to earthly life. Evade this hard doctrine, deny the meaning of death, and a culture becomes empty and tasteless, because spiritually dead."

Waugh kept a detailed diary of his military service, out of which was to come what Penelope LIVELY calls "the finest work of fiction in English to emerge from World War II." *The Sword of Honor* trilogy follows the war career of Waugh's alter ego, Guy Crouchback, Roman Catholic gentleman soldier, through *Men at Arms* (1952), *Officers and Gentlemen* (1955), and *Unconditional Surrender* (1961). Crouchback's counterpart is Trimmer, a former hairdresser who always abandons principles for self-advancement. The wily Trimmer, involved by chance in a publicity stunt gone awry, ends up a hero.

In the third volume Virginia, Guy's ex-wife, pregnant by Trimmer, persuades Guy to remarry her. She has the child, whom she sends away from London for safety, and then is killed by a bomb. The nobly behaving Crouchback ends up raising Trimmer's son as his own, while Trimmer escapes to South America unscathed. The good and noble suffer, and the evil and ignoble profit and prosper.

Waugh married Laura Herbert in 1937 and he fathered six children, one of whom was the writer Auberon WAUGH. Increasingly isolated from the modern world, he spent his last years in his country home. He never phoned when he could write, always wrote with a pen and ink, and refused to learn to drive.

Other Works by Evelyn Waugh

Black Mischief. Boston: Little, Brown, 1932.
Complete Stories of Evelyn Waugh. Boston: Little, Brown, 1998.
Edmund Campion. Boston: Little, Brown, 1946.

Works about Evelyn Waugh

Hastings, Selina. *Evelyn Waugh: A Biography.* Toronto: Sinclair-Stevenson, 1994.
Myers, William. *Evelyn Waugh and the Problem of Evil.* Boston: Faber & Faber, 1991.
Patey, Douglas Lane. *The Life of Evelyn Waugh: A Critical Biography.* Cambridge, Mass.: Blackwell, 1998.

Welch, Denton (Maurice Denton Welch)
(1915–1948) *novelist*

Born in Shanghai, China, to a wealthy British company director and his American wife, Denton Welch was sent to England for schooling when he was 11. That same year, 1926, his mother died. Her death greatly affected him, and he dropped out of school at 16, returning to the Goldsmith School of Art when he was 18. A second tragedy—a bicycling accident that left him permanently injured—inspired Welch to start writing. His frequently autobiographical writing combines surprisingly objective self-analysis with a penchant for specific, artistic description of external details.

Welch's best-known works are his three autobiographical novels: *Maiden Voyage* (1943), *In Youth Is Pleasure* (1945), and *A Voice Through a Cloud* (1950). His first novel, *Maiden Voyage,* tells the story of running away from school and being sent to Shanghai to live with his father. Critic Edith SITWELL observes: "As in all of Welch's novels, it is the precisely realized details of the author's physical and social surroundings that make the book such a remarkable journey." The following passage, which describes the opening of a crystal decanter, demonstrates Welch's extreme attention to the smallest details: "The prisms and roses seemed too sharp to touch and the glittering stopper was like a diadem. I pulled it up with the soft crunch and squeak of glass on glass, and smelt the whisky."

In Youth is Pleasure recounts the summer vacation of a sensitive 15-year-old boy who has just finished a miserable first year of school. Welch talks about his painful semirecovery from the bicycling accident that left him partially paralyzed in *A Voice through a Cloud.* Bedridden, he explores his own thoughts and feelings about pain as well as the relationships with his family and his doctor. Critic Jocelyn Brooke "can think of no writer who has described extreme physical and mental agony with a more appalling vividness."

Critic Matthew Louttit admires a different aspect of Welch's writing: "Welch writes about human feelings and motivations with an unblinking candour that we associate with a Sartre or Camus: his gaze on the world is of such clarity that he leads me to wonder what the greats of French literature could have achieved if they, like Denton Welch, were never tempted into intellectual posturing."

Other Work by Denton Welch

When I Was an Art Student. North Pomfret, Vt.: Elysium Press, 1998.

Weldon, Fay (1931–) *novelist, scriptwriter, playwright, nonfiction writer*

Fay Weldon was born in Alvechurch, Worcestershire, England, the daughter of a physician, Frank Birkinshaw and a writer, Margaret Birkinshaw. When her parents divorced, she grew up with her mother and sister in a world of women. Her early childhood was spent in New Zealand; she attended schools in Christchurch and, in her teens, in Hampstead, London. Weldon earned a master's degree (1954) and a doctorate (1992) from the University of St. Andrew's, and another doctorate from the University of Bath (1988). From 1954 to 1956 she worked in the information research department of the Foreign Office and did market research for the *Daily Mirror.* From 1960 to 1967 she was a successful advertising copywriter.

Weldon's literary career began in the mid-1960s. In addition to more than 20 novels, she has written radio, television, and film scripts; plays; and some nonfiction. She wrote the script for the award-winning first episode of *Upstairs, Downstairs* (1971). She married briefly in the 1950s and became a single parent to her son Nicholas. In 1960 she married antiques dealer Ronald Weldon, with whom she had three more sons. In 1976 the Weldons moved from London to Somerset. They divorced in 1994, and the following year Fay Weldon married her business manager.

Weldon has won several literary awards, including an *L.A. Times* award for fiction for *The Heart of the Country* (1987–88). She writes about women's experiences in a patriarchal world. Her fiction is labeled "feminist," but because her viewpoint remains very much her own and because she recognizes women's connivance in their victimization, her feminism is unorthodox. Her novels explore sex, marriage, infidelity, divorce, pregnancy, motherhood, abortion, housework, and thwarted careers. Though the battle of the sexes is the dominant theme, men usually play a secondary role in her novels, which often feature vividly developed female portraits. Thus, *Down among the Women* (1971/1972) is a novel about three generations of women, and *Praxis* (1978) is about four generations.

Female Friends (1975/1976) concerns one man's impact on the lives of three women—Chloe, Marjorie, and Grace—and *Life Force* (1992) focuses on a single man, Leslie Beck, who is obsessed with his masculinity and who makes love to most of the women in the book. *The Heart of the Country* (1987/1988) is a satire on suburban life that is viewed as Weldon's most feminist novel, with its theme of the objectification, or "commodification," of women. *The Hearts and Lives of Men* (1987/1988) was an enormous commercial success for the author.

The book for which Weldon is best known is probably *The Life and Loves of a She-Devil* (1983), which was televised in 1986 and filmed in 1989. The book is about a grotesquely ugly woman's revenge on her husband and his lover, a beautiful, rich, romantic novelist. From an inept housewife Ruth remakes herself into an irresistible multimillionaire. By the end she has completely surgically remodeled herself as a replica of Mary Fisher, her husband's lover, is able to dominate her husband totally, and finally reflects: "It was not a matter of male or female after all . . . merely of power. I have all, and he has none. As I was, so is he now." This is an ironic victory, however, for Ruth becomes everything she formerly longed to be but inwardly condemned.

Weldon's style is remarkable for a firm grasp of detail, deft dialogue, and wry sense of humor. She often alternates first-person present with third-person past narration. She is fascinated by the weird, as can be seen in her novel *Puffball* (1980), about a dangerous pregnancy and witchcraft, and in *The Cloning of Joanna May* (1989), which is about genetic engineering and takes place against the background of the Chernobyl disaster.

Since the 1980s Weldon's work has broadened as she has incorporated large social issues into her fiction, thus incurring criticism that her work has become more journalistic and polemical. Her tone has grown more acerbic and her vision more apocalyptic. Novelist and critic Anita BROOKNER praises Weldon as "one of the most astute and distinctive women writing fiction today."

Works about Fay Weldon

Barreca, Regina, ed. *Fay Weldon's Wicked Fictions.* Hanover, N.H.: University Press of New England, 1994.

Faulks, Lana. *Fay Weldon.* Boston: Twayne, 1998.

Sage, Lorna. *Women in the House of Fiction: Post-War Women Novelists.* New York: Routledge, 1992.

Wells, Herbert George (1866–1946)
novelist, short story writer, nonfiction writer

While H. G. Wells is often called the father of modern science fiction and has written many classics in the genre, he is also remembered for his comic, romantic, and dramatic novels and short stories. Whether he was writing about the distant future or his own England at the turn of the century, his work consistently expressed his hopes and fears for the human race.

Wells was born in Bromley, Kent, England, to Joseph Wells, a shopkeeper and professional cricket player, and Sarah Wells, who sometimes worked as a housekeeper. When he was seven he broke his leg and was laid up in bed for weeks. His father brought him books to help him pass the time, including works on natural history and astronomy. These ignited Wells's imagination, opened his mind to science, and offered him glimpses of places of which he had never heard.

When his father's business failed, Wells was forced to become a draper's apprentice, which he hated. Eventually, in 1883, he secured a position as a teacher/pupil at Midhurst Grammar School. A year later he obtained a scholarship to the Normal School of Science in London, where he studied biology under T. H. Huxley. Although Wells was interested in evolutionary theory, he soon lost interest in other studies and left school without a degree in 1887. He taught in private schools for four years, not taking his bachelor's degree until 1890. The following year he settled in London and married his cousin Isabel. In 1893, while he continued to teach, he began contributing short stories and drama reviews to local magazines. A year later he divorced Isabel and in 1895 he married Amy Catherine Robbins.

Wells's first novel was *The Time Machine* (1895). The "Time Traveler" tells his friend, the narrator, about the time machine he has built and about his adventures in the future. In the year 802,701 he finds two races of people: the Eloi, slight and peaceful, who live in a seeming garden paradise; and the beastly Morlocks, who live underground and feed on the Eloi. After escaping from this conflict, the Traveler flees further in time, eventually finding himself 30,000,000 years in the future on a dying Earth inhabited by giant crablike creatures. "I moved on a hundred years, and there was the same red sun—a little larger, a little duller—the same dying sea, the same chill air, and the same crowd of earthly crustacea creeping in and out among the green weed and the red rock."

The success of *The Time Machine* allowed Wells to devote himself full time to fiction writing. His next novel, *The Island of Dr. Moreau* (1896), tells of a scientist who attempts to perfect the human race by transforming animals into human creatures. Wells's darkest work, it served as a warning that human progress is not inevitable, that mankind shares much more with animals than it likes to admit. As the narrator, Prendick, says, ". . . only it seemed that I, too, was not a reasonable creature, but only an animal tormented with some strange disorder in its brain. . . ."

For the next few years Wells turned out some of the most enduring works of science fiction. *The Invisible Man* (1897) is the story of a scientist who goes mad with a sense of limitless power when he learns to make himself invisible. *The War of the Worlds* (1898) tells the exciting and disturbing story of a Martian invasion of Earth. *The First Men on the Moon* (1901) in some ways mirrored Jules Verne's earlier story of a trip to the Moon, but where Verne's rocket fails its mission, Wells's adventurers land on the Moon to find it inhabited by the antlike Selenites.

In addition to his novels, Wells also began in 1901 to write critical pamphlets attacking the British social order. In 1903 he joined the Fabian Society in London, which advocated a fairer British society by planning a gradual system of socialist reforms. Although he soon left the Fabians, he remained active in the political arena, meeting with world leaders, working for the League of Nations, and running for Parliament in the early 1920s.

In 1912 Wells sent a letter to Rebecca WEST in response to her negative review of his *Marriage* (1912), which advocated free love. The two soon began a 10-year affair that produced a son, the writer Anthony West.

In 1920 Wells published one of his most ambitious nonfiction works, *The Outline of History.* In it he stated that history was ruled by three ideas: the idea of science, the idea of one universal God of Righteousness, and the idea of a world policy. "The rest of the history of mankind is very largely the history of those three ideas . . . spreading out from the minds of the rare and exceptional persons and peoples in which they first originated, into the general consciousness of the race, and giving first a new colour, then a new spirit, and then a new direction to human affairs."

By the time Wells died, he had written more than 100 books and short stories. Whether readers see his canon of work as escapist fantasy or as socially conscious metaphor, both assessments are accurate. As Wells scholar Frank McDonnell observes, "the artist was never very far from the social planner and prophet."

Critical Analysis

When *The Time Machine* appeared, many books had been written about the idea of a utopia, or an ideal society that many believed was the inevitable culmination of the evolution of the human race. Some utopian novels projected that once machines had taken over the toil of life, people would be free to live in blissful luxury; others showed societies that had achieved perfection by rejecting technology.

The Time Machine presents both of these views and is critical of each. The efficient underground machines that run everything have reduced the people who service them into the monstrous Morlocks; and the peaceful Eloi of the garden surface are little more than passive, sickly children. "I thought of the physical slightness of the [Eloi]," the Traveler reflects, "their lack of intelligence and those abundant ruins, and it strengthened my belief in a perfect conquest of Nature. . . . This has ever been the fate of energy in security; it takes to art and to eroticism, and then come langour and decay." While many people felt that evolution would inevitably lead us to a utopia where the struggle for survival had ceased, Wells believed, as Darwin did, that without this struggle, the human race would die.

Critics have also been interested in the way Wells chose to tell his story. In most utopian tales, the narrator is met by a guide or historian who explains the new world to him and the reader. Not only does the Traveler have no such guide, but also no one in the future even speaks. The Eloi have a language, but it is much too rudimentary for them to tell the Traveler anything useful. "The Traveler is confronted with the future," writes Frank McConnell, "in much the same way the Romantic poet finds himself confronted with the inhospitable rockface of nature: a mute, gigantic, threatening, and absolutely uncommunicative presence, about which one can only speculate, only entertain notions."

The power of Wells's prose is evident throughout the novel but is particularly moving in one of the final passages as the Traveler journeys 30,000,000 years into the future, as Earth is dying and devoid of life: "It would be hard to convey the stillness of it all. All the sounds of man, the bleating of sheep, the cries of birds, the hum of insects, the stir that makes the background of our lives—all that was over."

Turning from his "scientific romances," in 1909 Wells published *Tono-Bungay*, which many consider to be his finest work. The book is yet another cautionary tale, this time set in Wells's own Edwardian England and dealing with the capitalist society that he believed was out of control and had turned England into a country of pointlessness and waste.

With *Tono-Bungay* Wells wished to write a classically British novel such as those by Charles Dickens. On the one hand, it is the semiautobiographical story of the narrator, George Ponderevo, a young, idealistic man trying to make his way in life and love. On the other, it is the story of George's uncle Edward, a scheming con man who strikes it rich with his invention of Tono-Bungay, a worthless cure-all that cures nothing. What Edward is marketing, in fact, is hope: "'We mint Faith, George,' said my uncle one day. . . . 'We been making human confidence ever since I drove the first cork of Tono-Bungay.'"

The strength of *Tono-Bungay*, according to Wells scholar Richard Hauer Costa, is that it successfully combines three roles that Wells assumed throughout his writing career: "the spokesman for a generation escaping from Victorianism; the scientific romancer who brought the Fourth Dimension and air-machine travel to the semi-educated man . . .; and the portrayer of warm human characters."

Other Works by H. G. Wells

Best Science Fiction Stories of H. G. Wells. New York: Dover 1994.
Seven Science Fiction Novels of H. G. Wells. New York: Dover, 1979.

Works about H. G. Wells

Costa, Richard Haver. *H. G. Wells.* Boston: Twayne, 1985.
McConnell, Frank. *The Science Fiction of H. G. Wells.* New York: Oxford University Press, 1981.
Smith, David C. *H. G. Wells: Desperately Mortal.* New Haven, Conn.: Yale University Press, 1986.
West, Anthony. *H. G. Wells: Aspects of a Life.* New York: Random House, 1984.

Wesker, Arnold (1932–   ) *playwright*

Arnold Wesker was born in London, England, the son of Joseph Wesker, a Russian-Jewish tailor, and Leah Wesker, a Hungarian kitchen worker. He dropped out of school at 16, but enrolled in the London School of Film Technique in 1955 to learn how to write film scripts. Critics classify Wesker with a group of English playwrights, including John OSBORNE and David STOREY, known as the ANGRY YOUNG MEN, who wrote about social problems in a realistic way. His plays are also known as "kitchen-sink" dramas, meaning they describe work and working people.

Wesker's first play, *The Kitchen* (1956), reflects his own experiences as a restaurant worker. The play uses the sometimes calm, sometimes insanely busy setting of a restaurant kitchen to explore interpersonal relationships among the workers. Critic Kenneth Tynan observes that the play "achieves something that few playwrights have ever attempted; it dramatises work, the daily collision of man with economic necessity, the repetitive toil that consumes that large portion of human life which is not devoted to living." A line from the play draws attention to the parallels of life in the kitchen and life in general: "This stinking kitchen is like the world—you know what I mean? It's too fast to know what happens."

After *The Kitchen,* Wesker wrote the trilogy of plays for which he became famous: *Chicken Soup with Barley* (1958), *Roots* (1959), and *I'm Talking about Jerusalem* (1960). He has described the trilogy, which is based on his own family, as being about "a family; on another level it is a play about human relationships; and on a third, and most important level, it is a story of people moved by political ideas in a particular social time." Critic T. F. Evans describes the trilogy as "an ambitious and impressive attempt to write about the times through which [Wesker] lived and to do it in a way that brings out the political significances of the period and the impact of politics on his family's life."

In his later plays, Wesker writes less about politics and more about what he calls "private pain," which he sees as a unifying force among people. Critics Glenda Leeming and Simon Trussler believe that "as dramatist and humanist, in concern for local colour and universal truth, [Wesker] is an Ibsen of our times—not least in determining to write as the times require, not as they or even his own inclinations entirely dictate."

Other Work by Arnold Wesker
The Plays of Arnold Wesker. New York: Harper & Row, 1976.

A Work about Arnold Wesker
Dornan, Reade W. *Arnold Wesker Revisited.* New York: Twayne, 1994.

West, Rebecca (Cicely Isabel Fairfield, Corinne Andrews) (1892–1983) *novelist, journalist, nonfiction writer, travel writer*

Rebecca West was born Cicely Isabel Fairfield in London. Her father, Charles, was a journalist specializing in politics and business, and her mother, Isabella, was a former pianist. West was especially close to her father and shared his enthusiasm for words. He would talk to her about his writing, and she began writing herself when she was very young. Her mother, too, loved to tell stories. West's childhood was happy until, in 1901, her father died. The remaining Fairfields moved to Edinburgh, where West threw her school into uproar by writing articles about woman's suffrage and poems about the death of God. When she was 16 she was diagnosed with tuberculosis, and her schooling was temporarily halted.

West trained briefly at the Academy of Dramatic Art, but her attempt at an acting career was fleeting. Next she tried her hand at journalism and immediately blossomed. Enthusiastic about advancing the cause of women's votes, she worked at the suffragette periodical *The Freewoman* for two years. Her first published article began with a bang: "There are two kinds of imperialists—imperialists and bloody imperialists." West feared her mother might become alarmed at the controversy her writing caused, so she assumed a pen name, choosing Rebecca West after an appropriately rebellious female character from Henrik Ibsen's play *Rosmersholm.*

A prolific and passionate journalist, West wrote for *The Freewoman, The Clarion, The Star, Daily News* and the *New Statesman.* In 1912 she wrote a scathing review of H. G. WELLS's controversial book *Marriage,* which advocates free love. The married Wells wrote to her, and that correspondence ironically began a 10-year affair between the two. She and Wells had a son, Anthony West, in 1914.

West published her first book in 1916, the first full-length literary study of the novelist Henry James. She then began work on her own first novel. She said later it cost her "buckets of blood and sweat" to produce *The Return of the Soldier* (1918). This novel describes the strange tangle of relationships among three women involved with a soldier who has lost his memory from shell shock. The editor Samuel Hynes called the book "a small masterpiece."

West's next novel was *The Judge* (1922), a novel about two generations of the women's suffrage movement. It begins with the sonorous lines, "Every mother is a judge who sentences the children for the sins of the fathers." West returned to the question of mother-child relationships in her biography *St. Augustine* (1933). This book takes a psychoanalytical approach, considering St. Augustine through the lens of his relationship with his mother.

West's most famous book is the epic travelogue *Black Lamb and Grey Falcon* (1941), a sprawling account of several trips she took to the Balkans in the mid-1930s. As such, it is a haunting evocation of a vanished landscape destroyed by World War II. The dedication on the first page reads in simple capitals, "To my friends in Yugoslavia, who are now all dead or enslaved." The book combines travelogue and history. Even today it is read by politicians attempting to understand the complex history of the Balkans.

After the war, West was commissioned to write a book on "Lord Haw-Haw," the Englishman William Joyce, who had joined the Nazi party and broadcast anti-British propaganda during the war. *The Meaning of Treason* (1949) examines Joyce's history as well as the wider question of a traitor's place in society. West was also commissioned to write reports on the postwar Nuremberg trials, gathered in *A Train of Powder* (1955).

West, who wrote over 20 books and countless articles and book reviews, was made Dame Commander of the Order of the British Empire (DBE) in 1959. She also published under the pseudonym Connie Andrews. She continued writing into advanced old age. William Shawn, editor of the *New Yorker*, declared that "Rebecca West was one of the giants and will have a lasting place in English literature. No one in this century wrote more dazzling prose, or had more wit." Her niece, Alison McLeod, said simply, "If Rebecca ever came back . . . it would be as a firework."

Other Works by Rebecca West

The Birds Fall Down. 1966. Reprint, London: Virago, 1986.
The Fountain Overflows. 1956. Reprint, London: Virago, 1984.
This Real Night. London: Macmillan, 1984.

Works about Rebecca West

Glendinning, Victoria. *Rebecca West: A Life.* New York: Alfred A. Knopf, 1987.
Rollyson, Carl. *Rebecca West: A Saga of the Century.* New York: Scribner, 1996.
Schweizer, Bernard. *Rebecca West: Heroism, Rebellion, and the Female Epic.* Westport, Conn.: Greenwood, 2002.

Westmacott, Mary

See CHRISTIE, AGATHA.

White, Jon Manchip (1924–) *novelist, nonfiction writer, screenwriter*

Jon Manchip White was born in Cardiff, Wales, to Gwilym White, a shipowner, and Elizabeth White. He is descended from a long line of seafarers and can trace his ancestry on his father's side back many hundreds of years. In his autobiographical work, *The Journeying Boy* (1991), White tells several fascinating stories about his ancestors, including that of Rawlins White, the owner of a fishing fleet who was burned at the stake for refusing to accept the Bible as the literal word of God.

Wales and the White family were hit hard by the Great Depression, called the Slump in Britain. Gwilym White's business suffered, and the family, which had been fairly well off, suffered a series of financial setbacks. Then, when White was about four years old, his father contracted tuberculosis. He later remembered that he and his mother would travel to visit his father in a sanatorium in Talgarth, Wales. They would spend the day with him, but the son was not allowed to touch his father for fear of contracting the disease.

When White was eight years old, his father was sent home from the sanatorium to die, and the boy was sent to boarding school in England to lessen the possibility that he might be afflicted with tuberculosis. He later remembered the pain of being taken away from his family: "There has never been any misery in my life that has matched the despair and the homesickness that I felt as a small boy banished to an institution in distant England." Yet he has also said that his English education served him well: "Over the years I have come to believe that the combination of Celtic nature and Anglo-Saxon nurture may be a useful one." His father died when White was in his early teens.

In 1941 White received a scholarship to study at St. Catherine's College at Cambridge. During World War II he interrupted his studies to enlist in the navy. Near the end of the war he joined the prestigious Welsh Guards, and on V-E day he met his future wife, Valerie Leighton, with whom he had two daughters.

After the war, White returned to Cambridge, where he took degrees in English, prehistoric archaeology, and Egyptology. In 1950 he moved to London, where he worked as a writer for the BBC (British Broadcasting Corporation). He did a brief stint in the British Foreign Service from 1952 to 1956, during which time he began to publish novels. His first, *Last Race,* was published in 1953. By the time he resigned from the foreign service to work full-time as a writer, he had published two additional novels and two nonfiction works, *Ancient Egypt* (1952) and *Anthropology.* During the next 10 years, he wrote screenplays, novels, and nonfiction.

In the mid-1960s White met literary critic Cleanth Brooks, who helped him find a position as writer-in-residence at the University of Texas at El Paso. He stayed at Texas from 1967 to 1977, when he accepted a professorship at the University of Tennessee at Knoxville.

A prolific writer, White has published more than a dozen novels, many of them mystery novels overlaid with fantasy. He has also published four volumes of poetry and more than a dozen nonfiction works, including *Diego Velazquez: Painter and Courtier* (1969) and *Everyday Life of the North American Indian* (1979). His most recent work is the autobiographical *The Journeying Boy,* in which he returns after 13 years to his boyhood home in Wales. This beautifully written memoir includes a history of Wales, an analysis of the Welsh character, a present-day look at Cardiff and the Welsh countryside, and a reminiscence of White's own boyhood and youth. The author writes with great passion about the rape of the land by the coal mining conglomerates and about the Welsh love of singing. White is still living in Tennessee.

Other Works by Jon Manchip White

Everyday Life in Ancient Egypt. New York: Putnam, 1964.
The Garden Game. Indianapolis: Bobbs Merrill, 1974.
Nightclimber. New York: Morrow, 1968.

White, T. H. (Terence Hanbury White)
(1906–1964) *novelist, poet, nonfiction writer*
T. H. White was born in Bombay, India, where his father was a civil servant. He was sent back to England for his education, then enrolled at Cambridge University to study English. White was extremely successful academically. While at university, he published his first book, *Loved Helen and Other Poems* (1929), a series of romantic poems. He wrote his first novel, *They Winter Abroad* (1932), about English visitors to Italy, while he was himself on holiday there.

After White finished his degree, he became an English teacher. During his teaching years he continued to pursue many interests, even learning to fly airplanes. He continued to write occasionally, but more for financial security than out of any real passion for writing. That all changed when he went to Scotland one Easter for a lonely fishing holiday. Relishing the chance to think in solitude, White realized he longed to give up his job and write full-time. In order to do so, he swiftly compiled a book from his various casual writings about hunting and travel experiences. This book, *England Have My Bones* (1936), was successful, and a publisher gave him a contract to finance serious full-time work.

As a student White had loved the Arthurian epic *Morte d'Arthur*. Written in the 15th century by Sir Thomas Malory, this medieval saga describes the mythical rise and fall of King Arthur and Camelot. White had written academic essays about the book, but now he dived into it from a new angle: He wanted to make it into a children's novel. This project was begun in *The Sword in the Stone* (1939), which describes Arthur's childhood and education before he realizes he is royalty. The wizard Merlyn finds unusual ways to teach him various life lessons, magically turning Arthur into various animals so he can learn lessons from these creatures. *The Sword in the Stone* was a huge success in both Britain and America.

The sequel *The Witch in the Wood* (1940) introduces the witch Morgause and her husband warrior King Lot. Immediately after becoming king, Arthur has to defend his realm against numerous aggressors. He succeeds in forging a nation from a mere set of warring clans, replacing famine and war with peace and cultured prosperity. He has allies in this project, and *The Ill-made Knight* (1941) records the triumphs and agonies of his most famous ally: Lancelot. But Camelot eventually succumbs to his enemies, and its downfall is described in *The Candle in the Wind*, written in 1940 and published in the collection *The Once and Future King* (1958).

Written during World War II, White's Arthurian novels are very much a product of their time. One might expect an Arthurian saga to glorify battle and war, but over the course of the war White came to realize that the Arthurian legend does exactly the opposite. King Arthur reflects at the end of his life: "The fantastic thing about war was that it was fought about nothing—literally nothing. Frontiers were imaginary lines." Describing *The Candle in the Wind*, White wrote to his Cambridge tutor, "I have suddenly discovered that . . . the central theme of Morte d'Arthur is to find an antidote to war."

The Candle in the Wind was the last Arthurian novel White published during his lifetime, but he had completed a fifth novel that he intended to close the saga. *The Book of Merlyn*, published in 1977, was written in 1941. White's publishers had originally resisted this addition to the series, and when in 1958 they collected his novels into one edition as *The Once and Future King*, *Merlyn* was omitted. In this fifth novel, Arthur meets various animals, none of whom war with each other. Merlyn educates Arthur about various political states by turning him, for example, into an ant (to teach him about totalitarianism). *The Book of Merlyn* was rediscovered and published after White's death.

White was a solitary man, spending much time living in wooded areas where he would hunt and fish on his own. He wrote books about this, including a book about falconry, *The Goshawk* (1951). He also wrote poetry and two nonfiction books, *The Scandalmonger* (1951) and *The Age of Scandal* (1950), a witty description of glamorous and depraved celebrities of the 18th century.

White was a prolific writer who remains best known for his Arthurian works, which the *Sunday Times* called "[m]agnificent and tragic, an irresistible mixture of gaiety and pathos." The *Times Literary Supplement* declared that these books "will long remain a memorial to an author who is at once civilized, learned, witty and humane."

Other Works by T. H. White

Book of Beasts: Being a Translation from the Latin Bestiary of the Twelfth Century. 1954, Reprint, New York: Dover, 1984.

A Joy Proposed: Poems. Athens: University of Georgia Press, 1980.

Letters to a Friend: Correspondence between T. H. White and L. J. Potts. Edited by François Gallix. New York: Putnam, 1982.

Maharajah and Other Stories. Edited by Kurth Sprague. New York: Putnam, 1981.

Works about T. H. White

Gallix, François. *T. H. White: An Annotated Bibliography*. New York: Garland, 1986.

Kellman, Martin. *T. H. White and the Matter of Britain: A Literary Overview*. Lewiston, N.Y.: Edwin Mellen Press, 1988.

Warner, Sylvia Townsend. *T. H. White: A Biography*. New York: Viking, 1968.

Williams, Charles (1886–1945) *novelist, poet, playwright, nonfiction writer, essayist*

Charles Williams was born in London to Walter Williams, a foreign correspondence clerk and entrepreneur, and Mary Williams, who eventually ended up supporting the family with her small art supply store. Williams attended St. Albans grammar school and for two years studied at University College, London, until financial straits forced him to abandon his education and go to work for the Oxford University Press, where he remained for 37 years.

Williams's position at the press brought him into close contact with T. S. ELIOT, C. S. LEWIS, and J. R. R. TOLKIEN. With the latter two he eventually formed the Inklings, a literary group whose members critiqued one another's writings. He published his first volume of poetry, *The Silver Stair* in 1912. By the end of his career he had produced a total of seven volumes of poetry, seven novels, seven biographies, and 15 plays.

Of all Williams's verse, his best known is the poetry sequence *Taliessin through Logres* (1938), which is based on the legends of King Arthur, told through the voice of Taliessin, Arthur's court poet. Much of the sequence focuses on Sir Galahad's search for the Holy Grail. Although some of the individual poems are filled with Williams's own inventions, others, such as "The Crowning of Arthur," render familiar parts of the myth in new, powerful, and complexly structured verse. This poem begins, "The king stood crowned; around the gate . . . Logres [Britain] heraldically flaunted the king's state" and goes on to catalog the reactions of such traditional Arthurian figures as Morgan le Fay and Lancelot at the coronation.

As a playwright Williams was an important contributor to the revival of religious drama in the early 20th century. Most of his plays show the influence of his involvement in the Christianity-tinged Hermetic Order of the Golden Dawn, which was given to the study of the occult and magic and whose members included William Butler YEATS and Algernon BLACKWOOD. Williams's *Thomas Cranmer of Canterbury*, the feature play of the Canterbury Festival in 1936, is a historical drama about the life of the 17th-century clergyman who became the archbishop of Canterbury and authorized Henry VIII's divorce from Catherine of Aragon as well as the king's marriage to Anne Boleyn. Cranmer also encouraged the persecution of Catholics, and the play's second act deals with his clash with Henry's daughter Mary, a Catholic who eventually burns him at the stake for heresy.

Williams's best-known work is his novel *Descent into Hell* (1937). While his earlier novels—*War in Heaven* (1930), a modern-day search for the Grail; and *The Greater Trumps* (1932), in which the misuse of a Tarot deck produces a killer storm that threatens the entire world—explore the meaning of salvation, *Descent into Hell* meditates on eternal damnation. Throughout the novel, characters interact with spirits as if they are real people, and in one of the book's most frightening moments they witness the dead digging themselves out of their graves with "earth heaving out of dark openings . . . in bursts and rushes—in a spasmodic momentum, soon exhausted, always renewed." One of the novel's central characters, the scholar Wentworth, is seduced by a succubus, a sexually alluring female demon, who tempts him into consciously choosing eternal damnation. At the end of the novel he is "drawn, steadily, everlastingly, inward and down through the bottomless circles of the void" into a world of horrifying and eternal isolation.

Williams was also a critic, essayist, and biographer. Among his most noteworthy nonfiction writing is *Reason and Beauty in the Poetic Mind* (1933), in which he argues that poetry must be structured; the essay "What the Cross Means to Me" (1943), in which he explains his view of an ultimately loving and compassionate God; and the biographies *Bacon* (1933), about the 16th-century philosopher Sir Francis Bacon, *Queen Elizabeth* (1936), and *Henry VII* (1937).

Although Williams is currently remembered primarily as an associate of Lewis and Tolkien, the scholar Agnes Sibley argues that he "puts into fresh, contemporary language the age-old truths about God, the soul, the mystic experience, sin and salvation" and offers his readers "not an escape from ordinary living, but an increasing understanding of its significance in eternal terms."

Other Works by Charles Williams

All Hallows Eve. 1945. Reprint, Laurel, N.Y.: Lightyear Press, 1993.
A Charles Williams Reader. Grand Rapids, Mich.: Eerdmans, 2000.

Works about Charles Williams

Howard, Thomas. *The Novels of Charles Williams.* 1983. Reprint, Fort Collins, Colo.: Ignatius Press, 1991.
Knight, Gareth. *The Magical World of Charles Williams.* Oceanside, Calif.: Sun Chalice Books, 2002.

Williams, Ella Gwendolyn Rees

See RHYS, JEAN.

Williams, Emlyn (George Emlyn Williams) (1905–1987) *playwright, screenwriter, memoirist*

Emlyn Williams was born in Motyn, Wales, to Richard and Mary Williams. His father supported the family working as a foreman in a steel plant. Williams had a religious upbringing overseen by his Calvinist mother. He learned English at age 10 (his family spoke Welsh at home), and a few years later, with the help of one of his teachers, he earned a scholarship to attend Christ Church College at Oxford, receiving his degree in 1927. He went on to have a notable career as a screenwriter, playwright, actor, and novelist who wrote psychologi-

cal thrillers that often drew upon his experiences as a boy growing up in the Welsh countryside.

Williams claimed that his inspiration for his work came from a range of everyday sources: "A theme occurs to me, half-subconsciously sometimes; my mind is set ticking by a book I have read, or even a chance remark, a news item, a face in the street." He earned his first acclaim as a dramatist for his play *A Murder Has Been Arranged*. This murder mystery tells the story of Maurice Mullins, who decides to kill his wealthy uncle for his inheritance. The ghost of the uncle, however, comes back and frightens the young man into confessing the murder to the family. The play received positive reviews during its performance in London in 1930.

Williams also became an actor during this period. He both acted in and wrote another murder mystery, *Night Must Fall* (1935), this time based on a 1929 case in which a man murdered his mother for insurance money by setting her on fire. In describing his inspiration for taking on this gruesome subject matter, Williams claimed, "I found myself wanting to write a play in which the audience knew as the curtain rose, that the murderer had not only 'done it' but was to be hanged for his crime."

In 1940 Williams's semiautobiographical *The Corn Is Green* debuted on Broadway. This story of a woman who sets out to provide a basic education to the children of Welsh coal miners was filmed in 1945 with Bette Davis and then remade for television with Katharine Hepburn in 1979.

During the late 1930s and early 1940s Williams established a reputation as a film actor and contributing screenwriter in movie thrillers such as *Dead Men Tell No Tales* (1938). He also acted in and wrote the screenplay for the patriotic film *This England* (1941) in support of the British war effort.

During the 1950s Williams toured in a one-man show in which he played Charles Dickens and then in the 1960s Williams turned his attention to writing his two-volume autobiography, *George: An Early Autobiography* (1961) and *Emlyn: An Early Autobiography* (1973). Taken together, these works tell the story of his childhood and early career. He also performed one-man shows based on the works of Charles Dickens and Dylan THOMAS.

Williams's prolific career earned him a reputation as both an actor and writer during his lifetime. He will be best remembered, however, for his success in writing mysteries that captivated critics and audiences alike. In describing his own ability as mystery writer, he simply claimed, "I invent." The *New York Times* review of his thriller *Night Must Fall* praised his ability to create realistic accounts of frightening events and circumstances: "When he is at his best . . . Mr. Williams can be morbidly terrifying."

A Work about Emlyn Williams

Harding, James. *Emlyn Williams: A Life*. London: Weidenfeld and Nicolson, 1993.

Williamson, Henry (1895–1977) *novelist, nonfiction writer*

Henry Williamson was born in Bedfordshire, England, the son of William Williamson, a bank clerk, and Gertrude Williamson. At age 18 he left school and joined the British army. After World War I he started writing with the goal of recreating the lives of his dead wartime comrades. He is best known for his books about nature; he wrote volumes about the landscape and wildlife of Devon, where he spent much of his life.

Tarka the Otter (1927), the story of an otter that Williamson raised, won the Hawthornden Prize for 1928 and became his most popular work. In it, Williamson's carefully observed, detailed descriptions show life from an otter's-eye view: "The shape of an otter loomed in the water, and the plaice swam down again in a rapid, waving slant, perceived by a one-eyed eel that was lying with its tail inside a bullock's skull, wedged in a cleft of rock." The writer J. W. Blench observes that Williamson's vivid description "enables the reader to enter into Tarka's inner world and to become more truly human by realizing that he or she is not isolated from the rest of creation."

In addition to several popular animal stories, Williamson spent a great deal of time on two semi-autobiographical novel groups: the four-volume *The Flax of Dreams* (1921–29) and the 15-volume *A Chronicle of Ancient Sunlight* (1951–69). These novels follow the lives of two boys from the English countryside through a stint in World War I and a stay in London. *A Chronicle of Ancient Sunlight* goes beyond mere descriptions of nature and the boy's life. The book argues the importance to a child's development of being out in nature and of having loving, understanding parents. Critic Mark Deavin adds: "Until the Second World War Williamson was generally regarded as one of the great English Nature writers, possessing a unique ability to capture the essential essence and meaning of the natural world in all its variety and forms."

Other Works by Henry Williamson

The Patriot's Progress: Being the Vicissitudes of Pte. John Bullock. 1930. Reprint, Gloucestershire: Sutton Publishing, 2000.
Salar the Salmon. 1972. Reprint, Boston: David R. Godine, 1990.

Works About Henry Williamson

Williamson, Anne. *Henry Williamson: Tarka and the Last Romantic Biography and Diary*. Gloucestershire, England: Sutton Publishing, 1997.
———. *A Patriot's Progress: Henry Williamson and the First World War*. Gloucestershire, England: Sutton Publishing, 1998.

Wilson, Angus (1913–1991) *novelist, short story writer, biographer*

Angus Wilson was born in Bexhill, Sussex, England, to William Wilson, a Scottish aristocrat and gambler, and Maude Johnstone Wilson. The family finances varied, depending on the father's success at gambling, and Wilson's childhood was spent living in a series of hotels and boardinghouses, experiences that he describes in his autobiography *Wild Garden* (1963). He received a B.A. in history from Oxford University in 1936. After graduating, he immediately began working for London's British Museum, where he remained, in various capacities, for 14 years.

Wilson's writing career did not begin until he was in his 30s, when a psychologist prescribed writing as therapy for depression. Simple freewriting gradually developed into short fiction. The stories in his first book, *The Wrong Set and Other Stories* (1949), immediately attracted critics' attention for its sharp, insightful look at middle-class life. The much-praised title story depicts a middle-class family divided when one of its members joins a leftist group—"the wrong set." The equally well-regarded "Realpolitik" revolves around the interaction of an anti-intellectual businessman and an antibusiness scholar.

Wilson was one of the first openly gay British writers, and his initial novel, *Hemlock and After* (1952), is based on his experiences. The adventures of homosexual novelist Bernard Sands serve as a vehicle to satirize both general society and the literary world.

The Middle Age of Mrs. Eliot (1958), which won the James Tait Black Memorial Prize, tells of Meg Eliot, an intelligent but domineering upper-middle-class woman who plunges into a world of isolation after the death of her husband. After a long recovery, she reemerges as an assertive and powerful yet less self-centered woman who finds strength in her independence. Near the end of the novel, before traveling to Asia, Eliot's homosexual brother David, whose partner recently died, attempts to persuade her to stay in England so that she may ease his loneliness. Eliot's response illustrates the extent of her recovery: "I know that loneliness and self-denial have made you somebody of strength and I will not destroy it. Nor, David—let me be honest—will I destroy myself."

The Old Men at the Zoo (1961) is set during a near-future war between Great Britain and an enemy European alliance. Despite the setting, little has changed for the middle classes, who remain the satiric target of the novel. In *Late Call* (1965) a retired hotel manager finds that the citizens of her new home in the English midlands lead empty,

desolate lives. The fortunes of the Matthew family are the focus of *No Laughing Matter* (1967); while *Setting the World on Fire* (1980), Wilson's final novel, traces the life of two brothers, Piers and Tom, from childhood to adulthood.

In addition to his fiction, Wilson also built a considerable reputation as a biographer. Both of his critical biographies, *The World of Charles Dickens* (1970) and *The Strange Ride of Rudyard Kipling* (1978), offer compelling insights into the lives of two of Britain's most prominent authors.

After establishing himself as an author, Wilson taught at a wide array of universities around the world, including UCLA, Yale, and Johns Hopkins University. He was named a Commander of the Order of the British Empire (CBE) in 1968 and was knighted by Queen Elizabeth II in 1980. The scholar Averil Gardner describes him as "the first important British writer of fiction to make his debut after the end of World War II" and writes that Wilson has amassed "a reputation of greatest distinction" for his "concern with character, manners, and morals with an ever-renewed alertness to the changing world and to new modes of fictional presentation."

Other Work by Angus Wilson
Anglo-Saxon Attitudes. 1956. Reprint, New York: Penguin, 1992.

Works about Angus Wilson
Conradi, Peter. *Angus Wilson.* Jackson: University Press of Mississippi, 1997.
Drabble, Margaret. *Angus Wilson: A Biography.* New York: St. Martin's Press, 1995.

Wilson, Colin Henry (1931–) *novelist, nonfiction writer*

Born in Leicester, England, the son of Arthur Wilson, a shoe factory worker, and his wife, Anetta, Colin Wilson left school at age 16 to become a writer. As a child he believed that he was different from others and declared himself a genius in an effort to transcend his working-class background. He is famous for being so dedicated to making a living from only his writing that he would sleep in a park at night and write by day in the British Museum Reading Room. Critic Nicolas Tredell believes that "a single idea drives all Wilson's work: that human beings are capable, by means of willpower and intelligent effort, of achieving a state of heightened consciousness which would raise them to the next level of human evolution." Other critics grouped Wilson with John OSBORNE and the ANGRY YOUNG MEN who questioned the status quo.

The Outsider (1956), Wilson's first book, is a nonfiction work that examines a common difference in a small group of people whose dissatisfaction with current scientific and existentialist thought makes them outsiders to society and even each other. The author uses examples from both fiction and the lives of famous artists to examine the lives of people who do not fit in to normal society. Critic Philip Toynbee called *The Outsider* "an exhaustive and luminously intelligent study of a representative theme of our time . . . a real contribution to an understanding of our deepest predicament," but other critics later dismissed the work as unsubstantiated.

Ritual in the Dark (1960), Wilson's first novel, recounts a socially and sexually eventful week in the life and existential development of its protagonist, Gerard Sorme. The author's next two novels, *The Sex Diary of Gerard Sorme* (1963) and *The Hedonists* (1970) also feature Sorme's discoveries while also exploring themes of the occult, violence, and the position of the artist in a society of nonintellectual people. Austin, a main character in both *Ritual in the Dark* and *The Sex Diary of Gerard Sorme*, reflects the author's own exploration of the self in society, as in the following lines from *The Sex Diary of Gerard Sorme:* "Austin was dimly, vaguely trying to follow his own deepest nature to some unheard-of form of self-expression."

Wilson also wrote several nonfiction works on the occult, the paranormal, murder, psychology, philosophy, and sexuality. Writer John A. Weigel believes that the context of modern thinking has "redefined Wilson's significance as a thinker who has persistently challenged pessimism and despair . . . as a freedom-espousing philosopher, [Wilson] chose for himself a big job, . . . to diagnose and to cure mankind's sickness."

Other Works by Colin Wilson
The Books in My Life. Charlottesville, Va.: Hampton Roads, 1998.
Rogue Messiahs: Tales of Self-Proclaimed Saviors. Charlottesville, Va.: Hampton Roads, 2000.

A Work about Colin Wilson
Tredell, Nicolas. *The Novels of Colin Wilson.* Lanham, Md.: Rowman & Littlefield, 1982.

Winterson, Jeanette (1959–) *novelist, short story writer, essayist, screenwriter*

Born in Manchester, England, Jeanette Winterson was adopted by evangelical Christians and raised in the nearby town of Accrington. She describes much of her childhood in her wryly comic, autobiographical first novel, *Oranges Are Not the Only Fruit* (1985). She recalls, for example, that she learned to read from the book of Deuteronomy and thus acquired an odd repertoire of animals for drawing at school. She also recalls that there were only six books in the house, but one of them in particular caught her attention: the medieval Arthurian saga *Morte d'Arthur.* However, reading anything but the Bible was regarded with suspicion.

Winterson's mother, a devout member of a local Christian sect, intended her to become a missionary, but adolescence brought complications as she began to fall in love with other girls. Her lesbianism outraged her church. Winterson writes about these experiences with a blend of vulnerability and understated wit. She left home at age 16 and supported herself with part-time jobs until she could enter Oxford University, where she studied English.

At 23 Winterson wrote *Oranges Are Not the Only Fruit* (1985), which was published three years later. This Whitbread Award–winning book slots fairy-tale flights of fancy alongside comic and poignant descriptions of childhood. That same year, Winterson published a lighthearted illustrated book, *Boating for Beginners* (1985). In 1987 she published the acclaimed novel *The Passion*. This fantastical tale describes the various adventures of a young man in Napoleonic France and a Venetian gondolier girl with webbed feet. The writer and critic Edmund White wrote in a review, "Magical touches dance like highlights over the brilliance of this fairytale." The novel won the John Llewellyn Rhys Memorial prize.

Sexing the Cherry (1989) is similarly a fantastical historical novel. The first page declares, "Every journey conceals another journey within its lines: the path not taken and the forgotten angle." The journeys of this novel, she continues, are "ones I might have made, or perhaps did make in some other place or time." These fantastical travels begin in 17th-century London. The *New York Times* noted that the novel "fuses history [and] fairy tale . . . into a fruit . . . of memorably startling flavor." *Sexing the Cherry* won the E. M. Forster Award.

By contrast, *Written on the Body* (1992) is set in contemporary Britain. This is the most melancholy of Winterson's works, for the protagonist, whose gender is never specified, is in love with a married woman who becomes increasingly ill. As the beloved becomes sicker, the novel becomes a lyrical catalogue of her body, with sad rapturous descriptions of her skin, her hair, and her bones.

Winterson is a prolific writer. *Art Objects* (1995) includes essays on language, literature, and culture. *The World and Other Places* (1999) is her first book of short stories. She has also written a television film called *Great Moments in Aviation* and television and cinema screenplays from two of her novels. Her recent collection of short stories, *The Powerbook* (2000), revolves around the strange profession of a fiction writer called Ali or Alix, who will write stories for people on demand. When Ali/Alix types the story into her laptop, the person who orders the story becomes the character.

Eclectic and eccentric, Winterson's books are a blend of history, fantasy, and metaphysical questions. The *Atlantic* described her as "a sorceress with language," and the *Boston Chronicle* wrote, "Her mind is a wonder that rewards exploration. . . . Winterson creates a beguiling world outside time and sense where the soul holds sway."

Other Works by Jeanette Winterson
Art and Lies. New York: Vintage, 1994.
Gut Symmetries. New York: Alfred A. Knopf, 1997.

Wodehouse, P. G. (Pelham Grenville Wodehouse) (1881–1975) *novelist, short story writer, playwright, lyricist, screenwriter*

Born in Guildford, Surrey, England, P. G. Wodehouse knew the British upper classes from the inside out; he could trace his lineage back 16 generations to the 13th century. His father was Henry Ernest Wodehouse, a civil servant in Hong Kong, and his mother was Eleanor Deane Wodehouse. He was born while his mother was back in England for a visit and was left there to be educated. In 1900, learning his father could not afford to send him to Oxford University, he went to work for a bank in London. Two years later he became a columnist for the London *Globe* and published his first book, *The Pothunters* (1902), a school novel that was first serialized in *The Public School* magazine.

Over the next 70 years Wodehouse turned out almost 100 books, wrote plays and screenplays, and even produced song lyrics ("Bill," set to Jerome Kern's music in *Showboat*, is his best-known song). He became one of England's most popular and successful writers. In 1914 he married Ethel Rowley. In 1947 they moved to New York City and subsequently to Long Island, New York. They became U.S. citizens in 1955.

In his fiction Wodehouse created a comic world populated by numerous memorable characters. He made his mark by gently satirizing the upper-class world he knew. His heroes are often not very bright, immature aristocrats. First and foremost in this category is Bertie Wooster, a wealthy, feckless young man who narrates his bumbling misadventures in a colloquial, breezy style. His problems are always set right by his imperturbable and almost supernaturally talented valet Jeeves in works such as *My Man Jeeves* (1919) and *The Code of the Woosters* (1938). A typical Bertie and Jeeves story, such as "The Inferiority Complex of Old Sippy," begins with Bertie's displeasure at Jeeves overstepping his authority on a minor matter: "And that was why, when Jeeves, wincing a bit, had weighed in with some perfectly gratuitous art-criticism, I ticked him off with no little vim. *Ne sutor ultra* whatever-it-is, I would have said to him, if I'd thought of it. I mean to say, where does a valet get off, censoring vases?" Bertie then gets into a ridiculous jam, from which Jeeves brilliantly extracts him, simultaneously gaining his own end (in this case, the destruction of the offending vase). Although the servant is so much more intelligent and capable than the master, however, Wodehouse never goes so far as to question the class structure.

Another of Wodehouse's most famous characters is Psmith, a loquacious, eccentric adventurer who appears in works such as *Psmith Journalist* (1915). In *Leave it to Psmith* (1923), he explains his unusual last name: "But it seemed to me that there were so many Smiths in the world that a little variety might well be introduced. . . . So I decided to adopt the Psmith. The p, I should add for your guidance, is silent, as in phthisis, psychic, and ptarmigan. You follow me?"

Lord Emsworth, who appears in novels such as *Blandings Castle* (1935), is an absentminded peer who devotes his time to raising his prize pig, the Empress of Blandings. Other notable Wodehouse creations include Lord Emsworth's brother, Galahad Threepwood; the ever-helpful Uncle Fred; Mr. Mulliner, a teller of tales about members of his family; and dozens of intimidating sisters, wives, and aunts. Wodehouse's prose, both narrative and dialogue, is justly esteemed by many, including Hilaire BELLOC, as the best in the language. Evelyn WAUGH, who dubbed him "The Master," observed, ". . . Mr. Wodehouse's world can never stale. He will continue to release future generations from captivity that may be more irksome than our own. He has made a world for us to live in and delight in."

Other Work by P. G. Wodehouse
What Ho! The Best of P. G. Wodehouse. London: Hutchinson, 2000.

Works about P. G. Wodehouse
Davis, Lee. *Bolton and Wodehouse and Kern: The Men Who Made Musical Comedy.* New York: James H. Heineman, 1993.
Donaldson, Frances. *P. G. Wodehouse: A Biography.* North Pomfret, Vt.: Trafalgar Square, 2001.

Woodcott, Keith
See BRUNNER, JOHN.

Woolf, Leonard (1880–1969) *journalist, editor, publisher, novelist, short story writer, nonfiction writer, memoirist*
Leonard Woolf, husband of Virginia WOOLF, was born in London to a middle-class Jewish lawyer, Sidney Woolf, and Marie de Jongh Woolf, who was Dutch by birth. Initially well-off, he suffered the economic consequences of his father's death when he was 12. Nevertheless he was schooled at St. Paul's and then at Cambridge University, where he became close friends with Thoby Stephen (brother of Virginia Stephen, who was to be Virginia Woolf), the writer Lytton STRACHEY, and the economist John Maynard Keynes. After graduation Woolf became an administrator in Ceylon (now Sri Lanka); his experience there soured him on British colonialism and changed his social and political views radically, from imperialist to socialist.

Returning to England, Woolf married in 1912 and resigned from the civil service. Shortly after they married, Virginia Woolf suffered a lengthy depression. Yet, as Louise de Salvo writes, "Once she recovered, she did not again suffer a major illness for twenty-four years and this was due, in part, to his care."

Early in his career Woolf wrote two novels: *The Village in the Jungle* (1913), based on his experiences in Ceylon; and *The Wise Virgins* (1914), based partially on his relationship with his wife.

However, neither was particularly well received. In 1917 the Woolfs founded the Hogarth Press, which would publish such writers as T. S. ELIOT, and they became leaders of the BLOOMSBURY GROUP. By 1920 Woolf was the editor of the journal *International Review* and was also writing on politics and foreign affairs for such highly respected periodicals as the *New Statesman,* the *Nation,* and the *Athenaeum.* He became secretary of the Labour Party Advisory Committee on International Affairs and ran unsuccessfully for a seat in the House of Commons in 1922. He also wrote *Empire and Commerce in Africa* (1920), an attack on European colonialism in Africa; and *Socialism and Cooperation* (1921), promoting the socialist cause.

In 1921 the Hogarth Press published three short stories of Woolf's as *Stories from the East.* One of these, "Pearls and Swine," attacked British imperialism by exposing racial prejudices: "Let 'em know you are top dog. That's the way to run an eastern country. I am a white man, you're black; I'll treat you well, give you courts and justice; but I'm the superior race, I'm master here." The story caught the attention of American literary agents, but they requested that Woolf tone down its realistic portrayal of racism.

In 1922 Woolf became lead staff writer for the *Nation,* and a year later Maynard Keynes bought into that journal and made Woolf literary editor. Most of the remainder of Woolf's life was spent on editing, working for socialist and Labour Party causes, and building the Hogarth Press into one of the preeminent publishing houses of its time.

In 1960 Woolf launched his most important writing venture when he published *Sowing,* the first volume of his autobiography. This book, an account of his first 24 years, is notable for its lyrical prose. It was followed by *Growing* (1961), the story of his life as a colonial administrator. Then came *Beginning Again* (1964), which details the Woolfs' courtship, marriage, and early years together. In *Downhill All the Way* (1967) he covers the founding of Hogarth Press and the writing and publishing of all of Virginia's major works. Woolf's autobiography concludes with *The Journey Not the Arrival Matters* (1969), in which he tells of the beginning of World War II, of Virginia Woolf's suicide, of life in wartime England, and of his later life. He finished *Journey* shortly before his death at the age of 80. Toward the end of the book he observes, "'It is the journey, not the arrival, which matters.'" Woolf's autobiography is not only valuable for its insights into the literary world of the first half of the 20th century, as well as for its record of the Woolfs' life together, but also for its literary merit. Woolf's writings, says critic Selma Meyerowitz, are "characterized by a synthesis of political consciousness, social conscience, and personal morality."

A Work about Leonard Woolf
Meyerowitz, Selma S. *Leonard Woolf.* Boston: Twayne, 1982.

Woolf, Virginia Stephen (1882–1941)
novelist, literary critic, essayist

Born in London, Virginia Woolf was the daughter of the noted man of letters, Sir Leslie Stephen, and his second wife, Julia Duckworth Stephen. The marriage produced three other children, brothers Adrian and Thoby and sister Vanessa, who became an artist and married art critic Clive BELL. The family divided their time between London and a summer home by the sea in Cornwall.

Woolf suffered from depression. The deaths of her mother in 1895, a half-sister in 1897, her father in 1904, and her brother Thoby in 1906 weakened her. Her marriage in 1912 to aspiring novelist Leonard WOOLF brought on an incapacitating bout of mental illness. "I married Leonard Woolf in 1912," she wrote, "and was almost immediately ill for three years." The marriage survived this rocky start, and Leonard supported, championed, and protected his wife through subsequent periods of depression until her suicide in 1941.

The Woolfs, along with Vanessa and Clive Bell, soon became the nucleus of the BLOOMSBURY GROUP, a loose-knit set of highly talented and intellectually brilliant people who almost all lived in the

Bloomsbury area of London. The Woolfs founded the Hogarth Press in 1917, publishing their own stories as a first venture. They subsequently built the press into a substantial force in the world of the literary avant-garde, publishing works by T. S. ELIOT, Katherine MANSFIELD, and Sigmund FREUD, among others.

Woolf's first novel, *The Voyage Out* (1915), depicts the literal and symbolic voyages in the life of the musician Rachel Vinrace. After publishing another relatively conventional novel, *Night and Day* (1919), which explores the role of women in modern society, Woolf shifted in 1922 to a more experimental style of writing in *Jacob's Room,* which is loosely based on her brother Thoby. This technique, "stream of consciousness," records the shifting inner thoughts of her characters. While time passes in her characters' lives, they may well be reliving memories of years gone by or projecting themselves almost simultaneously into the future, while still actively living in the present.

The Waves (1931), Woolf's most experimental novel and her fullest exploration of stream of consciousness, explores moments in the lives of six different characters. *The Years* (1937) describes a single family, the Pargiters, over the course of 50 years. *Between the Acts* (1941), her final and darkest novel, takes place in a single day at an English country house.

Woolf was also an accomplished critic and ardent fighter for women's rights. She worked as a critic and reviewer for many years, beginning with the *Times Literary Supplement* in 1905. In 1929 she published *A Room of One's Own,* one of the major documents of 20th-century feminist criticism. This exploration of "women and fiction" advocates female independence, suggests that great writers must have an androgynous mind, and traces a female literary tradition back to writers such as Aphra Behn, Jane Austen, and George Eliot. Woolf's two volumes of collected critical essays, *The Common Reader* (1925) and *The Common Reader: Second Series* (1932), reprint most of her best critical writing on topics ranging from the English classics to modern authors. She is widely acknowledged to be one of the greatest literary essayists in the English language and one of the most important feminists of the 20th century. According to scholar Eileen Barrett, "Woolf's writings are now essential to classroom and critical studies of modernism, women writers, feminist theory, and lesbian and gay studies."

Critical Analysis

The action of the novel *Mrs. Dalloway* (1925) takes place in a single day, yet through memory entire lifetimes elapse. Clarissa Dalloway is a middle-aged London socialite. Her character is contrasted with the shell-shocked war veteran, Septimus Warren Smith, who suffers at the hands of unfeeling and arrogant psychiatrists. Septimus suffers from delusions: "Why could he see through bodies, see into the future, when dogs will become men?" At the end of the novel, Septimus commits suicide, while Clarissa continues to live. Critic Jeremy Hawthorn has analyzed the theme of alienation in the novel: "We are given in the novel an extraordinarily powerful picture of men and women fighting a central inadequacy in their lives—the inadequacy of alienation—but we are shown no real way to escape from it."

Woolf's stream-of-consciousness technique is seen to best advantage in *To the Lighthouse* (1927), the novel many critics believe to be her finest. The core of the work concerns events in the lives of the Ramsay family. The novel is presented in three sections, the first of which takes place before World War I and the third after the war. Young James Ramsay wants to see the lighthouse near the family's summer home, is assured that he will by Mrs. Ramsay in section one, and does so 10 years later in section three. Dividing the two sections is a set piece called "Time Passes," which poetically compresses 10 years in the lives of the Ramsays, alternating meditations with bracketed statements of historical events. Critic Mitchell Leaska says of this passage, "No chapter in English or American prose fiction has yet surpassed this middle section in lyrical force or resonance." Whereas the outer sections of the work present events as seen and interpreted by the minds of the participants, the middle is presented as if by a disembodied spirit who observes the progressive ruin and decay of the house. Finally, what is left of the family returns after the war; tired from their journey, they go to sleep. The poet Conrad Aiken described the book thus: "Nothing happens, in this houseful of odd nice people, and yet all of life happens. The tragic futility, the absurdity, the pathetic beauty, of life—we experience all of this in our sharing of seven hours of Mrs. Ramsay's wasted or not wasted existence. We have seen, through her, the world."

Orlando (1928) is the story of a character who lives more than 400 years, participating in the affairs of Queen Elizabeth's court, English literary salons of the 18th century, and the Sultan of Turkey's court. The novel is Woolf's most radical and extended exploration of the constructed nature of gender roles. In the middle of the novel, the male courtier Orlando falls into a trance. When he wakes up, "He stood upright in complete nakedness before us, and while the trumpets pealed Truth! Truth! Truth! we have no choice left but confess—he was a woman." The change of sex does not change Orlando's fundamental identity: "Orlando had become a woman—there is no denying it. But in every other respect, Orlando remained precisely at he had been." Finally Orlando settles on being a woman in the 20th century. The Orlando of the last scene is clearly the image of the writer Vita SACKVILLE-WEST, whom Virginia had come to love passionately in the early 1920s.

Other Works by Virginia Woolf

Letters of Virginia Woolf. Edited by Nigel Nicolson and Joanne Trautmann. New York: Harcourt Brace Jovanovich, 1975–80.
A Passionate Apprentice: The Early Journals, 1897–1909. Edited by Mitchell A. Leaska. San Diego, Calif.: Harcourt Brace Jovanovich, 1990.

Works about Virginia Woolf

Barrett, Eileen, and Patricia Cramer, eds. *Virginia Woolf: Lesbian Readings.* New York: New York University Press, 1997.
Leaska, Mitchell. *Granite and Rainbow: The Hidden Life of Virginia Woolf.* New York: Farrar, Straus & Giroux, 1998.
Nicolson, Nigel. *Virginia Woolf.* New York: Viking, 2000.

Wyndham, John (John Beynon Harris)
(1903–1969) *novelist, short story writer*

Born John Wyndham Parker Lucas Beynon Harris in Birmingham, England, John Wyndham spent his early life in several different cities in Britain and was educated at various private schools. He tried his hand at many diverse jobs, including law, advertising, and even farming, and began writing short stories for American magazines in 1925. These were mostly sensational science fiction.

After World War II science fiction novels became popular, many of them exploring apocalyptic catastrophes that threatened human communities. Especially talented at writing this sort of tale, Wyndham produced *The Day of the Triffids* (1951). The novel begins with the narrator waking up to discover that nearly everyone else in the world has been struck blind—except him. To the narrator's horror, civilization crumbles. As one of the characters says, "You know, one of the most shocking things about it is to realise how *easily* we have lost a world that seemed so safe and certain." The novel is a masterpiece of restrained tension.

One of Wyndham's best-known works is *The Chrysalids* (1955), which is set in a postapocalyptic world where genetic mutation is rife and human society ruthlessly destroys anyone with a sign of genetic aberration. Churches recite slogans like "Blessed is the norm" and "Accursed is the mutant in the sight of God and man!" Women are sterilized, exiled, and sometimes killed if they bear mutated babies. The novel's narrator fearfully prays to be normal: "God, let me be like other people. I don't want to be different." But he has an abnormality: telepathy. The book is a scathing indictment of eugenics or the effort to ensure only people with certain genes survive.

Wyndham's novels are narrated in the first person, so the reader sees the narrator's bewilderment as he tries to make sense of a transformed world. Wyndham's most famous use of this device is in his novel *The Midwich Cuckoos* (1957), set in a small English village full of people leading bustling, ordinary lives. The village is so quiet that it is "almost notoriously, a place where things did not happen." Yet one strange day, the village of Midwich is cut off from the rest of the world for several hours. When contact is finally reestablished, it is soon discovered that every fertile woman in the village is pregnant. The novel describes the bewilderment and quiet fear of the next nine months in economical, calm, even humorous prose, and after nine months all the women give birth to eerie super-intelligent children with golden eyes and a terrifying ability to control people mentally. Wyndham creates an atmosphere of mounting strain. As one character says, "I feel that at any moment something ungoverned, and rather horrible, may break out." The novel, which builds to a shocking climax, became the film *The Village of the Damned* in 1960.

The *New York Times* declared in Wyndham's obituary that he "did more than any other British writer since H. G. Wells to make science fiction popular in this country . . . his plots, however fantastic, were characterized by inventiveness, clarity and a profound sympathy for mankind in the nuclear age."

Other Works by John Wyndham

Chocky. London: Michael Joseph, 1968.
Wanderers of Time. London: Severn, 1973.

Yeats, William Butler (1865–1939) *poet, playwright*

William Butler Yeats, an ardent Irish nationalist, was interested in Irish folklore, the occult, politics, poetry, and drama. He was born in Dublin to John Butler Yeats, a lawyer who became a painter, and Susan Pollexfen Yeats. Both his parents belonged to the Protestant land-owning minority of Ireland. His mother's family lived in Sligo, in the west of Ireland, and Yeats's experiences there provided him with a sense of the countryside, language, and concerns of the people that proved important in his work. By the time he had completed secondary school in Dublin in 1883, Yeats had decided to be an artist and a poet, but after a short attendance at art school he made the decision to focus on poetry alone.

While living in London for a time, beginning in 1887, Yeats became one of the founders of The Rhymers' Club, which included Ernest Dowson, Lionel Johnson, and Arthur Symons. Although he would later admit that the group was sometimes dull, he also enjoyed their discussions on various topics, especially poetry.

By now Yeats was publishing his own poetry, chiefly influenced by his time in Sligo and his interest in the current renaissance of Irish culture and folklore. Much of this verse appeared in his 1889 *The Wandering of Oisin and Other Poems.*

"The Stolen Child (1886, revised 1889) tells of a child lured from his home by faeries, while "The Madness of King Goll" (1887, revised 1888) is based on a legend about Goll, who goes insane while fighting pirates and then hides in the woods. In "The Lake Isle of Innisfree" (1890, revised 1892), the poet vows that

> *"I will arise and go now, and go to*
> *Innisfree,*
> *And a small cabin build there of clay*
> *and wattles made;*
> *Nine bean-rows will I have there . . .*
> *And I shall have some peace there."*

Yeats's poetry was further influenced by Edmund Spenser, John Donne, and the English romantic poets. He was also attracted to the religious mysticism of William Blake. He became increasingly interested in the occult and magic and joined both the Theosophical Society and the Hermetic Order of the Golden Dawn. He also became friends with fellow Irish mystic George ("A.E.") RUSSELL.

In 1889 Yeats met the fiercely nationalistic Irish activist and actress Maud Gonne, who inspired him to take a vigorous, active role in the Irish national cause. Deeply in love with Gonne, Yeats repeatedly proposed marriage, but she refused. For several years, much of his poetry featured her, as in "No Second Troy" (1910), in which he likens Gonne to Helen of Troy: "Was there another Troy for her to burn?"

In 1896 Yeats met Lady GREGORY and through her became interested in the theater. Three years later the two founded the Irish National Theatre Company. In 1904 the company's permanent home became the Abbey Theatre, for which Yeats was director and manager. The company put on a number of Yeats's own plays, which were generally filled with Irish nationalism and legend. In *Cathleen ni Houlihan* (1902) the title character, played initially by Maud Gonne and symbolizing an ideal Ireland of old, seduces a groom-to-be, who represents modern Ireland, into taking up arms against the English. Many of Yeats's plays were attacked as anti-Christian because he so often found his heroes among the ancient pagan Irish. His later plays were influenced by the Japanese Noh Theatre, to which American poet Ezra Pound introduced him.

The 1916 Easter Uprisings against English dominance in Ireland served as the inspiration for Yeats's poem "Easter 1916" (1920, 1921), written upon the death of various Irish rebels whom the poet knew personally. The following year, he married Georgie Hyde-Lees, who upon the couple's honeymoon supposedly fell into a trance and began writing out a series of messages from spirits. These writings came to play a vital role in assembling *A Vision* (1925, revised 1937), in which Yeats explains how imagination, history, and personality are related and how they are affected by different phases of the moon.

Over the last 15 years of his life, Yeats produced a great deal of poetry, most notably the collections *Michael Robartes and the Dancer* (1921), *The Tower* (1928), and *The Winding Stair and Other Poems* (1929), in which he wrestled with aging, the role of art, the changing world, love, madness, time, his health, and death. His *Collected Poems* appeared in 1950 (revised 1984).

Yeats's political career also continued and from 1922 through 1928 he served as a senator for the newly formed Irish free state. In 1923 he received the Nobel Prize in Literature.

Critical Analysis

"The Second Coming" (1920, revised 1921) is one of Yeats's most famous poems, written not long after the end of the Russian Revolution, World War I, and the struggle for Irish independence. All these events convinced the poet that the world as he knew it was crumbling and giving way to a new one. Both repelled and fascinated by this perceived disintegration, he opens the poem with the image of a falcon climbing ever higher in ever-widening circles that carry it beyond reach of the falconer's voice. To describe the bird's flight, the poet uses the word *gyre,* which is a circular or spiraling turn. For Yeats each cycle of history is represented by such a gyre. The loss of control by the falconer and the eventual breaking away of the falcon, an act which will end the gyre, shows that the present cycle is near its end: "Things fall apart; the center cannot hold."

The poet now wonders if the Second Coming of Christ is in the offing, for according to the scholar Richard Ellmann, in Yeats's philosophy "a new god comes to replace the old god . . . and every cycle is said to have its special deity." However, the speaker of the poem fears that the "god" of the Second Coming, preceded as he is by anarchy and bloodshed, may well offer the opposite of salvation. Thus, he imagines the approach of a sphinx-like creature. He despairs, asking, "what rough beast . . . Slouches toward Bethlehem to be born?"

In "Sailing to Byzantium" (1927) and "Byzantium" (1930, revised 1932) the ancient Byzantine Empire, an offshoot of the Roman Empire, symbolizes art and its unchanging nature as opposed to the constant alterations of the natural world. In *A Vision* Yeats writes that "in early Byzantium, maybe never before or since in recorded history, religious, aesthetic, and practical life were one, that architects and artificers [artists] . . . spoke to the multitude in gold and silver."

In "Sailing to Byzantium" the poet writes that youth is forever captured and preserved in the monuments and mosaics of the ancient Byzantines. It is not a land where the old belong. Indeed, the speaker cries out to the figures in the mosaics to "Consume my heart away . . . and gather me/Into the artifice of eternity."

The poet in "Byzantium" realizes that the world he sought in "Sailing" is a dead one, but it is also one that offers a spiritual purification from "[t]he fury and mire of human veins." A guide appears to lead the soul of the speaker into the unchanging world for which he yearns. At one point the poet experiences the purifying fires of Byzantium, "[a]n agony of flame that cannot singe a sleeve" because this fire is not of the real world. In the end, however, the speaker cannot escape the natural, changing world and is pulled back to blood and mire.

As the critic Edmund Wilson observes, "Yeats seems to be conscious from the first of an antagonism between the actual world of industry, politics, and science, on the one hand, and the imaginative poetic life, on the other." The Irish writer Seamus HEANEY writes, "Yeats as an artist in verse . . . would work long at shaping a poem, handling and testing a line until it pressed down with the greatest semantic density and conducted the right musical strain from the lines before and after. The evidence is . . . there in the perfected feel of the individual stanza."

Other Works by William Butler Yeats

The Autobiography of William Butler Yeats. 1916. Reprint, New York: Macmillan, 1995.
Yeats's Poetry, Drama, and Prose. Edited by James Pethica. New York: W. W. Norton, 2000.

Works about William Butler Yeats

Ellmann, Richard. *Yeats: The Man and the Masks.* New York: W. W. Norton, 1999.
Larrissy, Edward. *Yeats the Poet.* Upper Saddle River, N.J.: Prentice Hall, 1995.
Rosenthal, M. L. *Running to Paradise: Yeats's Poetic Art.* New York: Oxford University Press, 1994.

Yorke, Henry Vincent

See GREEN, HENRY.

SELECTED BIBLIOGRAPHY

Abrams, M. H., et al., eds. *The Norton Anthology of English Literature*. 7th ed., vol. 2. New York: W. W. Norton, 2000.

Adam, G. F. *Three Contemporary Welsh Novelists*. Bern, Switzerland: Francke, 1950.

Alexander, Flora. *Contemporary Women Novelists*. London: Edward Arnold, 1989.

Allsop, Kenneth. *The Angry Decade*. 2d ed. London: Peter Owen, 1964.

Arthurs, Peter. *Famous Irish Writers*. Belfast: Appletree Press, 1999.

Barron, Stephanie, and Wolf-Dieter Dube, eds. *German Expressionism: Art and Society*. New York: Rizzoli, 1997.

Bell, Vereen, and Laurence Lerner, eds. *On Modern Poetry: Essays Presented to Donald Davie*. Nashville, Tenn.: Vanderbilt University Press, 1988.

Bender, Todd K. *Literary Impressionism in Jean Rhys, Ford Madox Ford, Joseph Conrad and Charlotte Brontë*. New York: Garland, 1997.

Benstock, Bernard, and Thomas F. Staley, eds. *Dictionary of Literary Biography, British Mystery Writers 1920–1930*, vol. 77. Detroit: Gale, 1989.

Bleiler, E. F., ed. *Supernatural Fiction Writers: Fantasy and Horror*, vol. 1. New York: Scribner, 1985.

Bleiman, Barbara, ed. *Five Modern Poets: Fleur Adcock, U. A. Fanthorpe, Tony Harrison, Anne Stevenson, Derek Walcott*. New York: Longman, 1993.

Bloom, Clive, ed. *Gothic Horror: A Reader's Guide from Poe to King and Beyond*. New York: St. Martin's Press, 1998.

Bloom, Harold, ed. *Classic Fantasy Writers*. Broomall, Penn.: Chelsea House, 1994.

Bradford, Sarah. *The Sitwells and the Arts of the 1920s and 1930s*. Austin: University of Texas Press, 1996.

Brearton, Fran. *The Great War in Irish Poetry: W. B. Yeats to Michael Longley*. New York: Oxford University Press, 2000.

Coffman, Stanley K. *Imagism: A Chapter for the History of Modern Poetry*. New York: Octagon Books, 1972.

Daiches, David, ed. *The Penguin Companion to English Literature*. New York: Penguin, 1971.

Drabble, Margaret, ed. *The Oxford Companion to English Literature*. Oxford: Oxford University Press, 1985.

Drabble, Margaret, and Jenny Stringer, eds. *The Concise Oxford Companion to English Literature*. Rev. ed. New York: Oxford University Press, 1996.

DuBose, Martha Hailey. *Women of Mystery: The Lives and Works of Notable Women Crime Novelists*. New York: St. Martin's Press, 2000.

Dyson, A. E., ed. *Three Contemporary Poets: Thom Gunn, Ted Hughes, and R. S. Thomas.* London: Macmillan, 1990.

Gage, John T. *In the Arresting Eye: The Rhetoric of Imagism.* Baton Rouge: Louisiana State University Press, 1981.

Gorra, Michael. *After Empire: Scott, Naipaul, Rushdie.* Chicago: University of Chicago Press, 1997.

Graham, Desmond. *The Truth of War: Owen, Blunden, Rosenberg.* Manchester, England: Carcanet Press, 1984.

Groden, Michael, and Martin Kreiswirth, eds. *The Johns Hopkins Guide to Literary Theory and Criticism.* Baltimore: Johns Hopkins University Press, 1994.

Heim, Otto. *Writing along Broken Lines: Violence and Ethnicity in Contemporary Maori Fiction.* Auckland, New Zealand: Auckland University Press, 1998.

Johnstone, John Keith. *The Bloomsbury Group.* New York: Noonday Press, 1963.

Kemp, Peter, ed. *The Oxford Dictionary of Literary Quotations.* New York: Oxford University Press, 1998.

Lacey, Stephen. *British Realist Theater: The New Wave in Its Context.* London: Routledge, 1995.

Lane, Denis, ed. *A Library of Literary Criticism: Modern British Literature.* New York: Ungar, 1985.

Leitch, B. ed. *The Norton Anthology of Theory and Criticism.* New York: W. W. Norton, 2001.

Lovell, Mary. *The Sisters: The Saga of the Mitford Family.* New York: W. W. Norton, 2002.

Manganaro, Marc. *Myth, Rhetoric, and the Voice of Authority: A Critique of Frazer, Eliot, Fry, and Campbell.* New Haven, Conn.: Yale University Press, 1992.

Mann, Jessica. *Deadlier Than the Male: Why Are Respectable English Women So Good at Murder?* New York: Macmillan, 1981.

Marler, Regina. *Bloomsbury Pie: The Making of the Bloomsbury Boom.* New York: Holt, 1997.

McArthur, Tom, ed. *Concise Oxford Companion to the English Language.* New York: Oxford University Press, 1998.

Miller, Tyrus. *Late Modernism: Politics, Fiction, and the Arts Between the World Wars.* Berkeley: University of California Press, 1999.

Nasso, Christine, ed. *Contemporary Authors Permanent Series,* vol. 2. Detroit: Gale, 1978.

O'Connor, Theresa, ed. *The Comic Tradition in Irish Women Writers.* Gainesville: University Press of Florida, 1996.

O'Neill, Michael, and Gareth Reeves. *Auden, MacNeice, Spender: The Thirties Poetry.* London: Macmillan, 1992.

Ousby, Ian, ed. *The Cambridge Guide to Literature in English.* New York: Cambridge University Press, 1993.

Parini, Jay, ed. *British Writers: Supplement VI, Peter Ackroyd to A. N. Wilson.* New York: Scribner, 2001.

———. *British Writers: Supplement VII, Basil Bunting to Sylvia Townsend Warner.* New York: Scribner, 2002.

Parker, Peter, and Frank Kermode, eds. *A Reader's Guide to Twentieth Century Writers.* New York: Oxford University Press, 1996.

Pearce, Jon, ed. *Twelve Voices: Interviews with Canadian Poets.* Ottawa, Canada: Borealis, 1980.

Perkins, David. *A History of Modern Poetry.* Cambridge, Mass.: Harvard University Press, 1976.

Perry, Donna. *Backtalk: Women Writers Speak Out.* New Brunswick, N.J.: Rutgers University Press, 1993.

Rae, Patricia. *The Practical Muse: Pragmatist Poetics in Hulme, Pound, and Stevens.* Cranbury, N.J.: Bucknell University Press, 1997.

Raitt, Suzanne. *Vita and Virginia: The Work and Friendship of V. Sackville-West and Virginia Woolf.* Oxford: Clarendon Press, 1993.

Rosenbaum, S. P. *Victorian Bloomsbury: The Early Literary History of the Bloomsbury Group,* vol. 1. New York: St. Martin's Press, 1987.

Sage, Lorna, ed. *The Cambridge Guide to Women's Writing in English.* Cambridge, England: Cambridge University Press, 1999.

———. *Women in the House of Fiction: Post-War Women Novelists.* New York: Routledge, 1992.

Shattock, Joanne, ed. *The Oxford Guide to British Women Writers.* New York: Oxford University Press, 1993.

Staley, Thomas F., ed. *Twentieth-Century Women Novelists.* Totowa, N.J.: Barnes & Noble Books, 1982.

———. *British Novelists, 1890–1929: Traditionalists.* Detroit: Gale, 1985.

Stapleton, Michael, ed. *The Cambridge Guide to English Literature.* New York: Cambridge University Press, 1983.

Stringer, Jenny, ed. *The Oxford Companion to Twentieth Century Literature in English.* 2d ed. New York: Oxford University Press, 1996.

Sutherland, James. *The Oxford Book of Literary Anecdotes.* New York: Oxford University Press, 1975.

Taylor, John Russell. *The Angry Theatre.* New York: Hill and Wang, 1969.

Uroff, Margaret Dickie. *Sylvia Plath & Ted Hughes.* Urbana: University of Illinois Press, 1979.

Wachman, Gay. *Lesbian Empire: Radical Cross-writing in the Twenties.* New Brunswick, N.J.: Rutgers University Press, 2001.

Wagenknecht, Edward. *Seven Masters of Supernatural Fiction.* New York: Greenwood Press, 1991.

Wandor, Michelene. *Drama Today: A Critical Guide to British Drama 1970–1990.* London: Longman, 1990.

Welch, Robert, ed. *The Oxford Companion to Irish Literature.* New York: Oxford University Press, 1996.

Wilson, Colin. *The Craft of the Novel.* London: Gollancz, 1975.

Wullschläger, Jackie. *Inventing Wonderland.* New York: Free Press, 1995.

INDEX